PETER D'EPIRO

~

THE BOOK OF FIRSTS

Peter D'Epiro received a BA and MA from Queens College and an MPhil and PhD in English from Yale University. He has taught English at the secondary and college levels and worked as an editor and writer for thirty years. He has written (with Mary Desmond Pinkowish) *Sprezzatura: 50 Ways Italian Genius Shaped the World* (Anchor Books, 2001) and *What Are the Seven Wonders of the World? and 100 Other Great Cultural Lists—Fully Explicated* (Anchor Books, 1998), which has appeared in British, German, Russian, Lithuanian, and Korean editions. He has also published a book and several articles on Ezra Pound's *Cantos*, a book of translations of African-American poetry into Italian, and rhymed verse translations from Dante's *Inferno*. He has a grown son, Dante, and lives with his wife, Nancy Walsh, in Ridgewood, New Jersey.

ALSO BY PETER D'EPIRO

Sprezzatura: 50 Ways Italian Genius Shaped the World
(with Mary Desmond Pinkowish)

What Are the Seven Wonders of the World?
and 100 Other Great Cultural Lists—Fully Explicated
(with Mary Desmond Pinkowish)

THE
BOOK
OF
FIRSTS

THE
BOOK
OF
FIRSTS

150 World-Changing
People and Events

from Caesar Augustus
to the Internet

PETER D'EPIRO

ANCHOR BOOKS
A Division of Random House, Inc.
New York

AN ANCHOR BOOKS ORIGINAL, MARCH 2010

Copyright © 2010 by Peter D'Epiro

All rights reserved. Published in the United States by Anchor
Books, a division of Random House, Inc., New York, and in Canada
by Random House of Canada Limited, Toronto.

Anchor Books and colophon are registered trademarks
of Random House, Inc.

All of the essays in this collection are copyright by the
individual contributors.

Library of Congress Cataloging-in-Publication Data
D'Epiro, Peter.
The book of firsts : 150 world-changing people and events, from
Caesar Augustus to the Internet / by Peter D'Epiro.
p.   cm.
Includes bibliographical references.
ISBN 978-0-307-38843-8 (alk. paper)
1. History—Miscellanea.   2. Biography—Miscellanea.   I. Title.
D10.D47   2010
909—dc22
2009027573

Author photograph © Nancy Walsh
Book design by Rebecca Aidlin

www.anchorbooks.com

Printed in the United States of America
10 9 8 7 6 5 4 3 2 1

For Nancy

Si no'us vei, Domna don plus mi cal,
Negus vezer mon bel pensar no val.

(And if I do not see you, Lady mine,
No sight is worth your image in my mind.)

—Bernart de Ventadorn (fl. 1150–80)

Contents

Preface

WE ALL REMEMBER hundreds of key events in our lives that can be evoked by the casual question, "What was the first time you ever . . . ?" Depending on the rest of that question, we may find ourselves searching our memory banks for an incident decent or indecent, momentous or trivial, too pathetically droll to relate without laughter or too depressingly sad for words.

The first of anything in our lives acquires an aura all its own: the first time I spoke French in France, the first time I had an erotic dream, the first time I flew, the first time I got into a fight, the first award I ever won, the first time someone let me down.

If mundane firsts like these assume such importance in our eyes, the groundbreaking firsts of the mighty of the earth—its great heroes, artists, thinkers, discoverers, and villains—acquire something of the same magical glow as those of our private lives, except writ large. In their case, the firsts were not cosmically (or even locally) insignificant but represented audacious deeds never before seen on earth. If some of our private firsts determined the future course of our own lives, the historical firsts often determined, for better or worse, the fate of a large segment of the human race.

As in our own lives, the *very* first—such as the first discovery of gunpowder in China—might ultimately have less significance than another similar first at a different time and place—such as the first use of gunpowder in cannons in Europe, which allowed the rise of powerful and centralized European nations by denying local nobles the protection of formerly impregnable castles. Countries such as France, England, Spain, and Portugal were thus empowered to conquer, exploit, and some would say civilize, some would say terrorize, much of the rest of the world. Similarly, the printing press (first used in China) began to have its earth-shattering impact only after it was first used in Europe at a time when it fueled religious divisions, world exploration, the growth of a literate middle class, and the rediscovery of the ancient world. Likewise, the first voyages of Europeans to the Americas (Norsemen, c. 1000) produced nothing of lasting consequence, whereas Columbus's four voyages mightily diverted the course of subsequent history.

In attempting to understand human history as an organic development, we nonetheless impute a special importance to the first occurrence of a certain type of event, whether it be an invention, a philosophy, a literary genre, a geographic discovery, or a scientific breakthrough, because this helps us go back and determine which future aspects were already present ab ovo, which were gradual accretions, and which had intriguingly little to do with what came after. "Who (or what) was the first?" always implicitly carries within it the question, "Who (or what) was the first to make a *real* difference?"

Who was the first to sack the city of Rome? Write a sonnet? Take a picture? What was the first university? The first great novel of world literature? The first astronomical telescope? The first flying machine? These are the kinds of questions you'll find answered and explained in this book, which focuses on 150 of the most significant firsts that occurred in the first twenty centuries of the Christian (or Common) era.

The essays for each century are prefaced by a listing of all the who or what questions for that section, consecutively numbered throughout the book for a total of 150 questions, answers, and essays. The essays attempt to explain the answers engagingly and informatively, putting them in historical context and often aiming at clarification of the difference between the absolute first and the first that really mattered.

There's a certain pathos or poignancy to some of the firsts you'll read about, such as the first four-wheeled automobile consisting of a primitive engine plopped onto a stagecoach, or the paltry twelve-horsepower engine of the first airplane (see Questions 141 and 144). "If only they'd known what *we* know!" we like to say, but of course without thousands of pioneers like the ones in this book, we wouldn't know much of anything.

In *An Essay on Criticism*, Alexander Pope counseled wariness toward innovation:

> *Be not the first by whom the new are tried,*
> *Nor yet the last to lay the old aside.*

Conservative Mr. Pope was urging the writers of his time (1711) to exercise caution before adopting trendy new words too quickly, but most of us admire those brave souls who "boldly go where no man [or woman] has gone" and start something new for the rest of humankind to follow. Sometimes, however, the wisest course to pursue in the face of something new is to shun it, and examples of these firsts are liberally sprinkled throughout this book, as even a cursory glance at the table of contents will demonstrate. Those notorious firsts serve to remind us that much of what history considers worthy of recording is a succession of unspeakably cruel actions in the eternal saga of how *homo homini lupus est*—"man is a wolf to man."

Sometimes the process of sifting out a first is well-nigh impossible. Sigmund Freud observed that "every discovery is made more than once, and none is made all at once, nor is success meted out according to deserts. America is not named after Columbus." This sentiment was echoed and amplified by William F. Ogburn and Dorothy Thomas of Columbia University who, in 1922, compiled a list of 148 major scientific, mathematical, and technological discoveries that were made independently or more or less simultaneously by two or more persons. For examples in this book, see Questions 126 and 137.

I had originally planned a book featuring 301 very short essays, but I soon realized that before the essays could even get going, it was time for them to be ending. I carefully pared the number down to 200, where it stayed for quite a while, before I saw that the resulting book would be far too sprawling for a one-volume work. The next step was to bring the number of essays down to 175—and then whittle it down even further to 150. It still made for a long book, but I found that this number of topics was just about the bare minimum that would allow the contributors and me to provide a basic sense of the particular fragrance—or odor—of each century we cover.

With this aim in mind, I decided to allot either seven or eight essays to each of the twenty completed centuries of the AD era. Considerations of length and reader interest led me to aim for briefer and less detailed essays for the comparatively fallow years from 400 to 1000 than for the earlier and later centuries, but I have not always abided by my own rule. Nonetheless, it seemed natural that, as the essays approached our own tumultuous times, they should fill out a bit more, much as our waistlines have expanded in the most recent years.

Why does the book confine itself to the years 1 to 2000? Besides the advantage of round numbers—two thousand years, twenty centuries— that lends an air of mystifying symmetry to the book, it is undeniable that the start of the Christian era marks a dividing line not only in our chronology but also in the history of the human race. For better or worse, Christianity has been the dominant religion of Europeans—the peoples who were the impetus behind much of postclassical history by their gradual mastery of experimental science, technology, medicine, government and law, exploration, and, most of all, warfare. Their relentless and aggressive proselytizing, colonization, and imperialism have been matched only by their achievements in the arts that lend grace and refinement to life. And their conquest of North America eventually resulted in the creation of another military and cultural behemoth that has determined the course of much of world history for almost a hundred years.

But my main reason for banning the BC centuries from the book is the practical one of not having too many things stem back to the Sumerians, who created the world's earliest civilization way back in the fourth, third, and second millennia BC. The Sumerians invented a surprising number of important things we take for granted, such as writing, and if the Sumerians didn't invent it, you can be sure that some other very canny ancient civilization—Egyptian, Indian, Chinese, Cretan, Mycenaean, Etruscan, Hebrew, Greek, Roman, etc.—did.

Events that occurred so long ago are often poorly documented, if at all, and they rarely point to an individual or a specific date that can be associated with a first. To avoid bewildering generalities and, worse, an endless, recondite, hard-to-pronounce tour of Babylonian this and Syrian that, Phoenician this and Carthaginian that, Assyrian this and Hittite that, I decided to commence with the first century AD, which, presided over in the West by Caesar Augustus for its first fourteen years, presents a more recognizable historical epoch for our perusal.

While many of the earlier essays refer briefly to any BC antecedents that may exist, all the firsts in the questions are understood to mean "first in the AD era." Although the book is mostly about Europe and the United States, I have included as many firsts from other parts of the world as my limited space and even more limited knowledge allowed.

A book spanning so many centuries was not the place for a systematic account of the explosion of literary and artistic innovation and experimentation in the nineteenth and twentieth centuries. Adding essays on the Cubists, Futurists, and Dadaists, for example—not to mention Debussy, Stravinsky, Satie, Schoenberg, Baudelaire, Flaubert,

Proust, Kafka, Joyce, Pound, Eliot, etc.—would have extended this book far beyond any reasonable compass, and excellent resources on these movements and artists are widely available. Likewise, I was able to include only a sampling of the many inventions that have enhanced or detracted from our lives in the past several hundred years (see Questions 140, 141, 144, and 147). I have avoided topics dealing with sports, pop culture, or celebrities, leaving them to the experts in their respective fields.

"All men by nature desire to know," said Aristotle, and more and more of us are trying to escape the twin tyrannies of mindless entertainment and ubiquitous advertising by turning to one of humanity's perennial questions—"What happened before I was here?" I sincerely hope this book will provide at least the general contours of an answer and serve as an aperitif to stimulate the reader's hunger for further historical knowledge in greater depth and detail.

My favorite part of prefaces, even of books I haven't written myself, is the acknowledgments section. My mother, Virginia Ciavolella D'Epiro, has been an inspiration to me since she first drummed into my six-year-old head that "reading and writing are two of the most wonderful things in the world." Her steady, calm, and cheerful reassurance helped get me through the dispiriting moments that are inevitable in any long, challenging assignment.

Tom Matrullo, stalwart friend and intellectual companion of very long standing, has contributed mightily to this book (and my last two) in both the number of essays he expertly handled and in the constant e-mail pep talks and detailed feedback on this entire project.

My twice-monthly lunches with Wayne Guglielmo at Peppercorns (or, as we dubbed it, "*Les Grains de Poivre*") in Park Ridge, New Jersey, always expanded into three-hour discussions of this, that, and my various book woes. I owe to Wayne an epiphany—or at least a crucial breakthrough—in the winnowing process regarding the number of essays, as well as heaps of perceptive advice from one writer to another. Wayne and his gracious wife, Maria, also treated my wife, Nancy, and me to many a lavish dinner party during a very frenzied time for us.

My terrific agent, Rafe Sagalyn, steered me toward the concept of "firstness" at a time (December 2006) when I was floundering around in murkier waters. It's been a heartfelt pleasure working with my editor, Diana Secker Tesdell, whose advice on overall format and on ways to keep the content from ballooning out of control has been invaluable.

Nancy and I thank Bill Schaffner, MD, Professor and Chair of the Department of Preventive Medicine at Vanderbilt University School of Medicine in Nashville, Tennessee, for his help with Question 148. We are also grateful to Gregory House, MD, both in his original form and in his reincarnations as reruns and DVDs, for providing witty, urbane, and irreverent diversion from our daily scribal chores.

I thank Lynn and Arlene Austin, John Baranowski, Debbie Kaplan, Sally Kubetin, Fausto and Margaret Macera, Julia Muiño, Mary Desmond Pinkowish, Tony Vecchione, Bob and Roseann Vitale, and many other friends and family members for their good wishes during the book's incubation period.

I'm profoundly grateful to my team of distinguished contributors—Dante D'Epiro; Richard Jackson, PhD; Eric Lenk; Tom Matrullo; Kia Penso, PhD; Lisa C. Perrone, PhD; Joseph Sgammato; Nancy Walsh; and William A. Walsh, PhD—who have all graced this book with their distinctive voices (see pages 611–613).

My greatest debt is to my wife, Nancy Walsh, whose unflagging encouragement and loving support—not to mention her contribution of thirteen essays—made it all worthwhile.

Peter D'Epiro
June 10, 2009

FIRST
CENTURY

1 ⬧ *Who was the first Roman emperor?*

2 ⬧ *What was the first poetic handbook of Greek mythology?*

3 ⬧ *Who was the first Roman emperor to be assassinated?*

4 ⬧ *Who was the first pope?*

5 ⬧ *Who was the first known conqueror of Britain?*

6 ⬧ *Who were the first Christian missionaries?*

7 ⬧ *What was the first canonical Gospel to be written?*

8 ⬧ *When was the first recorded eruption of Mount Vesuvius?*

1 ∽ Who was the first Roman emperor?

Gaius Julius Caesar Octavianus, aka Augustus
(reigned 27 BC–AD 14)

LONG BEFORE THEY HAD AN EMPEROR, the ancient Romans had an empire. Beginning with Sicily, Sardinia, Corsica, and Spain, all wrested from Carthage in the third century BC, the Roman republic had strung together an imperial bastion of overseas possessions. By the time Octavian seized sole control of the Roman world by defeating his former ruling partner Mark Antony at the naval battle of Actium in 31 BC, the legions sent out from the Eternal City on the Tiber had conquered territories comprising most of Western Europe and great swaths of northern Africa, the Balkans, Turkey, Syria, and Judea. In the following year, Octavian converted the late Cleopatra's massively wealthy Egyptian kingdom into just another province of Rome.

After several generations of butchery in the successive civil wars between Marius and Sulla, Caesar and Pompey, the assassins of Julius Caesar (led by Brutus and Cassius) and the avengers of Caesar (led by Octavian and Mark Antony), and, finally, between Octavian and Antony, the Roman world was ready for peace and unity at just about any price. It received them from a cagey young man, handsome and intelligent but sickly and not overly courageous, who had the fortune of being Julius Caesar's great-nephew, adoptive son, and chief heir.

Caesar had been king of Rome in all but name, and that's why, in 44 BC, he was murdered at a meeting of the senate. Having thrown out their last king more than four centuries earlier, the Romans were fiercely proud of their republic presided over by magistrates elected for one-year terms. Not only had Caesar had himself declared dictator for life, he also affected an un-Roman monarchical demeanor with his purple robes, scorn for the senate, and godlike haughtiness. The Roman nobles feared Caesar, but they hated him even more.

The lesson was not lost on young Octavian (63 BC–AD 14). He graciously accepted from the senate the honorific *Augustus* ("revered, majestic, worthy of awe") on January 13, 27 BC, when, in a staged little drama, he offered to resign the extraordinary powers he had exercised since Caesar's death, and the senate made him a counteroffer he couldn't

3

refuse. But there would be no regal pretensions in the public manner or official status of Augustus. He was content to be *princeps civitatis*—first citizen—and *princeps senatus*—leader of the senate (hence the English term *Principate* for his regime). Meanwhile, he was lavished concurrently with the key offices of the old Roman constitution—consul, proconsul, tribune—which guaranteed his control of the civil government while fostering the illusion that he had restored the republic by acting only as a senior colleague of its traditional political leaders.

But Augustus's main basis of power, as commander in chief of Rome's armies, derived from his being proclaimed *imperator*, the origin of our word *emperor*. An *imperator* was, at first, a Roman military commander—the general of an army. Then the word was applied to a general who had been acclaimed by his soldiers after a victory and to a proconsul who held the military command of a province. But the power of an *imperator* was always meant to be limited in time and place.

When the senate eventually created Augustus *imperator* over the entire empire and for life, prefixing the title to his name, it officially sanctioned his control over all the military forces and foreign possessions of Rome, and this is why historians consider him the first Roman emperor. Subsequent emperors were invested with the same title, which required the armies of Rome to swear allegiance to them personally rather than to the state.

Vested with overall command of the Roman army, navy, provinces, and a large personal army guard, the Praetorians, Augustus convened the senate and initiated legislation that it rubber-stamped. He made and unmade senators, he handpicked cronies to govern the most critical territories of the empire in his name, and he deprived the popular assemblies of their legislative or veto powers. The old majestic formula for the twin pillars of the Roman state—*senatus populusque Romanus*, the Roman senate and people—had become a sham.

Though crafty and manipulative, Augustus, "that subtle tyrant" in Edward Gibbon's phrase, was ruthless during his reign only when he had to be, preferring to overlook petty affronts. He ruled the Roman Empire for more than forty years, during which he ushered in the era of peace known as the *pax Romana*, promoted family values (though failing signally with his own debauched daughter and granddaughter), and patronized the best writers of Rome's Golden Age. Virgil's *Aeneid*, Horace's patriotic odes, and Livy's epic history of Rome glorified the ancient Roman military and moral virtues that Augustus was attempting to resurrect. (No paragon of virtue himself, the Revered One and Father of His Country was addicted to women and dice.) His massive building program led him to boast that he had found Rome a city of brick and left it a city of marble. For his own dwelling, he chose a site above the ancient sanctuary where Rome's founders, Romulus and Remus, had supposedly been suckled by a she-wolf on the Palatine Hill. Augustus's residence was thus called the Palatium—the source of our word *palace.*

The emperor's last years were clouded by a catastrophic Roman defeat under the inept governor Varus in Germany, in which three legions—more than twenty thousand men—were cut down in AD 9. Augustus would bang his head against a door and shout, "Quinctilius Varus, give me back my legions!" After a favorite nephew and two grandsons died young, he reconciled himself to bequeathing his position—and Rome's twenty-five legions—to his stepson and adopted son Tiberius who, though a capable general and administrator, had always struck the emperor as too proudly aloof, morose, and temperamental to continue the Augustan constitutional charade. But Tiberius went on to have a long reign of his own (AD 14–37), and the sometimes admirable, sometimes deranged men known as Roman emperors succeeded to the throne until 476 in the Western Empire and 1453 in the Eastern or Byzantine Empire, besides inspiring Russian czars, German kaisers, and even an Italian ex-socialist known as *il Duce.*

In the account he himself wrote of his remarkable career, which was engraved on two bronze pillars in Rome and carved in stone throughout the empire, Augustus sometimes blusters like Shelley's Ozymandias: "In my triumphs there were led before my chariot nine kings or children of kings" and "Twenty-six times I provided for the people . . . hunting spectacles of African wild beasts . . . ; in these exhibitions about three thousand five hundred animals were killed." He also can't resist one final iteration of the big lie at the center of his administration: "After that time I excelled all in authority, but I possessed no more power than the others who were my colleagues in each magistracy."

The first, greatest, and longest-reigning of all the Roman emperors died in his mid-seventies in AD 14, in the month that had been renamed August in his honor, and he was promptly deified by the compliant senate. On his deathbed, he summoned his friends and, in the tradition of comic actors, asked for their applause if they thought he had played his part well in the farce of life.

Did the hypocritical role assumed by this political actor fool anyone? It all depends on your definition of *fool*. Roman aristocrats realized they could prosper by administering Rome and the empire in Augustus's name if they just threw a little sycophancy into their lives. The chief writers of the time obtained funds and farms from Augustus's cultural minister Maecenas, whose name has become synonymous with enlightened patronage. The soldiers got bonuses, while the common people got cheap food and gladiatorial games. And in those far-off days of children being seen and not heard, not one of them had ever dared shout out, "But the emperor has no clothes!"

2   What was the first poetic handbook of Greek mythology?

Ovid's Metamorphoses, *completed c. AD 8,*
one of the most influential books of all time

JUST BEFORE HIS BANISHMENT TO FRIGID, semibarbarous Tomis on the Black Sea coast by Caesar Augustus in AD 8 for an offense that may have involved the emperor's slutty granddaughter Julia as well as a sexy earlier work—a tongue-in-cheek seduction manual called *The Art of Love*—the Roman poet Ovid completed his *Metamorphoses*, a Latin poem of nearly twelve thousand hexameter lines. This treasure trove of Greek myths is thematically unified by the miraculous transformation of humans into beasts, birds, trees, plants, rocks, bodies of water, and even heavenly bodies.

Publius Ovidius Naso (43 BC–AD 17/18) set out to write a different kind of epic from the martial sagas of Homer and Virgil. His aim was to collect the most important Greek myths into a single narrative with the leitmotif that all is constant flux in the universe. The artistic problem was to keep the momentum going over a sprawling and varied terrain, which Ovid solved by weaving myths into other myths and quoting speakers who quote other speakers in a kaleidoscopic orgy of narration that never degenerates into a shaggy-dog story.

Ovid recounts about fifty myths in detail, such as that of Narcissus, who falls in love with his reflection in a pool while ignoring the proffered love of Echo (who pines away until only her voice remains), and the tales of the famous lovers Hero and Leander, Venus and Adonis, and Orpheus and Eurydice. The myth of Daphne, changed into a laurel tree to save her from rape by Phoebus Apollo, inspired one of Bernini's marble masterpieces, besides countless literary retellings. In some pruriently macabre lines from the tale, Ovid dramatizes the frustrated erotic desire of Apollo, the original tree hugger:

> *But Phoebus loves her even as a tree—placing his hand*
> *on the trunk, he feels a heartbeat beneath the bark,*
> *and taking the branches in his arms, as if they were human limbs,*
> *he kisses the tree, but the tree rejects his kisses.*

An immensely popular school text for teaching Latin and the myths at the heart of Western culture, the *Metamorphoses* became the secular bible of artists like Dante, Chaucer, Titian, Shakespeare, John Milton, and Ezra Pound. The 1567 translation of the poem into heptameter couplets by Arthur Golding, often referred to as "Shakespeare's Ovid," inspired the Bard's narrative poem *Venus and Adonis*, as well as the farcical playlet enacted by Peter Quince and his "rude mechanicals"— *The most lamentable comedy, and most cruel death of Pyramus and Thisby*—that provides *A Midsummer Night's Dream* with some uproarious humor. More recent manifestations of the book's perpetual appeal are the partial translation by Ted Hughes, *Tales from Ovid* (1997), and the dramatic adaptation, *Metamorphoses*, written and directed by Mary Zimmerman, through which Ovid made a big splash on Broadway in 2002 in a ninety-minute play staged around and in a large pool of water.

As far back as c. 700 BC, the Greek poet Hesiod had assembled myths on the genealogy of the gods in his *Theogony*. Ovid took his cue, however, from the Alexandrian Greek scholar-poet Callimachus (third century BC) who, in a long poem now almost entirely lost, the *Aetia* (*Causes* or *Origins*), explained certain cultural practices of his day by searching Greek history and legend for their ultimate explanations.

Ovid's more ambitious aim was to collect all the most noteworthy Greek myths and a number of Roman ones into a single narrative proceeding from the creation of the world to the transformation of the deified Julius Caesar into a star. In this poetic world, humans were often mere playthings of the gods. Did the hunter Actaeon, for example, do anything wrong when he stumbled on the goddess Diana stark naked in her bath deep in the woods? If not, why did she change him into a stag so that his own hounds would rip him apart?

The worldly-wise poet's main concern wasn't theological, however, since he believed in none of the old divinities, but psychological. He wanted to delineate the myriad ways that passion can lead to self-destructive behavior. Not all passion in Ovid is sexual. There is the fatal passion of the young Phaëthon to drive the heavenly chariot of his father, Apollo the sun god. In a similar tale, the boy Icarus forgets his father Daedalus's instructions about how to fly safely with wings of feathers and wax, plummeting into the sea after soaring too close to the sun. The tender tale of the hospitable old married couple, Philemon and Baucis, whose passion was to die at the same moment, ends with their being changed by the gods into an oak and a linden tree growing from a double trunk.

Another major theme of Ovid's book is that of hubris punished when mortals or lesser divinities offend the Olympian gods by daring to compete with them. Consider the sorry case of Marsyas, the satyr who thinks his piping sounds much better than Apollo's, thereby earning the punishment of being flayed alive—the subject of a gruesome canvas by Titian. Then there's Arachne, who boasts that she can weave better than Athena, the goddess of handicrafts. When Athena examines the girl's awesome work, she boxes her ears in a fit of envious rage, driving the desperate young woman to hang herself. In a questionable gesture of pity, Athena changes Arachne into a spider—the first arachnid ever and still a world-class weaver. Queen Niobe can't understand why her people worship the goddess Latona, mother of only Apollo and Diana, whereas she herself is the mother of *seven* handsome sons and as many lovely daughters. The reward for her presumption is to see her entire brood shot to death by the arrows of the divine siblings and to suffer transformation into a woman-shaped rock that still exudes moisture as if weeping tears of grief.

Though most of the love stories in the *Metamorphoses* feature heterosexuals, Ovid clearly relished those dealing with alternative lifestyles, such as the strange tale of Tiresias, who starts out a man, is changed into a sexually active woman for seven years, is changed back into a man—and vouches that sex is more enjoyable for women. Iphis, a girl who grows up as a boy, is transformed into a man so that she can marry the woman she loves. Caenis, raped by Neptune, begs to be changed into a man and becomes the warrior Caeneus. We also find in Ovid's poem the original hermaphrodite (Hermaphroditus, who is joined, literally, with the water nymph Salmacis); incest (Byblis falls in love with her brother, Myrrha with her father); pederasty (Jupiter's love for Ganymede, Apollo's for Hyacinthus); fetishism (the sculptor Pygmalion falls in love with his beautiful statue); and even bestiality (centaurs attempt to rape women; Queen Pasiphaë mates with a bull and gives birth to the monstrous Minotaur). With heady cocktails like these served up via the vivid storytelling that characterizes the poem, is it any wonder the *Metamorphoses* has been read avidly (and sometimes surreptitiously) for the past two thousand years?

3 ∾ Who was the first Roman emperor to be assassinated?

Caligula, the first certifiably insane Roman emperor, in January of AD 41

ALTHOUGH CALIGULA WAS THE GREAT-GRANDSON of both Emperor Augustus and Mark Antony, you'd never suspect it. This deranged young man became the third Roman emperor in AD 37 as the heir of his great-uncle and adoptive grandfather, Tiberius, but his numerous "behavior issues" guaranteed he wouldn't grow old in the job.

His real first name was Gaius, but as a child he acquired the nickname Caligula ("Little Boots") while growing up in army camps with his father, the great general Germanicus, who used to dress him up like a soldier, complete with the *caliga*, a military half boot. Tiberius was jealous of Germanicus, and when the famous general died young, perhaps of poisoning, many in Rome believed the emperor was behind it. Although there was no evidence for this, Tiberius certainly went on to dispatch Caligula's mother and two brothers, and he severely mistreated the young man himself, too.

Is it implausible that when the seventy-seven-year-old Tiberius lay on his deathbed in March of 37, Caligula was suspected of having administered a slow poison? Or of having refused him food after he woke up from a feverish coma? Or of having throttled him to death with his bare hands? In the version of the historian Tacitus, the sick old emperor had seemed to die, but when he inconsiderately woke up again, Macro, the commander of the Praetorian Guard, who was in cahoots with Caligula, ordered him to be smothered with his bed-clothes. While the truth may never be known, Caligula's presumed involvement might be viewed less as an assassination than as a way that an infirm Tiberius may have been "helped to die" in an ancient Roman version of euthanasia. Similar rumors had circulated about the death of Augustus, too, but there is no doubt that Caligula himself was the first Roman emperor to be openly murdered.

But what had Little Boots done to deserve it? The historian Sueto-nius says there was great rejoicing at his accession and that 160,000 animals were sacrificed in the first three months of his reign to help kick things off in grand style. Nonetheless, in addition to killing off a young cousin, who was also his joint heir, Caligula had a disquieting penchant for attending public executions, at which he might be heard bidding the officers in charge, "Make him *feel* that he's dying!" He held treason trials and apparently had men sawn in half. Once, when the people cheered the wrong team in the arena, he cried out that he wished they all had just one neck so that he could cut it off with one stroke. In a single year, he also managed to run through the bulging treasury that stingy Tiberius had left him.

Sexually omnivorous, Caligula committed incest with all three of his sisters. After debauching the wife of his henchman Macro, he ordered him to commit suicide. In fact, he compulsively borrowed other men's wives, sometimes even at their weddings, and then publicly critiqued the women's good and bad physical points and their sexual performances. Among the many men he had sex with was his brother-in-law, whom he later ordered to be killed.

Caligula disgraced his lofty office by appearing in public as an ath-lete and a performing artist (though perhaps he's to be commended for beating with his own hands anyone who talked during plays). He was so jealous of the fame of others—even dead writers—that he wanted to have the works and busts of Virgil and Livy banned from libraries. He planned to make his beloved horse, Incitatus, a consul of Rome. Even-tually he demanded to be worshipped as a god, setting up in his shrine his life-size golden statue, which was dressed exactly like his tall, pale, and spindly self every day. The least bad thing he seems to have done is a bit of cultural plundering in bringing an old Egyptian obelisk to Rome. (Now owned by the pope, it's the one in front of St. Peter's Basilica.)

Besides his obvious insanity, Caligula also suffered from severe epilepsy and incapacitating insomnia. After a little less than four years of him, some officers of his own guard and several Roman senators decided he had to go. One of the emperor's final provocations took place when he ordered a young actress to be tortured. A tribune of the Praetorian Guard, Cassius Chaerea, whom Caligula used to torment for his supposed effeminacy with obscene taunts and gestures, had to oversee the process and was disgusted by the woman's ordeal.

On January 24 of 41, when Caligula took advantage of an intermission in the day's theatricals to go wash up and have lunch, the conspirators were ready. As he stopped in a secluded corridor to chat with a song-and-dance troupe of foreign boys who were rehearsing, Chaerea stabbed him in the neck. When he fell to the ground, another Praetorian tribune, Cornelius Sabinus, plunged his sword into the twenty-eight-year-old emperor, followed by a number of other assassins. A centurion of the guard then swept through the palace, killing Caligula's fourth wife, Caesonia, and dashing their infant daughter's brains out against a wall. This first assassination of a Roman emperor by an army conspiracy, justified as it might have seemed to those behind it, established the precedent for numerous later military coups that eventually eroded the fabric of imperial government.

In the twentieth century, Caligula lent his name and notoriety to artistic creations as diverse as a play by the existentialist philosopher Albert Camus and a fancy porn flick by Bob Guccione of *Penthouse* fame. The main problem in evaluating Caligula is that almost all we know of him is derived from hostile ancient sources. Still, there must have been a kernel of horrific truth to the accusations if his reign became so indelibly associated with so many nasty episodes.

4 ∾ Who was the first pope?

St. Peter, considered by Catholics the first bishop of Rome,
AD 42–67

THE MAN WHO STARTED OUT LIFE as Shim'on Bar Yonah ("Simon Son of Jonah") was a fisherman living at Capernaum on the Sea of Galilee when he became a disciple of John the Baptist. His brother Andrew, a fellow fisherman and follower of the Baptist, led him to Jesus, who summoned the pair, his first apostles, to become instead "fishers of men."

We know that Simon was a married man and that, with James the Greater and John, he formed part of an inner circle among the twelve apostles of Jesus, being present at certain crucial events described in the Gospels. But his leadership of the group was firmly established when he became the first to assert that Jesus was the Messiah and the Son of God. In recognition, Jesus gave Simon a new name and some rather serious responsibilities:

> . . . you are Peter, and upon this rock I will build my
> church. . . . I will give you the keys to the kingdom of heaven.
> Whatever you bind on earth shall be bound in heaven; and
> whatever you loose on earth shall be loosed in heaven
> (Matthew 16:18–19).

In the Greek of the New Testament, the name translated as Peter is Petros, which means *rock*, corresponding to an original Aramaic word *kepa* with the same meaning, which Jesus presumably used in his own native language. (In fact, Peter is often referred to as *Kephas* or *Cephas* in the epistles of St. Paul.) And so the primacy of Peter in the Christian church, at least in the Roman Catholic view, is founded on a pun, that is, "You are now to be called Rock, and upon this rock I will build my church." But what did Jesus mean by the name change and the symbolism of the keys? Catholics claim that the absolute leadership and ultimate authority of the church were thus vested in Peter—and also in his successors as bishops of Rome, the popes.

But let's take a closer look at the man himself as presented in the New Testament. For someone whose name appears first in all four lists of the apostles recorded there, Peter sometimes comes across as a bit too impulsive, lazy, and cowardly to be a leader. When he sees Jesus walking on the water toward his boat, he tries to go meet him but panics when he starts sinking beneath the waves. At another time Jesus calls him Satan after Peter rebuked him for prophesying his passion and death. Peter was also one of the three apostles who couldn't keep his eyes open while Jesus went off to pray in agony in the Garden of Gethsemane. Jesus was particularly disappointed with him on that occasion, sadly reflecting that "the spirit is willing, but the flesh is weak." As a crowning indignity, Peter denies Christ three times "before the cock crows," but at least he goes off to weep in bitter remorse.

On the other hand, Peter makes a stout attempt to prevent Jesus' arrest when he draws his sword and cuts off a fellow's ear. After Jesus' death, he was the first to preach to the Gentiles, converting and baptizing the Roman centurion Cornelius and his household. After being thrown in prison by King Herod Agrippa I of Judea, he is said to have been miraculously released from his chains by an angel. The Scriptures even claim that Peter raised a woman named Tabitha from the dead. Two letters of the New Testament are traditionally attributed to Peter, but they're almost certainly not by him.

Although it's unknown exactly when and how Christianity first came to Rome, it must have antedated Paul's letter to the Romans (c. AD 56–58). We also learn from Suetonius's *Lives of the Caesars* that Emperor Claudius expelled Jews from Rome in 49 for making a ruckus over "Chrestus." Roman Catholic tradition claims Peter may have first visited Rome as early as AD 42 and established the Christian community there (thus acquiring the title of bishop, which at first meant "overseer"), though others say he arrived in the mid to late 50s, in 63—or perhaps even never.

Tradition maintains that Peter was executed on Rome's Vatican Hill in AD 67 (or 64) during a persecution of Christians under Nero, occasioned by the emperor's need of scapegoats to counter the unfounded rumor that he himself had set the great fire of Rome in July 64. While some Christians were ripped apart by dogs or coated with pitch to serve as human torches, others, like Peter, were nailed to crosses. Peter supposedly asked to be crucified head downward because he felt himself unworthy to die in the same way as Jesus. The Romans were also said to have beheaded St. Paul at approximately the same time, and thus the two martyrs share a feast day on June 29. What is called St. Peter's tomb may still be seen beneath the high altar in St. Peter's Basilica in Rome, and in 1968 Pope Paul VI announced, not without controversy, that the saint's relics had been discovered.

But how did we get from the simple fisherman of Galilee, whose master had said, "My kingdom is not of this world," to the pomp and majesty of latter-day popes who, as late as 1963, were crowned with the triple tiara and among whose titles are archbishop and metropolitan of the Roman province, primate of Italy, and patriarch of the West? Whereas other important early Christian centers could claim only one or another apostolic founder, Rome could point to Peter and Paul, the two towering figures of the nascent church. In time, the bishops of Rome (which was, after all, the capital of the Western world) came to regard themselves as supreme over all other bishops. This view was often resisted by other prelates, and fierce wars of words broke out, as in the mid-third century when Cyprian, bishop of Carthage, refused to accept the claim of Pope Stephen I that, as bishop of Rome, his authority was preeminent.

This claim was repeatedly articulated by Pope Leo I (440–61), who maintained that the leadership of the church had devolved from St. Peter to all later bishops of Rome. With the demise of the Western Roman Empire, papal authority in Rome increased, and popes began assuming the title of *pontifex maximus* ("supreme pontiff"), which had belonged to the chief priest of the old Roman pagan religion and was held by the likes of Julius Caesar, Augustus, and subsequent Roman emperors (whereas *pope* originally meant simply "father").

Pope Gregory I (590–604) established the medieval papacy as the hub of Christian authority, and Pope Boniface III in 607 was recognized as the one and only "Universal Bishop" by Byzantine emperor Phocas, reinforcing the view of Emperor Justinian eighty years earlier. When Pope Gregory II renounced his allegiance to the Byzantine emperor in 731, ending almost two centuries of nominal rule by a viceroy from Constantinople, the pope became ruler of Rome in name as well as in fact, and before the end of the century the papacy acquired vast holdings in Italy and military protection from Pépin and Charlemagne. With the death in 1115 of Countess Matilda of Tuscany, who left her lands to the church, the Patrimony of St. Peter was further enlarged.

In the later Middle Ages, popes like Innocent III (1198–1216) were powerful monarchs who enforced their will on Christendom by excommunicating recalcitrant individuals, declaring crusades against heretical groups, deposing disobedient rulers, and placing entire nations under interdict, depriving them of the sacraments. In the person of Pope Julius II (1503–13), Europe witnessed the vicar of the Prince of Peace leading his troops into battle on horseback to enlarge his papal kingdom, which was very much of this world. It was only in the nineteenth century that the pope lost his extensive Italian territories (known as the Papal States) and finally the city of Rome itself, though even today he remains absolute sovereign of Vatican City, the smallest independent state, as well as spiritual leader of the world's one billion Catholics.

5 ∾ Who was the first known conqueror of Britain?

Roman emperor Claudius, who believed in delegating, in AD 43

CLAUDIUS WAS THE MOST UNLIKELY CONQUEROR of anything. Perhaps afflicted with cerebral palsy, he went through life with the pathetic stammering, twitching, shuffling, and snorting that Derek Jacobi brought to the title role in the televised version of Robert Graves's *I, Claudius*. Long treated as the imperial family idiot, Claudius was actually an eccentrically pedantic scholar who, among other lost literary labors, such as an autobiography and a book on gambling, wrote histories of the Etruscans and the Carthaginians in Greek. After the murder of his nephew Caligula, the Praetorian Guards found the fifty-year-old Claudius cowering behind a curtain in the palace and acclaimed him emperor. After some resistance, the senate, which was considering restoring the republic, went along with the army's fait accompli.

Julius Caesar had been the first Roman to invade Celtic Britain, in 55 BC, and then again, in greater force, the following year, but these brief expeditions to the so-called ends of the earth were mainly undertaken to impress the folks back home, grab some booty, and deter the Britons from coming to the aid of their fellow Celts in Gaul, which Caesar was subduing. In AD 43, almost exactly a century later, Claudius decided it was time for Britain to join the empire.

Under the pretense of aiding a southern British king, Bericus (or Verica), who had been driven from the island by the dominant Catuvellauni tribe and taken refuge in Rome, Claudius moved four legions and their auxiliary troops—forty thousand men—to Britain under the command of Aulus Plautius. The actual casus belli was a desire to protect Roman Gaul from Celtic inroads from across the Channel, mingled with the ambition of Claudius to be seen in the same light as some of his more martial ancestors. The Roman army landed in Kent and pushed past the Medway to the Thames, meeting with some resistance on the way.

Within three months Plautius assured the emperor that the coast was clear, so Claudius headed for Britain, arriving in time to enter the enemy capital riding a war elephant. After spending all of sixteen days in Britain, he decided his work there was done—which was essentially showing his face in the war zone and receiving the formal surrender of eleven local tribes so that he could qualify for a triumphal procession in Rome. With the Catuvellauni duly defeated and their capital captured (where Claudius later had a temple built to himself), he declared the mission accomplished and moved on, though his army stayed behind. On his return to Italy from Britain, he celebrated by sailing through the harbor of Ravenna in a kind of vast floating palace and was hailed by the senate as "Britannicus." Within a few years, Rome extended its grasp to more than half of the island, and the Roman province of Britannia was born.

Back in Rome, Claudius, who was not devoid of cruelty and sadism, had his depraved third wife Messalina executed in 48. During his fourth and final marriage, to his own niece Agrippina, the aging and ailing emperor became increasingly uxorious. He died at age sixty-three on October 13, AD 54, perhaps from gobbling up a poisoned dish of his favorite food, mushrooms, served by his wife. Her motive was to secure the succession for her son, Nero, instead of Claudius's son (named, of course, Britannicus), who was predictably poisoned early in the next reign. The philosopher Seneca, whom Claudius had banished to Corsica for eight years, wrote a nasty squib on the dead emperor in which he is denied admission to Mount Olympus based on the hostile testimony of his step-grandfather Augustus.

In 60, during Nero's reign, Boudicca, queen of the British Iceni, led a rebellion against Rome after her people had been brutally treated, she had been flogged, and her two daughters raped by the conquerors. Plundering and razing the Roman settlements later known as Saint Albans and Colchester, not to mention the business center of Londinium, her forces massacred seventy thousand of the inhabitants and defeated the Romans in battle on numerous occasions. When her huge army was finally obliterated, she poisoned herself to avoid capture. Within about forty years of Claudius's invasion, by c. AD 84, Roman power was fully established in Britain after the victories of the general Agricola in the north and west.

Following several major attempts at conquest, over scores of years, the Romans decided that the wild Caledonians of what we call Scotland were better left to their own outlandish ways, and they never even bothered with Ireland. Much of Britannia (basically modern England and Wales) settled into a peaceful and prosperous urban-and-villa way of life based on the exportation of grain, tin, hides, pearls, and slaves. The Romans planted numerous cities and towns on the island, including the fashionable hot-springs resort of Aquae Sulis (Bath), and dug a splendid system of roads fanning out from London.

After about 350 years, Roman legions began pulling out of Britain to deal with barbarian onslaughts closer to home. In 410 Emperor Honorius officially urged the British to fend for themselves, leaving a power vacuum on the island that marauding Germanic tribes were quick to fill. It's believed that the fanciful tales of King Arthur may have originated in the actual struggles of a late-fifth-century Romano-Celtic military leader against the new wave of invaders.

6 ∿ Who were the first Christian missionaries?

St. Barnabas and St. Paul, who journeyed to Cyprus and Asia Minor in c. AD 45

IF WE THINK OF A MISSIONARY in its original meaning as someone who is *sent*, St. Barnabas would qualify as the first Christian missionary. When a Christian community had been founded in Antioch, Syria, by those fleeing persecution in Jerusalem after the stoning in c. AD 36 of St. Stephen, the first martyr, church leaders decided to strengthen the proselytizing efforts there by sending Barnabas. When he arrived in Antioch and saw the progress being made, he went to Tarsus to look for his friend Saul to help him out, and the two spent a year preaching in Antioch (c. AD 43), where, a few years earlier, the followers of Jesus had been dubbed *Christians* for the first time anywhere.

Barnabas was soon overshadowed as a missionary by his colleague, better known as St. Paul. Born with the Hebrew name of Saul and the Greco-Roman name of Paul in Tarsus, a city of Cilicia in Asia Minor, he was educated in Jerusalem and adhered to the strict Pharisee sect. The story of his conversion, sometime after AD 36–37 while he was on the road to Damascus to persecute Christians, is told three times in St. Luke's Acts of the Apostles. In each, he is thrown to the ground at the sight of an intense light and hears the voice of Jesus saying, "Saul, Saul, why are you persecuting me?" Though Paul subsequently did much of his preaching in synagogues, including those of Damascus, he came to see his mission as a God-appointed one to extend the message of Jesus to non-Jews, thus earning the appellation "Apostle to the Gentiles."

As such, he undertook, with various companions, three main missionary journeys through Asia Minor (modern Turkey), Macedonia, and Greece, establishing Christian communities in urban centers of the Greek-speaking Roman world. On the first journey, from c. 45 to 49, Paul and Barnabas are sent forth by the "prophets and teachers" of the church in Antioch, who are said to be inspired by the Holy Spirit to do so. After sailing from a seaport near Antioch, the pair arrive in Cyprus, Barnabas's native land. They preach only in synagogues, although Paul manages to convert the Roman proconsul Sergius Paulus.

When Paul and Barnabas eventually arrive at the city known as Pisidian Antioch in the interior of Asia Minor, Paul speaks of Jesus as the Messiah in the synagogue, and at first all goes well. On the following Sabbath, however, some of the Jews are angered by the crowds of Gentiles who turn out to hear Paul and Barnabas, so they drive the missionaries from the city. It's here that the pair decide to concentrate on preaching to the Gentiles, though at their next stop, Iconium, they speak in the synagogue and make many converts among both Jews and Gentiles, but they are ultimately driven out with a threat of stoning. In the nearby city of Lystra, after Paul heals a lame man, the Gentile crowds start calling him "Hermes" and Barnabas "Zeus" and attempt to offer animal sacrifices to them—which goes to show some of the dangers of preaching to pagan idol-worshippers. Meanwhile, some of Paul's enemies arrive from the other cities he had visited, and this time they do manage to stone him, leaving him for dead. After better successes elsewhere in Asia Minor, Paul and Barnabas retrace their steps to encourage the newborn Christian communities and then return to Syrian Antioch.

The two attend the so-called Council of Jerusalem (c. 48–49), where it's decided that neither circumcision nor Mosaic ritual laws should be imposed on Gentile converts to Christianity, beyond a few simple dietary and intermarriage prohibitions. Paul and Barnabas then quarrel over the competence of an assistant, John Mark, and go their separate ways with different companions.

On Paul's second missionary journey (c. 49–52), undertaken with Silas and later also with Timothy, he first revisits the Christian communities he and Barnabas had established and then moves into Macedonia, where, in Philippi, he founds the first Christian community in Europe (though there may already have been Christians in Rome at this time). He and Silas are beaten with rods by the Roman authorities in Philippi but released soon after their arrest when they're found to be Roman citizens. Paul makes many converts in the Macedonian city of Thessalonica but eventually has to flee to Athens, where he gives a speech mentioning the resurrection of the dead, at which some of the skeptical Athenians burst into laughter, though a few of them believe. After moving on to the Greek city of Corinth, where we discover that Paul's trade was that of a tent maker, he founds a church and then heads back to Jerusalem and Syrian Antioch.

Paul's third journey (53–58) takes him westward through the interior of Asia Minor until he reaches the coastal city of Ephesus, where he spends more than two years. It's here that the silversmiths of the town, which housed a temple of Artemis that was one of the seven wonders of the ancient world, stage a riot, because Paul's new teachings are ruining their business of making miniature silver shrines of the goddess. "Great is Artemis of the Ephesians!" they shout in all their unionized fury, but the town clerk finally manages to calm them down.

Paul decides it's high time to leave Ephesus, and after further adventures (including raising from the dead a boy who had fallen from a third-story window, tired of hearing Paul drone on all night), he arrives back in Jerusalem, where he encounters outraged Jews who claim he is undermining their religious practices. The remainder of Paul's story, as told in Acts of the Apostles, consists of arrests, trials, speeches, murderous plots, ingenious countermoves, an accusation that he is "a perfect pest," and various imprisonments. As a Roman citizen, Paul finally appeals to the emperor, who happens to be Nero.

And so, in the autumn of 60, Paul sets out for the imperial capital under Roman guard, but a storm at sea shipwrecks them on the island of Malta, where they pass the winter. Once in Rome, he spends two years under a lenient house arrest that allows him to preach to those who come to listen. Then he seems to have been set free to resume his travels, possibly even to Spain, but he is subsequently rearrested and again sent to Rome, where he is beheaded, perhaps in AD 67, during the same Christian persecution in the reign of Nero that ended the life of St. Peter.

Of the thirteen epistles attributed to Paul in the New Testament, almost half have been questioned as of doubtful authorship, but his major authentic works—such as his letter to the Romans and the two to the Corinthians—are significant for having been written before any of the canonical Gospels. As such, they preserve aspects of the Christian message that are prior to the four evangelists' accounts of the life and teachings of Jesus.

In the end, what are we to make of this learned Jewish convert who could quote the Greek poets, this dynamo of zeal who established and nurtured churches in major centers of the Roman Empire and who has been called the first Christian theologian? His fluent Greek epistles reveal him to be boastful, garrulous, self-important, obsessive, much too hard on fornicators, waspish against foes and rivals (though a loving friend), and a busybody of titanic proportions. He himself admits that he was not a trained speaker or physically strong or impressive, but listen to the litany of sufferings he endured for his faith (2 Corinthians 11:24–27):

> Five times at the hands of the Jews I received forty lashes
> minus one. Three times I was beaten with rods, once I was
> stoned, three times I was shipwrecked, I passed a night and a
> day on the deep; on frequent journeys, in dangers from rivers,
> dangers from robbers, dangers from my own race, dangers
> from Gentiles, dangers in the city, dangers in the wilderness,
> dangers at sea, dangers among false brothers; in toil and hard-
> ship, through many sleepless nights, through hunger and thirst,
> through frequent fastings, through cold and exposure.

In addition to his paean to love (1 Corinthians 13), which, despite being mouthed at countless exchangings of all-too-transient nuptial vows, still retains its sublimity unsullied—

> If I speak in human and angelic tongues, but do not have love,
> I am a resounding gong or a clashing cymbal. . . . If I have
> faith so as to move mountains, but do not have love, I am
> nothing. . . . Love is patient, love is kind. . . . It does not seek
> its own interests, . . . it does not brood over injury. . . . It bears
> all things, believes all things, hopes all things, endures all
> things. Love never fails. . . . So faith, hope, love remain, these
> three; but the greatest of these is love—

we also have Paul to thank for a pithy summation of a life worthily lived that only a fortunate few are able to claim on their deathbed: "I have fought the good fight, I have run the good race, I have kept the faith."

7 ∾ What was the first canonical Gospel to be written?

The Gospel of Mark, c. AD 65–75, the shortest of the four

THE LIFE OF JESUS has been called the greatest story ever told, and the Gospel of Mark is the first surviving account of it. Like the rest of the New Testament, it was written in Greek, and it was probably composed shortly before or after AD 70. Mark's text antedates the other three canonical Gospels, serving as the major source for those of Matthew and Luke and forming with them the so-called synoptics ("taken in at one view"), while John's Gospel, the latest to be written (c. 90–100), was based on different sources.

Although traditions identify the author of Mark's Gospel as an associate of St. Peter or as the John Mark whose lackadaisical attitude toward missionary work had angered St. Paul, we really don't know who wrote any of the Gospels. Mark's narrative may have been based on oral traditions about Jesus and perhaps a written record of his miracles. It appears to be addressed to Gentile Christians who were being persecuted, perhaps in Rome. Unlike the later Gospels, Mark's omits much of what we tend to associate with the life and teachings of Jesus—his birth, the Lord's Prayer, the Sermon on the Mount, and the Beatitudes—and its naive, spare, and primitive stories sometimes jar with the more familiar accounts of the other three evangelists.

For example, in the Gospel of Mark we discover a Jesus whose own relatives "set out to seize him, for they said, 'He is out of his mind'" (3:21). Despite the much later Catholic doctrine of Mary's perpetual virginity, Jesus is said to have four brothers and at least two sisters, though attempts have been made to see these as cousins or half siblings. And while the "Son of Man," as Jesus mysteriously calls himself, is acknowledged by Mark to be both the Messiah and the Son of God, he is also presented as a human being with very human emotions.

In addition, Mark's Gospel is eerily pervaded by malignant spirits; as in *Macbeth*, evil is everywhere, and Satan makes an early entrance in verse thirteen of chapter one to tempt Jesus in the desert. When Jesus begins preaching in his homeland of Galilee, he barely has time to announce his message of repentance and call his first disciples before he must exorcise a demon from a man in the synagogue of Capernaum. Mark even has the demon acknowledge Jesus as the Messiah, calling him "the Holy One of God." That same evening, Jesus is swarmed by "all who were ill or possessed by demons," and he duly cures them and also casts out "many devils." At one point, some scribes from Jerusalem think Jesus himself "is possessed of Beelzebub" and claim that "by the prince of demons he drives out demons." One unfortunate man is possessed by such a multitude of unclean spirits that they give their name as "Legion." After Jesus casts them out into a herd of swine (at their own request), about two thousand of the animals barrel down a steep bank and are drowned in the sea. When Jesus cures a boy whose symptoms we recognize as epilepsy, Mark has Jesus attribute the boy's condition to possession by a particularly stubborn demon.

Jesus' powers are presented somewhat inconsistently in the Gospel. While he is curing a paralytic, he is able to read the minds of hostile spectators, yet later, when a woman who has been hemorrhaging for a dozen years comes up behind him to touch his cloak, he realizes it only when he feels that "power had gone out from him," and he asks who did it. At one point, when Jesus is hungry and wants to eat some figs, he doesn't know beforehand that the tree has no fruit on it (or even that it isn't the season for figs), and he then curses it with barrenness.

To the amazement of the Jewish scribes and Pharisees, Jesus eats with "sinners and tax collectors," but this Gospel, written for Gentile readers, tends to minimize the importance of Jewish dietary, fasting, and Sabbath laws. According to Jesus, "The Sabbath was made for man, not man for the Sabbath" (2:27), and he casts an angry look at the Pharisees when they question his right to heal a man with a withered hand on God's holy day of rest. He seems to abrogate all Jewish dietary regulations when he teaches that "nothing that enters one from outside can defile, but things from within are what defile," identifying these latter things as evil thoughts, theft, murder, adultery, greed, and so on (7:1–23). In the district of Tyre, he even agrees to exorcise the daughter of a Gentile woman, and, in pointed opposition to Mosaic law, he forbids divorce.

Mark's Gospel contains only four of Jesus' parables but twenty of his miracles. Thus, he is shown calming the winds and sea with the words "Quiet! Be still!" He raises a twelve-year-old girl from the dead, although earlier he was incapable of working "a mighty deed" in his hometown of Nazareth because the people there rejected him as "the carpenter." He feeds five thousand people with five loaves of bread and two fish, and there are twelve baskets of food left over. He walks on the Sea of Galilee.

Some of the cures Jesus performs have the air of being magical (or primitively medical) rather than miraculous. Instead of healing everyone with a few words alone, as he does with the blind Bartimaeus (10:46–52), he cures a deaf man with a speech impediment by putting a finger in his ears and spittle on his tongue before giving the command, "Ephphatha" ("Be opened!"). He heals an unnamed blind man by putting spittle in his eyes and laying his hands on him, but when the man's newly acquired vision remains dim, Jesus puts his hands on him a second time to complete the cure.

Jesus' advice to the wealthy is to sell what they have and give to the poor, since "it is easier for a camel to pass through the eye of a needle than for a rich man to enter the kingdom of God" (10:25). (Although some have tried to explain this statement by suggesting that "The Needle's Eye" was the name of a small gate in Jerusalem that a camel could squeeze through only on its knees, there's no evidence that such a gate ever existed.) In the same vein, Jesus indignantly overturns the tables of the money changers and sellers of sacrificial doves in the temple—an act that did not endear him to the religious authorities in Jerusalem.

Indeed, Jesus predicts the utter destruction of the temple, and scholars have debated whether, at the time Mark wrote, the Romans had already destroyed it (AD 70). Jesus also foretells the imminent end of the world—"This generation will not pass away until all these things have taken place"—and his own coming in the clouds "with great power and glory." Yet he experiences a palpably human agony—"My soul is sorrowful even to death"—when he prays to God to remove the cup of suffering from him. After his arrest, Jesus claims to be the Messiah when examined by the council of the Sanhedrin, and this seals his doom.

The Gospel of Mark ends abruptly after Jesus' passion, death, and burial. Mary Magdalene and two other women visit Jesus' tomb on Sunday morning to anoint his body with spices, but they are surprised to see that the huge stone in front of the entrance has been rolled away and that a young man in a white robe (apparently an angel) is sitting inside. He tells them that Jesus has risen from the dead, that they should tell his disciples, and that they will see Jesus in Galilee. The women, "frightened out of their wits . . . said nothing to a soul, for they were afraid."

After this last verse, many editions of Mark's Gospel print a twelve-verse passage by an unknown writer that was appended at some later date in antiquity. In this, the risen Jesus appears first to Mary Magdalene, "out of whom he had driven seven demons." His apostles don't believe her when she tells them she has seen Jesus, nor do they believe two disciples who have also seen him. Jesus then appears to the apostles and reproves them before bidding them to proclaim the Gospel "to all creation." At this, he ascends into heaven and takes his seat "at the right hand of God."

Although some readers prefer the starkness (and priority) of Mark, his Gospel seems somewhat impoverished when compared with the vigor of Matthew's gripping narrative, the gentle humanistic touch of Luke's, or the austere portrayal of Christ, the God-Man as Greek Logos, in the Gospel of John.

There is a legend that St. Mark sailed into the Venetian lagoon long before there was a Venice and that an angel told him that someday his body would come to rest there. This prophecy encountered obstacles to fulfillment, since Mark was supposedly martyred and buried in Alexandria, Egypt, but the ingenuity of two Venetian sea captains ensured a happy outcome. While trading in Alexandria in about 828, these men persuaded the Christian wardens of the shrine where the body was located to substitute St. Claudian's remains for those of Mark so that the evangelist could be smuggled out of a Muslim land. The problem was that the Muslims were very fond of St. Mark, too, so a stratagem was employed to elude the vigilance of the customs inspectors. By stowing the body aboard ship in a tub covered with pickled pork, the captains sent the Muslim officials fleeing in horror.

Mark was thus brought to Venice and immediately became its patron saint, supplanting St. Theodore, who carried much less cachet. Only four years later, the first church of St. Mark was consecrated on the site of the present bejeweled basilica, where Mark's alleged remains rest beneath the high altar. The winged lion, St. Mark's symbol, is still ubiquitous in the city that went on to become the Queen of the Adriatic.

8 ❧ When was the first recorded eruption of Mount Vesuvius?

August 24, AD 79, destroying Pompeii, Herculaneum, and Stabiae

IT WAS "A CATASTROPHE which destroyed the loveliest regions of the earth," wrote seventeen-year-old eyewitness Pliny the Younger, when the top of Mount Vesuvius blew off during the afternoon of August 24 in the year 79.

By the first century AD, Vesuvius had been quiescent for almost eighteen hundred years, according to geological evidence, and the twenty-five thousand residents of the nearby city of Pompeii were unaware they were living on the southernmost slopes of a volcano. And although an earthquake had severely damaged the city in AD 62, they also were unaware of the connection between earthquakes and volcanic activity.

The young Pliny observed a peculiar cloud shaped like an umbrella pine over Vesuvius that fateful day from his uncle's residence in the town of Misenum on the northern arm of the Bay of Naples. His uncle, renowned naturalist and encyclopedist Pliny the Elder, commander of the Roman naval fleet in the district, had set out across the bay toward the mountain to have a closer look at the curious cloud—a fact-finding mission that soon became one of rescue, as word came of danger to those living nearer Vesuvius. By the time the elder Pliny reached the beachside town of Stabiae, four miles from Pompeii, debris was raining down from an eruption column estimated to have reached twenty miles into the sky.

In recounting the events of that and ensuing days in two surviving letters to his friend, the historian Tacitus, Pliny the Younger wrote that as his uncle sailed toward the volcano, "ashes were already falling, hotter and thicker as the ships drew near, followed by bits of pumice and blackened stones, charred and cracked by the fumes."

That first evening, across the bay in Misenum, young Pliny felt the earth shaking violently and could see that, on Vesuvius, "broad sheets of fire and leaping flames blazed at several points, their bright glare emphasized by the blackness of night." By morning the buildings in Misenum were tottering, and Pliny and his mother fled, along with a panic-stricken mob. According to his account, they witnessed the water being sucked away, leaving sea creatures stranded, and a "fearful black cloud, rent by forked and quivering bursts of flame" over the land. As the cloud approached, spreading darkness and spewing showers of ash, Pliny observed that "many besought the aid of the gods, but still more imagined there were no gods left, and that the universe was plunged into eternal darkness for evermore."

Despite ongoing quakes and the relentless downpour of ash, Pliny the Younger and his mother survived, unlike the elder Pliny, whose body was found when daylight returned on August 26. The towns of Pompeii, Herculaneum, and Stabiae were buried under ash, lava, pumice stones, rocks, and mud. More than two thousand died in Pompeii alone, many suffocating from exposure to toxic gases. Their remains lay forgotten beneath twenty feet of debris until the start of digging at Pompeii in 1748, when a detailed picture of daily life—and death—in a first-century Roman city began to emerge.

Excavations, which continue to this day, have revealed the remnants of temples to Apollo, Jupiter, and Isis; a large amphitheater in which gladiatorial contests were held; the Stabian Baths, dating from the fourth century BC; and an aqueduct, swimming pool, food market, and *lupanar*, or brothel, with its faded depictions of sexual acts over the women's tiny cells. The streets are straight, laid out in a typical Roman grid pattern and lined with what used to be shops and private houses. Delicate pastel-colored frescoes, portraits, and murals can be seen in many of the largest homes, while graffiti scratched onto street-side walls preserve a lively social commentary, with public announcements, electioneering, want ads, and facetious love notes.

Particularly popular with visitors to the city today are the House of the Faun, with its mosaic marble floors and bronze dancing faun (a copy of the original statue); the elaborately decorated House of Menander, in which a large assortment of silver objets d'art was found; and the House of the Golden Cupids, which features gold-leaf engravings of cupids on a painted bedroom wall.

But the eeriest sights are the plaster casts of Pompeians who died huddled against the deadly onslaught. In a technique developed by archaeologist Giuseppe Fiorelli in the 1860s, plaster was poured into the cavities left in the debris after the disintegration of the victims' bodies. In an area known as the Garden of the Fugitives, the final moments of thirteen adults and children are preserved, frozen in time as they attempted to flee their collapsed house and buried vineyards. Overall, more than a thousand such "bodies" have been found. Skeletal remains preserved at Herculaneum and unearthed only in the last few decades indicate that a large group of victims who were awaiting rescue by sea were instantly seared to death by a hundred-mile-per-hour superheated pyroclastic flow that caused their blood to boil and their skulls to explode.

Today, the Forum, which was the center of political, civic, and commercial life in Pompeii as in other Roman cities, is a vast expanse of ruined columns and walls. Mount Vesuvius looms four thousand feet high in the distance, clouds pluming its double peak. The volcano has hardly remained quiescent in the intervening centuries, regularly pouring lava down its slopes and hurling ash as far afield as Istanbul. More than three thousand were killed in an eruption in 1631. Its most recent, in 1944, buried several nearby villages and a fleet of B-52 bombers.

Some three million people currently live in the area considered to be at risk from Vesuvius, which is closely monitored by the Osservatorio Vesuviano in Naples. At present the volcano seems quiet, but its destructive capacity could be no clearer than in the silent streets of once-teeming Pompeii. In a poem composed in the shadow of Vesuvius in 1836, the great Italian pessimist Giacomo Leopardi invited the optimists and progressives of his day, so enamored of humankind's unlimited potential within a beneficent cosmos, to come see the devastation wrought by the mountain he calls "the exterminator," so that they can "witness just how much / loving Nature cares for us."

—*Nancy Walsh*

SECOND CENTURY

9 ~ Who was the traditional first inventor of paper?

Cai Lun, a Chinese eunuch, in 105

IT'S THANKS TO AN OFFICIAL at the court of Emperor He of China's Eastern Han dynasty that the page you're staring at isn't made of calf-skin or sheepskin parchment. And though our word *paper* is derived from *papyrus*, our paper has nothing to do with the papyrus reed, which was processed for writing in Egypt as early as 3000 BC but grows only in subtropical regions.

Archaeologists say that rag or hemp paper was first developed in China in the second century BC, but it may have been used for wrapping and packing rather than writing. In 2006, however, a scrap of paper made from linen fiber and covered with more than twenty Chinese characters, perhaps part of a letter, was discovered in an ancient rubbish dump in China and dated to 8 BC. But the Chinese were writing long before that—so what did they write on? Aside from various types of inscriptions on stone or metal, they used bamboo tablets or wooden strips, starting from about 600 BC, but these were so heavy and bulky that a single book or a daily pile of imperial state documents might weigh hundreds of pounds. Later, they also used pieces of silk, which were not only expensive but also difficult to write on.

An enterprising courtier named Cai Lun (c. 50–121), chief eunuch and director of the imperial Chinese workshops for manufacturing instruments and weapons, saw that the time was ripe for developing a new type of writing material that was light, easy to use, inexpensive, and able to be mass produced. His novel recipe seems to have called for the inner bark of the mulberry and other trees, hemp ends, linen rags, and even old fishnets. First, Cai Lun chopped up his materials, drenched them in water, and pounded them into a pulp. Then he spread them out as a thin sheet over a coarse cloth screen, which allowed the water to drain. The end result was a dry sheet of matted paper fibers remaining on the screen. Cai Lun's imperial master rewarded him for his useful invention with wealth and, eventually, the noble title of marquess.

Legend would have us believe that Cai Lun was at first mocked for his discovery, so he feigned death and had himself buried by friends in a coffin with a bamboo breathing tube. When his friends burned paper above the tube, Cai Lun sprang out of the coffin, scaring the wits out of those not in on the prank but also impressing them with the miraculous powers of his invention.

Perhaps more credible is the story told of his actual death, rather than his staged one. Embroiled in a court intrigue, the young Cai Lun served as the official interrogator of an imperial consort who realized things were looking grim for her and promptly committed suicide by poison. Many years later, in 121, when Emperor An—grandson of the late imperial consort—attained his majority and took over the reins of government, Cai Lun, now an old man, was ordered to report to prison. Instead, deciding to take a page (a paper one, no doubt) out of the imperial consort's book, he ended his life with poison. In his hometown in Hunan province there is a memorial hall dedicated to Cai Lun in which you can still see the stone mortar he used to pound his first paper pulp.

By the third century, Cai Lun's innovations in the content and manufacture of paper were diffused throughout China, and the availability of paper helped increase the general level of literacy and culture in the empire. The Chinese later added a sizing of glue or gelatin and a base of paste to Cai Lun's ingredients to increase the adhesiveness of paper and its ready absorption of ink.

By the seventh century, paper was in use in Korea, Vietnam, and Japan. The Arabs learned papermaking when, after their victory at the battle of the Talas River in Central Asia in 751, they required some Chinese prisoners of war who were adept at the art to reveal their secret skills. Baghdad became the site of the world's first paper mill in 794, and by 1150 the Moors had established Europe's first paper mill near Valencia, Spain. Paper spread to other parts of Europe when it was recognized as a less expensive alternative to animal-derived parchment or vellum, and this facilitated the greater circulation of books and ideas that characterized the High Middle Ages in the Western world.

10 ∾ Which emperor first criminalized Christianity in the Roman Empire?

Trajan, in a letter to Pliny the Younger,

c. 112

THERE'S NO DENYING that Nero made it hot for Christians in Rome when he was looking to blame the great fire of 64 on a minority that nobody loved. Yet his persecution had little to do with his victims' religious beliefs per se and was confined to the capital. Three decades later, Emperor Domitian, who had grown into a paranoiac murderer toward the end of his reign, may have persecuted some Christians for not participating in emperor worship, but many historians see no hard evidence for the specific victimization of Christians by this tyrant.

All sorts of beliefs about the early Christians circulated throughout the Roman Empire—that they were atheists (that is, nonbelievers in the gods of Rome), that they sacrificed infants on their altars and ate their flesh (a highly muddled notion of the Eucharist), and that they practiced group incest at their orgiastic gatherings (perhaps because they called one another "brother" and "sister" and participated in the agape, or love feast, in commemoration of the Last Supper). But eighteenth-century historian Edward Gibbon pointed to a major underlying factor when he stated that the early church was persecuted because it considered "every form of worship except its own as impious and idolatrous." This attitude, a legacy of Judaism, struck the Romans as a stiff-necked refusal to demonstrate a proper patriotism—or even basic loyalty. By the time of Emperor Trajan (98–117), we have the first documentary proof that the mere adherence to Christianity constituted a crime.

Trajan, the second of the five so-called Good Emperors, was also one of the ablest generals to rule Rome. In two hard-fought wars, he conquered Dacia (modern Romania with parts of Bulgaria, Hungary, and Moldova), bringing back to Rome five million pounds of gold and silver and commissioning a vast narrative of those campaigns to be carved in exquisite marble reliefs on a hundred-foot column still standing in a sprawling forum and market complex that he built with his plunder. At his death in 117, the empire was at its greatest extent, after his short-lived acquisitions of Armenia, Mesopotamia, and Assyria enabled the

Roman eagle to stretch its talons to the shores of the Persian Gulf. But in 111, when the province of Bithynia and Pontus in the north of modern-day Turkey was in political and financial turmoil, Trajan dispatched his friend, the litterateur and former consul Pliny the Younger, on a fact-finding tour of the troubled region, empowering him, as his personal representative and acting governor, to manage any problems he encountered.

Among the 121 items of official correspondence between the two men preserved in Pliny's letters, a pair of them (10.96–97) deal with how the troublesome sect of Christians should be handled. A number of persons charged with belonging to that religion have been brought before Pliny for trial, and he has a slew of questions for Trajan: How should they be punished? What kinds of investigations are warranted? Should young Christians be treated the same as older ones? Should those who retract their beliefs be pardoned? Is mere adherence to Christianity a punishable offense, or must there be wrongdoing?

But Pliny goes on to show his boss that he has already exercised considerable initiative. In the case of Christians brought before him who were not Roman citizens, he has ordered the execution of all those who refused to recant their faith, while sending citizens back to Rome for trial. On the other hand, he has released persons haled before him based on accusations in an anonymous pamphlet, but only after they have invoked the Roman gods, offered wine and incense to a statue of Trajan, and cursed the name of Christ. He has also seen fit to order the torture of two female slaves who were deaconesses to find out whether Christian rituals and celebratory meals were subversive in any way, but he discovered "nothing but a degenerate sort of cult carried to extravagant lengths." However, now that the number of accused Christians being brought to trial was growing fast—and the "wretched cult" was spreading from the towns into the rural districts, too—Pliny wanted to know how to proceed.

It's clear that no laws, senatorial decrees, or imperial edicts were in effect concerning these issues, since Pliny, an experienced lawyer who had held the consulship, would surely have known them. In his brief response, Trajan assures Pliny that he is doing the right thing in handling different situations differently, and he agrees that accused Christians who refuse to sacrifice to the gods must be punished with death. He also makes three further points that mitigate the rigor of his decision. First, Christians are not to be hunted out. Second, accused persons who deny being Christians and offer prayers to the Roman gods must be released. Finally, anonymous accusations must not be followed up on.

Since an imperial rescript such as this had the force of law, Trajan had finally established a government policy on this question—and it didn't bode well for Christians. Nonetheless, the number of Christian victims during the rest of his reign does not seem to have been very large.

In the early fifth century, the Christian historian Orosius enunciated what became a traditional view to the effect that the church had suffered ten persecutions under the Roman Empire, from the reign of Nero to the early fourth century, somewhat arbitrarily basing his round number on the ten plagues of Egypt. Yet it was only in 250–51, under Emperor Decius, that the organized and systematic persecution of Christians began and that loyalty oaths to the state religious cult were required of all on pain of death. One of the last persecutions was the fierce one that broke out in 303 under Diocletian, who destroyed churches, burned Scriptures, and condemned Christians to the mines or to a public death by torture.

Readers of Dante's *Paradiso* are sometimes surprised to find the soul of Trajan, the pagan persecutor of Christians, as a glorious saint high up in heaven with other just rulers, but the poet was following a curious medieval legend. The story is that the mighty emperor had once postponed riding out on a military campaign because he was implored by a poor widow, whose son had been murdered, to grant her justice before he set out. On learning of this virtuous deed, Pope Gregory I (590–604) prayed for the soul of Trajan, and God allowed the emperor to be raised back to life, but just long enough for him to repent of his sins and believe in Christ before sinking down into death a second time.

11 ∼ Who was the first comparative biographer?

Plutarch, in his Parallel Lives *of Greek and Roman statesmen and generals,*
c. 120

WE'RE FAIRLY ACCUSTOMED to comparative biographies of a pair of figures like Napoleon and Hitler or Hitler and Stalin, but the *Parallel Lives* of the Greek moral philosopher Plutarch (c. 46–c. 120) comprises a total of twenty-three paired biographies, in each instance an eminent Greek political or military figure being paired with a Roman counterpart (and followed, for most pairs, by a brief comparison), as well as four single lives. The fourteen-hundred-page tome commonly known as *Plutarch's Lives* has entertained, instructed, and inspired countless readers, including William Shakespeare, who mined it extensively for his description of Julius Caesar's murder, for example, and his gorgeous evocation of Antony's first sight of Cleopatra in her barge with its perfumed purple sails and silver oars.

Cornelius Nepos, a Roman author of the first century BC, was a forerunner of Plutarch in comparative Greco-Roman biography, but what remains of his biographical sketches is paltry and monotonous fare. At the rich banquet Plutarch sets out, we find not only extensive lives of Julius Caesar and Alexander the Great, paired as the two mightiest generals of antiquity, but also Demosthenes and Cicero as its greatest orators. Among the other titans we meet are the Athenian political leaders Pericles and Themistocles and formidable Romans such as the Gracchus brothers, Marius, Sulla, Pompey, Mark Antony, Cato, and Brutus.

According to the chronological order adopted in modern editions of Plutarch's book, we first find the stories of two mythic heroes, Theseus and Romulus, the founders of Athens and Rome, respectively, and two semilegendary figures, Lycurgus and Numa Pompilius, the lawgivers of Sparta and Rome. Adhering to tradition, Plutarch portrays Theseus as a slayer of monsters like the Minotaur and as a demigod who battles centaurs and beds Amazons. In the life of Romulus, we find all the familiar tales, such as how he and his twin, Remus, were suckled by a she-wolf, though Plutarch offers the alternative interpretation that the boys' adoptive mother was the real *lupa*, since the word can mean both "she-wolf" and "whore" in Latin.

The laws of the probably mythic Lycurgus were thought to have transformed the Spartan state into an armed camp, with military training in barracks beginning at age seven. Plutarch vividly describes how spartan the Spartans were in relishing their awful black broth and shunning any trade, moneymaking, or luxuries. He also gives examples of their laconic wit (the word *laconic* comes from the district of Laconia, of which Sparta was the capital), as when a Spartan refused to go hear a man who imitated a nightingale's voice with the explanation, "I've heard the nightingale itself." We would call Lycurgus's Sparta a totalitarian state, but Plutarch admires its leisured aristocratic warriors for their martial ardor, abstemiousness, and civic virtue, though he objects to their letting troops of young girls dance and exercise naked. Indeed, in his comparison of Lycurgus with King Numa the lawgiver, he praises the latter for enjoining on Roman women modesty, habitual silence, and abstention from wine, resulting in the "fact" that the first quarrel of any Roman woman with her mother-in-law occurred two centuries after Numa succeeded to the throne.

In the life of Solon, the Athenian lawgiver and reformer, Plutarch engages a fully historical personage. He preserves snippets of Solon's poems, including the inspiring line, "Each day I grow older and learn something new," and tells us how Solon repealed almost all of Draco's laws as too draconian. (Neither Plutarch nor I can resist interjecting Draco's explanation of why he punished most crimes with death: "Small ones deserve it, and I have no greater penalty for the more serious ones.") When mentioning that Solon forbade the export of any produce except olive oil, Plutarch explains how informers became known as *sycophants* (literally "fig revealers"), since they curried favor with the authorities by squealing on Athenians who traded in figs. He also tells an old chestnut about Solon and Croesus that he got from the Greek historian Herodotus; even though Plutarch suspects the two men lived at different times, he explains, "I cannot reject so famous and well-attested a narrative."

Plutarch's design, he tells us, "is not to write histories, but lives." His fascination with the quirks of character and the motivations of great men leads him to lovingly record their quips and bons mots, as when King Pyrrhus of Epirus, after winning a battle against the Romans but losing many of his own men, observed, "Another victory like that, and we're ruined." Even vicious traits can be useful for our moral instruction. When we discover that Crassus made an enormous fortune by snapping up the confiscated properties of Sulla's victims and buying for a song houses in Rome that were on fire and then having his army of slaves fix them up, we know that his other deeds will hardly edify us. From the fact that the young Julius Caesar laughingly warned a gang of pirates who had kidnapped him that he would execute them all someday—and then, after being ransomed, personally rounded them up and had them crucified—we learn to steer clear of ruthless egomaniacs, whose threats are as good as promises.

Plutarch's depiction of Alcibiades, the aristocratic statesman and superb general who started out as an über-celebrity in Periclean Athens and later plunged the city into disaster with an invasion of Sicily, is a masterpiece of characterization. We are told of his great physical beauty and charm, his bodily strength and gracefulness; even his lisping was attractive. Though he was a drunken carouser and a slave to his pleasures who engaged in various sacrileges with his friends (including breaking off the erect phalluses from most of the statues of Hermes in the city), no less a personage than Socrates loved him dearly.

Realizing that his first readers would know, from the pages of Thucydides, the role of Alcibiades in the political and military entanglements of the Peloponnesian War, Plutarch focuses instead on breathing life into his portrait of the man himself. He thus strings together anecdotes that reveal Alcibiades in all his troubling complexity, as when, during his teens, he once stopped by a grammar school to borrow one of Homer's works. The teacher answered that he had nothing by Homer, thereby earning a punch for his deficient educational standards. On another occasion, Alcibiades punched a very prominent Athenian in public just because he had told his friends he would do it, but when he went to apologize the next day, he was so contrite—even offering himself to be whipped—that the man forgave him and ended up giving him his daughter in marriage. When she later tried to divorce Alcibiades because of his countless infidelities, he swooped down on her as she stood before the magistrate and carried her home, with none of her family members daring to get in his way.

After the Athenians turned on him and sentenced him to death in absentia, he remarked, "I'll make them feel I'm alive," and began a series of rapid defections to the Spartans, the Persians, and back to the Athenians, fighting brilliantly for each side in turn until it hounded him into the ranks of one of the others again. Plutarch pairs this irrepressible force of nature with the dour and choleric (and probably mythical) Roman general Coriolanus, who nonetheless had a similar fate. After suffering exile, both men fought against their country and were finally killed by their treacherous hosts.

Plutarch served as a model for Greek biographers of the Byzantine Empire and European scholars of the Renaissance, reaching a much wider audience through the sixteenth-century French translation of Jacques Amyot, which Montaigne knew and loved. The translation of Amyot's version into English by Sir Thomas North became the main source for Shakespeare's *Julius Caesar*, *Antony and Cleopatra*, *Coriolanus*, and *Timon of Athens*. Like the American Founding Fathers, the French Revolutionaries—including the guillotined communist

"Gracchus" Babeuf—were awash in patriotic virtue culled from *Plutarch's Lives*, which even the far-from-martial Rousseau called his favorite book. Beethoven, Emerson, "Chinese" Gordon, Harry Truman—the list of Plutarch lovers through the ages is as lengthy and illustrious as his book itself.

12 ∿ What are the first surviving serial biographies of the caesars?

The biographies in The Lives of the Caesars *by Suetonius,*
c. 121

IN A LECTURE delivered during World War I, Freud complained that "thanks to their own discretion and the untruthfulness of biographers we usually learn very little of an intimate nature about our exemplary great men." We in our voyeuristic era can boast that, like Molière's Sganarelle, "*Nous avons changé tout cela*," but before we congratulate ourselves on what a long way we've come, we should reflect that Suetonius was already there in the second century.

Though Gaius Suetonius Tranquillus (c. 69–c. 140) was recommended in a letter by his close friend Pliny the Younger to Roman emperor Trajan as "a very fine scholar" and "a man of the highest integrity and distinction," he was also a man who, after Pliny had secured him an appointment as a military tribune, gave the position away to a relative. Later on, as a high-level imperial secretary, Suetonius had access to official archives that he used in composing his lives of the first dozen emperors, but he lost this privilege after Hadrian dismissed him in 122 because of a vague breach of court etiquette regarding Empress Sabina.

Among Suetonius's numerous lost works are books entitled *Lives of Famous Prostitutes* and *On Terms of Abuse in Greek*, which seem to evince a general interest in zesty topics. His aim in *The Lives of the Caesars* was not to provide a standard history of their reigns but to depict the men themselves as private individuals. As such, he recorded whatever anecdotes, rumors, or factoids he came across regarding their treatment of others or their sex lives as indications of their character and personality. How much is spurious, it is often hard to say, and some of his stories have been seen as little more than slanders concocted by the political or personal foes of the various emperors. Yet some of them are indubitably true.

Suetonius's typical biographical pattern comprises ancestry and birth, childhood and period before accession, wars fought, political and social life, private life, and death. Since he is chiefly known for the sensationalism and gossip that enliven his biographies, however, this essay will focus on those qualities that have made him more or less infamous through the ages.

The book begins with Julius Caesar, who was technically not the first emperor (see Question 1), though the title of "caesar" devolved on his successors. Suetonius records the story that the twenty-year-old Caesar was debauched by King Nicomedes of Bithynia—a tale that the more proper Plutarch omits from his "Life of Julius Caesar" but that our author clearly relishes. He reports that a colleague of Caesar thus referred to him in an edict as "the Queen of Bithynia" and that Cicero once interrupted Caesar (who was speaking in the senate of his obligations to Nicomedes) with the wisecrack, "Enough, please! We all know what *he* gave *you* and *you* gave *him* in return." When Caesar held his triumphal procession in Rome after conquering the Gauls, his men exercised their privilege of reciting bawdy songs about their general with a stinging taunt about Nicomedes' subjugation of the man who had subjugated Gaul.

But Caesar was also a notorious seducer of women, including, Suetonius charges, Brutus's mother (and perhaps his sister) and the wives of Caesar's partners in the First Triumvirate, Crassus and Pompey (who later became his son-in-law). In another of their ribald songs, Caesar's soldiers warned Roman men to lock up their wives, for "we bring you back the bald fornicator." One Roman politician summed up what his enemies felt about Caesar by referring to him in a speech as "every woman's husband and every man's wife." Caesar was also famous for considering the Roman treasury part of his own personal financial system, and Suetonius mentions how, during his first consulship, he stole three thousand pounds of gold from the Capitol and replaced it with the same quantity of gilded bronze.

The single most scandalous passage in Suetonius's book involves the pederastic activities of old Emperor Tiberius after he retired to Capri. From all over the empire, he had collected young men and women known as *spintriae* who were "experts in deviant intercourse" and whom he ordered to perform in front of him in groups of three. He also trained young boys, whom he called his "little fish," to nibble at him between his legs while he swam nude. In his bedroom he proudly displayed a mythological painting that featured the huntress Atalanta performing fellatio on Meleager, staunch hero of the Calydonian boar hunt.

Most of the unsavory details in the essays on Caligula and Claudius in this book were supplied by Suetonius and won't be repeated here (see Questions 3 and 5). Moving right along to the life of Nero, we learn that, when the emperor himself was singing or acting, no one was permitted to leave during the performances, with the result that some women gave birth during them and some men feigned death so that they would be carried out for burial. Nero also liked to go out at night in disguise to beat up people in the street—and knife them to death if they fought back. In the sexual sphere, Suetonius accuses him of raping a vestal virgin and of having a boy named Sporus castrated before going through a wedding ceremony with him. When they were borne through the streets in a litter, Sporus was seen to be dressed up like an empress. Subsequently, Nero himself became the "bride" of a freed slave named Doryphorus.

Nero was also accused of incestuous relations with his mother Agrippina—or at the very least he sought out a mistress who was a dead ringer for her. Later, tiring of his mother's domineering ways, he determined to do away with her. Three times he tried to have her poisoned, but the wily woman had previously taken an antidote on each occasion. He installed a rickety ceiling in her bedroom, but someone warned her about it. When he tried to drown her one night by having her sail home in a collapsible boat, she swam safely to shore. Finally, he had her stabbed but made it look like a suicide. When he went to claim the body, he examined her limbs and commented on their good and bad qualities while relaxing with a cup of wine. Suetonius also charges that, after dispatching one wife, Octavia, Nero killed his second spouse, Poppaea, by kicking her while she was pregnant (which may or may not be true) and that he ordered the Stoic philosopher Seneca, his former tutor, to commit suicide (definitely true).

Suetonius claims Nero was responsible for the great fire of Rome of AD 64 and that he sang an entire operetta on the burning of Troy in his tragic actor's costume while watching the conflagration from a tower and admiring the beauty of the flames (but see Question 4). Hardly a religious man, Nero despised all cults except that of a certain

Syrian goddess, but he eventually soured on her, too, and showed it by urinating on her statue. When mass army revolts finally constrained him to commit suicide at age thirty-two, he lamented his demise with the words, "What a great artist is perishing!"

Vitellius, emperor for only eight months in 69 before being butchered, had a reputation for both gluttony and cruelty. Suetonius explains that he managed to do justice to his daily regimen of three banquets, capped by an evening drinking bout, by relying on frequent emetics. To celebrate Vitellius's arrival in Rome, his brother threw a splendid bash at which seven thousand choice fish and two thousand game birds were served up. An enormous dish of food once ordered by Vitellius required that its constituents—the livers of pike, the brains of pheasants and peacocks, flamingo tongues, and eel sperm—be shipped to the capital from every corner of the empire. His cruelty was evident in that "he delighted in inflicting death and torture on anyone at all on the slightest pretext" and in the suspicion that he had his own mother starved to death when she was ill because a German prophetess had said he would have a long and prosperous reign, but only if his mother died before him.

The next emperor, Vespasian, is the subject of a well-known Suetonian tale. This thrifty man decided to increase state revenues by taxing the daily "intake" at Rome's public urinals, which was used by merchants to clean woolens. When his son Titus complained the tax was unseemly, Vespasian held to the young man's nose a coin that was part of the first day's take and asked him if it smelled bad. Titus said, "No," and his father snapped back, "And yet it came from urine." To this day, public urinals in Italy are called *vespasiani* in the emperor's honor.

Best to end with one of the more harmless stories told of Vespasian's other son, Domitian, the last emperor whose life Suetonius records. On first succeeding Titus to the throne, Domitian spent hours alone each day catching flies and stabbing them with a stylus. When someone once asked whether anyone was with the emperor, a court wag answered, "No, not even a fly."

The *Augustan History*, a fourth-century collection of brief lives of the later Roman emperors, was modeled on Suetonius, as was the ninth-century *Life of Charlemagne* by Einhard. On the other hand, a particularly egregious Suetonian legacy involves Gilles de Rais, better known as Bluebeard, who was hanged in 1440 for murdering dozens of children—if not several hundred—and who confessed that he had been inspired by reading the "Life of Tiberius."

13 ∽ Who built the first great Roman wall in Britain?

Emperor Hadrian, to keep out the Caledonians,
c. 122–26

EVER SINCE THE ROMAN CONQUEST of what are now England and Wales, the savage, red-haired, and gangly Caledonians of Scotland constituted the collective thorn in the collective flesh of imperial Britannia. In 84, the Roman general Agricola thrashed them, but little more than three decades later, the Ninth Legion was wiped out at York during a revolt.

Renouncing the expansionism of his predecessor, Trajan, Emperor Hadrian (117–38) withdrew the eastern boundaries of the empire to the Euphrates. He also set out on two extended tours of the empire with the intentions of satisfying his scholarly wanderlust and securing the frontiers of his realm, which comprised, according to Edward Gibbon, "the fairest part of the earth and the most civilized portion of mankind." Arriving in Britain in 122, he ordered a great wall built across one of the narrowest parts of England to protect Britannia from marauding Caledonians. From Wallsend, on the estuary of the Tyne, the wall eventually reached Bowness on the Solway Firth, running from the North Sea to the Irish Sea.

Hadrian's Wall was the largest Roman structure in the world. Constructed by soldiers of three Roman legions, it was seventy-three miles long and originally about fourteen feet high and ten feet thick. It was supplied with turrets every third of a mile and fortified gateways every mile with small detachments of men. Seventeen large forts were set into or erected near the wall for a total garrison of about nine thousand auxiliary troops. For most of its length, the wall had two outer faces of dressed limestone with a core of crushed rock; the rest was originally built with turf blocks and later redone in stone. A wide, deep ditch, flanked by earth mounds, was dug on both sides of the wall, and a military road ran roughly parallel to it. There were also three outpost forts north of the wall, as well as three regular legions stationed in Britannia to the south. The wall soon drew traders and even settlers to its environs.

Hadrian's successor, Antoninus Pius, moved the British frontier north and, in 142, began building a thirty-seven-mile wall about one hundred miles beyond Hadrian's bulwark. This Antonine Wall, a turf rampart erected on a stone foundation fourteen feet wide and supplied with a ditch and nineteen forts, ran between the Firth of Forth and the River Clyde in Scotland, north of modern Edinburgh and Glasgow. After fierce local rebellions in the 160s, the Antonine Wall was temporarily abandoned, and, at some time after 180, when the Caledonians invaded northern Britannia, the Romans retired to Hadrian's Wall.

In 211, Emperor Septimius Severus, old and ill, journeyed to Britain so that he could lead the ongoing fight against the Caledonians in person. After several bloody campaigns, he decided it would be easier to exterminate than subdue them, but before he could put his plan into effect, he died of gout at York. Almost a century later, Constantius Chlorus, the father of Constantine, died in the same northern city after a victory over the same perennial foes of the Romans.

Hadrian, brilliant and cultured builder of the Pantheon, his villa at Tivoli, and his splendid mausoleum (Castel Sant'Angelo), built his mighty wall in an attempt to fend off an unpleasant strategic reality. Despite the many times it was breached, the wall was abandoned by the Romans only when they left Britain in the early fifth century. In later ages, many of its stones were carted off for various building projects, including the monasteries at Jarrow and Lindisfarne, but we can still follow its snaky ruins through the idyllic British countryside, now that time has rendered its original purpose quite moot.

14 ∾ Who was the first philosopher-king?

Stoic Roman emperor and author Marcus Aurelius
(reigned 161–80)

IN PLATO'S REPUBLIC, Socrates says that the human race will never have respite from its evils until philosophers become kings or kings become philosophers. This hope led Plato to Sicily several times in the vain attempt to mold young Dionysius II of Syracuse into an enlightened ruler. Half a millennium later, Marcus Aurelius wrote a book in Greek entitled *Thoughts to Himself*—better known as the *Meditations*—which constitutes the remarkable spiritual testament of a Roman Stoic philosopher who became ruler of the most powerful empire of his day.

Founded by Zeno soon after 300 BC, Stoicism was essentially the code of personal and public virtue of high-minded Greek or Roman aristocrats like Cato and Brutus. Cicero was an admirer of Stoicism, and Nero's tutor Seneca was one of its most important authors. Epictetus (c. 55–c. 135), a Greek-speaking Stoic philosopher and teacher who began life as a Phrygian slave, inhabited the opposite end of the social spectrum, but the books pieced together by a student of his from lecture notes—the *Discourses* and the *Manual*—cast a potent spell on the young heir to the Roman throne and influenced much of the thought that later found its way into Marcus Aurelius's own book.

The stern Stoic creed was ideally suited to the times. Marcus's reign was marked by floods and earthquakes, dismal finances, Parthian wars, plague, insurrections, sedition, and barbarian incursions. At least part of the *Meditations* was written on the Danube, where he fought, year after year, against the onslaughts of German tribes like the Quadi and Marcomanni, and the aphoristic nature of his slim volume may be explained by the circumstances of its composition. The book was meant for his eyes alone, yet, as classicist Moses Hadas observed, "Marcus Aurelius in undress has nothing to be ashamed of."

He begins by acknowledging the lessons in proper living and thinking he received from numerous family members, teachers, and friends: "From my grandfather Verus I learned good morals and the government of my temper. From my father's reputation and my memory of him, modesty and a manly character." He strives to live always under the guidance of reason, never of his body and emotions, and his goals are calm and peace of mind from knowing that he adheres to duty in things great and small. Even rising at dawn, unpleasant as it is for him, is important because he has his allotted work to do. The chief thing is to live according to Nature, and for humans this means to live morally, rationally, and benevolently. All humans are like the different parts of one body, and if any of them wrong Marcus, they do it through ignorance and are thus to be pitied rather than hated. "Love mankind; follow God," he exhorts himself. Doing good is its own reward: "If it is not right, do not do it; if it is not true, do not say it."

Since God (or Zeus or Providence) rules the universe according to reason, even apparent evils have their function in a divine plan that short-sighted humans cannot perceive. Things that are neither morally good nor evil are termed "indifferent," and these are all the things we cannot control: good or bad health, wealth or poverty, political liberty or persecution, death itself. The only things we can control are our ideas about things—Hamlet expresses this as, "There is nothing either good or bad but thinking makes it so"—and our actions based on correct reasoning. Our minds must live in absolute freedom from external coercion (though our bodies may not), as well as from the more insidious tyranny of our misdirected desires, fears, and aversions. What makes us human is our reason and moral faculty; our bodies we have in common with the animals.

Marcus's ascetic book dwells most comfortably in the realm of abstract injunctions to virtue. It tends to shun the world of the five senses, except to decry it. To guard against gluttony, for example, the emperor deconstructs the delicacies set before him: "This is the dead body of a fish, and this is the dead body of a bird or of a pig; this Falernian wine is grape juice." His costly purple robe is really "some sheep's wool dyed with the blood of a shellfish." He demystifies sexual intercourse as "attrition of an entrail and a convulsive expulsion of mere mucus" (despite having thirteen children with his wife, Faustina). When he steps out of his bath, he notices "oil, sweat, dirt, filthy water, all things disgusting—so is every part of life and everything." His jaundiced eye, like Hamlet's, perceives "the rottenness of the matter which is the foundation of everything! Water, dust, bones, filth . . . "

An obsession with death and futility also runs through the book: "Hippocrates, after curing many diseases, also fell sick and died." Marcus tells himself not to act "as if you were going to live ten thousand years. Death hangs over you." Like the author of Ecclesiastes, he observes that "man's life is smoke and nothingness." He bids himself live every day as if it were his last—and the very last thought in the book is of death: "Make your exit, then, from the stage of life satisfied, for He who bids you depart is also satisfied." Marcus's exit at age fifty-eight, courtesy of smallpox, took place in a camp in what is now Vienna, where he was still battling the enemies of Rome.

With its pervasive gloom, the *Meditations* has sometimes been seen as a sophisticated version of whistling in the dark—as the author's deliberate divestment of all transitory things for the sake of avoiding suffering. It's no coincidence that Matthew Arnold, who reminds us in "Dover Beach" that the world "Hath really neither joy, nor love, nor light, / Nor certitude, nor peace, nor help for pain," considered Marcus Aurelius "perhaps the most beautiful figure in history." When in Rome, we can still see its last "Good Emperor" mounted on his war charger and extending his arm in serene (and weary) salutation.

In the end, Marcus Aurelius allowed paternal love to overrule his reason, naming his vicious young son as his successor instead of a far worthier man. Commodus (180–92), who claimed to be Hercules reincarnated, fought as a gladiator, slew wild beasts in the Colosseum, and was eventually poisoned by one of his innumerable concubines and then strangled to death in his bath by a wrestler sent to finish him off. The empire was now on a seriously wrong track from which it would only fitfully find its way back again.

Have there been other philosopher-kings? Some would cite the enlightened despots of the eighteenth century, such as Joseph II of Austria, Frederick II of Prussia, and Catherine II of Russia, but no potentate has ever produced a book quite like Marcus's, in which the responsibilities of a ruler are placed within a cosmic context of duties toward self, fellow humans, and God.

15 ～ What was the first great rabbinic compilation?

The Mishnah, c. 200, a Jewish law code forming the Hebrew portion of the Talmud

THE TORAH, THE FIRST FIVE BOOKS of the Hebrew Bible, is said to contain 613 *mitzvoth*—or commandments—of God. In the centuries following the return of the Jews from their Babylonian exile in 537 BC, the scribes (*soferim*) and, later, the learned rabbis (*tannaim*) interpreted the biblical commandments so that they could be applied to the living conditions of their time.

The resulting law code—the Mishnah ("teaching" or "repetition")—is the body of Jewish oral law, both religious and civil. The laws were memorized and transmitted orally to avoid diminishing the importance of the Torah itself, but at a certain point they became too unwieldy. Attempts to collect and systematize this body of laws were made by Hillel (c. 30 BC–AD 20) and Rabbi Akiba (died c. 132), but the work was completed by Rabbi Judah ha-Nasi ("the Prince," that is, head of the Sanhedrin, the high court of ancient Israel), who collated the traditions of the various exegetical schools and produced an authoritative text before the year 200—whether written or still only oral is not clear. Judah proclaimed his version to be the final codification—its text was now "closed" and thus became the standard collection of Jewish oral law.

The Mishnah, written in Hebrew, comprises six "orders" (*sedarim*) and a total of sixty-three tractates or treatises. Each treatise is divided into chapters—of which there are 523—and the chapters are subdivided into paragraphs. The six orders are *Seeds* (agricultural laws and rituals, but preceded by a treatise on prayers); *Festivals; Women* (marriage, divorce, and family relationships); *Damages* (civil and criminal laws); *Sacred Things* (sacrificial laws and the temple cult); and *Purities* (hygiene, ritually clean and unclean foods, modes of purification).

But the statements of the Mishnah itself were subjected to close analysis by the *amoraim* ("expositors," the rabbinical sages from c. 200–500) whose extensive oral commentaries, composed in Aramaic, came to be known as the Gemara ("completion"). Together, the Mishnah—the oral laws themselves—and the Gemara—the interpretation of the laws—form the Talmud ("study"). The two Talmuds are the Palestinian, completed c. 420 by scholars at the academy in Tiberias, near Haifa, and the Babylonian, completed c. 500, which is by far the lengthier and the more important—it is, in fact, *the* Talmud.

It's impossible to give more than a taste of the Mishnah here. In the treatise on prayer that introduces the first order (*Seeds*), we find the excellent advice that praying for things that have already occurred is futile—as when a man prays that his pregnant wife might have a boy.

The second order, *Festivals*, begins with a treatise on Sabbath regulations (*Shabbat*), which is the longest in the Mishnah dealing with a single topic. Here are the familiar prohibitions against working or even lighting or putting out a fire on the Sabbath. In *Shabbat* 16:8, we read "If a non-Jew lights a lamp on Sabbath, a Jew may make use of the light. But if he lights it for the sake of the Jew, it is forbidden." In the days before automatic light timers, the legal fiction of the *Shabbos goy* ("Sabbath Gentile") was resorted to in order to have electric lights turned on or off in Orthodox Jewish households on Friday nights. Though Jews were not allowed to actually ask the Gentile to operate the lights, nor to compensate him for it, there was the tacit understanding that the *Shabbos goy* (often a boy from the apartment building or neighborhood) would come in to do this on his own—and then pick up a coin that was left in a certain predetermined place.

The Passover regulations describe how, on the night before the feast begins, "a search for leavened food is conducted by the light of a candle." Unleavened bread (matzo) must be eaten during Passover, and, at the Seder meal, the son asks his father the four questions. On Yom Kippur, the Day of Atonement, "eating, drinking, washing, anointing, putting on sandals, and sexual intercourse" are forbidden.

The order of *Women* teaches that "no man may refrain from fulfilling the mitzvah [commandment] of: 'Be fruitful and multiply' (Genesis 1:28) unless he already has children. According to the school of Shammai, he must have two sons. According to the school of Hillel, a son and a daughter, for it is written, 'male and female he created them' (Genesis 1:27). If he marries a woman and lives with her ten years, and she bears no child, he is still not permitted to refrain from fulfilling the mitzvah." The Mishnah leaves nothing to chance: "A virgin should be married on Wednesday and a widow on Thursday." If things don't work out, however, the man can give the woman a *get*—a divorce document—not only for a serious cause like unchastity but "even if she has spoiled a dish for him." Here we have an early version of no-fault divorce, at least for the man.

Damages contains an interesting nonlegal treatise called *Pirke Abot* (*The Wisdom of the Fathers*) that preserves the favorite sayings and ethical maxims of the *tannaim*, such as "So long as a man talks overmuch with women he brings evil upon himself, neglects the study of Torah, and in the end Gehenna is his portion." Even with one's wife, idle chatter is to be avoided, since, as Moses Maimonides explains in his commentary on this text, "For the most part conversation with women has to do with sexual matters." So great is the injunction to study Torah that "he that does not learn deserves to die," whereas all the words of sages "are like coals of fire." Practical wisdom abounds in this treatise: "Do not appease thy fellow in his hour of anger; do not comfort him while the dead is still laid out before him . . . and do not strive to see him in his hour of misfortune." And when you really think about it, there are only four types of people: "One who says, 'Mine is mine and thine is thine'—this is the commonplace type. 'Mine is thine and thine is mine'—the boorishly ignorant. 'Mine is thine and thine is thine'—the saint. 'Mine is mine and thine is mine'—the wicked."

THIRD
CENTURY

16 ⌒ Who was the first emperor to grant Roman citizenship to all freeborn men of the empire?

Caracalla, "the common enemy of mankind,"
in 212

A GLANCE AT THE SCOWLING AND THUGGISHLY bearded features of his bust in the National Archaeological Museum of Naples is enough to convince us that Emperor Caracalla (211–17) was no bleeding-heart liberal. This was a man who, to avoid sharing the throne with his detested younger brother Geta, looked on as the twenty-two-year-old was stabbed to death, at his orders, while rushing into their mother's arms. Then he had all the inscriptions of Geta's name removed from the monuments of Rome—as may still be seen on the triumphal arch of their father, Septimius Severus, in the Forum. When the distinguished legal scholar Papinian refused to compose a formal defense of the murder, Caracalla had him beheaded in his presence, and a massacre of many thousands of Geta's supporters ensued. Shortly after promulgating his edict of citizenship, he butchered thousands in Alexandria, Egypt, because of mocking rumors circulating in the city that he was carrying on an incestuous relationship with his beautiful Syrian mother, Julia Domna.

Born Lucius Septimius Bassianus, this "common enemy of mankind," in Edward Gibbon's phrase, was renamed Marcus Aurelius Antoninus by his father on creating him junior emperor as a child. We know him by his nickname of "Caracalla" because of the long, hooded Gallic military tunic of that name that he wore instead of the Roman toga. But what would inspire a mass murderer like him to issue the Antonine Constitution, the edict named for him that conferred full Roman citizenship on all freeborn men living in the empire?

At first, only Roman patricians enjoyed the rights of citizenship—voting, serving as magistrates and priests, exercising the right of appeal, contracting legal marriages. Roman plebeians would have to wait until 337 BC for full civic rights. So prized was Roman citizenship during the republic that the Italian allies of Rome had launched the

Social War against her to attain it, finally achieving their goal in 90 BC. Julius Caesar had lavished Roman citizenship—and even admission to the senate—on wealthy Gallic chieftains and businessmen to secure their loyalty.

From the time of Augustus, however, Roman citizenship was extended only gradually to non-Italians in the empire, who were eager for tax exemptions and protection from arbitrary treatment by Roman magistrates. Under Claudius (41–54), it was extended to urban communities in the more Romanized provinces. Later emperors granted citizenship to entire favored communities, meritorious or aristocratic individuals, and army veterans on discharge from service. Certain favored municipalities received "Latin rights," which were an intermediate step between alien status and full Roman citizenship.

Caracalla's edict may have sprung from less than altruistic motives. After raising the soldiers' pay to consolidate their support, he doubled the inheritance tax, which only citizens paid, and then greatly increased the number of people who were liable to it by making citizenship universal except for men who had been born as slaves. (Freeborn women received the same limited citizenship rights as Roman women.) The new law also meant that all free male provincials were now technically required to serve in the army as conscripts or to pay a tax to escape service. On a less cynical level, the edict may have been intended to simplify and standardize the judicial, administrative, and financial functions of government. Nonetheless, according to classicist Donald R. Dudley, "Roman citizenship became universal when it was no longer a privilege but a burden." Now all the freeborn in the empire could look to Rome as their common fatherland, but the fatherland had become a tyranny.

At least Caracalla completed the luxurious public baths begun by his father that sat on twenty-seven acres and whose gargantuan ruins are still used as a backdrop for outdoor opera performances in the Eternal City. Far away from Rome, near Carrhae, where Caracalla had led his army on a futile expedition to conquer the Parthians—and where Crassus had been defeated and killed in battle against the same enemy almost three centuries earlier—the criminally insane emperor met his end at age twenty-nine, stabbed to death by an officer of his own bodyguard at the bidding of Macrinus, the Praetorian prefect who succeeded him on the throne.

17 ⮞ Who was the first King of Kings of the Sassanian (New Persian) Empire?

Ardashir I, shahan shah Eran,
reigned c. 224–41

FOR MORE THAN FOUR CENTURIES, the Parthians ruled the central core of the old Persian Empire that Alexander the Great had conquered and left to his squabbling successors. Under its Central Asian ruling family, the Arsacids, the ramshackle Parthian Empire handed the Roman Empire its share of defeats but never recovered from an invasion mounted by Emperor Caracalla in 216.

The coup de grâce was finally delivered to the Parthian state from within. Ardashir, or Artaxerxes, a petty king of a small region of Persia since 208, began conquering nearby provinces. This Sassanian ruler belonged to a Persian family named for an ancestor, Sasan. When Parthian king Artabanus V took notice of his vassal's growing power, it was already too late. Ardashir defeated his suzerain in two battles and finally killed him in a third in 224, following up his success by wiping out every member of the Arsacid royal family he could get his hands on.

Ardashir I then entered the old Parthian capital of Ctesiphon on the east bank of the Tigris and had himself crowned *shahan shah Eran* ("King of Kings of the Iranians") with the view of restoring the glories of the old Achaemenid dynasty of Persia, under kings such as Cyrus, Cambyses, and Darius. In 230, he thus invaded Roman Mesopotamia and laid claim to all Roman possessions in Asia. The young emperor Alexander Severus, accompanied as usual by his mother, Julia Mamaea, marched out to the eastern frontier and barely managed to dislodge the Persians. Returning in 238, Ardashir captured the strongholds of Carrhae and Nisibis from the Romans. Meanwhile, his conquests in the East enabled him to rule western Iran and southern Mesopotamia directly, and Afghanistan, Baluchistan, and Armenia through subject kings.

Ardashir also reestablished the ancient national Persian religion of Zoroastrianism. Rock sculptures in Iran still show him and the good god of the religion, Ormazd (Ahura Mazda), both on horseback, with the deity bestowing a giant ring of sovereignty on the king. Ardashir directed the Zoroastrian priests, the magi, to compile a written text of their oral scriptures, the Avesta, a project brought to completion in the following century. The king imprisoned those of his subjects who refused to embrace Zoroastrianism for one year to give them time to reflect. If they persisted in their obstinacy, they were executed.

Under Ardashir's son, Shapur I (241–72), the Sassanians defeated Roman armies, devastated Syria—sacking Antioch in 253—and terrorized southern Asia Minor. In 260, they even captured Emperor Valerian in a catastrophic defeat of the Romans at the battle of Edessa. Until the end of his life, Valerian, dressed in the imperial purple but weighed down with chains, had to serve as Shapur's footstool whenever the Persian king mounted his horse. Scholars have doubted the truth of this story, as well as the one maintaining that Valerian was ultimately flayed alive (or executed by being forced to swallow molten gold) and that his skin was filled with straw and put on permanent display in the main Persian temple.

The Sassanians attained their peak power in the reign of Khosrau II (590–628), who conquered Asia Minor and Syria and occupied Egypt, but he was defeated in 627 by Byzantine emperor Heraclius at Nineveh and murdered in the following year. Anarchy descended on the Sassanian Empire, which was so debilitated from chronic fighting with the Byzantines that it was ripe for plucking by the Arabs.

Muslim armies defeated the Persians in 635 and captured Ctesiphon two years later. The Sassanian dynasty was finally destroyed in 651, when its last king was assassinated. Iran soon embraced Islam, though the Zoroastrian Parsis ("Persians") fled to India, and even today about seventy thousand of them still practice their ancient religion.

18 ∿ Who was the first "barracks emperor" of Rome?

Maximinus, 235–38, formerly a Bulgarian shepherd, whose reign inaugurated an anarchic half century of Roman history

THE HALF CENTURY from 235 to 284 has been called "The Time of Chaos" in Roman history, with its usurpations (at least sixty men claimed the throne during this period), civil wars, assassinations, barbarian raids, famine, and pestilence. Farms were abandoned, cities were destroyed, trade stagnated, taxes skyrocketed, inflation soared, and the power of the senate dwindled.

The Roman soldiers of the third century were increasingly drawn from the very peoples that the frontier armies were defending the empire against. Less and less Romanized, they cared little for their duty to a faraway emperor, seizing the moment when a power vacuum in the capital or an access of prestige from a local victory could elevate one of their own to imperial rule. The understanding was that the newly created sovereign would lavishly increase their pay and lead them on pillaging expeditions against friend or foe. When he asked too much—or too little—of them, he was dispatched and another put in his precarious place. In the words of Roman historian Michael Rostovtzeff, "The empire became the chattel of the soldiers."

The "barracks emperors" were Roman military leaders of this era who seized supreme power in the field or were elevated to the throne by the army against their will. They were often uncultured and semieducated, or natives of backward provinces, like Maximinus Thrax ("the Thracian"), the first common soldier who rose through the ranks to become Roman emperor. Though Maximinus began life as a shepherd in what is now Bulgaria, his immense strength landed him a centurion's post under Emperor Septimius Severus, and he was later promoted to high army office under Alexander Severus.

This young emperor, with his mother in tow, came to Mainz in Germany, where a bridge had been built for a punitive expedition across the Rhine, and Maximinus commanded the army. When Alexander decided to buy off the Germans with annual cash subsidies, Maximinus's soldiers, appalled by this lily-livered behavior, broke into the emperor's tent in March 235, murdered him, his imperious mother, and his friends, and proclaimed their ferocious general as his successor. By now a hardened soldier with a ruffian's face and forty years of campaigning under his ample belt, Maximinus, "half barbarian and scarcely yet master of the Latin tongue," ascended the throne of Augustus, Hadrian, and Marcus Aurelius.

After massacring Alexander's surviving entourage, the burly new emperor used the bridge to good effect to ravage the German tribes on the far side of the Rhine. Besides quelling the plots of two usurpers—which he did expeditiously—he spent the rest of his brief reign fighting barbarians on the Rhine and Danube and bleeding the empire in taxes, confiscations, and extortions to pay his army.

In April 238, a revolt in Africa against these economic policies raised to the imperial purple Gordian I and II, an eighty-year-old senator and his son, who were subsequently confirmed as coemperors by the senate, which wanted men of its own kind in charge. When his son fell in battle against Maximinus's African supporters, Gordian Senior hanged himself with his belt after a reign of a mere three weeks. The senate promptly appointed two more senators, Pupienus Maximus and Balbinus, to replace them as joint emperors but also associated a junior colleague with them, the elder Gordian's thirteen-year-old grandson—Gordian III—as a sop to the people and the enemies of Pupienus and Balbinus.

Maximinus, who had never set foot in Rome, lumbered into Italy to deal with the crisis, but his army got bogged down besieging Aquileia in the northeast of the country and decided it was easier to kill him than continue fighting for his somewhat academic rights. Maximinus and his son, whom he had named coemperor, were assassinated in his tent, their heads sent to Rome, their bodies left for the animals. A few months later, Pupienus and Balbinus, who had started quarreling with each other and everyone else, were seized in their palace in Rome by the Praetorian Guard, tortured, and killed. The boy emperor Gordian III survived for almost six years, until he was done away with by his successor, Philip the Arab, who, in turn, was killed in 249, either by his own soldiers or while suppressing a revolt by his general Decius. So it went for the barracks emperors, at least ten more of whom (not to mention a bumper crop of usurpers) were slain by Roman troops in the period from 254 to 284.

The Roman Empire of this era even hatched a breakaway Gallic empire, lasting from 260 to 274 and consisting of Gaul, Britain, and part of Spain, with a gory succession of five separate emperors of its own. There was also a Palmyrene Empire (260–73), featuring a beautiful, brilliant, and belligerent Queen Zenobia and comprising Syria, Palestine, Egypt, and a chunk of Asia Minor.

Aurelian (270–75), the no-nonsense barracks emperor nicknamed "Hand on Sword" who built the massive walls of Rome, forced both the last Gallic Emperor, Tetricus, and Queen Zenobia, weighed down by golden chains and precious jewels, to grace his triumphal procession in Rome in 274. Nonetheless, he apparently gave Tetricus a government job in sunny southern Italy, and he allowed the learned Zenobia to retire to an estate in what is now Tivoli, whereas the royal captives of many previous "nonbarracks" Roman leaders were ritually strangled as sacrifices to Capitoline Jupiter shortly after the festivities were over. As for the magnanimous Aurelian himself, he was murdered in the following year by his own officers.

19 ◡ Where was the first Gothic raid into the Roman Empire?

Histria, on the Black Sea coast, sacked by the Goths in 238

PROMPTED BY THE CIVIL WARS and power grabs that broke out so frequently in the half century after the murder of Emperor Alexander Severus in 235, the Goths, a Germanic people who apparently originated in southern Sweden and migrated to the lower Danube and Black Sea region, started helping themselves to previously forbidden fruit. Their earliest attested raid into the territory of the Roman Empire occurred in 238, when they plundered Histria (on the Dobruja coast of modern Romania), a city founded by the Greeks and lying on the Black Sea just north of ancient Tomis, where the poet Ovid had been banished by Augustus long before (see Question 2).

The empire secured the withdrawal of the Goths by a subsidy, but this proved to be only the first in a series of Gothic raids in this region. In 249, it was the turn of Marcianople, a city just inland from the Black Sea. The following year, a Gothic king named Cniva and his army sacked a number of Balkan cities. In June 251, when Emperor Decius bested them and was trying to cut off their retreat, his troops were ambushed and routed, and he became the first Roman emperor to be killed fighting barbarians. Later in the decade, the Goths turned their attention to the northern coast of Asia Minor and its rich inland cities: Trebizond, Chalcedon, Nicomedia (burned down), Prusa, Apamea, and Cius.

Gothic destructiveness reached a new low in 262, when they burned the temple of Artemis at Ephesus on the western coast of Asia Minor, including its 127 marble Ionic columns, each sixty feet high and each said to be the gift of a different king. "The arts of Greece and the wealth of Asia," wrote Edward Gibbon, "had conspired to erect that sacred and magnificent structure," which was now wantonly destroyed a second time. (The first temple, one of the seven wonders of the ancient world, had been burned down in 356 BC by a lunatic named Herostratus, who wanted to become famous for his deed.)

Seaborne Gothic raids hit Rhodes and Cyprus in the Aegean, and, in a rampage that saw the plunder of Thebes, Argos, Corinth, and Sparta, even Athens itself was burned and sacked in 267 by the Goths

and Heruli. A probably apocryphal story relates that when books collected from libraries all over the city were heaped up and about to be
consigned to the flames, a Gothic chieftain stopped his men from setting fire to them, reasoning that as long as the Greeks were addicted to
study and learning, they would continue to make paltry warriors.

But the empire struck back with Emperor Claudius II (268–70), sur-
named Gothicus for his victory at the battle of Naissus (in modern Serbia) in 269, when he cut down fifty thousand of the mixed army of Goths
and Heruli, after which the remainder was finished off by plague and starvation. When the Goths resurfaced in the reign of Aurelian (270–75), this
emperor pursued them across the Danube, but after inconclusive fighting
ceded them the Roman province of Dacia (roughly modern Romania),
hoping it would serve as a buffer state to keep other roaming barbarians
on the far side of the river. The great Diocletian defeated the Goths in 289
and 291, and Constantine made peace with them in the 330s.

By the late fourth century, Goths who converted to Christianity
could read the Bible in their own language—*Atta unsar thu in himinam,
weihnai namo thein* ("Our Father, who art in heaven, hallowed be thy
name")—thanks to the translation efforts of Bishop Ulfilas. In the next
century, the western Goths—Visigoths—set up barbarian kingdoms in
Roman Gaul and Spain, and the eastern Gothic branch—Ostrogoths—
within Italy itself, when the exsanguinated Roman Empire of the West
finally succumbed to Germanic invaders.

20 ∽ Who was the first Manichaean?

Mani, a Babylonian prophet who had a vision of an angel,

c. 240

THE PROBLEM OF EVIL was a religious obsession in the third century, as
evidenced by the rise of various Gnostic sects, which attributed the creation of this fallen world of matter and the senses not to an all-good God,
but to some inferior being, often called the Demiurge. Manichaeism, a
syncretistic blend of Christianity, Zoroastrianism, and Buddhism, also
displayed Gnostic tendencies in that it offered esoteric knowledge that
could lead to personal salvation.

Mani, the founder of this world religion, was an Iranian born in

216 near Ctesiphon (not far from modern-day Baghdad) in Babylonia, which was still a province of the Parthian Empire. In a vision received when he was about twelve, an angel—"the Twin"—told him he was the last and greatest of the prophets and taught him divine truths. About a dozen years later, the Twin reappeared, ordering Mani to spread the message of the new faith.

Locating himself in the Christian tradition, Mani claimed that Jesus had been sent to restore the world to the way of light, but his apostles had strayed from his message, adhering to the false teachings of the Old Testament. In fact, it was an evil spirit pretending to be Jesus who had died on the cross. Now he, Mani, a true apostle of Jesus, had come into the world as the Holy Spirit, or Paraclete (the "Comforter" promised by Jesus in the New Testament), to set things right. From Zoroastrianism, the immemorial religion of the Persians, Mani took his dualistic view of the universe as a locus of perpetual warfare between good and evil. In his system, the supreme God (Zurvan) was pure light or goodness and identified with spirit, whereas evil partook of darkness and matter.

The two realms were at first distinct, though sharing a common boundary. Then the devil, a lion-headed, four-footed fish-bird, along with other demons whelped in darkness, invaded the kingdom of light. God thereupon produced a primal or original man who, with the help of five pure elements—mild air, living fire, cooling wind, clear water, and light—fought against the devil. But the devil, armed with his own five elements—smoke, heat, evil wind, vapor, and darkness—got the better of the primal man, and God had to come to the rescue. The damage was already done, however, since the primal man now also had the five dark elements within him—and he had been constrained to surrender his five good elements to the devil.

The mixed nature of the primal man stands for the conflicted material universe as we know it, with its clashing substrata of light and darkness, good and evil. The work of salvation consists of returning the particles of light trapped in the world of matter to their home in the realm of light, thus restoring the original separation of good and evil. But the actual creation myth itself is a lot livelier, incorporating demons—the Archons—who ejaculate at the sight of the naked Twelve Maidens, as well as female devils who have cosmic miscarriages. Think video game.

Next, two devils mated to produce the first humans, Adam and Eve, who nonetheless had some sparks of light within them, she less than he. The good angels—or Aeons—nurtured our first parents, instructing them and even sending the "real" Jesus to them. But Eve succumbed to the blandishments of a devil to produce Cain and Abel, and then lured Adam into the sin of sensuality, the result being their son Seth. And so the angels and demons warred for dominance over humanity, the demons tempting it to error via the false Mosaic religion, though Mani considered earlier Old Testament figures like Noah and Abraham to be true prophets, along with outliers like Zoroaster, Buddha, Hermes, and Plato.

The end of the universe will occur only after all the light imprisoned in this world of ours has been liberated. There is to be a Rapture of sorts, when the God of light, his Aeons, and the souls of all the elect, with Jesus as judge, will manifest themselves in all their radiant glory, before the universe is consumed in a conflagration (lasting 1,486 years) that will torment the sinners, to the delectation of the elect, and hermetically seal off the region of light and its happy denizens from the realm of darkness and its sinner-serried hell *per omnia saecula saeculorum.*

Add to this the convoluted tale of how a few dozen lesser gods had emanated from God and done various things to sundry demons, and you can begin to imagine the variegated lasagna that young Mani served up on his proselytizing debut on the coronation day of the Persian monarch Shapur I in 242. The King of Kings professed himself delighted with the novel religion but nonetheless urged Mani to depart on a long missionary journey.

Manichaeism eventually developed an elaborate church hierarchy, with a leader (Mani's successor), teachers, bishops, and elders. There were three chief classes of worshippers: a very few saints or elect (no sex, no meat, no wine, not much of anything except fruit), a great deal more auditors or catechumens, and a multitude of simple believers. The auditors had to serve, feed, and venerate the ascetic saints, who daily fought the battle of rescuing particles of light from the realm of matter. The light particles trapped in the saints' food—most often figs, as St. Augustine jeers—were released by digestion, so that they actually exhaled angels and even bits of God. The auditors didn't have to be nearly so strict, but they, too, had to avoid killing any living thing. Those who in this life had never purified themselves as members of the elect had to do so after death via the transmigration of souls.

Mani preached far and wide for three decades, but not long after he returned, the Magians, hidebound priests of the old Zoroastrian religion, prevailed on a new Persian king, Bahram I, to punish the heretic.

Bahram called Mani into his royal presence and, after scoffing at his pacifism and making slighting references to his healing powers, ordered him thrown into prison. In about 274–76, after a tormenting ordeal of twenty-six days, Mani was apparently either crucified or flayed alive, and his skin, stuffed with straw, was hung from the city gates as a warning to innovators. Of the eight books he left (one in Middle Persian, the rest in Syriac Aramaic), only fragments remain.

Yet Mani himself and his followers managed to spread his religion through much of the known world. From the Persian Empire Manichaeism branched out west to the Roman Empire, where Diocletian issued a death-penalty edict against it in 296 that failed to halt its diffusion. In Roman Africa, the young St. Augustine (354–430) lived as a Manichaean auditor for nine years, though after converting to Christianity he attacked Mani's religion as dangerously wrongheaded and ultimately tedious, claiming, "Their books are filled with long-spun-out tales of the heavens, the stars, the sun, and the moon."

The Cathars, or Albigensians, of the later Middle Ages were not actual followers of Mani, but their dualist beliefs had strong Manichaean tendencies. Eastward, the new faith planted deep roots in northern India, Turkistan, and western China, persisting until the thirteenth to sixteenth centuries. At the end of World War II, Ezra Pound, who had been imprisoned in an outdoor cage by the American army in Italy, began his *Pisan Cantos* with the image of Mani's suspended stuffed skin, likening it to Mussolini strung up by his heels from a gas station girder in Milan after being shot by Italian partisans.

21 ❧ Who was the first great master of Neoplatonism?

Plotinus, author of the Enneads, *c. 255–70*

ALEXANDRIA, CAPITAL OF EGYPT and a center of mathematical, religious, and metaphysical speculation during the third century, produced a thinker who created the last mighty system of ancient philosophic thought. Plotinus (205–70), a Greek-speaking Egyptian, studied in this city for eleven years with Ammonius Saccas, the self-taught founder of Neoplatonism who never committed his ideas to writing.

Settling in Rome in 244, Plotinus began lecturing on what he felt to be the true teachings of Plato (427–347 BC), which he claimed were being misrepresented. With its motto of "Back to Plato," his refined philosophy stressed the mystic and metaphysical aspects of Platonism rather than subtle argumentation or political thought. With Aristotelian, Pythagorean, Stoic, and Oriental admixtures, it went on to influence strongly the religious and philosophical thought of the Christian Middle Ages, especially regarding the nature of the Trinity. Plotinus's student and editor, Porphyry of Tyre, says at the beginning of his biography of his saintly and ascetic master, "He seemed ashamed to be in a body." Roman emperor Gallienus promised to help Plotinus establish in Campania an ideal Platonic city—to be called Platonopolis—but his advisers nixed the idea, regarding it as moonshine.

At the highest level of Plotinus's hierarchic structure of the universe is a triad of divinities: the One, Mind, and Soul. The ineffable, immutable, and impersonal One, or the Good, is the source of all being, yet is beyond being. In its superabundant Beauty, it emanates Mind or Intellect (*Nous*) and the infinite abstract Platonic Forms or Ideas contained in Mind. In its turn, Mind emanates Soul, which, as the World Soul, begets all individual souls and, at the lowest level of existence, sheer matter, impressing on it the Forms contained in Mind. Though the human soul is seen as imprisoned in the matter of the body, evil is viewed as a mere privation or absence of good.

Since everything ultimately stems from the One, everything strives to return to it, and for humans this involves escaping from the body and the senses by the mystical experience of ecstatic union, an annihilation of personal identity that recalls the nirvana of Buddhism. Plotinus is said to have achieved this vision of the One—"a flight of the alone to the Alone"—on only four occasions during the six years that Porphyry studied with him. Given this goal of Neoplatonism, classical scholar Albin Lesky observed, "Philosophy has become religion."

Neoplatonic ethics involved shunning materialism, religious wrangling, and political entanglements. The ideal was a life of study, contemplation, self-denial, and vegetarianism. "Man, when he commands not merely the life of sensation but also Reason and Authentic Intellection, has realized the perfect life." (Got that, dude?) But the ethical life is not directed only toward self-purification: "When one says 'God' without truly practicing virtue," writes Plotinus, " 'God' is nothing but a word." Those who live unrighteously will be reincarnated as lower life-forms until they finally ascend the ladder of being and are rejoined to the One.

Whereas Plato had disparaged art as the artist's copy of a copy (Nature, as an imperfect copy of the ideal spiritual Forms), and thus at several removes from ultimate reality, Plotinus saw it as the artist's creative expression of the cosmic Mind. Art is thus not a mere copy of Nature but a representation of the intellect of the artist, which partakes in some measure of the beauty and wisdom of the divine One and manifests it, however imperfectly, to others. The myths of the Greek gods are seen as allegories, and not, as in Plato, as blasphemous lies.

The doctrines of Plotinus are contained in the fifty-four treatises that constitute the *Enneads*—"The Nines"—so called because his writings were divided into six groups of nine treatises each when they were edited, reordered, and published c. 300–5 by Porphyry, who shared many of his master's ideas and on a single occasion even attained union with the One. However, beginning with the Syrian Iamblichus (c. 250–c. 330), Neoplatonism veered toward magic and superstition, numerological Neo-Pythagoreanism, occultism, Mithraism, demonology, and Oriental ritualism, rapturously bathing itself in ancient Chaldean and Egyptian "wisdom" in a kind of New Age mishmash.

In an ugly incident arising from factional strife between Archbishop Cyril and the civil governor of Alexandria in 415, the Neoplatonic philosopher, astronomer, and mathematician Hypatia, "the Divine Pagan" who lectured in the city and wrote lost commentaries on the algebraist Diophantus and the *Conics* of Apollonius of Perga, was pulled from her carriage and dragged into a church, where she was stripped naked and beaten to death with roofing tiles before her body was torn to pieces and burned by a savage Christian mob.

Yet many Neoplatonists of the time were or became Christians. St. Augustine imbibed many Neoplatonic ideas and passed them on to the early medieval church. The sixth-century Greek writings of an anonymous Christian author now referred to as Pseudo-Dionysius the Areopagite supplied Neoplatonic underpinnings to Christian cosmology via a ninefold series of angelic intermediaries (seraphim, cherubim, thrones, etc.) between the One and humankind that went on to influence Thomas Aquinas and other Christian, Jewish, and Muslim theologians.

An orgy of Neoplatonic thought marked the Renaissance. Marsilio Ficino (1433–99), head of the Platonic Academy at Florence, translated Plato and Plotinus into Latin and expounded Plato from a Neoplatonic slant to reconcile him with Christian doctrine. His contemporary Giovanni Pico della Mirandola imagined human potentiality as the power to sink to the level of beasts or insentient matter or to rise to the level of godhead. Edmund Spenser, the seventeenth-century Cambridge Platonists, and the Romantic poets and critics of later centuries all reveled in the heady doctrines of Neoplatonism, which placed a premium on the expressive powers of inspired poets and thinkers to create a radiantly beautiful cosmos of their own. Percy Bysshe Shelley expressed a quintessentially Neoplatonic view of the organic world as a messy thing when he wrote in *Adonais*, "Life, like a dome of many-coloured glass, / Stains the white radiance of Eternity."

Modern enthusiasts of Neoplatonism have included some well-known writers. In several late poems, William Butler Yeats conjures up Plotinus as the creator of an ascetic philosophy that wrongly undervalues the senses and sexuality—"bruising the body to delight the soul"—while remaining attractive for its spiritual and artistic transcendence. In Ezra Pound's "Canto XV," an Italian-speaking Plotinus ("*Andiamo!*") leads the narrator (as Virgil led Dante) out of a nauseating hell representing a nightmare vision of early-twentieth-century England. Later in the *Cantos*, various Neoplatonic philosophers are evoked for their identification of fire and light with the workings of Mind in the universe. Ever concerned with the delicate workings of his own mind, Gustave Flaubert read Plotinus to combat the crying jags of depression. And according to *Howl*, the "best minds" of Allen Ginsberg's generation studied, among other authors, Plotinus, presumably before being "destroyed by madness."

22 ∿ Who is considered the first Christian monk?

St. Anthony of Egypt, who went out to live in the desert in
c. 270

IF YOU DOUBT the medical hypothesis that severe caloric restriction can extend the human life span, consider St. Anthony (c. 251–356), who lived most of his life in the desert with very little food (but a huge amount of temptation) until age 105, and it couldn't have been due to great genes, because his parents died when he was a young man.

This Coptic-speaking Egyptian monk, variously called Anthony the Great, the Hermit, or the Abbot, has been regarded as the founder of Christian monasticism since the mid-fourth century. While *monks* (from Greek *monos*, "alone") is a generic term for people who withdraw from the world to live a religious life, it comprises two main subsets: *anchorites* (hermits or eremites—true solitaries) and *cenobites* (who live communally in monasteries). Anthony may be said to have originated anchoritic monasticism, in that his followers typically lived separately from one another in cells and huts and came together only infrequently for religious services.

Long before Anthony, there had been Buddhist monks, pagan Egyptian anchorites, and the Essene community in Judea, but these had little influence on Christian practices. What most inspired Anthony and zealots like him was the tradition that Christ, at the beginning of his ministry, had gone into the desert to be tempted by the devil for forty days and forty nights.

The story of Anthony's life, according to St. Athanasius, bishop of Alexandria, who knew him, is essentially as follows. He was born in Middle Egypt to rich Christian parents who left him and a younger sister orphans when he was about twenty. At church services, when he heard Gospel texts in which Christ exhorted his hearers to leave family and home and give all to the poor if they would have eternal life, Anthony took them as personal messages. In about 270, resolving on an ascetic life, he placed his sister with some Christian women in a kind of protoconvent and gave his wealth to the poor before going off to the outskirts of his town, where some hermits had already settled. After learning from each of them, Anthony went to live in an old tomb. There, he survived on bread and water and was beset by demons who flogged and clawed him mercilessly.

Determining to flee settled life altogether, he wandered out into the harsh desert, where he lived so austerely that Satan sent demons to tempt him with visions of the pleasures he had left behind. They offered him succulent food and assumed the forms of beautiful women, but Anthony defeated their diabolic wiles with arduous prayer. When the devils tried to terrify him with visions of a roaring and hissing menagerie of wild beasts, serpents, and scorpions, a light from heaven dispelled the visions, and the voice of Christ reassured him.

In about 286, Anthony crossed to the east side of the Nile and settled on a mountain called Pispir. He decided to shut himself up in a deserted Roman fort and lived there for twenty years, seeing no one and living on bread that was left for him twice a year and preserved more or less fresh. Emerging hale and hearty at age fifty-five, he found numerous admirers eager to imitate his way of life, so he began to preach, comfort the sick, and exorcise demons. Soon, there were five thousand followers living in caves, huts, and old pharaonic tombs. Like a true abbot, Anthony organized their living arrangements and preached sermons on the monastic life.

During a persecution of Christians in Alexandria in about 311, Anthony journeyed there in search of martyrdom but was disappointed in his goal, though he fearlessly ministered to many who were awaiting execution. When he returned, life at the old Roman fort had become much too crowded for Anthony's anchoritic taste, so he betook himself to Mount Colzim in the open desert near the Red Sea, about seventy-five miles east of the Nile, where he found an oasis with a spring and a few palm trees. He now undertook severe fasting, donned a hair shirt, and shunned all washing. He also determined to grow his own grain and herbs so that he wouldn't have to depend on others to bring him food.

Here an interpolated episode from St. Jerome's life of St. Paul the Hermit may not be amiss. At age ninety, Anthony heard a voice saying that there was an even holier man than he—Paul, who had been living in solitude in the desert for ninety years—so Anthony set out to find him. After meeting up with a centaur and a satyr, who may have been demons, he arrived at Paul's cave on the third day. As the first Christian hermit, Paul was reluctant to let Anthony in, but after many tears and entreaties he acquiesced. When it was time to eat, the raven that had been bringing Paul half a loaf of bread every day for sixty years showed up with a full loaf.

After their frugal repast, Paul told Anthony that God must have sent him to bury him—Paul was pushing 113—so he hoped it wouldn't be too much trouble for his visitor to go back home to get the lovely cloak that Bishop Athanasius had given Anthony and use it as his winding sheet. No problem, responded the nimble nonagenarian before scampering back to fetch the gift of Athanasius, who had been grateful to him for journeying to Alexandria several years earlier to speak out against the Arian heretics.

On his return, Anthony heard celestial singing and saw angels, apostles, and prophets bearing Paul's spirit up to heaven in the form of a shining star. Arriving at the cave, Anthony found the ancient hermit's body still kneeling in prayer. After reciting the offices of the dead, he wrapped Paul in the cloak and was helped to bury him by two devout lions who showed up to dig the grave with their strong paws.

Fifteen years later, on the day Anthony himself breathed his last in his cave on Mount Colzim, he bade his followers live every day as if it would be their last. Then angels came and conducted his soul to heaven.

Soon after, a monastery named for him arose on the site, where a Coptic Orthodox monastery still stands.

A follower of St. Anthony, St. Macarius the Younger, established a rule for Eastern monasticism, in which the most eminent name is that of St. Basil the Great. In about 341, St. Athanasius brought to Rome two Egyptian monks who, along with his later *Life of Anthony*, spurred the development of the monastic ideal in the West. St. Martin of Tours soon founded monasteries in France, and in the mid-fifth century popes Sixtus III and Leo I founded others in Rome. In the following century, the monastic movement began exercising a hegemony over learning and culture that it lost only with the advent of the Renaissance and the Reformation a thousand years later.

With his feast day on January 17, St. Anthony was venerated as a protector of farm animals from disease and was often portrayed with a pig at his feet, which may represent one of the shapes assumed by a devil who tempted him. The monks of the order of St. Anthony kept herds of swine that they allowed to roam freely and scavenge in the streets of medieval towns, where the pious regarded them as holy animals.

St. Anthony and his tribulations have been a favorite subject of painters from the young Michelangelo and Hieronymus Bosch to Salvador Dalí. In 1874, Gustave Flaubert published a droll closet drama on the theme, complete with a Queen of Sheba temptress and a trip to outer space with the old monk riding on the back of a flying devil. The Russian translation of Flaubert's *The Temptation of St. Anthony* was promptly banned by the czarist government as "detrimental to religion."

23 ⌒ Who were the first Roman tetrarchs?

Diocletian, Maximian, Constantius, and Galerius; joint Roman emperors, 293–305

AFTER BEING CATAPULTED to supreme power late in 284 as yet another in the long series of military commanders raised to the throne of Rome by his soldiers in the field (see Question 18), Diocletian soon demonstrated that, though born of ex-slave Dalmatian parents, he merited the historian Aurelius Victor's praise as a man "chosen emperor because of his wisdom." His reforms of the government, economy, and administration gave the reeling empire a fresh start and established the outlines of the early medieval world. The frontiers were stabilized, the barbarians kept in check, and challenges from usurpers greatly diminished—at least for a while.

In 286, Diocletian chose his tough military comrade, Maximian, originally a crude peasant from what is now Serbia, to be his partner—a fellow "augustus"—in ruling the Roman world. Seven years later, in 293, Diocletian determined to stabilize the imperial succession by creating two junior emperors—to be called caesars—to help him and Maximian, the two augusti, protect the frontiers and administer the vast empire. This elevation of Constantius and Galerius, two stalwart generals, created the Roman tetrarchy (Greek, "rule by four").

The wellborn Illyrian Constantius Chlorus—"Pale-Face"—had divorced his wife Helena, mother of Constantine, in 289 and married the stepdaughter of Maximian. Now, four years later, he was adopted by Maximian and made his caesar. Although Constantius's bust in Rome's Capitoline Museum makes him look as if he habitually sucked on lemons, he was apparently of an equable disposition. The ex-herdsman Galerius was appointed Diocletian's caesar, and he, too, was intimately bound to the alliance by having to divorce his wife and wed Diocletian's daughter. A contemporary porphyry statue of the tetrarchs, portrayed embracing, looted from the East and now embedded in an exterior corner of St. Mark's Basilica in Venice, shows how closely they were supposed to "stick together." Their cohesiveness was further emphasized by the fact that any law made by one of the emperors was issued in the name of all four. These were their respective spheres of influence:

The Original Tetrarchy

DIOCLETIAN: Eastern augustus	MAXIMIAN: Western augustus
Thrace, Egypt, Asian provinces	Italy, Spain, Africa
Capital: Nicomedia (in Asia Minor)	Capital: Milan
GALERIUS: Eastern caesar	CONSTANTIUS: Western caesar
Illyria to the Black Sea coast	Gaul, Britain
Protector of the Danube frontier	Protector of the Rhine frontier
Capital: Sirmium (in modern Serbia)	Capital: Augusta Treverorum (modern Trier, Germany)

The main purpose of this ancient "Gang of Four" was to quadruple the odds against any barbarian leader or Roman general who had notions of carving out territory within the empire for himself. But there was a downside. The establishment and maintenance of four opulent courts required enormous sums, and the strength of the army was raised by one-third to four hundred thousand men. The empire was now divided into a dozen dioceses and more than a hundred smaller provinces. The civilian administration was separated from the military in the provinces, so that the governor, no longer in charge of the provincial army, would be less likely to revolt, but this explosive expansion of the civil service system multiplied the costs of government.

Taxes soared to support a bloated bureaucracy. Farmers abandoned their land to avoid taxation—some of them becoming brigands—so that the government ended up owning much of the land and creating increasingly large estates, called *latifundia*, worked by *coloni* who were essentially serfs. Workers were frozen in their jobs down the generations, so that a plumber's son could only be a plumber. Even wage and price controls were attempted for a while (gastronomic example: no more than forty denarii could be charged for ten small songbirds or dormice). Many fled to the church to avoid this brave new Roman world, but Diocletian initiated the last—and fiercest—empire-wide persecution of Christians (303–11). He and Maximian adopted the demeanor, garb, and court protocols of Oriental kings and the cult status of gods. The senate became more like a social club for the wealthy than a force in the conduct of affairs, and the city of Rome itself became a backwater. As historian R. H. Barrow observes, "The price of security was the absorption of the individual by the state."

After Diocletian and Maximian celebrated a glorious triumph for all the victories they and their caesars had won over the years, they both abdicated on May 1, 305, in their respective capitals of Nicomedia and Milan, according to a decision foisted on Maximian. When the latter once urged his former colleague to reassume, along with him, the supreme power, Diocletian remarked that if Maximian could only see the wonderful cabbages he was growing with his own hands in his retirement, he wouldn't have made his futile suggestion.

Diocletian was doubtlessly eager to see his plan for orderly imperial succession work itself out before his eyes, and two new caesars were duly appointed after the former junior emperors had assumed the dignity of augusti. But civil wars soon broke out and continued for almost two decades. After Constantius, augustus of the West, died of illness in the summer of 306, his son Constantine was proclaimed emperor by his troops. The augustus Galerius accepted Constantine, but only as a caesar, while promoting the other caesar to the rank of augustus and appointing another junior colleague.

But now a fifth wheel, Maxentius, appended himself to the tetrarchy. As son of the bored retiree Maximian and son-in-law of chief boss Galerius, Maxentius (who was a dead ringer for the young Kirk Douglas, complete with cleft chin) had himself proclaimed augustus at Rome in 306. Soon this usurper's old father rushed back into the fray, assuming his position as augustus again. Diocletian's tetrarchy had swelled into a sexarchy.

After various battles, enforced suicides, resignations, new appointments, and natural deaths, the empire was once again headed by a foursome of monarchs, with Constantine and his brother-in-law Licinius soon teaming up against Maxentius and Galerius's nephew, Maximin.

Constantine invaded Italy and defeated Maxentius at the battle of Saxa Rubra a few miles north of Rome in late October 312, though his troops were outnumbered four to one. During the flight of his legions back across the Milvian Bridge, Maxentius drowned in the Tiber. In the East, Licinius defeated the feckless Maximin, who died soon afterward in August 313. With Licinius now ruling the East and Constantine the West, the two began angling for supreme power, fighting a series of wars that ended with the defeat and resignation of Licinius in 324 and his death at the hands of the ruthless Constantine the following year.

The laudable attempt to stabilize the empire and the succession by distributing power and responsibilities among a small group of men had led, after a single generation, to the emergence of a sole emperor who was even shrewder, tougher, and more farsighted than Diocletian.

FOURTH CENTURY

24 ∾ What was the first legal toleration of Christianity in the Roman Empire?

The Edict of Toleration of Emperor Galerius in 311

FOR EIGHT YEARS, toward the end of Diocletian's reign and continuing beyond it, Christians living in the Roman Empire endured the most severe persecution ever launched against them. By his edicts against the Christians, motivated by the desire to maintain a modicum of cultural unity in the empire but also to seize considerable assets, churches were burned down, legal protections were withdrawn, Christian assemblies were forbidden, and their sacred books destroyed. Beginning in 303, many Christians were tortured, and perhaps several thousand executed.

Then, on April 30, 311, one of the coemperors of that time, Galerius, who had originally incited Diocletian against the Christians, relented from his hatred of the church while suffering from the pain of bowel cancer or gangrene (see Question 23). The Edict of Toleration that Galerius published in Nicomedia in his name and those of his imperial colleagues Licinius and Constantine conferred legal recognition on Christians while asking them to pray for him, the empire, and themselves. He died a few days later.

The document allowed Christians "freely to profess their private opinions and to assemble in their meeting places without fear or molestation, provided always that they preserve a due respect to the established laws and government." It was an opportune decision, since by this time at least a tenth of the empire's inhabitants—six million out of sixty million—were Christians.

Two years later, a far more famous act of toleration was issued. By the so-called Edict of Milan (which may have taken the form of a series of letters instructing provincial governors on these matters), Constantine and coemperor Licinius, who had both already granted toleration and property restitution within their respective domains of the empire, now legalized Christianity—actually, all religions—throughout the remainder of the Roman world. This measure, dating from 313, led to the release of many Christians from imprisonment and slave labor, restored Christian property confiscated under Diocletian's decrees, and began a momentous shift in the balance of power in the empire, away from the adherents of an ancient Greco-Roman pagan aristocratic code and toward the worshippers of a carpenter's son who had died a criminal's death on a cross.

In the year before the Edict of Milan was issued, Constantine, who had grown up as a pagan, claimed to have had a vision of a cross of light in the sky, accompanied by Greek words meaning "by this sign, conquer," before facing his powerful rival Maxentius in battle. The emperor was inspired to make a monogram out of the first two letters (*chi* and *rho*) of Christ's name in Greek, and he blazoned this labarum on his soldiers' shields and battle standards on the day of his crucial victory over Maxentius and ever afterward. The new Christian convert, who had been an adherent of a solar cult, began building Christian basilicas in Rome soon after promulgating his edict of toleration.

It became readily apparent that Constantine intended to make Christianity the favored religion in the empire, providing the church with government funds and land grants and elevating bishops to prestigious appointments. The distinction between church and state grew increasingly blurred, especially after his defeat in 324 of his last imperial colleague, Licinius, who had begun persecuting Christians again. The capital city he named for himself and founded on the site of the ancient Greek city of Byzantium on May 11, 330—Constantinople, "the New Rome"—became the seat of a Greek Orthodox patriarch whose power and influence in the Christian world rivaled those of the bishop of Rome himself.

Though later dubbed "the Thirteenth Apostle" and revered as a saint in the Eastern Church, Constantine didn't evince too many Christian virtues. He executed his eldest son, Crispus, and several other troublesome relatives and had his wife, Fausta, killed by being locked in a steam bath. Some historians claim he legitimized Christianity grudgingly, mainly to increase the cohesiveness of the army, many of whose soldiers were now Christians. Some contrast the zeal of his Christian mother, St. Helena (who built shrines like that of the Holy Sepulchre in the Holy Land, where she claimed to have found the cross of Christ), with the dilatory behavior of Constantine himself, who was baptized only on his deathbed in 337. Yet the reason for his long delay may well have been the current belief that the sacrament conferred absolution of all sins committed up to that point. The ultimate irony regarding the empire's first Christian ruler was his deification as a pagan god by the Roman senate.

Whatever his motives for choosing to "make straight the ways of the Lord," whether politically calculating, sincerely personal, or a mixture of the two, Constantine succeeded in creating, according to historian Michael Rostovtzeff, "a new system which was to rule both East and West for many centuries—a monarchy by the grace of God." Its flip side, what may perhaps be called "a theocracy by the grace of the Roman emperor," was definitively discredited only in 1440, when the humanist scholar Lorenzo Valla proved that the document referred to as the Donation of Constantine—by which the emperor had supposedly bequeathed to the pope the western half of the Roman Empire—was actually a forgery, since the Latin in which it was written was not that of the fourth century. (It was composed four centuries later.) An apparently legal justification for the papacy's ancient claim to supreme political authority over the kings and other rulers of Europe had finally been undermined—by a scholar who went on to become apostolic secretary to Pope Nicholas V.

25 ∾ Who was the first Gupta emperor of northern India?

Chandragupta I (reigned c. 320–c. 330), whose dynasty presided over a golden age

IN ABOUT 308, a kinglet in Magadha (roughly modern Bihar in northeast India) made a smart marriage. His union with Princess Kumaradevi of the powerful Licchavi tribe extended the territory of their joint domains northward, perhaps into Nepal. By 320, Chandragupta and his son Samudragupta, with the help of the Licchavi, projected their power into the Ganges Valley states of northern India to create the first centrally administered Indian empire since that of the ancient Mauryas (321–185 BC). Chandragupta celebrated his prowess by declaring himself *maharajadhiraja*—"king of kings."

Samudragupta, "the Indian Napoleon," who killed or cowed more than twenty monarchs in his wars, acquired Pataliputra (modern Patna), which briefly became the Gupta capital, and exacted tribute from rulers in east Bengal, Assam and Nepal in the east, and the Punjab (in northwest India). On one of the magnificent gold coins of the era (the Guptas got their gold by selling as much as they could to the effete Romans), doughty Samudragupta is shown playing a harp. He is also said to have revived the ancient Vedic practice of sacrificing horses.

But it was Chandragupta II (380–415), called Vikramaditya ("Sun of Power"), who, around the year 400, ushered in the Golden Age of India by subsidizing poets, philosophers, artists, and scientists. Fahsien, a Buddhist monk from China who spent six years in India at this time and composed a journal of his travels, marveled at the wealth, freedom, security, and virtue of the Indians. He praised the free hospitals, the avid student and monastic life, and the charitable institutions he saw in the many bustling cities he visited. There was no capital punishment under the Gupta emperor: Criminals were fined, and recidivists merely had their right hands cut off. Fa-hsien mentioned that, except by the untouchable Chandalas, no living creatures were killed in the country—by the law of ahimsa—and no booze was sold in the markets.

Also a warrior in his own right, Chandragupta II did his share to extend the Gupta Empire until it covered the vast expanse from the Bay of Bengal in the east to the Arabian Sea in the west, and from the Himalayas down to the central Deccan Plateau. Yet the chief delight of this monarch was in attracting gifted men to his court at Ujjain, including those later called the Nine Gems, of whom the most illustrious was the Sanskrit poet Kālidāsa, who, on the basis of his three extant plays, has been overenthusiastically dubbed "the Indian Shakespeare."

Kālidāsa's most famous play, the *Shakuntala*, usually considered the poetic and dramatic masterpiece of India, is named for the foster daughter of a hermit whose tranquil existence is shattered when King Dushyanta arrives in his chariot during a hunt, promptly falls in love, marries her in secret, and regrets that he has to rush away to his capital on urgent business—slam, bam, thank you, ma'am. He leaves a ring with her, and a holy man tells her the king will remember her as long as she safeguards it. Shakuntala gives birth to a boy and sets out to find the king but loses the ring while bathing in a river. When she arrives at court, the king fails to recognize her and sends her packing, but after a fisherman brings him the ring, which he'd found in a fish's belly, Dushyanta's memory is miraculously restored, and, after several highly improbable adventures, father, mother, and son are all providentially reunited. Goethe loved the play and, in his *Faust*, imitated its convention of having the stage manager appear as a character in the prologue.

In another play by Kālidāsa, the divine nymph Urvashi agrees to marry mortal king Pururavas—with the proviso that she never wants to see him naked. When she espies him in the buff and flees back to heaven, the king's insane grief knows no bounds, but the mismatched lovers are brought together at the end.

During the reign of Chandragupta II, the *Bhagavad Gita* ("The Song of the Lord"), the Hindu philosophical poem in seven hundred verses centering on the dialogue between the god Krishna and the reluctant warrior Arjuna, assumed its final written form, though perhaps it was first composed hundreds of years earlier. The work is embedded within the gargantuan martial epic, the *Mahabharata*, the longest poem ever written at more than two hundred thousand lines, which, along with the slightly less massive *Ramayana*, also received canonical written form at this time when Hinduism was gradually replacing Buddhism as the major religion of India.

This was also a period of refined and sensuous sculpture and of sublime Buddhist art—especially the gracefully serene statue of the *Buddha of Sarnath* and the frescoes of the Ajanta temple caves in central India, though the Gupta rulers do not appear to have directly patronized these works. Astronomy and mathematics flourished, and Chandragupta II issued a single code of law for his domains. The twenty-two-foot-high, six-ton Iron Pillar of Delhi, which many attribute to his reign, remains almost totally uncorroded after sixteen hundred years.

Toward the end of the next reign, that of Kumaragupta I (c. 415–c. 455), the "Huna"—the Ephthalites, or White Huns—first started ravaging northwest India. Strenuous resistance during the following reign staved off the empire's final dissolution until the mid-sixth century, though petty Gupta kings clung to power for several hundred more years, and traders and Buddhist missionaries disseminated Gupta cultural norms far beyond the subcontinent to Burma, Thailand, Indochina, the Malay Peninsula, and Indonesia.

26 ❧ Who was the first Santa Claus?

*St. Nicholas of Myra (flourished c. 325), whose gifts
of gold saved three girls' virtue*

IT IS A STRANGE METAMORPHOSIS indeed that transformed a fourth-century Greek-speaking bishop of Myra on the southern coast of modern-day Turkey into, well, Santa. Aside from this iconic distinction, St. Nicholas can claim to be a patron of sailors, children, travelers who worry about thieves, Russia, Greece, Sicily, the Italian port city of Bari, scholars, pawnbrokers, and prostitutes.

He was said to be born in a city of Asia Minor to wealthy Christian parents, and the legends that later accrued to him claimed that, on the very day of his birth, he stood up in his bath, joined his hands, praised God, and decided to breast-feed only once on Wednesdays and Fridays to teach himself to fast. Much later, as an orphan with Christian charity in his heart and a massive patrimony on his hands, he came to the rescue of a widower who had lost all his riches and feared he would have to make prostitutes of his three young daughters to keep them all from starving.

Nicholas hit on the stratagem of taking a handful of gold, wrapping it in a handkerchief, and somehow delivering it anonymously to the desperate family. The moon, shining brightly on an open window, pointed the way—he threw the golden gift in and ran. The father, who saw it land at his feet, used it as a dowry to marry off his eldest daughter. You know the rest—Nicholas, in true fairy-tale fashion, does the same for the other two daughters, but on the third occasion the father was on the watch for him and thanked him profusely, though Nicholas made him promise not to mention anything to anyone. Some say the three balls in front of pawnshops do not hark back to the Medici banking family but to St. Nicholas's three pouches of gold.

Then he took a sea voyage to Palestine during which he brought back to life a sailor who had fallen overboard. Naturally, when a storm later arose, the sailors all prayed to him, and he calmed it. On returning home, Nicholas settled in the city of Myra, where, after the bishop died, the priests had a vision ordering them to choose as their next leader the first man to show up at church the following morning, who—you guessed it—was Nicholas. They made him bishop and never had reason to regret their choice. He saved the people from a dread famine during which he happened to stay at the inn of a man who used to kidnap children and feed them to his guests. Immediately divining what manner of food the wicked man had set before him, Nicholas went to a tub of salted meat, made the sign of the cross over it, and three little children who had been pickled in it came back to life, safe and sound. So runs the legend, an uneasy amalgam of Hans Christian Andersen and the Brothers Grimm.

Perhaps you're wondering how St. Nicholas, who was buried in a church in Myra after his death sometime in the mid-fourth century, came to reside in a silver casket in the crypt beneath the altar of the Basilica di San Nicola in Bari, on the southeastern coast of Italy. The short answer is that some intrepid merchants of Bari, on their way back from a wheat delivery to Antioch in 1087, stopped in Myra, absconded with Nicholas's body (despite the protestations of its Greek Christian guardians and thanks to the insouciance of the city's Muslim overlords), and stored it in a wine cask until their glorious return home. The grateful Baresi soon built a splendid basilica fit to receive the remains of a holy man who, ever afterward, has been known as St. Nicholas of Bari.

Every year, on St. Nicholas's feast day, December 6, priests of his basilica extract a flask of an oily substance—called *manna*—that is supposedly exuded from his bones. Since it is believed to have miraculous powers, it is distributed to those who need miracles most, and thus Bari remains the home of one of southern Italy's most illustrious shrines, where many pilgrims still wend their way.

St. Nicholas's penchant for discreet gift giving (combined with the ancient Roman custom of giving presents at the winter festival of the Saturnalia) may lie behind his later habit of leaving gifts secretly for young people, first on the eve of his feast day, and then a few weeks later on Christmas. The Dutch brought this tradition of *Sinterklaas* with them when they settled in what later became New York City, and the saint's name underwent its change to Santa Claus by the time Washington Irving mentioned him in his early-nineteenth-century tales about Dutch New York. The 1823 poem "A Visit from St. Nicholas," long attributed to Clement Clarke Moore but possibly by Henry Livingston, featured most of the trappings we associate with Santa—reindeer, the descent and ascent via the chimney, the sack of toys for sleeping children who have hung up their stockings, the jolly old coot with the twinkle in his eye, the white beard, and "his little round belly, / That shook when he laughed, like a bowlful of jelly"—though the name Santa Claus is not used in the poem. In 1841, Prince Albert introduced the first Christmas tree to England from his native Germany, where the St. Nicholas story had long been assimilated to old Norse and Teutonic legends.

German-American caricaturist and cartoonist Thomas Nast did much to fix the image of Santa Claus in popular consciousness, drawing him annually for thirty years, beginning in 1863. Then, in the 1920s, the Coca-Cola Company began glomming on to Santa's image in its ads, and it's never let go. "At this time," according to a recent company posting under Coke Lore, "many people thought of Coca-Cola as a drink only for warm weather. The Coca-Cola Company began a campaign to remind people that Coca-Cola was a great choice in any month."

27 ❧ What was the first ecumenical Christian council?

The Council of Nicaea, 325, which condemned the teachings of Arius on Christ's nature

FROM THE BEGINNING, to be a Christian meant to accept the mission of Jesus of Nazareth as divinely ordained by the God of the Jews, but the precise nature of Jesus himself—prophet? Messiah? Son of God? God incarnate?—began in the third and fourth centuries to exercise the ingenuity of the church's subtlest thinkers: the Greek-speaking, philosophically sophisticated prelates and clerics of the Eastern Roman Empire. For a mere hint of the problems involved, consider that the same New Testament that contained these statements pointing to the divinity of Jesus:

> *the only Son, God, who is at the Father's side* (John 1:18)
>
> [Thomas the Apostle to Jesus]: *My Lord and my God!* (John 20:28)
>
> *He is the true God and eternal life* (1 John 5:20)

also presents Jesus as saying of himself

> *a man who has told you the truth I heard from God* (John 8:40)
>
> *for the Father is greater than I* (John 14:28)

*But of that day and hour [the end of the world] no one knows,
neither the angels of heaven, nor the Son, but the Father alone*
(Matthew 24:36).

In about 318, Arius (c. 250–336), a Christian priest in Alexandria,
Egypt, began promulgating his doctrines on the nature of Christ: that
Jesus Christ, though an exalted semidivine being and Son of God, had
been created by God out of nothing; that there was a time when he had
not existed; that he inhabited his human form like a veil of flesh, rather
than being truly human; and that though he had created the heavens
and the earth (and the Holy Ghost), and was the intermediary between
all of creation and God, he was not of the same nature and substance as
God, to whom he was inferior (as the earlier theologians Tertullian and
Origen had maintained). Arius's superior, Alexander, archbishop of
Alexandria, removed him from his post and excommunicated him, but
Arius had broad backing for his views.

Emperor Constantine, fresh from defeating in 324 his last rival,
Licinius, for authority over the entire empire, east and west, was dis-
turbed by the rifts in the Christianity he hoped would bring ever-
increasing unity of religious thought and practice to his vast domains.
After failing to get the two sides to agree over what he considered tri-
fling differences, he decided to resolve the issue by convening the first
Christian ecumenical ("worldwide") council, which was supposed to
bring together bishops—all expenses paid—from all over the empire to
Nicaea, a small town not far from Constantinople.

About 250 bishops heeded his summons, almost all from the
Greek-speaking Eastern Christian world. Hardly any of the Western
bishops could see what all the pother was about, but Pope Sylvester I,
too infirm to attend, sent two priests as his representatives.

The council opened in either May or June of 325 with preliminary
sessions in the main church of Nicaea and the chief hall of Constantine's lakeside palace—some of the attendees hobbling in on crutches
or maimed and scarred from the not-too-distant anti-Christian persecutions. When the emperor himself arrived, clad in imperial purple and
gold cloth covered with precious gems, and mounted his golden throne,
you can be sure the real business of the council began.

Soon the Nicene Creed was drawn up, representing a revision of an
earlier creed and succinctly embodying what became the orthodox
statement of belief, to the effect that Jesus Christ was begotten of the

Father (*not* created); was himself God and was of the same substance as—*homoousios*—the Father; that God created all things in heaven and earth through the agency of Christ, who became incarnate as man, and as such suffered and died, rose from the dead on the third day, ascended into heaven, and would return to judge the living and the dead. The creed anathematized (formally cursed) those who said there was a time when Christ did not exist or that he was of a different substance from the Father.

Most of the bishops at Nicaea had never thought very deeply about some of these hairsplitting issues, but almost all of them, with the encouragement of Constantine, who wanted a consensus, soon subscribed to the notion that God the Father and Christ were consubstantial, that is, they shared the same divine substance or essence. Arius and two bishops who refused to accept the Nicene Creed were exiled and anathematized, and Arius's writings, now officially heretical, were consigned to the flames. A legend expects us to believe that Bishop Nicholas of Myra—we're talking Santa Claus here (see Question 26)—gave the septuagenarian Arius a swat upside his head that knocked him out of his chair.

The council also addressed the issue of when to celebrate Easter (the first Sunday after the full moon following the spring equinox) and passed twenty canon laws, including one that forbade any clergyman to live with a woman other than his mother, sister, aunt, or "any person who is above suspicion" (though the council declined to vote on a measure mandating clerical celibacy), and another law forbidding clergymen to lend at interest. The council came to an end on either July or August 25 with a superb feast hosted by Constantine, who also lavished gifts on the attendees.

Nonetheless, now that Pandora's box had been opened, rival points of view sprang up. Various clerics maintained that Christ was totally unlike the Father (*anomoios*), or sort of similar to him (*homoios*), or perhaps even of a similar substance with him (*homoiousios*). It may seem that between this last compromise position and the orthodox one of *homoousios*, there's only an iota of difference—which there literally is—but much depended on that extra *i*. Was Christianity just another version of pagan polytheism or of Neoplatonism (see Question 21), complete with its own demigod, or did it have at its heart an austere mystery asserting that humankind's salvation was personally accomplished by God himself, rather than a created being? When the equally divine nature of the Holy Spirit was asserted by later councils, the church had its dogma of the Trinity intact: one divine substance—one God—in three divine persons.

In later years, Constantine flip-flopped twice on his pro-Nicene position after meeting with smooth-talking Arius, but on the second occasion, after being restored to Christian communion at Constantinople, the old heresiarch died suddenly on the very day of his triumph. As described in grisly terms by a fifth-century church historian, Arius, while walking through the streets of the capital, suffered a massive hemorrhagic bowel evacuation that expelled his small intestine and other viscera. Some later historians, among them Edward Gibbon, smelled foul play on the part of Arius's ecclesiastical enemies.

Constantine's deathbed baptism was performed by the Arian bishop Eusebius of Nicomedia, whose influence at court may have led Constantine's son Constantius II to embrace Arianism ardently and protract the seething—and often violent—religious conflict into the next generation and beyond. In just the years 342–43, more Christians were murdered by other Christians than the Roman authorities had killed in all their persecutions.

At the second ecumenical council, held at Constantinople in 381, Jesus was declared to possess a truly human soul, and at the Council of Chalcedon, the fourth ecumenical council, in 451, Jesus was pronounced to be a "hypostatic union," being both true God and true man and containing within himself two complete natures, divine and human, in one person. Further councils addressed other Christological heresies that had sprung up, including Nestorianism (Christ exists as two persons rather than as two natures), Monophysitism (Christ has only one nature—divine), and Monothelitism (Christ has only one will, as opposed to the orthodox view positing two wills, one for each nature).

Several later Roman emperors professed or supported Arianism, not to mention various barbarian tribes who converted to Arian Christianity, such as the Goths, Vandals, Burgundians, and Lombards. Persecutions and counterpersecutions over a doctrine that the church had branded a heresy at the Council of Nicaea thus persisted three centuries after the death of its founder, fueling countless whirligigs of human futility.

28 ∽ What was the first major battle in the West in which cavalry was decisive?

The battle of Adrianople, in 378, which pitted the Romans against the Goths

BETWEEN A ROCK AND A HARD PLACE—or, for the classically inclined, between Scylla and Charybdis—is where the Germanic nation of Visigoths found itself in the spring of 376. On one side, the Goths were being harried by the nightmarish Huns, while on the far shore of the Danube, which impeded their panicky flight, they could see the camps of the Roman legionnaires who, just a few years earlier, had launched three waves of punitive expeditions deep into Gothic territory.

Pleading to the Roman soldiers patrolling the mile-wide river in ships, like souls in Hades begging to be ferried across the Styx, the Visigothic hordes were relieved to learn that Emperor Valens had finally granted their request to settle as farmers in the fertile lands of Thrace, a province south of the Danube in what is now Bulgaria. Of course, the men would all have to be disarmed before entering the empire, and yes, they would have to sign up for a major war Valens was concocting against the hated Persians—and, oh, they would have to give hostages to ensure their good behavior—but these were all standard immigration policies for allowing groups of barbarians into the empire.

In the frenzied, day-and-night crossings of the Danube that followed, most of the tens of thousands of Visigoths managed to hold on to their weapons. The Roman generals in charge of the new denizens of the empire began appropriating for their own profit the supplies earmarked for the Goths while providing the starving refugees with dogs to be used as food in exchange for their children—one dog for each Gothic child who would then be sold as a slave.

The following spring, when it was time to move the immigrants south to their new homes, riots broke out after further instances of insolent cruelty and outright treachery by the Romans. The Visigoths, joined by Ostrogoths (who, denied admission to the empire, had stealthily crossed the river anyway), and by slaves, escaped convicts, and Gothic countrymen who were already enrolled in the Roman army, went on an extended rampage in the eastern Balkans, "a foul orgy of rapine and slaughter, bloodshed and fire," according to the ancient historian Ammianus.

Since these doughty barbarians defeated or held their own against the forces sent against them, Valens himself decided to march his Eastern field army of about thirty thousand west from Syria to squash the rebellion. Although his colleague and nephew, Gratian, emperor in the West, was hurrying east to join up with him, Valens, who underestimated the number of Goths he had to deal with, preferred to win a great victory that would be untarnished by his coemperor's aid.

On August 9, 378, near Adrianople, in modern-day European Turkey, the army of Valens chased down the Gothic infantry host, which may have been as large as that of the Romans. Led by their crafty chief, Fritigern, the Goths at first tried to sue for peace and then managed to stall for time, while the Roman forces—hungry, thirsty, and tired after marching a dozen miles—waited in formation, in all their arms, in the blazing summer sun.

The Gothic foot soldiers, well-rested, took up their positions in front of their circle of wagons, which held their families and possessions. While the Roman cavalry of the left wing was still at least partly en route, and the Visigoths anxiously awaited the arrival of their mainly Ostrogothic horsemen, who were out on raids, some archers and horsemen on the Roman side impulsively attacked, starting a melee.

The Roman infantrymen on the left advanced too far toward the wagon circle, so that when the Gothic cavalry descended on the scene like a thunderbolt, they were cut off and killed, while the rest of the Roman infantry found itself unprotected on the left flank by its absent or fleeing cavalry. The Gothic horsemen drove into the exposed Roman flank while the Gothic infantry crashed against its front. The Romans were so hemmed in that they couldn't even move their arms to defend themselves while being hacked to death, trampled by horses, shot with arrows, and pierced with javelins. When they finally managed to retreat a short distance, they were surrounded by the Gothic cavalry, which continued the slaughter until a moonless night put an end to it. Two-thirds of the Roman army—about twenty thousand soldiers—had perished in the worst military disaster of the imperial era. St. Ambrose pronounced the battle of Adrianople "the end of the world."

As for foolhardy Emperor Valens, either he was struck down by an arrow and died on the field or he was seriously wounded, brought to a nearby farmhouse, and burned to death when the Goths set fire to it. In neither version was his body ever recovered.

In the aftermath, the Goths attempted to capture Adrianople—and even mighty Constantinople itself—and only their ignorance of how to conduct a siege saved those cities from destruction. Meanwhile, the Romans responded to the ongoing threat by massacring their young Gothic hostages and even the Gothic soldiers in their own army.

Valens's successor in the East, Theodosius I, after failing to bring the Goths to heel, finally made peace with them late in 382, recognized them as military federates of Rome, assigned them lands in Thrace, and handed out plum jobs to their leaders. Within a decade of the battle of Adrianople, he was leading a mixed army of Goths, Alans, and Huns against an imperial usurper in the West, but, as historian Michael Grant reminds us, the situation of the empire after Adrianople was "unprecedentedly and indeed fatally grave." There was now, in effect, a Germanic state within the state.

Cavalry had played the decisive role in this major European battle, and from this point on, the assault power of the broad human wall of Roman infantry, advancing inexorably with shields interlocked and bristling spears, began to give way to deployments of heavy cavalry for delivering the main shock or knockout blow to enemy troops. Soon, armored horsemen were carving proto-European states out of the former Western Empire, while the heavily armored cavalrymen—the cataphracts—of the Eastern Empire helped keep its enemies at bay for another millennium.

To complete the evolution of armored horsemen into the aristocratic leaders of the new sociopolitical world of feudalism, think of Frankish horsemen gradually metamorphosing into French knights, of King Arthur's legendary retinue assuming all-too-real form as Richard the Lionheart's mounted crusaders, of how the Vulgar Latin *caballus*— "horse"—gave rise not only to the word *cavalry* but also *chivalry*, and of how the Spanish *caballero* still means "gentleman."

29 ∾ Who first made Christianity the official religion of the Roman Empire?

Emperor Theodosius I, in February of 380

AFTER THE REIGN of CONSTANTINE THE GREAT (see Question 24), Christians in the Roman Empire experienced one more relatively mild persecution, initiated by Constantine's nephew, Emperor Julian, who wanted to replace the upstart religion with the venerable Greco-Roman worship of the gods and goddesses, at least among the ruling classes. His measures consisted mainly of reopening pagan temples and revoking the material privileges and seizing the wealth that had accrued to the church. All Julian gained for his efforts was the sobriquet of "the Apostate" and the spuriously attributed lament, "Thou hast conquered, O Galilean," while dying in battle against the Persians after a very brief reign (361–63).

In February of 380, a year after coming to the throne of the Eastern Empire, Theodosius I "the Great" (379–95), a pious Christian, decided to stamp out the internecine conflict then raging within the church. He began with an edict declaring that the true Catholic Christian faith—the creed of Pope Damasus I and of Peter, bishop of Alexandria, not that of the Arians (see Question 27)—was to be the official religious belief of the Roman Empire:

> [L]et us believe in one God—Father, Son, and Holy Spirit—in equal majesty and in a holy Trinity. . . . [A]s for the others, since we judge them to be foolish madmen, we decree that they be branded with the ignominious name of heretics. . . . They will suffer . . . the punishment of our authority.

Seeking to extirpate Arianism in its hotbed of Constantinople, he also deposed the city's Arian bishop. After a serious illness in the fall of 380, Theodosius finally had himself baptized as a Nicene Christian and, in the following year, convened at Constantinople the second ecumenical council so that the bishops of the empire could provide religious sanction to his anti-Arian measures.

Theodosius continued issuing edicts against Arians and other heretics, but in April of 390, after his general Botheric and several guards were murdered during a riot over a charioteer sports hero in the Greek city of Thessalonica, he retaliated by authorizing a massacre in which seven thousand Thessalonians were indiscriminately killed while sitting in the arena. Ambrose, the powerful bishop of Milan, forbade Theodosius the sacraments, and even entry to the church, until the emperor atoned for his horrendous sin. After eight months of public penance, Theodosius was finally admitted to communion by Ambrose on Christmas, and the chastened ruler issued an edict forbidding the carrying out of a capital sentence until a cooling-off period of at least thirty days had elapsed.

After this experience, in which shame and humiliation heaped bitterness on remorse, Theodosius outlawed the old pagan creed. On February 24, 391, spurred on by Bishop Ambrose, he ordered the Greco-Roman temples to be shut down and the revered oracle of Apollo at Delphi to be silenced. In November of the following year, he forbade the worship of the pagan gods in any form, public or private. The temple of Serapis in Alexandria—the Serapeum—called by Ammianus "the most magnificent building in the whole world" next to those on Rome's Capitol, was destroyed, along with the Library of Alexandria, by a Christian mob led by Bishop Theophilus. The temples that escaped destruction or looting by local fanatics were turned into museums. The austere College of Vestal Virgins in Rome was disbanded. After a history of almost twelve hundred years, the Olympic Games were abolished in 393. The final victor in the ancient games was an Armenian boxer named Varastad.

In September of 394, Theodosius defeated a usurping rival emperor, Eugenius, who, though ostensibly Christian, had become the standard-bearer for die-hard adherents of the traditional cults. It was now the Christians' turn to persecute the pagans, and they did so with gusto. Prominent pagans like Libanius and Symmachus fought back with learned orations, but their sun had finally set.

Christianity, still a minority religion in the empire as a whole (though the cities were largely Christian), had triumphed because of the principle much later enunciated as *cuius regio, eius religio*—the ruler decides the religion. Theodosius was also partly actuated by the same political motives that had led Constantine to issue his Edict of Milan in 313. Both rulers had detected in Christianity an esprit de corps, adamant defense of its beliefs, and stiff-necked opposition to all other creeds, which, if co-opted into the machinery of Roman power and administration, would help preserve the empire from further sociopolitical disintegration. It remains remarkable that, less than seventy years after it was first tolerated by Roman law, the Christian faith was proclaimed the state religion of the empire.

Theodosius died in Ambrose's arms in Milan in January 395, and the staunch bishop of Milan went on to eulogize the emperor in his funeral oration.

30 ⌒ What is the first surviving European cookbook?

The Latin collection De re coquinaria, ascribed to Apicius, late fourth century

PETRONIUS'S SATYRICON PROVIDES US with a colorful description of a Roman dinner party, satirizing a vulgar Nero-era extravaganza that begins with "elegant hors d'oeuvres" of dormice sprinkled with honey and poppy seeds. This course is followed by a large boar on a platter with "little piglets made of cake" arranged around it. When it is sliced open, a flock of thrushes flies out.

The remarkable eating habits of the Romans, or at least the elite among them, are also on view in a collection of recipes called *De re coquinaria* ("On Cooking"), credited to Marcus Gavius Apicius, a renowned epicure who lived during the reign of Tiberius early in the first century AD.

Apicius was said to have been "an exceedingly rich voluptuary" who spent a fortune on keeping his belly full. When he had only ten million sesterces left, he committed suicide by drinking poison at a banquet rather than face the dire prospect of scaling back his conspicuous consumption.

He is said to have established a cooking school and originated many of the five hundred recipes that were collected in the late fourth century. This assemblage has come down to us through a number of manuscripts, although the true origin of many of the recipes is uncertain. Differences in style and the numerous repetitions suggest the likelihood of multiple sources, possibly from ancient Greece, and, indeed, the chapter titles are in Greek.

The recipes are divided into ten chapters according to subject. The introductory chapter includes instructions on the preparation of various drinks, including spiced wine, vermouth, and a honey refresher for travelers. Special wines flavored with rose petals or violets serve as laxatives. Subsequent chapters address the preparation of meats, fowl, fish, legumes, vegetables, and sauces. The collection is thought to be the remains of a much larger work, and thus it lacks recipes for desserts and baked goods, at which Roman cooks excelled.

The recipes presume considerable knowledge and experience, since no quantities are provided for the ingredients and instructions are vague. A favorite component was a sauce called garum, made from fish guts left out in the sun to putrefy. The Romans loved garum—it was their ketchup, mustard, relish, and steak sauce rolled into one. Pliny the Elder said of it that "scarcely any other liquid except unguents has come to be more highly valued." More than four hundred of the Apician recipes include sauces made with garum.

Many herbs and spices are used in the elaborate recipes, as are fruits and nuts, both fresh and dried, along with lots of honey and vinegar. Boiled eel, for example, is cooked with pepper, lovage, dill, celery seed, coriander, mint, rue, pine nuts, honey, vinegar, wine, and oil.

Exotic birds figure prominently. A recipe that can be used for either flamingo or parrot involves parboiling the bird in water, salt, vinegar, and dill, and then adding leeks and coriander. An accompanying sauce contains coriander, cumin, pepper, mint, rue, dates, and vinegar. Tasty dumplings are created by lightly roasting "choice fresh pheasants," dicing the meat, mixing it with forcemeat made of the fat and trimmings, and adding a seasoning of broth, wine, and pepper. The mixture is formed into spoon dumplings and poached in water seasoned with garum. An ostrich ragout contains dates, pepper, mint, vinegar, and, of course, garum. When it comes to meatballs, nothing beats peacock meat.

The approach followed by the author(s) of *De re coquinaria* is decidedly practical, reflecting the challenges of cookery in the days before refrigeration. The problem of strong, "goatish-smelling" birds is managed by treating them with pepper, lovage, mint, sage, honey, vinegar, wine, and broth, and then baking them encased in dough. Meat can be kept fresh by immersing it in honey, while fried fish can be preserved by pouring hot vinegar over it.

De re coquinaria was first printed in Venice in 1483, soon followed by publication in Milan and a second printing in Venice. The book subsequently went through fourteen Latin editions.

In the introduction to his English translation of 1936, Joseph Dommers Vehling goes to some length to justify the ways of the Romans, asserting that the "proverbial excesses" and "gastronomic insanity" of Nero and other wastrels were rare occurrences. He points out that only the very wealthy could indulge in such self-gratification. The vast majority of Romans were "poor and shiftless," their existence consisting of "grind and drudgery," and their meager diets certainly did not include flamingo, pheasant, or ostrich.

He offers a spirited defense of the health-enhancing qualities of the Apician diet, declaring, for example, that modern science has "vindicated" garum and likening it to cod liver oil. "The ancients, it appears, knew 'vitamin D' to exist," he claims.

Vehling also advocates continued interest in these ancient recipes, assuring the reader, "If you care not for the carnal pleasures in Apician gastronomy," or for garum, for that matter, "there is still something healthy, something infinitely soothing and comforting—educational—in the perusal of the old book. . . . A jolly fellow is Apicius with a basketful of happy messages for a hungry world."

—*Nancy Walsh*

31 ∿ What is the first surviving book-length autobiography?

St. Augustine's Confessions, *c. 397–400*

MANY WHO HAVE NEVER PICKED UP Augustine's *Confessions* have come across his famous prayer to God in that book: "Give me chastity and continence, but not yet!" The mordant irony of his quip reminds us that the author had been a professor of Latin rhetoric in Carthage, Rome, and Milan. Indeed, his way with words, as much as his message, has drawn countless readers to his book. Both form and content resonated with T. S. Eliot, who, in *The Waste Land*, alluded to these words of Augustine: "To Carthage then I came, where a cauldron of unholy loves sang all about mine ears." Rhetorical flourishes abound in the *Confessions*, from simple repetition—"I was not yet in love, but I was in love with love"—to elaborate antithesis, as when, looking back on when he studied Virgil's *Aeneid*, Augustine marvels that he wept over the fictional heroine Dido's death, "because she killed herself for love, when all the while amid such things, dying to you, O God my life, I most wretchedly bore myself about with dry eyes." Regret for wasted time receives classic phrasing in the words "*Sero te amavi, pulchritudo tam antiqua et tam nova, sero te amavi!*" ("Too late have I loved you, O Beauty so ancient and so new, too late have I loved you!")

But Aurelius Augustinus (354–430), who probably dictated most of his book in the midst of his myriad other responsibilities as bishop, would have downplayed its rhetorical polish, since he composed the first surviving book-length work that tells the story of one's own life—especially the inner life—to encourage others to set out on their quest for God. The *Confessions* recounts Augustine's exploration of his own soul, revealing how, when shipwrecked on the shoals there, he turned his gaze outward and upward to God and discovered that "in Thy good pleasure lies our peace." Keeping in mind the story of St. Paul's trajectory from persecutor of Christians to propagator of Christ's message, Augustine framed his spiritual autobiography as an extended prayerful confession to God of his various transgressions.

We learn that Augustine was born in the coastal town of Thagaste in Roman North Africa to a pagan father, Patricius, and a devout Christian mother, Monica, who was instrumental in her son's later conversion. Her clinginess, especially after she was widowed, is conveyed with a mischievous touch: "For she loved me to be present with her, after the custom of mothers, but much more than many mothers."

Augustine makes much of his youthful addiction to sex and other former vices now considered mere foibles—berating himself, for example, for going along with some boys who steal pears from a tree for the sheer sake of stealing—though his definition of peer pressure, according to which "it is shameful not to be shameless," is still a useful insight. His early amatory adventures are tormented by the usual concomitants of "jealousy, and suspicion, and fear, and anger, and quarreling." In what would be considered a miracle today, a book of Cicero's sets him ablaze with desire for wisdom and philosophy at age eighteen. He also describes his many years of wandering in the intellectual mazes of Manichaean and Neoplatonic thought before his conversion (see Questions 20 and 21).

In one of the book's most moving passages, Augustine evokes his inconsolability at the death of a dear friend, and in one of its most currently relevant, he complains of the wretched behavior of his students in Carthage. (In Rome, the students were better behaved but cheated him of his pay.) For thirteen years he lived with an unnamed lover who bore his son Adeodatus when Augustine was still only a teen. Later, while waiting for his respectable fiancée to reach minimum age, he dismissed his first mistress—with grief and woe on both sides—but promptly took another.

While teaching in Milan, then seat of the Western Roman Empire, Augustine was captivated by Bishop Ambrose's preaching, first for its style, then for the substance. By degrees he drew nearer to Christianity. One day, tormented by his spiritual crisis, he had flung himself beneath a fig tree in his garden when he heard a child's singsong voice saying over and over, "Take and read! Take and read!" (*tolle et lege*), as if in some game. On going into his house, he took up the New Testament and opened the book at random to a passage from St. Paul exhorting the renunciation of various sins of the flesh and the acceptance of Christ. After resigning his professorship, he retired to a villa outside Milan to consider religious and philosophical issues with some associates. The upshot was that, along with his son Adeodatus and a close friend, Augustine was finally baptized on Easter Eve in 387, when he was thirty-two.

All thoughts of marriage forgotten, Augustine decided to move back to Thagaste. Monica, who had been overjoyed at living to see her son's conversion, died of fever in Ostia, the port of Rome, while they were waiting for a ship. Back in his native town, Augustine founded a small monastic community where he lived with his fellow monks, including Adeodatus, who soon died, however, at age seventeen. In 391, Augustine was forcibly made a priest by demand of the admiring faithful in the neighboring city of Hippo, whose bishop he became five years later. The book ends with many chapters—almost two-fifths of the volume—concerned with philosophical speculations on form and matter, the nature of memory, time and how it relates to God's eternity, biblical exegesis, and praise of the creator.

In hundreds of sermons and a bookshelf of other works, Augustine went on to expound the orthodox doctrine of the Trinity, the church's theory of original sin, and his notion of the indispensable role of God's grace in human salvation. His massive philosophy of history and government from a Christian viewpoint, *The City of God*, posits the direct providence of God in guiding the course of human affairs. He died at age seventy-five in 430, at the beginning of the long siege of Hippo by the Vandals under Genseric. Along with Ambrose, Jerome, and Gregory the Great, Augustine was afterward declared one of the Doctors of the Latin Church and is usually considered the greatest of the four, not least for having pricked the consciences and instructed the piety of vast numbers of common readers with his *Confessions*.

When we come to another lengthy autobiography of the same title, written almost fourteen centuries later, we are at the antipodes from Augustine's book. That eminently readable saga of human perversity and perverseness describing the formation of Jean-Jacques Rousseau, the first modern neurotic, became the model for the ubiquitous contemporary memoir as confessional narrative of abuse and victimization—a literary phenomenon to which Augustine would no doubt have applied his phrase, "this disease of curiosity."

FIFTH
CENTURY

32 ∾ What was the first Latin translation of the Old Testament made directly from the Hebrew?

St. Jerome's Vulgate, the Old Testament portion of which was completed in 405

IN HIS YOUTH the Christian scholar and Doctor of the Latin Church we know as St. Jerome (c. 345–420) had been an avid student of the pagan Latin classics, whose formal beauties made the style of Scripture seem insipid to him by comparison. Then he had a dream in which Christ seemed poised to consign Jerome's soul to hell because, instead of a Christian, he had been a Ciceronian. Jerome decided to devote the rest of his life to sacred rather than profane literature, convinced that the values expressed in pagan writings were detrimental to the soul's salvation and that his love of authors such as Cicero and Virgil was inspired by the Father of Lies.

The man who became one of the most learned of his day was born in the Balkans to Christian parents and received an excellent education in Rome, but, in opposition to the urbanized welter the Roman Empire had become, he made an ideal of asceticism and the reflective life. From 373 to 379 he lived as a hermit in the Syrian desert, where he began studying Hebrew and became a priest.

Now proficient in Latin, Greek, and Hebrew, and familiar with several other learned languages, he was called to Rome, where he worked for three years as secretary to Pope Damasus I, who asked him to revise the chief Latin translation of the New Testament for use in the Western Church. Jerome did so by about 384, but the new pope was not especially fond of him. In addition, for a tireless encomiast of virginity and a Juvenalian critic of the loose morals of the women of his day, Jerome certainly enjoyed female company, keeping an assemblage of rich Roman widows and virgins around him, teaching them Hebrew and the Scriptures. On being accused by the local clergy of improper relations with one of them, he found it expedient to depart from Rome.

After arriving in Bethlehem in 386, where he founded a monastery and a convent, he perfected his Hebrew with Jewish teachers. He now sought to complete his revision of the Old Latin translation of the Christian Scriptures by turning to the Old Testament. After revising several books, however, he determined that a new Latin version based on the original Hebrew text was called for, not just a patching up of the Old Latin translation, which had been done by many different hands and was often inaccurate. Further, it had been based on the earlier Greek translation of the Old Testament, the Septuagint (c. 250–c. 100 BC), and was thus the translation of a translation.

The herculean task Jerome had set himself of translating the Hebrew Bible afresh took the better part of a dozen years (c. 393–405). In the process, he made use of several learned rabbis for determining fine points of translation and interpretation, as well as the funds of his steadfast Roman lady friends to pay his staff of assistants.

The new translation met with considerable resistance. Hidebound opponents, many of them former friends of Jerome, refused to accept novel wordings of familiar passages that had been drilled into them from childhood. Some believed that the translators of the Greek Septuagint had themselves been inspired directly by God and that it was thus heresy or blasphemy to base the Latin version on the Hebrew original rather than the Greek version. They all soon felt Jerome's wrath via polemical diatribes that made his translation even less popular, but his feisty, quarrelsome personality, which, in the tradition of the ancient Romans, mingled personal invective with refutation of a foe's position, delighted in demolishing all those foolhardy enough to disagree with him. Yet, as erudite a figure as St. Augustine, though opposed to the translation project, said of him, "What Jerome is ignorant of, no human being has ever known."

Although it took quite a few more centuries for Jerome's translation of the Bible, later named the Vulgate ("disseminated" or "common"), to supersede the other Latin translations, his version was instrumental in shaping medieval or "church" Latin, which is looser in structure—and much easier to read and write—than the Ciceronian Latin that Jerome had cut his teeth on. The book has also had an incalculable influence on the development of European poetry, in both Latin and the vernacular tongues.

The Vulgate went on to be one of the first books printed in the Western world and, in 1546, the Council of Trent proclaimed it the official Catholic translation of the Bible. The revised Vulgate, published in 1592, remains the standard version of the Western Church.

St. Jerome, who died at a goodly age in Bethlehem in 420, has often been portrayed in art as a scholar hard at work in his study with a well-behaved lion for a house cat, based on a legend of his having extracted a thorn from a grateful lion's paw. The gratitude of the Latin Church to Jerome may be gauged by its enshrinement of the monumental text that he practically lost his sight in producing.

33 ⌣ Who first sacked the city of Rome?

Alaric and his Visigoths, in late August of 410

ACCORDING TO PLUTARCH, the ancient Gauls first crossed the Alps into northern Italy in search of wine. They must have liked it, because they ended up staying. Eventually, they moved down the peninsula to devastate a Roman army and capture Rome itself, traditionally in 390 BC. Many civilians had fled; many who hadn't were massacred. The Gauls pillaged for months and burned much of the city down but were unable to seize the Capitol—the legend is that the cackling of Juno's sacred geese alerted the garrison that an enemy detachment was sneaking up by night. The Gallic leader Brennus finally agreed to leave Rome on receipt of a thousand pounds of gold. When the Romans protested against the crooked scales being used to weigh out the payment, Brennus flung his sword into the balance while shouting with barbaric glee, "*Vae victis!*"—"Woe to the conquered!"

For eight hundred years, no foreign enemy ever took Rome again. Even audacious Hannibal, who had led his victorious army to Rome in 211 BC, moved off without making the attempt. But six centuries after Hannibal's time, in AD 395, a young Romanized Goth of noble birth—an educated man who spoke fluent Latin—was angered at not having been promoted to the rank of Roman general. As commander of Visigothic auxiliaries, Alaric had helped win a critical battle for the late emperor, Theodosius the Great, in what is now Slovenia, but he was nonetheless being sent east, still in charge of his barbarian contingent.

He decided to revolt against his ungrateful Roman masters by leading his Visigoths in an invasion of Thrace, extending his field of operations in the next few years to Greece, where he sacked the port of Athens and some major cities. The empire responded in the person of

Stilicho, the part-Vandal supreme military commander in the West, who landed a naval force in Greece, driving Alaric's army north into the mountains of Epirus. When, in 402, the Goths took the war home to Italy, Stilicho defeated them twice but refrained from finishing them off. In the meantime, Alaric's siege of Milan persuaded the eighteen-year-old emperor Honorius to transfer the Western capital to the much more easily defended city of Ravenna, then surrounded by marshes and swamps.

Alaric began playing off the two halves of the empire against each other, managing to extort privileges from both. In 407, he threatened to invade Italy again unless he received four thousand pounds of gold. Stilicho, intending to sic Alaric on a usurper in Gaul, advised the government to buy him off, but the imperial court started suspecting its general's motives and turned against him. Convinced that Stilicho was planning to seize the vacant Eastern throne, Honorius had him beheaded in August of 408—and ordered the slaughter of the wives and children of his barbarian auxiliaries in the Roman army, who had been detained as hostages. These mad acts deprived the Western Empire of its outstanding general and swelled Alaric's ranks by many thousands of furious deserters whose family members had been murdered in cold blood.

When the Gothic army entered Italy and its demand for gold was refused, Alaric besieged Rome, for the first of three times, in the winter of 408. The city sent out an embassy that issued threats of Rome's countless defenders. "The thicker the grass, the more easily mowed," was Alaric's contemptuous reply. When asked what he wanted, he told them all the gold, silver, and other precious items his men could cart off—plus all the barbarian slaves.

"But what will you leave *us*?"

"Your lives."

After money and goods exchanged hands, Alaric moved off to Tuscany, where an enormous number of barbarian slaves fled their masters to join his forces. Again he demanded gold, grain, and the position of commander of the Western imperial forces, the last of which proved to be a stumbling block. Besieging Rome once again, he demanded grain and part of the Danube valley in what is now Austria for settling his followers, but this was refused. For the second time, Alaric's blockade of the Tiber prevented food from entering the city. People ate rats; some slaughtered their infants for food. Unburied bodies piled up and led to pestilence. Alaric even set up his own rival emperor for a while, but nothing seemed to work.

After fifteen years of battling the Romans, the forty-year-old Alaric was wearying of his futile negotiations with Honorius. When he abandoned the siege and moved his troops to Ravenna for further talks, a Gothic general named Sarus, leading a band of his followers in Roman employ, made a sudden attack on Alaric's men and cut down a goodly number of them. Rightly or wrongly interpreting this as treachery on Honorius's part, Alaric yet again headed for Rome, arriving on about August 20 of 410.

Rome's Aurelian Wall, constructed more than a century earlier, was a mighty bulwark—twelve feet thick, fifty feet tall in places, and twelve and a half miles in circuit—that defended the half-million inhabitants of the city, but at midnight of August 24, slaves sympathetic to the invaders' cause threw open the Salarian Gate, and the Goths poured into Rome, sounding their battle trumpets. For the next three days, the ancient capital of the Western world was plundered by foreign troops for the first time since the Gauls took the city. Like many of his Visigothic followers, Alaric was a Christian (though of the Arian persuasion), and so he spared the old St. Peter's and churches and church vessels in general. The chief targets were the palaces of the aristocrats, which were looted and wrecked. None of the great public buildings were destroyed, but the plunder carried away by the invaders was of astonishing proportions.

As for Alaric, he caught a fever—perhaps malaria from his summer sojourn near Rome—and died before the end of the year in southern Italy as the Goths vainly tried to cross over to Sicily on their way to North Africa. It is probably a myth that the Busento River was diverted to bury Alaric secretly in its bed with priceless treasures looted from Rome, maybe even the gold vessels from the temple at Jerusalem. After the river was steered back into its usual channel (the story says), the Roman captives who had done the digging were all killed so that the location would remain unknown. Bereft of their incomparable leader, the Visigoths agreed to fight the Vandals and other German barbarians on behalf of the Roman government, which then settled them in Aquitaine, where they eventually formed the first barbarian kingdom within the bounds of the empire.

There were to be more sacks of Rome, notably by Genseric and his Vandals in 455, whose two-week destructive spree gave us the word *vandalism*; Totila and his Ostrogoths in 546; the Saracens in 846; Robert Guiscard and his Normans in 1084; and Charles V's German, Italian, and Spanish mercenaries in 1527, who killed, pillaged, and desecrated during eight days of unspeakable violence.

By contrast, the slaughter during Alaric's sack of the city in 410 was kept to a minimum. Yet even so, and despite Rome's having long ceased to be the capital of the empire, the events of 410 seemed to herald the end of the world to many at the time. St. Augustine spent thirteen years on *The City of God* to show that the sack of Rome was not due to its relatively new adherence to Christianity but to the inscrutable will of God, whereas his disciple Orosius threw together in a single year a plodding history of the world demonstrating that far worse catastrophes had struck before Christian times. Nonetheless, barely six years after Alaric, the poet Rutilius Claudius Namatianus addressed Rome in glowing terms: "You have made a city of what was formerly a world." But now a formerly excluded barbarian world had begun to find its way to the city's threshold, and after Rome's spectacular eclipse in the early Middle Ages, it would take some very determined Renaissance popes to lift it back into the first rank of cities again.

34 ❧ Who was the first Christian missionary to Ireland?

St. Patrick, traditionally in 432, but possibly several decades later

TRADITION HAS IT THAT, in the year 432, the future St. Patrick traveled from war-ravaged Roman Gaul to Armagh in the north of Ireland, where he established a church and began fulfilling his long-standing dream of spreading Christianity among the warring Irish tribes. Much of what we know of him is from a document he wrote in rustic Latin shortly before his death, the *Confession*, in which he tells the story of his life and missionary work.

Born as Patricius into a middle-class Roman family in Banna Venta Berniae, somewhere in Britain around the year 390 (though all dates in his life are conjectural), he received only a modest education before being captured by raiders and taken into slavery in Antrim, Ireland, where he endured six years of misery—solitude, cold, and hunger—as a herder of pigs enslaved to a chieftain named Miliucc. It was on the side of a mountain known as Sliabh Mis that this formerly irreligious youth took to prayer, day and night, and found comfort from the spirit he felt burning within him.

According to the *Confession*, one night during his captivity he awoke from a dream, hearing a voice tell him that his days of being famished were over and that he was going home. "Look, your ship is ready," the voice said.

Miliucc's lands were far from the sea, but Patricius set out to find his way, allegedly walking some two hundred miles until he came upon a ship, probably in the southeast near Wexford, ready to sail for the Continent. Initially rebuffed by the ship's captain when he sought to embark, he was ultimately allowed on board by a crew member.

When they reached Gaul (in modern France), they found scenes of widespread devastation and starvation, since the Romans were battling the barbarians at the time. Patrick was taunted by the sailors for his faith in a God who failed to provide sustenance for them—until they came across a feast in the shape of a herd of pigs.

Patrick continued to wander for several years, finally making his way home to Britain, where he was welcomed by his parents, who begged him not to leave them again. The visionary young man stayed for a time but became more and more aware of a *vox Hiberionacum*, "the voice of the Irish," speaking to him in dreams and pleading with him to come and walk among them again. Accordingly, he left for a monastery in Auxerre, in northern France, where he supposedly prepared for the priesthood for many years and was ultimately ordained.

At this time, pockets of Christianity already existed in Ireland, and these early believers petitioned the church authorities to appoint a bishop. In 431, Pope Celestine I accordingly elevated his deacon Palladius to this rank, dispatching him as a guardian of orthodoxy for the fledgling Irish flock. The perceived danger was the heresy of Pelagianism, which had erupted among British Christians.

Pelagius (c. 354–after 418) was an ascetic probably born in the British Isles who asserted, in contrast to other church authorities such as Augustine and Jerome, that there was no original sin and that humans could work out their own salvation, even without the benefit of God's grace or Christ's death on the cross, by proper use of their own free will in choosing good rather than evil. The task of Palladius, first bishop of Ireland, was to prevent the spread of these unorthodox notions. He was not, however, a missionary, whose primary goal would be conversion of the heathen.

That responsibility fell to Patrick, who had maintained his determination to return to Ireland throughout his years at the monastery in Gaul. His opportunity came soon enough, since Palladius died within a year of reaching Ireland, and Patrick was ordained as his successor bishop, setting forth to save the souls of the people who had enslaved him.

Patrick's impact on his adopted country was rapid and profound. Tradition holds that he established churches and monasteries through the northern, eastern, and central parts of the country, with his own bishopric at the old city of Armagh, formerly a center of pagan worship. Of his successful missionary work he wrote in the *Confession*, "I am greatly God's debtor, because he granted me so much grace, that through me many people would be reborn in God, and soon after confirmed, and that clergy would be ordained everywhere for them."

Important changes were seen as more of Ireland became Christianized. Tribal warfare and human sacrifice became less common, and the Irish slave trade, whose victim Patrick had been in his youth, eventually ceased. Latin was widely adopted in the monasteries Patrick established. Irish monks copied, illuminated, disseminated, and thus preserved many Greek and Roman manuscripts that would otherwise have been lost. As missionaries, they also played an important role in rechristianizing and recivilizing the Continent after the barbarian invasions had done their worst.

Patrick is thought to have died in 461 (though perhaps as much as three decades later) and to have been buried by the cathedral in County Down, along with the two other patron saints of Ireland, St. Brigid and St. Columba. Little credence is given today to the more fanciful legends about him, such as his expulsion of the snakes from Ireland or his use of the shamrock to teach the concept of the Holy Trinity. His feast day of March 17 is celebrated, most notably in New York City, with parades, boisterous revelry, and the wearin' of the green, and also as a day on which everyone, regardless of heritage, can be lucky enough to be Irish.

—*Nancy Walsh*

35 ❧ Who led the first Germanic settlers to Britain?

Traditionally, the brothers Hengist and Horsa in 449

AFTER THE ROMANS PULLED THEIR LEGIONS out of Britain early in the fifth century to help defend Italy from invading Goths, Germanic-speaking marauders soon flocked to the southern and eastern shores of the island. The Romanized Celts, or Britons, who were left behind were no match for the ruthless bands of warriors that moved in for the kill.

As far back as the mid-third century, Saxon pirates had been raiding the coasts of Britain, and toward the end of that century the Romans had devoted a fleet to defending their province of Britannia against them. But after the withdrawal of the Roman army—the traditional date is 407 or 410—the typical springtime hit-and-run attacks of the Germanic tribes increased in frequency and morphed into something ominously different, especially in the quarter century from 425 to 450.

The Anglo-Saxon Chronicle records that in 443 the Britons asked Rome for help against the savage raids of the homegrown Picts and Scots from up north, but the Romans had their hands full with Attila the Hun. Then Vortigern, a Celtic chieftain who probably had firsthand experience of the fighting prowess of the continental Germanic tribes, summoned them to help him against the Picts, offering them the Isle of Thanet in Kent (southeast Britain) for their settlement.

The foreign warriors dutifully sailed across the North Sea in three longships and drove off the Picts whenever they met them in battle, but they also sent messages home to send more help and to consider two things: the Britons' worthlessness in battle and the excellence of the land.

You can be sure that reinforcements arrived, traditionally in 449, led by the Jute brothers Hengist and Horsa—the Horse Brothers, we might call them, since Hengist means "stallion" and Horsa is just "horse." These Jutes, who hailed either from northern Denmark (Jutland) or the coastal region of the Netherlands (Frisia) and claimed to be the great-great-grandsons of the crafty god Woden, brought over warriors from the kindred Germanic tribes of Angles (from southwest Denmark) and Saxons (from the mouth of the Elbe on the German coast).

While Vortigern and the Horse Brothers might be legendary figures, the invasion force was not.

The new arrivals predictably ganged up with the Picts against the Britons and demanded more land and provisions. Horsa is said to have died fighting against Vortigern in 455, when the Britons were slaughtered by the Saxons at Aylesford in Kent. In 457, according to *The Anglo-Saxon Chronicle*, the forces of Hengist and his son Aesc killed four thousand Kentish Britons in battle. The survivors abandoned Kent and fled to London, and Aesc became the first of a line of Kentish kings. In 480, the Britons were again defeated at the battle of Portsmouth Harbor in the south. Hengist, if he ever actually lived, died in 488.

A respite from the Britons' string of military failures may have been achieved in about 500, when they supposedly defeated the Saxons at the battle of Badon. Their leader, the personage we call King Arthur, may have been an actual Romano-Celtic general (definitely not a king) who checked the invaders for a while. But the ongoing Germanic conquest meant ravaged land, razed buildings, and dead or enslaved Britons. Most of the more than one hundred Roman towns in Britain, such as fashionable Bath, were destroyed, burned, or abandoned, and so were the villas. The heathen farmers, fishermen, and pirates who were subduing Britain were neither city people nor suburbanites. They were also uninterested in acquiring Christianity.

The Celtic-speaking natives retreated west and north into Wales, Cornwall, and Scotland—*flugon tha Engle swa swa fyr* ("They fled the Angles as from fire")—and many immigrated to the Continent, especially after about 525, to bring their name and Breton language to Brittany. The Germanic warriors called the Britons *wealas*—"foreigners"—giving us the word *Welsh* and the name *Walsh*.

Within 150 years of the invasion of Hengist and Horsa, the Anglo-Saxon heptarchy—the seven kingdoms—had taken shape, comprising the Jute kingdom of Kent; the Saxon kingdoms of Sussex, Wessex, and Essex; and the kingdoms of the Angles, namely Northumbria, East Anglia, and Mercia. The Angles eventually had the honor of giving their name to *England* and *English*.

The Angles, Saxons, and Jutes spoke mutually comprehensible dialects of West Germanic, a linguistic family that also gave rise to modern German and Dutch. The Roman rulers' Latin had never replaced Celtic among the majority of Britons, but the effect of both languages was minimal on Anglo-Saxon at its earliest stage. A few

Celtic words survived, such as *Kent*, *London*, *York*, *Thames*, *Avon*, and the *Cam-* in Cambridge. A Latin word that was borrowed by the Celts and passed on to the Anglo-Saxons is the common place-name suffix *-caster* or *-chester* (Latin *castra*, "camp" or "town"), as in Lancaster or Manchester.

The Anglo-Saxon, or Old English, period of English lasted from c. 450 to c. 1150. The language, in four major dialects, had a vocabulary of sixty thousand words, of which 85 percent have died out, being replaced mostly by Latin, French, or Danish loanwords. Yet English still derives many of its simplest words from Anglo-Saxon: *man*, *wife*, *child*, *house*, *meat*, *grass*, *leaf*, *good*, *high*, *strong*, *eat*, *drink*, *sleep*, *live*, *fight*, *one*, *two*, *head*, *blood*, *hand*, *eye*, *nose*, *heart*, *mouth*, *tooth*, *dog*, *cow*, *lamb*, *sheep*, *ox*. It is a dizzying thought that the rude Germanic dialect barked out (or should we say "neighed"?) by the likes of "Stallion" and "Horse" managed to evolve into the glorious instrument of Shakespeare, Milton, and the King James Bible, as well as the supple, infinitely adaptable world language of today.

36 ∾ Who were the first inhabitants of the Venetian lagoons?

Refugees from Attila's attack on Aquileia, Italy, in 452

UNDER ATTILA, the Huns and their subject peoples launched raids on the Western Roman Empire from their staging ground in Hungary from 441 to 453, terrorizing the Balkans, Gaul, and northern Italy. Having already carved out a powerful state in Central Europe after defeating the Ostrogoths and other Germanic tribes in the late fourth century, they were now drawn to the wealth of the Western Empire, spurred on by the military prowess of their leader, "the Scourge of God" who called himself "King of the Huns, Goths, Danes, and Medes," to undertake a major assault against the dying behemoth that was Rome.

Besides, in 450, a Roman princess, Honoria, half sister of Emperor Valentinian III, had sent Attila her ring—and a plea for help—after being disgraced for an amorous indiscretion, and the wily Hun chose to interpret the gift as an offer of marriage. The latter stages of his invasion of the Western Empire were thus justified as an attempt to take possession of his bride. After all, hadn't Honoria's imperial mother, Galla Placidia, been briefly wed to a barbarian—Athaulf, king of the Goths? But after Attila was memorably checked in Gaul by the Roman general Aëtius and his Visigothic allies at the exceptionally bloody battle of Châlons in June of 451, he retreated east to ravage northeastern Italy.

One of the cities there, Aquileia, among the richest of the empire, had already been sacked in 402 by Alaric and his Visigoths (see Question 33), who had returned to besiege it unsuccessfully in 408. Some inhabitants of that part of the peninsula had fled from the Gothic hordes to the mudflats and sandy islets of what came to be called the Venetian lagoon, but most of them had returned to the mainland when the barbarian threat had receded. A traditional story relates that the city of Venice was officially founded at noon on March 25, 421, on the islands of Rialto, but its authenticity is suspect.

Attila's arrival in the same mainland area in 452 was the signal for another widespread evacuation. Again, many residents of Aquileia fled about fifty miles southwest to the Venetian lagoon as the Huns prepared to lay siege to the city. The attackers had no easy time of it. After three months, they had still gotten nowhere as a result of fierce resistance. At last, when his army was on the verge of giving up, Attila noticed that the storks that had nested in the gables of the city's houses were flying away with their young—a sure sign, he informed his superstitious rabble, that the prescient birds realized Aquileia was doomed. Their spirits reinvigorated, the Huns manned their battering rams and other siege engines to force their way into the city in the next day or two and proceeded to burn and devastate it so thoroughly that it later became difficult even to figure out where it had once stood.

Attila went on to spare the city of Rome at the earnest entreaties of Pope Leo I and died of a hemorrhagic stoke in 453 after an exceptionally bibulous celebration of his wedding night. (The bride was *not* Honoria.)

Meanwhile, the refugees from Aquileia and neighboring areas began to consider that permanent residence in the Venetian lagoon would provide a safe haven from the fury of mounted nomadic pastoralists who knew little, and cared less, about the sea. At first, the mainland inhabitants fled to a dozen islands near the shore, but because of malaria from the stagnant water there, they moved farther out into the lagoon. One of their first tasks was to ferry boatloads of sand to their marsh-grass islands to prevent them from flooding during high tide. By the year 466, their representatives met with those of a lagoon community in Grado, not far from the site of Aquileia, to confer on matters of self-government.

But perhaps Venice is a lot older than previously thought. A stone walkway discovered on the island of Torcello, a half hour's boat ride northeast of Venice and closer to the mainland, has been dated to the second century AD, and a recent theory has posited a Roman origin for Venice a century earlier. Certainly, the ancient Romans were a practical people—and superb engineers—who liked to make the very most of the territory their hard-won conquests had brought them.

By 523, the scholarly monk and statesman Cassiodorus was comparing the residents of the Venetian lagoon to seabirds living on the waters and lauding their ships, abundant fishing, and lucrative salt trade. A massive influx of refugees arrived in the lagoon as a result of the Lombard invasion of northeast Italy in 568, and of these the majority stayed. Venice had a long way to go before it became the seafaring empire of fabulously wealthy merchant princes who, according to Wordsworth, held "the gorgeous East in fee." Yet the lagoon dwellers soon began putting down roots in their wondrously improbable new home in the form of many millions of wooden piles driven into the marshy terrain of the 118 little islands that came to constitute the Most Serene Republic of Venice.

37 ∾ Who was the first barbarian king of Italy?

Odoacer, who deposed Emperor Romulus Augustulus on
September 4, 476

DURING THE LAST FEW DECADES of its existence, the Western Roman Empire was a sorry spectacle. The Germanic army chief Ricimer made and unmade emperors at will. The Western provinces had all fallen away—Britain to the Anglo-Saxons, North Africa to the Vandals, most of Gaul and Spain to the Visigoths. The empire was a welter of Goths, Huns, Franks, Burgundians, and other barbarians too numerous to specify.

In 474, Julius Nepos was appointed Western emperor by the Eastern emperor and chose as commander of the army a half German named Orestes who had been, of all things, Attila the Hun's Latin secretary. In the very next year, Orestes took up arms against his benefactor, who fled to Dalmatia, where he was murdered in 480. Realizing that the snooty Roman aristocrats would never consent to have a part-barbarian emperor, Orestes had the idea of elevating to the throne his son, Flavius Romulus, a handsome boy of about fourteen whose mother was a Roman.

On October 31, 475, Romulus was installed as a puppet emperor at the Western capital of Ravenna, where he soon acquired the nickname Momyllus ("Little Disgrace") to rhyme with his pretentious name of Romulus. The soldiers, unimpressed by the cute teen, dubbed him Augustulus—meaning "Little Augustus" or "the Tiny Emperor." The Eastern Emperor Zeno the Isaurian refused to acknowledge the young usurper at all.

But now it was payback time for Orestes, who had promised his German troops one-third of the land of Italy in exchange for their support. On his refusal, their leader Odoacer, the senior military officer of Orestes and chief of the Germanic Heruli, had himself proclaimed king by his men on August 23, 476. He chased Orestes down at what is now Pavia, which was captured and sacked, and ordered him beheaded. Odoacer proceeded to depose Romulus Augustulus on September 4, the traditional date for the end of the Western Roman Empire. Edward Gibbon suggested that "instead of inquiring *why* the Roman Empire was destroyed, we should rather be surprised that it had subsisted so long."

Taking a shine to the polite young ex-emperor, Odoacer gave him a large pension and set up him and his mom at the stupendous villa built near Naples many centuries earlier by the gourmandizing Roman general Lucullus. Nothing is known of the later life of Romulus Augustulus.

Odoacer (476–93) was shrewd enough to send the imperial insignia to Zeno, who became, in effect, the first Byzantine emperor, since the Roman Empire now had no more East and West. The new king of Italy thus subordinated himself to the emperor and also retained the entire Roman administrative apparatus, while making sure that he and his soldiers grabbed enough land to set themselves up as a rival landowning class to the old aristocratic families.

Things went well in Italy for about a dozen years, until Emperor Zeno grew weary of Odoacer and wary of an Ostrogothic king and warlord, Theodoric, who had long been stirring up trouble in the Balkans. Zeno decided to dispatch Theodoric against Odoacer.

The king of Italy tried to stop the Ostrogoths at the Isonzo River but was defeated there on August 28, 489—and even more badly at Verona on September 30. Odoacer fled to Ravenna, where, except for occasional sallies, he remained holed up for several years. Since the situation was deteriorating for all concerned, Theodoric and Odoacer agreed on terms. Soon afterward, the Ostrogoth lured Odoacer to a banquet by promising to share the rule of Italy with him and then slaughtered him with his broadsword, right after he made a toast, on the ides of March of 493.

On this treacherous note was inaugurated the Ostrogothic Kingdom of Italy under Theodoric the Great (493–526), the mightiest Goth of them all. Once again, recourse was had to the legal fiction that the new king was answerable to the Byzantine emperor.

Having spent ten years as a young man in Constantinople, Theodoric venerated Roman civilization, though he apparently had never learned to write. He protected the statues in Rome from being pillaged, continued the ban on intermarriage between Romans and Goths, permitted the senate to meet, and appointed learned men as his chief ministers. Although he brought a third of a century of true peace and prosperity to Italy, he disgraced his last days by ordering the cruel execution of the Roman statesman Boethius (c. 480–c. 525), perhaps the greatest scholar of his time and author of *The Consolation of Philosophy*, a Latin work in prose and sonorous verse that was translated into English by King Alfred the Great (or at his bidding), Geoffrey Chaucer, and Queen Elizabeth I.

The Ostrogothic Kingdom of Italy came to an end in 553, after the eunuch Byzantine general Narses defeated King Teia, who was killed in battle near Naples. The peninsula was not politically united again until 1870.

38 ∾ Who is considered the first king of France?

Clovis I (reigned 481–511), founder of the Merovingian dynasty of French kings

IN ABOUT 428, A GROUP of Salian Franks, a nation of Germanic barbarians, began taking control of what is now northern France in what was then the moribund Roman Empire. Its ruling Merovingian house made its capital at Tournai in Belgium and took its name from the possibly mythical Merovech (448–56).

At age fifteen, Clovis, putative grandson of Merovech, succeeded his father Childeric I as king of these Western Franks. In the same year of 481, he seized Reims and had himself crowned there, setting a more-than-millennial precedent for the site of future French coronations. It was at Reims that the young pagan king met Clothilde, a Christian Burgundian princess whom he married in 493.

Long before his nuptials, Clovis had already made his mark, when in 486 his troops annihilated those of the last Roman governor of Gaul, Syagrius, at the battle of Soissons, later making sure to have Syagrius executed. This victory doubled the size of Clovis's kingdom, extending it south to the Loire, and within another decade he had brought all northern Gaul beneath his sway.

But in 496, after he rode out to meet the invading Germanic nation of Alamanni near Cologne, there was a rocky start to the battle. Clovis prayed to the Jesus that his wife was always talking about, and things turned around fast in his favor. On Christmas that year, grateful for his mighty conquest, he and three thousand of his men were baptized into Catholic Christianity by Archbishop Remigius (Rémi) of Reims, who supposedly bade him, "Worship what you have burned [the holy images in churches], and burn what you have worshipped [images of pagan gods]." The scene has been re-created in paint and stone innumerable times by French artists, and in the nineteenth-century painting done for the Panthéon in Paris, Clovis is portrayed as a mustachioed and long-haired "blond beast," as well he might have been, since he made a point of personally slaying in public any soldier whose behavior had offended his sensibilities. Perhaps Bishop Avitus, in a surviving letter to the king, had his tongue in his episcopal cheek when he referred to him as "Your Most Subtle Humility."

In 507, with the help of the Burgundians, Clovis defeated the Arian Visigoths under Alaric II (and killed him with his own hands) at a battle near Poitiers in west-central France. The God of the Catholics brought the walls of the Goths' city of Angoulême tumbling down for him without even the requisite trumpet blasts as in the case of Jericho. Clovis then chased the Visigoths out of Aquitaine and beyond the Pyrenees into Spain.

Next, he persuaded the son of his ally King Sigibert the Lame of the Ripuarian (Rhine River) Franks to kill his father. That done, he split the skull of the treacherous son with his trusty double-headed ax and lied to the Ripuarian chieftains at Cologne about his role in the sordid affair. The chiefs proclaimed Clovis their new king with a suitably barbaric clashing of swords on shields and booming beery yawps. Lifting their Machiavellian monarch high over their heads on a shield, they paraded him around for all to admire. The chronicler of these events—St. Gregory of Tours—draws a curious moral: "Day in, day out, God submitted the enemies of Clovis to his dominion and increased his power, for he walked before Him with an upright heart and did what was pleasing in His sight."

Clovis went on to defeat some rival Salian Franks in battle, had their king and his son beheaded, and took over their kingdom. Demonstrating impeccable Gallic taste, he made Paris his capital in 507, though the City of Lights covered less than twenty-five acres in those days. The next year, he annexed the Visigothic Kingdom of Toulouse. He split open the skulls of quite a few kings who were related to him and took over their territory, resorting to this type of statecraft more and more as time went on. At the end, he became so paranoid about ambitious kinsmen that he tried to lure any remaining relatives into his power by lamenting to his assembled people that he had no relations to come to his aid in case of troubles.

In about 510, Clovis promulgated the Salic law code, which contains such Solomonic distinctions as setting the fine for stealing a suckling pig at 120 denars, but reducing the penalty to 40 denars for making off with "a pig that can live without its mother." Anyone caught stealing a bull got fined 1,800 denars, but anyone caught stealing a bull belonging to the king needed to shell out 3,600 denars. Regarding the wergild paid for a slaughtered man, the sons were to get half the money with the remainder to be shared among the nearest relatives. Trial by ordeal or combat was written into numerous laws.

The code's stipulation that women could not inherit land was later deviously manipulated to deny the claims of various candidates to the French throne through the maternal line. Shakespeare dramatizes the situation in *Henry V*, where a paraphrased sentence from Clovis's code and its translation are metamorphosed into blank verse: "'*In terram Salicam mulieres ne succedant*,' / 'No woman shall succeed in Salic land'" (1.2.38–39)—that is, in France.

Clovis died in 511 at age forty-five after a reign of thirty years and was buried in Paris. He divided his kingdom among his four sons, and though it was briefly reunited under one of them, Lothar I, he in turn bequeathed it to four sons of his own. The Merovingian line of France persisted, with increasing degradation, debauchery, bloodlust, and ineptitude, until 751.

Although Clovis was the first king to unite all the Frankish peoples, he and his subjects were never able to substitute their Germanic language for the Latin that had flourished in Gaul for many centuries and that eventually morphed into French. Yet, in honor of this founder of the French monarchy, his original name of Chlodwig ("famous warrior") gave rise to such common subsequent monikers as Louis, Ludwig, Luigi, and Luis.

39   What was the first great schism between Western and Eastern Christian Churches?

The Acacian Schism of 484–519

IN 482, THE BYZANTINE EMPEROR, Zeno the Isaurian, issued the *Henoticon* ("Unity"), a religious formulary instigated by Acacius, the patriarch of Constantinople. This document was an attempt to heal a massive rift that had arisen in the Eastern Church between the Catholics and the Monophysites, who taught that Christ had only one nature, the divine. The compromise statement failed to satisfy the hard-liners on either side, especially Pope Felix II, who ascended the papal throne in 483.

Pope Felix was displeased because the *Henoticon* did not condemn Monophysitism forcefully enough, while it attempted to clarify the nature of Christ without due deference to the teachings of the Council of Chalcedon (451), which had set out the Catholic viewpoint—that Christ has two natures, human and divine. After the Catholic patriarch of Alexandria, who had been banished, complained to the pope, Felix sent legates to Constantinople with orders to summon Acacius to Rome. The legates were detained as soon as they arrived and forced to receive communion from Acacius in a liturgical function that recognized various Monophysite leaders as legitimate Eastern prelates. As a result, the pope deposed and excommunicated Patriarch Acacius, and the patriarch responded in kind.

The first great schism between the Western and Eastern Churches lasted thirty-five years until a Catholic emperor, Justin I, came to the Byzantine throne. Pope Hormisdas then sent his *Formula*—a list of demands that had to be met before reconciliation with Rome could take place. The pope required Eastern bishops to renounce Monophysitism and its past and current adherents and accept the teachings of the Councils of Ephesus (431) and Chalcedon on the nature of Christ. The patriarch of Constantinople and all the bishops of his see agreed to abide by these terms, and the two churches were reunited on Easter Sunday, March 24, 519, though major disagreements soon cropped up again.

Another major schism took shape in 858, when Byzantine Emperor Michael III "the Drunkard" deposed and banished Ignatius, the patriarch of Constantinople, for refusing the sacraments to Bardas, the emperor's uncle and prime minister, who had divorced his wife and was living in incestuous sin with his son's widow. Bardas chose the professor and scholar Photius, a layman, as the new patriarch. After Ignatius appealed to Rome, Pope Nicholas I demanded that Photius be deposed in 863. When he was ignored, he excommunicated Photius, who, in turn, excommunicated the pope in 867 at a council he and the emperor had summoned, which also condemned as heretical the Western insistence on clean-shaven priests and clerical celibacy.

The Catholic Fourth Council of Constantinople (869–70) condemned Photius, but the Eastern Church bounced back with the Orthodox Fourth Council of Constantinople (879–80), which restored Photius (after he had been deposed and banished by a new emperor), condemned Pope Nicholas I (who was long dead), and declared against the "*Filioque*" ("and from the Son"), referring to the attempt of Catholics to insert that phrase into the Nicene Creed. Catholics believed that the Holy Ghost proceeded from the Father and from the Son, whereas the Eastern Church asserted that the Holy Ghost proceeded from the Father *through* the Son but not *from* him.

The final schism between the Roman Catholic and Eastern Orthodox Churches was fueled by Eastern resentment of papal encroachments on the political aspirations and religious independence of the Byzantine Empire. It was triggered in 1053, when Michael Cerularius, the patriarch of Constantinople and an advocate of Orthodox independence from Rome, began denouncing the use of unleavened bread in the Western Eucharistic rite, as well as the old chestnuts of clerical celibacy and the *Filioque*. He ordered the Latin-rite churches in his see to use Greek in their services and adopt the Greek liturgy. When they refused, he ordered the churches closed and their clergy excommunicated.

He was answered by a tract of the French cardinal Humbert of

Silva Candida that was provocatively entitled *Against the Slanders of the Greeks*. Pope Leo IX then dispatched the cardinal to Constantinople as his legate to see whether things could be patched up, but Humbert found the Greek prelates adamant in their refusal to submit to the pope—and Cerularius wouldn't even meet with him.

In the meantime, the pope died, and on July 16, 1054, the cardinal decided to take matters into his own inexorable hands by convoking a formal meeting in the cathedral of Hagia Sophia at which he excommunicated Cerularius and his recalcitrant clergy. The patriarch retaliated by excommunicating the cardinal and his fellow legates at a Holy Synod. And that was *that*, although the Catholics had the satisfaction of seeing Cerularius deposed and exiled by a new Byzantine emperor in 1058.

There was a temporary and insincere effort to unite the churches in 1439, as a result of the Council of Ferrara-Florence, when the East wanted the West's military aid against the encroaching Muslims, but the attempt soon fizzled. In 1964, Pope Paul VI met with Patriarch Athenagoras in Jerusalem, and in the following year, in simultaneous ceremonies, the two leaders presided over formal ceremonies that revoked the mutual excommunications of nine centuries earlier. In 2006, Pope Benedict XVI visited Patriarch Bartholomew I, but the division between the Western and Eastern Churches persists, now thoroughly ingrained after so many centuries of separate cultural and institutional development.

SIXTH CENTURY

40 ~ Who first developed the Christian calendar?

The scholarly monk Dionysius Exiguus in 525

IT HAD ALWAYS BEEN DIFFICULT to figure out the date of Easter, the most important of Christianity's movable feasts. In the Western Church, which declared Easter to be the first Sunday after the first full moon after the spring equinox, it could fall between March 22 and April 25. In the year 525, a learned monk of Rome—perhaps the abbot of a monastery—set out to refine the church's method of calculating the date of Easter.

Dionysius Exiguus (usually translated as "Dennis the Short," but *Exiguus* is probably a name taken in self-deprecation—"Of Small Account") was an astronomer and mathematician, as well as an expert in Greek, Latin, and church law, and thus abundantly qualified for the task he set himself. When his laborious undertaking of providing revised Easter tables was finished, he had determined the dates for a total of ninety-five years, but in the process he numbered the years themselves with reference to the Incarnation of Jesus, viewed by Christians as the central event of human history. The current system dated its year 1 from the accession of Emperor Diocletian (our year 284), and Dionysius thought it wrong that Christians should number their years from the coming to power of a notorious persecutor of Christians. Yet the system appealed to many at the time because they preferred to see in it a reference to "the Era of the Martyrs."

When Dionysius set out to determine in what year Jesus was born, he found some clues in the Gospels. For example, he knew from Luke 3:1 and 3:23 that Jesus was thirty years old in the fifteenth year of Tiberius's reign (our year AD 30, counting Tiberius's first full regnal year as AD 15). He thus determined that the Incarnation (conception) of Jesus had taken place 525 years before his own time, corresponding to March 25, 1 BC (or AD 1—there is disagreement), and marking the beginning of the Christian era.

Dionysius's AD system (for *anno Domini*, "in the year of the Lord") had a few problems with it. In the Gospel accounts of Matthew and Luke, Jesus is said to have been born while Herod the Great of Judea was still alive and kicking—but Herod died in the year we call 4 BC. Thus, according to the chronology devised by Dionysius, Jesus' *calendrical* birth was set at least four years—perhaps even five or six years—after his *actual* birth. In addition, the proposed new calendar went directly from the year 1 BC to AD 1, omitting a year 0. That's why the twenty-first century, for example, will go from 2001 to 2100, and not from 2000 to 2099.

The Roman scholar Cassiodorus, a friend of Dionysius, used AD dating in a work of his in 562, but the system didn't catch on in the rest of Europe until the eighth to the tenth centuries. It took even longer—until the seventeenth century—for the BC ("before Christ") system to become widespread for dating events before the birth of Jesus. The hoary Roman AUC system ("*ab urbe condita*"—"from the founding of the city [of Rome]" in our year 753 BC) was still often used until that time for dating ancient occurrences. Other common methods were the "year of the world" system (which used the Jewish calendar to date events from what we call 3761 BC, the supposed year of the creation of the world) and a system using the birth of Abraham (traditionally in October of 2016 BC) as its base year.

In our day, the BC/AD system is in general use except in parts of the Muslim world, though the abbreviations BCE for "Before Common Era" and CE for "Common Era" are sometimes substituted. Yet the politically correct avoidance of referring to Christ, even indirectly in an abbreviation, cannot alter the fact that our years, common as they may be, still have his conception and birth as their point of departure—whether or not, thanks to an oversight of Dionysius Exiguus, Christ was actually born four or more years before the era named after him.

41 ~ What was the first event of the Middle Ages?

St. Benedict's founding of the monastery of Monte Cassino, south of Rome, in 529

YES, IT'S A SILLY QUESTION with a somewhat subjective answer, but it gets us to think about what event most fully sounds the death knell of the Greco-Roman ancient world. A number of the candidates for this defining event feature Roman emperor Constantine the Great: the so-called

Edict of Milan in 313, by which Christians were allowed to practice their religion; his convening of the Council of Nicaea in 325; and his consecration of the city of Constantinople in 330 (see Questions 24 and 27). Some would consider the turning point between antiquity and the medieval world Theodosius's establishment of Christianity as the official religion of the Roman Empire in 380; others locate it in the sacks of Rome in 410 or 455 or in Odoacer's deposing of Romulus Augustulus, the last Roman emperor, in 476 (see Questions 29, 33, and 37). A few see the death of the ancient world emblematized in the torture and execution of Boethius—"the Last of the Romans"—at the hands of Theodoric the Ostrogoth in 524, and the birth of a new order in the medieval "bestseller" *The Consolation of Philosophy*, written by Boethius while he languished in prison. Many cite Justinian's closing of the Neoplatonic Academy in Athens, one of the last strongholds of paganism in the Byzantine Empire, in 529.

But if one occurrence has to bear this extraordinary symbolic burden, it should be another event that took place in 529: St. Benedict's founding of Monte Cassino, the motherhouse of the Benedictine order. Although monasteries had existed in Western Europe for almost two hundred years, it was here, only eighty miles south of the ancient capital of the empire, that Benedict of Nursia formulated the *Benedictine Rule*, established a seminal library, and founded the first religious order in the West. Benedictine monks would go on to play a crucial role in keeping a modicum of literacy and learning alive during the war-ravaged Dark Ages by teaching within their own walls, sending out missionaries, and copying manuscripts of pagan classical works and early Christian texts in their scriptoria. Because of this cultural domination of Western Europe, the long period from the founding of Monte Cassino to the mid-twelfth century has been called "the Benedictine Centuries."

When Benedict led his monks fourteen hundred feet above the valley of the Liri River, they found at the summit of Monte Cassino a temple of Apollo and a grove of Venus, both still venerated by local *pagani*, but not for very much longer. The extent to which the lingering values of Greco-Roman paganism were due to be subverted is apparent right from the first chapter of the *Benedictine Rule*, in which we read of monks "waging their war under a rule and an abbot." But this is hardly a war that Alexander the Great or Julius Caesar would recognize as such. The monks' fight is "against the devil" and "against their own bodily and spiritual vices." When Benedict goes on to refer to "single combat," he means not that of spear-wielding princes like Hector and Achilles, but of hermits, who fight their purely spiritual battles in solitude.

The traditional Greco-Roman emphasis on oratory in political and legal forums was replaced by communal prayers at set hours of the day and night and enforced monastic silence at most other times. Greco-Roman aristocratic pride—in family, race, class, country, and, most of all, self—gave way to the central monastic virtue of humility. The classical right of a citizen to accumulate property and bequeath it to his family ceded to the Benedictine order's prohibition of private ownership of anything by any monk, whether he was a freeman or serf. For patriotism was substituted religiosity; for Greek *areté* and Roman *virtus*, a communitarian ethos; for this world, the next.

The monastery of Monte Cassino was pulverized on February 15, 1944, by furious Allied bombing that sought to root out German troops. Rising from its ashes after World War II for the fourth time in its history, it still houses monks of the Order of St. Benedict.

42 ∽ What was the first complete codification of Roman law?

Byzantine Emperor Justinian's Corpus Iuris Civilis, *completed in 534*

EMPEROR THEODOSIUS II had codified Roman imperial law up to his own day, but by the time Justinian I the Great (r. 527–65) came to the Byzantine throne, almost a century's worth of further enactments were not represented in the Theodosian Code of 438. Justinian, whose main goal on achieving power was to wrench Italy and the rest of Western Europe from barbarian hands, decided his program of conquest should proceed in tandem with his plan to update, overhaul, and streamline the bulky system of Roman law, which he aimed to reimpose on the West. In addition, lawsuits would be easier to resolve—and frivolous ones would be prevented from coming to trial—if the statutes on the books were devoid of inconsistencies, obsolete enactments, and massive redundancy.

While Justinian called on his general Belisarius to oust the Vandals from North Africa and the Ostrogoths from Italy, he ordered his chancellor Tribonian to head a commission for making a new compilation of Roman imperial law. Building on the Theodosian Code and two earlier compilations, Tribonian's group finished its monumental task in only a year, but by the time the new code—or *Codex Justinianus*—appeared in 529, it was already obsolete because Justinian had made so many laws in the interim.

Tribonian went back to work, and another *Codex*, divided into twelve books and incorporating the new laws, was published on November 16, 534. It contains about 4,700 statutes, beginning with the reign of Hadrian (117–38), rather than with the year 312, as in the Theodosian Code, with its 2,529 imperial enactments.

In the meantime, Justinian had asked for the development of two more components in the unified code of law that he envisioned: a textbook of law and a collection of the writings of the classical Roman jurists. The *Institutes*, an elementary textbook of civil law for first-year students, was thus duly drafted by Tribonian and two of his commission members in 533. Based on similar earlier works, especially one by the jurist Gaius, it had the force of law.

The *Digest* (sometimes called the *Pandects*), a product of the indefatigable Tribonian and a team of sixteen legal experts, was the stupendous response to Justinian's request for an exposition of law not covered in the *Codex* and based on the legal opinions of the most famed Roman jurists. By the end of 533 the *Digest* stood forth in all its glory—here, divided among fifty books, were 9,142 passages culled from the opinions and interpretations of thirty-nine jurists spanning more than three centuries, but mostly from the great age of legal learning, AD 100–250. Two jurists, Ulpian and Paulus, together account for more than half the bulk of the *Digest*, but hefty contributions were also made by Papinian, Pomponius, and Gaius. The compilers were instructed to paraphrase, smooth out inconsistencies, leave out superfluous verbiage and obsolete or superseded parts of the law, and in general edit the passages as they saw fit. This work, too, had the force of law.

These three texts (the second edition of the *Codex*, the *Institutes*, and the *Digest*) are often grouped with the *Novellae*—152 later enactments of Justinian, mainly in Greek—to form the monumental collection known as the *Corpus Iuris Civilis* (Body of Civil Law), or simply the Code of Justinian. Weighing in at considerably more than a million words, the Code would give the professors and students at the law schools of Constantinople and Berytus (Beirut) plenty to think about, but at least they would be able to approach their studies more systematically.

As with the Theodosian Code, Christianity as defined by the church of Rome was written into the law, though the overlordship of the emperor was asserted even in religious and ecclesiastical matters. Justinian's Code prescribed death for Manichaeans (see Question 20) and severe penalties for Christian heretics. The punishment for rape or homosexual acts was death, but citizens convicted of a capital crime had the right of appeal.

For just a taste of the opinions on torts in the *Digest*, here are Pomponius on theft and Ulpian on libel:

> If I give something of mine to you, believing it to be yours, whereas you know that it is properly mine, the better view is that this is theft on your part if you did this intending to profit dishonestly (47.2.44).

> If someone composes, writes, or publishes something tending to bring another into hatred, ridicule, or contempt . . . he will be declared to be untrustworthy so that his word cannot be given in court, nor can he make a will (47.10.5).

To avoid a new morass of interpretations, commentaries on Justinian's Code were forbidden. A huge problem, however, was the fact that the laws were in Latin, whereas the Byzantine Empire was Greek-speaking. Only in the ninth and tenth centuries did a Greek compilation, the *Basilica*, appear, which folded the *Codex* and the *Digest* into a single legal code.

After serving as the law for the Byzantine Empire and the reacquired parts of Italy and North Africa, the Code of Justinian was rediscovered as a treasure-house of ancient Roman jurisprudence with the revival of law studies in the West, beginning in eleventh-century Italy (see Question 79). It thus became the ancestor of the legal systems of most of continental Europe, as well as of the canon law of the church.

43 ∾ Where was chess first developed?

India, c. 550, though the date is largely conjectural

ALTHOUGH WE CAN say for certain that this brainy game was not invented by King Solomon or Aristotle, the first origins of chess remain irrecoverable. This much seems plausible: An early form of the game developed in India, probably in the sixth century, perhaps significantly earlier.

Persian and Arab sources attribute its origin to India, and a charming Persian tale recently dated to the early seventh century tells how, during the reign of the great Sassanian king of Persia, Khosrau I (r. 531–79), an embassy arrived from a northern Indian king bearing magnificent gifts but also a serious challenge embodied in a puzzle involving a chessboard and elaborately carved chessmen. If the Persians could figure out how the game was played and the pieces moved, the Indian king would pay them tribute. If not, he would demand tribute from the Persians. The Persian king asked for a week to solve the problem, but after his courtiers failed to do so, the dream interpreter and sage counselor Buzurjmihr figured it out in a day and a night. He then invented *nard* (backgammon) and led a delegation to the Indian king with his own challenge to explain the new Persian game—which the Indians couldn't do.

The earliest form of chess that we know was an Indian board game simulating war and called by the Sanskrit word *chaturanga* ("four arms"), referring to the Indian army as traditionally divided into war elephants, chariots, cavalrymen, and infantry. It was played on an 8-square-by-8-square unicolored board, though sometimes a 9-by-9 or 10-by-10 board was used.

The sixteen pieces, often made of ivory, stood for the four "arms" of the army plus the king and his minister. The raja was the king (who became the shah in Persian); he moved like our chess king. The *mantri* was the minister (or counselor), the weakest piece, moving only one square diagonally, but he eventually gave rise to the queen, the strongest piece in chess. The *gaja* (elephant), the distant ancestor of our bishop, moved two squares diagonally, jumping over the intervening square. The *ashva* (horse) became our knight, and the *ratha* (chariot) became the rook, both moving like the modern pieces. The *padàti* (foot soldier) marched forward like the lowly pawn but without any initial two-square advance. The object of the game was to mate the opposing king. A player who stalemated his opponent lost the game.

The Indian *chaturanga* became the Persian game called at first *chatrang* and then, by the Arabs, *shatranj*, which gave rise to modern chess. In *shatranj*, a player could win by checkmating the king or capturing all the other pieces. In the eighth century, chess spread across the Islamic world, arriving in Christian Europe before 1000 (whereas *chaturanga* seems to have arrived in China independently in about 750).

Chess was trendy enough to be prohibited by a council at Paris in 1213 and an edict of Louis IX in 1254, during the same century that the first checkered boards came into use. In 1474, William Caxton published the first chess book in English, *Game and Playe of the Chesse*, a translation of a thirteenth-century book written by an Italian Dominican friar. Only in the fifteenth century did the queen and bishop acquire their strong modern powers. In the next century, castling, en passant capture, and the two-square pawn advance helped inaugurate the modern game, and Gioacchino Greco became one of the first chess professionals. The French master François-André Philidor wrote a highly influential book on chess strategy in 1749.

The Persian word *shah*, after various permutations in Arabic, Old Spanish, Old French, and Middle English, gave us our word *check*, as in "to check the king." The term for winning the game by stalling the king, *checkmate*, comes from the Persian *shah mat* ("the king is stymied, blocked, thwarted," though most authorities claim it means "the king is dead"). The word *chess* itself is from Old French *esches*, the plural of *eschec*, which meant "check"—and is the ultimate source of our word *checkers*.

44 ∾ What is the first surviving tell-all memoir about royals?

Procopius's Secret History *about the Byzantine rulers Justinian and Theodora, c. 550*

THE ULTIMATE *CHRONIQUE SCANDALEUSE* was written by the greatest historian of his time, a senatorial aristocrat who left a detailed narrative in Greek of Justinian's Persian, African, and Gothic wars. Procopius, legal secretary and adviser to Justinian's chief general Belisarius, had accompanied the latter on his campaign against the Vandal kingdom of North Africa and his first expedition against the Ostrogothic kingdom of Italy, singing the praises of his martial patron in his *History of the Wars*. And then, in 550, he wrote a book much later given the generic title of *Anecdota* ("Unpublished"), which is now known as the *Historia arcana* (*Secret History*).

This work is a 150-page hatchet job on the reign, wife, and court of Justinian I "the Great." Even Procopius's former idol, Belisarius, comes off as a dim-witted cuckold, repeatedly duped by his depraved wife, Antonina, and her royal enabler, Theodora. We don't know what prompted Procopius's splenetic attack, but his book is the dead albatross around the neck of Justinian, the conqueror, builder, and codifier of Roman law (see Question 42).

We learn in the *Secret History* that four years after becoming sole ruler, Justinian was faced with tumultuous riots that nearly cost him his throne. In an enmity that had originated in the brawls of chariot-racing fans at Constantinople's Hippodrome and degenerated into urban gang warfare, the emperor allied himself with the faction known as the Blues, traditional enemies of the Greens.

Procopius describes with distaste the "Hun haircuts" sported by the Blues, who clipped their hair short on top but let it grow very long in the back and never trimmed their beards and mustaches. Their cloaks, trousers, boots, and accessories were also "Hun style." When Justinian executed some of their leaders, the Blues briefly joined forces with the Greens in a five-day rampage of murder and arson directed against any and all. The Nika riots (named after the shouted slogan of *Nika!*—Conquer!) were brutally extinguished by Belisarius, who led three thousand veteran soldiers in a massacre of thirty thousand Greens in the Hippodrome.

But insurrections like this were only the most obvious evidence of how, under Justinian, the empire was going down the tubes. Rich Arian heretics were despoiled, ex post facto pederasts (especially those of the Green faction) were castrated and exhibited in public parades, astrologers were whipped and displayed around the city on camelback, senators were accused of disloyalty and stripped of their possessions.

Justinian himself is described as not bad-looking but a dead ringer for an earlier odious tyrant, Roman Emperor Domitian. As for his character, Procopius does not shrink from calling the great man "a moron" but qualifies his generalization by claiming he was also "deceitful, devious, false, hypocritical, two-faced, cruel, skilled in dissembling his thought . . . a liar always," a faithless friend and a treacherous enemy who, the author ventures implausibly, was responsible for more murders and war fatalities than in all of previous history—a trillion people, in fact, a myriad myriads of myriads. Procopius even attributes the devastating earthquakes and plague that assailed the empire to divine displeasure or diabolic powers.

Then he moves on to an uncensored account of the early life of Theodora. The woman who went on to become joint ruler of the Byzantine Empire was the middle child of three sisters whose Cypriot father was known as "the Bearkeeper," since he was in charge of the wild beasts that did battle in the amphitheater of Constantinople. After his death, the mother of the young girls put them on the stage or in brothels to earn their daily bread.

As opposed to the cultured, high-class hookers the Greeks called *hetaerae*, Theodora became a common whore. Not for her the accomplishments of the flute or harp—or even your basic belly or lap dance— no, Theodora was just the acting-troupe trollop who excelled in scenes of low comedy or striptease because she had a gift for mimicry and was utterly shameless. Often slapped around on the stage for comic effect, she kept the audience in stitches by raising her skirt to put her wares on view. Sometimes, in a loftier vein, she would enact a version of the myth of Leda and the swan that involved geese pecking at barley grains that slaves had strategically sprinkled on her naked body.

Procopius assures us that Theodora often went picnicking with ten or more young men with whom she would have sex throughout the night—and then take on their servants, too, "perhaps thirty in number." She once simulated sex with a projecting corner of the dining couch in the house of an illustrious gentleman. In the book's most notorious phrase, "she flung wide three gates to the ambassadors of Cupid," but regretted that nature had not supplied her with a fourth.

Frequent pregnancies were countered with frequent abortions (though the one child that slipped through, a son who returned as a teen after she was empress to claim his share of the good things in life, was never seen or heard of again). After a stint as mistress of a Byzantine governor in North Africa, the young Theodora worked her way back to Constantinople plying the only trade she knew.

This was the woman whom the forty-three-year-old Justinian, acting emperor for his dithering uncle Justin, chose as his twenty-something bride. First, however, he had to concoct a statute repealing the prohibition against senators like him marrying actress/prostitutes like Theodora, and old Justin duly signed it into law a few years before leaving what our tabloids might refer to as the Justinodora in charge of the Byzantine Empire.

In Procopius's weirdest charge, he accuses the royal pair of being devils in disguise, maybe even vampires. He relates how Justinian's mother mentioned something about a demon as her lover when she conceived her son. Visitors to the palace described how Justinian's head seemed to vanish at times and then reattach itself to his body. A holy monk once saw Satan seated on Justinian's throne, and the emperor himself hardly ate, drank, or slept, but "was possessed by the quenchless lust of a demon." The young Theodora's lovers declared they were sometimes chased out of her bedroom by a devil that wanted to take their place.

According to Procopius, the empress took excessive care of her bod: long, luxurious baths before breakfast; after breakfast, rest. She loved to eat and drink just about anything, and she slept a lot, both day and night. She kept even top officials cooling their heels in her antechamber, and once they entered, they often just managed to throw themselves on their faces, kiss her feet, and then bolt out again since, unless she told them to speak, they had to keep their mouths shut. When she was feeling frisky, Theodora and her eunuchs would prepare some mocking little ditty—on a vexing hernia problem, for example—and spring it on some visiting dignitary.

Theodora died in 548 before she turned fifty, predeceasing her husband, who survived into his eighties, by seventeen years. In Justinian's church of San Vitale in Ravenna, the crowned royal couple (who never visited the city) are depicted in stunning mosaic portraits on the apse walls, along with officials and attendants. The emperor looks very determined and capable, and Theodora is as Procopius described her: "fair of face" and "somewhat pale," but with eyes that were "dazzling and vivacious." Indeed, she is majestically beautiful, with her cascade of huge pearls and purple robes, holding out a gift chalice. Despite the vicious smears of the *Secret History*, both husband and wife are considered saints by the Eastern Orthodox Church.

The fickle historian's last work, *On Buildings* (c. 558–60), is an extravagant paean in honor of Justinian's multifarious construction projects, crammed with fulsome flattery of the emperor. Maybe Justinian had rewarded Procopius in the interim—or perhaps the book was a command performance, and the author could not well afford to be coolly objective.

45 ∾ Who was the first important historian of the Franks (the early French)?

Gregory of Tours, author of History of the Franks,
c. 575–94

THE SPARE-TIME HISTORIAN Gregory of Tours (c. 539–94), whose day job for twenty-one years was to serve as bishop of that city and who went on to be canonized by the church, came from a distinguished Gallo-Roman family of senatorial rank that had produced many prelates. He was supposed to be tiny, but he comes across as a courageous though modest man whose misfortune it was to live in a barbarous age and who set down in spirited but sometimes ungrammatical Latin his portrait of La Belle France in its untrammeled cultural infancy. Although Gregory monkishly opens his history of the Franks with the creation of the world and other biblical events, he quickly lands in his own century and begins regaling us with the deeds of the Merovingian kings of France at a time when they were still Frankish louts (see Question 38).

A nightmarish horror flick could be based on Gregory's book, replete as it is with countless wars, treasons and treacheries, assassinations, arsons, rapes, lootings, floggings, charges of witchcraft, burnings at the stake, breakings on the wheel, beheadings, mutilations, strappados, and wooden splinters hammered beneath fingernails and toenails. Interrogations never seem to be conducted without the use of torture. Men accused of crimes are often cut to pieces on the spot rather than allowed to burden the penal system. On rare occasions, though, the Merovingians are almost negligently soft on crime, as when some would-be assassins of King Childebert II merely have their ears and noses sliced off before being released to become objects of ridicule. Literary critic Erich Auerbach wrote of Gregory's *History*, "Reading it, we almost smell the atmosphere of the first century of Frankish rule in Gaul."

Gregory calls his sovereign, King Chilperic I of Soissons (Neustria), "the Nero and Herod of our time." This ruler's perennial reminder to his judges was, "Those who disobey my orders must have their eyes torn out." A debauched and gluttonous man, he also wrote bad Latin verses and lousy church music, had his second wife garroted in bed, and made nasty fun of bishops. Bishop Gregory can barely conceal his schadenfreude while recounting Chilperic's murder by stabbing in 584: "Blood immediately streamed both from his mouth and through the gaping wound, and that was the end of this wicked man."

But the most incorrigibly villainous star of the book is Chilperic's third wife, Queen Fredegund (d. 597). Originally a serving-woman who became Chilperic's concubine, she had his half brother, King Sigibert I, knifed to death in 575 and schemed to kill her husband's sons by his first wife. She tried to dispose of the third and last by sending him to a town in which dysentery had broken out; when that failed, she had him stabbed to death and his girlfriend and the girl's mother tortured.

Once, to put an end to a feud that had devastated many families, she had the last three surviving feuders invited to a banquet, made sure they got stinking drunk, and then placed three axmen behind them where they sat on the same couch to decapitate all three in unison. She had a bishop stabbed to death in his own cathedral at Rouen for speaking truth to power. When one of the town leaders rebuked her for the sacrilege, she asked him to have a friendly drink of absinthe mixed with wine and honey—"a favorite drink of the barbarians," Gregory informs us—but this one was laced with poison. The number of people she had tortured to death, including a bunch of Parisian housewives, can only be hinted at here.

Fredegund's bloodiest machinations were often motivated by her determination to protect the throne of her son Chlothar II (584–629), Chilperic's posthumous child for whom she acted as regent, in the turbulent dynastic struggles among the various Frankish kinglets. A number of her assassination attempts were unsuccessful, however, as when she sent a group of men (headed by a fellow named Baddo) to assassinate King Guntram. Having already murdered King Sigibert years earlier, Fredegund sent two priests to stab Childebert II, his son and successor, with poisoned daggers after drugging the clerics with a potion to make them brave, but they, too, were caught beforehand. When the priest whom she sent to kill Sigibert's widow, Brunhild, failed to do so, she had his hands and feet lopped off.

On a more mundane level, Gregory records how Fredegund turned against her daughter Rigunth because she had blossomed into a little slut. The two of them "frequently exchanged slaps and punches," but on one occasion Fredegund tricked her daughter into reaching inside a huge treasure chest and then slammed the lid down on her neck and leaned heavily on it, setting poor Rigunth's eyes starting out of her head. Luckily, servant girls burst in and rescued the young lady from

certain death. Gregory himself once had to face trial for slandering Fredegund (supposedly spreading the rumor that the bishop of Bordeaux
was her lover), but he somehow managed to come away unscathed.

It must be admitted that Gregory's book has the lamest beginning
of any major history—"A great many things keep happening, some of
them good, some of them bad"—but we have to make some allowances
for an author who has been dubbed "the Herodotus of barbarity." As
Auerbach reminds us, "When Gregory writes, the catastrophe has
occurred, the Empire has fallen, its organization has collapsed, the culture of antiquity has been destroyed."

46 ∽ Who was the first Christian missionary to Anglo-Saxon England?

St. Augustine of Canterbury, who arrived in Kent in 597

ALTHOUGH CHRISTIANITY MAY HAVE FIRST COME to England in the late
second or early third century, it was all but extirpated after the fifth-
century invasions of Angles, Saxons, and Jutes (see Question 35). The
man who reintroduced it there, thus earning the appellation "Apostle to
the English," was the Roman-born monk Augustine. The pope who
picked him for the job was his fellow Roman and monk Gregory I the
Great (590–604), true founder of the medieval papacy, who possessed,
according to British historian G. M. Trevelyan, "the genius of a Caesar
and the organizing care of an Augustus."

A famous anecdote tells how, when still in his mid-thirties, Gregory
was walking through the Roman Forum one day and saw some handsome
blond-haired English slave boys who were being sold. On learning they
were pagan *Angli*, he is said to have remarked, "*Non Angli, sed angeli*"
("not Angles but angels") and determined to go convert them, but his plan
fell through. It was only several decades later as pope that he was able to
commission Augustine, the prior of the monastery Gregory had established in his family's palace on the Caelian Hill, to journey to England
with about forty followers and attempt to save the English heathens.

Augustine and his group set off in June of 596, but well before they
got to England, they lost heart at the thought of traveling to, in historian
Bede's words, "a barbarous, fierce, and pagan nation." When Augustine
returned to Rome to plead their case, Gregory reassured him, named

him abbot of his followers, and exhorted them all to soldier on. After wintering in France, the missionaries arrived in 597 on the Isle of Thanet, which was then separated by a channel from the Kentish mainland of southeast England.

The immediate object of their expedition was Aethelberht I (r. 560–616), king of the Jutes in Kent and overlord of England south of the Humber. This most powerful English ruler of the time was married to Bertha, daughter of a Christian Frankish king. She had come to Britain accompanied by a Frankish bishop who served as her spiritual adviser and conducted services for her and her entourage in a church built during the Roman occupation. These favorable conditions for reintroducing the Christian faith to England may have prompted Pope Gregory to send his mission.

Aethelberht, who was still a pagan, received the group courteously but told them to stay on Thanet while he conferred with his people. When he returned a few days later to summon the strangers, they approached in procession behind a silver cross and a likeness of Jesus painted on a board. They prayed, sang a litany, and, at the king's invitation and via interpreters, preached to him and his court. Aethelberht liked what he heard but said it was asking a lot to expect his people to abandon their traditional faith. Nonetheless, he reassured the missionaries that they would not be harmed, that they would be given everything they needed and a place to live in his capital of Canterbury, and that they could preach openly and try to make converts—which they did.

Soon the king himself was won over by Augustine and, on Christmas Day of 597, a reported ten thousand of his people were baptized. Canterbury became a center of Christianity, and churches were built or restored. Augustine made a brief trip to the Continent to be consecrated archbishop of all England by the archbishop of Arles.

In sending a messenger to inform Gregory of his spectacular success, he also asked the pope about a series of issues that had arisen: what to do about the different liturgical practices of the surviving Celtic Church in Britain, how to punish thieves who rob churches (fines for some, beatings for others, replied the pontiff), which family members are prohibited from marrying each other, and even sexual conundrums such as whether a man may enter church after having intercourse if he hasn't washed yet and whether priests can say Mass on the morning after they've had erotic dreams. To the question of whether a menstruating woman should be permitted in church, Gregory sensibly answered yes, since "the workings of nature cannot be considered culpable."

In 601, Augustine received from Gregory his pallium, a sashlike vestment attesting his status as archbishop, as well as several helpers, including Mellitus and Paulinus, and useful gifts such as church vessels and vestments, relics, altar coverings, and books. He was also given authority to create other bishops and install metropolitan bishops at London and York, each with a dozen bishops under his supervision. As for the native bishops in the western and northern parts of Britain, Gregory gave Augustine authority over them, but these Welsh and other Celtic prelates refused to surrender their long-established liturgical traditions and relative independence from Rome. Augustine consecrated Christ Church, Canterbury, as his see in 603.

In a letter sent to Abbot Mellitus before he journeyed to England, Pope Gregory wrote, "Tell Augustine that he should by no means destroy the temples of the gods, but rather the idols within those temples. . . . For, if those temples are well-built, they should be converted from the worship of demons to the service of the true God." This moderate policy would encourage the former heathens "to flock more readily to their accustomed resorts," thus smoothing the transition to Christianity. The pagan practice of sacrificing oxen to the Germanic gods should thus be replaced with church-sponsored festivals in honor of martyrs, complete with feasting, for "if the people are allowed some worldly pleasures in this way, they will more readily come to desire the joys of the spirit."

In 604, the East Saxons were converted by Mellitus, who was consecrated bishop of London by Augustine. In that same year, Augustine died, after having converted all of Kent and consecrated Laurence as his successor as archbishop of Canterbury.

The Roman Catholic faith soon spread over south and central England. In 627, Paulinus, the metropolitan of York, converted King Edwin of Northumbria, but after Edwin was killed in battle six years later, paganism reasserted itself in the north. Missionaries of the Celtic Church now came to Scotland and Northumbria from Iona, the Celtic monastery that had been founded in 563 by the Irish monk and prince St. Columba on a small island off the western Scottish coast. His disciple St. Aidan of Iona converted Northumbria, beginning in 635, and founded the monasteries of Melrose and Lindisfarne. Long resistant to Christianity under its pagan king Penda, the central English kingdom of Mercia was finally converted in 659. The differences between Celtic and Roman Christianity, in matters such as determining the date of Easter and the procedure for baptism, were decided in favor of the Roman position at the Synod of Whitby in 664.

SEVENTH CENTURY

47 ∾ What is the first surviving English love poem?

"The Wife's Lament," an Anglo-Saxon poem,
c. 500–700

"THE WIFE'S LAMENT," to use the modern title it was given, is a short elegiac poem in which a woman bemoans the loss of her husband and the sorrow of her solitary life in exile. As with other Anglo-Saxon poems, its origins are lost in the abyss of time, and it has been preserved in a manuscript probably written many generations, if not centuries, after its composition by an anonymous poet. The sole extant manuscript is part of a priceless collection of Anglo-Saxon poetry known as the *Exeter Book*, donated by Bishop Leofric (d. 1072) to the library of Exeter Cathedral in England.

"The Wife's Lament" is spoken by an unidentified woman who cryptically describes her loss and grief, leaving unanswered many questions as to why she and her husband have been separated, what part his kin have played in her misfortune, whether they have turned the husband against her, and why she has been exiled. It is also unclear whether a second man figures in the narrative.

The vagueness of the events and personae in the poem has resulted in much critical speculation and disagreement, with some suggesting that the speaker is an allegorical religious figure, a deceased woman, or even a man, but these interpretations have been largely discounted. Although the woman's lament may seem puzzling, the missing pieces may have been well understood by its original audience. The woman's soliloquy may have been part of a larger heroic story quite familiar to them, or it may have represented a stock dramatic situation chiefly valued for its emotional content but not requiring further explanation. Here is a version in modern English that preserves some of the alliteration of the original:[1]

The Wife's Lament

Full of sorrows I sing this song of myself
and tell of my plight, rehearsing the tale

---

[1] Translated by Peter D'Epiro.

of the hardships I bore since coming of age,
both the old and the new, but none worse than now.
How bitter the pain of my journeys to exile!
        First my lord departed, far from his people,
over welter of waves. Dreamless at dawn,
I knew not where my lord might abide.
I fared forth in search of men who might seek him—
poor I, friendless exile—because of my woes.
Then his kinsmen began to take secret counsel
as to how they might best keep us always apart,
so that we two dwelt far away in the world—
our life was most wretched and I always longing.
My lord himself then bade me remain here,
though I had few loved ones at all in this land,
few friends who were loyal. My spirit is sad.
        Just when I had found someone so suitable,
he showed himself hard-souled and mirthless in mind,
hiding his heart and considering crime.
Blithe in our bearing, both of us vowed
that nothing would part us except death alone,
naught else—and now that vow is worth naught.
It is now as if the friendship we shared
had never existed. Far or near I must
bear with the feuding of my much-beloved.
        I was commanded to live in a grove in the woods,
under an oak-tree, hard by an earth-cave.
Old is this earth-hall, and I am all longing;
these dales are so dim, these hills are so high,
bitter bastions of old overgrown with briars,
joyless abodes—so often I feel here
the lack of my lord. There are friends on earth,
loving and living and sharing their beds,
while I at dawn make my way all alone
under the oak-tree, hard by the earth-cave.
There I must sit all the long summer's day,
there I must weep for my journeys to exile,
all my adversities. Never can I
grant any respite to cares of the mind
nor the longing that seized me in life.

A man who is young must be sober-minded,
and, hardy of heart-thought, must also possess
a blitheness in bearing, despite all his breast-cares,
his sorrows' afflictions. Let him look to himself
for his world's winsomeness. May my friend be cast out
far off from all people—may my friend have to sit
beneath stony cliffs berimed by the storm,
my weary-souled lover, surrounded by water
in a dreary dwelling; there he will suffer
multitudes of mind-cares, remembering too often
a dwelling more delightful. Woe to him who must
with longing abide for someone beloved.

As the earliest extant English love poem, "The Wife's Lament" stands at the head of a glorious tradition whose highlights include Geoffrey Chaucer's *Troilus and Criseyde*, the Elizabethan sonnet sequences of Sir Philip Sidney and Edmund Spenser, John Donne's metaphysical lyrics, and, nearer our time, the poems chronicling William Butler Yeats's unrequited love for Maud Gonne. An abiding irony is the fact that the most celebrated love poems in the language— Shakespeare's sonnets—were almost all addressed to a man, including the one beginning with the famous question, "Shall I compare thee to a summer's day?"

—*Nancy Walsh*

48 ❧ Where were the first civil service examinations instituted?

China in 606 during the Sui dynasty

FROM ANCIENT TIMES, Chinese scholars gave private lessons to boys whose families hoped they could thus qualify for government positions. The first tentative steps toward establishing a civil service based on merit examinations were taken under Wu-ti (140–87 BC). This Han dynasty emperor also revived the study of Confucian texts, made them central to Chinese education and religion, and literally had them carved in stone. From the early second century AD, examinations were held sporadically to identify qualified candidates for China's burgeoning imperial bureaucracy, but the first emperor to institute civil service testing (the *keju* system) was Yang Jian of the short-lived Sui dynasty (581–618), who decreed in 606 that applicants for public office had to show satisfactory examination results instead of being recruited solely on the recommendation of government officials.

During the early Tang dynasty (618–907), the exams were made strictly competitive and were offered at set intervals. They came in three main levels of difficulty, corresponding to local, provincial, and national competitions, each successive level qualifying the successful candidate for higher government positions. Under the Song dynasty (960–1279), provincial and national examinations were held every three years. Males of any age were eligible to sit for the tests, though sons of merchants and artisans were sometimes excluded. Many a grizzled old aspirant kept taking the test in the hope of joining the ranks of the scholarly elite before he died. A man who passed the provincial exam was termed a *juren* ("recommended man") and was allowed to sit for the national examination. If he passed the grueling test held at the capital, he became a *jinshi* ("presented scholar") and was eligible to become one of the highest ministers of state.

By the fourteenth century, the national examinations held in Beijing lasted twenty-four to seventy-two hours. Test-takers had to schlep their own food, bedding, and chamber pots, sometimes from the other end of the empire. They were then locked into one of thousands of tiny, dark, grimy cells for the duration of the test. By the mid-eighteenth century, this system was being criticized and satirized. The extremely bloody Taiping Rebellion (1850–64), a civil war in which twenty million perished, was led by Hong Xiuquan, a failed candidate for the civil service who claimed to be a younger brother of Jesus. The examinations were abolished as hopelessly archaic only in 1905, after a history spanning, with some interruptions, thirteen hundred years.

What did these fabled tests cover? For the most part, especially from 1313 until the demise of the system, successful candidates were those who had thoroughly memorized and studied the ancient texts known as the Four Books and the Five Classics, most of them erroneously ascribed to Confucius (c. 551–479 BC) as either author or editor. The Four Books were *The Analects of Confucius* (the philosopher's discourses and dialogues as compiled by his disciples), *The Great*

Learning, *The Doctrine of the Mean*, and *The Book of Mencius* (a philo-sophical work by Confucius's greatest follower). The Five Classics comprised *The Book of Poetry* (an anthology of 305 poems), *The Book of Documents* (or *History*), *The Book of Changes* (*I Ching*), *The Book of Rites*, and *The Spring and Autumn Annals* (a history text). By age fif-teen, each boy who was lucky enough to attend school had memorized these nine books—a total of 431,286 Chinese characters.

Though the top-level national examinations also tested candidates on the political problems of the times, the *keju* system chiefly demanded that they be able to write highly formalized essays on topics pertaining to this varied Confucian lore (and the commentaries thereon) and also to compose poems on assigned topics. The ideal test-taker was thus a scholar-gentleman who could demonstrate how thoroughly he had imbibed the letter and spirit of the Confucianism that formed the intel-lectual and spiritual core of Chinese culture. This philosophy stressed ethical teachings—responsibilities and respect toward society and indi-viduals, decorum and ritual in social and religious observances—rather than metaphysics, abstruse theology, or science. Civil service examina-tions were also given in the specialized fields of law, military skills, and other areas.

Potential test-takers required leisure for intense study and money to buy books and pay tutors. An old scholar might offer his tutoring ser-vices for a modest fee, or several families might pool their resources to hire a teacher for their sons. The boys started learning at dawn and con-tinued till late afternoon, except in summer, during which they were dismissed at noon to go work in the fields. Since the bamboo rod was never spared, the memorization of texts and the lessons in calligraphy, essay writing, and verse composition progressed at a brisk trot, if not a gallop.

Of the two million test-takers each year, not more than 2–5 percent passed. Some who failed the tests killed themselves, and suicide among unsuccessful students remains a problem in East Asian cultures. Despite many safeguards, applicants found ingenious ways to cheat, though the penalty was often severe: corporal punishment, banishment, or even execution.

Successful candidates—later called "mandarins" in the West, after their dialect of Chinese—often grew arrogant and obnoxious, like some of the members of any charmed circle. Yet the examination system allowed men of even modest means and plebeian origin to enter government service and rise high in it. It also prevented the government from being monopolized (and threatened) by powerful cliques of aristocrats, plutocrats, or military men, though the wellborn were, as usual, overrepresented. Will Durant may have been exaggerating only slightly when he wrote that, as a result of the Chinese civil service system, "the national mind and ambition were turned in the direction of study, and the national heroes and models were men of culture rather than masters of wealth."

49 ∽ Who was the first Muslim?

Muhammad, who in 610 had a vision of the angel Gabriel

THE WORD *ISLAM*, related to the Arabic *salam* ("peace"), is the condition of having made peace with—or submitted to—God (Allah), and a *Muslim* is "one who submits" to the will of Allah. Although the line of twenty-five prophets mentioned in the Koran, sometimes referred to as "Muslims before Muhammad," runs from Adam through Noah, Abraham, Ishmael, Isaac, Moses, and David, and on to John the Baptist and Jesus, Muhammad is considered "the Seal of the Prophets," the last and greatest of them, the final revealer of Allah's teachings and thus the first Muslim properly so called.

Muhammad (c. 570–632), born in Mecca, an oasis and important commercial center in western Arabia, was the posthumous child of Abdullah, a member of a poor but noble family of the powerful Quraysh tribe. After his mother, Amina, died while he was still a child, his grandfather and then an uncle served as his guardians. As he matured he came into contact with Arabian Jews and Christians, though the majority of his countrymen, to his distress, were polytheistic idol worshippers. Muhammad worked as a caravan trade manager for Khadija, the widow of a rich merchant, and at age twenty-five he married his forty-year-old employer. Although he later went on to take ten other wives, Muhammad lived monogamously with Khadija, who became his first convert, during the remaining twenty-six years of her life.

In the month of Ramadan of 610, the forty-year-old Muhammad went to the cave of Hira on Mount Noor near Mecca to meditate, when he heard the voice of the archangel Gabriel (Jibril) exhorting him to be the messenger of Allah, the one true God who had "created man from a clot" and "taught man what he knew not" (Koran 96:1–5). After this "Night of Power," Muhammad had revelations for more than twenty years, during which the text of the Koran (Qur'an, "recitation") was delivered piecemeal to him by Gabriel. This book, regarded by Muslims as the eternal uncreated Word of Allah, was dictated by Muhammad to a scribe, since he is said to have been illiterate, and then preached to his family and friends, who became his first followers.

Muhammad's proselytizing over the next dozen years won converts but also met with resistance and ridicule from his fellow merchants and traders—polytheists who profited from the thriving pilgrimage trade centered on the Kaaba and other Meccan shrines. In 622, he was forced to flee toward Medina—"the city," at that time an agricultural oasis named Yathrib, some two hundred miles northeast of Mecca. Since Muhammad's hegira ("emigration, flight") marks the beginning of the Muslim lunar calendar, AD 622 corresponds to AH 1 (Latin, *anno Hegirae*).

In the following year, Muhammad, supported by two hundred followers from Mecca, made peace between warring clans of farmers in Medina who agreed to join forces under the protection of Allah. Firmly established as a religious and military leader, he raided a Meccan caravan in 624 but, with a force only one-third the size, had to face an army of a thousand sent out from his native city to punish him. This difficult first victory at the battle of Badr was followed by a defeat at the hands of Meccan soldiers on Mount Uhud near Medina, during which Muhammad was wounded.

When an army of ten thousand was dispatched from Mecca to Medina several years later in retaliation for ongoing caravan depredations, the Muslims defended themselves against the cavalry and camel attack with a deep trench they had dug in front of the city, and a terrible wind that blew from over the Red Sea for three days and nights persuaded the invaders to return home. Muhammad authorized the beheading of about seven hundred members of a Jewish tribe of Medina who were accused of treachery in this fight; their families were enslaved and their wealth confiscated.

By January of 630, Muhammad and his army of followers were in a position to return in force to Mecca, which they conquered against little resistance. After entering the city in triumph and sparing the populace for its opposition, he and the people removed all the idols from the Kaaba, the small cube-shaped stone shrine said in the Koran to have been built by Ibrahim (Abraham) and his son Ismail (Ishmael), and rededicated it to Allah.

A few years later, complaining of a severe headache, Muhammad died in the hut of his wife Aisha in Medina on June 8, 632, having won for Islam almost the entire Arabian Peninsula, which had previously been a collocation of warring tribes. Historian William H. McNeill has written, "Never before or since has a prophet won such success so quickly; nor has the work of a single man so rapidly and radically transformed the course of world history." And Machiavelli was surely thinking primarily of Muhammad when he declared that "all armed prophets have conquered."

Like Orthodox Judaism, Islam is a strict monotheism that looks to its holy book and religious traditions to guide all aspects of life, forbids the consumption of pork or blood, bans the creation of images, and practices circumcision (though this is not mentioned in the Koran). In addition, the use of alcohol or other intoxicants, gambling, and the charging of interest on loans are forbidden to Muslims.

Besides angels, Islam believes in the existence of jinn, invisible creatures of smokeless fire who may be either good or evil; the leader of the evil jinn is Shaitan (Satan). It also teaches that the prophet Isa (Jesus), who spoke in his cradle and created real birds out of clay as a child, was not the Son of God—Allah has no sons—and that he did not die by crucifixion but was taken away by Allah, who left a shadow or criminal in his place.

The official version of the Koran was issued by Uthman, the third caliph, in c. 650. The sacred book of the Muslims comprises 114 suras (chapters) arranged according to length (longest first), 6,239 verses, and 77,934 Arabic words, making it about four-fifths the length of the New Testament. Memorized by millions across the world, it is used as a textbook of religion, law, morality, and language skills, much as Homer long remained the centerpiece of ancient Greek education. Its classical Arabic cadences are said to be miracles of euphonious rhythmic prose and rhetorical splendor.

The Five Pillars of Islam, incumbent on all Muslims, are the confession of faith ("There is no god but Allah, and Muhammad is his Prophet"), prayer five times daily facing Mecca, obligatory charity, fasting during the daylight hours of the holy month of Ramadan, and the pilgrimage (hajj) to Mecca at least once, for those who possibly can. Jihad ("striving") is another duty, but its primary meaning is to strive after the ethical and spiritual life enjoined in the Koran, not only to fight against infidels in defense of Islam: "And whoever strives hard, he strives only for his own soul" (29:6).

With Islam came increased charity toward widows and orphans, a modicum of justice toward slaves, the outlawing of infanticide, the right of women to own and inherit property, and the obligation of relatives of those unintentionally killed to accept a blood price instead of exacting revenge. Yet Islamic law, or Sharia, prescribes fierce punishments for sexual and other transgressions: stoning for adultery, the death penalty for homosexuality, a hundred lashes for fornicators (24:2), and the loss of one or both hands for theft (5:38).

After the day of judgment, a seven-gated hell of fire awaits the evil and the unbelievers. The Islamic paradise, described as a luxuriant garden abode filled with sensual delights, including the virgin houris, is often interpreted allegorically as a blissful condition in which the faithful who have adhered to the teachings of Islam will behold Allah for all eternity.

50 ∾ Who was the first caliph?

Abū Bakr, Muhammad's father-in-law, who became
leader of the Muslims in 632

MUHAMMAD LEFT BEHIND NO SONS or clearly designated successor at his death in Medina, Arabia, on June 8, 632 (see Question 49). Ali, his first cousin and son-in-law (husband to Muhammad's daughter Fātimah), was his closest surviving male kinsman, but it remained unclear whether the succession should be hereditary or based on consensus. In a contentious meeting, the elders of the Muslim community passed over Ali, choosing instead the pious Abū Bakr (c. 573–634), the wealthy Meccan father of Muhammad's child bride, Aisha, as the first caliph ("successor"), or leader, of the Muslim theocratic community. Although the Islamic rank and file immediately approved the choice, Ali made his submission to Abū Bakr only after several months.

The first caliph had been the closest friend and a very early convert of the prophet. A cloth merchant, he had traveled with the young Muhammad on caravans to Syria, been beaten and persecuted for his propagation of the new faith, and served as the prophet's sole companion on the hegira from Mecca to Medina. He had fought as a warrior and military leader in numerous battles for nascent Islam, and, during Muhammad's final illness, was appointed by him to lead the congregation of Medina in public prayers. A description of the caliph that can be traced back to his daughter speaks of "fair skin, thin, emaciated, with a sparse beard, a slightly hunched frame, sunken eyes, and protruding forehead." He went by the nickname of Abū Bakr—"father of the camel foal"—because of his love of these desert animals. More significant, he initiated the first permanent Islamic expansion beyond Arabia.

After Muhammad's death, several Arabian tribes that had accepted Islam decided they owed no allegiance or tribute to his successor. Calling on the great general Khalid ibn al-Walid, the caliph soon launched military campaigns that brought the rebellious tribes (some with copycat prophets of their own) back into the Muslim fold, saving the entire enterprise from splintering into historical inconsequence.

Abū Bakr next made the momentous decision to send his armies northward. These forays were not undertaken solely to propagate Islam abroad but also to acquire booty and tribute so that his restless and devout nomadic warriors could support themselves (and the rest of Arabia) without fomenting political and religious schisms at home. Devastating attacks on Mesopotamia, then part of the Persian Empire, and a victory over the forces of Byzantine emperor Heraclius in southern Palestine in July of 634 capped off the first caliph's reign. He died on August 22, 634, after slightly more than two years in office, and was buried beside Muhammad in Medina.

Among the many sayings attributed to Abū Bakr, who spent much of his wealth in ransoming slaves, are the following:

Do not deceive or be faithless even with your enemy.

If an ignorant person is attracted by the things of the world, that is bad. But if a learned person is thus attracted, it is worse.

Youth is not restored by the dyeing of your hair.

For the story of the mighty conquering caliphs who followed Abū Bakr, see Question 51. Here, we'll skip ahead to highlight some of the intellectual glories—and the violent end—of the caliphate under the dynasty of the Abbasids, who ruled the Muslim world from 750 to 1258 from their pleasure-loving metropolis of Baghdad, after its founding by al-Mansur in 762. The next caliph, al-Mahdi (775–85), accepted the authority of the ulema—the legal and religious specialists of Islam—to act as judicial arbiters in vexed issues of the Muslim law of Sharia, thus confirming the caliph in his role of political and military leader rather than as spiritual heir of the prophet.

Under al-Mansur's grandson, Harun al-Rashid (786–809), Baghdad became the most prosperous and splendiferous city in Islam. His reign marked the apogee of the Abbasid caliphate in both international trade and cultural attainment at a time in which numerous ancient Greek scientific works were being translated into Arabic. A talented and learned man himself, al-Rashid presided over a brilliant court rife with poets, dancers, doctors, artists, and comedians—in fact, all manner of scholars, wits, and entertainers. He also figures as the caliph in *The Arabian Nights* who orders that the seven voyages of the fictional Sinbad the Sailor be inscribed on parchment in letters of gold for the delight of future ages.

Al-Rashid's son Mamun (813–33) continued the vast translation program that was to prove crucial to the intellectual and scientific revival of Europe in later ages. Under Mamun and later caliphs, the medical writings of Hippocrates and Galen, some of the works of Plato and Aristotle, Euclid's *Elements*, Ptolemy's *Almagest*, and other works on logic and mathematics, as well as Persian, Syriac, and Sanskrit texts, were rendered into Arabic. Muslim scholars thus came to be possessed of the finest scientific knowledge available at the time, which, after physicians like Rhazes, philosophers like al-Farabi, and dozens more had added to it, they passed on to Western Europe via their Spanish and Sicilian domains. There, retranslated into Latin, seminal Greek works, as enriched by original Islamic contributions, formed the substratum of the advances in logic, mathematics, medicine, geography, and natural science that marked European thought in the later Middle Ages, the Renaissance, and the seventeenth century.

But the gradual fragmentation of the caliphate was evident in Spain's independence under its own rulers as early as the mid-eighth century. In 929, Abd al-Rahman III founded the Umayyad Caliphate of al-Andalus (Spain) with its magnificent capital of Córdoba, which housed seventy libraries and served as another great center of translation. The Fatimids, a family claiming descent from Muhammad's youngest daughter, Fātimah, established at their capital of Cairo yet another rival caliphate (909–1171) over North Africa, Egypt, Syria,

Palestine, and Sicily. Then the Seljuk Turks arrived from the east to carve out a vast realm from Central Asia to Turkey, ruling as sultans and emirs.

The Abbasid caliphate itself came to a shuddering end in 1258 with the death of hundreds of thousands in the destruction of Baghdad by the Mongol general Hülegü Khan, who had Caliph al-Mustasim trampled to death by horses. After this debacle, Abbasid "shadow caliphs" ruled as ceremonial religious figureheads in Egypt under Mamluk sultans for several hundred years, followed by a long line of Ottoman sultans, who adopted the title of caliph, for four hundred years more, until the caliphate was finally abolished by the Turkish National Assembly in 1924.

51 ∽ What was the first nation outside Arabia to fall to Islam?

Iraq, whose conquest by Muslim forces was virtually complete by 634

IF THE CONCEPT OF BLITZKRIEG had been current in the seventh century, the newly Islamized Arabs would certainly have applied it to their conquest of much of the Middle East, which they won by charging furiously into battle on horses and camels during the first few caliphates (see Question 50). Within a century of Muhammad's death in 632, the Islamic Empire was twice the size of that of Alexander the Great or the Romans.

The Byzantine and Persian Empires, whose territories bordered on Arabia, had been warring against each other from 602 to 630, and were further debilitated by recent outbreaks of plague. In 633, Abū Bakr, the first caliph, sent Khalid ibn al-Walid—"the Sword of Allah"—to capture the capital city of Al-Hirah in Iraq, which was the wealthiest province of the Persian Empire and seething with resentment against its overlords. After four victories for his eighteen thousand troops in as many battles, Khalid received the surrender of Al-Hirah in May and went on to capture two more Iraqi cities. By January 634, after the battle of Firaz, Iraq had effectively become the first province of the Islamic Empire. Abū Bakr also began wrenching the rich and fertile province of Syria from the Byzantine Empire but died before its conquest.

Omar I (634–44), the father of one of Muhammad's wives who became the martial second caliph, was appointed by Abū Bakr to succeed him. It was during Omar's reign that Damascus, Syria, fell to Khalid ibn al-Walid after a siege in 636, the same year that saw a catastrophic defeat of the counterattacking Byzantine army of Emperor Heraclius at the Yarmouk River (in present-day Jordan). Omar's forces also defeated the Persians near Kufa, Iraq, and in 637 the main Persian army was trounced, and the empire's capital of Ctesiphon, near Baghdad, was captured. Keeping in mind the Koran's injunction that "there is no compulsion in religion" (2:256), the victorious Muslims allowed "People of the Book"—Jews and Christians—in the conquered Byzantine and Persian territories to practice their own religion, provided they paid an additional annual tax. Although many chose to convert, Muslim leaders knew that mass conversions would result in massively reduced revenues.

The Byzantine Empire was soon rocked by more defeats. Jerusalem surrendered to the Muslims in 638 after a four-month siege. Syria and Palestine, assailed by a Muslim army of thirty thousand, were now almost entirely in Arab hands, and in 639 Syria received its first Muslim governor, the general Muawiya. Then the Byzantine province of Egypt was invaded and conquered within a few years. After a decade of rule that saw a massive expansion of the fledgling Islamic Empire, Omar was assassinated by a Persian slave in the mosque at Medina.

Uthman (644–56), the elderly third caliph, belonged to the powerful Umayyad family of Mecca. During his tenure, the remainder of the Sassanian Persian Empire was seized, and its last shah was killed in 651 (see Question 17). Uthman also presided over the incursion of Muslim armies into Armenia, Asia Minor, North Africa, and Cyprus before being murdered by mutinous soldiers while praying in his house in Medina.

By the time of Caliph Al-Walid I (705–15), the Islamic Empire stretched from the Indus Valley to the Iberian Peninsula. The Muslim invasion of Spain began in 711 under the Berber general Tariq, whose seven thousand troops landed at Gibraltar and defeated Roderick, Spain's last Visigothic king. Both Seville and the capital, Toledo, fell in the following year, and much of the rest of Spain and Portugal was subdued within another two years. By 718, Muslim armies had pushed through the Pyrenees into France. Subsequent centuries saw the consolidation of Islam in Central Asia, as well as the conquest of the Balkans under the Ottoman Turks, accounting for the large native-Muslim populations in countries such as Albania and Bosnia, which form part of the 1.25 billion adherents of Islam worldwide.

52 ∾ Who was the first English poet known by name?

The Anglo-Saxon poet Caedmon, who composed his
"Creation Hymn" in
c. 670

WRITING IN LATIN about six decades after the event, Bede tells the story of how an elderly herdsman for a Yorkshire monastery—a man with the Celtic name of Caedmon—used to be embarrassed by the lack of a social skill considered crucial in seventh-century Anglo-Saxon England. Whenever he happened to be at convivial gatherings (Bede's Anglo-Saxon translator calls them "beer-feasts"), and the harp would be passed around so that each guest could sing a song, Caedmon would slip away because he didn't know how to extemporize a little ditty.

On one such occasion, after he had slinked off to the stables to look after his cows and make his bed there, he dreamed that a man bade him sing. When he protested that he couldn't, the man insisted again, and Caedmon asked what he should sing about.

"Sing the beginning of creation," came the answer.

In his dream, Caedmon composed a short poem, in strict Anglo-Saxon poetic style, that was an expansive paraphrase of the very first verse of Genesis: "In the beginning God created the heavens and the earth." When he awoke, Caedmon discovered he clearly remembered his poem, which went like this:

> *Nu sculon herigean   heofonrices Weard,*
> *Meotodes meahte ·   ond his modgethanc,*
> *weorc Wuldorfaeder,   swa he wundra gehwaes,*
> *ece Drihten,   or onstealde.*
> *He aerest sceop   eorthan bearnum*

> *heofon to hrofe,   halig Scyppend;*
> *tha middangeard   monncynnes Weard,*
> *ece Drihten,   aefter teode,*
> *firum foldan,   Frea aelmihtig.*

This is literally what it means, phrase by phrase:

> *Now we must praise   the Guardian of the heaven-kingdom,*
> *the might of the Measurer   and his mind-plan,*
> *the work of the Glory-father,   when he of every wonder*
> *—the eternal Prince—   established the beginning.*
> *He first shaped   for the children of earth*
> *heaven as a roof,   the holy Creator;*
> *then middle-earth   the Guardian of mankind,*
> *eternal Prince,   afterward arranged*
> *for men on earth,   the Lord almighty.*

Note that each verse of the original is divided by a major pause into two half lines of varying length that are bound together by a strongly accented alliteration (words beginning with *h* in the first line here, *m* in the second, *w* in the third, and so on, sometimes with a vowel sound alliterating with other vowels, as in the initial *e* and two initial *o*'s of line four). The poem luxuriates in synonyms for God (the eight capitalized nouns), emphasizing his centrality in the act of creation, and it moves from the heights of his "heaven-kingdom" down to the "middle-earth" on which we, also his creatures, have our home.

The poem, which has come down to us in many separate manuscripts, is here transcribed in the Old English of the West Saxon dialect, though Caedmon originally wrote in the slightly different Anglian (Northumbrian). The English of 670 was obviously very different from ours, and the word order was much looser, but we can still pick out quite a few words that, though somewhat exotic-looking, have given rise to similar words in modern English: *Nu* (now), *sculon* (shall, should), *heofon* (heaven), *Weard* (ward), *meahte* (might), *ond* (and), *weorc* (work), *faeder* (father), *wundra* (wonder), *sceop* (shaped), *eorthan* (earth), *hrofe* (roof), *halig* (holy), *tha* (then), *monn* (man), *aefter* (after), and *aelmihtig* (almighty).

Caedmon went on to continue his poem about the creation as told in Genesis, and when St. Hilda, the abbess of Whitby Monastery, where

Caedmon worked, was told of his newly acquired power of verse composition—and made further trial of it—she came to believe it was God-
given. She persuaded him to become a monk and continue producing
paraphrases of biblical texts in the style of the traditional Anglo-Saxon
bards (the scops), thus providing texts for religious instruction and edification in a poetic format that the English people loved as part of their
ultimately Germanic cultural patrimony (see Question 35).

Bede tells us that, in addition to Genesis, Caedmon later composed
verse paraphrases of Exodus and other Old and New Testament narratives. Although longish Anglo-Saxon poetic texts on these subjects
have come down to us, they were not written by the gifted monastic
herdsman. Of the authentic work of the first English poet we know by
name, all that remain are the nine starkly majestic lines of "Caedmon's
Hymn."

53   Who first used Greek fire?

The Byzantine navy against the invading
Arab fleet near Constantinople, 674

INCENDIARY WEAPONS HAVE been used since ancient times, with com-
bustibles such as liquid pitch, sulfur, charcoal, and naphtha propelled
against foes by catapult, flaming arrows, and other more ingenious
means. But the concoction first dubbed "liquid fire," "maritime fire," or
"artificial fire," and then "Greek fire" during the Crusades, was used to
spectacular effect during two early Muslim attempts to conquer Constantinople, the capital of the Byzantine Empire of the Greeks.

Caliph Muawiya I planned to capture Constantinople by attempting to storm the fabled walls of the city and starve it into submission
with a naval blockade. The Muslims had a much bigger fleet than their
adversaries when they sailed into the Sea of Marmara in 674, but the
Byzantine navy had a surprise for them.

A Syrian architect named Callinicus, who had fled his homeland
after the Muslim conquest and settled in Constantinople, had created a
secret weapon for the Byzantines, or at least had shown them how it
could be used effectively in war. What became known as Greek fire was
a highly flammable viscous liquid or gel that stuck to surfaces and

couldn't be extinguished with water—in fact, it floated on water, setting
ablaze whatever crossed its path. Greek fire may have included naphtha,
or distilled petroleum (think gasoline), sulfur, rock salt, pine resin, and
perhaps quicklime, but the exact formula remains unknown, largely
because the Byzantine emperors kept the formula top secret for many
years.

The Byzantines began using this fiery weapon against invading
Arab troops in the form of earthenware hand grenades, or they catapulted it into enemy lines in large pots, but by far the most destructive
deployment of it occurred at sea. With siphons or huge pumps mounted
on the decks of their galleys, Byzantine sailors shot jets of the burning
liquid at enemy ships through long metal pipes and flexible tubes that
could be aimed. The results were devastating, since only sand, vinegar,
or, less plausibly, urine was said to be effective in putting the fires out.
When Arab boarding parties were sent against Greek vessels, they
would be greeted by blasts of Greek fire in their faces.

Whether Greek fire had to be ignited as it streamed from the tubes
or burst into flame on contact with air or water is uncertain, but the tac-
tical advantage it gave the Byzantines was surely equivalent to their
being miraculously provided with flamethrowers or napalm. In later
times, the ends of the tubes were decorated with the horribly grinning
faces of sculpted wild beasts to add to the horror.

After their first taste of Greek fire at sea off Cyzicus, their base
about eighty miles from Constantinople, the Muslim forces went into
winter quarters there, but they sallied out again each summer to harry
the capital until 678. Each time, starvation took a massive toll in the
Arab army in the face of the stalwart ramparts of the city. In 677, many
Muslim ships were incinerated with Greek fire in a sea battle, the
retreating Arab fleet was savaged by a storm, and the Byzantine navy
chased the straggling vessels back to Syria, destroying whatever was
left of their armada. After the loss of at least thirty thousand men,
Caliph Muawiya was ready to sign with Byzantium a peace treaty for
thirty years.

About forty years later, in 717, the Muslims were back, dispatched
this time by Caliph Sulayman. This second Arab siege of Constantinople took the form of a massive sea-and-land blockade in which most of
the invading army succumbed to cold, starvation, or massacre by fierce
Bulgarian allies of the Byzantines, and almost all of the twenty-five
hundred ships and boats of the Muslims were either destroyed by Greek

fire or sunk by another cataclysmic storm. The defense of the city was ably conducted by Emperor Leo III the Isaurian, and after more than a hundred thousand Muslim troops perished, the next caliph, Omar II, pulled the remnant out of harm's way in 718. This crushing defeat saved Eastern Europe from Muslim invasion for the next seven centuries.

Although the Byzantine emperors treated the formula for Greek fire as a state secret, the Muslims eventually managed to develop a variant of the weapon for themselves. They used it tellingly against the crusaders, one of whom described it roaring like thunder as it blazed through the night like a fiery-tailed dragon. The Byzantines themselves used Greek fire to destroy an invading Russian fleet in the tenth century, as well as in subsequent frays, but the development of gunpowder at last made the fearsome incendiary obsolete.

EIGHTH CENTURY

54 ～ What is the first surviving epic poem in a European vernacular language?

Beowulf, composed in Anglo-Saxon, c. 700–50

SEVERAL DECADES AGO, college survey courses in English literature would sometimes be facetiously referred to as "*Beowulf* to Virginia Woolf." In this sense, *Beowulf* functions as our *Iliad*, since it stands at the head of English literature, as Homer's poem does for the Greeks, and also since it deals with the martial exploits of a national folk hero.

But the characters of *Beowulf* are Scandinavian rather than English, and the action takes place in Denmark and Sweden, the Germanic homes of the people who had conquered England in the mid-fifth century (see Question 35). The deeds recounted in *Beowulf* reflect heathen Norse legends of the early sixth century, while the poem itself was likely composed, perhaps orally, in the first half of the eighth century by an anonymous Christian. It was finally written down around 1000, surviving in a single manuscript. Before being committed to writing, Anglo-Saxon poems were preserved and circulated by singers called scops (pronounced "shopes" or "shops"), who chanted them to the accompaniment of the harp in the halls of aristocratic warriors.

At over three thousand lines, *Beowulf* is by far the longest Anglo-Saxon poem—and the sole epic—to have come down to us, besides being the earliest extant European verse epic in a nonclassical language. Yet this venerable work has not been accorded universal respect. "The story is commonplace and the plan is feeble," said literary scholar W. P. Ker in 1912. A decade later, literary critic J. Middleton Murry called *Beowulf* "an antediluvian curiosity," and to classicist Gilbert Highet in 1949 it was "a rude and comparatively unskilled poem." While studying at Oxford, Kingsley Amis pronounced it "a crass, purblind, infantile, *featureless* HEAP OF GANGRENED ELEPHANT'S SPUTUM."

The plot of *Beowulf* is mind-numbingly simple, but the considerable allure of the poem resides in the details—the thumpingly accented Anglo-Saxon alliterative verse (see Question 52), the poetic kennings (metaphorical paraphrases), and the dialogue and narrative that embody the values of a primitive heroic age, when valor, loyalty, resignation to fate, and mutual succor were the only weapons for survival in a no-man's-land of barbarous warriors inciting constant strife in their pursuit of plunder and vengeance.

The poem begins with a long-standing problem faced by the king of the Danes, old Hrothgar. At night, a demonic monster from the watery depths named Grendel, the spawn of Cain, invades his magnificent mead-hall by the sea, Heorot, and makes off with some of his warriors, or thanes, and no one can put a stop to it. The young hero Beowulf, whose father's life Hrothgar had once saved by paying "blood money" on his behalf, hears of these difficulties from across the seas in Geatland (southern Sweden) and sails with a band of fourteen warriors to take care of business.

After a welcoming feast brimming with mead and bright with song, Hrothgar's retainers leave the hall, while Beowulf and his men await Grendel's visitation. Soon the fiend breaks in and mauls a warrior, bolting down huge morsels of him and lapping up his blood until he has quickly devoured all of him, down to the hands and feet. When he grabs Beowulf, however, who has the strength of thirty men, Grendel realizes he's in trouble. Struggling frantically to free himself from the hero's inexorable grip, the monster rips his own arm out of its socket so he can flee howling in panic to die in his fenny home. Beowulf nails the oversize bloody limb and shoulder beneath the roof of Heorot.

That night, at a joyful celebration, the young victor and his men are splendidly rewarded, but disaster strikes again when, in the absence of Beowulf, Grendel's monstrous mother comes to exact vengeance by snagging Hrothgar's dearest friend and dragging him off to a horrible death. When Beowulf returns, he plunges into the sea pool where the monsters live, descending for the best part of a day as slithering snakes and sea beasts attack him. Finally, in a deep underwater cave, he slays Grendel's mother after a desperately fierce fight, espies Grendel's corpse nearby, beheads it, and swims back up to the surface with his new trophy, which four of his men can barely carry to Heorot.

Many years later, when Beowulf has reigned as king of the Geats for a half century, a fifty-foot dragon guarding a fabulous hoard of gold and gems is outraged that someone has dared steal a jeweled goblet from the treasure. Flying by night, it wields its flaming breath to burn down Beowulf's hall and his people's homes. The old hero decides to take on the dragon and succeeds in dispatching it with the help of a young retainer, but he himself is poisoned by his foe and dies soon afterward. The poem ends with Beowulf's blazing funeral pyre. J. R. R.

Tolkien, in a seminal article of 1936, explained that the tragedy of the poem was thus structured around "a contrasted description of two moments in a great life, rising and setting."

The *Beowulf* poet emphasizes the contrast between the peace, warmth, light, and community of Heorot—where a generous king, "the ring-giver," showers his loyal thanes with gifts—and the horror, cold, darkness, and isolation of Grendel's lair. Yet in this Norse world awash with doom, new perils are always on the horizon. Beowulf is a deliverer from the forces of evil and chaos, cleansing Heorot of their polluting presence, but the poet also informs us that the famed hall is fated to be burned down in war someday. The Danes may rejoice over the slaying of Grendel and his mother, but they don't realize that vengeful enemies will swoop down on them once King Hrothgar is dead. Beowulf himself prophesies that after his death, Franks, Frisians, and Swedes will attack and dispossess his people.

One of the beauties of *Beowulf* is the use of poetic kennings—stock phrases that garb everyday nouns in fanciful guise. Thus, the sea is the "whale-road" (*hron-rad*) or the "swan-road" (*swan-rad*), and the ship that sails it may be called the "seafarer" or the "foamy-necked." A battle is sometimes referred to as a "sword-storm," and the dragon in the poem as the "twilight-spoiler," since it wreaks havoc at night. These handy reusable metaphors also figure in theories of the oral-formulaic nature of the poem's composition, as does the use of entire stock phrases like "*Thaet waes god cyning!*" ("That was a good king!"), which is used twice in *Beowulf*.

An important critical debate has centered on the role of Christianity in the poem and how it affects the interpretation of the characters and incidents. Is Beowulf an ideal leader, possessing even some attributes of Christ in that he sacrifices his life for his people while offering thanks to what seems to be a Christian God—"the Lord of all" and "the Glory-King"? Or is he a noble pagan whose life of tragic futility is bound to a dying code that stresses only earthly fame and glory—a man who is praised for, among other things, never having killed a comrade during a drinking bout? Is the dragon's gold treasure, which Beowulf asks to look upon before he dies, a symbol of the Christianity that, in the poet's time, had already conquered England? Or is the dragon's jealous guarding of the hoard merely a reproach against the miserliness of rulers who, unlike Hrothgar and Beowulf, are stingy with their thanes?

Some scholars think the Christian elements and allusions are monkish interpolations foisted onto the text of a preexisting pagan poem, whereas others, like Kemp Malone, believe that the author, "devout Christian though he is, finds much to admire in the pagan cultural tradition which, as an Englishman, he inherited from ancient Germania." Either way, *Beowulf* repays close attention, and with Seamus Heaney's spirited verse translation, printed with facing Anglo-Saxon text, the interested reader can occasionally glance at the original and gain some appreciation of the aural, stylistic, and metaphoric richness of the poem.

55 ❧ Who initiated the first iconoclast persecution?

Byzantine Emperor Leo III, who banned religious images in 726

WE TEND TO USE the word *icon* metaphorically these days, often with reference to someone like Madonna, but to Christians of the medieval Byzantine Empire icons were religious images (of someone like the original Madonna), and those who advocated smashing them were the original iconoclasts (literally "image-breakers"), very distant forebears of the trendy nonconformists of today.

But why would anyone want to destroy religious images? Among other biblical texts, this verse of the first commandment seems to forbid *all* representational painting and sculpture: "Thou shalt not make unto thee any graven image, or any likeness of any thing that is in heaven above, or that is in the earth beneath, or that is in the water under the earth" (Exodus 20:4). But since the context of this apparent prohibition is a warning against "other gods," and since the graven images and likenesses are forbidden expressly from the viewpoint of idolatry—"Thou shalt not bow down thyself to them, nor serve them"—most Christian thinkers believed that religious pictures and statues were permitted, as reminders of the sacred persons they called to mind, as long as the images did not become objects of adoration or worship in themselves.

Yet some Christians regarded religious icons superstitiously, as if they were endowed with miraculous or magical powers of their own. In the Byzantine Empire of the early eighth century, the faithful often treated icons as their pagan ancestors had treated the idols of Greek mythology. Religious images were kissed, honored with incense, sung and prayed to, or used to heal the sick or prevent the spread of floods or fires. Some even chose icons as godparents for their children.

Practices such as these helped convince Emperor Leo III the Isaurian (716–41) that the use of icons had crossed the line into idolatry and may have been a stumbling block to the conversion of image-abhorring Jews and Muslims. In an edict of 726, he ordered his soldiers to remove religious statues and pictures from churches and destroy them. Church murals were to be covered over with plaster, and crucifixes were to be replaced by plain crosses without the figure of Christ on them. He even vainly commanded Pope Gregory II to carry out his iconoclastic policies at Rome and in the Western Church.

Thus began the long, disruptive, and destructive strife known as the Iconoclast Controversy, which assailed Christendom in two major waves, adding up to more than a century of *odium theologicum*. Monasteries were destroyed, and some monks were tortured and executed, since they and the common people were the most ardent supporters of icons (so-called iconodules or iconophiles), whereas many influential Byzantine prelates and most of the army were iconoclasts. Soon, a rival iconodule emperor was proclaimed in Greece, although he was promptly captured and beheaded.

When Leo's son, Constantine V (741–75), came to the throne, he prosecuted the war against the iconodules even more vigorously than his father. In 753, he convoked a church council of iconoclast bishops and clergymen to legitimize his view that icon veneration was heretical. Later, he also condemned the use of relics and praying to saints. The churches were now adorned with pictures of fruits, flowers, and birds, so that they looked like grocery stores or pet shops. Constantine blinded a patriarch of Constantinople and beheaded another; he ripped out the eyes and tongues and lopped off the noses of recalcitrant monks and turned monasteries into army barracks. Not many of his subjects were brokenhearted when he died fighting against the Bulgars in 775. He was posthumously branded with the nickname "Copronymus" ("Shit-Name") because he had supposedly defecated in his baptismal font. In the following century, he was exhumed and his remains flung into the sea.

This first wave of iconoclastic persecutions ended in a victory for the iconodules in 787, after the Seventh Ecumenical Council (Second Council of Nicaea) was called by Irene, coemperor and regent for her young son, Constantine VI. This synod of more than three hundred bishops reversed Leo III's ban on icons, ruling that the veneration (*not* the adoration) of religious images and of the crucifix was permitted, and it also called for the restoration of desecrated monasteries.

Twenty-seven years after the council, iconoclastic fever broke out again in 814 and persisted for a grueling twenty-eight years until 842. The second iconoclast persecution was essentially a replay of the first. The main characters changed, but the ideological stances and the toll of senseless suffering (scourgings, brandings, exiles, imprisonments) remained much the same, and again the iconodules prevailed after the iconoclasts were finally excommunicated.

On Sunday, February 19, 842, the icons were triumphantly brought back into churches in processions all over the Byzantine world, and the "Feast of Orthodoxy" was instituted as an annual reminder of the religious travails that had bitterly divided the church for so long. The spiritually charged gold-leaf icons created by the artists, craftsmen, and monks of the empire over many following centuries have taken their place among the chief glories of Byzantine art.

During the early years of the Protestant Reformation, iconoclastic riots broke out in various European cities, and a noted orgy of Puritan iconoclasm occurred during the English Civil War in the mid-seventeenth century. In contrast, the always down-to-earth Martin Luther thought the Protestant iconoclasts of his time were, quite simply, fanatics.

56 ∾ What was the first full-length work of English history?

The Ecclesiastical History of the English People *by St. Bede the Venerable, 731*

ASIDE FROM A FEW BRIEF VISITS to other monastic houses, St. Bede (c. 673–735) lived from age seven in the double monastery of Wearmouth-Jarrow in his native northern England. His first teacher, Abbot Benedict Biscop, was a cultured churchman who made many trips to the Continent and Rome to bring back to his monastery Latin and Greek books, religious paintings, church vestments, craftsmen to build in stone, and methods of liturgical chanting. Bede, ordained a priest at thirty, devoted his life to study, teaching, and voluminous writing—almost forty books, most on the interpretation of Scripture, but also several biographical, scientific, and technical works. The title of "Venerable" was given to him not for the advanced age he attained—he died at sixty-two—but for his wisdom and knowledge.

Considered by historian of science David C. Lindberg "doubtless the most accomplished scholar of the eighth century," Bede is chiefly remembered for writing the first book-length work on English history. This magnum opus, *Historia ecclesiastica gentis Anglorum*, completed in 731, is an account of the progress and vicissitudes of Christianity in England from its beginnings under the Romans until shortly before Bede's own death.

No mere chronicler, Bede weaves a coherent, thoughtful, and detailed story, focusing on the successes and adversities of holy Christian men and women as they came in contact with the beneficence or intransigence of various rulers all over the island. As such, his book naturally abounds in saints' tombs, persecutions and martyrs, miracles and heresies, inspiring sermons, monks and virgins, prophetic dreams, methods of calculating the date of Easter, demonic possessions, the calming of tempests at sea by pouring holy oil on the waves, lapses into idolatry, the appointment of bishops and archbishops, heavenly lights in the sky, and harrowing visions of the afterlife vouchsafed to a man who died and came back to life the next day.

Despite Bede's inclusion of the obligatory monkish legends, this "Father of English History" was a diligent historian by the standards of his age. He prefaces his book with an account of how extensively he relied on earlier writings (such as a Latin jeremiad on the woes of the English by St. Gildas, which Bede calls a "tearful discourse"), the memories of older men, and a network of correspondents who supplied him with information and documents. Bede is one of the earliest writers to use the AD (*anno Domini*) system of dating events from the birth of Christ (see Question 40).

Among the most memorable episodes of Bede's narrative are those dealing with the sanguinary arrival of the barbarian Angles, Saxons, and Jutes; the reintroduction of Christianity into southeast England by St. Augustine of Canterbury; and how the simple herdsman Caedmon became an Anglo-Saxon poet (see Questions 35, 46, and 52).

A typical saint's legend in the book is that of the posthumous miracles of St. Cuthbert, a monk and hermit who was made bishop of Lindisfarne in 685 and about whom Bede composed several works. It seems that eleven years after Cuthbert's death, when his fellow monks exhumed him for reburial, "they found the body whole and incorrupt as though still living and the limbs flexible, so that he looked as if asleep rather than dead," and his garments appeared spotless and new (4.30). After they placed the body in a coffin aboveground, many miraculous healings were effected with his garments and remains.

One of them occurred when a young monk who had a tumor growing on his eyelid rubbed a relic of Cuthbert's hair against it. Later that day, as the monk himself informed Bede, the tumor and deformity disappeared without a trace (4.32). Another monk who had been stricken with paralysis prayed earnestly before Cuthbert's coffin and then fell into a deep sleep in which he saw a hand rest on his painful head. He woke to find himself totally cured (4.31). In another work, Bede relates that Cuthbert's relics healed him of an unspecified condition affecting his tongue while he was writing about the saint's miracles. Such was life—and the writing of history—at a time when, as Matthew Arnold wrote, "The Sea of Faith / Was . . . at the full."

Perhaps the most poetically beautiful passage in Bede's book occurs when King Edwin of Northumbria summons a council of his chief advisers in 627 to decide whether the kingdom should accept Christianity. One of his nobles urges Edwin to embrace the new religion with these words:

> The present life of man upon earth, O king, seems to me, in comparison with that time which is unknown to us, like to the swift flight of a sparrow through the house wherein you sit at supper in winter, with your ealdormen and thanes, while the fire blazes in the midst and the hall is warmed, but the wintry storms of rain or snow are raging abroad. The sparrow, flying in at one door and immediately out at another, whilst he is within, is safe from the wintry tempest; but, after a short space of fair weather, he immediately vanishes out of your sight, passing from winter into winter again. So this life of man appears for a little while, but of what is to follow or what went before we know nothing at all. If, therefore, this new doctrine tells us something more certain, it seems justly to deserve to be followed. (2.13)

And so King Edwin and his nobles, and many of the common folk of Bede's own Northumbria, were converted to Christianity.

Bede's *History* was one of the four Latin books later translated into Anglo-Saxon by, or at the behest of, King Alfred, and it also supplied much of the early historical data for *The Anglo-Saxon Chronicle*. It can still while away a long winter evening for the history buff.

57 ∿ What was the first decisive defeat of the Muslims in Western Europe?

The battle of Tours (or Poitiers), 732, in which they were beaten by Charles Martel

SOMETIME AROUND 718, the Christian Visigothic king Pelayo defeated the Muslims, who had conquered almost all of the Iberian Peninsula, at Covadonga in northwest Spain, founding there the kingdom of Asturias, which never fell to Islam. This battle seems to have been a minor encounter, however, and many of Pelayo's achievements are more legendary than historical. In a major foray beyond the Pyrenees into what is now southern France, the Spanish Muslims attempted to conquer the duchy of Aquitaine in 721 but were stopped by a surprise attack of Duke Eudes the Great (aka Odo) at the battle of Toulouse. Yet only four years later the Muslims sacked Autun, all the way in central France.

Then, in 732, exactly one hundred years after the death of Muhammad, Abd al-Rahman, the emir (governor) of Muslim Spain and a proven general, led an experienced cavalry force of about thirty thousand (perhaps many more) across the western Pyrenees, gunning for Duke Eudes, who had allied himself with a renegade Muslim deputy governor. The Islamic forces sent the pickled head of the renegade to the caliph in Damascus, slaughtered almost all the troops of Eudes in southwest France near Bordeaux (which was thoroughly pillaged), and then headed north, sacking forts, burning churches, and hoping to catch up with the fleeing Eudes.

The king of the Franks at this time was one of the *rois fainéants* ("do-nothing kings") of the later Merovingian dynasty (see Question 38). Fortunately for the Franks, the mayor of the palace (chief minister) and de facto ruler was Charles Martel ("Hammer," the nickname he earned as a result of the battle of Tours). Duke Eudes now appealed to this formidable warrior for help, which Charles promised on condition of his submission to the Franks. Meanwhile, the emir was on the road to Poitiers, with the ultimate goal of sacking the fabulously wealthy abbey and pilgrimage shrine of St. Martin of Tours.

After Charles force-marched his troops by mountainous backways to a point somewhere between Poitiers and Tours in west-central France, Emir Abd al-Rahman was surprised to discover this army of veteran Frankish and Burgundian infantrymen, perhaps thirty thousand strong, overlooking his position from a wooded hill above. The Muslim army was also not outfitted for the late October weather of Northern Europe.

The battle of Tours (sometimes called the battle of Poitiers) began with the opposing forces skirmishing for a full week before the emir decided to attack—which meant unleashing armored cavalry charges uphill and around trees. Charles's heavily armed soldiers formed a large square phalanx and absorbed the successive impacts of the horsemen, who thrust and slashed at them with long lances and swords. The Frankish line was breached at certain points, but the tall sturdy warriors in their thick mail refused to break ranks.

The encounter lasted an entire day—perhaps two—but when the Muslim horsemen heard that Frankish scouts were seizing the slaves and vast plunder stowed in their tents, some squadrons broke away to defend their loot. This looked like a mad retreat to the rest and, in the ensuing confusion, the emir himself was surrounded by Frankish troops and hewn down. At the loss of their brave leader, the remaining horsemen fled, and many were killed.

Night put an end to the fighting, but when the Franks woke early the next morning to resume it, they saw that their foes' tents were still there but their owners had departed for Spain. The Muslims had received such a severe drubbing—losing perhaps ten thousand men—that they determined the better part of valor was discretion. Charles decided not to pursue the enemy—a sure sign his forces had taken a good beating themselves, though Christian sources claim he lost only fifteen hundred men.

The battle of Tours has traditionally been viewed as a great turning point in history, when the advance of Islam into Christian Europe north of Spain was permanently halted. Thus it appeared to Edward

Gibbon, as well as to English military historian Sir Edward Creasy, who listed it among the fifteen decisive battles of the world in an 1851 book. Some contemporary historians, however, have pooh-poohed Tours as a mere skirmish, or the defeat of a raiding party, or just one of many similar earlier and later battles pitting Christians against Muslims in France, such as Charles's resounding victories in Provence several years afterward.

Nonetheless, it seems that a large Muslim army was decisively and memorably checked at Tours—Arab writers called it "the deadly battle" and "the disgraceful overthrow"—and there was no later serious attempt to conquer territory in Northern Europe for Islam. Nor was there any other European force capable of withstanding another Muslim onslaught if Charles had lost the battle.

Yet the Muslims retained a foothold and launched attacks on the far side of the Pyrenees for almost three more decades in the Languedoc region of southern France, which they had conquered in 720–24 and ruled from their capital at Narbonne. In 759, however, they lost even this remaining territory in France to Charles Martel's son, Pépin the Short. As for Spain and Portugal, their *Reconquista* would require more than seven hundred years—until 1492—when the last Muslim ruler of Granada surrendered his kingdom.

58 ∾ Who was the first world-class Chinese poet?

The Tang dynasty's enfant terrible,
Li Po, 701–62

IN THE MID-EIGHTH CENTURY, China, the world's most powerful and cultivated empire, was home to fifty-three million people and contained almost two thousand cities. Its capital of Changan was the largest city in the world with a population of two million, three dozen imperial palaces, and a red-light district teeming with dandified gentlemen and fashionable young women who painted their eyebrows green.

The merchants of the Silk Road and intrepid sea traders hauled in luxuries and delicacies from all corners of the known world to cater to the cosmopolitan sensibilities of an urbane upper class, while native artists created masterpieces in ceramics and porcelain. The Tang dynasty (618–907) also saw the most magnificent flowering of Chinese poetry. Almost fifty thousand poems by about twenty-three hundred poets have survived from this era, including more than a thousand poems by Li Po (701–62), though many of these may not be authentic.

A selection of twenty-nine poems in French translation introduced Li Po's work to the Western world in 1862. In English, Joseph Edkins published his translation of twenty-four poems in 1890, and Herbert A. Giles a series of twenty-one in 1898.

But the Chinese poet's reputation in the English-speaking world was clinched in 1915 when Ezra Pound's *Cathay* appeared, containing his free translations of seventeen Chinese poems, eleven of them by Li Po. Pound's imagistic free verse was a perfect vehicle for this poet, especially in "The River-Merchant's Wife: A Letter," in which a simple young wife writes with desperate longing to her absent husband; "Lament of the Frontier Guard," which resonated poignantly during World War I; and the exquisitely crafted "Exile's Letter," in which the disillusioned middle-aged poet wistfully recalls the intellectual camaraderie, peripatetic life, and ecstatic conviviality shared with a generous and loving friend who is now a thousand miles away.

Not all Sinophiles have been as enthusiastic as Pound about Li Po. Only four years later, Arthur Waley, who translated two dozen Li Po poems into English, complained of his "endless restatement of obvious facts" relating to "the impermanence of human things, as opposed to the immutability of Nature." He also quoted an eleventh-century Chinese scholar who claimed Li Po's "intellectual outlook was mean and sordid, and out of ten poems nine deal with wine or women." But for Tu Fu (712–70), often regarded as China's greatest poet, his dear older friend Li Po was "the poet unrivaled," whom he celebrated in more than a dozen works.

Li Po (or Li Tai-po), "the Bright One," received his name because on the night of his birth his mother dreamed of the planet Venus. Apparently born in Chinese Turkestan, he grew up in Sichuan in southwestern China. By age ten, he had mastered the Confucian books of *Odes* and *History* and many other classics and was already writing verse. As a young teen, he went to live in the mountains as a Taoist recluse for several years, and his expert swordsmanship—which may have resulted in several deaths in his self-appointed protection of the helpless— contributed to the braggadocio he occasionally affected: "I am strong enough to meet ten thousand men."[1] Friends said that "he ate like a hungry tiger" and "his big voice could be heard in heaven."

His first wife left him, taking their children, because of his lack of ambition—he never condescended to take the civil service examination that was crucial to government appointment (see Question 48)—and maybe he was thinking of her when he wrote, "It is three years since you went. The perfume you left behind haunts me still." In another poem, he writes about his young children who have been growing up during the three years since their father has seen them. The peach tree he planted is now "as tall as the tavern roof," and he sees in imagination his daughter plucking a flowering branch from it, while his little boy now comes up to his sister's shoulder.

But Li Po, who went on to seek marital bliss with three other women, preferred at this time to console himself by becoming one of the "Six Idlers of the Bamboo Valley," whose occupation was, according to an unimpeachable eleventh-century source, "daily drinking till they sank to the ground." He also met the younger poet Tu Fu and lived with him as with a brother for a while, sleeping off hangovers under the same blanket and walking hand in hand during the day. At age twenty-five, Li Po began his long peregrinations up and down China, dashing off his remarkable poems with aristocratic sprezzatura.

By the time he made his way to Changan, he was in his early forties. Emperor Hsüan-tsung, an avid patron of the arts, was so pleased with an ode Li Po presented that he seasoned the poet's soup for him with his own hands and gave him a position in the Hanlin Academy. Once, during an unscheduled command performance at court, Li Po was brought in so drunk that the emperor's men had to dash cold water on his face to sober him up. That was enough help for him to improvise a brace of odes on the beauty of the chief imperial concubine, Yang Kuei-fei, the jewel of the three thousand palace women. The emperor himself played a jade flute while a singer performed Li Po's songs.

Yet the poet spent much of his time drowsing in wineshops as a member in excellent standing of the capital's "Eight Immortals of the Wine Cup." In a poem about the group, Tu Fu marvels at his friend's prodigious facility, especially when under the bacchic inspiration of wine: "As for Li

---

[1] All quotations from the poems of Li Po and his contemporaries are from *The Works of Li Po, the Chinese Poet*, translated by Shigeyoshi Obata (New York: Paragon Book Reprint Corporation, 1965; 1935).

Po, give him a jugful, / He will write one hundred poems." Listen to another of the "Immortals," Tsui Tsung-chi, on the subject of Li Po:

> *I clapped my hands at your enchanting utterances;*
> *We talked metaphysics; we bubbled with laughter.*
> *You expounded the vicissitudes of the past dynasties,*
> *And made visible the exploits of kings and conquerors.*
>
> *A knap-sack on your back, filled with books,*
> *You go a thousand miles and more, a pilgrim.*
> *Under your sleeve there is a dagger,*
> *And in your pocket a collection of poems.*
> *Your eyes shine like luminous orbs of heaven*
> *When you recite your incomparable songs and odes.*
> *You sip wine and twang your lute strings*
> *When the winter's breath congeals the crystalline frost.*

The inevitable court intrigues followed. One story says that when Li Po had the chief eunuch pull off his shoes when he himself was too drunk, the official poisoned Yang Kuei-fei's mind against him. Promotions never seemed to come Li Po's way, and after three years at court he was restless. At last, the emperor gave him some gold and allowed him to leave. As the poet wrote to three of his fellow "Idlers of the Bamboo Valley," who had also been disillusioned with government service, "When the hunter sets traps only for rabbits, / Tigers and dragons are left uncaught."

His insatiable wanderlust kept him journeying for the rest of his life—a fellow poet likened him to "a god in exile." Always in quest of new encounters with old friends, he braved the craggiest of China's mountains—"The road to Shuh is more difficult to climb than to climb the steep blue heaven"—and followed the meandering courses of its mighty rivers.

Like a Chinese Omar Khayyám, Li Po weaves many verses on the drinking life, imagining a dead rice-wine brewer still plying his craft in the life beyond: "But since there's no Li Po on the Terrace of Night, / To what sort of people do you sell your wine?" In another poem, he laments how he must drink with only the moon and his shadow for company, neither of which can imbibe along with him. He addresses numerous carpe diem poems to young virgins to make much of their time and to those of his fellows who don't drink enough according to his own lights:

> *Do you not see high on yonder tower*
> *A white-haired one sorrowing before his bright mirror?*
> *In the morning those locks were like black silk,*
> *In the evening they are all snow.*

The poet's solution is simple: "Kill the sheep, slay the ox, and carouse! / Truly you should drink three hundred cups in a round!"

A leitmotif of Li Po's verse is the (often drunken) farewell to a departing friend. It was a time of punishing journeys over a vast empire in quest of advancement, appointment to office, or artistic recognition— a time of extended job searches lasting, as in our own day, well into old age. In a typical departure poem, the friend slowly vanishes at the end, leaving only vacant Nature and a melancholy Li Po behind.

Another recurrent theme is the suffering brought about by an expanding empire's endless wars: "Ravens and kites peck at human entrails, / Carry them up in their flight, and hang them on the branches of dead trees." During the rebellion of An Lu-shan, a Tatar military governor, which began in 755 and lasted for the rest of Li Po's life, Changan was brutally sacked and thirty-six million Chinese died or were left homeless or unaccounted for in eight years of unspeakable chaos.

After Li Po joined the staff of a southern prince who later rebelled against the emperor, the poet was imprisoned by the imperial authorities for several months and condemned to death. His sentence was commuted to banishment—"Oh, the long road of a thousand miles to Yeh-lang! / The westward journey made me old"—but he was soon pardoned in a general amnesty. By now ill, he made his way back from exile and resumed his roving but died while visiting a relative. Legend has it that the poet whose works were often drenched in moonlight died drunk when he fell over the side of a pleasure boat, trying to embrace the moon's reflection in a river.

But Li Po's artistry lives on, as he himself intuited in a poem about a painted silk screen that contains lines eerily anticipating Keats's "Ode on a Grecian Urn":

> *How many years since these valley flowers bloomed*
> *To smile in the sun?*
> *And that man traveling on the river,*
> *Hears he not for ages the monkeys screaming?*
> *Whoever looks on this,*
> *Loses himself in eternity . . .*

59 ∿ Which was the first European Renaissance?

The Carolingian Renaissance, 776–877

THE SO-CALLED CAROLINGIAN RENAISSANCE, associated with the reign of Charlemagne and his immediate successors, preceded the so-called Ottonian Renaissance (tenth century) and the so-called Renaissance of the Twelfth Century, which in turn preceded "the real one"—the Italian Renaissance of c. 1350–c. 1600—and its generalized European imitation.

Charles the Great (742–814), or Charlemagne, the eldest son of Pépin the Short, ruled as Frankish monarch from 768 to 814, having become sole king when his brother Carloman died in 771. From 776, when he first invited several learned Italians to his court, until the end of the reign of his grandson Charles the Bald in 877, Western Europe enjoyed a rebirth of enthusiasm for classical achievements in literature and the arts.

A burly, blond, and blue-eyed German giant with a walrus mustache and an appetite for meat roasted on spits, Charlemagne was the fiercest warrior Europe had produced since the days of the Romans. Astride his outsize white stallion, he crushed Bavarians, Saxons, Avars, Slavs, Danes, and many others, and had himself crowned king of the Lombards with their Iron Crown after defeating and deposing their last monarch, Desiderius. In his spare time, he contracted four marriages and disported himself with at least a half-dozen concubines.

Despite this busy schedule, he was determined to make the palace school at his capital of Aachen (Aix-la-Chapelle), Germany, into more than just a semibarbarous finishing school for royal children by staffing it with some of the best minds of Europe. He started by summoning Peter the Deacon of Pisa and Paulinus (later patriarch of Aquileia) to his court in 776, and he himself began studying Latin grammar under the former.

Charlemagne's broader aim, in a Europe still without universities and wallowing in ignorance and illiteracy, was to establish an educational center that could serve as the model for new schools in the cathedrals and monasteries that would educate the clergy and promising young scholars throughout his kingdom. As he later noted in a directive to the abbot of Fulda, he had received letters from pious monks "whose sentiments were sound but whose speech was uncouth." He thus urged all clergymen to study Latin literature so that they might learn to speak the language correctly and "be able more easily to penetrate the mysteries of the holy Scriptures," which were available only in the Latin of the Vulgate Bible (see Question 32).

The crowning acquisition for Charlemagne's palace school was Alcuin (c. 735–804), a Northumbrian deacon and scholar who had studied with a student of the Venerable Bede (see Question 56) and was the headmaster of the famed cathedral school in York, England. In 782—the same year that Charlemagne ordered the beheading of 4,500 rebellious Saxon leaders in Germany who had reneged on their forced conversion to Christianity—the Frankish king persuaded Alcuin to journey to Aachen to head his assemblage of scholars. Another prize catch that year was the Lombard scholar Paul the Deacon, whom Charlemagne later nominated as abbot of the great Benedictine monastery at Monte Cassino, Italy, where Paul may have composed his valuable *History of the Lombards*.

But Alcuin was the chief literary figure in Charlemagne's program of reviving classical and biblical studies. Besides poetry and hundreds of edifying epistles, he wrote on theological subjects, helped prepare a revision of the Vulgate, and developed a question-and-answer catechism for teaching the rudiments of the Christian faith. He also compiled a book of fifty-three arithmetical word problems entitled *Propositions for Sharpening Youths*. In 796, after more than a decade at court, Charlemagne nominated him to be abbot of the monastery of St. Martin in Tours, and it appears that under the gentle Alcuin's influence, the king abolished the death penalty for paganism in the following year.

The palace school at Aachen was intended chiefly for nobles, their children, and the clerics of the royal chapel, but even some studious young commoners were admitted. Charlemagne and his family studied along with the others—the king himself deigning to learn rhetoric, logic, arithmetic, and astrology from Alcuin, who wrote the basic textbooks for several of these subjects. When the royal family journeyed throughout the kingdom, the school moved along with it.

The teachers and students spoke and wrote in Latin, the common learned tongue of Europe. Though Charlemagne's native language was Frankish, he spoke Latin fluently and understood some Greek, but, having started too late in life, he never learned how to write, despite keeping wax tablets under his pillow so that he could practice.

Soon after 791, the palace school was graced with the arrival of

Einhard, a tiny Frankish noble who became Charlemagne's friend and adviser. Einhard was dazzled by Alcuin, whom he considered "the most learned man in the entire world," though he himself went on to compose the most lustrous literary gem of the Carolingian Renaissance, his Latin *Life of Charlemagne*. This charming book took as its model the brief biographies of the first twelve Roman emperors by Suetonius, especially the "Life of Augustus" (see Question 12).

The monks of Charlemagne's scriptorium at Aachen and numerous monastic centers throughout the kingdom performed the invaluable service of collecting and copying ancient manuscripts, preserving almost the entire corpus of Latin literature that has survived into our times, as well as the works of the church fathers. They wrote in an elegant and easy-to-read rapid script called Carolingian minuscule, which gave us the lowercase alphabet we still use.

In about 792, Charlemagne began work on the Palatine Chapel in Aachen, now part of the city's cathedral. With its octagonal dome and variegated marble interior, it was the creation of Odo of Metz, the first Northern European architect known by name. The chapel was modeled on San Vitale, Justinian's sixth-century Byzantine church that had impressed Charlemagne on his visits to Ravenna. Its Roman-inspired solid-bronze doors were cast at the foundry built by Charlemagne at Aachen, but its marble columns had to be shipped north from Rome and Ravenna. Pope Leo III consecrated the chapel to the Virgin Mary in 805, and Charlemagne was buried there nine years later. Another large-scale work of this time was a short-lived five-hundred-foot-long wooden bridge built over the Rhine near Mainz.

Although Charlemagne drew to his court Greek artists fleeing from the iconoclast persecutions in the Byzantine world (see Question 55), not many frescoes and mosaics of the time have survived. We do have many carved ivory plaques—exquisite reliefs, often imitating ancient paintings, that were used as elaborate book covers. Among the most precious artistic creations of the age are its marvelously illuminated manuscripts whose lavish miniatures imitated themes and styles from ancient Roman and early Christian art. Charlemagne also brought papal singers from Rome to instruct his scholars and clerics in liturgical chanting, and the first postclassical musical notation system may have been developed at his court.

Charlemagne's son and successor Louis the Pious (814–40) and his grandson Charles the Bald (843–77) both continued the practice of attracting intellectual luminaries to their courts. The latter was host to the most eminent Western European scholar of the ninth century, John Scotus Erigena (fl. 850–75), an Irishman who knew Greek well—an anomaly for his place and time. In addition to his own controversial Neoplatonic philosophical works, Erigena translated several books from Greek into Latin, including *On the Celestial Hierarchies*, a treatise on the nine orders of angels that provided later theologians with much of their lore on this arcane subject. The original was erroneously attributed to Dionysius the Areopagite, who, as an Athenian convert of St. Paul, was said to have benefited from Paul's eyewitness account of what he had seen when he was rapt into heaven. Making this angelic vision available to the Western world was among the last major literary achievements of a minirenaissance that had begun with the educational vision of a man who never quite managed to learn how to write.

60 Where did the first overseas Viking raid occur?

The coast of southern England, c. 789

IF YOU CAN INTUIT anything about a people from their most characteristic nicknames, what can you say about the Vikings, whose annals include enlightened rulers like Erik Blood-Axe and Thorfinn the Skull-Splitter? Or consider the sentimental fool who was teasingly dubbed "Child-Friend" because "unlike the other Vikings, he did not throw babies into the air and catch them on the end of his spear." Today he'd be on Prozac for having lost his zest for living. Also keep in mind that our word *berserk* comes from the Old Norse for "bear-shirt," which was the unarmored bear-hide outfit in which certain crack troops of the Vikings would rush into battle, howling like frenzied animals, foaming at the mouth, and biting the edges of their iron shields.

The Northmen, Norsemen, or Norse were North Germanic peoples who settled in the Scandinavian countries of Norway, Sweden, and Denmark. When they had their plundering hats on, they were usually called Vikings, perhaps from the Old Norse *vik*, the creek, fjord, or inlet from which the lurking raiders emerged, or from the Old English *wic*, the name for the temporary camp they inhabited while on expedition.

Their extensive native coastlines helped mold them into excellent fishermen, traders, and pirates. Famines in inhospitable climates and population pressures stemming from polygamous earls made the Norse head out to sea to trade in furs or purloin the crops and cattle of their less belligerent neighbors across the water—especially the strange, tonsured beings known as monks, whose gold church vessels and jeweled artistic treasures were sure to warm the icy cockles of pagan Viking hearts.

After keeping their piracy to themselves in the Baltic, the Vikings began, in the late eighth century, to turn their attention and their long-ships toward the British Isles. Their first overseas raid occurred in c. 789, when three boats with perhaps several hundred Norwegian Vikings "from the land of the robbers" came ashore near Portland, in modern Dorset, on the southern coast of England, during the reign of Beorhtric, king of the West Saxons. When the king's reeve Beaduheard rode up to ask the strangers why they had come and, thinking they were traders, tried to direct them to the royal manor, they killed him and made their escape.

It must have seemed like an isolated incident until 793, when the monastery on the island of Lindisfarne off the northeast English coast was attacked and, in the words of *The Anglo-Saxon Chronicle*, "the harrying of the heathen miserably destroyed God's church . . . by rapine and slaughter." Then the floodgates opened, with raids repeatedly launched against the British Isles and northern France. In 794, the double monastery of Wearmouth-Jarrow, which had earlier housed the Venerable Bede, was sacked and the monks dispatched to their eternal reward, with the following year witnessing an assault on the monastery island of Iona. In rapid sequence, the coast of western Scotland, south Wales, the Isle of Man, and the Irish coast were all hit, and islands off the coast of Aquitaine were devastated in 799.

The Vikings had not failed to notice that the British Isles and the Frankish Empire were lacking in sea power. The marauders who arrived in their seventy-five-foot-long oak vessels also depended on surprise. Often their victims had less than an hour to brace themselves from the time that Viking sails were spotted over the horizon. The shallow-draft Norse ships allowed warriors to scramble in and out fast, and their thirty-two oarsmen could soon put distance between their sleek crafts and any lumbering tubs sent in pursuit.

It didn't take too many huge Viking hauls for copycat attacks to proliferate. Soon even some of the girlfriends came along for the fun. In 842, there was "great slaughter in London . . . and Rochester." In

851, Danish Vikings entered the Thames estuary and sacked Canterbury and London. The West Saxon king Aethelwulf managed to defeat them and drive them off, but they returned with a vengeance. By the late ninth century, northern and eastern England was occupied by the Danes, who terrorized the kingdoms of Mercia, East Anglia, and Northumbria, then inhabited by pious monks and peaceful Christian farmers instead of the Anglo-Saxon warriors of old (see Question 35).

By 852, a Norse kingdom of Dublin had been established. Among other Irish cities founded by the Norse are Cork, Limerick, Waterford, and Wexford. Vikings settled the Scottish island groups of the Shetlands, Orkneys, and Hebrides, as well as northern Scotland itself.

On the Continent, an especially murderous assault occurred in Nantes in 845. With the crews of sixty-seven ships, Ragnar the Dane sailed into the Seine, defeated the Frankish army of Charles the Bald, hanged 111 prisoners of war on an island in the river to discourage further resistance, and plundered Paris on Easter Sunday. Charles agreed to hand over seven thousand pounds of silver to rid himself of Ragnar and his men in this first recorded instance of "Danegeld" being paid.

Historian Gwyn Jones rightly observes that "Ireland, England, France were the Vikings' Mexico," but these restless Norsemen (who gave their name to Normandy) wandered much farther afield than their immediate neighborhood—to Spain, Iceland, Greenland, the Byzantine Empire, and Russia—even fighting against Arabs and briefly settling in North America. During the Viking era, it wasn't only the Christians who had occasion to pray, "From the fury of the Norsemen, O Lord, deliver us!"

61 ❧ Who was the first emperor in the West since the fall of the Roman Empire?

Charlemagne, who ruled as emperor of the
Western Roman Empire, 800–814

ON APRIL 25, 799, some impolite Roman enemies of Pope Leo III tried to blind him and cut out his tongue. Escaping, the stricken pontiff fled to Charlemagne's camp at Paderborn, Germany, and urged the mighty king of the Franks to come to Rome, where in due course the papal foes were brought to justice. When Charlemagne visited St. Peter's church on Christmas Day of 800, the grateful Leo supposedly surprised him by crowning him "emperor of the Romans." The ruler of the Byzantine Empire—the redoubtable Irene of Athens, who called herself emperor, rather than empress—was outraged that a Germanic barbarian had dared sully her title, but a successor of hers recognized Charlemagne's rights in the West a dozen years later in exchange for a chunk of territory along the Adriatic coast.

As several of his predecessors had done, Pope Leo had merely cast his lot with the Frankish ruler against both the Byzantine emperor and his own Italian enemies. But this revival of the imperial ideal was to set papal Rome at the center of future maelstroms arising from foreign troops descending into the peninsula to legitimize their sovereign's claims to be "Roman emperor" (see Question 73). On the other hand, Charlemagne's allowing himself to be crowned by the pope could be interpreted to mean that the emperor was subservient to Christ's vicar on earth. (That's one of the reasons Napoleon crowned *himself*.)

Charlemagne had already tried to imitate, from a very respectful distance, the cultural glories of the ancient Roman Empire (see Question 59). His real genius, however, was for commanding large armies of peasant infantries and lordly cavalries that he led into the field just about every spring, when the vassals he had rewarded with land repaid their sovereign by mustering troops in their territories. His conquests brought the Frankish Empire to its greatest extent, embracing most of modern France, western Germany, Switzerland, the Low Countries, Italy as far south as Rome, and strips of a few other nations—a huge centralized domain. His decrees were transmitted to its farthest reaches through missives known as capitularies, dealing with both church and state matters, and pairs of *missi dominici* (royal envoys), who traversed the 350 counties of the empire to announce new edicts to local assemblies, size up local officials, and hear complaints against them.

In capitularies sent to Saxony after the Council of Paderborn in 785, on the Christianization of the wild Saxons, we obtain a glimpse of the state of civilization in the far eastern part of the empire: "If anyone is deceived by the devil, and believes after the manner of pagans that some man or some woman is a witch and eats people, and if because of this he burns her or gives her flesh to someone to eat or eats it himself, let him pay the penalty of death." Capitularies following the Synod of Frankfurt in 794 include a more genial reminder that "priests, deacons, monks, and clerics should not go into taverns to drink"—and indeed Charlemagne was as much the head of a Christian theocracy as he was the supreme secular lord to whom every male subject age twelve or older had to pledge fealty.

Despite Caliph Harun al-Rashid's gift of an elephant, mutual hostilities with the Muslim world minimized contacts in that direction and kept Charlemagne's realm a continental empire. As historian Henri Pirenne wrote, "Without Muhammad, Charlemagne would have been inconceivable," meaning that a Northern European "Roman emperor" made sense only in a world in which the entire southern Mediterranean littoral and almost all the coastline of Spain had fallen to Islam. The old Roman Empire's maritime traffic and commerce had essentially disappeared, though Charlemagne's attacks on the Slavs somewhat reinvigorated Danubian trade routes to Constantinople.

Charlemagne's empire was thus a rural society in which serfs worked the nobles' land alongside slaves who had been captured in war. This Frankish feudal system had its origins under Charles Martel (see Question 57) but was carried much further during his grandson Charlemagne's reign. The needs of its agrarian barter economy were met by a new silver coinage that divided a pound of silver into 240 deniers.

This was the relatively crude but extensive and unified empire that Charlemagne bequeathed at his death, on January 28, 814, to his son Louis the Pious (814–40) and that his quarreling grandsons split into three parts in 843. Soon, however, a rich cycle of medieval legends and sagas grew up around the first Frankish emperor, vying with those woven about Alexander the Great and King Arthur. Lusty old Charlemagne was even declared a saint in 1165, and in the *Paradiso* Dante sees him in the heaven of Mars, among the warriors for the faith—though a levelheaded eighteenth-century pope demoted him to "blessed" status.

NINTH
CENTURY

62 ⮑ Who was the first Scandinavian ruler to convert to Christianity?

King Harald Klak of Denmark, in 826

MORE THAN A CENTURY PASSED between the unsuccessful first Christian mission to Denmark by the Northumbrian Willibrord in 715 and the arrival of Archbishop Ebo of Rheims, who was sent by Frankish emperor Louis the Pious in 823 and made some converts. But the first large-scale conversion occurred three years later, when a Danish king known as Harald Klak, driven from his country by rivals for the throne, came as a suppliant to Louis.

The emperor promised his help if the pagan Harald agreed to accept Christianity. The upshot was that Harald, his wife, and four hundred Danish men and women of his following were baptized near Mainz in 826 and that Louis presented Harald with a county in Frisia on the northern German coast.

Returning to Denmark that same year with Louis's backing, Harald took with him the young missionary monk Anskar (801–65), the indefatigable "Apostle of the North" who eventually became the patron saint of Denmark. Anskar and his group of monks started a small Christian school for a dozen boys in the important market town of Hedeby at the southern end of Jutland. King Harald, however, was permanently driven from Denmark in the following year, at least partly because of his newly acquired religion, and returned to his Frisian territories. The monks left, too, but the seed of the Gospel had been planted in Scandinavia, the only remaining stronghold of paganism in Western Europe.

In 849, Anskar, now a middle-aged archbishop, returned to Denmark. Harald Klak's successful rival, King Horik I, allowed the missionary to build a church in Hedeby, and his successor permitted Anskar to build one in Ribe on the southwest coast of the Danish peninsula, but it was destroyed during a pagan backlash in 888.

And so the matter stood until Harald Bluetooth became king of Denmark in c. 950. In contrast to his staunchly pagan father, Gorm the Old, Harald converted to Christianity in c. 960. A twelfth-century altar carving in East Jutland still shows the cadaverously thin king standing naked and waist-deep in a barrel-like baptismal font as he receives the sacrament from a bishop named Poppo. In Harald's time, the bishop of Bremen preached in Denmark, churches were erected, three bishoprics were established, and a pagan grove notorious for human sacrifice was abandoned. Harald also set up an eight-foot-high, intricately carved memorial boulder in Jelling, Jutland, which features the earliest representation of Christ in Scandinavia. In a runic inscription on the stone, he rightly claims that he had "made the Danes Christians."

As for Norway, King Hakon the Good, who was brought up as a Christian in England, vainly tried to bring his religion to his country in the mid-tenth century. At the same time, our cosmetically challenged friend, Harald Bluetooth of Denmark, began staking his claims to the Norwegian throne and helped Christianize the territories he won in the south and east of the country, though the north and west remained imperturbably heathen.

Then, in 995, Olaf Tryggvason, a young man of royal blood who had been sold into slavery and done a stint abroad as a Viking raider, was supposedly converted to Christianity by a prophetic hermit on an island off the coast of Cornwall. Returning to Norway, he was acclaimed king and set about spreading his new religion by founding the first church in that nation, by importing English priests as missionaries, and by threatening and cajoling, but he died in battle in 1000 after only five years as king.

The true bringer of Christianity to Norway was Olaf Haraldsson, who as a young man was baptized in Rouen in c. 1013 and fought his way to the Norwegian throne a few years later. He built many churches, but his main method of dealing with pagans who refused to convert was to blind, maim, or kill them and destroy their heathenish idols. By the time of his death in battle in 1030, Christianity had taken hold in most of the country, and by 1100 all but the most remote hinterlands of Norway had accepted the faith. This redoubtable king is now known as St. Olaf.

Sweden, the last Scandinavian nation to be Christianized, benefited like Denmark from the labors of Anskar, who made a first brief mission to the trading center of Birka in 829 and built a church there. After pagans expelled the Christians in 845, Anskar returned in c. 850 and was kindly received, but acceptance of Christianity was still a long way off.

Finally, after a century and a half, King Olaf Skötkonung and his Swedish court were converted in 1008, but as late as 1075 or 1080, Adam of Bremen described a gold-adorned pagan temple and its rituals at Uppsala. The statues of three gods were enthroned there: Thor the thunder god flanked by an armed Odin and the fertility god Frey, endowed with a huge phallus. Every ninth year at the spring equinox, the Swedes would gather to propitiate their gods with the blood of sacrifices for nine days. The victims had to be males and included a man, a stallion, a dog, and five others each day. The seventy-two corpses were suspended from the branches of trees in a sacred grove and allowed to putrefy. In about 1087, not long after Adam wrote, the temple was destroyed.

The abolition of human sacrifice was just one of the benefits Christianity brought to Scandinavia, others being fellowship in the dominant political and social world of Christendom, the gradual ending of the slave trade, acquisition of the Latin literary treasures of ancient Rome and the church, and, one suspects, a gradual refinement of manners and mores. But the splendidly gloomy world of old Norse mythology, fortunately preserved for us in the Icelandic *Eddas* of the thirteenth century, evaporated with the advent of the "pale Galilean."

Gone forever were Brynhild and her Valkyries, who brought slain Viking heroes to Valhalla, where they cut one another to pieces every day, were healed again to carouse the night away, and then got up the next morning to do it all over again; the three Fatelike Norns, oracular ancestresses of *Macbeth*'s "Weird Sisters"; Yggdrasil, the great ash tree supporting the universe; the incestuous Signy, her brother Sigmund, and their son Sigurd (Wagner's Sieglinde, Siegmund, and Siegfried); Thor, the muscle-bound, red-bearded god with the enormous appetite who flew in a goat-drawn chariot flinging his hammer Mjöllnir at uncouth giants and trolls, and who was once forced to dress up as the love goddess Freya; the chief god Odin, who never consumed anything but wine, traded an eye for wisdom, hung wounded on a tree for nine days and nights in exchange for the lore of runes, and stole the poetry-inspiring skaldic mead from the giants; Loki, the malicious being whose delight was to torment the gods; Baldur, the god killed by a sprig of mistletoe flung into his heart at Loki's instigation but who will rise from the dead again; Ragnarok, the day of doom, when the gods will lose their apocalyptic battle against the giants and the forces of evil; and the prophecy that, after Ragnarok, a new heaven and a new earth will arise.

63 ❧ Which king first united all of England?

King Egbert of Wessex, who managed it briefly from 829 to 830

THE PERIOD IN ENGLISH HISTORY from roughly 600 to 800 is called the
heptarchy ("rule of seven") because seven main kingdoms took shape
after the Anglo-Saxon conquest of England: Wessex, Essex, Sussex,
Kent, East Anglia, Mercia, and Northumbria. The first of these and the
last two eventually became dominant, Northumbria for much of the
seventh century; Mercia for most of the eighth, culminating in the reign
of Offa the Great (757–96); and finally Wessex, from the later years of
King Egbert. This warrior laid the groundwork for his kingdom to
assume leadership in the long fight against the Viking invaders, a
struggle that forged the unity of the English nation in the early tenth
century.

A descendant of the royal family of Wessex in south-central
England, Egbert (c. 775–839) returned from exile at Charlemagne's
court to seize the throne of his ancestors in 802, perhaps with the formidable emperor's backing. Not much is known about the early years of
his reign, but in 815 he devastated the territory of the Britons of Cornwall. His greatest victory, however, came a decade later when, at the
battle of Ellendune, in Wiltshire, he put an end to the long ascendancy
of Mercia (in central England) by trouncing the forces of King Beornwulf, who may have initiated hostilities.

Following up on this success, Egbert sent an army with his son
Aethelwulf to attack the small southeastern kingdom of Kent, where he
had dynastic claims. Aethelwulf did his work so well that Egbert was
soon recognized as Kent's new king, and the bordering kingdoms of
Sussex and Essex—all the rest of southern England that had formerly
been subject to Mercia—decided it was wise to submit to him, too. In
the same year or the next (826), East Anglia rebelled against Mercian
domination and asked for Egbert's protection; when the Mercian king
Beornwulf attacked East Anglia, he was defeated and killed.

In 829, Egbert, now ruler of all England south of the Humber,
thought the time was ripe for conquering once-mighty Mercia itself
and, in the process, he drove out the new Mercian king, Wiglaf. Extending his march into Northumbria, Egbert accepted the submission of that

kingdom's ruler, who may have capitulated without a fight. Recognized as overlord of the seven kingdoms of the heptarchy, Egbert was now, in effect if not in name, king of England.

But in the very next year, Wiglaf came back to recover the Mercian throne and thumb his nose at Egbert. For one brief shining moment there had been unity, but *sic transit gloria mundi*. It would take another century for the nation to unite under King Athelstan.

As it was, Egbert had his own troubles. He was bested by the invading Danes in 836, though he managed to defeat them when they returned two years later. The man whose name often appears first in lists of the kings of England died in 839.

During Egbert's long reign in Wessex (802–39), Viking attacks increased in number and severity, with the brunt being borne by Northumbria, East Anglia, and Mercia. Wessex became the rallying point for defense against the barbarous heathen invaders who threatened to swallow up the entire island. Indeed, after two centuries of harrying and settlement within England, the Danes succeeded in placing three of their countrymen on the English throne (1016–42) and endowing the language with a slew of common words such as *skin*, *skirt*, and *sky*, and *they*, *their*, and *them*.

Egbert's son Aethelwulf sensibly allied Wessex with its old enemy Mercia to fight against the Danes. As for Egbert's grandson—the famed Alfred, who was the only surviving native-English king—he was gladly accepted as overlord by all the English who had not yet been subjugated by the Danish foe.

64 ❧ What is the first surviving text in a Romance language?

Two brief passages in Old French in the Oaths of Strasbourg, *842*

AT THE DEATH of Charlemagne's son Louis the Pious in 840, Louis's eldest son, Lothair, succeeded him as emperor of the West. Lothair's brothers, Louis the German and Charles the Bald, began squabbling with him over the succession and their respective patrimonies, and in 841 their forces gave him a major drubbing at the battle of Fontenoy.

After their victory, Louis and Charles formally ganged up against the emperor at a ceremony at Strasbourg in the presence of both their armies. First, in the languages of their troops (Old High German and proto-French), the brothers aired their grievances against Lothair ("he's devastating our people by burning, pillaging, and murdering"), and then they swore eternal fidelity to each other in opposition to their despised older sibling.

Although the contemporary chronicler reports the speeches in Latin, he opts for a touch of authenticity by providing the original version of the oaths that each brother made in the language of the other's army. Speaking first, Louis the German delivered himself of this highly peculiar specimen of Old French—the earliest surviving document in a Romance language:

> *Pro Deo amur et pro Christian poblo et nostro commun salva-*
> *ment, d'ist di in avant, in quant Deus savir et podir me dunat,*
> *si salvarai eo cist meon fradre Karlo, et in adiudha et in cad*
> *huna cosa, si cum om per dreit son fradra salvar dist, in o quid*
> *il mi altresi fazet; et ab Ludher nul plaid numquam prindrai*
> *qui, meon vol, cist meon fradre Karlo in damno sit.*

> (For the love of God and for the Christian people and our com-
> mon salvation, from this day forward, to the extent that God
> will give me the wisdom and power, I shall protect this brother
> of mine Charles, both with aid and anything else, as by rights
> one ought to protect his brother, in which he would do the
> same for me; and I shall never make any pact with Lothair
> that, of my own free will, would harm this brother of mine,
> Charles.)

What looks like a hodgepodge of Latin, French, Provençal, and Spanish illustrates the transition from the spoken Vulgar Latin of the ancient Roman Empire to something that would eventually coalesce into French. The grammatical endings of Latin are any which way (*Pro Deo amur* instead of *Pro Dei amore* and *meon fradre* for *meum fratrem*) or have dropped off altogether (*salvament* and *vol*). Extensive conso-nantal substitutions have occurred—*b* or *v* for *p* (*poblo* for *populo* and *savir* for *sapere*), *d* for *t* (*podir* for *potire* and *fradre* for *fratrem*), and *z* for *c* (*fazet* for *faceret*)—and vowel changes may be detected in words like *amur* for *amore* and *cosa* (modern French *chose*, thing) from Latin *causa.* In short, it's a mess, but it's a first tentative step on the long road to Voltaire, Baudelaire, Flaubert, and Proust.

Oh, yes, Charles the Bald gave his oath in proto-German, but since we have third-century runes that preserve specimens of North Germanic and portions of Bishop Ulfilas's fourth-century translation of the Bible into Gothic, a branch of East Germanic, the ninth-century Old High German preserved for us in the *Oaths of Strasbourg* is relatively anticlimactic.

After the rousing oaths of the brothers, each army swore, in its own vernacular, that if its lord violated his oath, it would never support him against the other one. The public display of fraternal amity apparently worked well, because in the following year, 843, Louis and Charles extracted the Treaty of Verdun from their brother, Lothair. By this agreement, Lothair was to retain his title as emperor and rule over northern Italy, Burgundy, and the Low Countries; Louis was to rule over much of what became Germany; and Charles was to receive most of what became France. So much for Charlemagne's unified Frankish Empire (see Question 61).

65 ～ Who was the first major Muslim philosopher?

Al-Kindi (c. 800–870), "the Philosopher of the Arabs"

WITH THE METEORIC RISE of the Muslim Empire in the century after Muhammad's death, the Arab world came in contact with some of the world's richest civilizations, especially in Syria, Egypt, Iran, and northwest India (see Question 51). By far the most fruitful cultural discoveries they made were the key texts of ancient Greek philosophical and scientific knowledge. Beginning in about 800 and continuing unabated for two centuries, the masterworks of the greatest Greek thinkers—such as Plato, Euclid, Ptolemy, Galen, and especially Aristotle—were translated into Arabic and exerted a galvanizing effect on a civilization that had formerly relied almost exclusively on the Koran for its worldview.

Aristotle (384–322 BC) had written magisterially in almost every field of inquiry in his day. The first major original thinker to emerge in

Islam was a polymath, like his master Aristotle and many later Muslim scholars. Abu Yusuf Yaqub ibn Ishaq al-Kindi (c. 800–70) was born in Basra, Iraq, and lived in Baghdad at the court of the Abbasid caliphs al-Mamun and al-Mutasim, the epicenter of Muslim learning (see Question 50). Of almost three hundred treatises attributed to al-Kindi, only sixty to seventy have survived, but we marvel at his astounding range: metaphysics, logic, cosmology, psychology, ethics, politics, mathematics, medicine, optics (in which he devised an influential theory of light radiation), astronomy, astrology, meteorology, and music—among other disciplines. At Baghdad, he oversaw the work of an important group of translators from Greek.

Given his intellectual milieu, it is not surprising that he became interested in reconciling the thought of Aristotle with that of Plato—the two major Greek philosophers, representing the summit of human reasoning—so that their combined wisdom could be used to elucidate the more obscure theological doctrines of Islam, a project that would also preoccupy medieval Jewish and Christian thinkers vis-à-vis their respective religions. This was easier then than now because both Plato and Aristotle were interpreted from a Neoplatonic viewpoint, largely because of the misattribution to Aristotle of texts that had actually been written by the Neoplatonists Plotinus and Proclus (see Question 21).

Al-Kindi's own Neoplatonic bent is evident in his most important work, *On First Philosophy*, in which he asserts that God is a simple "One" and thus admits of no descriptions by language. Even if God is said to be loving, wise, powerful, etc., his unity breaks down into multiplicity, which is the defective nature of every other being in the universe: "Thus the true One possesses no matter, form, quantity, quality, or relation. . . . It is therefore only pure unity, nothing other than unity." This seemed to imply that the attribution of qualities to God in the Koran was to be interpreted allegorically rather than literally.

Following the lead of the Christian Neoplatonist John Philoponus, al-Kindi parted company with Aristotle's belief that the world was eternal, since the creation of the world by God at a specific moment that gave rise to both time and motion was the dogmatic stance of Islam as well as Christianity. Even more central to Christian and Muslim orthodoxy was the conviction that the world would have an end (and a Judgment Day), whereas Aristotle thought it would continue on its merry way forever.

More interesting was al-Kindi's acceptance of the Platonic notion of recollection. This was the belief that we can intuit the eternal Forms or Ideas of things and abstract qualities—the chairness of chairs, the concept of Justice—not because we abstract from our sensory perceptions of external reality, but because we remember the Forms themselves from the preexistence of our souls before they were infused into our bodies at birth. Wordsworth phrased it thus a millennium later:

> *Our birth is but a sleep and a forgetting:*
> *The Soul that rises with us, our life's Star,*
> *Hath had elsewhere its setting,*
> *And cometh from afar . . .*

In a less lofty vein, al-Kindi wrote an influential book that helped spread the use of what became known as Hindu-Arabic numerals in the Middle East and eventually Europe. He also taught mathematical rules for determining the desired amount of each component in compound drugs as part of his broader attempt to enlist mathematics as a handmaiden in the healing arts of health and medicine.

Al-Kindi's association with the Mutazilites, a group of philosophically minded theologians who shared his belief that no attributes could be predicated of God and who also declared that the Koran was created in time and thus not eternal, may have contributed to the animosity of certain professional rivals of his. As a result of their insinuations, Caliph Mutawakkil seized al-Kindi's personal library and may have had him beaten, but the old scholar apparently got his books back, if not his dignity, before his death a decade later.

The roll call of Muslim thinkers who immersed themselves in the thought of Aristotle as a living legacy that could point the way to truth, even in the realms of religion and morals, culminated in two of the most illustrious philosophers in the medieval pantheon. The Persian scholar Avicenna (980–1037), besides profoundly influencing Christian theologians such as Albert the Great and Thomas Aquinas and the Jewish Aristotelian Moses Maimonides, became the outstanding medical authority of the Middle Ages. His *Canon of Medicine* remained the standard European textbook on the subject until the mid-seventeenth century.

But the greatest—and virtually the last—of the Muslim Aristotelians was the Spanish philosopher Averroës (1126–98). Besides serving as a judge and the court physician at Córdoba, he became known in the West simply as "the Commentator," since he wrote more than three dozen detailed commentaries on Aristotle's works. Yet in 1195 he fell into disgrace, and his philosophical works were burned, perhaps because of his many unorthodox views, such as his denial of individual immortality and of creation ex nihilo.

Almost eighty years after the death of Averroës, a number of his philosophical disciples at the University of Paris, the center of Christian theological speculation, were embroiled in serious charges of heresy and irreligion. In 1277, the bishop of Paris condemned 219 propositions—he called them "loathsome errors"—that were rampant at the university, many of them stemming from Averroistic doctrines. The minimum penalty for the unrepentant teaching of, or mere listening to, any of the propositions was excommunication. Even some of the ideas of the recently deceased Aquinas appeared on the bishop's lengthy list.

Nonetheless, a generation later, the highly orthodox Christian poet Dante placed the souls of Avicenna and Averroës among the "philosophical family" headed by the exalted shade of Aristotle—"the master of those who know"—in the limbo of virtuous heathens in Canto 4 of his *Inferno*, and he imagined the soul of Siger de Brabant, the most prominent Christian Averroist of his day, in the lofty heights of the heaven of the theologians in Canto 10 of his *Paradiso*.

66 ∿ Who were the first successful Christian missionaries to the Slavs?

*Saints Cyril and Methodius, "the Apostles of the Slavs,"
who journeyed to Moravia in 863*

THE SLAVIC PEOPLES were latecomers to Christianity. The first to be converted were the Moravians, who lived in what is now the eastern Czech Republic, and the reason they were Christianized by missionaries from the Byzantine Empire rather than from the West reflected the tangled skein of politics at the time.

Latin-speaking German missionaries had already been mousing around in Greater Moravia, but Prince Rastislav considered them stooges of the Frankish emperor Louis the German (see Question 64), who had attacked his nation in 855 but failed to subjugate it. In 862,

Rastislav turned to the Byzantine emperor, Michael III the Drunkard, requesting men who could convert his people to Christianity in their own language of Old Slavonic (a proto-Slavic tongue).

The young scholar Constantine (c. 827–69), dubbed Cyril ("lordly") probably after his death, was already a veteran of a politico-religious mission to the Muslim caliph and a missionary journey whose unrealized goal was the conversion of the Khazars, a Turkic people of Central Asia whose ruling class had converted to Judaism a few generations earlier. Cyril was an expert linguist—besides his native Greek, he knew Latin, Arabic, Hebrew, and the language of the Khazars—and one of his acquisitions was Slavonic, possibly because of his frontier-region birthplace, Thessalonica in northern Greece.

The emperor conveyed Rastislav's request to Photius, the learned patriarch of Constantinople who had been Cyril's teacher. Realizing that his former student—a philosopher, theologian, Slavonic speaker, and now a monk—would be an ideal choice for the mission, Photius suggested that Cyril take with him his older brother and fellow monk and scholar Methodius (c. 815–85).

With the ruler of the nation on their side, the brothers made such rapid progress in converting the Moravians that they soon organized a seminary for training priests. They also translated parts of the Bible and several liturgical books into Slavonic, and these are the earliest remaining specimens of any Slavic language.

Cyril is often credited with devising the Cyrillic alphabet that is named after him, but he may have only modified with some extra letters and signs the earliest Slavic alphabet, Glagolitic, which was partly based on Greek letters, so that it could accommodate Slavic sounds that had no counterpart in Greek. Some scholars, however, claim the brothers actually developed the Glagolitic alphabet themselves. The later Cyrillic alphabet, much more closely based on Greek letters and the ancestor of alphabets used for writing Russian, Ukrainian, Bulgarian, Serbian, Mongolian, and many other languages, was invented in the early tenth century, possibly by Cyril's students, and named in his honor.

The brothers began celebrating Mass in the local language, now often called Old Church Slavonic or Old Bulgarian. Within a few years, the German ecclesiastical hierarchy in Moravia complained to the pope that they were conducting services and administering the sacraments in a pagan tongue instead of the sanctioned liturgical languages of Latin or Greek. Summoned to Rome, Cyril and Methodius convinced Pope Adrian II that they had no heretical or heathenish motives, so he granted them permission to continue ministering to the Slavs in their own idiom.

Cyril died soon afterward in 869 and was buried in Rome. Methodius, elevated to the rank of archbishop, turned to the task of Christianizing Slovakia and Serbia, but he was soon swept up in a bitter turf war with the bishop of Salzburg and the German Church. In 870, he was summoned to a synod at Ratisbon, Bavaria, by Louis the German and his bishops, where he was deposed, maltreated, and thrown in prison.

In the same year, Louis the German's son Carloman of Bavaria received Prince Rastislav from the hands of his treacherous successor in Moravia, his nephew Svatopluk. The unfortunate Rastislav was blinded and imprisoned in a Bavarian monastery, where he soon died.

Methodius was luckier. After almost three years in captivity, he was released by the intercession of Pope John VIII and returned to his missionary work among the Slavs, this time concentrating on the Bohemians and the Poles in Moravia, but the Germans wouldn't let him be. Soon a Frankish priest named Wiching was denouncing him to Rome, claiming Methodius had heretical notions and was desecrating the liturgy by conducting services in Slavonic. Déjà vu all over again.

So Methodius hauled himself down to Rome again in 880, and Pope John said the vernacular liturgy was fine with him, but the aging archbishop, having had his fill of the Germans, is said to have headed for Constantinople, where he and a few other scholars completed translating the Bible into Slavonic. He died in 885, apparently having returned to Moravia.

Wiching, who succeeded Methodius as bishop, decided it was time to turn back the clock by banning the detested Slavonic texts and liturgy and rounding up two hundred of Methodius's disciples. After these men were exiled, many of them drifted to Bulgaria, where Boris I had accepted baptism in 864. It was probably in one of the two literary academies founded by Boris that the Cyrillic alphabet was developed.

Needless to say, the new pope, Stephen V, promptly banned the use of Slavonic in the liturgy, but we'll leave the last word on the Apostles of the Slavs to another pontiff—the first Slavic pope, John Paul II, in his 1985 encyclical *Slavorum Apostoli*, written in the eleven hundredth year after Methodius's death:

Rightly therefore Saints Cyril and Methodius were at an early date recognized by the family of Slav peoples as the fathers of both their Christianity and their culture. In many of the territories . . . although there had been various missionaries, the majority of the Slav population in the ninth century still retained pagan customs and beliefs. Only in the land cultivated by our Saints, or at least prepared by them for cultivation, did Christianity definitively enter the history of the Slavs during the following century.

67 ∾ What was the first important Russian state?

Kievan Rus, under Prince Oleg,
c. 882

IN THEIR EPIC age of raiding and settling abroad, the Danish and Norwegian Vikings went west and north, and the Swedes went east and south. Vikings from Sweden were the most enterprising in the conflux of peoples that constituted the nucleus of Russia. The trading posts they founded across the Baltic pointed them on their way south into what became Russian lands by the early ninth century. In 839, Swedish traders reached Constantinople, and Swedish Vikings presumed to attack the city in 860, plundering some suburban monasteries.

The seagoing Swedish barbarians found it relatively easy to control the major Russian waterways down to the rich and civilized Byzantine and Muslim empires in the south. They eventually captured the commercial route running from the Baltic mainly along the Dnieper to the Black Sea and thence to Constantinople, as well as the more easterly one running from the Gulf of Finland mainly along the Volga to the Caspian and thence by camel train to Baghdad, capital of the Abbasid caliphate and emporium for the caravan trade routes to China (see Question 50). "The Vikings were pirates," wrote economic historian Henri Pirenne, "and piracy is the first stage of commerce."

As far back as the sixth century, East Slavic tribes moved into the forests of the future Ukraine and settled the valley of the Dnieper as farmers and fur traders harried by nomadic Khazars and other predatory tribes. Into this unsettled world erupted the people from the north known as the Rus (a Finnish word for Sweden) who gave their name and something more to Russia. The Rus, an amalgam of mainly Swedish and some Finnish warrior-traders who later coalesced with local Slavs, began building fortified trading posts along the river routes. At the head of the long line of Rus adventurers stands the semilegendary Rurik, a Swedish Viking who had made his bones raiding in Western Europe.

In 859, according to the twelfth-century *Russian Primary Chronicle*, the Rus imposed tribute on the Slavs and other tribes but were driven out after a few years. Soon, however, what with the Slavs fighting the Finns, and the depredations inflicted by Khazars and Pechenegs, the local tribes begged the Rus to send them a prince to rule over them and bring peace.

Three brothers responded to the call, the eldest Rurik becoming the ruler of the northern trading settlement of Novgorod ("new fort") in about 862. He and his Viking fighting force, called Varangians ("followers," a name for Scandinavian trader-warriors in Russia), lost no time in making themselves masters of the natives, selling them as slaves (the word *Slav* giving rise to *slave*) and living off the produce of their land.

According to the traditional account (which has been challenged on many grounds, including that of telescoping events), Rurik was succeeded at Novgorod by his kinsman Oleg, who ruled as regent for Rurik's young son Igor. Moving against southern Russia in about 882, Oleg seized Kiev from Khazar control and united it to Novgorod, founding a state known as Kievan Rus that absorbed settlements like Smolensk, as well as a large hinterland inhabited by tributary Slavic tribes.

In 907, Oleg led a fleet against Constantinople in a show of strength sufficiently impressive to extract a commercial treaty from the city guaranteeing free baths and eats to the men of the "great prince of the Rus." It also provided for the hiring of Rus mercenaries, the beginning of a practice that resulted toward the end of the century in the formation of the Varangian Guards, special fighting units of the Byzantine emperor.

But when they weren't fighting, we must imagine the Rus blithely collecting honey, beeswax, furs, and slaves from the surrounding forests to exchange them (always armed with axe, sword, and knife) for the silks, wine, fruits, spices, glass, and gold artifacts of the southern empires, conveying them to their far northern homes and even beyond into Western Europe. Their open-air copulation with slave girls before selling them might lead to the hasty conclusion that we are dealing with uncouth heathens, but a pious cast of mind is evinced by their prostration before idols with earnest pleas to send them wealthy traders who would not haggle.

Prince Igor, supposedly the son of Rurik (perhaps actually the grandson), succeeded to the rule of Kiev in 912. Late in his reign, he, too, tried his hand at attacking Constantinople—which the Rus referred to simply as Mikligarthr ("the Great City")—but his ships were strafed with Greek fire (see Question 53). Undeterred, he returned three years later in 944 and was able to wrench a commercial treaty from the Byzantines that gave the Rus their own suburban quarter as a summer residence and lots of free food, but they in turn had to avoid entering the city in packs of more than fifty, leave their weapons at home, fight against the Bulgars when the emperor saw fit, and, above all, go back to Kievan Rus each fall. Igor himself was assassinated for collecting tribute from a subject tribe twice a month instead of just once.

Igor's widow Olga converted to Christianity in 955, but her son Svyatoslav, said to have been born when she was sixty and her husband seventy-five, remained a staunch pagan. A contemporary described him as rather savage and gloomy-looking, with bushy brows, snub nose, long mustache, and shaved skull except for a lock of hair on one side.

During most of Svyatoslav's reign (945–72), Olga looked after domestic affairs while he led his Rus forces in battle, destroying the army of the Khazars, sacking their capital on the Volga, and putting an end to their empire. He ripped into Volga Bulgars and Danubian Bulgars but succumbed in the end to an ambush near the Dnieper by the nomadic Turkic Pechenegs, who made a drinking cup of his famed bald skull.

The fifth grand duke of Kiev, St. Vladimir the Great (980–1015), brought nascent Russia into the welcoming arms of Byzantine Christianity when he married Anna, sister of the Greek emperor, in 988. He chose Slavonic rather than Greek, however, as the liturgical language of his church (see Question 66), which was spiritually Greek but linguistically Slavic.

His successor, Yaroslav the Wise (1015–54), brought the power of Kiev to its greatest level and adorned the imperial capital with churches and other splendid edifices, but in the century after his death the state fragmented. First Novgorod and eventually Moscow inherited its preeminence among Russian principalities, as ravenous enemies engulfed

Russia from all sides in the later Middle Ages. Kievan Rus, the kernel
of modern Ukraine, Russia, and Belarus, disintegrated into more than a
dozen warring petty states in the later eleventh century and was sacked
by the Kipchak Turks in 1203. A generation later, in 1240, the magnificent city of Kiev, one of the largest in the world, was plundered and
burned to the ground by the Mongols. The modern city has been the
capital of an independent Ukraine since 1991.

68 ∾ Who built the first regular English navy?

King Alfred the Great of Wessex in 896

IN 850, THE VIKINGS who sailed to England as part of a mighty fleet of
350 ships abandoned their old practice of returning to Denmark each
year, wintering in the country for the first time on the Isle of Thanet in
Kent (see Question 60). The following spring, they stormed Canterbury
and London. East Anglia was devastated in 866, the year in which the
Vikings began leaving their ships in stockades and stealing horses to
bring their murderous plundering to the interior.

Soon the northern city of York was captured, the Northumbrian
kingdom overthrown, north Mercia overrun, King Edmund of East
Anglia tortured to death, and the London mint used for stamping Danish coins. The stereotype is of Vikings swinging two-handed battle-axes
over their heads, but some of the more exotic realities included their
fiendish torment of "the blood-eagle"—hacking away the victim's ribs
from his spine and then pulling his lungs out and spreading them on his
back like wings. On the English side, some flayed their captured Viking
enemies and nailed their skins to church doors.

This was the world inherited by Alfred of Wessex (849–99; r.
871–99). He was handsome and smart, but may have suffered from
epilepsy, apparently having a seizure at his own wedding feast. Despite
his lifelong infirmity, he became a tough, tenacious, and intrepid warrior, and no other English monarch has more deserved the honorific
"Great," first accorded him in the sixteenth century.

By 871, the Danes had begun attacking the southern kingdom of
Wessex, where young Alfred fought alongside his brother, King
Aethelred, in a series of rapid-succession battles that they mostly lost

but that must have been Pyrrhic victories for the enemy. In one of them, Aethelred appears to have been fatally wounded, and Alfred came to the throne by choice of the witenagemot (the assembly of nobles and prelates), since his brother's sons were infants, and those were no times for a child-king. With most of eastern and central England lost to the Danes, the nine battles that the men of Wessex fought south of the Thames that year prevented the entire nation from falling into enemy control. Though the new king was so badly beaten at Wilton that he had to buy off the foe with a payment of Danegeld, the gumption he and his soldiers had shown persuaded the Vikings to turn their attention elsewhere for five years.

During the next invasion of Wessex, Alfred's fortunes plummeted to their nadir in January of 878, when the Danes caught him completely off guard with a midwinter raid. His kingdom collapsed—many of his subjects fleeing overseas, others becoming quislings, and Alfred himself escaping to the lake island of Athelney, in Somerset, with a small band of followers. According to legend, the king took refuge incognito in a swineherd's cottage. While he was sitting by the stove sunk in melancholy thoughts over his lost kingdom, the cakes that the swineherd's wife had put in began to burn. Seeing the smoke as she entered the room, the woman bellowed, "You don't bother turning the cakes, but you're quick to eat them when they come hot from the oven!" Accepting the justice of her rebuke, the king silently turned the cakes.

The reality is even more incredible. In the spring, Alfred managed to rally his mounted thanes and loyal peasant foot soldiers as he passed through Somerset, Wiltshire, and Hampshire. Engineering a surprise attack on the Danish army under King Guthrum at Edington, in Wiltshire, he "destroyed the Vikings with great slaughter," according to Alfred's biographer, his chaplain Asser. He pursued the remnant to their stronghold and besieged them for two weeks, until they were starving so dreadfully that they agreed to give him hostages.

The subsequent Treaty of Wedmore required Guthrum to accept Christianity (Alfred joyfully became his godfather) and withdraw from Wessex into East Anglia. A later treaty defined the boundary between Alfred's domains and what became known much later as the Danelaw—the part of England settled by the Danes and, later, the Norwegians, delimited by a wobbly diagonal from London northwest to Chester. This included almost the entire eastern portion of the nation (most of Essex, East Anglia, northeast Mercia, and Northumbria). At that point, half of the Viking army in England decided to take advantage of the confused political situation in the Frankish Empire to raid France for many years to come, whereas the others settled in the Danelaw as farmers and traders with a bit of discretionary pillaging.

Accorded some respite from war, Alfred turned to repairing the woeful state of literacy in his kingdom. He invited the best scholars in Britain to his court, including the Welsh monk and later bishop Asser, who wrote a Latin biography of Alfred modeled on Einhard's *Life of Charlemagne* (see Question 59), and, like Charlemagne, Alfred reached out to scholars overseas. He exhorted bishops to make sure their clerics learned Latin, and he built schools so that at least the sons of the well-to-do learned to read. He ordered illiterate nobles to either learn to read or resign from their offices.

Alfred also saw to it that, among others, four highly influential books were translated from Latin into the Anglo-Saxon of the people (perhaps helping translate some of them himself): Pope Gregory the Great's *Pastoral Care* on the duties of prelates; Boethius's *Consolation of Philosophy*, one of the most popular books of the Middle Ages; Bede's *Ecclesiastical History of the English People* (see Question 56); and Orosius's *Universal History*. He also inspired the compilation of *The Anglo-Saxon Chronicle*, a major source for English history to 1154, and compiled a law code, choosing the best statutes from his country's past and omitting the rest.

By the time that major Viking invasions of England resumed, Alfred had reorganized the peasant levies; half of the eligible men would be on active military service at any time, and the rest remained home awaiting call-up, so that there would be an armed force in the field at all times. He had also created a system of fortified towns throughout his kingdom. In 886, Alfred reoccupied, walled, and garrisoned London, and all Englishmen not living under the domination of the Danes accepted him as their king (see Question 63).

Viking sea power was the key to their mobility and swiftness, and Alfred had used his own ships against the enemy as early as 875. Ten years later, his sailors succeeded in capturing sixteen Viking ships but were defeated on their way back by a different Danish naval force. Then, in 892, several hundred Viking ships transported to Kent the army that had been raiding France, and another army with eighty ships entered the Thames. Alfred finally managed to block this armada up on the Lea River north of London and capture or destroy its ships, but it was clear that he needed to confront the ongoing Viking naval threat more directly.

In 896, while the Danish fleet was harrying the southern coast of Wessex, King Alfred built the first regular English fleet, a decision for which he has been dubbed "the Father of the English Navy," although the monarch under whom that famed fighting force would start projecting a more-than-local power would be Shakespeare's queen, Elizabeth I. Alfred's warships were apparently very large, some with sixty oars or more, but also faster and steadier than the enemy ships. The king suggested innovations in the design so that, in the words of *The Anglo-Saxon Chronicle*, "they were built neither after the Frisian fashion nor after the Danish but as it seemed to himself that they could be most serviceable."

That same year, the last of that particular war, he sent nine of his new ships after a Danish squadron of six that was raiding his southern coast again and captured five of them in a minivictory at sea that distantly presaged a thousand more momentous naval encounters in England's future. When Alfred died a few years later in 899, he left his capable son, Edward the Elder, to carry on the protracted struggle of the kings, soldiers, and sailors of Wessex against the attacks of the Vikings.

TENTH
CENTURY

69 ∾ Who was the first pope of the Pornocracy?

Sergius III, 904–11, who initiated the papal era of "Rule by Harlots"

THE MOST SORDID ERA of the papacy, the sixty years spanning the reigns of Sergius III (904–11) to John XII (955–64), has been labeled by a pejorative referring to a family of female popemakers who secured the election of their favorites in order to maintain political power in a purulently corrupt Rome and to control the wealth of the church. Compared with the Pornocracy—Greek for "Rule by Prostitutes"—the reign of the Renaissance Borgia pope, Alexander VI, seems downright pious.

The prelude to our era may fittingly begin in 897, when Pope Stephen VI exhumed the body of Pope Formosus (891–96) to put it on trial at the so-called Corpse or Cadaver Synod. Dressed in his papal regalia, Formosus (Latin for "handsome") was placed on a throne and harshly questioned by the prosecutorial Stephen himself. The dead pope was duly convicted of various canonical crimes, all his acts were declared void, the three fingers he had used for blessing were chopped off, and his naked body was flung into the Tiber, but fishermen salvaged and buried it. This was too much even for the unruly Roman mob, which rose up against Stephen and threw him into prison, where he was smothered with a pillow.

Five very brief papal reigns intervened between Stephen VI and Sergius III, but we must now shift our attention to Theophylact, consul (that is, prince) and senator of Rome, keeper of the papal treasury, and leader of the Roman troops, and especially to his wife Theodora and their daughters Marozia and the younger Theodora. The Theophylacts were the dominant family of Roman nobles, and installing one of their own creatures as pope meant running the whole lucrative show until a rival pontiff took over.

The elder Theodora saw to it that her husband's kinsman was elevated to the papacy as Sergius III in 904 (seven years after his first election, when he had been immediately chased out of Rome) and that her beautiful fifteen-year-old daughter Marozia (c. 890–c. 932) became the new pontiff's mistress. Sergius took the precaution of having his predecessor, Leo V, strangled in prison, as well as an antipope (a rival claimant to the papal office) named Christopher. Having been wowed as a spectator at the Cadaver Synod of 897, he dug up Pope Formosus again, found him just as posthumously guilty as Pope Stephen had, and ordered the dead man's head chopped off. After Sergius's death, Theodora wangled the elections of both Anastasius III (911–13) and Lando (913–14).

The next pope, John X (914–28), is said to have been Theodora's lover. Be that as it may, he certainly owed his election to her. In gratitude, he made her a "senatrix"—female senator—of Rome, an honor he also conferred on her daughters. It was during his reign that Marozia contracted the first two of her three marriages: to Alberic I, duke of Spoleto, and to Guido, marquis of Tuscany; she later married Hugo of Provence, king of Italy. Pope John X is famed for personally leading the military forces of central Italy in a Christian league against Saracen invaders from the sea. In a bloody battle in 915, the warrior-pope routed the Muslims near the Garigliano River in central Italy, preventing them from advancing north to Rome.

In 927, Marozia and her husband Guido organized the ouster of John X to clear the way for her own papal candidate, Leo VI. Both he and his successor, Stephen VII (928–31), were Marozia's puppets. As for John X, he died imprisoned in Castel Sant'Angelo or, according to the prevailing custom, was strangled there.

After Stephen VII, it was the turn of Marozia's twenty-one-year-old son (perhaps by Pope Sergius III) to succeed to the throne of St. Peter as John XI (931–36), but her son Alberic II by her first husband imprisoned her in about 932, while her third husband, Hugo, flew the coop. Marozia died within a few years without ever regaining her freedom. Is it any wonder that a very young Ezra Pound had considered writing what he later called "a jejune trilogy" about her?

Some Pornocracy-era stories may well be tainted by the partisanship of a major historical source for this mostly dead-zone century, the Lombard bishop Liutprand of Cremona. Liutprand attended the synod of prelates at Rome in 963 that deposed his bête noire, Pope John XII, and, as a protégé of the German emperor (see Question 73), he hated the arrogant Roman nobles and the fickle urban populace.

With that caveat in mind, we turn to this John XII (955–64), the most colorful of all the Pornocrats. A grandson of Marozia, he assumed the pontifical dignity at age eighteen and did his best to earn his sobriquet of "the Christian Caligula" (see Question 3). Bishop Liutprand claims the teen pope turned the Lateran Palace into "a brothel and resort for harlots" where he committed incest with his niece and impregnated his father's mistress.

Liutprand quotes the evidence of "all the citizens of Rome" to the effect that Pope John was so besotted with a widow that he made her "governor of many cities" and presented her with golden crosses and chalices. The randy pontiff also put a dent in the pilgrimage trade because women stopped journeying to the sacred places of Rome for fear of a pope who took "female pilgrims by force to his bed—wives, widows, and virgins alike." His taste in women ranged from aristocrats—"thin as reeds from dieting"—to "common buxom strumpets."

At the synod of 963, summoned by the German emperor, the charges brought by the prelates against Pope John (who was on the lam at the time) ranged from the amusing to the shocking: celebrating Mass without receiving communion, ordaining a deacon in a stable, going hunting, selling bishoprics for cash, setting houses on fire, having sex with a pair of sisters, fatally blinding his spiritual adviser, lethally castrating a cardinal. The pope drank wine "for love of the devil" and shot craps while invoking Jupiter, Venus, and other non-Christian deities.

His Holiness replied by threatening to excommunicate all his accusers—basically the entire hierarchy of the Italian church—but, because his grammar was poor, he worded his statement, "You have no power to ordain no one." His pedantic foes countered with a word-maven gotcha: "We always thought, or rather believed, that two negatives make an affirmative."

When a new pope, Leo VIII, was proclaimed, John tried to bribe the Romans into murdering him, but the best they could do was chase Leo out of the country. John's vengeance had to slake itself on clerics who had testified against him: a cardinal who had his right hand cut off, a bishop who was scourged, and a notary who lost his tongue, two fingers, and his nose. But when it rains, it pours—John soon died of a stroke sustained while debauching a married woman. (Other sources say the husband beat him up so badly that he died three days later.) The pope's last inspirational gesture was to refuse the sacraments.

Things continued on this mavericky trajectory for a while longer. John XIII (965–72) was the son of the younger Theodora. Antipope Boniface VII is alleged to have strangled another papal grandson of Marozia, Benedict VI, in 974. Ten years later, the same antipope murdered John XIV.

Finally, in 999, the brilliant French scholar Gerbert, the most distinguished Western mathematician of his time, became pope as Sylvester II (999–1003) and presided over the first millennium in 1000. Having studied in Muslim Spain, he helped introduce Hindu-Arabic numerals into Christian Europe, and he also invented a mechanical clock and a steam-operated organ. A man like this was so unusual at the time that he was thought to be a wizard with magical powers or even someone who had sold his soul to the devil.

Legends also developed around the figure of a supposed ninth-century Pope Joan, who fooled everyone into thinking she was a man but revealed the true state of affairs by giving birth while traveling through Rome in a procession. A possible source of the totally fictitious tale was the fascination exerted on the popular imagination by the mother-daughter team of popemakers, Theodora and Marozia.

70 ❧ What was the first federated monastic order?

Cluny, founded in 910, eventually embracing hundreds of monasteries

WHILE PAPAL ROME was wallowing in degradation (see Question 69), the building of a new monastery in the hills of Burgundy, France, provided the impetus for a spiritual renewal and ecclesiastical reform that profoundly influenced the religious, cultural, and political life of Europe over the next several centuries.

In a charter dated September 11, 910, William the Pious, count of Auvergne and duke of Aquitaine, and his wife, Ingelberga, founded a monastery that was to be under the Benedictine Rule (see Question 41), dedicating it to the apostles Peter and Paul. They bestowed on it their town of Cluny, "with the court and demesne manor, and the church . . . the dwellings, indeed, the chapels, the serfs of both sexes, the vines, the fields, the meadows, the woods, the waters and their outlets, the mills, the incomes and revenues, what is cultivated and what is not, all in their entirety." They installed Berno, abbot of Gigny, as the first abbot of Cluny (910–27) and its dozen monks. Subordinate only to the pope, the abbot of Cluny was to be independent of the local bishop, and his aristocratic patrons also attested he would be "subject neither to our yoke, nor to that of our relatives, nor to the sway of any earthly power." Soon, existing Benedictine houses, as well as new monasteries, were incorporated into the Congregation of Cluny.

Since its founding in the sixth century, the Benedictine order had consisted of autonomous monasteries, each following the Rule of St. Benedict but electing its own abbot and maintaining its independence. Cluny, by contrast, was headed by an abbot who appointed all the priors of the Cluniac member monasteries. The abbots of Cluny—all belonging to noble families of the locale—were absolute rulers of their daughter houses and gradually ranked second only to the pope in ecclesiastical power and prestige. They annually visited each of the subordinate houses in person or through deputies, and each man wishing to join a Cluniac monastery had to be approved by the abbot and spend at least a few years at the motherhouse itself. Eventually, representatives from each house would attend an annual chapter presided over by the abbot. Such a high level of centralized oversight made it difficult for lax or corrupt houses to continue along on their same old sinful paths.

Cluny was fortunate in that seven of its first eight abbots were men of exceptional sanctity, culture, and energy. Its second abbot, Odo, established a code of discipline for the Cluniac houses that hearkened back to the ancient ideals of St. Benedict's Rule, with its vows of poverty, chastity, and obedience. He reformed monasteries in France and Italy, personally bringing his code even to the great Benedictine motherhouse of Monte Cassino.

In the following century, St. Hugh the Great, the eldest son of a count, became abbot of Cluny at age twenty-five, exercising this function for the next sixty years. Involved at the highest levels in many delicate and convoluted peace negotiations in Europe, he supported his friend Pope Gregory VII in the Investiture Controversy against the right of secular rulers to appoint church officials, and he preached the First Crusade along with the former Cluny monk, Pope Urban II (see Question 82). In 1089, he initiated work on the Romanesque abbey church of Cluny, which, with its five naves and length of 555 feet, was the largest church in Christendom before the building of the new St. Peter's Basilica in Rome during the Renaissance. Dedicated in 1131, the magnificent church fell victim to the destructive ardors of the French Revolution.

By the twelfth century, Cluny comprised 314 monasteries all over

Europe and even in the Holy Land. Its last great abbot, Peter the Venerable (1122–56), summoned a chapter of twelve hundred monks from
the Cluniac houses who drafted a constitution of seventy-six statutes to
regulate all aspects of monastic life. Peter also had the Koran translated
into Latin in about 1141 as an aid to Christian missionaries in the conversion of Muslims.

Abbot Peter fell out with his famously ascetic and mystical friend,
St. Bernard of Clairvaux, leader of the austere Cistercians, on how
much learning was proper for a monk. Bernard thought that praying
and working in the fields were how monks should spend all their time,
whereas Peter stressed the importance of education. The library of 570
volumes at Cluny was considered massive by twelfth-century Christian
standards. Nonetheless, study of the ancient pagan classics was often
frowned upon in Cluniac houses, too. According to historian Charles
Homer Haskins, "If a monk wanted a book during the hours of silence,
he made a sign of turning the leaves; if he wanted a classical book, he
scratched his ear like a dog." Perhaps the best deed of Peter the Venerable was his providing sanctuary for the hounded theologian Peter
Abelard after his condemnation at a church council.

The Congregation of Cluny entered into a long decline in the mid-
twelfth century, partly because monasteries abroad were increasingly
reluctant to submit to French abbots. New orders carried on the work of
monastic reform—St. Bernard's Cistercians, the Carthusians, Augustinian canons—and the rise of the friars in the early thirteenth century put
an entirely novel type of cleric on the European stage (see Question 92).

71 ∾ Where was gunpowder first used in battle?

China, at the battle of Lang-shan Jiang, in 919

GUNPOWDER MAY HAVE BEEN INVENTED by Chinese Taoist alchemists
searching for an elixir of immortality in the mid-ninth century—or perhaps a century and a half earlier, but very little is unambiguous about the
deadly compound's early history. At first, the Chinese employed this
combination of sulfur, saltpeter (potassium nitrate), and charcoal for fireworks, treating skin diseases, and as an insecticide, but some historians

of science have cited a specific time and place for the earliest military use of gunpowder.

During the Five Dynasties and Ten Kingdoms era of Chinese history (907–60), a river battle in 919 pitted the small southern coastal kingdom of Wuyue against its larger neighbor, the kingdom of Wu, in which each side mustered about five hundred small ships. At this battle of Lang-shan Jiang, the men of Wuyue came equipped with bellows-operated flamethrowers for projecting a gasoline-type substance—*huo yao* ("fire oil")—but, as opposed to the earlier Greek fire (see Question 53), they apparently used a slow-burning gunpowder match to ensure a continuous spewing of flame. The new weapon did what it was supposed to do—four hundred Wu ships were destroyed and thousands of men captured.

The Chinese went on to develop explosive bombs utilizing gunpowder by about 1000, hand grenades by the mid-twelfth century, primitive gunpowder-propelled rockets (used against invading Mongols) in 1232, and the first cannons late in the thirteenth century.

These exciting innovations were brought west by Mongols, Arabs, and Saracens. In the mid-thirteenth century, Roger Bacon is said to have couched in anagrams his formula for gunpowder, and other names associated with the development of this explosive in Europe are the possibly mythical Marcus Graecus writing in Italy and the probably mythical Berthold Schwarz writing in Germany.

Although at the beginning of *King John*, Shakespeare has the king warn the French ambassador, "The thunder of my cannon shall be heard," that particular sound wouldn't be heard anywhere in Europe for at least another century. It was only in the 1320s and 1330s that early cannons were used in Italy, and these were more likely to kill their own gunners than the enemy. The English used tiny, ineffective cannons in 1346 at Crécy during the Hundred Years' War, but by late in the century cannons were widely employed against castles and walled towns—as well as knights in armor. In the 1430s, cast-iron cannonballs began to replace earlier ones made of stone. It's ironic that by the time European traders and adventurers began bullying China in the sixteenth century, the Chinese had to rely on the Portuguese to manufacture their cannons and teach Chinese soldiers how to use them.

After European nations had been blasting one another with cannons for several hundred years, a certain ordnance fatigue set in among their brightest lights. John Milton ascribes the invention of cannons to

Satan himself in Book 6 of *Paradise Lost* (1667). During the epic battle in heaven between the angelic and demonic hosts, the poet—an old blind survivor of a bitter civil war—describes how thousands of angels are knocked off their feet at the discharge of a cannon, giving Satan the opportunity to crack jokes about the foe's choice of a strange time for dancing.

Almost six decades later, Jonathan Swift imagines Gulliver describing gunpowder and cannons to the gigantic king of Brobdingnag, informing him

> that a proper Quantity of this Powder rammed into a hollow
> Tube of Brass or Iron . . . would drive a Ball of Iron or Lead
> with such Violence and Speed, as nothing was able to sustain
> its Force. That the largest Balls thus discharged, would not
> only destroy whole Ranks of an Army at once, but batter the
> strongest Walls to the Ground, sink down Ships, with a Thou-
> sand Men in each, to the Bottom of the Sea. . . . That we often
> put this Powder into large hollow Balls of Iron, and discharged
> them by an Engine into some City we were besieging, which
> would rip up the Pavements, tear the Houses to pieces, burst
> and throw Splinters on every Side, dashing out the Brains of
> all who came near.

Far from being tempted when Gulliver offers to teach him how to acquire these technological marvels for his own belligerent purposes, the sage sixty-foot-tall ruler of Brobdingnag "was amazed how so impotent and groveling an Insect as I (these were his Expressions) could entertain such inhuman Ideas." The horrified king goes on to say that he would rather lose half his kingdom than make use of "those destructive Machines" of which "some evil Genius, Enemy to Mankind, must have been the first Contriver." Gulliver is warned, on pain of death, never to speak of them again.

72 ∾ What was the first general legislative assembly in Europe?

The Icelandic Althing, in 930

TOWARD THE END of the Dark Ages, the lands of Northern Europe began to form national assemblies. Oddly it was Iceland—a remote, recently populated volcanic island with no indigenous legal tradition— that in 930 first laid the foundation for a commonwealth ruled by a general assembly. The reasons have much to do with how Iceland first acquired a settled population.

Reports of an island northwest of Ireland had been in the air ever since Pytheas, a Greek traveler of the third century BC, claimed to have seen such a land, a six-day sail from Britain, where night lasted only two to three hours. He called it Ultima Thule—the end of the world.

In 825 an Irish monk, Dicuil, described the island as a summer vacation spot for priests, some of whom were apparently still visiting around 871, when the first intentional settler, a Viking from Norway named Ingolf Arnarson, arrived. He alighted at a place he called Reyk-javík ("Smoky Bay") because of its many thermal springs.

Ingolf was on the cusp of a sea change for Iceland. Soon thousands of settlers arrived—many from Norway, thanks to the expansionist wars of King Harald Fairhair in the latter half of the ninth century. After Harald triumphed at the battle of Hafrsfjord in c. 890, many chiefs and landowners chose to relocate rather than submit—and Iceland was wide open. Others arrived from the Orkney Islands and parts of Scotland, fleeing Harald's lengthening reach.

By the time Ingolf's son Thorsteinn came of age, farms and fisheries were scattered across Iceland. Townships grew, each consisting of perhaps a score of families who shared fishing rights and pasturelands, took care of the poor and infirm, and, as far as they were able, mutually ensured against catastrophic losses of livestock and farmhouses. Following a Northern European model that originated around 800, Iceland's heads of households would meet in a local assembly, called a *thing*, from the Old Norse for "appointed time."

At the core of these districts were the chieftains, called *godar*, who owned substantial land (claimed by getting there first) and who, before the introduction of Christianity in 1000, were the keepers of temples dedicated to Odin, Thor, Freya, and the other Norse gods. Independent farmers were legally obliged to belong to a chieftaincy, but allegiance did not depend on vicinity—they were free to follow any chief and, in turn, the *godar* were permitted to expel followers.

The right to a voice in the assembly was restricted to male heads of households; no women or workers, whether free or slave, had a role in the political system. There weren't many slaves in any case—there were no aboriginal natives to exploit—and the farming conditions were such that a man consumed as much as he produced. So instead of a clannish set of nobles living off ground rent as in the old country, chiefs here worked their land like everyone else.

With a few local *things* in place, the question soon arose of the feasibility of a general assembly to address a host of concerns, such as the lack of any shared law code. Bear in mind that Iceland was relatively isolated. In one of its great *Eddas*, the "Havamal," the hardships of the traveler were keenly appreciated:

> *He hath need of fire, who now is come,*
> *numbed with cold to the knee;*
> *food and clothing the wanderer craves*
> *who has fared o'er the rimy fell.*

Perhaps such conditions made Icelanders more sensitive to the benefits of a sturdy social fabric.

In the 920s, one of the *godar*, Ulfljot of Lon, was sent back to Norway, where, with the help of his uncle, he adapted the West Norwegian Gulathing Law to the needs of Iceland. While he was gone, his foster brother traveled around Iceland to garner support for a general assembly and find a suitable place for it.

In 930, about forty chiefs from all over the land met at Blaskogar, near the eastern bound of Ingolf's estate. There they saw beautiful Lake Thingvallavatn in an open plain, at the edge of which rose an elevated outcrop of dark rock. The scene is a natural wonder: Fissures around the lake reveal that the tectonic plates of Europe and the Americas are pulling apart there. Divers in the Great Atlantic Rift say the water is so clear they have visibility to well over three hundred feet.

By a quirk of fate, Blaskogar's owner had murdered his servant, and his land had passed into common ownership. Renamed Thingvellir

("Assembly Plains"), it was declared the site of the general assembly, or *Althing*.

From the rocky outcrop that became the "Law Rock" (*Lögberg*) anyone could address the assembly, which combined legislative and judicial duties. With no king or army, each citizen was entrusted with executive power to enforce the law. Since the laws were not written down until the thirteenth century, the essential (and sole) government official was the Law Speaker (*lögsögumaður*), who had to recite from memory one-third of the law code to the assembly for each of three years, and then, if he was reelected by the *godar*, to start over. The first Speaker was Ulfljot; the first law enacted, Ulfljot's Law.

The Althing met annually. For two weeks each summer, Thingvellir was where important matters were addressed, news from all over was shared, and laws were crafted by the Law Council (*Lögrétta*). This consisted of the chieftains, who sat in a circle, each with an adviser in front of him and one behind him, thus creating three concentric rings presided over by the Law Speaker. Later, Catholic bishops became members of the Council, with status equal to that of the chieftains. Besides establishing customs, the Council also curbed ambitions, offsetting the power struggles among its independent peers.

One of these struggles arose shortly after the first Christian missionaries arrived in 981. The earliest of these, the German Thangbrand, baptized a few chieftains but also reportedly killed a few recalcitrant heathens. Within twenty years the devotees of the old gods were at such loggerheads with the Christian converts, who had the active backing of King Olaf Tryggvason of Norway, that the matter came before the Althing. Both sides swore they would not live together under the same law, and Christians demanded a separate law of their own. The question was left to Thorgeir the Law Speaker, who was still a pagan, to decide.

Thorgeir lay down under his cloak for an entire day and night, and then rose to say, "It will prove true, if we break the law in pieces, that we break the peace in pieces too." And so at Thingvellir in 1000, what the sagas call the "Change of Ways" came to pass: Thorgeir declared that all Icelanders should be baptized in the Christian faith. Sacrificing to the old gods was not outlawed, so long as it was kept private, and certain practices, including the exposing of infants and the eating of horseflesh, were briefly allowed before finally being abolished.

That spirit of independence-with-compromise persisted at Thingvellir. In 1022, the Althing accepted a trade agreement with the king of

Norway that gave Icelanders rights to all the wood they wanted from the royal forests. But two years later, when the same king asked for the off-shore isle of Grimsey as a mark of Iceland's esteem, the Law Council, ever mindful of the grasping legacy of Harald Fairhair, refused. "With law is our land built," they responded.

Although the commonwealth period ended in 1262, when a badly fractured Iceland submitted to the Norwegian king, the Althing continued to conduct business of state at the Law Rock until 1798. Laws adopted by the Lögrétta were subject to the king's assent, and legislation initiated by the king required the consent of the Council.

Besides its governmental function, the meeting of the Althing served as the social gathering of the year. An old law book, *Grágás*, mentions tanners' and peat-cutters' booths, and the sagas sing of beer-brewers and food-sellers. Men looked for wives, merchants hawked their wares, sword-sharpeners sharpened, clowns clowned, beggars begged, and ale-makers kept the assembly guests in good spirits. It's not too much to say that in addition to its legal groundwork, the foundation of Iceland's culture, language, and literature was established at Thingvellir, and the heart of the people still beats from that riven plain.

—*Tom Matrullo*

73 ∽ Who was the first Holy Roman Emperor?

Otto the Great of Germany, ruled as emperor 962–73

"NEITHER HOLY NOR ROMAN NOR AN EMPIRE" was Voltaire's caustic quip about the Holy Roman Empire, which succeeded the Frankish Western Empire established by Charlemagne in 800 (see Question 61). Its founder, Otto I (912–73), was elected as the second German king of the Saxon dynasty at age twenty-four after the death in 936 of his father, Henry the Fowler, who had subdued Lorraine, Bohemia, Schleswig, and the Slavic lands east of the Elbe.

Otto began his reign by reducing rebellious German duchies and other states to submission. Through his marriage to Adelaide, widow of King Lothair II of Italy, he styled himself "King of the Lombards" and forced the new Italian king, Berengar II, to pay him homage.

In 955, at the battle of Lechfeld, near Augsburg, Bavaria, Otto soundly defeated the Magyars. These nomadic horsemen from the east had arrived, under their leader Arpad, in what is now Hungary in the late ninth century, pushing the Serbs and Bulgarians south of the Danube and launching dozens of terribly destructive cavalry raids into Germany, Moravia, France, and Italy throughout much of the tenth century. They calmed down after being Christianized under the first Hungarian king, Stephen I, in 1000.

The fame of Otto's momentous victory induced Pope John XII to summon his aid against King Berengar and his son Adalbert, who had their eyes on the Papal States of central Italy. Otto duly crossed the Alps, had himself crowned king of Italy, and rescued the pope, who rewarded his German savior by crowning him Roman emperor of the West on February 2, 962.

As soon as Otto had receded into the Nordic mists, the twenty-something pope double-crossed him with Berengar and Adalbert and tried to form an alliance with the Byzantines and even the Magyars, claiming the emperor had reneged on his promise to restore the lands of the exarchate of Ravenna to the Holy See. Otto hastened back to Rome and had John deposed after a synod that he summoned in 963 (see Question 69), at which, though he might have been emperor enough, and even holy enough, he certainly wasn't Roman enough to address the assemblage in Latin, having his chief ecclesiastical fart-catcher, Liutprand, bishop of Cremona, do the bloviating for him, rather than croak out something unintelligible in Saxon. The prelates proceeded to elect a new pope, Leo VIII, a layman and chief notary of the church who just happened to be the nominee of the emperor.

The Romans, feeling bearded in their den, dispatched troops to attack the emperor on his way back to Germany, but they were beaten off. At least they managed to send Leo packing and brought back their depraved young pope, John. After the latter's untimely death, they elected Benedict V, whom Otto deposed after a month, restoring his man Leo. On this trip down to the Eternal City, Otto made the citizens solemnly promise they would never elect another pope without "the consent and approval of the august Caesar Otto, the lord emperor."

By this time Otto was so sick of Roman politics that when the city rebelled against him in 966, he let his soldiers sack it. Having formally united Italy to his empire, he campaigned against the Byzantines and Saracens in the southern part of the peninsula, seeking to bring it under his control, but all he did was leave pickings for the Normans, who moved in at the beginning of the next century. Although Otto had no luck bringing France into his empire, Mieczyslaw I, prince of Poland, submitted to him and accepted Christianity in 967, and the king of Denmark also acknowledged him as suzerain before the emperor's death in 973.

In the so-called Ottonian Renaissance during the reigns of Otto and his immediate successors, some notable churches were built, and the miniaturists of the island monastery of Reichenau left behind superb examples of their artistry. At the cathedral school of Bruno the Great (Otto's brother, who was duke of Lorraine and archbishop of Cologne), Bruno taught Greek and philosophy, attracting scholars and importing books from Italy and the Byzantine Empire. The learned nun Hroswitha (c. 935–c. 975) of the Benedictine convent of Gandersheim has been called the first German poet, the first female playwright, the first postclassical playwright, and the second-favorite author (after Boethius) of Ignatius J. Reilly in John Kennedy Toole's comic masterpiece *A Confederacy of Dunces* (1980). Hroswitha's literary output includes six Latin prose comedies inspired by Terence and a minor verse epic on the deeds of Otto I.

Otto II (973–83), crowned coemperor with his father by Pope John XIII in 967, was married to the Byzantine royal princess Theophano, who brought her hypercivilized Greek ways to Ottonian Germany. Like his father, Otto tried to oust the Byzantines and Arabs from southern Italy but was seriously defeated. He managed to secure the election of Pope John XIV before dying in his palace at Rome at age twenty-eight.

When Otto III (983–1002) came of age, he elevated his cousin to the papacy as Gregory V, the first German pope—who promptly returned the nepotistic favor by crowning Otto emperor. When Gregory fled to Germany after the Romans threw him out, Otto rushed back to Rome and suppressed the "Roman republic" that had been established against him, executing its leader Crescentius and mutilating an antipope. After Gregory's death, the young emperor chose as pope his former teacher, the brilliant scholar Gerbert of Aurillac, who became the first French pontiff as Sylvester II (999–1003). Three years later, Otto had to flee his splendid palace on the Aventine after yet another Roman revolt, dying near Viterbo at age twenty-two, succumbing, it seems, to malaria. The Romans claimed he was poisoned by Crescentius's widow after she had seduced the emperor to accomplish her nefarious purposes.

In the later eleventh century, the papacy took a firm stand against the long-established practice of secular rulers appointing the bishops and abbots in their realms—not to mention the popes—treating them much like other political officials. The Investiture Controversy reached a notorious climax during the blizzards of January 1077, when Holy Roman Emperor Henry IV (whose father had deposed three popes) stood barefoot in the snow and dressed in a penitential hair shirt for three days outside a castle at Canossa, seeking forgiveness from Gregory VII after the pope had excommunicated and dethroned him.

Henry was forgiven, but he soon retaliated by attacking Rome. The first phase of the long struggle between popes and emperors over "lay investiture" ended a half century later when the emperor pledged to cease investing bishops with their rings and staff, insignias of their office—though he and other secular rulers still often appointed them. The battle between papal and imperial claims continued for hundreds of years more, and even in 1809 French emperor Napoleon annexed the Papal States and took Pius VII prisoner.

The most illustrious Holy Roman Emperors of the Hohenstaufen dynasty were Frederick I Barbarossa (1155–90), who battled valiantly against popes, the great city of Milan, and its Lombard League; and Frederick II (1220–50), the "Wonder of the World," who conducted protracted wars against various popes. The empire was long dominated by the house of Hapsburg, whose mightiest emperor, Charles V (1520–56), was also king of Spain and lord of a goodly portion of the earth.

When Adolf Hitler referred to his regime (1933–45) as the Third Reich, he was thinking of the empire inaugurated by Otto I (and lasting until Napoleon deposed Francis II in 1806) as the First Reich, and of Otto von Bismarck's empire under Kaiser Wilhelm I from 1871 as the Second Reich (which ended after Wilhelm II fled to the Netherlands in 1918 after World War I). The longevity of the reichs decreased drastically as time went on—less than 850 years, then less than 50, and then barely a dozen, though Hitler had predicted the third would last a thousand.

74 ∽ Where was the first medical school in medieval Europe?

Salerno, an Italian city south of Naples, in c. 985

BY THE SECOND HALF OF THE TENTH CENTURY, the southern Italian coastal city of Salerno, long a cosmopolitan trade nexus and health resort, had become a renowned center of the physician's art that drew on a variety of medical traditions. Dubbed *Civitas Hippocratica* ("City of Hippocrates") for the ancient Greek "Father of Medicine," Salerno had acquired, by the end of that dark century, a fame that stretched as far as northern France.

Medical practice at Salerno—initially less an organized school than an assemblage of skilled physicians—represented a significant shift from the monastic medicine that had become dominant with the rise of Christianity. In their infirmaries, monks relied on techniques such as bloodletting and bathing, along with the emetics and purgatives of folk and herbal medicine, but they also emphasized the necessity of prayer and penitence, with illness being considered a sign of divine displeasure.

The early Salernitan practitioners took a more secular approach, becoming known for their practical skills learned through apprenticeship rather than for any systematic theoretical or academic medical knowledge. During the eleventh century, however, a nascent medical literature began to appear. Among the first manuscripts was the *Passionarius*, possibly by Gariopontus, containing translated works of the Greco-Roman physician Galen (second century AD). Another early manuscript was a treatise on gynecology, known as the *Trotula*, which is thought to have been at least partly written by a woman of that name who practiced and taught at Salerno and which became a standard medieval text on women's health.

In about 1070 Constantine the African arrived at Salerno, possibly at the invitation of Alfano, the city's archbishop. Constantine had gathered many medical texts in his travels through the Islamic world, and after a short stay at Salerno he took up residence at the nearby Benedictine abbey of Monte Cassino. There he translated into Latin as many as thirty-seven medical works, including the *Prognostica* and a treatise on acute illness by Hippocrates with commentaries by Galen; works by Byzantine Greeks; and treatises on diets, fevers, and urine written in Arabic by the Jewish physician Isaac Israeli ben Solomon (died c. 932).

Constantine also translated parts of the *Pantegni* (*The Universal Art*) of tenth-century Persian physician Haly Abbas. This first introduction of Islamic science to the West opened up vistas of ancient Greek technical knowledge that had been lost in the European Middle Ages but recovered and expanded on by Muslim scholars. Constantine's efforts facilitated the gradual resurgence of science in medieval Western medicine. As Paul Oskar Kristeller observed in his seminal 1945 article on Salerno, "After the middle of the twelfth century the translations of

Constantine became the common property of the Salerno school and even the center of its medical teaching."

Through the twelfth and early thirteenth centuries the school continued to grow in influence and sophistication with the development of a structured core curriculum called the *Articella* ("Little Art"). The *Articella* followed an educational model incorporating commentaries on authoritative texts such as the *Aphorisms* and *Prognostica* of Hippocrates. This approach, widely practiced in the Middle Ages in disciplines such as law and theology, represented a shift in the Salernitan form of instruction from the practical to the theoretical, scholastic, and philosophical.

Strongly contributing to the philosophical dimension of Salernitan medicine at this time were the writings of Urso of Calabria (died 1225). Urso's writings included conventional medical texts but also treatises exhibiting deep familiarity with some of the newly translated writings of Aristotle. This early promulgation of Aristotelian conceptions represents a further contribution of Salerno to the overall development of medieval European science and philosophy.

Far from being overly bookish, the curriculum at Salerno also included anatomical study based on the dissection of animals (usually pigs, which were considered anatomically similar to humans)—a learning technique in abeyance since the end of antiquity. Roger Frugardi's influential *Practica chirurgiae* (c. 1170) became the standard surgery text at Salerno, including instructions on how to suture lacerated intestines and repair skull fractures. The prescriptions of medical school dean Nicolas were collected in his *Antidotary*, which became a popular medieval pharmacopoeia.

The thirteenth century marked the beginning of the decline of the medical school of Salerno, although it was only during that time that the school achieved organized legal status. In 1231, Emperor Frederick II ruled that the granting of a medical license required candidates—which could include women and Jews—to pass a public examination before the Salerno professors. Requirements he added a decade later stipulated a prerequisite of three years' study of logic before the initiation of a five-year medical training course that had to include surgery.

During the thirteenth century, medical curricula began appearing in other European universities, including those in Paris, Bologna, Montpellier, and Padua. It also was during this century, at the very latest, that the most famous of the Salernitan texts was compiled, the *Regimen sanitatis Salernitanum* (*Salernitan Guide to Health*), written in Latin verse. A free translation of this work by Sir John Harington in 1608, adapted for his English audience and his king (James I), contains the following eternally sage advice:

> *The Salerne school doth by these lines impart*
> *All health to England's King, and doth advise*
> *From care his head to keep, from wrath his heart,*
> *Drink not much wine, sup light, and soon arise,*
> *When meat is gone, long sitting breedeth smart:*
> *And after noon still waking keep your eyes.*
> *When moved you find yourself to Nature's needs,*
> *Forbear them not, for that much danger breeds,*
> *Use three Physicians still; first Doctor Quiet,*
> *Next Doctor Merry-man, and Doctor Diet.*

—*Nancy Walsh*

75 ∾ Who was the first European to sight the Americas?

Bjarni Herjolfsson, a Norse trader, in 986

MIGRANTS FROM EASTERN ASIA crossed the Bering land bridge down into the Americas as early as the Clovis culture of thirteen thousand to twelve thousand years ago—perhaps even a millennium earlier—but Europeans were comparatively tardy arrivals in the New World. Although hoary legends tell of Irish sailors settling in what is now Nova Scotia in about 875, the first semireliable traditions of European visitations to the Americas are enshrined in the often imaginative *Saga of the Greenlanders* and *Saga of Eric the Red*, written two to three centuries after the events they describe.

It's best to start with Eric the Red. Outlawed from Norway for murder, he fled to Iceland (see Question 72) and was banished thence for three years for another series of killings. This repeat offender had heard tales of a shoreline sighted to the west a half century earlier, so he sailed off in that direction in about 982 and, after about five hundred miles, discovered a land mass he euphemistically named "Greenland"—a land of glaciers with a pair of sheltered fjords in the southwest bordered by grassy areas and some scrubby growth on the hillsides.

The part of Greenland Eric stumbled on was uninhabited by pesky humans but abundant in bear, fox, caribou, and birds. He stayed for his term of three years and then headed back to Iceland. At the dubious prospects of a "green land" in the west, twenty-five ships manned by hardy souls fleeing the cramped conditions and ever-threatening famine of the habitable parts of Iceland sailed with Eric in 986. Only fourteen of the ships arrived, laden with about 450 settlers and a supply of domestic animals, but Eric's settlement eventually included almost two hundred farms.

It so happened that a Norwegian ship owner named Bjarni Herjolfs-son, who traded between his country and Iceland, put into port in the lat-ter country but learned that his father, with whom he used to spend the winters, had joined Eric the Red's expedition to Greenland. Bjarni and his men set off in pursuit but got blown way past their destination until they saw in the west a flat shoreline covered with woods—we call it Labrador—and, heading north, they gazed on mountains hemmed in by glaciers. Although Bjarni and his crew were the first Europeans to sight America, they didn't realize the momentousness of their discovery—and had a cargo to unload—so they didn't go ashore. After turning around, they arrived in Greenland four days later.

To Eric the Red's son Leif Ericson, the story of how Bjarni spotted a new land west of Greenland must have been more than a twice-told tale, because he ended up buying his ship and pointing it in the same direction. In about 1001, Leif—later known as Leif the Lucky—led a crew of thirty-five on a voyage of discovery to the unknown land Bjarni had glimpsed from a distance.

Soon, Leif and his men were shouting the Norse equivalent of "Land, ho!" when the southern part of Baffin Island hove into view, though their subsequent disappointment on going ashore is memorial-ized in the name they gave it—"Flatstone Land." Embarking again and coasting farther south, they were less displeased with Labrador, thick with forests, which they thus dubbed "Markland" ("Woodland"). Finally, they put in at a place they called "Vinland" ("Wineland" or "Vineland"), where they decided to winter.

They found grass pastures for their animals, timber for building, and huge salmon. It was a place of wild grapes and self-sown wheat—and no frosts during the winter—which might accord with an unusually temper-ate season in Nova Scotia or New England, unless Leif's settlement was farther south. Long Island Sound? Some have even speculated about Georgia or Florida. The so-called Vinland Map, published with tremendous hoopla by Yale University Press in 1965, can't help us at all, because it's quite probably a forgery.

The only unequivocal site of a Viking dwelling found in the New World is at L'Anse aux Meadows at the northern extremity of Newfoundland. This could have been Leif's settlement only if those "wild grapes" were some sort of mountain cranberry that grows that far north. Eight or nine housing sites were excavated at L'Anse aux Meadows in 1961–68, and the few Norse artifacts found there were carbon-dated to about the right time.

Leif and his men returned to Greenland the following summer. The next expedition to the Americas was led by Leif's brother Thorvald, who sailed there in 1002 in Leif's ship with a crew of thirty. They found Leif's settlement, but Thorvald was shot dead with an arrow in a scuffle with the natives, whom the Norse called *Skraelings* (perhaps meaning "dwarves," "screechers," or "ugly little creatures"), described as small people with big eyes, broad cheeks, and "ugly hair on their heads." Though apparently a name for the Eskimos they encountered in various places, *Skraelings* seems to have been applied to American Indians, too. Thorvald's men stayed the winter and returned to Greenland in the spring.

Several years later, Thorfinn Karlsefni arrived in Greenland on a trading expedition from Iceland and married the widowed Gudrid Thorbjarnardottir, who had been a daughter-in-law of the late Eric the Red. Thorfinn's goal was to found a colony in Vinland, so with three ships, about 160 men and women, and a goodly amount of livestock, he sailed to Labrador and then down the coast to Leif's settlement.

During a summer when Thorfinn and his group camped on a southern bay that they named *Hop* ("Estuary"), Gudrid gave birth to a son, Snorri Thorfinnson, the first child born to Europeans in America. The Skraelings were unfriendly, though they seemed greatly interested in trading furs and pelts for the Norsemen's milk and red cloth. Finally, they launched an attack en masse from their boats, which drove the settlers back to Greenland after three mild but grapeless winters in Vinland.

Little Snorri's family soon relocated to Iceland, where his descendants included three bishops. After being widowed a second time, Gudrid supposedly made a pilgrimage to the Continent and died as a nun at Snorri's farm in Iceland.

Yet another expedition to Vinland involved Freydis, the sister of Leif and Thorvald. When a nasty dispute arose between her followers and the band of thirty settlers led by Icelandic brothers named Helgi and Finnbogi, Freydis egged on her husband and his followers to murder the brothers and their men—and then she herself, a chip off the old block of Eric the Red, axed to death the five women of the rival group. When they returned to Greenland the next spring, Freydis told Leif that the others had stayed in Vinland—which was technically accurate—but when he found out the truth, Leif solemnly cursed his homicidal sister and her children.

And so, by about 1020, the Viking adventure in the Americas was largely over. Although Greenlanders may still have sailed to Markland to fetch timber and furs as late as the mid-fourteenth century, historian Daniel J. Boorstin sums up the entire experience as follows: "What is most remarkable is not that the Vikings actually reached America, but that they reached America and even settled there for a while, without *discovering* America."

ELEVENTH CENTURY

76 ∽ Who first developed solmization (*do, re, mi*, etc.)?

The Italian monk Guido of Arezzo, c. 1024

ACTUALLY, I LIED: It was *ut, re, mi,* etc., that Guido invented. He got the names of the notes—*ut, re, mi, fa, sol, la*—from the initial syllables of the half lines that make up the first stanza of an eighth-century Latin hymn to John the Baptist written by Paul the Deacon. In this work, each nonitalicized syllable below fell on a higher successive tone of the hexachord, the first six notes of the major scale (c, d, e, f, g, a):

> Ut *queant laxis* re*sonare fibris*
> Mi*ra gestorum* fa*muli tuorum,*
> Sol*ve polluti* la*bii reatum* . . .

(So that your servants can, with unrestrained voice, sing the wonders of your deeds, remove the guilt of our tainted lips!)

The initial letters of "*S*ante *I*ohannes," the next words in the text, which directly address St. John, later gave us the name of the note *si*, which was eventually changed to *ti*, just as *ut* was later changed to *do* and *sol* to *so* in many countries for reasons of euphony. The singing of vocal exercises to these syllables is termed *solfeggio* or *solfège,* names deriving from *sol* and *fa*, just as *solmization* itself is derived from *sol* and *mi*.

The background to this development was the difficulty of teaching monks and cathedral singers the Gregorian chant, which was named for Pope Gregory the Great (590–604), though it probably coalesced about two hundred years after his time. This official music of the Roman Catholic liturgy was a monodic plainchant, meaning that the same notes were sung by all the voices. Although the Arabs had developed a system of musical notation in about 700, and the French manuscript called *Musica enchiriadis* ("Handbook of Music") used Latin letters for notation in c. 870, the most common system in Europe by the early tenth century was notation by means of neumes (from the Greek for "breaths").

Looking like accent marks placed higher or lower over words to be sung, neumes indicated in a slapdash way whether the pitch was rising or falling. This crude way of reminding singers of the direction their voices should go was better than nothing, but the specific pitches had to be laboriously memorized for each individual piece of music—and the church had a vast repertoire of hymns and liturgical songs.

Enter the Benedictine monk Guido of Arezzo (c. 991–1050), a composer, choirmaster, and theorist of liturgical music who is sometimes called "the Father of Modern Music." Building on insights gleaned from a French musical treatise, he and a fellow monk named Michael began to experiment with the teaching of music at the northern Italian monastery of Pomposa on the Adriatic coast.

Their success was such that Guido became something of a celebrity in the locale, and the envy of the other monks caused him to depart for the city of Arezzo, southeast of Florence, in about 1025. Bishop Theodald of Arezzo gave him a job training singers of the cathedral school and asked him to write a book on musical theory. The resultant *Micrologus de disciplina artis musicae* (*Manual of the Art of Music*) in twenty chapters included discussions of early polyphony and was used as a standard European text for several hundred years.

Guido's major innovation, however, was a protomodern system of musical notation. In his day, two lines were sometimes used to indicate the range of pitch within a composition—a red line to indicate the note now known as F and a yellow or green line to indicate C, and the aforementioned neumes were placed at varying distances from them to roughly indicate pitch. Guido added a black line between F and C and another black one above C to create the first four-line musical staff (the current five-line staff first appeared in 1200). He thus made use of his lines—as well as the spaces between them—to place letters indicating the specific notes. He continued to mark the C and F lines—the C would appear above the F for a song with a high melody, and the reverse would be the case for a lower melody. His symbols for these notes have now become our treble and bass clefs. Following on Guido's notation, square notes appeared in the thirteenth century, the ancestors of our oval ones.

Now that musical intervals could be clearly indicated with Guido's notation and four-line staff, music could be learned much more rapidly—and composed and preserved much more efficiently—than in the past. It became possible to learn an enormous amount of music and even to sight-read. Whereas a church singer might take a decade to train in the past, Guido's methods allowed it to be done in a year or less. His achievements also permitted and encouraged the rise of polyphony in the eleventh century, since complicated musical lines and parts could now be set down graphically with precision and clarity.

In about 1030, Pope John XIX invited Guido to Rome, and the pontiff himself became his first music pupil there. The details of Guido's later life are extremely hazy, but some accounts have him returning to Arezzo, perhaps to the nearby monastery of Avellana, where he may have died as its prior in 1050. The Guidonian hand, a drawing of a hand marked with the names of tones to facilitate memorization of the scale, was devised in its modern form after Guido's time, though he may have used a similar mnemonic.

The music historian Stuart Lyons has recently claimed that while Guido took the words for his solmization from the Latin hymn to John the Baptist, he found the music for it in a southern French manuscript that featured a series of dots and dashes to indicate the melody over the words of the ancient Roman poet Horace's "Ode to Phyllis" (*Odes* 4.11). Though Lyons says the melody was not necessarily composed by Horace himself in the first century BC, it is an interesting hypothesis that ties together two Italian artists eminently gifted with musicality who lived an entire millennium apart.

77 ∾ Who first developed movable type?

The Chinese printer Pi Sheng, c. 1041–48

SEE-108

PRINTING IS AN ANCIENT ART that began with the creation of designs on textiles or the reproduction of signatures on official seals. As early as the third century, the Chinese invented what we erroneously call "India ink" for making well-nigh indelible images for these purposes.

Wooden block printing was long the norm in China and other Eastern nations. An image or text was carved into a block of wood, which was then laid flat with the carved surface facing up and covered with ink. Paper or a textile was placed over the block and tamped down with a brush to make the impression. For written texts, each word had to be incised into the block, which then became useless except for printing that same page. Every later occurrence of the same word in a text had to be individually carved anew.

During the Tang dynasty (618–907), Chinese Buddhists practiced printing on a fairly large scale because they believed that reproducing their sacred texts and holy pictures garnered karma. The wooden blocks were sometimes replaced by copper plates in Japan as early as the late eighth century and in China by the tenth.

The world's oldest surviving printed book—in actuality, large printed sheets of Buddhist scripture pasted together to form a scroll— is the *Diamond Sutra*, whose creation with wooden blocks can be dated precisely to May 11, 868. An inscription attributes the book to a certain Wang Chieh in memory of his parents.

For the next three centuries, the Chinese government monopolized printing, outlawing any private use. In 953, the Confucian classics and numerous commentaries on them were printed in 130 volumes (see Question 48). Several decades later, the entire Buddhist sacred canon was printed in 5,048 volumes comprising 130,000 pages. Not to be outdone, the Taoists printed 4,000 volumes of their own lore in 1019.

But what we call "movable type" promised significant advantages over block printing, since individual characters of type could be created once and used repeatedly. During the Song dynasty (960–1279), a man named Pi Sheng first used movable type made of clay in c. 1041 to 1048, after an unsuccessful effort with wooden movable type. First, he cut his clay characters very thin and hardened them in fire. Then he arranged the types, carved side up, next to one another in an iron frame which, when it was full, he set down on an iron plate covered with pine resin, wax, and ashes.

Heating the plate slightly and then pressing the types down flat with a wooden board made them all stand even in the frame; when the waxy mixture cooled, the types remained in this position, creating a neat and uniform impression on the paper. When the page was printed, Pi Sheng heated the plate again, causing the types to disengage so they could be removed and used again. While copies were being made of one page, other workers set the next page of type.

The problem was that Chinese, lacking an alphabet, had more than forty thousand individual characters representing its words, each requiring its own separate type. Even when all these had been laboriously prepared (and common words would require multiple copies of type), the problem of accessing them readily—and then filing them away again—created a logistical nightmare. Pi Sheng's invention thus failed to revolutionize printing in China, which largely kept using carved wooden blocks or metal plates for each page of text. The earliest development of movable metal type, in Korea, did not occur for almost two more centuries.

In all these developments, Europe lagged far behind. In fact, it may have been another Chinese invention utilizing printing—playing cards, originating in the tenth century and migrating westward by the late fourteenth century—that first got Europeans interested in a technological process that turned their world upside down when it exploded on the scene (see Question 108).

78 ∽ Who was the first Norman king of England?

William the Conqueror, who ruled the country from 1066 to 1087

IN AN ATTEMPT to get the Viking Northmen to stop raiding deep into French territory, King Charles III the Simple made a virtue of necessity in 911 by allotting them as a fief part of what was later named "Normandy" after them. The marauders had already conquered that coastal swath of northern France, and their chieftain Rollo agreed to swear fealty to the French king. Within a century, the Normans had accepted Christianity, developed their own dialect of French, intermarried with French women, and shed at least some of their old piratical ways.

Across the Channel in England, almost three decades of Danish rule came to an end in 1042. Back from his long exile in Normandy came Edward the Confessor (r. 1042–66), son of the feckless English king Aethelred the Unready and Emma, daughter of a former duke of Normandy. Ultra-pious and French-speaking, the new king Edward soon surrounded himself with Normans, antagonizing powerful nobles—especially the greatest of them all, Earl Godwin of Wessex, who nonetheless gave him his daughter Edith in marriage.

King Edward never produced an heir—perhaps his marriage was a chaste one—and as early as 1051, when he was not yet fifty, he reportedly promised his second cousin—William, Duke of Normandy—the succession to the English throne in exchange for support against his tyrannical father-in-law, Earl Godwin, and his brother-in-law Harold Godwinson.

William, a direct descendant of Rollo, was the bastard son of Robert the Magnificent, Duke of Normandy, and Herlette, a tanner's daughter. Physically daunting, he was among the toughest warriors of his time, having fought rebellious barons to hold on to his dukedom despite his illegitimate birth. But in the years since that promise to William, King Edward had come to an understanding with Harold Godwinson, the new earl of Wessex. On his deathbed, Edward named Harold—the preeminent warrior of the kingdom—as his successor, and on the following day, January 6, 1066, the witenagemot (the assembly of nobles and prelates) approved the nomination and had the earl crowned king of England as Harold II. This was despite the story that Harold had sworn a solemn oath to William two years earlier that he would not seek the English throne—in fact, that he would help William obtain it.

Duke William had the eager backing of the pope, an opponent of the house of Godwin, as well as the support of many Continental noblemen. During the spring and summer of 1066, armies and fleets assembled on both sides of the Channel, but then an unexpected invasion of northern England sent King Harold and his men scurrying north.

The perpetrator was the last mighty Viking warrior, King Harald Hardrada ("Stern Ruler") of Norway, who had fought stoutly from Russia to Denmark, with stops in Poland, Bulgaria, Sicily, and elsewhere. He, too, had some convoluted claim to the English throne, but despite initial victories against local forces in his surprise attack with about three hundred ships and nine thousand men, Harald was killed in the destruction of the Norwegian forces at the battle of Stamford Bridge near York on September 25—though at a very heavy cost to King Harold's English army.

Meanwhile, when stubborn winds finally allowed him to sail, Duke William crossed the Channel and made an unopposed landing on September 28 in southern England. When Harold heard the news a few days later, he headed south again, covering the two-hundred-mile march back to London in less than a week. There, he hurriedly gathered what forces he could before setting out after William.

The king took up his position on a hill six miles from Hastings, protecting the main road to London, sixty miles away. At the top of this ridge, later named Senlac Hill, Harold's seventy-five hundred infantry-men looked down on a formidable Norman center of heavy cavalry flanked by Breton and French light and heavy infantry, probably eighty-five hundred men in all. For a while, the English wall of shields withstood the enemy's cavalry charges, but the experienced Norman horsemen and archers took an increasingly heavy toll as the day progressed.

The *Bayeux Tapestry*, created at the bidding of William's half brother Odo, the fighting bishop of Bayeux, to celebrate the conquest of England, has been thought to depict the manner of the forty-four-year-old King Harold's death late that afternoon—shot in the eye with an arrow. His two brothers were killed, too, as well as his corps of loyal retainers, who died to a man, while the surviving members of the local militia fled under cover of nightfall.

William headed for London, destroying a few villages in the vicin-ity to show he meant business. Fairly soon, the leaders of England sub-mitted, and London invited him to be crowned king on Christmas Day in Westminster Abbey, which had been consecrated by King Edward only a year earlier. A small band of hardened warriors had seized a country of a million and a half people.

Though he kept the country's efficient judicial system and com-mon law intact, William the Conqueror replaced the entire English ruling class—nobles, as well as bishops and abbots—with his own Nor-mans in a system of feudal fiefdoms based on knightly obligations to fight for the king. He savagely repressed rebellions, especially one abetted by an invading Danish fleet in 1069. In his subsequent "harry-ing of the North," he and his horsemen massacred everyone they could find between York and Durham. Throughout the nation rose grim castles, of timber at first, later of stone. William's famed Tower of Lon-don overtopped the city walls, reminding independent-minded Lon-doners of who was in charge.

An entirely typical feature of William's reign was the Latin *Domes-day Book* (pronounced as if *Doomsday*, which is apparently what the landowners associated with the arrival of the king's agents). Compiled in 1086, it was a vast census and survey of English landed property for the purposes of royal taxation and settlement of land disputes. William died the following year at age fifty-nine from injuries while assaulting the French town of Mantes and was succeeded by his son, the ram-bunctious William Rufus.

The linguistic effects of the Norman conquest were profound and far-reaching. Anglo-Saxon became for several centuries the language of peasants and slaves, while Latin and Norman French were the languages of the church and the new aristocracy, respectively. Over the next 350 years, ten thousand French words came flooding into England, many dealing with the pursuits and perquisites of the upper classes: military words such as *war, peace, battle, victory, defeat, army, general, sergeant, corporal*; words relating to government, such as *parliament, crown, palace, nation, prince, duke, count, baron, tower, dungeon, prison, justice, jury, verdict, innocent, plaintiff*; words dealing with art, such as *poet, literature, verse, comedy, tragedy, artist, color*; words about cooking, such as *beef, sausage, pork, mutton, venison, poultry*; and many others dealing with religion, fashion, and hunting.

Almost two centuries had elapsed since the conquest when Henry III first used English as well as French in a proclamation of 1258, but by 1300 English was emerging as the language of the ruling classes again. The simple Germanic vocabulary of English, teeming with monosyllables, had been immeasurably enriched by "refined" French terms, producing a language abounding in synonyms and capable of expressing the subtlest shades of meaning.

After the conquest, England lost its place in the Scandinavian orbit of nations and was realigned with the Continent, especially with France. Along with a strong infusion of martial valor, it received from the Normans more than a smidgen of their higher French civilization, though this latter quality should not be overstated. The Christian Normans were not far removed from the ruthlessness of their Viking forebears. The Conqueror's forest laws against poaching were ferocious—and consider the "enlightened" curtailment of the trade in slaves (who represented 9 percent of the population) and the abolition of capital punishment in two of William's statutes:

> I forbid any one to sell a man beyond the limits of the country. . . .

> I forbid that any one be killed or hanged for any fault, but his eyes shall be torn out or his testicles cut off.

And the close relations now established between the ruling families of England and France, as complicated by future princely inter-marriages, would set the stage for the Hundred Years' War, which dragged on intermittently between the two countries from 1337 to 1453.

79 ∽ Which was the first university?

The University of Bologna, traditionally dating from 1088

ALTHOUGH THERE WERE many university-type towns in the ancient world—Athens, Alexandria, Rome, Antioch, Beirut, Constantinople—in which students pursued higher education in law, rhetoric, or philosophy, they were not the sites of organized institutions with established curricula, faculties, colleges, regular examinations, and a hierarchy of degrees. Neither was this true of various schools of higher learning in the Muslim world, such as those established at Cairo and Córdoba in the tenth century.

What we associate with a full university—Salerno remained solely a medical school (see Question 74)—first developed in the city of Bologna, a mercantile center on a main road leading from Florence to northern Italy. At Bologna, the rising merchant class supported the establishment of a center of learning specializing in the intricacies of the law.

The role of the first European universities was to provide advanced training in law, medicine, or theology to men who had studied in the cathedral or monastery schools, which were geared toward producing churchmen. The medieval Latin word *universitas* originally denoted a corporation or guild of any type and was later narrowed in meaning to refer to an association of professors and students.

At Bologna, the professors' guilds were called *collegia* and were mainly concerned with controlling admission to the ranks of those licensed to teach—the *magistri* and *doctores*. The "universities" were at first the guilds of the students, who formed into four or more groups by broad ethnic origin, though at one point there were only two: for students from "this side of the Alps" and those from "beyond the Alps."

These organizations were important because, as foreigners to the city, the students had no legal rights. All they could do was band together and threaten to leave the city if the locals charged them too much for food, rent, and books. Since many of the students were already practicing lawyers in their twenties and thirties, they also managed to control the teachers at Bologna—no skipping chapters in the textbook, no extra vacation days, no tardiness or late dismissals from class—by threatening to boycott their lectures, at a time when students paid their professors directly. In addition, they assigned student committees to evaluate the teachers.

Though earlier centers of legal studies existed in several Italian cities, none grew into a university until much later, whereas by 1119 the law school in Bologna was already referred to as "the Learned." Its excellent medical faculty, which is still producing physicians, arose c. 1150, but one mustn't think of an early European university in terms of a campus with austerely impressive buildings, since, for many more centuries, professors would teach in their own homes or rent a hall in a large building such as a convent.

The University of Bologna eventually developed a school of theology and a faculty of the arts in which the traditional seven liberal arts were taught: the trivium, consisting of grammar (mainly classical Latin literature), rhetoric, and logic, leading to the quadrivium of arithmetic, geometry, astronomy (mainly astrology), and music. Students pursued the liberal arts for five or six years before taking oral examinations and receiving a master's degree, which prepared them for teaching the arts or for moving on to advanced study in a professional field leading to a doctorate in law, medicine, or theology.

But it was as a school of jurisprudence that Bologna became "*alma mater studiorum*" ("fostering mother of studies") and earned worldwide fame. There the study of law first became distinct from the rhetorical analysis of legal texts and the drawing up of legal documents. What allowed Bologna's astounding success in this field was the recent rediscovery of the complete text of Justinian's *Corpus Iuris Civilis*, the massive sixth-century compilation of ancient Roman law (see Question 42). A sign of Europe's awakening from its long cultural slumber during the Dark Ages was the eagerness with which it made this body of Roman law the basic text for legal studies in the following centuries, as opposed to the earlier Germanic law codes, such as those of the Visigoths and Lombards.

In 1076, a man named Pepo, "bright and shining light of Bologna," became the first eminent legal scholar to teach there. He was followed by Irnerius, "the Lamp of the Law," who began lecturing on the law in 1088, the traditional date for the founding of the university. He was the first of the great Bolognese legal glossators, who resuscitated Roman law in depth and detail by carefully glossing the meanings of difficult or technical words in the margins of the *Corpus Iuris*, explaining knotty passages, and interpreting them in light of the entire body of Roman statutes and legal doctrines. Students flocked to Irnerius's lectures, since he first taught the *Corpus Iuris* as a whole and not just in extracts or epitomes.

Gratian, a student of Irnerius and professor at Bologna, compiled the *Decretum*, a collection of canonical (ecclesiastical) law. Consisting of thiry-eight hundred decrees of popes and church councils with Gratian's commentary, it first appeared in c. 1140 and within a decade began attracting commentaries of its own.

The so-called Four Doctors succeeded Irnerius as glossators at Bologna: Bulgarus, Martinus Gosia, Hugo de Porta of Ravenna, and Jacobus de Voragine. All of them doubled as advisers to Holy Roman Emperor Frederick Barbarossa, who was pleased to offer a charter of rights and privileges to Bologna's students in 1158, since there they learned to cite Roman imperial law as a prop to his lifelong struggles against the northern Italian communes and the church.

By about 1250, the Florentine scholar Accursius (Francesco Accorso), the outstanding legal mind of his century, had compiled the vast *Glossa ordinaria*, which summarized the entire tradition of the Bolognese glossators and remained an authoritative legal text for centuries. His son Francesco also became a renowned legal scholar at Bologna (though Dante placed him in his *Inferno* for being a sodomite), and Accursius's daughter may have been one of the first women to teach there, at a time when Bologna may have had about six thousand students. From Italy, Roman law spread throughout much of the Continent from the twelfth to the sixteenth centuries.

Other universities soon followed Bologna's lead. Montpellier was an early center of medicine and later of law, when Placentinus arrived there from Bologna sometime after 1160. The nucleus of the University of Paris, founded c. 1150–70, was the cathedral school of Notre Dame. Paris soon became the premier university of Europe in theology and philosophy, with distinguished teachers such as Albert the Great, Thomas Aquinas, and Roger Bacon.

Oxford University was founded as a spin-off from Paris in c. 1167, though historian Charles Homer Haskins claimed, "As compared with Paris and Bologna, Oxford in 1200 was only an inchoate university." Nonetheless, it wasn't inchoate enough to avoid a town-and-gown riot in 1209, when a student supposedly killed a woman, and the town-ies hanged several students in retaliation. This trouble caused several thousand students to leave Oxford, some of whom migrated to Cambridge, where another famed university soon arose.

Bologna's educational innovation was here to stay, as universities continued to proliferate by scission and imitation. By the end of the Middle Ages, there were at least eighty of them in Europe. This is a paltry number compared with the four thousand colleges and universities of the United States—though it's doubtful many of these would remain open long if, as in medieval universities, all lectures and textbooks were in Latin, and the students were allowed to speak and write only in that universal language of learning.

80 ∽ Who were the first Assassins?

Members of a Muslim sect that included political killers,
organized in 1090

MARCO POLO, who supposedly journeyed by the forlorn Persian headquarters of the Assassins, has left a jumbled account of its founding leader, a diabolically mysterious figure he calls "the Sheikh of the Mountain." It appears that, in a hidden valley there, the sheikh had planted a garden of earthly delights, complete with "fair ladies and damsels." All the young recruits to his cause would be drugged unconscious with liquid hashish and left to awaken in the garden, where they soon believed themselves to be in paradise itself. After an interval, they were drugged again and made to awaken in the sheikh's castle, but their thoughts remained hell-bent (so to speak) on paradise alone. Henceforth, they would fanatically embrace any suicide mission—which always involved murdering the sect's foes—since those who died fighting for the faith would be assured of going directly to paradise again.

Other versions of the story, mostly brought to Europe by returning crusaders, tell of how the hashish was used by the killers to give themselves courage before going out on missions—or supplied to them as a reward for a mission accomplished. A variant told how the pleasure induced by hashish was supposed to prefigure the joys of paradise, thus spurring on the young men to risk their lives.

The group these tales refer to—the Assassins (from the Arabic *hashishin*, "users of hashish")—was originally a Muslim religious sect founded in 1090 in Persia and soon spreading to Iraq and Syria. The Assassins terrorized the authorities in that part of the world for almost two centuries, murdering whichever political, religious, and military enemies their grand masters sent them against.

But first a little backstory. By the mid-eleventh century, the main split in the Muslim world was between the Abbasid caliphs in Baghdad and the rival Fatimid caliphs in Cairo, who controlled Egypt, North Africa, Palestine, and Syria. In 1055, Togrul Beg, founder of the Seljuk Turkish Empire (c. 1080–1243), seized Baghdad and set himself up as sultan, while leaving the caliph in place as a figurehead. Besides Iraq, Togrul Beg's empire included Persia and parts of eastern Turkey and Central Asia.

The next sultan, Togrul's nephew Alp Arslan ("Valiant Lion"), routed the Byzantine army at the battle of Manzikert in eastern Turkey in 1071. Under his son, Malik Shah (1072–92), the rest of Asia Minor (which we might as well start calling Turkey at this point) was conquered from the Byzantines, and Syria and Palestine were wrenched from the Fatimids. It was during the last few years of this reign that the Assassins came into being, since they adhered to the Muslim Shiite sect of Ismailis, whereas the newly dominant Seljuk Turks were Sunni Muslims.

The founder of the Assassins was Hasan-i Sabbah, a Persian leader of the Ismaili sect. Hasan was supposedly a schoolmate of the poet-astronomer Omar Khayyám (whose *Rubaiyat* became part of the English literary canon through Edward FitzGerald's nineteenth-century translation), as well as of his future victim Nizam al-Mulk, but this is almost certainly a legend. After a peripatetic early life, Hasan and a few followers seized the mountain fortress of Alamut ("Eagle's Nest") in northwest Persia in 1090. There he trained young men to follow his commands unhesitatingly, especially when it came to murdering the Seljuk Turkish oppressors and persecutors of the Ismailis.

Hasan's putative schoolmate Nizam al-Mulk became the brilliant and industrious vizier (prime minister) of Turkish sultan Malik Shah. In about 1090, Nizam wrote in Persian *The Book of Government*, a guide for rulers in which he excoriated the Ismailis as threatening the unity of the Muslim state. Two years later, an Assassin approached him in the guise of a suppliant and stabbed him to death.

As a Shiite, Hasan initially supported the Shiite Fatimid caliphate in Cairo, but when the caliph al-Mustansir died in 1094, he and many other Persians cast their lot with Nizar, the deposed elder brother of the new caliph. This schism between the Nizaris and the Fatimids prompted the Assassins to add the latter to their hit list. After Nizar and his son were killed in an Egyptian prison, an infant grandson was supposedly sneaked away to Persia to be raised by Hasan.

Did Hasan-i Sabbah drug his followers? The founder of the Assassins was an ascetic, writing in a memoir, "I saw that the Nizari group was God-fearing, pious, abstinent, and anxious about drink; and I dreaded drink." A man that concerned about violating a religious prohibition against alcohol—and who executed one of his sons for drunkenness—would probably not push intoxicants on his followers. Hashish would also not be the drug of choice to give someone before sending him out on a difficult mission, so its connection with the sect may well be a myth.

Nizari Ismailis were referred to as "hashish users" by other Muslims, it seems, to associate them with disreputable practices, much as the pillars of society in the 1960s referred to hippies as "drug-crazed junkies"—not that the Assassins were love, peace, and happiness types. Nonetheless, the moniker stuck. Dante used the word *assassin* to mean a hired killer in his *Inferno* in the early fourteenth century, and the first English usage can be traced back to 1603.

After the establishment of Assassin headquarters at the Alamut castle, numerous strongholds sprang up in Persia and Iraq, from which disguised killers would emerge to bring down their quarry in public places, such as mosques, with as little collateral damage as possible. The Assassin sect comprised secret agents, infiltrators, spies, propagandists, and lay brothers, as well as the famed killers of generals, statesmen, and even two caliphs.

The movement flourished in Syria in the early twelfth century, when their grand master was called the *Sheikh al-Jabal*—"Mountain Chief"—a title the crusaders brought home with them as "Old Man of the Mountain." Christian victims of the Assassins included Raymond II of Tripoli in 1152, a patriarch of Jerusalem, and, perhaps at the bidding of Richard the Lionheart, Conrad of Montferrat, king of Jerusalem, in 1192. But even the greatest Muslim warrior of the twelfth century, the chivalrous Saladin, sultan of Egypt and Syria, had two close encounters of the wrong kind with Assassins in 1176 and came to terms with them, probably using the "enemy-of-my-enemy-is-my-friend" argument.

At Alamut, Hasan-i Sabbah died in 1124 after thirty-four years of rule and was succeeded by seven other grand masters. One of them, Hasan II (1162–66), proclaimed himself the son of Nizari's grandson, who had been brought as an infant from Egypt, and was duly murdered. The last was Khwurshah, who, expecting clemency, surrendered Alamut to the Mongols under Hülegü in 1256 and was soon hanged. As late as 1271, Prince Edward of England, later King Edward I, was wounded with a poisoned Assassin dagger, but within two years the Syrian Assassins were destroyed by Baybars I, the mighty Mamluk sultan of Egypt and Syria.

The Assassins are long gone, though Nizari Ismaili Muslims live on as a religious group. Their leader in 2009 was the billionaire Aga Khan IV, whom they consider their forty-ninth imam in succession to Ali, son-in-law of Muhammad (see Questions 49 and 50).

81 ⌘ What was the first chanson de geste?

La Chanson de Roland (The Song of Roland), *c. 1095–99*

THE EARLIEST OF ALMOST A HUNDRED surviving French chansons de geste (medieval epic or heroic tales), *The Song of Roland* is also reputed to be the best. This patriotic Old French epic of slightly more than four thousand lines, divided into stanzas of varying length whose verses are linked by assonance rather than rhyme, pits the treachery of Roland's stepfather, Ganelon, against the chivalric and feudal values of fighting for God, religion, country, king, and fellow aristocrats.

The Song of Roland has a historical core. The greatest king of the Franks, Charlemagne (age thirty-six at the time and not, as in the poem, "two hundred years and more"), responded to the plea of three Muslim princes of Spain, including the governor of Saragossa, to check the expanding power of Emir Abd al-Rahman, who had subjugated two-thirds of the Iberian Peninsula (see Questions 57 and 61). But when Charlemagne arrived with an army of twenty-five thousand, the Muslim conspirators decided he was too dangerous to let into Saragossa. When Charlemagne tried to quarter his army among the Christian Basques of Pamplona, they told him what he could do instead, so he destroyed their city.

As the Frankish army headed back to France, the incensed Basques set an ambush at the wooded top of the mountain pass of Roncesvalles (or Roncevaux) in the Pyrenees. On August 15, 778, they managed to slaughter the rear guard of the army, including a leader named Roland—Hruodlandus, to give him his Latinized Germanic name—who was "lord of the Breton Marches" (Brittany). Writing three centuries later, the anonymous French poet of the chanson substituted the Muslim overlords of Spain for the Christian Basques in the role of sneaky enemy of the French Christians, but as literary scholar Erich Auerbach reminds us, "For audiences of the eleventh, twelfth, and thirteenth centuries the heroic epic was history."

In the poem, Roland is imagined as Charlemagne's young nephew and the mightiest warrior of the Christians, who have been waging what amounts to a religious war against Muslim Spain for seven years, capturing all of it but Saragossa, held by King Marsilius. The Muslims are presented as heathenish idolaters—and invariably treacherous—so that when Marsilius offers peace and promises to journey to France in a month's time to convert to Christianity, Roland's advice is to fight on, whereas Ganelon moves to accept the king's offer.

We find out later that Roland and his stepfather, Ganelon, hate each other because of property conflicts, but at this point we see their animosity in action. After Roland volunteers for a highly risky assignment and is turned down by Charlemagne, who dotes on him—did Roland know he would be refused?—he proceeds to nominate his stepfather for it. The job is that of serving as envoy to King Marsilius, who has beheaded the last pair of ambassadors from the French. As if to say, "You want peace with this man? Go get it yourself," Roland laughs in Ganelon's face when his furious stepfather swears vengeance if he ever makes it back.

Indeed, events reveal that Ganelon would have been slain by Marsilius if he hadn't offered to betray his own people—not that he needed an extra incentive. Ganelon's plan is to arrange for Roland; his closest friend, Oliver; the warrior-archbishop Turpin; and the rest of the Twelve Peers (or paladins)—the war hawks of the Frankish army—to be appointed to the rear guard, where they can be surprised and killed by Marsilius's troops. To get the main body of the army setting out for France, Ganelon advises Marsilius to send the French king treasure, hostages, and false promises of ruling Spain as a vassal of Charlemagne and of coming to France to convert. Once Roland is dead and gone, Ganelon is sure Charlemagne will lack the will to turn back and renew the fight.

After Ganelon returns with the treasure and false assurances from Marsilius, he promptly nominates Roland for the leadership of the rear guard, the most dangerous post in the army on its march back to France. Now it's Roland's turn to rant and rage, but even the weeping Charlemagne is unable to veto an assignment that seems eminently reasonable to the rest.

When Marsilius and his hundred thousand followers swoop down on the twenty thousand men of the rear guard—now that Charlemagne and the main body of the French army are a hundred miles ahead—you can be sure that Roland, Oliver, Archbishop Turpin, and the rest of the Twelve Peers perform wondrous—nay, miraculous—feats of arms on horseback, but the sheer numbers of the enemy begin attritting their forces.

Now, besides his sword Durendal, Roland's prize possession is a marvelous ivory horn called the Olifant, carved from an elephant's tusk and adorned with gold and jewels. Three times Oliver begs him to sound a blast on the horn to summon Charlemagne, but Roland scorns to call for help: "Now God forbid that man alive could say / I ever sounded my horn for these pagans!" Like Shakespeare's Prince Hal, he wants only "we happy few" to share the glory of a victory against such overwhelming odds, but, unlike Hal, he miscalculates.

When only sixty of his men are left alive, Roland wants to sound his horn. Three times he asks Oliver if he should, but his friend counters each time that it would be shameful to resort to the horn now that all is lost, and the only result would be Charlemagne's witnessing of the needless carnage caused by Roland's folly.

At the bidding of Archbishop Turpin, however, who wants revenge and decent burial for the men, Roland finally blows the horn three times—one blast so mighty that it bursts the veins in his temples. Soon only he, the archbishop, and a warrior named Walter de Hum remain—and the Muslims still have forty thousand horsemen—but the trio fight on so valiantly that the enemy flees after killing Walter, as well as Roland's and Turpin's horses from beneath them.

Though Roland and the indomitable archbishop are left in possession of the field—technically, they "won"—the latter soon dies of his grievous wounds, and Roland collapses in a swoon. A bit of unintentional comedy occurs when a Muslim warrior, thinking Roland is dead—after all, his brains are running out his ears—tries to steal his sword. Reviving, Roland brings his Olifant crashing down on the hapless man's skull, knocking the eyes out of his head and smashing the mouth of the famed horn in the process.

When death is imminent, he holds out to God his right glove—which the angel Gabriel comes down to accept and, with two other angels, he bears Roland's soul directly to heaven. Ezra Pound saw fit to smirk at the stagy death scene of the hero, who expires with hands folded in prayer: "Perfect chivalric pose, perfect piety!" For all his martial prowess and love of "sweet France," Roland's dunderheaded self-conceit has destroyed the Peers, the twenty thousand men entrusted to him, and his own life.

Understanding everything now that the horn has sounded, Charlemagne orders Ganelon arrested and hastens back into Spain, destroys the remainder of the army that slaughtered Roland's men, and, with the help of the busy angel Gabriel, splits open the skull of Emir Baligant, who has futilely come to the aid of his coreligionists with an enormous host drawn from all quarters of the Muslim world. The French king buries the dead of Roncesvalles, converts or kills all one hundred thousand inhabitants of Saragossa, and makes sure the widowed queen of Marsilius (who dies of wounds earlier dealt him by Roland) is conveyed to France to accept Christianity "willingly." The simplistic philosophy of the poem may be summed up in the line, "*Paien unt tort e chrestiens unt dreit*" ("Pagans are wrong, and Christians are right").

As for Ganelon, he is quartered—a horse is tied to each limb and whipped until the foul traitor is torn apart—and the thirty family members who agreed to be sureties for him are hanged. At the end of the poem, the angel Gabriel informs the cosmically weary Charlemagne that he must now carry the religious war into Syria—a premonition of the Crusades that would soon engulf the Middle East.

Roland went on to have a long shelf life as a romantic hero in the person of Orlando, the protagonist of the Italian Renaissance epics *Orlando Innamorato* (*Roland in Love*, 1495) by Matteo Maria Boiardo and *Orlando Furioso* (*Roland Crazed by Love*, 1516–32) by Ludovico Ariosto. In *The Song of Roland*, the hero is too busy slaughtering the enemy to have a love life, though we are told that his fiancée, Aude, falls into a lethal swoon when Charlemagne breaks the news to her that Roland will not be coming home.

82 ∽ What was the First Crusade?

*A war in which Europeans captured Jerusalem and other
Middle Eastern territories, 1096–99*

"DEUS VULT"—God wills it. With this acclamation, roared by the bishops assembled to hear Pope Urban II speak at the Council of Clermont in November 1095, the First Crusade was launched. Word spread quickly through Western Europe that the pope had called on the faithful to rally to the defense of Christians in the East. Over the next year, tens of thousands of Franks (as Western Europeans were collectively called) knelt to take up the cross. By the time the First Crusade reached its improbable climax less than four years later, it had not only liberated Jerusalem from Muslim rule but also carved out an entirely new Latin dominion in the Holy Land—*Outremer*, or "Land Beyond the Sea"— that would endure for nearly two centuries.

Plans for a crusade to liberate Jerusalem had been percolating at the papal court for at least a decade. The rise of the Seljuk Turks, recent converts to Islam who had arrived in the Near East from Central Asia a half century before, had thrown the region into turmoil. The Seljuks had disrupted the pilgrim traffic to Jerusalem, which had been tolerated by the Holy Land's previous Arab rulers—and lurid tales of massacres began to circulate in the West. In 1071, at the battle of Manzikert, the Seljuks had also inflicted a crushing defeat on the Byzantine Empire, which had remained on the defensive ever since.

When envoys from Emperor Alexius I Comnenus arrived in Italy in March 1095 to seek the pope's help in securing Western military aid, Urban II was quick to seize the opportunity. An alliance with the Byzantines would not only improve the chances of the crusade's success but would also give the papacy leverage in its bid to reunify the Roman and Greek Churches, which had split in the Great Schism of 1054.

Modern historians have variously characterized the First Crusade as a cynical papal power play, a war of feudal conquest, and an early example of European colonialism. The First Crusade was all of these things. But it was first and foremost a holy war—Christendom's answer to Islam's jihad.

Between the seventh and the tenth centuries, roughly two-thirds of the Christian world had been conquered by the armies of Islam, from Syria in the East to Spain in the West (see Question 51). But starting in the early eleventh century, a newly confident Western Christendom, which had emerged from the Dark Ages and was experiencing a period of remarkable demographic and economic growth, began to push back. By the time of the First Crusade, the Genoese, Pisans, and Venetians had wrested control of the Mediterranean sea-lanes from the Muslims; the Normans had driven them from southern Italy and Sicily; and the tiny Christian kingdoms of León, Castile, and Aragon, led by the great warrior prince El Cid, had begun the *Reconquista* of Spain (see Question 89).

Along the way, the counteroffensive acquired the character of a holy war. Although they are not numbered in the history books, many of these earlier expeditions were, in fact, crusades, encouraged and blessed by the church, which was only too happy to channel the restless energy of the Frankish nobility into a greater cause than fratricidal violence. By the late eleventh century, the crusading ideal had permeated Western Europe's popular culture and captured the imagination of its warrior caste. The perfect knight was no longer just a loyal vassal but also a defender of Christendom. It is no coincidence that the first and greatest of the medieval chansons de geste, *The Song of Roland*, whose eponymous hero fell battling the infidel at the mountain pass of Roncesvalles, was written at about the time the First Crusade was launched (see Question 81).

None of this means that the participants in the First Crusade were indifferent to worldly power. Ambition and greed steered its course from start to finish. Yet, to an extent difficult to imagine in today's secular West, the participants were also motivated by religious zeal. For most of the rank-and-file knights who joined the expedition—among them the anonymous author of the *Gesta Francorum (Deeds of the Franks)*, our most important eyewitness account—the crusade was a pilgrimage, and the only goal that mattered was the liberation of Jerusalem, the earthly manifestation of the heavenly city. While the opportunity to plunder was a welcome bonus, the crusaders' ultimate reward was in heaven, of whose attainment they were assured by a plenary indulgence, a kind of "get-out-of-hell-free card" that the pope granted to all who took up the cross.

The crusaders departed for the East in several waves—the first being the so-called People's Crusade, which was assembled without papal approval. An ill-equipped and untrained rabble comprising the flotsam and jetsam of feudal society, it was led by a charismatic French monk known as Peter the Hermit. Its progress through Europe was punctuated by occasional atrocities, including the massacre of Jews in the Rhineland in what was Europe's first large-scale pogrom. When Peter and his followers finally arrived at Constantinople, the staging ground for the crusade, the Byzantines were horrified. According to Anna Comnena, the emperor's daughter and author of the *Alexiad*, a highly erudite history of her father's reign, it was as if "all of the barbarians who lived between the Adriatic and the Straits of Gibraltar had migrated in a body to Asia." Alexius had them ferried across the Bosporus in August 1096, whereupon they were promptly slaughtered by the Turks—with only a handful (among them the resourceful Peter) escaping to tell the tale.

When the regular crusading forces reached Constantinople the following winter and spring, the Byzantines were once again in for a surprise. Alexius had wanted bands of mercenaries that could be enlisted under the command of his own generals. What he got were four large armies, each loyal to its own leaders. Among these were some of Western Europe's most redoubtable feudal lords: Robert, the count of Flanders; Godfrey of Bouillon, the duke of Lorraine, together with his brother, Baldwin of Boulogne; Raymond of Saint-Gilles, the count of Toulouse; and Bohemond, the prince of Taranto. The arrival of Bohemond was particularly alarming, for he was the son of the great Norman adventurer Robert Guiscard, the scourge of Byzantium, who had chased not only the Muslims but also the Byzantine Greeks from southern Italy.

Amid mutual suspicions, a deal was struck. The Byzantines agreed to lend the crusade military and logistical support, and in return the Franks swore oaths that any territories they conquered that had once belonged to the empire would be returned to it. Amazingly, the deal held for a while. The crusade's first objective—Nicaea, a strategically important Anatolian city—fell to a coordinated Greek and Frankish assault in May 1097 and was dutifully handed over to the imperial authorities. But as the host marched southward, the conquests became more arduous, the stakes grew larger, and dissensions erupted—not just between the Franks and the Byzantines, but among the Franks themselves. By the time the crusaders reached Antioch, the gateway to Syria and Palestine, the deal had collapsed amid mutual accusations of perfidy. The crusaders received little in the way of additional support from Alexius—and the pope never got his reunification.

From this point on, the Franks acted as free agents. Baldwin of Boulogne struck out on his own to conquer Edessa, which became the first of several crusader states. The rest of the host invested Antioch, which fell in June 1098 after an epic eight-month siege that became a favorite subject of later chansons de geste. Although the road to Jerusalem now lay open before them, the crusaders' departure was delayed for another six months as Bohemond and Raymond of Saint-Gilles vied for possession of the captured city. In the end, Bohemond prevailed, adding "Prince of Antioch" to his titles.

When the crusaders at last arrived before Jerusalem, they fasted and marched barefoot in solemn procession around its walls before busying themselves with building siege engines. The final act came on July 15, 1099. All sources agree that there was much weeping and rejoicing among the Franks when the city was captured—as well as a great slaughter of Muslims and Jews. As soon as some semblance of order was restored, the crusaders made their way to the Holy Sepulchre, where, the author of the *Gesta Francorum* tells us, they worshiped in fulfillment of their vows. Once again there was a quarrel over possession of the prize, and as an interim measure Godfrey of Bouillon took the unassuming title of "Defender of the Holy Sepulchre." When Godfrey died a year later, his brother Baldwin succeeded in crowning himself king of Jerusalem.

In time, the Franks learned to coexist with the much more numerous Muslim population they ruled; some even went native, learning Arabic and adopting local customs. Yet the existence of the crusader states always remained precarious. They were continuously threatened by the Seljuks, who remained ensconced in Damascus, just a short march to the north, as well as by the Fatimids, who controlled Cairo to the south. Their survival hinged on the support of the Italian maritime republics, whose navies had helped consolidate the conquest of Outremer and continued to provide a vital lifeline to the West. It also came to depend on the fabulous wealth and military prowess of the Hospitallers, Templars, and Teutonic Knights, autonomous crusading orders that were founded to defend the Holy Land.

But in the end this wasn't enough. Despite eight other major crusades mounted to relieve beleaguered Outremer during the twelfth and thirteenth centuries, the crusader states succumbed, one by one. Edessa, the first to be founded, was also the first to fall in 1144. Jerusalem was reclaimed by the Muslims in 1187 and Antioch in 1268. A few port cities held out longer—Tripoli until 1289 and Acre, the last crusader toehold on the Asian mainland, until 1291. Some of the crusading orders went on to find new missions. The Hospitallers fought a centuries-long rearguard action against the Ottoman Turks, the Seljuks' successors, retreating first to the island fastness of Rhodes, then to Malta, where they ruled until Napoleon ousted them in 1798. The Teutonic Knights returned to the West, where they became shock troops in the campaign to Christianize the pagan fringes of Northern and Eastern Europe. But Outremer had vanished forever.

Textbooks often describe the First Crusade as a great turning point in the history of the West. In reality, it was merely an exceptionally dramatic episode in the long seesaw struggle between Christendom and Islam that stretched from the battle of Tours (see Question 57) to the battle of Lepanto and beyond. The First Crusade did not, as historians once thought, jolt Western Europe out of the Dark Ages by bringing it into contact with the Muslim world's more advanced civilization. In fact, the causality was just the reverse: It was the revival of Western Europe during the eleventh century that made the First Crusade possible. The crusade's conquests, moreover, were ephemeral. Medieval Christendom's counteroffensive turned the tide of history in Italy and Spain, but not in the Holy Land. All that remains of Outremer are the imposing ruins of the crusaders' fortresses—preeminent among them the mighty Krak des Chevaliers in Syria, the stronghold of the Hospitallers and perhaps the most magnificent structure of its kind in the world.

—*Richard Jackson*

TWELFTH CENTURY

83 ✒ Who is considered the first troubadour?

Guillaume IX of Aquitaine, 1071–1127, whose eleven surviving
poems are mostly bawdy

NO LESS AN AUTHORITY on everything than Friedrich Nietzsche asserted that "love *as passion*" was a creation of "the Provençal knight-poets, those magnificent and inventive men . . . to whom Europe owes so much and, indeed, almost itself." In another context he included Provence with four other places—Paris, Florence, Jerusalem, and Athens—"where genius found its home."

Though troubadours soon sprang up in northern Spain (from where Arabic influences helped shape Provençal verse and song) and northern Italy, the majority hailed from Provence—or, rather, the south of France in general. Flourishing from the late eleventh to the late thirteenth century, they were the first to create a large body of lyric poetry in a European vernacular, the Romance language variously referred to as Provençal, Occitan, or langue d'oc.

Their collective name of *troubadour* derives from the Provençal verb *trobar* ("to find, invent, or compose"). These poets, often of aristocratic birth, composed lyrics that would be set to music, sometimes by themselves, but often by professional musicians. The poems were sung to musical accompaniment by *joglars*, a word related to our word *jugglers*, since the joglars sometimes entertained audiences at the castles of lords and knights by less sophisticated means, including working with performing animals.

We have more than 2,500 poems in Provençal from the hands of more than four hundred troubadours (including a score of women *trobairitz*), and about three hundred of their original monophonic melodies survive. Three common types of Provençal lyric (all of whose names are accented on the last syllable) were the *canso* (a love song of five or six stanzas with a short envoi), the *sirventes* (a satiric or political poem), and the *tenso* (a poetic "duel" between two poets). Others were the *balada* (a dance song), the *pastorela* (a seduction poem featuring a knight and a shepherdess), the *alba* (a song of lovers parting at dawn), and the *planh* (a lament for a dead lord or better times).

The poet we call by his French name, Guillaume (William), was in his own language Guilhem, the seventh count of Poitiers and the ninth duke of Aquitaine and of Gascony, lord of almost all southwestern France. Grandfather of Eleanor of Aquitaine, successively queen of France and of England, he became through her the great-grandfather of another aristocratic poet, Richard the Lionheart. The earliest known troubadour whose songs have survived, Guillaume was also thus the first European lyric poet in a postclassical language. In his capacity as warrior, though, he was a bit deficient, leading a belated and disastrous crusade in 1101–2, during which his second wife, Philippa, ruled Aquitaine in his stead.

Hardly a staid and reserved nobleman, Guillaume was what Ralph Kramden would have called "a regular riot." In one of his lost songs, he joked about opening up a mock nunnery at Niort, where the women would be trained in debauchery. His fights with the church got him excommunicated twice. On the first occasion, he chose merely to exile the excommunicating bishop, since to have run him through with his sword would have done him the favor of sending his soul to heaven. In the second case, he scoffed at a papal legate who solemnly adjured him to put aside a married noblewoman he had installed in his castle at Poitiers. "A comb will curl your hair," he shouted at the bald cleric, "before I give up my mistress"—and he proceeded to marry his son and heir to the woman's daughter, while his humiliated wife retired to an abbey. Guillaume's *vida* (a brief, anonymous thirteenth-century bio) claims that "for a long time he wandered about the world seducing women"—though "the world" is an exaggeration.

Of the poems written by Guillaume, the eleven that have come down to us are often humorous and sometimes coarsely obscene. Most seem to have been thrown together for the snickering delight of his drinking buddies rather than for performance at entertainments with highfalutin ladies present at his splendid court at Bordeaux. In these poems, women are seen as straightforward sex objects, as in "*Companho, faray un vers tot covinen*" ("My friends, I'll write a poem for the occasion"), in which we learn that

> *I have two noble horses for my saddle.*
> *They're excellent in battle, full of mettle.*
> *But I can't keep them both—they hate each other.*

He greatly regrets this, especially since his "mounts" are actually named N'Agnes and N'Arsen (*N'* standing for *Na*—"Lady"), and he asks his companions which of these ladies he should keep. In the last stanza, he boasts that the castles that the ladies and their husbands live in belong to him, since the men are his vassals. This puts a different spin on why his two "mares" may be so compliant toward Guillaume.

In "*Companho, tant ai agutz d'avols conres*" ("My friends, I've had my fill of sloppy seconds")—a complaint against men who keep a tight rein on their wives—Guillaume spouts his signature line: "*Pero dirai vos de con cals es sa leis*" ("But I'll tell you guys about cunt— what its law is"). This "law" turns out to be that, just as when woods are judiciously pruned of a tree now and then, two or three spring up in its place, so, though other things "decrease when taken from, cunt grows and thrives." The moral is much like that of Chaucer's Wife of Bath, who compares her lubricious private parts to a blazing lantern: There's plenty to go around for all, no matter how many others light their candles at her "*queynte,*" so why should her doddering old husband complain? In another poem with the same theme, Guillaume warns a woman's strict guardians that, if she can't have any "strong wine," she'll find a way to drink water—that is, she'll just have sex with servants around the house rather than with fine fellows like himself.

Guillaume tells a stirring tale of fortitude under pressure in "*Farai un vers, pos mi somelh*" ("I will make a poem while I'm dozing"). Walking along in Auvergne, he meets N'Agnes and N'Ermessen, the wives of two noblemen, who stop to ask who he is. Slyly, he stammers back like a mute: "*babariol, babariol, babarian.*" Happy at finding a man who could never tattle on them, the women take Guillaume home, set him in front of a roaring fire, feed him several capons with excellent wine to wash them down, and have him strip naked—but also decide to run a test before doing anything rash. Suddenly producing a big scary "*gat ros*" (red cat) with massive whiskers, they yank its tail to make it attack our poet, who suffers the agony of more than a hundred scratches in silence but proves beyond a reasonable doubt that he's incapable of speech. In a fitting conclusion to this locker-room bullshit story, Guillaume informs us that he stayed with the ladies for eight days:

> Listen up now to how many times I screwed them:
> exactly one hundred and eighty-eight times,
> so that I almost broke my breeching strap
> and my harness, too.
> And I can't even begin to tell you
> how bad it hurt . . .

Another poem opens with Guillaume's boasts of his mastery in matters of love—he's the top dog, alpha male, macho stud—and everybody knows it. The little ladies never spend a night with him without begging him to stay the next day, too. In fact, he could set up shop and make a living with this skill of his. Nonetheless, he confesses to a recent isolated episode in which he lost his nerve, and the lady complained that, "My lord, your dice are small." But after Guillaume adjusted the position of her "gaming table," he rolled against the table—hard—and certainly won the toss.

In his few surviving songs written for a mixed audience, the incipient conventions of courtly love are in evidence (see Question 87). These poems have the same object in mind—*con*—but they go about pursuing it more subtly than in the poems where the speaker is a swaggering blowhard. Since the court ladies expect gentlemanly behavior and refined language from their lovers, Guillaume agrees to play along. He proclaims himself his lady's vassal, warns her he will die if he doesn't win her love, and shivers and trembles in amatory pain.

Guillaume's loveliest poem, "*Ab la dolchor del temps novel*" ("With the sweetness of the new season"), features a springtime opening that soon became conventional among the troubadours, with the trees turning green again and the birds singing "in their own Latin," and every young man's fancy turning to . . . well, you know. The poet recounts how, after the end of a lovers' quarrel—when their love was like a hawthorn branch that had trembled in the rain and frost all night but has warmed its leaves in the next day's sun—his lady renewed her pledge and gave him a ring. This happy turn of events prompts him to send a prayer winging its way to God, "that I might live long enough / to get my hands beneath her mantle." Others may talk at length of love, but he and his lady have "its hunk of bread and the knife to cut it with."

"*Pos de chantar m'es pres talentz*" ("Since I feel a great need to sing"), the only poem of Guillaume's for which the music has survived, is a valediction to his country and his former joyous gaiety as he goes off to fight the Moors in Spain (1120–23)—leaving his young son at war and renouncing his frivolous past while asking God to receive his soul. The first of the troubadours died in 1127 at age fifty-five.

Some of his greatest successors include the master lyricist Bernart de Ventadorn; the superb technician Arnaut Daniel, inventor of the sestina; and the warrior-poet Bertran de Born, whose spirit Dante sees in the *Inferno* holding his severed head in his hand like a lantern and about whom Ezra Pound wrote two of his finest short poems, "Sestina: Altaforte" and "Near Perigord." The most gifted of the Italian troubadours was Sordello, who figures prominently in Dante's *Purgatorio* and inspired a long narrative poem by Robert Browning. Dante himself tried his hand at eight lines of Provençal verse in Canto 26 of the *Purgatorio*, where he honors the soul of Arnaut Daniel, being tormented in fire for lustfulness, by allowing him to speak his native tongue in the only non-Italian passage of the entire *Divine Comedy*. Another poet being purged of his lustful sins there, the Bolognese Guido Guinizzelli, the initiator of the *dolce stil nuovo*—"the sweet new style" that influenced Dante's early verse—refers to the troubadour Arnaut as "*il miglior fabbro*" ("the better craftsman"), a compliment that T. S. Eliot, six centuries later, passed on to Ezra Pound in his dedication of *The Waste Land*.

84 ◆ What was the first Western erotic memoir?

Peter Abelard's The Story of My Misfortunes, *c. 1134*

A YOUNG WOMAN GETS PREGNANT, and an incensed relative exacts a horrible revenge from her seducer. This is not an uncommon story, except that the star-crossed lovers in this case were the greatest philosopher of the twelfth century, dubbed "the Socrates of Gaul," and his lovely and precocious pupil—a student of Latin, Greek, Hebrew, and theology—who was about twenty years his junior. Peter Abelard (1079–1142) was so brilliant that a professor at Paris offered him his chair in return for the privilege of studying with him as his student, and Héloïse (c. 1098–1164) was so enamored of her genius seducer that she begged him not to marry her lest it ruin his philosophic career.

"Erotic memoir" is a stretch. Abelard's *The Story of My Misfortunes* is actually a book-length consolatory letter addressed to a troubled friend in the form of an intellectual autobiography with an erotic memoir (of sorts) at its heart, but it is well to remember that this was the "Age of Ovid," when even monks treasured the ancient amatory poet's complete works (see Question 2). When Abelard's work came to the attention of Héloïse, she wrote to her long-absent husband in Latin, initiating the series of seven lengthy letters that figure among the most fascinating documents of the era.

As Abelard tells us in *The Story of My Misfortunes (Historia calamitatum mearum)*, written in Latin in about 1134 when he was in his mid-fifties, he was the eldest child of a noble Breton family. Renouncing the life of a knight for that of a peripatetic scholar—"I fled utterly from the court of Mars that I might win learning in the bosom of Minerva"—he later often used military terms to describe his countless intellectual "battles."

Arriving in Paris, the intellectual capital of Europe, Abelard studied with the master of the cathedral school of Notre Dame, the philosopher William of Champeaux, whom he defeated in disputations and finally so overwhelmed (Abelard is lying here) that he forced him to change his position on the problem of universals—"the most vexed one among logicians"—dealing with whether abstractions such as the church, mankind, or truth actually exist (William's position) or are merely verbal constructs (Abelard's view). After a hiatus in his home country caused by an illness stemming from his "immoderate zeal for study," Abelard returned to Paris and so utterly confounded his old master, who was now a bishop, that William's former pupils abandoned him and flocked to Abelard's philosophy lectures. This, he boasted, was the origin of both his fame and the envy it always brings in its train.

After William of Champeaux, Abelard studied with Anselm of Laon, whose "miraculous flow of words" was "contemptible in meaning and quite void of reason"—and started cutting his lectures, thus earning the hatred of that "venerable coward." Although not a theologian, Abelard entered that field on a dare by concocting overnight a splendid lecture on the murkiest prophetic passage of Ezekiel, and he began to achieve "glory" and prosperity from his teaching in both philosophy and theology.

By now Abelard was apparently a canon of Notre Dame—a member of the minor clergy and thus expected to be celibate—but since he had come to regard himself "the only philosopher remaining in the whole world," he began to "loosen the reins on desire." Having often espied the young student Héloïse, who lived with her doting uncle Fulbert, also a canon of Notre Dame, Abelard managed to secure a position as the girl's live-in tutor to gain access to her. Her beauty and learning, he claimed, "made her the most worthy of renown in the entire kingdom." As for the new tutor himself, "so distinguished was my name, and

I possessed such advantages of youth and comeliness, that no matter what woman I might favor with my love, I dreaded rejection of none."

So far, Abelard sounds like a writer of courtly romances, someone like Chrétien de Troyes, but he soon puts an edge on his narration that makes it an ancestor of the bawdy French fabliaux, saying of Canon Fulbert, as if he were a foolish husband devising his own cuckoldry:

> He entrusted her wholly to my guidance, begging me to give
> her instruction . . . whether by day or night, and to punish her
> sternly if ever I should find her negligent of her tasks. In all
> this the man's simplicity was nothing short of astounding to
> me; I should not have been more smitten with wonder if he
> had entrusted a tender lamb to the care of a ravenous wolf.

Héloïse's uncle had, in effect, given her tutor "free scope to my desires" and every opportunity "to bend her to my will with threats and blows if I failed to do so with caresses." Abelard seems to relish telling us that "under the pretext of study we spent our hours in the happiness of love. . . . Our speech was more of love than of the books which lay open before us; our kisses far outnumbered our reasoned words. Our hands sought less the book than each other's bosoms. . . . If love itself could imagine any wonder as yet unknown, we discovered it."

Even a blockhead like Fulbert caught on after several months and dismissed Abelard, but the lovers continued to meet secretly—perhaps even being caught together, as it "once happened with Mars and Venus"—and Héloïse soon became pregnant. Abelard managed to steal her away from her uncle's house and send her to live with his sister in Brittany, where Héloïse gave birth to a son. An index of the intellectual ferment of the times is the fact that the new mother named her child Astrolabe after an astronomical instrument.

By this time, with Abelard approaching age forty and Héloïse about twenty, they married at his insistence in an attempt to appease Fulbert—perhaps also to make an "honest woman" of Héloïse, to make sure she wouldn't be married off to someone else, and to legitimize their son—but Abelard insisted that the marriage be kept secret "so that I might suffer no loss of reputation thereby." After the simple ceremony, the lovers separated.

But Canon Fulbert, who served as a witness at the wedding, became enraged that the hushed-up arrangement meant that his own personal and familial shame would continue. He began spreading news of the marriage, which Héloïse vehemently denied and was promptly punished for. Abelard thus had her conveyed to the convent of Argenteuil, where she had studied as a girl, and little Astrolabe was sent to Abelard's sister.

Furious that his beloved niece had been forced to become a nun, Canon Fulbert convinced several of his kinsmen to attack Abelard as he lay sleeping one night. As the philosopher himself phrased it, "They cut off those parts of my body with which I had done that which was the cause of their sorrow." Two of the men were caught—one was Abelard's bribed servant—and they were subjected not only to castration, as he was, but they also had their eyes gouged out for good measure. After this, Abelard became a Benedictine monk at the royal abbey of Saint-Denis, writing that "for my sensuality, I lost those things whereby I practiced it."

Héloïse had been against the marriage, later assuring Abelard that she would rather have been his concubine than the wife of Caesar Augustus. "God knows I never wanted anything from you but yourself," she wrote.

Abelard's troubles continued. Among the most famous of his many books, *Sic et non (Yes and No)* was a compilation of passages from the church fathers that seemed to contradict one another on 158 issues like "That to God all things are possible—or not," "That a lie is permissible—or not," and "That it is lawful to kill a man—or not" without any attempt by the author to resolve the contradictions. "By doubting we come to inquiry, and by inquiry we perceive the truth," he declared in the preface, but his invitation to apply dialectical methods to the resolution of thorny theological problems was largely decried by his contemporaries. In 1121, his treatise on the Trinity was condemned as heretical and burned at the Council of Soissons. He also had to leave his monastery to flee the wrath of his fellow monks, who resented him for pointing out that their beliefs about their exalted founder, Saint Denis, were confused and unhistorical. Embracing a solitary life near Troyes, Abelard was soon swamped with eager students, however, so he resumed teaching at the oratory he had built for himself out of reeds and stalks, and which his followers rebuilt in stone and wood. He named it the Paraclete in honor of the Holy Spirit as Comforter.

Then, in about 1126, he was chosen abbot of the monastery of Saint Gildas in his native Brittany, whose monks, with their mistresses and children, he considered "far more savage than heathens and more evil of life." This is as far as *The Story of My Misfortunes* takes us, but we know that after years of futile attempts to reform the monks, he fled when they tried to poison him and waylay him on the road. Meanwhile, when Héloïse and the nuns of Argenteuil were turned out of their convent in 1129, Abelard arranged for her to become prioress at the Paraclete oratory, which still belonged to him, and to settle her nuns there. For a time he served as abbot of the new religious group, ministering to Héloïse and the others as their spiritual guide.

By 1136, he was teaching in Paris again, but his appeal to reason as the best means to arrive at truth arrayed against him mystics and contemplatives like Bernard of Clairvaux (1090–1153), who feared that the rationalistic Scholastic philosophers and their newfangled logical tools were undermining religious belief and the authority of Scripture and the church. In ethics, Abelard taught that a clear conscience about one's deeds absolved a person of guilt even if his or her actions were deemed wrong by traditional codes of behavior.

Under pressure from St. Bernard, the Council of Sens condemned Abelard's *Theology* as heretical in 1141. After appealing in vain to the pope, Abelard was officially silenced and spent most of the short span of life left to him at the famed monastery of Cluny (see Question 70), where he made his peace with Bernard. Peter Abelard died in the priory of St. Marcel on April 21, 1142, at age sixty-three. His wife, Héloïse, outlived him by twenty-two years.

In 1557, all of Abelard's voluminous works were placed on the Church's *Index of Prohibited Books*, but the story of his tragic love has inspired artists and writers through the ages. Alexander Pope's proto-Romantic poem *Eloïsa to Abelard* (1717), based on the famous series of letters exchanged by the aging former lovers, was considered by medievalist Étienne Gilson to be one of the finest embodiments of Héloïse's indomitable spirit: "Even here, where frozen chastity retires, / Love finds an altar for forbidden fires." More than a century ago, historian Henry Adams conjured up the sad magic of their story by claiming that "the twelfth century, with all its sparkle, would be dull without Abelard and Héloïse."

The ill-fated pair are said to be the oldest denizens of Père-Lachaise Cemetery in Paris, where lovers and the lovelorn still leave letters on their elaborate nineteenth-century monument. Legend says that when Héloïse was placed in the same tomb with Abelard, his dead arms enfolded her.

The most brilliant thinker of the twelfth century was also a noted Latin poet and musician. In addition to lost love songs that he wrote for Héloïse—which he asserted were "widely known and have been sung in many lands"—he composed hymns for the Paraclete after Héloïse became the abbess there and an "Epithalamica" for bride and bridegroom. Six *planctus* (laments) of his also survive, one of them with his original music. In his "Lament of David for the Deaths of Saul and Jonathan," Abelard seems to be speaking for himself when he has David exclaim, "How empty, how brief / I now perceive joys to be!"

85 ∾ What was the first major building in the Gothic style?

The royal abbey of Saint-Denis, France, rebuilt by
Abbot Suger, 1137–44

A NEW TYPE OF ARCHITECTURE THAT arose in northern France in the twelfth century—simply called *opus modernum* ("modern work") by contemporaries—was later dubbed "Gothic" in disparagement by Italian Renaissance artists and scholars, such as the first great art historian, Giorgio Vasari, who spoke of its "barbarous German style," which "has polluted the world." For German philosopher Arthur Schopenhauer, to consider Gothic architecture as the artistic peer of the ancient Greco-Roman style was "a barbarous presumption that must not for one moment be allowed."

For us jaded postmoderns, however, the emphatic verticality of the towers, spires, and soaring interior spaces of Gothic cathedrals, as if aspiring toward the heavens, can evoke nostalgia for the serene convictions of the Age of Faith. We marvel at these magnificently complex structures that required centuries to complete, were the pride of their communities, and often remained until the nineteenth or twentieth century the tallest edifices in their locales. By comparison, our sky-scraping steel-and-glass cathedrals of Mammon seem to be no more than gigantic reflecting mirrors of what the Preacher called "vanity of vanities."

Suger (c. 1081–1151), the man usually credited with first refurbishing a church in the Gothic style, became in 1122 the abbot of the renowned Benedictine monastery of Saint-Denis, north of Paris. Born poor in that very area, he nonetheless became a schoolmate, lifelong friend, sage counselor, and biographer of French king Louis VI "the Fat" and also a protector of Peter Abelard, to whom he granted permission to leave the monastery after the controversial philosopher earned the other monks' enmity by shattering some misconceptions about their founder (see Question 84).

This founder was the third-century martyr Saint Denis, the first bishop of Paris, who, after being decapitated in Montmartre by the Romans, supposedly picked up his head and walked several miles with it, setting it down where he wished to be buried. In about 630, King Dagobert I endowed a monastery at the site of Denis's shrine, but it was the abbey church completed by Charlemagne in the eighth century that became "the Westminster Abbey of France"—the final resting place of all but three of its kings after Hugh Capet (r. 987–96), founder of the Capetian dynasty, was buried there. Though Denis was the patron saint of the French throne, by Abbot Suger's time the abbey church dedicated to him—"the sacred altar of the fatherland," to use later French grandiloquent terms—was in a sorely dilapidated state.

Far from springing into action, Suger took thirteen long years to collect the funds he envisioned needing for rebuilding the church according to his grandiose plans. Having spent more than a year in Rome, he knew what grandiose was. Having read widely, he fancifully took Solomon's Temple in Jerusalem and Justinian's Hagia Sophia in Constantinople as his "models." Having pondered what he mistakenly took to be Saint Denis's writings (and fortunately ignoring Abelard on this point), he became obsessed with their emphasis on light as a visible manifestation of the invisible God. A lover of precious gems and gold and all things beautiful for their symbolic import and usefulness in elevating the mind toward the truth and beauty of God, he adopted as his catchphrase "from the material to the immaterial."

Finally, in 1137, he got down to work. The Romanesque style, which flourished during the eleventh and twelfth centuries, had used the rounded Roman arch as a basic structural device and adopted late Roman barrel vaults and thick stone columns, which allowed large basilicas to be built. Now, with the help of the best stonemasons, sculptors, painters, and other craftsmen from near and far—including Arabic glassmakers—Suger, though no architect himself, was ready to rebuild his abbey church on a much more epic, lavish, and sumptuous scale.

Starting with the western facade, he carved out and embellished with relief sculpture three stone portals to replace the old tunnel-like entrance, fitted them with bronze doors, and surmounted them with a large stained-glass rose window, the first of its kind. The tower remaining on the right lost its mate in 1846, when cracks in its structure required it to be taken down. The crenellated parapets at the top of the facade call to mind a fortified castle of God.

In 1140, Suger embarked in a new direction that would enable him to build higher, greatly enlarge the interior to accommodate the hordes of pilgrims, and let more light into his church. Concentrating on the apse, or east end of the church behind the main altar, he built a double ambulatory, decked with semicircular chapels, around the new choir. Here he made use of pointed arches (which he may have seen in Normandy) in conjunction with narrow stone ribs rising in a skeleton of scaffolding thrown diagonally across the vaulted ceiling. This allowed the ribbed vault to rest on slender pillars and columns rather than on massive stone walls.

Wall space was thus freed up for tall windows of mostly blue and red stained glass that bathed the interior and the mosaic floor in a jewel-like colored light. Rich and poor alike could now ponder the biblical and allegorical stories narrated on the windows in a much more luminous and striking form than in Romanesque murals. Suger may have been the first to depict the Tree of Jesse—the ancestors of Christ—in visual form, and there was also a Moses window. "The dull mind rises to truth," he had inscribed on a door of his church, "through that which is material."

On a main altar bedizened with gold and gems rested a golden chalice weighing 140 ounces and set with jacinth and topaz when the new church was dedicated on June 11, 1144, with Louis VII, Queen Eleanor of Aquitaine, and scores of archbishops, bishops, and nobles in attendance. For Suger, who wrote of "my delight in the beauty of the house of God," a sole architectural regret was his inability to procure for Saint-Denis some columns he had admired in the Baths of Diocletian at Rome.

The highest duties of state soon called Suger away from his labor of love. From 1147 to 1149, he served as regent of France, while Louis VII participated in the disastrous Second Crusade. The greatly elongated nave and the transepts of Saint-Denis were completed in mature Gothic style in the following century. Long afterward, the church was sacked and severely damaged by a mob during the French Revolution and later restored by Eugène Viollet-le-Duc.

The life span of Gothic was c. 1100 to 1500, its most prized structures rising in France, England, Germany, and Spain. Soon after Suger's work at Saint-Denis, the bishop of Paris started construction on Notre Dame (1163–1345), which art historian Kenneth Clark deemed "not perhaps the most lovable of cathedrals, but the most rigorously intellectual facade in the whole of Gothic art." Those who have seen it will not soon forget its double 200-foot-high towers with their tall mullioned windows, the three deep portals, the rose windows, the 110-foot-high nave vault, and the flying buttresses spidering off from the structure.

In the national archives of France in Paris, one may still see Suger's last will and testament, drawn up on June 17, 1137, just as he was beginning work on Saint-Denis, in which the mighty abbot looked back on his rise from a peasant background: ". . . *valida Domini manus me pauperem de stercore erexit . . .*" ("the strong hand of the Lord raised me, a beggar, from the dungpile"). This powerful image may shed some light on a later statement describing his thoughts while gazing on the glittering high altar of the church he had built:

> I see myself dwelling, as it were, in some strange region of the universe which neither exists entirely in the slime of the earth nor in the purity of Heaven, and that, by the grace of God, I can be transported from this inferior to that higher world.

86 ❧ Who was the first Plantagenet king of England?

Henry II, 1154–89, the first of a line of fourteen English monarchs

OUT OF THE OFTEN TURBULENT LIVES and reigns of the fourteen Plantagenet kings of England, William Shakespeare wove nine of his ten history plays—*King John*, *Richard II*, *Henry IV* (2 plays), *Henry V*, *Henry VI* (three plays), and *Richard III*—and Christopher Marlowe chipped in with a tragedy about the ill-fated Edward II. The era of the Plantagenets (1154–1485) saw crusades, baronial rebellions, Scottish wars, the Hundred Years' War, the Black Death, a fierce peasants' revolt, usurpations, royal murders, and the War of the Roses between the Lancastrian and Yorkist houses of the Plantagenets.

Shakespeare's failure to set a play during the reign of Henry II, founder of the Plantagenet dynasty, was somewhat compensated for by three later plays dealing with Henry's strife with Thomas Becket, as imagined by Alfred Tennyson, T. S. Eliot, and Jean Anouilh, as well as a 1964 film adapted from Anouilh's play featuring Richard Burton as Becket and Peter O'Toole as his angry and vindictive king.

The man who became Henry II was a son of Matilda (daughter of Henry I) and thus a great-grandson of William the Conqueror (see Question 78). His father was Geoffrey, the great count of Anjou, who acquired his nickname of Plantagenet ("Sprig of Broom") from his sporting a sprig of yellow broom plant tucked into his helmet. As a child and young man, Henry witnessed the martial efforts of his mother to enforce her claims to rule in England against her cousin King Stephen (1135–54), who, as son of the Conqueror's daughter Adela, had usurped the throne from Matilda, the designated heir of Henry I.

A year before Stephen died, Henry invaded England and extracted a promise from him that, in return for being allowed to live out the rest of his life as king, he would name Henry as his successor, and so, in 1154, twenty-one-year-old Henry Plantagenet became one of the most powerful rulers in Europe on acquiring the English crown.

England wasn't his only holding by far. From his father, who had died a few years earlier, Henry had received Normandy, Anjou, Maine, and Touraine. As heir to his brother, he got Brittany. As a result of his marriage with the famed Eleanor of Aquitaine, whose marriage with French King Louis VII had been annulled, Henry gained Aquitaine, Poitiers, Gascony, and Guienne—and the fierce enmity of King Louis. In fact, Henry held more French territory than the French king, ruling all of western France down to the Pyrenees.

The early years of his reign were spent in bringing to heel Scotland, Wales, and Brittany. Among his first foreign initiatives was a request to Pope Adrian IV to allow him to invade Ireland, a policy to which the pontiff—aka Nicholas Breakspear, the first and only English pope—gleefully acquiesced: "And may the people of that land receive thee with honor, and venerate thee as their master; provided always that the rights of the churches remain inviolate and entire, and saving to St. Peter and the holy Roman Church the annual pension of one penny from each house." After many other distractions, Henry led his troops to Ireland sixteen years later and forced the Irish kings and Norman and Welsh warlords already ensconced there to recognize him as their overlord.

In domestic affairs, Henry oversaw and took a personal role in the administration of justice and the reform of criminal procedure. Relying on legal scholars who had studied civil and canon law in the budding universities on the Continent (see Question 79), he struck at the power of feudal courts in favor of royal ones and created circuit judges to travel into the shires. His judges adopted the methods rather than the authoritarian substance of Roman law, laying the groundwork for a law that would be "common" to all of England and based on the procedures and precedents of Henry's central courts.

Among Henry's signal accomplishments was the introduction of a jury system to replace the ancient tradition of trial by ordeal or combat, although these early jurors were summoned as witnesses who could testify on the facts of cases rather than as neutral evaluators of evidence presented to them. Another form of jury was that of presentment, ancestor of the grand jury, by which respectable men of a locale were called on to testify regarding "whether in their . . . township there be any man who . . . has been charged or published as being a robber or murderer or thief; or any one who is a harborer of robbers or murderers or thieves."

The first great tragedy of Henry's reign swallowed up Thomas Becket (c. 1118–70), chancellor of England and close friend of the king. A willing and sometimes unscrupulous tool of Henry, he surprised his royal master when, on being appointed archbishop of Canterbury in 1162, he resigned the chancellorship against Henry's wishes, donned the habit of a Benedictine, and reoriented his chief allegiance toward the church and the pope.

The casus belli was Henry's demand that Becket support his proposal to reform how members of the clergy were tried for serious offenses. During Stephen's anarchic reign, churchmen accused of a felony—and note that there were a hundred murders by English clerics within a decade in those days—were tried in ecclesiastical courts, in which the punishment was often comparatively lenient. Henry wanted clerics to be charged in a secular court, handed over to a church court for trial, and, if found guilty and stripped of office, sent back to a lay court for sentencing and punishment.

At first, Becket acceded to the *Constitutions of Clarendon* (1164), in which Henry outlined what he claimed had been the customary procedures for trying clerical felons under his grandfather Henry I, and for managing relations between church and crown. Then, after Pope Alexander III refused to approve the *Constitutions*, Becket also retracted his support for them. Henry's outraged reaction was to strip the recalcitrant archbishop of his estates and revenues and banish his friends. Becket fled to the Continent, spending six years in a pair of austere French monasteries.

After the pope threatened to put England under interdict in 1170, Henry allowed the archbishop to return, but the stiff-necked prelate, who didn't know the meaning of compromise, soon publicly excommunicated some of the bishops who had supported the king. Four Norman knights who took literally Henry's frustrated outburst—"Of the cowards that eat my bread, is there none that will rid me of this upstart priest?"—slipped away from court to do what they thought was their sovereign's will. On December 29, they cornered Becket in his own cathedral of Canterbury and, after an angry verbal tussle, hacked his brains out on the steps of the altar.

Europe was shocked by the sacrilege. Thomas Becket was canonized in 1173, and his cathedral and tomb at Canterbury became an international pilgrimage site. In the following year, a barefoot King Henry knelt at the spot of the murder and submitted to scourging as penance for his share of the guilt. More than two centuries later, Geoffrey Chaucer imagined a group of English pilgrims who told tales on their leisurely way to Canterbury, "the hooly blisful martir for to seke," and the easy pace at which such pilgrims urged their horses ultimately gave us our verb *canter*. Finally, the cult of St. Thomas Becket was officially discountenanced by Henry VIII, who pulverized the shrine and supposedly burned the saint's remains.

Becket's successful fight for the right of clerics to be tried and punished by ecclesiastical courts degenerated in later times to the practice of letting men accused of crimes claim "benefit of clergy" simply by proving they could read (since literacy was uncommon in laymen). Because the text chosen for the test was generally the same—Psalm 50 of the Vulgate (51 in other Bibles)—those who could read or had merely memorized this "neck verse" (since it often fended off the penalty of hanging that the king's court would have imposed) were considered clergymen and thus often got off with light punishment, if any, for crimes like theft, rape, and murder.

The latter part of Henry's reign was envenomed by family problems. Queen Eleanor, eleven years older than he and embittered by his infidelities, roused their sons against him—Ezra Pound claimed the British climate had ruined her—and paid the price by a long imprisonment ended only by her husband's death. The king's heir, Prince Henry, who had been crowned king during his father's lifetime, led an unsuccessful revolt and died in 1183. The king then supported his youngest and most inept son, John, as his successor, but another son—Richard the Lionheart—ganged up with King Philip Augustus of France in an invasion of England in July 1189. Henry, prematurely old and worn out at fifty-six, died soon after discovering that his beloved John had secretly joined the forces arrayed against him.

A Japanese proverb claims that "the great man has no seed." One of the ironies of English history is the fact that the first and most powerful of the Plantagenet monarchs was succeeded by his two surviving sons, Richard I (1189–99) and John (1199–1216), who seemed to vie with each other for the appellation of their country's worst king.

87 ～ What was the first treatise on courtly love in Christian Europe?

Andreas Capellanus's The Art of Courtly Love, 1184–86

IN DAYS OF YORE, HIGHBORN young women were cloistered and chaperoned at all times, and marriages among the well-to-do were prearranged agreements in which the feelings of the bride and groom were not necessarily taken into account. Against this backdrop, a new sensibility in European aristocratic life first appeared in the south of France in the twelfth century, as more women began to rule inherited lands on their own or in a husband's absence. The result was a novel cult of romantic love that, though almost entirely a literary convention, profoundly affected the way the upper classes viewed love between the sexes.

At a time when many knights and nobles were off on crusade, the castles and aristocratic courts of southern France became magnets for a new class of poets, the troubadours, who, often noble themselves, provided more sophisticated entertainment than the jugglers, acrobats, buffoons, and animal trainers of an earlier day (see Question 83). Their intricate lyrics in Provençal, set to music and sung, were often addressed to an unattainable ladylove whose identity was disguised under a pseudonym known as a *senhal* ("signal"). The lady of the castle and each member of her entourage could wonder whether she was the object of the poet's secret admiration. The complex code that developed—first termed "courtly love" by literary scholar Gaston Paris in 1883—may have been a poetic fiction, but it was one of the most powerful and far-reaching ever devised.

Many of the leitmotifs incorporated into this "system" can be traced back to the Roman poet Ovid (see Question 2). His *Art of Love* (ostensibly a seduction manual), the *Remedies for Love*, and the lyrics collected under the title *Amores* became urtexts of courtly love, especially for readers not attuned to the irony with which the poet had laced his handbooks for fools. Ovid's lovers are the idle and bored upper classes of Rome whose frivolous behavior in amatory matters becomes the focus of his satirical vision. He thus describes extramarital love affairs in terms of warfare under Cupid, a demanding generalissimo who requires all sorts of proofs from a man courting a woman, such as spending long, cold, moping nights on her doorstep, sighing and languishing a great deal, and growing gaunt and pale from loss of appetite and sleep.

In the twelfth century, the troubadours seized on these notions, perhaps combining them with the conventions of the love poetry of the Spanish Muslims. With the encouragement of great ladies like the beautiful and sophisticated Eleanor of Aquitaine (c. 1122–1204)—the most powerful woman of her time, who married two kings in succession and maintained a splendid court at Poitiers—and her daughter Marie, countess of Champagne, the troubadours sang of *fin' amors* ("refined love") as well as of the earthier variety, and the addressee was almost always a married noblewoman. The poems often made use of metaphors drawn from the feudal society in which they were written, as in these lines of Bernart de Ventadorn:

> *Good lady, I request of you nothing more*
> *than that you should take me as your servant,*
> *for I shall serve you as my own good lord,*
> *whatsoever be the wages that I earn.*
> *Look, here I stand, ready for your command . . .*

This lady receives the promises of service and loyalty usually reserved for a feudal overlord, and indeed the troubadour sometimes addresses his lady as *midons* ("my lord"), while he styles himself her vassal or *drutz* ("faithful lover"). The vocabulary of theology was similarly mined for metaphors of "worship" and "adoration" of the lady, at a time when the cult of the Virgin Mary was elevating the mother of Jesus to the status of a deity.

Aside from possible antecedents in Muslim Spain, the earliest treatise on courtly love is Andreas Capellanus's *De arte honeste amandi*, literally *On the Art of Loving Honestly* but usually translated as *The Art of Courtly Love*. Andreas "the Chaplain" seems to have exercised this role at the court of Countess Marie de Champagne from 1181 to 1187, but his book was intended to mirror the perfervid atmosphere of her mother Eleanor's court at Poitiers about a decade earlier.

Though probably commissioned by Countess Marie for the amusement of those of her courtiers who could understand Latin, Andreas's book informs us that a certain Walter, a noble young friend of the author, begged him for written instructions on how to manage his first serious crush. Walter got much more than he bargained for—a two-hundred-page tract seasoned with more than a pinch of Gallic wit. Like a new Ovid, from whom he quotes copiously, the worldly chaplain proceeds to teach his friend how best to navigate the shoals of love.

Andreas starts by defining love in this context as "a certain inborn suffering derived from the sight of and excessive meditation upon the beauty of the opposite sex, which causes each one to wish above all things the embraces of the other." The male lover "begins at once to lust after [the woman] in his heart . . . to pry into the secrets of her body, and he desires to put each part of it to the fullest use." Get the picture? (Nonetheless, men who lust after every woman they see are compared to shameless dogs and asses.) The true lover is always fearful—of being rejected, discovered, betrayed—and the affair is always adulterous and secret.

Certain age limitations restrict those who may love. Girls younger than twelve and boys younger than fourteen are excluded, as well as men over sixty and women over fifty. For sixtysomething men, beset with "various difficulties" and "various ailments," the only remaining consolations are food and drink.

Among the precepts scattered through the book is the warning to women to avoid choosing fops as lovers, opting instead for excellence of character, and to men that "a woman who puts all her reliance on her rouge usually doesn't have any particular gifts of character." A woman who "desires to sate her lust with many" is to be shunned, "unless you are so potent at Venus's trade that you can satisfy her," but "that would be harder for you to do than to dry up the oceans." Peasant women, being naturally shy, need "a little compulsion."

The learned chaplain insists that the only legitimate way of acquiring a lady's love is for the man to prove his worth by means of eloquence, which turns out to mean grandiose promises, lies, blandishments, and sophistries. Although the specific approaches depend on the respective social classes of the lover and the lady, it is interesting that none of the men in the eight extended dialogues that form the core of the treatise— elaborate verbal schemata for getting into a woman's pants—is successful in his suit.

Andreas's gentle ridicule is apparent in how, despite the men's windy and subtle arguments—redolent of the new pettifogging Scholastic logic and dialectics—the women, untrained in such lore, nonetheless see right through it. The dialogues are spiced with side debates over whether "pure" love (a kind of nude embrace and nothing else) is nobler than "mixed" love and whether men who are content to indulge only in "the solaces of the upper part" are preferable to those who also seek "the solace of the lower part."

We also come upon an authoritative list of thirty-one "Rules of Love," among which are these:

1. Marriage cannot be pleaded as an excuse for refusing to love [meaning you can't use the excuse "No, thanks, I'm married"].

2. A person who is not jealous can never be a lover.

16. At the sudden and unexpected prospect of his ladylove, the heart of the true lover invariably palpitates.

17. A new love affair banishes the old one completely.

27. A lover can never have enough of the solaces [you know what *these* are] that his beloved may offer him.

The book also describes what the Italians later called a "*questione d'amore,*" a debate on the fine points of problems arising from love. The decisions in these "cases" were rendered by a high-ranking member of the "court of love"—someone like Eleanor or Marie. Here, for example, is one handed down, according to Andreas, on May 1, 1174, in a court of "a great many ladies" presided over by the countess of Champagne, who thus delivers her verdict: "We declare and we hold as firmly established that love cannot exert its powers between two people who are married to each other."

Only in Book 3, "The Rejection of Love," which concludes the work, does Father Andreas take off his carnival mask, as it were, to advise his friend Walter to eschew the kind of love he's been describing in the preceding 150 pages. He reminds him of Christian teachings on the evils of fornication and undermines the airy-fairy nonsense propounded in the first two books by dwelling on all the vices of women that a long tradition of misogynistic and antifeminist literature had rendered canonical: avarice, miserliness, envy, slanderousness, greed, deficiency of wisdom, gluttony, fickleness, deception, disobedience, arrogance, foul temper, hatred of all other women, pride, mendacity, drunkenness, loud- and blabber-mouthedness, wantonness, and an utter inability to resist any kind of evil.

In short, Andreas tries to terrify Walter against having anything to do with women of any sort. To us, this seems to constitute a schizophrenic reversal on the part of the genial author of the earlier sections of the treatise, but Andreas seems to have been indulging his young friend with au courant worldly fripperies in Books 1 and 2, only to set him up for a rude awakening in Book 3, in which he tells him that if he chooses to pursue "the delights of the flesh," he now has the guide he requested, but he will be deprived of "the grace of God, the companionship of the good, and the friendship of praiseworthy men." The debonair love manual gives way to a homily and, at the very end, a memento mori.

Andreas's book was widely popular during the Middle Ages, especially after it was translated into French, Italian, Catalan, and German. The cult of courtly love, like the broader ideal of chivalry, is often seen as having exercised an ennobling and civilizing influence on crude knights, who became less enamored of hacking one another to pieces with broadswords or battle-axes and began acquiring spoonier ladies and better manners (*courtesy* originally meaning the behavior that became de rigueur in noble courts).

Whatever its social effects, courtly love gave rise not only to the lyric poetry of the troubadours, but also to that of the northern French trouvères, the German minnesingers, and Dante and the Italian *stilnovisti*. It inspired courtly romances like those of Chrétien de Troyes, long allegorical poems like *The Romance of the Rose*, and tragic tales in verse and prose celebrating the passion of famed lovers such as Tristan and Iseult, Lancelot and Guinevere, and Troilus and Cressida. The supreme sonneteer Petrarch and his myriad imitators throughout Europe kept courtly love alive for many centuries to come.

Though mocked even in their own heyday, the conventions of romantic love received their definitive deflation at the hands of nineteenth-century über-ironists like Gustave Flaubert. Here the master of *le mot juste* punctuates Rodolphe's first ardent vows to Madame Bovary with the barked background cries of a speaker awarding prizes at an agricultural show:

> "And I've stayed with you, because I couldn't tear myself away, though I've tried a hundred times."
> "Manure!"
> . . .
> "And so I shall cherish the memory of you."
> "For a merino ram . . ."
> . . .
> "No, say I shan't! Tell me I shall count for something in your thoughts, in your life?"
> "Pigs: Prize divided!"

88 ∽ Who established the first Japanese shogunate?

Yoritomo of the Minamoto clan, 1192–99

IN *TOTEM AND TABOO*, Sigmund Freud quotes from a description of the Japanese emperor's routine in about 1700. The emperor, considered the direct descendant of the Shinto sun goddess, Amaterasu, is forbidden to touch the ground with his sacred feet, so he must be borne aloft everywhere. The sun is not worthy to shine on his head, and his hair, beard, and nails are too holy to be cut. Freud, drawing on the anthropological researches of Sir James Frazer, explains that the office of the priest-kings of primitive societies was often eventually split up into that of a religious icon, who shunned all contact with the world outside his bubble and whose life was a nightmare of taboos, and that of a secular ruler, like the Japanese shogun, whose function was to whip reluctant men and recalcitrant matter into some semblance of shape.

The emperor of Japan, called *Tenshi* ("Son of Heaven"), *Tenno* ("Heavenly King"), and, less commonly, *Mikado* ("August Gateway"), resided at Kyoto ("Capital of Peace"), a city of half a million that rivaled the Chinese capital of Changan in sophistication and remained the imperial residence for more than a thousand years. For centuries, the Fujiwara family was the real power behind the throne, but with increasing luxury came the inevitable concomitant of decadence, and by the mid-twelfth century Japan was being ripped apart by civil wars among its provincial warrior families, especially the Taira and Minamoto.

When these noble clans, both descended from emperors, first clashed in 1159, the Taira were victorious. They miscalculated, however, in sparing the young sons of the Minamoto leader Yoritomo (1147–99) and his half brother Yoshitsune. As adults, the brothers joined a vast rebellion in 1180—termed the Gempei War—during which Yoritomo entrusted several crucial battles to the younger Yoshitsune, a military genius (and future hero of Kabuki plays). Yoshitsune defeated the Taira in the battle of Yashima Island in March 1185 and, a month later, annihilated them in the great sea battle of Dannoura, in which the Taira child emperor Antoku drowned. After the Minamoto brothers quarreled, however, Yoshitsune was forced to commit suicide in 1189 by the treacherous son of a Fujiwara leader with whom he had taken shelter.

With the Taira clan out of the way, Yoritomo used his private army of vassals, samurai, and retainers to set up what was later called a *bakufu* (a tent—that is, military—government) at Kamakura, a seaside village ten miles south of modern Tokyo. The *bakufu* was an administration separate from, though nominally subordinate to, Emperor Takahira's court at Kyoto, featuring its own system of councils and departments, including officers sent out to the provinces to enlist troops, collect taxes, administer justice, and keep the Minamoto vassals and other feudal lords in check. This Kamakura era of Japanese history extended from 1185 to 1333.

In 1192, Yoritomo, whose tentacles had extended their reach throughout the Japanese islands, became first to receive from an emperor the title of *seii taishogun* as a permanent and hereditary military dictator of the entire empire. The *seii taishogun* ("barbarian-subduing generalissimo"), often shortened to *shogun*, was at first merely a general appointed by the emperors to deal with inroads of border chiefs or other military emergencies, much as in the Roman republic dictators were appointed for a maximum of six months to deal with a specific crisis. The first to receive the title in that older sense was the late-eighth-century military leader named Sakanoue Tamuramaro, who defeated the Ainu of the north.

Now, with Yoritomo as the new-style shogun, an aristocratic caste of warriors, our endlessly parodied samurai ("sword-bearers"), rose to prominence. The old civil aristocrats at the emperor's court in Kyoto lost much of their power to these fighting men from the provinces who grew mighty in the same way the Sicilian Mafia was to do—by offering strong-arm protection in return for tribute and privileges. The samurai, with the terrifying masks of their facial armor and their horned helmets, lived by a martial code of absolute loyalty to their lords and of suicide by seppuku or hara-kiri—disembowelment—in defeat, shame, or solemn protest, or as a method of joining a dead lord to serve him in the beyond.

Shogun Yoritomo also supported Buddhism, patronizing the sculptor Unkei and his team of assistants, who carved imposing Buddhist statues for the ancient capital and religious center of Nara. Yoritomo died in 1199 at age fifty-two as a result, said his enemies, of a throw from his horse, which had shied at the apparition of the vengeful ghost of his dead brother Yoshitsune.

Both of Yoritomo's sons succeeded him as shogun, and both were assassinated. The following shogunate—more precisely, regency—was that of the Hojo family (1203–1333), to which Yoritomo's widow, Masako, belonged. Nine members of the Hojo clan ruled as successive regents for puppet shoguns, who, in turn, supposedly ruled for the figurehead emperors. After the second of Yoritomo's sons, Sanetomo, was murdered in 1219, the Hojo assumed full control.

During this time, the Japanese monks Eisai and Dogen returned from China with the tenets and teachings of Chan Buddhism—called Zen in Japan—which proved highly attractive to the samurai because of its austerity and self-discipline. Later in the century, the Mongol rulers of China mounted two invasions of Japan, in 1274 and 1281—the latter a massive armada of perhaps 3,500 ships and 140,000 men. Both met with the fierce resistance of the samurai but were doomed chiefly by typhoons that destroyed the invading fleets. Hence arose the tradition that a kamikaze—a "divine wind" sent by native Shinto gods—had protected the Japanese islands, just as kamikaze pilots were supposed to do almost seven centuries afterward.

The tail end of the next long shogunate, the Ashikaga of Kyoto (1338–1573), was marred by civil wars, though Japan was subsequently unified in 1591 by the imperial regent and chancellor Hideyoshi. Nicknamed "Monkey-Face" for his ugliness, Hideyoshi was also styled *Taikun*, from the Chinese for "Great Prince," which became a traditional title of shoguns and gave us our word *tycoon* in the nineteenth century.

The third and last shogunate, the Tokugawa, arose in 1603 under the formidable Ieyasu, who defeated other daimyo (provincial lords) and forbade the practice or preaching of Christianity in 1614, two years before his death. Like Louis XIV enfeebling his territorial magnates by requiring them to become courtiers at Versailles, the shoguns required the daimyo to spend every other year at the shogun's court at the new capital of Edo (modern Tokyo). The emperor, still in residence at Kyoto, was totally deprived of power, becoming, in effect, the chief fashionista for the aristocracy. The xenophobia and anti-Christian decrees of the Tokugawa aimed to keep firearms out of the hands of the daimyo, as well as safeguard native Japanese traditions and prevent a European takeover, as was happening in parts of China.

Then, in 1853 and again in the following year, American warships under Commodore Matthew C. Perry entered Japanese waters to wrench from the Tokugawa shogunate commercial treaties guaranteeing trading rights. This breach of Japan's self-imposed isolation prompted even the traditionally silent imperial court to issue a call to the nation to melt its temple bells into guns. The resultant domestic turmoil led to the abdication of the last shogun, Yoshinobu, in 1867, and the restoration of imperial rule on the following January 1 under Emperor Mutsuhito, who called his reign the *Meiji* ("Enlightened Government"). Rapid industrialization followed.

When the emperor abolished feudalism in 1871, the samurai joined the ranks of the unemployed. Many of them, however, partook in the creation of a modern nation while retaining their traditional mindset and installing their divine emperor in Edo, city of the shoguns, which they renamed Tokyo. With a rallying cry of "Enrich the country and strengthen the army," their descendants became the generals and other officers who transformed Japan into the nation that defeated Russia; prostrated China, Korea, and Taiwan; overran French, British, and Dutch colonies in East Asia; and, on December 7, 1941, awakened the sleeping lion that was the United States.

89 ∽ What is the first surviving Spanish epic?

The Poema de Mio Cid (The Poem of the Cid),
probably late twelfth century

THE NATIONAL HERO OF SPAIN, Rodrigo (Ruy) Díaz de Vivar (c. 1043–99), was known in his lifetime as *Mio Cid*, ultimately from the Arabic *Sayyidi* for "my lord." Of the numerous sagas that grew up around his martial exploits, the greatest was the folk epic known as the *Poema* (or *Cantar*) *de Mio Cid*, the first monument of Spanish literature.

The poem tells of the Cid's successful quest to regain the trust and affection of his king. Against the backdrop of *La Reconquista*, the centuries-long conquest of Muslim Spain by Christian princes, the honor and fealty of the Cid toward a lord who had unjustly exiled him are contrasted with the betrayal and insulting of the Cid by the despicable infantes of Carrión.

Consisting of 3,730 lines composed by an anonymous Castilian minstrel in the late twelfth or very early thirteenth century, the poem has survived in a single manuscript copy. Like the French *Song of Roland*, by which it was influenced, *The Poem of the Cid* eschews rhyme, making use instead of assonance at the ends of lines to form 152 stanzas of widely varying length (see Question 81). Of the twenty-nine characters in the poem, twenty-five have been identified as historical.

The historical Ruy Díaz, born into the minor nobility in the village of Vivar, near the city of Burgos in north-central Spain, was educated at the court of Burgos and knighted at age sixteen. The shifting alliances of the petty kingdoms of the times, both Christian and Muslim, required him to fight against Moors under his king, Sancho II of Castile—and sometimes with Moors against Christians. The intrepid Cid became Sancho's military chief and received his affectionate nickname of *Campeador* ("Champion," "Campaigner," "Battler").

When Sancho's brother and bitter enemy succeeded him as King Alfonso VI of Castile, the Cid, who had fought against him, now became a simple vassal, though he was allowed to marry Alfonso's cousin, Doña Jimena. Nonetheless, the Cid's unauthorized military raids in Muslim lands that were under Alfonso's protection—and the charge of embezzlement of tribute money that was made by some influential nobles whom he had bested on the battlefield—persuaded Alfonso to banish the Campeador twice, first in 1081–87 and then in 1089–92.

In 1085, Alfonso captured the Moorish city of Toledo and made it his capital, but in the following year Emir Yusuf ibn-Tashfin of the Almoravid dynasty of Morocco defeated him. Needing help, Alfonso recalled the Cid, but the latter did little fighting, since he had set his sights on winning the wealthy Moorish kingdom of Valencia on the east coast of the peninsula. He began besieging the city in 1092 and entered it in triumph in 1094, halting Almoravid expansion. Soon after the Cid's death in Valencia in 1099, the city fell to the Almoravids once again and was not reconquered by the Christians until 1238.

The Poem of the Cid is divided into three long *cantares*, or parts. The first *cantar* opens with the Cid, banished by King Alfonso, hastily departing his deserted palace in Vivar, with its pegs devoid of fur tunics and cloaks and its perches bereft of falcons and hawks. Entering Burgos with his sixty knights, he finds a ghost town whose silence is broken only by a nine-year-old girl who ventures out of a locked house to inform him that the king's awe-inspiring writ had preceded him, threatening anyone who lodged the Cid with confiscation of his property and loss of "the eyes of his face"—"*los ojos de las caras.*"

A brave citizen of Burgos, Martín Antolínez, provides the Cid and his men with bread and wine and joins them in their exile, not caring "*un figo*" for what he's leaving behind. Although the Cid has only his horse and armor, adventurous souls soon throw in their lot with him. It torments him to have to leave his wife and two young daughters behind at a monastery as he rides out to earn his livelihood by fighting in Moorish territory.

The Cid obtains some ready cash for paying his followers by a ruse worthy of Odysseus. He orders that two big chests be filled with sand and offered to the moneylenders Rachel and Vidas, along with the story that they are packed solid with gold (and are thus too heavy to take with him) and the stipulation that they not be unlocked and peered into for a full year. Meanwhile, many more men swell the ranks of the banished Campeador's private army. He captures the Moorish town of Castejón and takes Alcocer by a wily stratagem. After stoutly defeating a Moorish army—and selling Alcocer—he makes sure to send King Alfonso thirty horses, fully caparisoned, each with a sword hanging from the saddle.

In the second *cantar*, the Cid and his 3,600 men capture Valencia after a ten-month siege, and he sends Alfonso a hundred more horses, with the request that the king allow his wife and daughters to join him in his newly conquered city. The Cid's men slaughter an invading army of fifty thousand under King Yusuf of Morocco, the latter barely escaping the wrath of the Cid's right arm, dripping with blood down to his elbow. The Cid sends Alfonso Yusuf's captured tent with its gold tent poles—and yet another two hundred horses.

The mollified king now extends his pardon, and a reconciliation takes place in which the Cid shows his total submission by getting down on all fours and pulling up a mouthful of grass with his teeth: "*las yerbas del campo a dientes las tomó.*" At the request of Diego and Fernando, the infantes ("heirs," "princes") of Carrión, Alfonso agrees to marry off the Cid's daughters, Doña Elvira and Doña Sol, to the brothers, though the Cid expresses reservations about the match with the young men who are so absurdly proud of their aristocratic lineage.

With his newly acquired sons-in-law ensconced in Valencia, the Cid is taking a nap one day when his pet lion escapes. His men gather round to protect their sleeping lord, but the infantes almost soil themselves with fear, hiding ignominiously behind the Cid's couch and a filthy winepress. The Cid wakens, grabs the lion by the scruff of the neck, and leads it back into captivity. When he calls for his sons-in-law, they refuse to respond. Discovered cowering, they immediately become the laughingstock of the Cid's men, no matter how sternly he attempts to stifle the ridicule.

This risible scene cinematically opens the third *cantar*. The infantes proceed to demonstrate their cowardice anew in the victory of the Cid's forces over the invading hordes of King Búcar of Morocco, whom the Cid dispatches with a blow of his sword straight down on his helmet and continuing south to his waist. The infantes run away in battle but make up stories about their valor. Misinterpreting a remark of the Cid as mockery—and wilting under the open mockery of the army—the infantes huffily depart with their wives for their beloved Carrión.

On the way home, the infantes decide to humiliate the Cid for the episode of the lion by beating his daughters with straps and slashing them with their spurs, leaving them for dead in an oak grove. A nephew of the Cid who had been sent to keep an eye on the infantes saves the women's lives.

The outraged Cid asks for justice from Alfonso. At a court of justice held at Toledo, the infantes are required to give back two splendid swords and all the money they had received from the Cid. Calling the brothers "treacherous dogs" at the assemblage, the Cid arranges for his henchmen to challenge his sons-in-law to trials by combat, in which they are humiliatingly defeated. The marriages are annulled, and the Cid accepts offers to marry his daughters to the crown princes of Navarre and Aragon.

The poem portrays the Cid as a redoubtable warrior—impressive in the long, terrifying beard he has sworn to keep unshorn during his banishment—but also as a humane leader who treats his soldiers as equals. He is shown acting not only as a consummate soldier but also as a dutiful vassal, friend, husband, father, and Christian. The epic abounds in realistic touches and avoids the supernatural—at most, the angel Gabriel appears to the Cid in a dream—as opposed to the frequent angelic visitations and sundry religious paraphernalia of *The Song of Roland*.

The Cid figures in a later incomplete Spanish epic, *Mocedades de Rodrigo* (*The Youth of Rodrigo*), and also appears as a character in *Las almenas de Toro* (*The Battlements of Toro*) of the great Spanish playwright Lope de Vega. Pierre Corneille's tragedy *Le Cid* (1636), often seen as inaugurating modern French drama, was based on yet another Spanish play and not on the *Poema de Mio Cid*, since the latter was first published only in 1779. After a long night of relative obscurity, a major medieval masterpiece finally saw the light of day.

The *Poema* was soon hailed by English and German authors and scholars, such as Robert Southey, who called it the most Homeric poem in spirit since the *Iliad*; Henry Hallam, who saw it as the greatest post-classical work to appear in Europe before Dante's *Divine Comedy*; and Friedrich Schlegel, who considered it a superb embodiment of the Spanish character. In the twentieth century, the early episodes of the poem were deftly evoked in Ezra Pound's "Canto 3," and the Spanish national epic has survived even a 1961 film version starring Charlton Heston and Sophia Loren.

THIRTEENTH CENTURY

90 ∾ What was the first sack of Constantinople?

The sack during the Fourth Crusade in 1204

EVERY SCHOOLCHILD USED TO LEARN that Constantinople fell to the Ottoman Turks in 1453. For a thousand years, the "queen of all cities," capital of the Eastern Roman Empire (aka the Byzantine Empire or Byzantium), had been the guardian of classical learning, preserving the heritage of Greco-Roman literature, art, science, and law even as Western Europe sank into barbarism. It was also the great bulwark of Christendom. Over the centuries, its armies halted the advance of successive waves of Asiatic invaders, from the Persians and Arabs to the Avars and Bulgars, sheltering Western Europe and allowing it to develop in relative security as it emerged from the Dark Ages.

What is less well known is that the sack of Constantinople in 1453 was neither the first nor the most fateful. The Byzantine Empire that fell to the Turkish sultan Mehmed II was already an enfeebled state living on borrowed time (see Question 109). It may have given up the ghost in 1453, but the blow that crippled it had been struck two and a half centuries earlier in 1204 during the Fourth Crusade. It is one of history's great ironies that the crusader host, originally assembled to liberate the Holy Land from Muslim domination, ended up sacking Christian Constantinople, dismembering the Byzantine Empire, and paving the way for the Turkish conquest of large parts of Europe.

The story of the Fourth Crusade, with its Machiavellian twists and turns, reads like a medieval whodunit. The central figure in the tale is Enrico Dandolo, the aging doge of Venice, who masterminded the crusade's diversion to Constantinople and, though half-blind and in his eighties (some sources say nineties), personally led the assault on its walls. There is some scholarly debate about whether Dandolo planned to conquer Byzantium from the outset or merely seized the opportunity when it arose. Either way, the result was the same: At a single stroke, he transformed the republic of Venice from a rising commercial power into the capital of a Mediterranean maritime empire.

The story begins in 1198, when Pope Innocent III called for a new crusade to recapture Jerusalem, which a decade earlier had fallen to the

Muslim armies of Saladin after nearly a century of Christian rule (see Question 82). Inspired by the charismatic preacher Fulk of Neuilly, many prominent Frankish barons took up the cross. (The term *Franks* refers to all Western Europeans, though most of the barons were in fact French.)

In the spring of 1201, the barons sent envoys to Venice to arrange maritime transport for an army of 33,500. The embassy, headed by Geoffrey de Villehardouin, marshal of Champagne and author of the eyewitness account that is our principal source for the crusade, struck a deal with Dandolo—or, more precisely, took the deal that was offered and signed on the dotted line. Venice agreed to build, man, and provision a fleet large enough to transport the crusaders, as well as provide fifty heavily armed galleys at its own expense "for the love of God." The price: eighty-five thousand marks, roughly twice the combined annual income of the kings of France and England. The host was to gather in Venice a year later in June 1202, at which time the fleet would be ready and payment due in full.

The host mustered in Venice on the appointed date, but rather than 33,500 knights and men-at-arms, barely one-third of the expected number showed up. From this moment on, the fate of the crusade was in Dandolo's hands. When it became clear that the smaller force could not scrape together more than a fraction of the sum owed Venice, Dandolo offered to defer repayment of the debt (defer, not forgive—he drove a hard bargain) if the crusaders would help the Venetians recover Zara, a rebellious dependency on the Dalmatian coast that had put itself under the protection of the king of Hungary. The Frankish barons hesitated. After all, Zara was a Christian city—and the king of Hungary had himself taken up the cross. But in the end, they overcame their scruples, the fleet sailed, and Zara was captured and sacked in November 1202. When the news reached Rome, the pope excommunicated the entire host.

While the crusaders were wintering at Zara, an embassy arrived from Alexius Angelus, son of the Byzantine emperor Isaac II, who had lost his throne a few years before in a palace coup. The crown prince promised to pay two hundred thousand marks and lend military assistance to the crusaders—provided they first took a small detour to Constantinople, deposed the usurper Alexius III, and restored his own family to the purple. He also promised to reunite the Roman and Greek Orthodox churches, which had split in the Great Schism of 1054 (see Question 39). Villehardouin, with touching naïveté, seems to regard the turn of events as a happy coincidence. But the proposed deal almost certainly came as no surprise to either Dandolo or Boniface de Montferrat, the crusade's titular leader, who himself had close family ties to Byzantium.

However the deal came about, it seemed to solve everyone's problems. It suited the Franks, who could now hope to repay their debt to the Venetians. It suited the papacy, which had long sought to reassert Roman primacy over the Greek Church. Innocent III did a quick about-face, lifted the excommunication, and gave the expedition his blessing. Above all, it suited the Venetians. For more than a century, La Serenissima's merchants had enjoyed extensive trading privileges in the Byzantine Empire that gave them a virtual monopoly over its maritime commerce. In recent years, however, Venice found its position threatened. It faced fierce competition from the upstart Genoese and Pisan maritime republics—and growing hostility from the Byzantines. In 1171, all Venetian merchants had been temporarily expelled from the empire—and in 1182, a Greek mob had massacred the inhabitants of the Venetian quarter in Constantinople. The deal presented an extraordinary opportunity to put Venice back on top.

The crusader fleet appeared before Constantinople in June of 1203. After negotiations failed to produce results, the crusaders stormed the city. The main attack was launched against Constantinople's seawalls by the Venetian galleys, with Dandolo, in full armor, the first to leap ashore. The city fell, Alexius III fled, and Isaac II emerged from a dungeon beneath the imperial palace to reclaim the throne, with his son, now proclaimed Alexius IV, as coemperor. The crusaders then withdrew across the Golden Horn to await the promised payoff.

The new emperors, however, found that the imperial treasury was almost empty—and their debt impossible to repay. In desperation, they imposed burdensome taxes that infuriated the Byzantine nobility and alienated the populace. In January 1204, Isaac II and Alexius IV were deposed in a new palace coup. The first act of the new emperor—yet another Alexius, this one nicknamed Murzuphlus on account of his thick eyebrows that met in the middle—was to repudiate the debt to the crusaders.

Thus we arrive at the denouement. In a stirring oration, Dandolo persuaded the Franks that the only possible response to the Byzantines' perfidy was to seize the city and empire for themselves. Although the crusaders' second assault on Constantinople was more fiercely resisted than the first, the city nonetheless fell on April 13, 1204. The three-day sack that followed was a notoriously savage affair, even by medieval standards. In comparison with these creatures "who bear the cross of Christ upon their shoulders," writes Nicetas Choniates, a Byzantine historian who lived through the carnage, "even the Saracens are merciful and kind."

The affair was also extremely lucrative. "So much booty," wrote Villehardouin, "had never been gained in any city since the creation of the world." Both the Franks and the Venetians plundered, but only the Franks wantonly destroyed. The Venetians selected the finest of the imperial and ecclesiastical treasures, crated them up, and shipped them back to Venice, which as a result possesses one of the finest collections of Byzantine art in the world. Much of the loot ended up adorning St. Mark's Basilica, including the four horses formerly perched above its main portals (and now, replaced by copies, housed within the church's museum). The only full-scale equestrian bronzes to survive from antiquity, they are thought to have stood in the Hippodrome of the Byzantine capital since the days of Constantine and the city's founding.

When order was finally restored, the Franks and the Venetians partitioned the empire in accordance with the terms of a sworn pact executed prior to the sack. Dandolo shrewdly conceded the emperorship, and hence the semblance of power, to the Franks. The emperor, however, was little more than a figurehead handpicked by Dandolo, and the doge of Venice was in any case exempted from paying him homage. The Franks also acquired a collection of disconnected feudal principalities carved out of the empire—and the thankless job of skirmishing with the Byzantine Greeks, who set up rival states in Nicaea, Epirus, and Trebizond, each of which claimed to be the legitimate government in exile.

For its part, Venice got exclusive trading privileges, extraterritoriality, and an unbroken string of fortified naval bases stretching from the Adriatic to the Black Sea that long outlasted the new Latin Empire itself. The Byzantines recovered Constantinople in 1261 with the help of Genoa, Venice's archrival. But Venice held on to its last naval base, Spinalonga in Crete, until 1718.

Although the Latin Empire was short-lived, the Fourth Crusade cast a long shadow over subsequent history. Instead of healing, it hardened the schism between Eastern and Western Christendom. It also fatally weakened the Byzantine state, which never recovered more than a fraction of its former territories or power. After 1261, the restored

Byzantine Empire managed to survive for nearly two more centuries by cleverly playing off the Genoese against the Venetians. With each passing year, however, the Turkish noose was drawn ever tighter.

—*Richard Jackson*

91 ⮞ Who was the first ruler of the Mongol Empire?

Genghis Khan, ruled 1206–27

THE FAVORITE PASTIME OF GENGHIS KHAN, founder of the Mongol Empire, was "to crush my enemies and hear the lamentation of their women." Christians called his Mongol soldiers *Tartars* (from the Tatars, the name of a tribe that Genghis exterminated), assimilating the word to Tartarus, the classical underworld of diabolically fierce torments for egregious criminals.

Genghis began life as Temujin (1162–1227), a member of a royal Mongol clan who spent his youth on the run from or imprisoned by his enemies. By cunning, a steely will, and shifty alliances, he managed to gather a large army that he used to destroy his aristocratic foes and enslave or annihilate the tribes he had issues with.

In 1206, after uniting the thirty-odd tribes of the nomadic Mongols ("the brave men"), the burly, middle-aged Temujin was proclaimed "Genghis Khan" ("Universal Ruler") by tribal leaders at their holy place of Karakorum on the Mongolian steppe. A fearsome amount of koumiss—fermented mare's milk with a kick to it—and boiled mutton must have been consumed on the occasion. Soon, however, most of the inhabitants of Eurasia would have little to celebrate, for the Mongols, in the words of historian William H. McNeill, "came as a horde of fierce and barbarian warriors, prepared to treat their human victims as they treated animals rounded up in their annual great hunts: domesticating or slaughtering them as circumstances might dictate."

Under Genghis, Mongol warriors exploded onto the world scene during a century-long expansion that would plant their yak-tailed banners over an area stretching from Korea to the Adriatic. Among the earliest victims were Turkestan and northern China, then known as Cathay.

Vicious raids destroyed the Turkish Muslim Khwarezm Empire of Persia and Central Asia by 1220. In 1223, it was the turn of southern Russia, where a defending army was routed at the battle of the Kalka River. Genghis led his last campaign against the Hsi Hsia kingdom of the Tibetan-speaking Tanguts, which fell in 1227, the year of his death. His armies remained undefeated after two decades of warfare, and his empire, extending from the site of present-day Beijing to the Caspian, was divided among three sons of his principal wife under the suzerainty of their brother Ögödei, who was the first Mongol ruler to style himself *khagan* ("great khan").

What made the Mongols such successful conquerors? Their superbly mobile light-cavalry archers used stirrups and saddle-steadying cruppers that enabled them to shoot their armor-piercing arrows with lethal accuracy in any direction while they continued to ride. Their heavy cavalry then swooped in with lance and mace to finish off the survivors. Far from being a mass of undisciplined savages, the Mongol army was highly organized and trained, using couriers and scouts to maintain communications and coordinate movements over enormous distances between columns of their invading forces. Its tactics of wide encirclement enabled it to close a huge noose around its foes until the battle became, to mix the metaphor, like shooting fish in a barrel. The Mongols also excelled in the feigned retreat that elicited pursuit and ended in the ambush and slaughter of the unwary enemy.

Contact with the highly developed civilizations of China and Islam taught the Mongols how to batter down walls and resistance with mangonels—catapults for hurling massive stones. Perhaps their chief weapons were their own indefatigable hardihood and their use of terror to paralyze opposition by indiscriminate massacres even of defeated or unarmed populaces.

Genghis's successor Ögödei (r. 1229–41) established his capital city at Karakorum and proceeded to swallow up, in 1234, the Jin Empire of the Manchurian tribes of northern China. He conquered Korea in 1236 and sent his nephew Batu Khan to ravage Russia. Batu sacked and burned Russia's largest city, Kiev, in 1240 (see Question 67) and, in the following year, invaded Poland, torching Cracow and defeating a Polish-German army at Liegnitz in Silesia. Hungary was next; Buda and Pest were sacked, and sixty thousand men of the army of King Béla IV were killed. Raiding parties had reached the outskirts of Vienna when Batu learned of the great khan Ögödei's death in

Mongolia and withdrew to establish his virtually independent khanate at Sarai on the Lower Volga.

In addition to Batu's new realm, named the Golden Horde (from the gold brocade covering his residence and "horde" from the Turkic for "camp" or "court") and comprising southern Russia and Eastern Europe, two other main khanates developed: that founded by Genghis's son Chagatai in Central Asia and the ilkhanate ("lesser khanate") of the Middle East under Genghis's grandson Hülegü. The titular head of the entire empire was the great khan, who ruled directly over Mongolia, China, and Korea.

Güyük, son of Ögödei, was great khan only from 1246 to 1248 but helped himself to Tibet in the interim. His successor, Möngke (r. 1251–59), a grandson of Genghis, sent his brother Hülegü to suppress a rebellion in Persia with one hundred fifty thousand men, including subject warriors and a thousand artillerymen from China. Hülegü dutifully wiped out the Assassins (see Question 80) and established his ilkhanate in Tabriz in 1256. In 1258, he devastated Baghdad for forty days, massacring eight hundred thousand in the process of overthrowing the doddering Abbasid caliphate (see Question 50). When the last caliph, al-Mustasim, surrendered during the siege, he and his sons were sewn inside rugs and trampled to death by horses, since the Mongols could be superstitiously finicky about spilling royal blood. Before his death in 1259, Möngke annexed what later became known as Thailand and Vietnam, as well as Korea.

Like Batu before him, Hülegü withdrew east with most of his army when great khan Möngke's death sparked a succession crisis. After Damascus and Aleppo had fallen to the Mongols, the Mamluk sultan of Egypt defeated the diminished Mongol forces at Ain Jalut near Nazareth in 1260 and drove them from Syria, saving the heartlands of Islam from conquest.

In 1260, Kublai Khan, yet another grandson of Genghis, became the new ruler of the Mongol Empire. After a journey from Venice that took three and a half years, Marco Polo reached Kublai's capital of Khanbalik or Daidu (present Beijing) in 1275 and made sure to visit his summer palace of Xanadu (Shangdu) in Inner Mongolia, with its "stately pleasure dome" of gilded canes. Marco was in his service from 1275 to 1292, marveling at his use of paper money and claiming that "all the emperors of the world and all the kings of Christians and Saracens combined would not possess such power or be able to accomplish so much as this Kublai, the Great Khan."

Kublai overthrew the Southern Song dynasty of China and, in 1279, founded his Yuan dynasty (1279–1368), thus reuniting the north and south of the country for the first time since 907. Only two years later, he lost more than one hundred thousand men in a typhoon during his second attempt to conquer Japan—the largest catastrophe ever to befall a Mongol force (see Question 88). An invasion of Java also came to ill, and Mongol expansion ceased after Kublai's death in 1294.

Sprawling from Korea to Hungary, the Mongol domain was more than six times larger than the Roman Empire. It was the vastest continuous land empire the world has ever seen—second in size only to the British Empire—but it fell apart rapidly in the fourteenth century, especially after the Black Death ravaged half its people (see Question 99). A spasmodic last gasp occurred when Timur, or Tamerlane (1336–1405), a Turkic vizier of the Chagatai khanate, seized power and left behind pyramids of human skulls as he stormed through Mesopotamia, Persia, Turkey, Russia, and northern India in an attempt to restore the Mongol Empire. Meanwhile, a Chinese Buddhist monk had led a revolt that drove the detested Mongols beyond the Great Wall, becoming the first emperor of the Ming dynasty in 1368. Twenty years later, the Chinese destroyed the former Mongol capital of Karakorum, and Timur died of plague in 1405 while attempting to conquer Ming China for himself.

92 ⟳ Who were the first friars?

The Franciscans, founded by Francis of Assisi; recognized in 1209

MEDIEVAL MONASTIC ORGANIZATIONS WERE ENORMOUS wealth attractors. The rapid growth of Cluny (see Question 70) and St. Bernard's propagation of the Cistercians in the twelfth century could be casebook studies at Harvard Business School. Whenever a group with a wise administrator organized under a rule (*regula*) to work and pray, money followed. Some monasteries supported themselves by selling the fruits of their agriculture or viniculture; many received bequests and endowments from aristocrats who hoped to secure a good place in the next world.

After 1200, however, something else seemed called for. Monks could work, write, and pray in mountaintop abbeys, but towns and cities were filling with disenfranchised poor, and heresy was rife. In the face of deep poverty, the lifestyles of abbots, bishops, and priests seemed opulent and out of touch with the spiritual and material needs of a growing portion of the flock.

As if in response to this need, four orders of friars (Latin *fratres*, "brothers") arose in the thirteenth century with an object at variance with monastic seclusion: They were to plunge into the world armed with nothing but their mission to do the Lord's work among men. Some would do physical labor, and others would teach. With no property or means of support, they were to beg their daily bread and a place to sleep from those to whom they ministered—hence the term mendicant (that is, "begging") orders.

First to be recognized by the church was the Order of Friars Minor ("little brothers"), founded by a little man from Assisi. Francis received Pope Innocent III's verbal blessing for his band of twelve men in 1209 after, it is said, Innocent dreamed he beheld the future saint holding up the Lateran Basilica. Pope Honorius III confirmed the order, also known as the Gray Friars because of the color of their robes, in 1223.

In 1215, a Castilian later known as St. Dominic obtained papal authorization for his Order of Preaching Friars (or Black Friars), which was tasked specifically with defending the true faith against heretics, including the Albigensians of Languedoc. In 1245, the Carmelites, or White Friars, originally a contemplative order in the Holy Land, reformed as mendicants. Several other small monastic groups united as mendicants under the name of Augustinians (Austin Friars) in 1256. All four orders of friars were recognized at the Second Council of Lyons in 1274, which suppressed several other would-be mendicant organizations.

The crux of mendicant rules was the renunciation of property. In the storied life of St. Francis, this embrace of "Lady Poverty" took a number of forms. There was the famous moment when Francis, formerly Assisi's life of the party, publicly stripped himself naked in order to follow his heavenly father instead of his earthly father, a wealthy merchant. There are the charming moments when birds, fish, rabbits, and all of nature relate to Francis as kin, because, like the lilies of the field, none of them owned a thing.

But Francis was possessed to go further. To scorn the right to possess was to be ravished by all the ills flesh is heir to. Asked where perfect joy is to be found, he replied:

When we knock at the door, and the doorkeeper comes in a rage and says, "Who are you?" and we say, "We are two of your friars," and he answers, "You lie, you are rather two

knaves . . . begone!" and he . . . makes us stay outside hungry
and cold all night in the rain and snow . . . and if he . . . issues
forth with a big knotted stick and seizes us by our cowls and
flings us on the ground, and rolls us in the snow, bruising
every bone in our bodies; if we, thinking on the agony of the
blessed Christ, endure all these things patiently and joyously
for love of Him . . . in this is found perfect joy!

Likewise, when St. Dominic was being abusively threatened by
heretics who asked if he feared death, he offered a reply worthy of Jef-
frey Dahmer:

I would have begged you, he said, not to have slain me suddenly, but little by little to have hewn limb from limb, one after
another, and then that you would show before my eyes my
body parts cut to pieces, and then that you would leave my
body so lying, fouled in my blood, without having slain me as
you wished.

Led by these "two princes," as Dante has St. Thomas Aquinas, the
greatest Dominican, so honor them in the *Paradiso*, the mendicants
grew by leaps and bounds. When Francis died in 1226, his friars numbered five thousand; by 1280, there were two hundred thousand little
brothers spread over eight thousand monasteries across Europe. They
remain the largest Roman Catholic order and were the first to sail to
America (with Columbus) and travel to China (Friar Odoric, in about
1318). The other orders experienced similar momentum, spreading the
Gospel far and wide. An Englishman in 1240 described a group of
Dominicans thus: "Shod only with the gospel, they slept in their clothes
on mats, and laid stones for pillows under their heads."
About 150 years later, another Englishman offered this depiction:

A friar there also was, wanton and merry,
A limiter—a very important man.

By the time Geoffrey Chaucer immortalized Friar Hubert riding on the
way to Canterbury, the begging men of God had become a literary and
social type rich in traits of hypocrisy, decadence, and corruption.
"People were beginning to regard poverty as a social evil instead of an
apostolic virtue," wrote historian Johan Huizinga.

If Francis had sought to literally imitate Christ by becoming a walking Sermon on the Mount, many of his later followers were less faithful to the letter. The friars had become past masters at finding ways to divert revenue streams that were formerly the sole province of priests and other churchmen. Indeed, Chaucer's portrait reads like a point-by-point subversion of Francis's own rules:

FRANCIS: All the brothers are to wear inexpensive clothing, and they can use sackcloth and other material to mend it with God's blessing.

HUBERT: *But he was like a provost or a pope.*
Of double worsted was his semi-cope
And rounded like a bell straight from the mould.

FRANCIS: Those who must may wear shoes.

HUBERT: *For though a widow had no shoes to wear,*
So pleasant was his greeting to her ear
He always got a farthing before he went.

FRANCIS: I strictly forbid the brothers to receive money in any form either directly or through an intermediary.

HUBERT: *For if one gave, he dared to boast outright,*
He knew the man had truly been contrite.
For many a man there is so hard of heart
He cannot weep, for all that it may smart.
Therefore, instead of weeping and of prayers,
Men can give silver to the impoverished frères.

FRANCIS: I strictly order all the brothers to avoid suspicious meetings or conversations with women and to stay out of the convents of nuns.

HUBERT: *His sleeve was always stuffed with little knives*
And pins and things to give to pretty wives. . . .
And he could flirt as well as any pup.

Chaucer drew upon an already abundant literary tradition of images of devious and venal friars. In *The Romance of the Rose,* the hypocritical character Faux-Semblant ("False-Seeming") is presented as a Franciscan; *Piers Plowman* gives us a friar named Penetrans Domos ("Home Penetrator"); and in Boccaccio's *Decameron* a worthless crook reinvents himself as Friar Alberto of Imola, who convinces a gullible Venetian beauty that the angel Gabriel wishes to enjoy her nocturnal caresses—but would like to use the humble friar's body to consummate the sacred union, if she wouldn't mind. (She didn't.)

For many in the fourteenth century, the legacy of Francis and Dominic had been profoundly betrayed; the scabrous denouement of Chaucer's *Summoner's Tale* was mere poetic justice (see Question 103). Francis's radical way of following Christ led to fissures within the church as well. Other orders had enjoined their individual members to embrace poverty, but their communities were allowed to own property. Each follower of Bernard owned nothing, but the order had accumulated a fortune in lands, buildings, and endowments.

Francis disrupted the entire system. Neither individual friars *nor the order* was to own anything. The only source of means was begging, according to the Spirituals, those Franciscan friars who adhered to the belief that Jesus and the apostles owned nothing (in contrast to the Conventuals, who took a more moderate approach). If someone gave a house or land to the order, what was given was the mere use; the property remained in the owner's hands and, if he died, it went to the pope.

At the time of this dispute, the popes were living a princely life in Avignon, France, provoking criticism from the Spirituals, who promoted a more basic Christianity. Pope John XXII (1316–34), in particular, was not pleased to think he reminded people of Croesus. He argued with legal precision that if the Friars Minor had permanent use of a house or land, any meaningful distinction between use and outright ownership was obliterated. What's more, if they continued to argue with him, they just might qualify as heretics.

To which the Franciscan William of Ockham (1288–1348), one of the most brilliant philosophers of his own or any other time, countered that the legal sense of "property" was inappropriate to his order. As with Adam and Eve before they bit into the forbidden fruit, friars enjoy the use of things by "natural right." Such right has no standing in a court of law, being more like a permission that can be revoked at any time. Further, he suggested it might be the pope who was behaving heretically in ruling against the Spirituals.

This was bold. Fearing imprisonment and possible execution,

Ockham and other Franciscan leaders fled to Germany and lived out their lives under the protection of the Holy Roman Emperor.

Later, another potent critic of church corruption arose in Germany when Martin Luther, a former Austin friar, traced mendicant corruption back to Francis's vow of poverty. "The evil friar's life began early," he wrote, "when people, under color of piety, abandoned temporal matters."

—*Tom Matrullo*

93 ∾ What was the first guarantee of rights exacted from an English king?

The Magna Carta, wrested by his barons from King John in 1215

WHEN HENRY I, youngest son of William the Conqueror, ascended the English throne in 1100, he faced a host of political challenges, including hostility from his earls and barons due to rampant corruption during the reign of his brother, William II. To placate them, the new king issued the Charter of Liberties, a fourteen-point declaration in which he pledged himself to "end all the oppressive practices which have been an evil presence in England"—among them, royal interference with the church and marriages, as well as excessive and arbitrary taxes and death duties.

Though the Charter of Liberties was the forerunner of the Magna Carta, its issuance was a political ploy by Henry for currying favor with his nobles and other subjects. The charter was never enforced and largely ignored throughout the following century, but by the time John became king in 1199, the barons were again restive and not likely to be satisfied by a mere show of concessions.

The early years of John's reign were marked by disputes with the French king and Rome. The death of the archbishop of Canterbury in 1205 led to a confrontation between John and Pope Innocent III, in which the king sought to increase his power over the English Church by appointing his own candidate rather than the choice of one of their own by the monks of Canterbury or the papally sanctioned Stephen Langton. The conflict between king, pope, and clergy resulted in John's expulsion of the recalcitrant monks from his realm and his branding of

Langton's supporters as public enemies. The pope retaliated by placing England under interdict of the sacraments in 1208 and by excommunicating the king in the following year.

By 1213, however, with John increasingly fearful that he would be deposed and England invaded by Philip II Augustus of France at the behest of the pope, he decided to accept Langton and allow the Canterbury exiles to return. Moreover, he handed over England and Ireland as papal fiefdoms, renting them back from the pope for one thousand marks a year.

This act of surrender outraged the English barons, who had grown increasingly disgruntled, not only with the king's abusive treatment, but also with his political blunders. The enormous English holdings in Normandy, Brittany, Anjou, Maine, and Touraine had been retaken by Philip in 1204 following a disputed marriage contract, and John allied himself with Otto IV of Germany and the princes of Flanders with the goal of bringing these wealthy, income-generating lands back under his control.

But John and his allies were decisively defeated in France by Philip at the battle of Bouvines in 1214. The English king demanded yet more taxes from his subjects to recoup his losses, increasing scutage fees (payments in exchange for avoidance of military service) and imposing massive inheritance duties on some of his nobles. By the spring of 1215, the barons had rebelled and were besieging John's castles, and at Northampton on May 5 they formally renounced their fealty to the king. Twelve days later they arrived in London, where they were allowed free entry.

Negotiations with the king and clergy ensued, with Archbishop Langton encouraging the barons to model their demands on the old Charter of Liberties. But the nobles went far beyond the vague generalities of the earlier document and their own complaints against the king, essentially addressing the whole system of governance. The resulting Articles of the Barons can be considered the earliest European written constitution.

On June 15, 1215, the king met with the barons and prelates at Runnymede, a meadow beside the Thames, and affixed his great seal to the document that became known as the Magna Carta—"the Great Charter." For the first time in English history, the ruler had been forced to grant the demands of the ruled and acknowledge that English law was binding even on the king. Moreover, the rights and safeguards exacted from John were not limited to the barons but included all freemen.

After a preamble, in which the king greeted his officials and loyal subjects, the Magna Carta contained sixty-three clauses dealing with numerous practical concerns of a feudal society. For example, the "relief" (payment made by a feudal tenant on his inheritance of an estate) was established at one hundred pounds for a baron's or an earl's estate and one hundred shillings for a knight's. Underage heirs were guaranteed receipt of their inheritance on attaining majority without payment of relief. Widows were also guaranteed their inheritance and could not be forced to remarry if they did not wish to do so. The goods of any freeman were to be disposed according to his will and, if he died intestate, would be distributed to his heirs.

Checks placed on the king included the requirement that he levy only reasonable profits from his estates and pay for their upkeep with revenues they generated. Also, he would not be allowed to seize a baron's landholdings as repayment of a debt if the baron possessed sufficient other "goods and chattels" to discharge it. Furthermore, certain wrongs that John perpetrated on his subjects would be undone: "All fines made with us unjustly and against the law of the land, and all amercements [punishments] imposed unjustly and against the law of the land, shall be entirely remitted."

Further clauses stipulated that merchants be allowed to transact business without the imposition of arbitrary tolls and fees and that they (and all freemen) be allowed passage into and out of the kingdom without interference. Weights and measures were to be standardized throughout the realm.

Judicial rights also were prominent in the Magna Carta. Fixed law courts were to be established, and fines were required to be proportionate to offenses. Only judges, not officers of the crown, could try crimes. Several of the most renowned clauses set forth what we now refer to as the rights of habeas corpus and due process, stating that courts may make inquiries as to the whereabouts of a prisoner, that no one may be put on trial without reliable witnesses, and that "no freeman shall be arrested or imprisoned . . . except by the lawful judgment of his peers or by the law of the land."

But the most direct challenge to the king in 1215 was the "security clause"—number 61: "The barons shall elect twenty-five barons of the kingdom to observe and hold, and cause to be observed, the peace and liberties we have granted and confirmed to them by this Charter." In other words, the twenty-five most powerful barons could overrule the king if they disagreed with his actions and could seize the crown's castles, lands, and possessions under the feudal practice of distraint, which permitted the seizure of property as payment of debt or other claim. In effect, they could declare war on the king if he refused to accede to their wishes. Moreover, this council of twenty-five, created for the good of the state rather than as a tool of the king, represented an early form of parliament (see Question 96).

King John submitted to the barons' demands on June 15 but subsequently requested the ruling of Pope Innocent, who declared the Magna Carta null and void on August 24, stating that John's agreement to the document had been coerced. Innocent also asserted that since John had ceded his kingdom as a papal fiefdom in 1213, he was a vassal of the pope and incapable of entering into binding agreements without papal approval. Civil war ensued between John and the rebellious nobles, who now favored Prince Louis of France, but within a year John was dead of dysentery, and the English forces supporting his nine-year-old son, soon crowned as Henry III, drove out the invading French troops.

The Magna Carta was reissued by court councillors in 1216 and 1217 and by Henry III himself in 1225 after he had come of age. For the next two hundred years, each subsequent king reconfirmed the 1225 charter.

Four copies of the original 1215 Magna Carta exist. One is held at the British Library and another at Westminster Palace, both in London. A third is on display at Salisbury Cathedral, and a fourth is owned by Lincoln Cathedral. The Lincoln copy, lent for the 1939 New York World's Fair, was held for safekeeping in Fort Knox for the duration of World War II.

Today the Magna Carta is often considered the historic prototype of later declarations of law and liberty, such as the French Declaration of the Rights of Man and of the Citizen, issued in 1789, and the United States Constitution and Bill of Rights, with its Fifth Amendment assertion that "No person shall be . . . deprived of life, liberty, or property, without due process of law."

When the American colonists rebelled against England, they were fighting for rights and liberties exacted by the Magna Carta that had evolved into common law for all Englishmen, colonists included. Like King John's barons, they took up arms for what they perceived as the violation of these rights and liberties by an unjust and tyrannical king.

—Nancy Walsh

94 ❧ Who launched the first papal Inquisition?

Pope Gregory IX against the Albigensians (Cathars)
of southern France in 1233

In July of 1209, the learned, aristocratic, and iron-willed Pope Innocent III (1198–1216), "the Augustus of the Papacy," sent an army of twenty thousand on a crusade. The enemy was nowhere near the Holy Land—or even in Constantinople (see Question 90)—but relatively close by in southern France, where as many as a third of the people had fallen prey to a religious belief that had little to do with Christianity. By the end of the holy war, which dragged on for twenty years until 1229, whatever dregs remained of the exquisite culture of the Provençal troubadours were stomped into the dirt, the luxury-loving cities and towns of the Midi impoverished, and the nobles and populace converted into either the dead victims or living despisers of the church and the northern kingdom of France (see Question 83).

The goal of the crusaders was the elimination of the Cathars, a sect that had spread throughout the southern French lands often loosely referred to as Provence, Languedoc, Occitania, or the Midi. A bloody landgrab ensued on the part of the French nobles of the north, who thrilled at the prospects of a crusade against their southern counterparts. The pope had promised that conquered territories would belong to the victors—besides plenary forgiveness of sins and guaranteed places in the heavenly mansions above.

What prompted Pope Innocent to pull the trigger was the murder in 1208 of a papal legate to the heretical south by vassals of Count Raymond VI of Toulouse (r. 1194–1222), one of the most powerful nobles of Western Europe, who had been excommunicated in the previous year and, for his supposed complicity in the assassination, was to be publicly scourged in the following year. In the war's first major military operation, at Béziers in 1209, the ecclesiastical leader of the crusade, Abbot Arnold of Citeaux, may never actually have responded, when asked by the victorious French soldiers how to tell apart the Cathars from the Catholics, "Kill them all! God will know his own." Nonetheless, the town was sacked, most of the population slaughtered—twenty thousand men, women, and children—and the city burned to the ground. Carcassonne was next; the city was taken, the inhabitants massacred, and four hundred heretics burned. In 1213, the pious, ambitious, and brilliant military leader of the crusade, the French nobleman Simon de Montfort, routed a large army at the battle of Muret, in which King Peter II of Aragon, fighting for Occitania, was killed, and fifteen to twenty thousand southern soldiers were either cut down or drowned in the Garonne.

Soon after Simon was appointed lord of all the conquered realms of the south, he was killed in 1218 by a woman flinging a stone down on his head from the walls of Toulouse, which he was besieging. The lands, including the county of Toulouse, were temporarily wrenched back by the southern nobles but subsequently ceded to the king of France.

The Cathars (from the Greek for "pure ones"), also called Albigensians from the southern town of Albi, weren't so much a Christian heretical sect as the followers of a non-Christian religion that ultimately derived from the Manichaeans of ancient Persia and the Eastern Roman Empire (see Question 20). Sprouting up in the Midi in the early eleventh century, probably brought there by traders and, afterward, crusaders who may have picked up shards of Manichaean-like beliefs from the Bogomils in the Balkans, Catharism constituted a separate church in southern France by 1160 with adherents and sympathizers ranging from the lowest to the very highest strata of society. It was a dualistic religion that claimed God had created only spirit, whereas everything in the material world, including human bodies, was the work of a sinister deity. Humans were considered to be souls trapped in evil bodies.

The religion was divided into a large body of *credentes* (believers), whose lives were sometimes shockingly dissolute, and a tiny cadre of *perfecti*, who were practically worshipped as divinities. The *perfecti* were ascetic priests—no meat, no sex, no money—who could administer the all-important *consolamentum* (consolation), a laying on of hands that forgave all a person's sins and guaranteed reception into heaven, if no further transgressions occurred. Since most *credentes* postponed receiving the *consolamentum* until they were on their deathbeds, many whooped it up until then.

The Cathars taught that Christ was a creature, believed the Old Testament was the Scripture of the evil God, embraced the doctrine of the transmigration of souls (hence their vegetarianism), were fiercely anti-clerical, criticized the greed and worldliness of prelates and monks, saw the material world as inherently corrupt and worthless, encouraged suicide, and often lived hypocritical lives dedicated to lechery, gluttony, inebriation, and other fun things, relying on their last-minute sacrament to make up for a lifetime of debauchery.

Needless to say, the Catholic Church was aghast, Innocent III considering the Cathars "worse than the Saracens." Beginning in the late twelfth century, an episcopal Inquisition had signally failed to root them out, largely because the local bishops were often absentee potentates with other matters on their minds. What was needed was a troop of professional, full-time, well-trained inquisitors. In 1233, after the crusade had also failed to eradicate the heresy, Pope Gregory IX (1227–41) appointed Dominican friars to carry out the first papal Inquisition.

The order had recently been founded by the future St. Dominic to teach, preach, and combat the Albigensian heresy (see Question 92), and he himself spent a dozen years doing so in the Midi. The fact that many members of the order were fanatics is conveyed by a contemporary pun on their Latin name of *Dominicanes*—"followers of Dominic"—and *Domini canes*—"the Lord's hounds."

The modus operandi of the inquisitors, who were responsible only to the pope, was to lure into their clutches people with a guilty conscience or a spotty past by preaching a fire-and-brimstone sermon that ended with the offer of a "grace period" of a week or so during which heretics could confess, recant their doctrinal errors, and receive the penance imposed on them—to go on a pilgrimage, go fight in the Crusades, carry a cross around their parish, forever wear two crosses on their garments, do charitable work, or recite certain prayers at specified times.

Those who did not surrender themselves and were later found guilty of heresy might be imprisoned in unspeakably foul oubliettes or handed over to the secular authorities to be burned at the stake, on rare occasions in large groups, as the first pair of papal inquisitors did with 210 victims at Moissac in 1234. In a notorious case, an old woman on her deathbed was tricked into revealing herself as a heretic by a bishop impersonating a Cathar and transported in her bed to the stake, bound to it, and immolated. Innumerable bodies were dug up and burned or dragged through the streets for having housed the souls of heretics.

Once engulfed by the inquisitorial system, self-accusers had to name names if they wished to be let off the hook. Enormous lists of suspects were thus compiled, each follow-up investigation spawning the names of new suspects until entire communities of possible heretics were available for the inquisitors' cherry-picking of the most promising cases. The inquisitor was prosecutor, jury, and sentencing judge. The accused had no right to face their accusers. The use of torture against tight-lipped heretics was authorized by the bull *Ad extirpanda* of Pope Innocent IV in 1252, though it was doubtlessly resorted to earlier. In short, the Inquisition initiated a system of police-state-style justice that eventually blossomed into the show trials, kangaroo courts, political purges, extracted confessions and denouncements, and deliberate creation of community-wide panic, suspicion, and terror for ideological ends that characterized much of the depressing twentieth century. Its modern literary embodiment is not only the chapter from Dostoyevsky's *The Brothers Karamazov* entitled "The Grand Inquisitor"—a fable in which Christ himself, appearing in Seville during the Spanish Inquisition, is arrested and accused of heresy—but also Franz Kafka's modern classic of justified paranoia, *The Trial*.

The nobles of the Midi rebelled in 1240 and 1242, but in 1244 the mountaintop fortress of Montségur in the Pyrenees, headquarters of the Cathar resistance since 1231, capitulated to the northern French armies after a ten-month siege. The result was the mass burning of more than two hundred of the surrendering Cathars who did not recant their faith and the destruction of their stronghold. In 1271, all of Languedoc passed into the hands of the French crown.

In 1320, an inquisitor bishop, Jacques Fournier, later Pope Benedict XII, interrogated people in the small village of Montaillou for suspected adherence to Catharism. The transcripts, published in the mid-twentieth century, furnish an unsurpassed view not only of Cathar beliefs but also of the daily activities of average people in the Middle Ages. That latest round of inquisitorial activities seems to have crippled Catharism, which limped along, however, until the end of the fourteenth century.

The infamous Spanish Inquisition was established by papal approval in 1478 under the authority of the *Reyes Católicos*, Ferdinand and Isabella (see Question 111). The Spanish inquisitor general, Tomás de Torquemada, promoted to grand inquisitor in 1487 by Pope Innocent VIII, sent about two thousand to the stake in his career. It was this Spanish version of the inquisitorial institution that was mainly in Voltaire's mind when he defined it as "an admirable and thoroughly Christian invention to make the pope and the monks more powerful and a whole kingdom hypocritical."

95 ∽ Who wrote the first sonnets?

The Sicilian poet and court official Giacomo da Lentini, c. 1233

IN CANTO 24 OF THE *PURGATORIO*, Dante sees the soul of an earlier Italian poet doing penance for the sin of gluttony and uses the occasion to deliver himself of a little disquisition on what made his own love poetry so much better than that of his interlocutor—and of Giacomo da Lentini and yet a third Italian poet who is mentioned: the fact that Dante was truly inspired by the emotion of love, almost as if he were taking dictation from its personified god, whereas the others were mere imitators.

Indeed, the poetic style of Giacomo da Lentini (d. c. 1250), designated by his birthplace in east-central Sicily, is often pedestrian and drab and his syntactical structures shaky. The conventionality of his verse, which rings slight changes on the clichéd tropes of the Provençal troubadours, reminds us that Giacomo and his colleagues of the so-called Sicilian School of poetry—the earliest to write in Italian—were true amateurs. They all held down demanding day jobs as judges, chancellors, magistrates, and other busy officials for the Italian-born Frederick II—called "the Wonder of the World"—the erudite Holy Roman Emperor and king of Sicily whose brilliant roving court was often based in Palermo from about 1220 to his death in 1250. Frederick's courtiers (and the king himself and his sons) dabbled in love poetry, especially in the form of the long, elaborate song known as the canzone, but writing poems remained for them an aristocratic refinement that rounded them out as accomplished gentlemen. Indeed, Giacomo was known as "the Notary," a position vastly more prestigious than its modern counterpart.

Almost a third of about 125 surviving poems from the Sicilian School are by Giacomo da Lentini, many more than by any of his colleagues. He seems to have been the leader of the group, which included several other poets of considerable talent (not all Sicilians, but also including southern Italians and Tuscans). His greatest gift to posterity, however, was the invention of the intricately rhymed, fourteen-line poems known as sonnets ("little songs"), the first of which may well have originated as a stanza of an unfinished canzone that was then prized for its succinctness and cultivated as a separate form.

In an Italian sonnet's first eight lines (the octet), a problem is posed or a situation established, which is then resolved, completed, contradicted, or commented on in the last six lines (the sestet). A common Italian rhyme scheme is *abbaabba cdecde*, but there are many variations. About twenty-five of Giacomo's sonnets have survived, though not in their original Sicilian dialect but in later Tuscanized versions.

Many of his sonnets are marred by frigid conceits: He's saturated with love—like a water-soaked sponge; he's like a plucked lily when he's away from his lady, rapidly fading away; like a moth to the flame, he doesn't fear being consumed by his love, which will, in fact, renew him, as self-immolation did for the legendary phoenix. He's tiresome when he mentions the *viso* ("visage") of his lady in each of a sonnet's first nine lines, but he's positively juvenile when he uses the word or its derivatives in all fourteen lines of another poem, sometimes as often as three times in a single line. This sort of thing prompted literary historian Francesco De Sanctis to refer to the "insipid ingenuities" of Giacomo's verse and led John Addington Symonds to decry the Sicilian School's "elegant and artificial monotony."

But Giacomo left behind at least two admirable sonnets. In both, his rhyme scheme is *abababab cdcdcd*, which my translations do not preserve, though in the first I've introduced a few rhymes to suggest some of the music of the original.

> *I've resolved in my heart to serve my God*
> *so that I'll go to Paradise someday,*
> *that holy realm where, I have heard men say,*
> *the happiness and joys endure forever.*
> *But without my lady I'd not want to go—*
> *the one with the blond head and the bright face—*
> *because, without her, I could not rejoice,*
> *separated from my lady in that place.*
>
> *I do not say this with the implication*
> *that I would want to sin with her up there,*
> *but only to look upon her noble bearing,*
> *her lovely visage, and her tender gaze.*
> *For it would be a mighty consolation*
> *to see my lady residing there in glory.*

The following sonnet by Giacomo revolves around not only the beauty of precious stones, which invites comparison with that of the poet's lady, but also their "virtues," in the medieval sense of special properties possessed by gems, often medicinal or magical. One of the virtues of heliotrope, for example, was its supposed ability to confer invisibility on the wearer. In translating this sonnet, I have avoided all rhyme.

> *Neither diamond, nor emerald, nor sapphire,*
> *nor any other precious gem or stone—*
> *not topaz, jasper, onyx, nor red rubies,*
> *not heliotrope, packed full with magic virtues,*
> *not amethyst, nor any fine-cut garnet—*
> *which is a very sparkling sight to see—*
> *could claim a modicum of all the beauties*
> *that my ladylove bears within herself.*
>
> *She far exceeds in virtue every jewel,*
> *resembling more, instead, a star of splendor,*
> *with her serene and radiant joy in love,*
> *lovelier far than any rose or flower.*
> *May Christ grant her life and gaiety,*
> *increasing her great worthiness and honor.*

Poems like these influenced the Bolognese circle of poets led by Guido Guinizzelli, which, in turn, profoundly inspired the Tuscan movement in verse that Dante dubbed the *dolce stil nuovo* ("sweet new style"), of which he himself and his older friend Guido Cavalcanti were the most brilliant representatives.

Sir Thomas Wyatt (1503–42) introduced the sonnet form to England, translating or imitating the sonnets of Petrarch (1304–74) and other Italian sonneteers. The English sonnet, sometimes called Shakespearean after its most famous practitioner, generally consists of fourteen lines of iambic pentameter with a rhyme scheme of *abab cdcd efef gg*. Structured as three quatrains and a couplet, the English sonnet often packs an epigrammatic punch into its final two rhyming lines.

The craze for writing sonnet sequences was never more pronounced than during the Renaissance, drawing inspiration from Petrarch's *Canzoniere* (*Songbook*), 366 poems (including 317 sonnets) mainly about his love for Laura. England saw Sir Philip Sidney's *Astrophel and Stella*, Edmund Spenser's *Amoretti*, Shakespeare's 154-poem sequence, and many others, while Italy, France, Spain, and Portugal also spawned an abundance of them. Other first-class sonneteers in English included John Donne, John Milton (who also wrote five sonnets in Italian), William Wordsworth, John Keats, Dante Gabriel Rossetti, Gerard Manley Hopkins, and William Butler Yeats.

It's curious that the two outstanding English sonnets about the sonnet form itself are both, in form, Italian sonnets. The first, written by Wordsworth in 1807, explains why the poet does not feel confined by the sonnet's brevity:

> *Nuns fret not at their convent's narrow room;*
> *And hermits are contented with their cells;*
> *And students with their pensive citadels;*
> *Maids at the wheel, the weaver at his loom,*
> *Sit blithe and happy; bees that soar for bloom*
> *High as the highest Peak of Furness-fells,*
> *Will murmur by the hour in foxglove bells:*
> *In truth the prison, into which we doom*
> *Ourselves, no prison is: and hence for me,*
> *In sundry moods, 'twas pastime to be bound*
> *Within the Sonnet's scanty plot of ground;*
> *Pleased if some Souls (for such there needs must be)*
> *Who have felt the weight of too much liberty,*
> *Should find brief solace there, as I have found.*

More somber, majestic, and abstruse is Rossetti's introductory sonnet to his 101-poem sequence, *The House of Life* (1881), in which the final lines imagine a sonnet serving as a substitute for the coin traditionally paid by the newly dead to Charon to ferry them across the river of the underworld:

> *A Sonnet is a moment's monument—*
> *Memorial from the Soul's eternity*
> *To one dead deathless hour. Look that it be,*
> *Whether for lustral rite or dire portent,*
> *Of its own arduous fullness reverent;*
> *Carve it in ivory or in ebony,*

As Day or Night may rule; and let Time see
Its flowering crest impearled and orient.

A Sonnet is a coin; its face reveals
The soul—its converse, to what Power 'tis due—
Whether for tribute to the august appeals
Of Life, or dower in Love's high retinue,
It serve; or, 'mid the dark wharf's cavernous breath,
In Charon's palm it pay the toll to Death.

96 ～ Which English parliament first included town representatives?

Simon de Montfort's Parliament, 1265

DESPITE ICELAND'S ALTHING HAVING BEEN the first European legislative assembly in 930 (see Question 72) and the *cortes* of the king of León, Alfonso IX, having been the first to include commoners in decision making in 1188, it was England's lawmaking body that earned the name "the Mother of Parliaments." The sobriquet does not refer to temporal priority but to the English parliament's global role in the growth of representative government, where it grew at all.

In England before the Norman conquest (see Question 78), the witenagemot (or witan) harked back to the Germanic councils of nobles who advised the king. After the conquest, the Curia Regis ("King's Court") took its place, consisting of the great feudal landholders and, later, the king's professional advisers. In 1213, however, toward the end of the troubled reign of King John, a Great Council of barons and churchmen met at Saint Albans and issued a first draft of the Magna Carta (see Question 93). The long reign of the pious Henry III (1216–72), who succeeded his father John at age nine, was marked by chronic and often violent disputes with his nobles, who had asserted themselves during Henry's minority.

Meetings of the Great Council began to be summoned fairly regularly from 1254 onward, sometimes even twice or three times in a year, for a total of twenty-three assemblages during Henry's reign. These are often considered the first English parliaments—literally "talks" or "parleys"—during which the barons frequently refused to pay taxes demanded by the king and aired their disagreements with Henry's policies.

One of Henry's more harebrained schemes was his agreeing to finance a costly war over the Sicilian succession in exchange for the pope's making Henry's son Edmund king of the island. The parliament he called to request more funds for the cockamamie plan was his seventh and met at Oxford on June 11, 1258. Later acquiring the nickname of "the Mad Parliament," this assembly was attended by about a hundred barons, who showed up armed, under the leadership of the king's disaffected brother-in-law, French-born Simon de Montfort, 6th Earl of Leicester and son of the like-named leader of the Albigensian Crusade (see Question 94). This was the first parliament to which commoners—knights of the shire who represented counties—were summoned, though they were not required to be elected.

After Parliament adjourned, the barons drew up the Provisions of Oxford, which, in return for a pledge of financial aid to their cash-strapped monarch, stipulated that power was to be exercised jointly by the king and a fifteen-member baronial privy council and that Parliament, which would monitor the council, had to be convoked three times a year. Henry capitulated but, after the pope quashed the agreement in 1261, he repudiated it.

Open warfare now broke out with his barons, still led by Simon de Montfort, who had experienced enough of Henry's dithering and double-crossings to realize he was unfit to rule. In the process of soundly defeating the royal forces at the battle of Lewes, in Sussex, in May of 1264, Simon captured Henry and his heir, Prince Edward Longshanks, and began ruling the country in Henry's name.

With the backing of reform-minded barons, the citizens of London, and some of the clergy, Simon soon called a parliament without Henry's approval—often referred to as "de Montfort's Parliament"—that included not only the barons of Simon's faction and the higher clergy but also two knights from each county and two burgesses (townsmen) from each of the major towns, representing the rising class of merchants.

The composition of de Montfort's Parliament, which met from late January to mid-February of 1265, reflected a need to broaden and deepen his support in the realm. The knights and burgesses representing their communities were also for the first time required to be chosen by election, and therein lies the historic importance of this parliament for the future development of representative government in England.

In May, however, young Prince Edward escaped from his uncle Simon and, rallying royalist forces and Welsh nobles after the baronial party had split into factions, outmaneuvered, defeated, and killed Simon at the battle of Evesham in August of 1265.

During the reign of Henry's son, Edward I (1272–1307), once an ally of his brilliant uncle, Parliament was established as the fundamental body for conducting public business, and the English feudal system began its long fade-out. A tall, handsome, strong, redoubtable soldier who had crusaded in Egypt and Syria, Edward also became a renowned legal reformer—later known as "the English Justinian" (see Question 42)—for the epochal statutes he passed through his parliaments regarding property transfers, church lands, the police system, regulation of trade, debt collection, and other administrative matters.

In Edward's incessant search for funds for his military campaigns, this "Hammer of the Scots" convened a total of forty-six parliaments, including his famed "Model Parliament" in late November to early December of 1295. Edward recognized the importance of gaining the support of the emerging middle class for his rule—and his proposed taxes—especially since in 1290 he had expelled England's Jews, who had served as the nation's principal moneylenders but had been impoverished by the sacking of their communities during the Barons' Wars of Henry's reign.

Edward's Model Parliament is sometimes falsely considered the first in which every estate was represented (that was de Montfort's Parliament of 1265). The Model Parliament comprised two archbishops, eighteen bishops, seventy abbots, seven earls, forty-one barons, seventy knights, and two hundred burgesses from the boroughs and citizens from the cities, as well as representatives of the minor clergy. The numerical superiority of the knights and burgesses, taken together, must in no way be deemed to offset the power and influence of the lords spiritual and temporal, yet, from this time forward, the summoning of commoners to Edward's parliaments became more regular. "His object was not to limit the royal power or to subject it to the will of the commonalty," wrote historian G. M. Trevelyan. "His object was to make the royal power more efficient by keeping it in constant touch with the life of the governed."

After 1320 (during the reign of Edward II), commoners were

always summoned to Parliament, which divided into two houses—
Lords and Commons—within a few decades. Later in the fourteenth
century, Parliament began initiating legislation on its own (in contra-
distinction to royal initiatives) in the form of bills that became laws—
acts of Parliament—if the king assented to them. In the following
century, bills also had to pass through both houses to become law.

James I, first English monarch of the Stuart dynasty, held a theory
about the divine right of kings that cost his son Charles I his head in
1649 in his battle against Parliament, which temporarily overthrew the
monarchy, and cost his Catholic grandson James II the throne after the
Glorious Revolution of 1688–89, which definitively established parliamentary sovereignty. In the eighteenth century, a revival of absolutism
under George III led to major problems with the American colonies
(see Questions 128 and 129). The opening lines of Percy Bysshe Shelley's "Sonnet: England in 1819" evoke the disgusted mood of English
liberals after almost sixty years of George's reign:

> An old, mad, blind, despised, and dying king,—
> Princes, the dregs of their dull race, who flow
> Through public scorn,—mud from a muddy spring,—
> Rulers who neither see, nor feel, nor know,
> But leech-like to their fainting country cling,
> Till they drop, blind in blood, without a blow . . .

FOURTEENTH CENTURY

97 ◆ *Who was the first modern painter, according to Giorgio Vasari?*

98 ◆ *What was the first Italian epic poem?*

99 ◆ *What was the first appearance of the Black Death in Western Europe?*

100 ◆ *Who was the first modern man?*

101 ◆ *Who was the first university teacher of Greek in Western Europe?*

102 ◆ *Who completed the first translation of the Bible into English?*

103 ◆ *Who was the first world-class English poet?*

97 ∽ Who was the first modern painter, according to Giorgio Vasari?

The Florentine artist Giotto
(c. 1266–1337)

SUDDENLY, THERE WAS GIOTTO.

From history's perspective, the effect of Giotto di Bondone on Italian painting at the beginning of the trecento (as art historians call the 1300s in Italy) was as abrupt as that sentence, bringing about a revolution in style that changed the look, the feel, and indeed the very goals of religious art well within his own lifetime, opening the door to the Italian Renaissance. In his epochal *Lives of the Artists*, Giorgio Vasari (1511–74) claimed that Giotto's innovations had "brought back to life the true art of painting," paving the way for a long line of illustrious successors (see Question 105).

Giotto was born in or near Florence at the height of the Byzantine tradition in medieval European painting, in which the human forms of Christ, the Virgin, and the saints were, by rigid Eastern convention, presented in flat, highly stylized forms that emphasized their sacredness rather than their humanity. Gone were the natural shapes and faces of antiquity: The Greco-Roman art of realistically imitating the human body had been lost hundreds of years earlier in the rubble and confusion of the Dark Ages. Suddenly, Giotto broke this mold and began painting figures that appeared rounded, clearly grounded within an organized space, and with faces that could have belonged to one's friends and neighbors. The natural representation of men and women had returned to painting.

Giotto's achievement is made clear by comparing him with Giovanni Cimabue (c. 1240–1302), the most acclaimed artist of the day (and Giotto's teacher, according to Vasari). Both artists painted huge fresco crosses that can still be seen in Florence. In Cimabue's *Crucifixion* (now in the Museo dell' Opera di Santa Croce) the image of Christ follows familiar Byzantine conventions: The head is large and tilted unnaturally to the side, the arms form a straight line on the horizontal crosspiece, and the trunk angles outward to the right on the vertical spine of the cross, defying gravity and several other standards of reality, but serving—in the medieval artist's view—the higher function of inspiring awe in the presence of the supernatural. We see a man but are never allowed to forget that this man is God.

Giotto's *Crucifix* in the church of Santa Maria Novella presents the viewer with a far more human Christ. The arms are not straight, but pulled down by the weight of the hanging body. The belly sags. The head hangs downward, not sideways. We may be seeing the Son of God on the cross, but Giotto reminds his Christian audience that their God was also a man.

Similar differences inform Cimabue's and Giotto's versions of the Madonna: Byzantine stiff figures with conventionally tilted heads in Cimabue's *Enthroned Madonna and Child with Angels and Prophets* versus softer, natural-looking representations of human beings in Giotto's *Ognissanti Madonna*. (Both paintings may be seen in Florence's Uffizi Gallery.) Often cited as a telling advance in technique is Giotto's rendering of clothing: Here robes drape gracefully around the figure of Mary as they did on Greek and Roman statues. In contrast, Cimabue's Virgin is dressed in the familiar Byzantine style, with brilliant gold highlights where every fold of her cloak would be, resulting in a hard, metallic look. We have the impression that Giotto's Madonna, if she chose, could rise from her throne silently, whereas Cimabue's glistening Madonna would clank.

The impact of Giotto's new realism was memorably recorded by his contemporary Dante Alighieri: "In painting, Cimabue thought to hold / The field, but now Giotto is all the rage, / So that the other's fame has been eclipsed" (*Purgatorio* 11.94–96). Giovanni Boccaccio would later write in his *Decameron* that the art of painting, which "had lain buried for many centuries," had been revived by Giotto. This admiration for Giotto's role as an innovator was reechoed by Italian artists throughout the Renaissance, culminating in Vasari's famous assessment of his historic contribution.

Had Giotto's art sprung full-blown, like the Venus of myth? Adumbrations of perspective in Cimabue and flashes of the Greco-Roman style in the Roman painter Pietro Cavallini (c. 1240–c. 1330) may have had an influence but do not seem to account for the giant leap forward in foreshortening, perspective, and solidity—the sheer representational success—in Giotto's works. For a likelier source, we must turn to sculpture, specifically the revolutionary pulpit in the Baptistery of St. John in Pisa created by Nicola Pisano in 1260. Its lifelike faces and figures, carved in bas-relief, may be contrasted with the elongated bodies and serene faces executed not too many years earlier for the Gothic cathedral at Chartres, enchanting in themselves but clearly idealized in the medieval manner. Pisano ushered in the Greco-Roman naturalism that would be the mark of Renaissance statuary. In Giotto's rounded figures that skillfully created the illusion of three-dimensionality on flat surfaces, painting caught up with sculpture.

We know virtually nothing about Giotto's personal life. From legal documents, it is clear that he traveled all over the Italian peninsula executing commissions for both church and secular leaders. Most of these works have not survived. In addition, questions of attribution attach to many of the extant paintings. Were the famed frescoes in the Basilica of St. Francis in Assisi—where Giotto may have received his first public notice in the 1290s—done by Giotto alone or with the help of workshop assistants? Unlike modern critics, Giotto's contemporaries may not have put so fine a point on it.

Of the generally unquestioned works, the most magnificent are found within the Scrovegni (or Arena) Chapel in Padua. In the early years of the trecento, the Paduan nobleman Enrico Scrovegni wished to build a family chapel on the former site of a Roman amphitheater, reportedly in expiation for the sins of his father, a notorious usurer. (Apparently too little, too late for Dante, who was soon to place the elder Scrovegni in the seventh circle of his *Inferno*.) Commissioned to decorate the interior in the difficult medium of fresco, which requires the artist to paint on still-wet plaster, Giotto produced his masterpiece: an elaborate narrative cycle painted in luminous colors depicting the process of God's redemption of the human race, from the events leading up to the birth of the Virgin, through the public life of Jesus, to the Crucifixion and beyond. The visual story unfolds like a graphic novel, with three levels of panels "reading" left to right around the church, while the entire entrance wall is covered by a giant fresco of the Last Judgment.

Visitors to the Arena Chapel today may first experience the sense of being surrounded by an air of peaceful harmony, and their eyes may be drawn up to the blue vaulted ceiling studded with stars. Then the frescoes begin offering up their delightful dramas. In the opening panels, a sad Joachim, the future father of Mary, is rejected by the temple priests for being apparently unable to sire children and makes a touching bid for sympathy from shepherds in the countryside. The quizzical rustics cannot hide their uneasiness over this unexpected visit, unlike their animals—a dog and sheep—who welcome him warmly. (Their joyful greeting may reflect the influence of the passionately venerated St. Francis of Assisi [c. 1181–1226], whose life was a subject for Giotto's brush throughout his career and whose humane, compassionate sensibility informs his works.) In a later panel, a solid, rounded Joachim draped in a cloak that convincingly hugs his form dreams his wife will bear a child. He is seated on solid ground, the same on which two shepherds are realistically standing. The result is not a Byzantine presentation of figures floating symbolically within the spiritual air of faith, but a true scene: human beings arranged in groupings within a solid landscape. Such scenes form the basis of Giotto's reputation as a superb visual dramatist.

This narrative cycle, filled with a cast of characters drawn from life, anticipates the richly diverse populations within the frameworks of Boccaccio's *Decameron* and Chaucer's *Canterbury Tales* (see Question 103). Giotto was certainly a fan of humanity. His paintings are populated by ordinary persons with delightfully familiar faces and shapes that evoke not awe but sympathy and involvement: a portly innkeeper in *The Marriage at Cana*; a shepherd tending to a skittish camel in the *Adoration of the Magi* while all others are transfixed by the divine newborn; neighbors holding their noses in *The Raising of Lazarus*; and dozens more. As never before, worshippers were able to identify with the subjects painted on their church walls. Giotto's apparent efforts to draw his audience into his paintings raised a bar that would not be lowered for hundreds of years.

The Betrayal of Christ is a masterpiece of action and human drama. Judas's saffron cloak, wrapped around Jesus in a treasonous embrace, dominates the center of the painting and leads us into the central moment—in dramatic terms, the turning point—in the story of the Passion, just after the kiss of betrayal. Judas's lips are caught still puckered, but Christ's are not. Instead, he fixes on Judas a deep, comprehending gaze. The pair are enveloped by disciples, soldiers, and spectators, while torches, staffs, and spears wave overhead. In cinematic terms, Giotto presents both the long action shot and the quiet close-up within the same frame, capturing the moment unforgettably.

In *The Lamentation*, Christ's dead body lies horizontally across the bottom of the panel, supported by women and surrounded by mourners with powerfully grieving faces. Overhead, in a remarkable invention, distraught, wailing angels fly hither and yon, like birds circling a calamity below, helpless to intervene.

To first-time viewers, these church frescoes might seem primitive—closer to Grandma Moses than to Michelangelo—but only by the later standards for which Giotto himself blazed the trail. They need no apology. Indeed, if the Sistine Chapel is the glorious Easter of the Renaissance, then the Arena Chapel, with its dazzling moments of drama and beauty, is its humble, endearing Nativity.

In 1334 an adoring Florence placed Giotto in charge of its public works, with a special focus on the city's cathedral-in-progress. During the last few years of his life, he worked on a design for a campanile adjacent to the church—now one of Florence's most familiar sights. Since only his plan for the base was used, visitors walking by "Giotto's tower" today can view his original design at street level. Giotto himself lies buried within the cathedral, reportedly in the spot closest to his bell tower.

—*Joseph Sgammato*

98 ～ What was the first Italian epic poem?

Dante's Divine Comedy, *c. 1306–21*

IN HIS *DIVINA COMMEDIA,* the first and greatest Italian epic, Dante portrays Italy not as the "mistress of provinces," as once in the days of ancient Rome, but as the madam of a bordello, welcoming any and all comers, domestic or foreign, who are allowed to manhandle her for their own nefarious purposes as long as they pay up. Dante's native city of Florence and the corrupt papal city of Rome are lashed in the harshest terms—the former for harboring nothing but "envy, greed, and pride" and being highly renowned in Hell, the latter for being the biblical whore of Babylon, selling holy offices for gold.

Regarding other cities of Italy, Italians love to quote Dante's invectives against Pisa (he prays the Arno may get blocked up and drown every single soul in the city), Genoa ("People alien to every good custom and brimful of all corruption, why aren't you driven from the earth?"), Bologna (its citizens are greedy and prone to pimping), Siena (full of airheads and spendthrifts), Lucca (all of its officials are crooks), Fiesole (whose "ungrateful and malignant people" planted its bad seed in Florence, rendering it a "pile of manure"), Pistoia ("Why don't you just go incinerate yourself?"), and so on. Dante also pillories popes, princes, kings, and emperors. Literary critic Harold Bloom has rightly described him as "brazen, aggressive, prideful, and audacious beyond all poets, before or since."

It's hardly because his poem is funny—though it sometimes is—that Dante Alighieri (1265–1321) called it his *Commedia* (the epithet *Divina* first appearing in a 1555 Venetian edition), but because it begins with terrifying dangers threatening a Christian Everyman pilgrim—Dante himself as the protagonist of his poem—yet ends happily, indeed blissfully, with his beatific vision of God. *The Divine Comedy* takes us on a grand tour of the cosmos in order to show us how men and women deal with sin and evil in widely varying ways and thus come to merit eternal salvation or damnation in the afterlife.

Although the poem incorporates many religious, philosophical, and scientific beliefs that are now outdated, most of its 14,233 lines in one hundred cantos remain perennially fascinating because of Dante's numerous encounters with the souls of famous and not-so-famous sinners, penitents, and saints as he pursues his journey from earth down into the circles of Hell in the *Inferno* (the first part of the poem), up the terraces of towering Mount Purgatory (the second part), and finally into the successive spheres of heaven in the *Paradiso*, to end up in the empyrean in God's immediate presence, beyond all time and space.

In the fiction of the poem, which is set in the year 1300, Dante is granted the grace to try to save his soul from damnation by visiting, while still alive, the world beyond the grave and profiting from what he sees. He thus becomes the hero of his own epic as a new Christian Aeneas or Ulysses seeking his true country and home—paradise.

From the very first lines of the poem, we are plunged into a dramatic situation:

> *Midway along this life we journey through,*
> *I found myself in a dark wood, astray,*
> *For the right path was wholly lost to view.*

When three wild beasts suddenly appear, symbolic of various types of sinfulness, Dante is overwhelmed with fear. To the rescue comes a ghost—the shade of the ancient poet Virgil, author of the *Aeneid*, the Roman foundational epic that also involved a journey to the underworld.

Virgil explains how Dante's great love, Beatrice, who is now a saint, urged him to go to Dante's aid. But the only way for Dante to save himself from the evils that beset him is to experience firsthand the degradation of the lost souls he will meet in Hell with Virgil's sage guidance. Then he will learn how suffering and purgation can cleanse the soul of its evil propensities when the two poets climb the mountain of Purgatory together and converse with the souls doing penance there for their participation in the seven deadly sins. At its summit, Beatrice herself will appear to Dante and conduct him through the various heavenly realms so that he may learn the ways of virtue from the many saints he will encounter and experience the crowning vision of the Holy Trinity, the ultimate goal of his quest.

The *Inferno* has always remained the most popular of the poem's three parts, and this discussion will focus on it. Here Dante makes the penalty fit the crime according to a wittily ironic version of the Old Testament *lex talionis* ("an eye for an eye"). His imaginative and often devilishly cruel punishments must be understood, however, as poetic concretizations of interior states. For example, in the episode involving Paolo and Francesca, in-laws who began an adulterous affair while reading about Lancelot's seduction of Queen Guinevere, the two former lovers are blown across the starless sky of Hell by eternal tempests that symbolize their helplessness while living in the throes of their uncontrolled sexual passion, which led to their death.

Farther down in Hell, Dante speaks with the soul of the politician and suicide Pier delle Vigne, who had done violence to his own body, and now his soul is trapped within a bush that's periodically ripped apart by bird-women Harpies. The feces of the sewerlike ditch in which the flatterers must wallow are merely the emblem of people whose words had been shit. The false counselor Ulysses is totally enveloped by a huge tongue of flame that calls to mind how he used to hide his true purpose by crafty words that burned like fire. A divisive stirrer-up of strife, the Provençal troubadour Bertran de Born has been divided from his own head, which he carries by the hair in front of him like a lantern. Traitors, whose sin was cold and premeditated, are punished by being planted in a lake of ice at the bottom of Hell, and there Dante sees enormous Satan himself at the very center of the earth—and of the universe—the farthest point from God in the poet's Ptolemaic cosmos.

The characters in Hell—even the wishy-washy ones—all remain "full of themselves," forever trapped by the faulty existential choices they made in life. Some are still extremely nosy about what's happening on earth, and their interactions with Dante epitomize their former vices and obsessions. A few, however, still bear traces of nobility of soul, like Ulysses, who tells Dante that he reminded his crew on their disastrous last sea voyage, "You were not made to live your lives like beasts, / But to follow paths of virtue and of knowledge." Some still thrive on heroic gestures, like the arrogant Florentine aristocrat, warrior, and heretic Farinata, rising from his fiery tomb "as if he held all Hell in great disdain," whereas others still make obscene gestures, like the sacristy thief Vanni Fucci, who makes "the figs" with his hands and screams, "Take them, God! I'm aiming them at *you*!"

There are a number of popes in Dante's Hell, and, in a way, the overarching villain of the entire poem is Boniface VIII (1294–1303), who was serving as pontiff at the time the poem is set. Dante makes St. Peter say of him and of papal Rome, in the highest realms of the *Paradiso* (27.22–26), "the one who usurps my place . . . has made of my tomb a sewer of blood and stench." In the *Inferno*, Dante tells the story of how Boniface begged the foxy old Romagnole condottiere-turned-friar Guido da Montefeltro for advice on how to destroy his enemies. "Promise big, but deliver small" was Brother Guido's succinct answer, so the pope told his foes, who were holed up in their stronghold of Palestrina, that he would declare an amnesty if they surrendered; when they did, he razed their city to the ground. But Boniface outfoxed Guido, too, by assuring him he could grant absolution in advance for his fraudulent advice—though when Guido died, a fierce devil promptly arrived to carry him off to Hell.

In an earlier episode of the *Inferno*, we come across the simoniac pope Nicholas III (1277–80), planted upside down in a tight round crevice in the rock with just his wildly flailing legs exposed and the soles of his feet on fire. In a bit of Dantesque black comedy, we learn from Nicholas himself that both Boniface VIII and a subsequent pontiff, Clement V (1305–14)—who was pope while Dante was actually writing the *Inferno*—will land upside down in that exact spot after death, Boniface first reaming Nicholas down out of sight into the depths of the hole and then Clement doing the same to Boniface almost eleven years afterward in a kind of corrupt-pope sausage factory. Was Dante being objective, or was his treatment of Boniface influenced by the fact that the wily pope had ruined Dante's life, having set in motion the series of events that led to the poet's perpetual banishment from Florence on trumped-up political charges and his subsequent condemnation in absentia to be burned alive?

The farther down Hell we go, the worse the sinners, the sins, and the punishments get—and the less pity Dante has for them. Toward the bottom, he rips out tufts of hair from the head of a notorious Florentine traitor who's fixed in a lake of ice with just his head exposed (which Dante had "accidentally" kicked). He promises the treacherous Fra Alberigo, also fixed in the ice and with his eyes frozen over, to remove the ice from his eyes (at least till they freeze over again) if he would say what he had done to deserve his fate. But after Dante hears the damned friar allude to the sordid tale of how he murderously betrayed his own brother and nephew at a feigned banquet of reconciliation, he decides to leave Alberigo's eyes as they are—"and it was courtesy to be a boor to him." As for the Genoese Branca Doria, who had treacherously murdered his father-in-law, Dante was eager to place him in Hell, but since Branca was still alive, the poet claimed he saw the man's soul already being punished down there in the lake of ice—and that the person who still seemed to be eating and drinking as Branca up on earth was a mere zombie animated by a devil.

The *Inferno*, however, is only the first third of Dante's "medieval miracle of song"; more than 9,500 lines of the *Purgatorio* and the *Paradiso* follow. The Florentine poet's haughty scorn for human pettiness and inertness, his fierce loves and hates, his consummate literary craftsmanship, the fantastic epic similes, the architectonic construction, the inexhaustible variety of his fluent phrasing and rhymes, his detailed and minutely observed natural images, his ability to create convincing fictional worlds even in the heights of heaven, his grandeur, terror, sublimity, and psychological astuteness, his superb handling of religious, literary, mythological, and historical materials and themes—and even his occasional rollicking or bathroom humor—make of Dante, according to literary scholar Ernst Robert Curtius, "the poet who is the first among the Moderns to rank with the great classics of antiquity."

There were to be noteworthy Italian epics after Dante—especially Boiardo's *Orlando Innamorato*, Ariosto's *Orlando Furioso*, and Tasso's *Gerusalemme Liberata*—but none would capture the imagination of Italians (or the rest of the world) on a level remotely approaching the *Divina Commedia*. The masterpiece of a man unjustly exiled from his native Florence for the last nineteen years of his life remains, along with Homer's epics and a handful of tragedies by Shakespeare, in the top echelon of the world's poetic creations.

99 ⌒ What was the first appearance of the Black Death in Western Europe?

An infected Genoese ship at Messina, Sicily, in 1347

IN OCTOBER OF 1347 a Genoese trading ship arrived at the harbor of Messina in Sicily, having sailed from the Black Sea emporium of Caffa with a cargo that included flea-infested vermin and a crew of dead and dying sailors. Rumors had been circulating among Europeans of a terrible pestilence in the East, accompanied by fires, hail, and winds and depopulating vast stretches from India to China and Asia Minor, but they had not felt threatened, because they were unaware of the nature of contagion. The arrival of that ill-fated ship in Messina, however, soon followed by other vessels from the Levant putting in at Venice and Genoa, signaled the introduction to Europe of the greatest plague the world had ever known. Some four years later, when the first outbreak of the Black Death abated, one-third to one-half of the population of the Continent had perished.

Scholars now believe the plague had first erupted in Central Asia fifteen to twenty years earlier, possibly in Mongolia, and then spread along the trade routes through Turkey and Greece to Constantinople and Egypt. In the spring of 1348 the full force of the plague hit Europe, its arrival coinciding with an earthquake that devastated buildings and villages from Naples to Greece. Moreover, it followed a half century of food shortages and other hardships, possibly caused by overpopulation, that left many weakened and vulnerable.

As 1348 progressed, the pestilence crossed France from Marseille, and from Normandy traveled across the Channel into southern England. The following year saw it spread through Germany and the northern British Isles, and by the end of 1350 it had reached Eastern Europe and Scandinavia, where a ghost ship with a dead crew and a cargo of wool drifted until running aground near Bergen in Norway. By the close of 1351 the plague had spread to Russia and then gradually faded out, although intermittent outbreaks continued until the early eighteenth century.

Known at the time as "the Great Mortality," the Black Death was an infection caused by the bacterium *Yersinia pestis*, found in the digestive tract of fleas and in the bloodstream of the fleas' hosts in endemic areas. When their usual host, *Rattus rattus*—the black or ship rat—dies off, the fleas seek other sources of nutrition, including humans.

Infection with *Yersinia pestis* after the bite of a flea, as the unlucky of Southern Europe quickly discovered, can cause egg- or apple-size swellings known as buboes in the armpits and groin. Late in the disease, the skin becomes blackened from internal bleeding and subcutaneous hemorrhages, and some have argued that this feature of the disease was the source of the term "Black Death." Others suggest that the expression, which first appeared in the 1830s, referred to the dark gloom that settled on victims as they faced death. In any case, most victims of bubonic plague died within a week.

An even more lethal variation was the pneumonic form of the plague, which spread via bloody respiratory secretions. People who acquired this form, characterized by fever and coughing up of blood, often expired in three days or less. Some of the affected went to bed unaware they were infected and died before morning.

As the disease spread across Europe, it typically persisted in a given area for four to six months and then disappeared, only to resurface elsewhere. Because even the most sophisticated physicians at the time had no notion of vector-borne disease, they had no means of prevention or control. They recommended the burning of aromatic substances thought to purify the air, which they believed was poisoned, and they relied on therapeutic measures such as bleeding, purging, and lancing of the buboes—all to little avail.

Various public health measures were also enacted. The first boards of health were established in 1348 in Venice and Florence, where the practice arose of quarantining—the isolation of the possibly infected in hospitals for forty (*quaranta*) days. Despite these efforts, about six hundred people perished each day in Venice, dying so rapidly that the living were unable to keep up with burials. Bodies were often dumped in mass graves or left in the streets to putrefy—and further spread the disease.

The true death toll of the bubonic plague is unknown and varied by area, but estimates range from twenty million deaths across Europe to two hundred million worldwide. A disease that within days wiped out entire families, villages, and districts in such a horrifying fashion inspired terror and revulsion, especially given the medieval belief that such a calamity could only result from God's wrath.

Penitential efforts to appease the divinity included processions of flagellants, sometimes in groups of hundreds, dressed in sackcloth and covered in ashes, beating themselves with whips to reenact the suffering of Christ and his expiation of human sin. The leaders of these groups eventually began challenging the very authority of the church, assuming the duties and powers of priests and stirring up further unrest and property destruction among the distraught populace. In response, Pope Clement VI decreed in 1349 that flagellants should be dispersed and arrested, while King Philip VI of France outlawed public flagellation.

Medical authorities developed a different explanation for the pestilence. Medieval medicine, strongly influenced by Arab traditions, was less under the control of church doctrine than other aspects of life, and incorporated astrological and planetary influences. The medical faculty at the University of Paris determined that the plague was the result of a peculiar conjunction of Saturn, Jupiter, and Mars on March 20, 1345, which had polluted the atmosphere. This became the official explanation, but the common people continued to consider their horrible fate as the wages of sin.

Survivors also sought someone to blame for the catastrophe that had befallen them, finding a convenient target in the Jews, who were already often reviled for their refusal to accept Christ and their participation in moneylending. Rumors spread that the Jews had poisoned the wells used by Christians, and that they kidnapped, tortured, and drank the blood of Christian children. In France, Switzerland, Germany, and Spain many Jews were tried and burned at the stake, while others were slaughtered by mobs. Lepers were also targeted.

The terrors of the disease and the ensuing societal disruptions had profound psychological consequences for the surviving population. *The Decameron* of Giovanni Boccaccio, written during the plague years in Florence, described these effects. "Diverse apprehensions and imaginations were engendered in the minds of such as were left alive," Boccaccio wrote, observing that some shunned all contact with the sick and tried to live temperately and in seclusion. Others recklessly caroused and drank in taverns and inns "with an entire disregard of rule or measure," singing, laughing, and mocking everything. Still others followed a middle course, becoming neither excessively restrained nor overly dissipated and going nowhere without fragrant herbs, flowers, and spices on their persons "to comfort the brain with such perfumes, because the air seemed to be everywhere laden and reeking with the stench emitted by the dead and dying. . . ."

In the aftermath of the plague, important socioeconomic changes began to occur. The drastic depopulation meant a shortage of labor, which resulted in rapid increases in peasants' and laborers' wages. Land was vacant and devalued, and tenants' rents fell as landowners struggled to maintain cultivation. Some peasants were emboldened, but wage demands were strongly resisted by the authorities. In England, the Statute of Laborers of 1351 froze wages at levels seen before the plague and was partly responsible for the attack on the English feudal system known as the Peasants' Revolt of 1381.

Dissatisfaction with the church also grew because of the inability or refusal of some priests to provide comfort and relief in the plague years, during which vast numbers died without benefit of the sacraments or prayers. But survivors also experienced uncertainties about God, questioning what possible purpose the scourge of the plague could have served. In *A Distant Mirror: The Calamitous 14th Century*, historian Barbara W. Tuchman wrote as follows:

> If a disaster of such magnitude, the most lethal ever known, was a mere wanton act of God or perhaps not God's work at all, then the absolutes of a fixed order were loosed from their moorings. . . . Once people envisioned the possibility of change in a fixed order, the end of an age of submission came in sight; the turn to individual conscience lay ahead. To that extent the Black Death may have been the unrecognized beginning of modern man.

—Nancy Walsh

100 ∾ Who was the first modern man?

Petrarch, 1304–74 (at least according to Ernest Renan)

FRANCESCO PETRARCA WAS DUBBED "the first modern man" by the French historian and philosopher Ernest Renan in his 1852 doctoral thesis, *Averroës and Averroism*. There, in a section on Petrarch's detestation of both the teachings and the contemporary followers of the widely influential twelfth-century Muslim philosopher Ibn-Rushd (Averroës), Renan justifies his view of the Italian poet and humanist by saying that

he initiated, among the Latin peoples, a refined notion of
ancient culture, source of all our civilization. . . . Despite their
admiration for antiquity, the Middle Ages never understood
what was most vibrant and fertile about it. Petrarch, on the
other hand, was truly an ancient. He was the first to evince a
certain nobility, generosity of spirit, and openness to life that
had disappeared from the world since the triumph of
barbarism.

It may seem strange that Renan justifies calling Petrarch the first
modern by claiming he was an ancient in spirit, but many thinkers of
the mid-nineteenth century still shared the Renaissance humanist viewpoint that the era from the sack of Rome in 410 (see Question 33) to the
first glimmerings of an ancient revival in mid-fourteenth-century Italy
constituted, in Petrarch's words, "a Dark Age." By viewing life more
like the ancient Romans, Petrarch, the first major humanist and inaugu-
rator of the Italian Renaissance, was also paradoxically the first modern
individual—no longer captive to the excessive religiosity, narrowness
of mind, distrust of sensory experience and pleasure, and unenlightened
weltanschauung of monkish medieval Europe.

Indeed, Petrarch loathed materialistic Averroists, Scholastic philosophers, logic-chopping Aristotelians, astrologers, and physicians,
lumping them all together as pedantic charlatans. When a young Venetian Averroist mocked St. Paul and Augustine in Petrarch's house, the
poet, who remained a sincere Christian his entire life, grabbed him by
his gown and threw him out. In another incident in Venice in 1367, four
young, skeptical Averroists referred to him as an ignoramus, spurring
the greatest scholar of his age to relocate huffily to Padua.

Born in the Tuscan city of Arezzo in 1304, Petrarch lived as a boy
in Provence, where his father, banished from his native Florence for
political reasons, served as a lawyer at the papal court then resident in
Avignon. As a young man, Petrarch quit his hated law studies, which his
father had made him pursue, opting instead for the life of a professional
man of letters, the first of modern Europe, and dandifying his appearance by curling and perfuming his reddish brown hair, which later
turned prematurely gray.

From his first sight of Rome in 1337, Petrarch fell in love with the
remnants of its imperial past and began writing his *Africa*, an epic in
Latin hexameters about Rome's titanic clash with Hannibal in the

Second Punic War. Although he never finished it, the fragmentary poem earned him an honor from King Robert of Naples that was to be the high point of his public life. Dressed in a purple cloak given him by the king, Petrarch was crowned with laurel as "Poet Laureate" on Rome's Capitoline Hill on April 8, 1341, by a dear friend who was also a Roman senator. The sixteenth-century humanist Paolo Giovio claimed that Petrarch had been the first to resurrect European letters "from their Gothic grave," since the poet's elegant Latin style represented a vast improvement over the cruder church Latin that had long been predominant.

Because he took minor ecclesiastical orders as a young man to be eligible for church benefices, Petrarch couldn't marry, but he did father a son and a daughter out of wedlock. His chronic guilt over sins of the flesh caused him to keep a scorecard of "how many times" from 1344 to 1349, tallying his results on the endpapers of, significantly, his copy of the letters of Abelard and Héloïse (see Question 84).

In his youth, Petrarch's wanderlust took him to northern Italy, France, Flanders, Germany, and Switzerland as a cultural tourist, and in 1345 he discovered manuscripts of letters by Cicero to Atticus, Brutus, and Quintus Cicero. A pioneer of textual criticism, he initiated the humanist searches for venerable ancient manuscripts that lay forgotten in monasteries. He was a hero-worshipper of the ancient Romans—especially Scipio Africanus, Julius Caesar, Cicero, Virgil, and Seneca—writing Latin biographies of more than a score of them. Parts of his long poem in Italian, the *Trionfi*, are essentially a litany of classical names strung together in a paean to his beloved ancient Romans—"a people armed with iron and with valor."

Petrarch even addressed Latin letters to some ancients as if they were his contemporaries, taking Cicero to task, for example, for his unseemly reentrance into the maelstrom of political life in old age instead of pursuing philosophical pleasures at his country estates. His rediscovery of Cicero's letters led him to make a collection of his own multitudinous Latin letters to his friends. Petrarch's immersion in Roman literature and history enabled him to avoid the anachronistic blunders of earlier admirers of the ancient world, who saw the mighty Roman consuls and politicians as more or less like the knights and barons of their own feudal world.

His obsession with fame for literary achievement harks back to the ancients, as in Horace's proud claim "*non omnis moriar*"—"not all of me will die"—as opposed to the often anonymous artistic creations of the Middle Ages. Petrarch's *Secretum meum* (*My Secret*) consists of three imaginary dialogues between himself and his favorite Christian thinker, St. Augustine (see Question 31), focusing on the poet's spiritual malaise and melancholy and positing an unresolved dilemma between a life of love, poetry, and fame versus one of Christian self-abnegation and humility.

Petrarch's passion for the glories of ancient Rome explains his enthusiasm for Cola di Rienzo, a visionary whose overthrow of the rule of the Roman barons and the pope and attempted revival of the ancient Roman republic took place in May of 1347. Petrarch was one of the first Italians to view patriotism as a peninsular rather than a localized sentiment, as in his famous canzone "Italia mia," in which he exhorts the Italian princes to throw out the barbarous German mercenaries who were ravaging the nation.

But it was as the creator of the modern lyric or love poem that Petrarch garnered an undying fame, which stemmed from his exquisitely wrought poems in Italian rather than the scholarly Latin products of his lucubrations. His *Canzoniere* (*Songbook*) comprises 366 poems, the great majority being sonnets about his unfulfilled love for a woman he calls Laura (perhaps Laure de Noves, married to an ancestor of the Marquis de Sade). In these much-imitated poems (see Question 95), we observe an introspective modern sensibility tormented by myriad passions and torn between classical and medieval views of physical love. The poet realizes his adulterous lust is morally suspect, but he's helpless to abandon it, since his stormy emotions are always at war with his reason. His frequent puns on Laura and the laurel, symbolic of the poetic fame he craved, led Leonardo da Vinci to quip that the reason Petrarch loved laurel so much was that "it goes well with sausages and thrushes."

"Nothing but weeping lasts upon this earth!" Petrarch laments, and indeed his beloved Laura died in the Black Death in 1348 (see Question 99). Roughly the last third of the *Canzoniere* is written after her death, which provides a new impetus for the poet's pining in his mellifluously smooth and musical verse. As with the English Romantic poets, some of Petrarch's loveliest poems make use of bird imagery. When he visits Laura's girlhood haunts, he wonders, "Is this the nest in which my lovely phoenix / Acquired both her gold and rosy plumage?" In another lyric, he identifies with the plaintive song of the nightingale, "mourning perhaps her young ones or her mate." In yet another, he is "lonelier than any sparrow on a roof." World-weariness and angst characterize most of the collection, and in the very last poem, a sublime hymn to the Virgin

Mary, the poet concludes, "My whole life has been nothing more than anguish."

In his "Epistle to Posterity" (1351), often considered the first modern autobiography, Petrarch parades his personality while indulging in some shrewd self-analysis and a good deal of undisguised boasting: "The greatest kings of this age have loved and courted me." Commenting on his works as a whole, Renaissance scholar Paul Oskar Kristeller concluded that Petrarch "talks about a variety of things and ideas, but essentially he always talks about himself." What could be more modern than that?

Petrarch was ahead of the curve in understanding the crucial importance of learning ancient Greek for acquiring a broad humanistic culture, though he himself failed in that endeavor (see Question 101). Yet his staunch belief in the value of classical literature for forming character and morality persisted in some Western circles until the very concepts of "character" and "morality" were derided as scare-quotishly passé by decon and pomo professors.

The movement he initiated, which involved placing the multifaceted human personality at the center of creative aspiration, made possible the profound introspection of the last great humanist, Michel de Montaigne, and ended in the self-obsession of the Romantics and Moderns. Anticipating by several centuries Alexander Pope's assertion that "the proper study of Mankind is Man," Petrarch saw the conflicted human condition itself as the central problem of existence, and that insight was his true passport to immortality. The poet and biographer Morris Bishop summed him up like this: "Petrarch is frequently termed the first modern man. I would go further; I would call him one of the eternal men."

101 ∽ Who was the first university teacher of Greek in Western Europe?

Leonzio Pilato, who taught at the University of Florence, 1360–62

IN ABOUT 1350 THE ITALIAN POET PETRARCH, an avid devotee of classical Latin poetry, received a precious gift from his friend the Byzantine ambassador: a copy of Homer's epics in Greek. He responded with a letter of profound gratitude for "the genuine and original text of the divine poet, the fountain of all invention." Just one small problem: "Alas!

Homer is dumb, or I am deaf; nor is it in my power to enjoy the beauty which I possess."

At that time, knowledge of ancient Greek was extremely rare in Western Europe. A few years before receiving the manuscripts, Petrarch had met Barlaam of Seminara, a Byzantine ambassador and humanist at the papal court in Avignon, France. It was Barlaam—a native of Calabria, in southern Italy, where many still spoke the Greek vernacular of their ancestors—who first inspired Petrarch and his friend Giovanni Boccaccio with the desire to hear the fountain of poetry sing in his own voice. But Barlaam, caught up in theological controversies in the Eastern Orthodox Church, couldn't stay to teach.

It fell to another Calabrian to offer Italy the first faint notes of Homeric song. In 1360, Leonzio Pilato, a Greek speaker with little appreciation of Latin, was on his way to Avignon when Boccaccio invited him to stay at his home in Florence. The famed author of *The Decameron* managed to get the Florentine republic to pay Pilato an annual stipend to teach at the *Studium Generale* (the incipient University of Florence, then boasting fewer than twenty teachers), thus becoming in 1360 the first professor of Greek in Western Europe.

Pilato was physically and socially repugnant—Petrarch couldn't abide him, referring to him as "a great ox." Historian Edward Gibbon offers a memorable description:

> His countenance was hideous; his face was overshadowed with black hair; his beard long and uncombed; his deportment rustic; his temper gloomy and inconstant; nor could he grace his discourse with the ornaments or even the perspicuity of Latin elocution. But his mind was stored with a treasure of Greek learning.

He made a rough Latin prose translation of the *Iliad* and the *Odyssey* for Boccaccio, who also picked his brain for enough lore of the pagan gods to eventually fill a lengthy and influential treatise entitled *On the Genealogy of the Gods of the Gentiles*. But Pilato, ever inconstant, taught in Florence for only three academic years (1360–62) before departing for Constantinople. Charged by Petrarch to forage for classical manuscripts there, he apparently recovered some tragedies of Euripides and Sophocles. However, during a storm on his return voyage in 1366, having had himself tied to the ship's mast like Odysseus nearing the island of the Sirens, Pilato was struck dead by lightning just outside the Gulf of Venice. Petrarch might well have lamented the loss of the manuscripts more than that of their bearer.

The voices of ancient Greek poetry in Italy went silent for another generation. But events were taking a turn that would soon bring learned Greeks to Italy and other cultural centers of Europe in greater numbers. By 1400 the Byzantine Empire was crumbling, under siege from the Ottoman Turks, and many natives looked to Italy for refuge.

The scholar who caused the first widespread revival of interest in Greek was Manuel Chrysoloras, who arrived in Italy in 1391 as an envoy of the Byzantine emperor. While in Venice negotiating Western assistance for the beleaguered empire, he gave Greek lessons to Cosimo de' Medici's future tutor, Roberto de' Rossi, who raved about his teacher to Coluccio Salutati, the chancellor of Florence. In 1396 Salutati invited Chrysoloras to teach Greek grammar and literature at the University of Florence.

In his classes, Chrysoloras used *schedographia*, a method of analysis previously unknown in Italy. After reading a passage aloud he would comment on it while explaining the nuances in the language and meaning. Chrysoloras also translated Homer's works and Plato's *Republic* into Latin. His *Erotemata civas questiones*—the first basic Greek grammar in use in Western Europe—was published in 1484 and widely reprinted. It was later used by Thomas Linacre at Oxford and Desiderius Erasmus at Cambridge.

Many others arrived in Chrysoloras's wake. When the aged Gemistus Plethon attended the Council of Florence in 1439, his lectures on the differences between Plato and Aristotle ignited a fervid enthusiasm for Plato that led to the founding of Florence's Platonic Academy under Marsilio Ficino. Sigismondo Malatesta, Lord of Rimini, held the old Platonist in such esteem that he later stole Plethon's remains while he was fighting in the Peloponnese and had them interred in a stately sarcophagus in his Tempio Malatestiano.

Before Chrysoloras left Florence in 1400 to teach in Bologna, Venice, and Rome, his lectures had reached the ears of many of the foremost humanists of the Renaissance, including Salutati, Guarino da Verona, Leonardo Bruni, Poggio Bracciolini, Ambrogio Traversari, Giacomo d'Angelo da Scarperia, and Palla Strozzi, inciting a frantic effort to rescue the texts of ancient Greece before it was too late. Guarino and Giacomo d'Angelo spent five years in Constantinople studying

Greek and collecting enough manuscripts to fill two trunks. The loss of one of these by shipwreck caused Guarino such distress that his hair turned gray in a single night.

Guarino's efforts were exceeded by those of Giovanni Aurispa, who scoured Constantinople for venerable Greek writings, returning to Venice in 1423 with 238 manuscripts—the largest single trove of ancient texts to reach the West up to that time. All of Plato, all of Plotinus, all of Proclus were there, along with much of Pindar and other poets, Greek historians, some of Aristotle, and, the crown jewel, a tenth-century codex salvaging seven plays by Sophocles and six by Aeschylus—the only known manuscript in the world containing them. Aurispa was so impoverished by his labors that he was forced to pawn the entire collection in Venice to pay his shipping costs, but Cosimo de' Medici redeemed the manuscripts and brought both them and Aurispa to Florence, where the texts of his collection were widely copied out by the humanists.

As the Byzantine Empire collapsed, more refugees arrived. When John Argyropoulos came to Italy in 1456 on a diplomatic mission, he was offered the opportunity to teach in Florence. He accepted and remained in Italy until his death in 1487.

Another Greek, Basilios Bessarion, became a Roman Catholic cardinal and kept refugees from Constantinople busy transcribing manuscripts at his palazzo in Rome. In 1469, reasoning that Venice had the most stable government in Italy, he gave the city his entire eight-hundred-volume collection, which thus became the nucleus of the Library of San Marco. One of his students from Asia Minor, John Lascaris, who later taught at Florence at the invitation of Lorenzo de' Medici, returned from Mount Athos in 1492 with about two hundred manuscripts.

It was largely because of the presence of Cardinal Bessarion's library in Venice that one of the giants of Renaissance publishing, Aldus Manutius, chose to establish his printing house there in 1493. Aldus had studied Greek at Ferrara under Guarino da Verona and continued his humanist studies with his friend Giovanni Pico della Mirandola.

Aldus aimed to secure the literature of Greece by committing its chief masterpieces to type. Gathering a small army of Greek scholars and scribes from among the four thousand or so expats then in Venice, and conducting his business entirely in spoken and written Greek, he issued the first volume of his edition of Aristotle in 1495, with four more volumes completing the work in 1497–98. Aristophanes appeared in 1498; Thucydides, Sophocles, and Herodotus followed in 1502; Xenophon's *Hellenica* and Euripides in 1503; Demosthenes in 1504. War slowed production, but in 1508 came the minor Greek orators, and in 1509 the lesser works of Plutarch.

After another lull owing to war, Aldus brought out an edition of Plato in 1513, which included an eloquent preface comparing the miseries of Italian warfare with the peace of the student's life. Pindar, Hesychius, and Athenaeus followed in 1514. Toward the end of his life Aldus began an edition of the Septuagint, the first to be published, which appeared posthumously in 1518. His successors continued his work with first editions of Pausanias, Strabo, Aeschylus, Galen, Hippocrates, and Longinus. Thanks to the combined energies of the Greeks and the Italian humanists, much of the extant corpus of ancient Greece was recovered, edited, and published within 170 years of Boccaccio's fateful encounter with Leonzio Pilato.

Not only did the West reap enormous intellectual, literary, and even scientific benefits from the rediscovery of Greek language, literature, and learning, but the entire realm of pagan knowledge—once considered benighted and in need of illumination from Scripture—now became a source of cultural and philological insights bearing even on fundamental matters of theology.

The reversal goes to the heart of Renaissance humanism. In the days of Barlaam and Leonzio Pilato, the papacy used Greek speakers to monitor the Eastern Orthodox Church and combat its heresies. By the time Aldus was rolling out his sublime editions, proto-Reformation thinkers were using their knowledge of classical Greek to understand Scripture better. In 1516, Erasmus published a Latin translation of the Greek New Testament that aimed both to remove errors in the text that had long caused interpretive controversies and to recapture more of the letter and spirit of early Christianity. Ironically, he prepared himself for that delicate task by faithfully translating Euripides' *Hecuba* and *Iphigenia in Aulis*.

—Tom Matrullo

102 ∾ Who completed the first translation of the Bible into English?

John Wycliffe and associates, 1380–82

THE FIRST COMPLETE BIBLE to appear in English was produced by followers of a Catholic priest whose legacy so perturbed the church hierarchy that, forty-four years after his death, the pope ordered his bones to be dug up, burned, and hurled into a river.

John Wycliffe of Yorkshire (1324?–84) was so spare of body that a contemporary called his appearance "wasted, and not strong." In 1345 we find him studying at Balliol College, Oxford, where he developed a reputation for uprightness and quotability—people of rank were said to have "clung to him," copying down his sayings. His predecessors there included independent-minded clerics such as the scientist Roger Bacon and the philosopher William of Ockham, whose challenges to papal authority led to charges of heresy and exile. Wycliffe soon showed abilities in natural science, mathematics, philosophy, and ecclesiastical law, but his first love was theology. After obtaining his doctorate of divinity in 1372, he began writing about the relationship of church and state—a hot topic at the time, as the pope happened to be dunning England for unpaid feudal tribute.

Wycliffe believed that the ultimate authority for Christians was not the pope, but Scripture, and that the Roman Catholic clergy had gone seriously astray by failing to follow the Gospel's example of Christ and the apostles. Indeed, he went so far as to declare that if the clergy ostentatiously abused its ecclesiastical property, the king was required to take it from them. This thinking might have influenced how his contemporary Geoffrey Chaucer depicted certain of the debased clerical characters in *The Canterbury Tales*, such as the Friar:

> *He was an esy man to yeve penaunce,*
> *Ther as he wiste to have a good pitaunce.*

> *(He was an easy man at giving penance,*
> *Wherever he knew he'd gain a good pittance.)*

Not surprisingly, the first to express unhappiness with this line of thought were the monks who held possessions. Even less surprisingly, Wycliffe's thinking interested the royals, particularly John of Gaunt, Duke of Lancaster, who, as young King Richard II's uncle, was the most powerful man in the kingdom. In 1377, when Wycliffe was summoned to St. Paul's Cathedral "to explain the wonderful things which had streamed forth from his mouth," Gaunt stood at his side and made a fiasco of the proceedings by arguing with the bishop of London over whether Wycliffe should sit down or remain standing.

Wycliffe then published several tracts even more radical in tone, emphasizing the primacy of Scripture and reform of clerical orders. He wrote, for example:

> We ought to believe in the authority of no man unless he say
> the Word of God. It is impossible that any word or any deed of
> man should be of equal authority with Holy Scripture. . . .
> Believers should ascertain for themselves what are the true
> matters of their faith, by having the Scriptures in a language
> which all may understand.

He raised questions about indulgences and the Eucharist and argued that there should be no clergy above elders and deacons. He began sending out pairs of "poor priests"—unconsecrated laymen who lived in poverty, spoke to the people in English, and laid stress on the priority of the Bible over church authority. These wandering laymen, who acquired the abusive name *Lollards* for their habit of reading Scripture aloud, garnered large popular support, which provoked a strong response from the church. Although Wycliffe seems not to have been involved with the Peasants' Revolt of 1381, he and the Lollards were said to be linked to the violent upheaval. He was briefly imprisoned, given a stern warning, and expelled from Oxford.

Wycliffe retired to his parish, where he and others, including Nicholas of Hereford, John Purvey, and perhaps John Trevisa, worked on giving the people a Bible they could read for themselves (nobles already had a French translation). By 1382, two years before Wycliffe died, they had completed a very basic English translation. The Gospels are believed to be Wycliffe's own work, and the entire effort has a rough-hewn style as a result of his emphasis on preserving even the word order of St. Jerome's Latin (see Question 32). In 1388, Purvey offered a revised version that smoothed and clarified rough patches. Here's a sample from the Wycliffe and Purvey versions of the first two verses of Psalm 1:

> Wycliffe: Blisful the man, that that went not awei in the coun-
> seil of unpitouse, and in the wei off sinful stod not; and in the
> chayer of pestilence sat not, But in the lawe of the Lord his wil;
> and in the lawe of hym he shal sweteli thenke dai and nygt.

> Purvey: Blessid is the man, that gede not in the councel of
> wickid men; and stood not in the weie of synneris, and sat not
> in the chaier of pestilence. But his wille is in the lawe of the
> Lord; and he schal bithenke in the lawe of hym dai and nygt.

The advent of the English Bible was a major event. While the Gospels had been translated long before—and Aelfric had paraphrased the first seven books of the Old Testament—the Old English of the tenth century was as foreign to Englishmen of Wycliffe's time as the Latin of the Vulgate. And while those earlier translations were accomplished under church guidance, Wycliffe's project had no such auspices and soon met with intense resistance. "The jewel of the clergy has become the toy of the laity," cried his opponents, and churchmen said the translation was riddled with errors.

The impetus for reform initiated by Wycliffe was not easily dispelled. Lollards popularized secret reading circles in which the words of the vernacular Scripture were interpreted directly, no longer subject to the doctrinal claims of the pope or the councils. Friction between Lollards and the church sharpened until a number of Lollard leaders were declared heretics and burned at the stake. Wycliffe himself was posthumously declared a heretic at the Council of Constance in 1415. His bones, disinterred from his parish churchyard, were incinerated and flung into the River Swift in 1428.

But the ripples of his reforming impulse continued to widen. In Bohemia, Jan Hus, preaching in his congregation's native Czech, fervently embraced Wycliffe's ideas. After Hus was burned at the stake in 1415, the Hussites fought on to create an independent religious community recognized by the emperor and the pope. Martin Luther's thinking went beyond Wycliffe's, but certainly drew on his work.

Despite the church's efforts to suppress Wycliffe's Bible, more copies survive today—more than two hundred manuscripts—than those of any other medieval text. What he set in motion came to fruition more than two centuries later in the magnificent King James Bible of 1611. In between, many other versions appeared, most notably that of William Tyndale, an Oxford scholar whose translation from the Greek Septuagint led to his being garroted and burned at the stake in 1536. Tyndale's version supplied the basis for many later ones. Indeed, you can trace the evolution of biblical grandeur in a single phrase:

Vulgate: *Dixitque Deus: Fiat lux, et facta est lux.*

Wycliffe (early): And God said: Be made light, and made is light.

Wycliffe (later): And God said: Light be made; and light was made.

Tyndale: Than God sayd: let there be lyghte and there was lyghte.

King James: And God said: Let there be light; and there was light.

The first English Bible to be printed was Coverdale's (1535), followed by the Great Bible (1539). Then came the Geneva Bible (1557), used by the Pilgrims; the Bishops' Bible (1568), which Shakespeare read; and the Douay-Rheims (New Testament, 1582; Old Testament, 1609), which was authorized by the pope. Wycliffe's translation was first printed only in 1731.

A large portion of the King James version—83 percent by one study—is indebted to Tyndale. As for Wycliffe, many familiar phrases have "streamed forth from his mouth," including "For many be called, but few be chosen," "He that is not against us, is for us," "Suffer ye little children to come to me," and "A prophet is not without honour, but in his own country."

—*Tom Matrullo*

103 ∾ Who was the first world-class English poet?

Geoffrey Chaucer, "The Father of English Poetry,"
c. 1342–1400

GEOFFREY CHAUCER—English courtier, diplomat, and royal official—would have merited his worldwide fame even had he written only the tragic courtly-love romance set during the Trojan War, *Troilus and Criseyde* (1381–86), which literary critic Harold Bloom considers "one of the handful of great long poems in the language." After that, however, he went on to write *The Canterbury Tales* (1386–99), one of the most formidable literary masterpieces in any language.

Chaucer's last major work is a sprawling four-hundred-page magnum opus, most of it in iambic pentameter couplets, though some of the tales are in rhyme royal and other poetic forms, and two are in prose. In the frame of the poem, the narrator and twenty-nine other men and women ride out in April on a pilgrimage from the Tabard Inn in Southwark, across the Thames from London, under the leadership of its Host, toward the shrine of St. Thomas Becket at Canterbury (see Question 86), about fifty-five miles to the southeast. To while away the time, they decide to tell stories along the way, and the original schema called for each pilgrim to tell two stories on the way to Canterbury and two on the way back—120 tales in all. Chaucer never actually managed to get his group to the shrine, however, and only twenty-four tales were told (three of them left unfinished), though the work does possess a definite beginning and an end.

The pilgrimage was a natural medieval metaphor for the journey of human life toward its ultimate goal of heaven, but Chaucer's human comedy is replete with mankind's foibles, sins, and vices, as well as its virtues. Among his pilgrims we find the entire gamut of Chaucer's world except the top echelons of the nobility and the church: a knight, middle-class professionals, lower-class rogues, idealized ecclesiastics and corrupt or worldly ones, men and women, young and old, learned and ignorant. "Here is God's plenty," said John Dryden of this crew after modernizing some of their tales from Chaucer's Middle English.

The 858-line General Prologue is a masterly introduction to the cast of storytellers via successive portraits of some depth and detail as depicted by the genial and enthusiastic but naive narrator—Chaucer the Pilgrim—who is considerably less astute than his ironic creator and ready to be impressed by his fellow pilgrims' apparent aptness for the roles they play in society or church. Nonetheless, he does have his occasional little joke, as with the Man of Law, who seemed busier than he was, and he sees through the nastiest customers, like the Miller, Reeve, Summoner, and Pardoner.

By cleverly matching the tales to the tellers and exploiting some of the antipathies between the pilgrims, such as the animosity between the Miller and the Reeve, and the Friar and the Summoner, Chaucer adds dramatic tension to his poem, as when he has some of the pilgrims tell tales as rejoinders to others, whether well-intentioned or malicious. The stories themselves represent a wide variety of medieval genres that Chaucer often subverts for comical, ironic, or satirical effects, and since quite a few of his pilgrims are scoundrels—or at least sorely in need of the spiritual benefits that pilgrimages were thought to afford— quite a few of the tales are bawdy or scatological, and these are the ones we tend to remember most fondly.

Giovanni Boccaccio's epic, *Teseida*, was the source of Chaucer's initial story, *The Knight's Tale*, a 2,250-line chivalric romance set in ancient Athens. The action involves two young knightly cousins and sworn brothers vying ridiculously—and ultimately violently—for the love of the "fair Emelye," who, for most of the time, is unaware of their existence. The absurd courtly lover behavior of these two young fools is satirized by the Knight who tells the tale, a devout, middle-aged warrior who places little importance on externals like his horse or his clothing. Thus, the truly chivalrous Knight is made to narrate a story exemplifying the destructive effects that uncontrolled passion has on chivalric ideals, possibly to alert his son, the Squire, "a lovyere and a lusty bacheler," to the dangers of the path he's treading. In fact, when we finally get to read it, *The Squire's Tale* turns out to be a piece of meandering fantastical fluff that's politely terminated midstory by the opportune intervention of the pilgrim called the Franklin.

The earnest Matthew Arnold saw Chaucer as deficient in "high and excellent seriousness," and, indeed, Chaucer's genius in this work is most evident in the comic tales. The second story told on the pilgrimage is a fabliau—a short, vulgar, often obscenely comic tale with bourgeois or lower-class characters. It is narrated by the drunken, brawny, and red-bearded Miller, who rudely demands to go next instead of the Monk, as a down-to-earth response to the Knight's ethereal courtly love story.

A foppish courtly lover, Absolon, goes to the window of a frisky young married woman to mouth sweet nothings to her while he thinks her husband is away. Alison, who is with a lover, tells Absolon to pucker up and be quick if he wants to kiss her. Throwing the window open in the dark, she sticks her naked ass out, and Absolon kisses this rather than her lips. "Tehee!" Alison titters as she claps the window shut.

Bent on revenge, Absolon comes back prepared. This time when he calls out to Alison for another of those delicious smackeroos, her boyfriend thrusts *his* bare ass out the window—and gets a red-hot coulter (the blade in front of a plowshare) stuck up it. Meanwhile, the woman's dim-witted cuckold of a husband, a carpenter, is ridiculed in the tale's subplot. The Reeve, a pilgrim who is the overseer of a manor, being a carpenter by trade, takes umbrage.

The Reeve's Tale, another fabliau, is thus motivated by an angry and spiteful old man's attempt to get back at the Miller. It features a mistaken-identity plot in which a miller has his wife and young daughter debauched by two crafty young men he allows to spend the night in his one-bedroom home.

The notorious Wife of Bath, still lusty and vivacious though considerably past her prime, talks freely about her "*bele chose*" in telling the story of her five marriages in the lengthy prologue to her tale. She judges her first three husbands as good—rich old men who let her do as she pleased. The fourth had a mistress, so she tormented him in turn by making him jealous. The fifth she loved, but she was forty and he was twenty and always reading aloud to her from an antifeminist "book of wikked wyves." When she tires of this one night and clouts him in the face, he belts her back so hard that he thinks he's killed her. After this knockdown, she gets him to burn his book and let her do as she wishes. Now, after his death, she's on pilgrimage to meet husband number six. The moral of the story she finally goes on to tell—an Arthurian wish-fulfillment fairy tale—is that marital woes can be avoided only if husbands submit to their wives. At the end, she prays to Jesus to send women meek young husbands who are good in bed.

The merrily wanton and avaricious Friar, who "knew the tavernes wel in every toun," as an enemy of the Summoner (a rival type of church official), tells a story in which a summoner is tricked by a devil into swearing away his soul but is not at all concerned, instead taking the opportunity to teach the devil himself a few tricks about how to swindle people. In retaliation, the ugly, pustuled, and revoltingly lecherous Summoner slams the Friar in the prologue to his tale, which parodies a pious old legend that told how, on going to heaven and seeing no friars there, a newly minted saint had asked why—and was shown how thousands upon thousands of them were all nestled by the Virgin Mary beneath her cloak. In the Summoner's version, a friar has a vision of hell in which he sees none of his colleagues and, on asking whether they enjoy a special grace in this matter, is shown Satan's ass—bigger than the sail on a huge ship—from which twenty thousand friars swarm out like bees, fly around hell a bit, and then creep back into their "nest."

This is only the first act of the Summoner's revenge. His tale is a fabliau in which a dying old man tricks a corrupt friar, who is hoping for a rich gift, into swearing that he will share it equally with his twelve fellow friars and then tells him to search under the bedclothes for it, "bynethe my buttok." When he does, the friar's groping hand is greeted by a fart more explosive than was ever emitted by a horse drawing a cart.

After he's thrown out of the house, the friar, as infuriated as a wild boar, stalks off to the house of the village lord, whom he finds at table. He demands justice, but the assembled company is more intrigued by how the friar might fulfill his solemn oath to share the aromatic bequest with his brethren. The lord's squire drolly offers a solution. He suggests that a cartwheel with twelve spokes be brought into the lord's hall, under which each of the friar's companions shall kneel with his nose firmly against the end of a spoke and the friar himself shall stick his nose upright beneath the wheel's hub. Then the sick old man shall be propped up over the center of the wheel and encouraged to fart, thus distributing the sound and stink equally, except that the friar himself shall have "the first fruyt." The hilarious ending manages to be blasphemous, too, in that the cartwheel was often represented in medieval depictions of Pentecost, with the tongues of divine fire poised over the heads of the twelve apostles.

Harking back to the main theme of the Wife of Bath's prologue and tale, the Clerk of Oxford, a scholarly young student preparing for the priesthood, tells a Job-like allegorical tale of the trials, tribulations, and ultimate reward of patient Grisilde (Griselda)—a wife who stolidly puts up with a number of sadistic "tests" by her husband. *The Clerk's Tale*, whose original version was the final tale in Boccaccio's *Decameron*, so impressed Petrarch that he translated it into Latin, and this was Chaucer's main source (see Question 100).

The Merchant's Tale, a fabliau with the moral that men should avoid marriage, is the cynical response of the Merchant, who has recently wed "a shrewe," to the Clerk's presentation of the "ideal" wife. The tale, a masterpiece of misogyny featuring a grotesquely repulsive old cuckold named Januarie and his unfaithful young wife, May, exemplifies the notion that a woman can brazenly talk her way out of anything—even, as in this story, when her husband catches her in flagrante with her lover up in a pear tree in his own backyard.

The Pardoner, a seller of indulgences who is perhaps the most corrupt of the pilgrims because he actually boasts of the tricks he plays in the name of religion, is apparently a eunuch: "A voys he hadde as smal as hath a goot. / No berd hadde he, ne nevere sholde have." Although the narrator thinks he might be "a geldyng or a mare," the Pardoner claims to "have a joly wenche in every toun," sings fashionable love songs, and sports trendy clothes. Yet his true delight is to trick his gullible auditors into buying pigs' bones as miraculous relics after admiring things like a piece of the sail of St. Peter's fishing boat and the veil of the Virgin Mary (just a plain old pillowcase).

The Pardoner's Tale, an exemplum about how "the love of money is the root of all evil," stars three juvenile delinquents who kill one another out of greed. It's an example of the kind of sermon the Pardoner preaches to scare his audience into charitable giving for the sake of their souls, but of course he keeps the money for himself. His brazenness and hypocrisy overreach themselves, however, when, after boasting to his fellow pilgrims in great detail about how he cozens simple souls, he tries to get the pilgrims themselves to buy his phony wares. The Host, not your shrinking-violet type, gives the con man his comeuppance, responding that he'd sooner cut off the Pardoner's testicles and enshrine them in a hog's turd—a taunt especially meant to rankle a man who's probably been castrated. The Pardoner is speechless with anger, but the Knight intervenes to make the Host and Pardoner kiss and make up.

The last of the Canterbury stories, *The Parson's Tale*, is a vast and boring prose sermon on the sacrament of penance and the seven deadly sins and their remedies, but it does comment on the various vices exemplified by many of the pilgrims and their tales. It is Chaucer's call to serious matters after dallying long in the realms of the world, the flesh, and the devil.

According to the Reverend W. W. Skeat, the great philologist who produced a standard edition of Chaucer, "The poet had good cause to regret such Tales as those of the Miller, the Reeve, and the Merchant," and indeed Chaucer did append a "Retraction" to his book that retracts just about all his writings, including the nastier of the tales told on the road to Canterbury. There is little reason to see it as other than a medieval convention—a stereotypically pious conclusion to a long work whose individual parts may not all have been very chaste, moral, or decorous. Despite his saucy reputation, Geoffrey Chaucer, the first truly world-class English poet, was to be surpassed by only one other— William Shakespeare—in the six centuries since his time. He was buried in 1400 in Westminster Abbey, where his tomb later became the nucleus of the "Poets' Corner."

FIFTEENTH CENTURY

104 ∾ Who was the first Renaissance architect?

Filippo Brunelleschi, builder of the dome of the cathedral of
Florence, 1420–36

THE MAN WHO SOLVED THE PROBLEM of placing a dome atop Florence's cathedral was thought to be mad and was carried bodily from the assembly at which he first described his plan.

Filippo Brunelleschi (1377–1446) was a short, feisty fellow given to practical jokes, ingenious mechanisms, and secretive research. Everyone in Florence knew he was clever—hadn't he convinced Manetto the woodworker through a diabolically intricate ruse that Manetto was not himself but someone else entirely? But this was a serious matter: No domes had been built in the Western world since antiquity. All Brunelleschi's knowledge of architecture, engineering, and persuasion would be needed to win the trust of the Florentines for the job of constructing the largest cupola in the world.

But that's not the half of it. Brunelleschi in fact has so many firsts to his name that, were he alive today, he'd keep a platoon of patent lawyers busy. Besides inventing the methodology of the dome and the machines to build it, he's credited with uncovering the laws of mathematical perspective. In architecture, he designed the earliest Renaissance buildings, applying rules and techniques of construction lost since the fall of Rome. He holds the world's first patent—a design for an amphibious paddleboat to transport marble (it sank, submerging much of his fortune); he attempted to hydraulically engineer an attack on Lucca; and he invented an alarm clock, worked on military fortifications, and created fanciful theatrical machinery.

Although he started out as a goldsmith, Brunelleschi was interested in every form of representational art, whether in paint, metal, or stone. His first venture into public art ended in spectacular defeat after he entered the 1401 competition for a most prestigious commission: the first set of bronze doors for the baptistery of the cathedral of Florence.

Many artists joined the fray, but in the end it came down to Brunelleschi and his archrival, Lorenzo Ghiberti. Brunelleschi's sample panel was more daring and original, alluding to an ancient Roman statue called *Lo Spinario* ("Boy with Thorn"), but it seemed unrefined. Various pieces of the panel had been molded separately and bolted to the back plate. Ghiberti, on the other hand, produced an elegant sculptural telling of the same tale—the sacrifice of Isaac—cast in one fluent bronze piece.

According to his first biographer, the judges asked Brunelleschi to share the labor with Ghiberti, but he refused, wishing to be in sole charge of the work. Not long afterward, he and his sculptor friend Donatello left for Rome, where he spent years studying the Baths of Caracalla, the Colosseum and Forum, the aqueducts, the Appian Way, and other Roman constructions, reverse-engineering them to divine their innermost secrets. Filling long strips of parchment with cryptic codes and Arabic numerals, not yet commonly used in Europe, he took detailed measurements of architectural elements—indeed, it was Brunelleschi who first determined the proportional rules governing the Doric, Ionic, and Corinthian orders.

He particularly studied the largest dome up to his own time, that of the Pantheon, which, offering no visible signs of support, caused people to mutter that it had been built by demons. He saw how its 142-foot-wide concrete dome had a thickness of twenty-three feet at its perimeter that tapered to just two feet at the center. He excavated and examined building materials, scrutinizing the ways ancient architects had distributed the structure's internal compressions and tensions, and noting how those stresses had caused jagged cracks in the dome.

All the while he knew that one day the Florentines would need an architect to span the vast 143.5-foot diameter of their cathedral's octagonal chancel—a project begun in 1296. Born practically in the shadow of Santa Maria del Fiore, Brunelleschi had watched the building proceed, with plenty of opportunity to observe the hoists and other construction machines. He knew the day would come when all that would be left would be the staggering problem of the dome.

The call came in 1418, inviting all architects who wished to compete for the project to submit models. Brunelleschi was something of a dark horse—a goldsmith with virtually no architectural accomplishments to point to. Indeed, he was best known for having demonstrated the principles of single-point perspective several years earlier. On a small panel, he had applied geometric rules to depict the Baptistery of San Giovanni and the surrounding piazza as seen from the doorway of the cathedral. Then he drilled a small hole through it precisely at the vanishing point. When one stood in the doorway and looked from behind the image through the hole at a mirror, it was said to be impossible to tell whether one was seeing a reflection of Brunelleschi's image or the real scene.

The dome would not be built with illusionary tricks, however. As everyone knew, the masonry of such a structure would have to be supported by some sort of framework, or centering, as it was being built. Centering was used at the time even for small arches. As the vault neared completion, its bricks would incline at a sixty-degree angle to the horizontal. The problem was, an entire forest would need to be imported to build such a large supporting framework. For the parsimonious city fathers, one key question for the candidate architects was how they planned to minimize the costs of the centering.

No one was prepared for Brunelleschi's astounding solution, which was to do away with centering completely. The proposal was greeted with more than the usual Florentine skepticism, especially when he refused to explain in any detail how it could be done. Indeed, things became so heated, says Giorgio Vasari, that Brunelleschi became an object of ridicule:

> As he grew warm in explaining his ideas, they doubted him
> the more, and held him to be a mere chattering fool. And when
> they had bidden him depart several times and he would not go,
> he was carried out by force, all supposing him to be mad.

When no proposal achieved consensus, Brunelleschi was summoned to reveal the secret of his solution. As the story goes, he challenged them to a wager: Let the architect who could make an egg stand on end on a flat piece of marble win the commission. After all the other contestants failed, he simply cracked the egg on the bottom and stood it upright. When his rivals said anyone could have done that, Brunelleschi pointed out that anyone who saw his plans would also know how to vault the cupola without centering.

Brunelleschi's model proved to be deeply detailed, containing two self-supporting vaults—one within the other, for lightness and strength. It included openings for wind and light, internal staircases, lights, chains, herringbone brick patterns, gutters to handle rain, and myriad solutions to foreseeable problems of the task, including a canteen where the workers' meals could be prepared high in the scaffolding. Behind all this lay his grasp of Roman construction techniques. In 1420, he was awarded the contract but was told he had to work with, of all people, Lorenzo Ghiberti. And he was given the go-ahead to build only the first fifth of the dome without centering, on a trial-and-error basis. After that, his entire responsibility would be reviewed.

So great was Brunelleschi's ardor for the task that he agreed. For the next sixteen years, the dome rose under his relentless eye, helped by machines he invented, which were, according to Frank D. Prager, "centuries ahead of the technical understanding of the time." Leonardo da Vinci, who later saw some of these machines in the workshop of his teacher Verrocchio, sketched them and mistakenly got credit for having invented them.

In the end, four million bricks—thirty-seven thousand tons' worth—seemed to defy gravity, ascending 295 feet into the sky without the use of any wood support. On March 25, 1436, Pope Eugenius IV consecrated il Duomo, which has ever since defined the skyline of Florence. Brunelleschi's controversial plan for the lantern above the dome—a large, complex work of art in itself that brings the total height to 375 feet—was accepted and the first stone laid in 1446, shortly before he died.

Brunelleschi completed few other buildings, but each offers evidence of an imagination deeply versed both in the formal language of architecture and in the science behind it. Based on two simple geometric modules—the cube and the hemisphere—the Ospedale degli Innocenti, or Foundling Hospital (begun 1419), with its nine round arches offered a lightness and openness unknown amid the towering spires and close, curving streets of Florence. The long loggia created the first great public space of modern urban design, its sober dignity keyed to human rather than divine dimensions.

The architectural elements of the hospital were of gray stone set off against cream-colored walls. Known as *pietra serena*, this stone was also used in the Old Sacristy of San Lorenzo, which Brunelleschi designed for the father of Cosimo de' Medici, as well as in the church of Santo Spirito and the Pazzi Chapel—mature works that demonstrate a breathtaking erasure of the architectural forms of the Middle Ages.

If the Corinthian columns and capitals of the Foundling Hospital, along with its windows surmounted by pediments, its fluted pilasters at each end of the loggia, and its geometric proportions, made clear reference to classical antiquity for the first time in Florence, the round dome atop the precise square of the Old Sacristy constitutes, according to art historian Frederick Hartt, "the first Renaissance space that could actually be entered."

But even that was merely a vestibule to the crowning achievement commissioned by the Pazzi family, the chapter house of the church of Santa Croce. In that small chapel, the clear geometric principles of structure, the hemispherical arches and Corinthian pilasters, the square panels of the barrel vaults, and the round dome that seems to float over the arches provide a complex harmony of forms so sweetly tempered as to suggest the pure play of formal intelligence at work—a play of reason which, like the music of the spheres, might almost be audible to an intellect properly attuned.

—*Tom Matrullo*

105 ❧ Who was the first Renaissance painter?

Masaccio, who created the frescoes for Florence's
Brancacci Chapel in
c. 1424

WHEN MICHELANGELO WAS A TEEN, his nose was crushed in a scuffle with another young art student in the Brancacci Chapel in Florence, where the two were studying the revolution in art wrought by a certain Tommaso Cassai.

Cassai, better known as Masaccio (1401–28), was the first indisputably great painter of the Renaissance. And just as Michelangelo's nose remained disfigured for life, so was his sense of figure ever after marked by his experience of Masaccio's art.

Tommaso was born in 1401 in a small town near Florence. Ten years after his father died in 1406, his family moved to Florence itself, where he acquired the nickname of "Masaccio"—"Tom the Big Slob." According to art historian Giorgio Vasari, people called him this because he was so preoccupied with his art that he demonstrated complete carelessness about his clothes, money, and all such quotidian matters.

The known facts of his life are few. Masaccio joined one of the seven major craft guilds in Florence in 1422, identifying himself as a *pictor*—"painter." Six years later, in the autumn of 1428, he was dead. Between those dates he created, with astounding speed of artistic development, an original approach to representing human forms in space by the means of perspective, light, and narrative power.

Some of these advances are already present in one of the earliest works attributable to him, the *Virgin and Child with St. Anne* (c. 1424), which he worked on with Masolino ("Little Tom"), an older and, at the time, better-known painter. Although much of the painting reflects the delicate Gothic manner of Masolino, a closer look shows that the angel at the upper right differs from the rest of them: His face, hand, and wings have a volume reminiscent of Giotto (see Question 97). Then—and this is unlike Giotto—the main figures, the Virgin and Child, are bathed in light from a single source. In addition, Christ looks like he's been working out with Hercules, and St. Anne's left hand, in motion, seems to generate spatial depth around it. It's as if a three-dimensional figure were seeking to escape from the picture plane.

Florence in the early fifteenth century was a noisy maelstrom of artistic energies. The bronze doors of the baptistery were taking form in Ghiberti's workshop; the largest dome since antiquity was rising over the cathedral under Brunelleschi's cantankerous eye (see Question 104); Donatello was resurrecting classical forms in stone—and demanding that they speak—while the early humanists were giving Homer, Plutarch, and many other ancient Greeks greater currency in Latin.

Masaccio could not but be inspired by daily contact with such innovations. Hearing what Donatello and Brunelleschi had to say about their protracted artistic investigations in Rome may have convinced the painter to journey there, probably in 1423. He soon acquired commissions, producing many works lost in later turbulent times.

The *Enthroned Madonna and Child*, created for an altarpiece in Pisa in 1426, suggests what Masaccio learned from his friends and from Rome. Mary sits deep within the encompassing space of a solid-looking throne, and her massive figure seems palpable beneath the blue cloth, which is contoured to her form in folds of shadow and light. The classical columns depicted on her chair invest it with the grandeur of an ancient multitiered temple. Two angels are nearly squeezed out of the frame by the monumental throne, while two others play lutes—one intently listening to the melody—as the Christ Child munches unceremoniously on grapes held in both fists.

In 1424 Masaccio was back in Florence, commissioned with Masolino to create a series of frescoes for the Brancacci Chapel in the church of Santa Maria del Carmine—works whose revolutionary visual storytelling prompted art historian Kenneth Clark to describe them as "the grandest of all testimonies to the dignity of man." Here, with an astonishing rapidity demanded by the technique of wall painting, Masaccio produced scenes that would constitute a virtual master class in narrative depiction for an "endless stream" of European artists, as Vasari put it, for centuries.

How fast did Masaccio work? Analysis of the *Expulsion from the Garden of Eden* on the upper left wall of the chapel showed that the entire tragic image was painted in four *giornate*—a *giornata*, or "day's work," being the area of wet plaster that could be painted and expected to dry in one day. The stricken figure of Adam—from departing feet to thumbs jammed over eyelids shamed shut—was completed in a single *giornata*.

Masaccio's rendering of the story of *The Tribute Money* runs along an inner wall. Here, the original Gospel narrative is broken into a kind of triptych, but Masaccio has stripped away the ornamental Gothic frame that traditionally separated three such scenes. The story, which tells how when a Roman tax collector demanded payment, Christ ordered St. Peter to catch a fish in the lake, take the coin out of its mouth, and give it to the collector, begins in the real space emanating from the central grouping, moves to the fishing episode on the left, and then finally to the right, where Peter pays up. The naturalized scene, governed by both aerial and mathematical perspective, is illuminated by single-source light against a backdrop of Tuscan mountains and scudding clouds. While Christ is at the vanishing point of lines converging from the architecture on the right, it is the character of Peter, with his furrowed face and expressive gestures—whether he's pointing, or grappling with the fish's mouth from an uncomfortable squat, or pressing the coin into the palm of the dandified tax official with utter disdain—that breathes life into the narrative.

In 1427 Masaccio was commissioned to paint a fresco of the Holy Trinity for the church of Santa Maria Novella in Florence. In some ways this austerely majestic work, twenty-two feet high, recapitulates the course of his artistic odyssey. For one thing, it is supposed to produce the illusion of an actual side chapel for anyone entering the nave of the church. The faux pilasters, cornice, and barrel vault, rendered with Brunelleschi's mathematical precision, allow the dimensions of the illusory chapel to be measured. If real, its vault would be seven feet wide by nine feet deep.

The Trinity is located within that illusion, flanked by the vivid figures of Mary and John the Apostle, who in turn are flanked, a step lower, by the married couple who were the painting's donors. "Before Masaccio had created his two donors," wrote art historian Michael Levey, "no painter in Florence had achieved such lifelike portrayal of people."

Above the donors and saints, the crucified Christ, at the center, is in the same forward plane as Mary and John. The small mound at the base of the cross is precisely at the spectator's eye level. Above all the figures, God the Father does the impossible: We see that he stands on a ledge at the back of the chapel—his feet are actually visible—yet his head appears to be in the same plane with Christ's head and the Holy Spirit, and his hands support the horizontal axis of the cross. What's more, while all else is handled according to the rules of perspective, the Trinity itself is seen not from the spectator's point of view below, but straight on, without foreshortening, thus violating the rigorous system that everything else in the painting obeys.

This enigmatically simultaneous invocation and denial of the realistic human view makes more sense as we read the rhyming Italian inscription in Roman capitals over the skeleton resting on the faux sarcophagus below:

> *IO FU GIA QUEL CHE VOI SIETE E QUEL CHIO SON VOI ANCO SARETE*
>
> *(I was once what you are, and what I am you also will be.)*

Alive, we are confined to the reality of Brunelleschian three-dimensional perception, but afterward we are face-to-face with the impossible.

Not long after Masaccio died at age twenty-seven—some said he was poisoned in Rome, where he'd returned in 1428—awareness of his accomplishment gathered momentum, and not only in Florence, but also in the rest of Italy and much of Europe. Numerous subsequent visions, like that of the Sistine Chapel ceiling, testify to the ineradicable influence of his priceless gift.

—*Tom Matrullo*

106 ❧ Who was the first Medici ruler of Florence?

Cosimo de' Medici, who deftly pulled the strings of government, 1434–64

WHAT IF YOU LIVED IN Florence in the early fifteenth century—a small, vibrant city shaped by a strong republican ethos and filled with proud families, upstart citizens, brilliant scholars, and artists of genius—and happened to inherit the largest banking fortune in Europe?

If you're Cosimo de' Medici, you go about your business, pruning your pear trees and telling your family and friends, "Envy is a plant you must not water."

In 1429, on the death of his father, Giovanni, the forty-year-old Cosimo took charge of a holding company that included silk and wool factories as well as the bank, inheriting an estimated 180,000 gold florins. In that day, less than a thousand florins would buy a nice palazzo.

The Medici ran a *banco grosso*. As the largest financial institutions of the time, these mercantile banks possessed vast accumulations of capital that were used to fund major government projects and international trade. Based in Florence, Cosimo's bank had offices in Venice, Rome, Genoa, and Basel, as well as correspondents throughout Europe. The network brought Cosimo, who already had a reputation both for business acumen and diplomatic discretion, the most up-to-date, intimate intelligence of world affairs.

This kind of power required all of Cosimo's considerable wits to thrive in a contentious Florence, which had been ruled for generations by an oligarchy of families who controlled the large guilds. One day, four years after taking charge of the bank, Cosimo was jailed and threatened with execution by a faction led by Rinaldo degli Albizzi, who had long hated the Medici. To him, Cosimo was an upstart who profited from loans helping to fund the city's war against Lucca even as he joined discontented Florentines in deploring the war and its noble ringleaders, including Rinaldo. Besides, the plans drawn up for their fortresslike new palazzo on Via Larga proved that the Medici had ambitions unworthy of republican citizens.

Cosimo dodged execution with a bribe of a thousand florins. Later he wrote: "They had little spirit, for if they had insisted on more money, they might have had ten thousand florins and more to deliver me from danger." Citizen Cosimo—the wealthiest man in Europe, richer than the pope—went into exile to the mournful good-byes of peasants offering gifts. His friend Donatello quit Florence in disgust. With Cosimo went his bank, and soon the city's middle class, taxed for the nobles' war, was sensible of the loss. A year later, the people joyfully welcomed Cosimo back, having driven the politically inept Rinaldo into permanent exile.

The banker's first task was clear: He had to find a way to maintain the forms and living image of republican freedom while ensuring that the exercise of civil liberties did not prevent his huge financial operation from doing business safely and with minimum political stress.

His solution was remarkable, involving stern measures at first— many of the most troublesome nobles, including the humanist patron Palla Strozzi, were banished, never to return. At least one popular military man, Baldaccio d'Anghiari, was stabbed and hurled from a window of the government offices in Palazzo Vecchio. But Cosimo, urging his sons "to exercise intellect no less than force," preferred subtler modes. Gradually, key nodes within the political network of Florence came into his patient hands. He gained control of the *accoppiatori*, the elections board that determined, based on typically byzantine rules, who was eligible to run for office. No need for active politicking when all the candidates come from a preselected pool. To an angry rival, Cosimo once explained that "you and I will act like two big dogs who, when they meet, smell one another and then, because they both have teeth, go their ways."

As a major benefactor of the city, Cosimo held sway over the credit markets. He famously built up his social capital, helping untold numbers of businessmen who remained bound to him by ties of gratitude and honorable debt. But the obverse was also infamously true. Many of Cosimo's wealthy enemies met economic ruin thanks to adjustments to the tax law, which he wielded, according to historian Francesco Guicciardini, "like a dagger."

From 1434 until Cosimo's death in 1464, the creaky constitutional components of the Florentine republic moved with a purposive finesse that allowed the city to prosper. Without ever holding public office, he formed and transformed alliances with the major states of Italy, switching

support from Venice to Milan and contriving a balance of power formalized in the Peace of Lodi of 1454. When he wasn't overseeing the bank or
functioning as the uncrowned prince of the city, he was endowing some of
the leading minds and hands of the day with the means to build, paint,
compose, redact, and sculpt what we know as the Renaissance.

Cosimo's role in the arts and sciences was more than that of mere
patron. He attracted a circle of early humanists—men like Niccolò Niccoli, Carlo Marsuppini, Giannozzo Manetti, Leon Battista Alberti, and
Ambrogio Traversari—who turned with passion toward the recovery
and editing of the key works of Cicero and other Roman authors.

At the Council of Florence—an effort, bankrolled by Cosimo, to
reconcile the Greek and Roman Churches—he met the Greek Neoplatonist Gemistus Plethon and heard him lecture on Plato, whose work
was then largely unknown in the West. From that encounter came generous funding for the Platonic Academy of Florence, an influx of priceless Greek manuscripts, and masterly Latin translations of the entire
corpus of Plato by Cosimo's protégé, Marsilio Ficino, which began to
blast away at the Aristotelian foundations of European learning.

While Michelozzo designed Palazzo Medici, and Benozzo Goz-
zoli its Chapel of the Magi, Brunelleschi built the church and Old Sacristy of San Lorenzo, and others worked on the abbey of Fiesole and the
monastery of San Marco, in the last of which Cosimo, using the eight-
hundred-volume collection of his late friend Niccoli as the nucleus,
created the first public library of the modern world. Lippo Lippi, Fra
Angelico, and Donatello enjoyed his patronage, and for him the famed
humanist Poggio Bracciolini wrote *On Nobility*, which argues that the
sole nobility is that of personal merit. Nothing better fit Cosimo's plain
style—disdainful of external shows while combining "big dog" tenac-
ity with the powers and sensibilities of a prince.

Cosimo died at age seventy-five, reportedly while reading a Platonic dialogue. He left the Medici fortune in the hands of his sickly son,
Piero the Gouty, fearful that his family would be vulnerable from every
side. He left behind no overt dynastic base or inherited title, and as if
honoring that, the people inscribed on his tomb in San Lorenzo the
same honorific that Rome had bestowed on Cicero and Augustus: *Pater
Patriae*, "Father of His Country."

The later adventures of the family—from Lorenzo the Magnificent
to popes Leo X and Clement VII to Catherine and Marie de' Medici—
were many and varied, ranging from its expulsion from Florence in

1494 to the attainment of royalty and the very highest offices of the church. Across three centuries, their fortune helped shape the fortunes of Europe.

—Tom Matrullo

107 ⌒ Who was the first "Universal Man"?

Leon Battista Alberti (1404–72), scholar, architect, author, athlete, churchman, musician, etc.

LEON BATTISTA ALBERTI STEPS FROM THE SHADOWS of the Middle Ages as the first Renaissance man, according to no less an authority than historian John Addington Symonds, who called him "the very type of those many-sided, precocious, and comprehensive men of genius who only existed in the age of the Renaissance." Jacob Burckhardt went further, saying of Alberti, "Among these many-sided men some who may truly be called 'all-sided' tower above the rest." Although many prefer to think of Leonardo da Vinci as the perfect embodiment of an all-sided or universal man, Leon Battista Alberti, who lived a half century earlier, mastered even more fields of endeavor.

Look where you will in Alberti's work, it bristles with innovation—his own or someone else's. Were he alive today, he'd be contributing to or reporting on new developments among the digerati, as well as in science, architecture, the fine arts, public affairs, and literature, and even that would not do justice to the range of his interests and accomplishments.

Born in Genoa in 1404 as Battista (he prefixed it with *Leon* later in life), he came from an old Florentine banking family that had been exiled from its native city by oligarchs jealous of the increasing power of merchant-bankers like the Alberti and the Medici (see Question 106). His father, a wealthy businessman, taught him mathematics and sent him to a school in Padua which, in its emphasis on oratory—the rhetorical adeptness of Cicero rather than the Scholastic logic of Aristotle—reflected the burgeoning influence of the early humanists.

Apparently a bit of a showoff, Alberti trained himself to leap over a man's head from a standing position and to master wild horses. At twenty he composed the *Philodoxeos*, a comedy in Latin verse which, as late as 1588, was published by the prestigious Aldine Press as the "discovered" work of an ancient Roman playwright.

To support himself—he was cheated of his patrimony after his father's death—Alberti obtained a doctorate in canon law, graduating from the University of Bologna in 1428. Within a few years he became a secretary in the papal chancery and took holy orders. He is said to have hated the law, and the varied writings he went on to produce betray little evidence of his connection to the church. Many are dialogues in the manner of Cicero, engaging the secular world of business and management, while others are technical treatises about art and method.

Quite a few of his works, including his first published treatise, *On the Family* (1432), were composed in Italian to serve a growing urban public that did not have the benefit of a classical education. The characters were often drawn from life, including his own family, yet reflect generic advice about dealing with the ups and downs of fortune, acquiring an education, and managing a household that can be found in works by Seneca or Cicero. As a guide, Alberti was pouring old wine into new skins.

But Florence made him a purveyor of new wines as well. He arrived there as part of the papal legation in 1434 (though he might have visited the city earlier, in 1428) and instantly registered the shock of the new. It was there that he first made his mark as a writer and thinker, a result of his firsthand encounter with the extraordinary intellectual and artistic life of the city. There was much to absorb, from Brunelleschi's vast dome and his demonstrations of linear perspective, to Donatello's reinvigorated classical figures, to Ghiberti's bronze *Gates of Paradise*, to Masaccio's dramatic—and mathematically rigorous—frescoes (see Questions 104 and 105).

The result was *On Painting*, the first postclassical treatise on art, published in Latin in 1435, then rewritten in Italian and rededicated to Brunelleschi. Alberti describes it thus:

> You will see three books: the first, all mathematics, concerning the roots in nature which are the source of this delightful and most noble art. The second book puts the art in the hand of the artist. . . . The third introduces the artist to the means and the end.

The treatise reflects a peculiarly Albertian synthesis of practical and rhetorical elements. Painting, elevated to a liberal art, is conceived as an expressive performance that has much to learn from the skills of ancient oratory. Like a Cicero of line and color, the painter chooses his subjects and arranges them to produce a unified emotional impact on his "audience." But since painting contains a "divine force," the painter should interrogate nature. Alberti drew upon mathematics and a penchant for method, as well as on his observations of the Florentine avantgarde, in offering detailed "how-to" guidance for painters.

Alberti is justly credited with first putting into words a set of procedures for creating paintings that obey the geometric rules of single-point perspective. He also urges painters to study anatomy, explore the psychological effects of color on the observer, and attend to aesthetic principles of harmony. The coming generation of artists—Paolo Uccello, Piero della Francesca, Raphael, and especially Leonardo—would apply Alberti's original insights to achieve new levels of technical and emotive virtuosity.

Practically nothing in the fertile early quattrocento was safe from Alberti's curiosity and pedagogic bent. Although not trained in music, he was an organist whose compositions were admired by learned musicians. His friendship with Paolo Toscanelli, a Florentine mathematician and cosmographer whose maps were used by Columbus on his first voyage (see Question 111), led to applications useful in astronomy and geography, and engendered Alberti's influential treatise on surveying and mapping the city of Rome.

He moved easily among the leading courts of his day. At the Este court in Ferrara, he was urged to revive the study of architecture, leading to his *De re aedificatoria* (*Ten Books on Architecture*). The publication of this work, with its assimilation of ancient practices and engineering into a comprehensive modern discipline, came just as a host of large-scale Renaissance building projects, including the reconstruction of St. Peter's, were getting under way. In his last two decades Alberti himself became a practicing architect, designing, among other noted works, the Tempio Malatestiano in Rimini (with its Roman triumphal-arch motif), the facades of the Palazzo Rucellai and Santa Maria Novella in Florence (with its famous S-curved volutes, which had no ancient precedent), and the church of Sant'Andrea in Mantua.

In his spare time, he dabbled in optical devices that could create moving scenes and composed dozens of other works, including several poems and misogynist comedies, a manual on cryptography, another on math games, a study of sculpture, the first grammar of Italian, and a panegyric to his dog. He is said to have foretold certain events,

including the deaths of popes. A recent scholarly edition of his complete works fills twenty-four volumes. He died in Rome in 1472.

Alberti's artistic legacy lags behind his success as a prescient dissem-
inator. Giorgio Vasari said he was better known for what he wrote than for
the work of his hands; Symonds described his poetry as that of "a man
largely gifted, but not born to be a singer." Doing many things first that
others would do better, he was a significant harbinger of glories to come.
Let his Italian compatriot Francesco De Sanctis have the last word:

> Whoever measures Alberti by the quantity of his works, or by
> the scope of his fields of knowledge, must recognize him to be
> as miraculous a genius as he was considered to be in his own
> day. Certainly he was the most cultivated man of his time, and,
> in his interests, the complete epitome of his century.

—Tom Matrullo

108 ᧧ Who invented the first mechanical printing press?

The German goldsmith Johannes Gutenberg,
c. 1450

SEE-77

WHEN HISTORIAN EDWARD GIBBON called printing "an art which
derides the havoc of time and barbarism," he was referring to the
products of mechanical presses that used movable metal type and first
made the reproduction of texts and images rapid and relatively inexpensive. Although the Chinese created the world's first dated printed
book as early as 868—a Buddhist scroll called the *Diamond Sutra*—
and invented movable wooden and ceramic type by the eleventh century, their lack of an alphabet with a manageable number of characters
impeded the success of printing (see Question 77). The same problem
beset the Koreans, who later developed movable metal type. In addition, rather than a press mechanism, early Asian printing relied on
brushing behind each sheet of paper to make the other side receive the
impression from an inked surface in a time-consuming technique that
often produced uneven or smudgy results.

By the late fourteenth century, Europeans were printing from carved wooden blocks or metal plates—an inefficient method that was better suited to images like those on playing cards than to the discursive tomes medieval authors loved to churn out. A European pioneer with movable type may have been Laurens Janszoon Coster in Haarlem, Holland, in about 1430. Paper, an ancient Chinese invention (see Question 9) that had long before been introduced into Europe by the Arabs, was also on hand. It took a German goldsmith, however, to find a practical, comprehensive solution to the increased demand for information by the literate merchant classes, who wanted more books for less money than could be supplied by even the most efficient lay or monastic scribes.

Johannes Gutenberg (c. 1398–1468), born with the surname Gensfleisch ("Gooseflesh"), preferred to assume the name of the family's house in Mainz. Son of a patrician of the city, he was exiled in the strife between the patricians and the guilds, settling in Strasbourg (now in France), where he worked as a goldsmith and also started experimenting with new printing techniques in the 1430s and 1440s.

No books surviving from Gutenberg's time list him as publisher. We know him mostly from the court records of various lawsuits brought against him. The paper trail from one such proceeding in Strasbourg in 1439 refers to many important components of modern printing—such as types, stockpiles of metals, forms—leading some to believe Gutenberg may have been experimenting with movable metal type by 1438 or earlier.

Gutenberg's process seems to have begun with hand-carving into the end of a metal punch a character—a letter or punctuation mark—that was used to stamp its impression into a small copper plate (or matrix). The matrix was placed, raised side down, into a rectangular holder or mold that was filled with molten lead, tin, and antimony. When the metal cooled, a rectangular stick of durable type had been produced with the character in relief at the bottom. Repeating the process supplied the many identical copies of characters that printers needed for speedily setting type into forms that would enable them to print individual pages. Some scholars, however, have recently speculated that the ability to duplicate many copies of characters from the same matrix was a refinement that occurred only after Gutenberg's death.

When arranged face up in a form or text block, the type was inked and a sheet of paper pressed down on it with the uniform pressure imparted by a flat piece of wood forced down by a screw-type mechanism, which was ultimately an adaptation of a winepress. But the ink had to adhere evenly to the raised metal type, which traditional water-based inks did not do. Influenced by the linseed-oil-based varnish that Flemish painters used for their pigments, Gutenberg created his own linseed-oil, carbon-based ink, which also included copper, lead, and titanium. When one sheet was printed, it was removed and hung to dry while another was inserted, enabling a worker to print three hundred to five hundred sheets a day.

Back in his hometown of Mainz, Gutenberg may have used these techniques to print a number of early works, including a German poem and the *Constance Mass Book* in about 1450. In 1454, he printed a letter of indulgence issued by Pope Nicholas V, the earliest surviving European printed text bearing a date. He may also have printed some Latin grammars, various other letters of indulgences, and an appeal to Christians against the Turks by Pope Calixtus III in 1455 (see Question 109).

In 1450 and again in 1452, he borrowed a significant amount of money from Johannes Fust, with whom he entered into a partnership in the latter year. Impatient for returns on the venture, Fust sued Gutenberg in 1455 and was awarded the amount of the two loans plus compound interest, as well as rights to the printer's equipment and processes.

It was just at this time that Gutenberg was printing his masterpiece: the magnificent two-volume Bible in the Latin Vulgate translation (see Question 32). Though not the first printed book in the Western world, this double-folio Gutenberg Bible of 1,282 double-columned pages, with its rounded Gothic Textura font and elegant drop capitals illuminated by hand, is one of the most prized and finely crafted. Also known as the 42-line Bible (from the number of lines on the great majority of its pages) or the Mazarin Bible (after a richly illuminated copy found in 1760 in the library of French statesman Cardinal Mazarin), Gutenberg's most famous work had a press run of about 180 copies, of which one-quarter were printed on vellum and the rest on Italian paper. Forty-eight copies survive, eleven of them in the United States. The even rarer 36-line Gutenberg (or Bamberg) Bible, once thought to have been produced earlier than the 42-line Bible, is now known to have been printed in 1457–59.

Fust must have made a handsome profit on the Gutenberg Bibles, but we don't know how Gutenberg himself fared. The exquisite Latin Psalter of 1457, with hundreds of two-color initial letters, also must have been the fruit of Gutenberg's labors, though it was printed by Fust and his new partner, his son-in-law Peter Schöffer (Gutenberg's ex-foreman, who testified against him in the trial of 1455). The Psalter was the first printed European book to list the name of its publisher—Fust and Schöffer—and to contain a typographical error, right in the second word of the colophon: "*spalmorum*" for "*psalmorum*" ("of psalms").

When Mainz was sacked in 1462 by its martial archbishop, Adolph II of Nassau, the various printers who had set up shop there were sent scurrying throughout and beyond Germany, and Gutenberg himself fled to the Hessian town of Eltville. In 1465, however, the archbishop awarded him an annual pension of grain, wine, and a suit of courtly clothes, creating him a "gentleman of the court." Perhaps Gutenberg didn't die destitute, as formerly thought, but it is known that he was stricken blind before his death in 1468.

Even before Gutenberg died, two Germans fleeing from Mainz produced the first book printed in Italy—Cicero's treatise *De oratore*—at Subiaco, east of Rome, in 1465. About four years later, another pair of Germans established a press in Venice, which soon became the European capital of printing, especially after Aldus Manutius, the greatest printer of his age, began printing affordable pocket-size editions of the Greek and Latin classics (see Question 101). Three Germans set up the first French printing press at the Sorbonne in Paris in 1470. In 1472, the first printed edition of Dante's *Divine Comedy* appeared in Foligno, Italy.

About two years later, the first printed book in English, *The Recuyell [Collection] of the Historyes of Troye*, saw the light of day in Bruges, Belgium. The printer was William Caxton (c. 1422–91), a wealthy English merchant who had translated the original French work into English and, overwhelmed by the demand for it, went to Cologne to study printing and then set up a press in Bruges, where he had worked as a businessman.

After printing a book in English on chess and four books in French at Bruges, Caxton established the first printing press in England at Westminster in 1476. The next year he brought out the first dated book printed in the country, *Dictes and Sayenges of the Phylosophers*, a translation from French by Anthony Woodville, Earl Rivers. Caxton printed the first definitive edition of Chaucer's *Canterbury Tales* in 1478 (see Question 103), and in 1485 he edited and printed *Le Morte Darthur*, an epic retelling of nearly all the French Arthurian tales in magnificent English prose that Sir Thomas Malory had completed in prison in 1470. Oxford University's press, established in 1478, specialized in more scholarly books.

Scribes and copyists continued to produce Latin books by hand in the luxury trade, competing with incunabula ("in the cradle")—what we call books printed before 1501. The printing press, however, encouraged the development of books in the European vernaculars because many middle-class readers couldn't read Latin. Soon, even discriminating book collectors like the Medici and the popes began adding printed books to their precious manuscript collections. In 1455, there were about one hundred thousand books in all of Europe. By 1500, there were about nine million.

The rapid adoption of the printing press, which made the diffusion of information and knowledge so much easier and more affordable, ushered in not only a European Renaissance but also a religious Reformation (see Question 113). Martin Luther, who made superb use of the Gutenberg revolution to divulge his ideas and his classic German translation of the Bible, said, "Printing is an art that deserves our praise as the supreme clarion of the world. It is the most precious gift of the German lands." He would have been shocked to learn that media theorist Neil Postman, speaking at a meeting of the German Informatics Society in 1990, argued that in making modern science possible, printing "transformed religious sensibility into an exercise in superstition."

109 ∾ Who was the first Muslim overlord of Constantinople?

Ottoman sultan Mehmed II the Great, who ruled it from 1453 until his death in 1481

IN 330, ROMAN EMPEROR CONSTANTINE established his new capital of Constantinople on the site of the ancient Greek city of Byzantium, strategically located at the southern mouth of the Bosporus, the portal to the Black Sea. After the fall of the Western Empire in 476, the city became the capital of the vast Eastern—or Byzantine—Empire, but after numerous Arab, Persian, Slavic, and Italian conquests of its territories and the advent of the Seljuk Turks, the empire was tottering. In 1204, the Venetians,

French, and other Western Christians infamously sacked Constantinople, making it the capital of a Latin Empire that survived for two generations before reverting to Greek rule (see Question 90).

The Ottoman Turks succeeded the Seljuks—whose power had been broken in the mid-thirteenth century by the Mongols—as the Muslim nation that continued to snip away at the incredibly shrinking Byzantine Empire. The first conquest of their own fledgling empire was Bursa in northwestern Asia Minor (now Turkey) in the 1320s, during the last days of the founder of the dynasty, Sultan Osman I (or Othman, hence "Ottomans"). In 1354, the Ottomans captured the fortress of Gallipoli, their first European possession. Seven years later, they took Adrianople (Edirne) in southeastern Europe and soon made it their new capital, giving them a bead on Constantinople itself, about 150 miles to the east.

This new European power, which defeated the kingdom of Serbia at Kosovo in 1389 and trounced an army of crusaders at Nicopolis in 1396, had the wind knocked out of its sails—and its sultan caged—by the Turkic conqueror Tamerlane (Timur the Great) in 1402. Nonetheless, by this time, Bulgaria had also fallen to the Ottomans, who went on to capture the second-largest Byzantine city, Thessalonica, in 1430.

Mehmed (Muhammad) II (1432–81), later known as Fatih ("the Conqueror"), had an early taste of absolute power when his father, Sultan Murad II, abdicated in his favor when the boy was only twelve. Murad came out of retirement to destroy a Hungarian-led crusading army at the battle of Varna in 1444 but was persuaded to return to his full government duties in 1446 after a revolt of the elite foreign troops known as Janissaries.

In the meantime Mehmed acquired a wide culture, studying Latin and Greek with the Italian humanist Cyriacus of Ancona and being trained in traditional Muslim lore and science by other scholars. On his father's death in 1451, he took over the empire for a second time. His dream was to become a new Caesar, donning the mantle of the Byzantine—then called "Roman"—emperor, even if by this time the dominion under the direct rule of Constantine XI Palaeologus (1404–53) had been reduced to a sliver of land on the European side of the Bosporus—essentially, the city of Constantinople itself. To protect his rear, Mehmed concluded peace treaties with Hungary and Venice. To control the Bosporus and prevent grain convoys from reaching Constantinople from the Black Sea, he built, about six miles north of the city, the fortress later known as Rumeli Hisari.

The Ottoman sultan was only twenty-one years old when, on April 5, 1453, he signaled the start of the attack on the city of fifty thousand, which, though still splendid, was but a wraith of its former self. Mehmed's forces comprised at least one hundred thousand men and about 125 ships and smaller vessels, supported by fifty cannons, including the world's largest, a twenty-seven-foot-long piece forged by a Hungarian named Orban. Constantinople at this time could be thought of as a triangle protected on its western, or land, side (the base of the triangle) by a triple wall and a ditch a hundred feet deep, on the southern side by a seawall on the Sea of Marmara, and on the northern side by the Golden Horn, a fortified inner harbor to which access from the Bosporus was denied by an iron chain stretching across the harbor mouth from the city to the northern suburb of Galata.

Two sides of the triangular city, those lying on the water, were thus inaccessible to the Turkish onslaught, and the land walls were formidable, though constructed a thousand years earlier by Roman emperor Theodosius II. Almost four miles in length, they were manned by defenders who disgorged so many stones, arrows, lances, bullets, artillery shots, and searing liquids that the Muslim attackers were slaughtered in huge numbers. Unlike the seven thousand Christian soldiers of the garrison—of whom two thousand were foreign troops, mostly Genoese and Venetians—the Turks had many thousands to spare, and their ships outnumbered the Christian fleet by at least five to one.

The rest of Europe, embroiled in its own conflicts, provided little aid to the besieged city, with the heroic exception of four large ships, three Genoese and one Greek, loaded with food, wine, oil, soldiers, and sailors that set out from the island of Chios, a colony of Genoa, and fought their way through the blockading Turkish fleet. Bristling with weapons, the relief ships raked the attacking enemy with artillery, missiles, and projectiles, and sprayed them with Greek fire (see Question 53) before slipping into the inner harbor.

Desperately needing to open a second front, Mehmed ordered a platform of planks laid down and greased with the fat of sheep and oxen north of the walls of the Genoese colony of Galata (sometimes called Pera). He then commanded that about seventy of his smaller vessels in the Bosporus be hauled ashore, set on rollers, and dragged by men and pulleys—with the aid of wind in the sails—about ten miles overland, in the course of a single night, until they splashed into the waters of the Golden Horn and opened up the city to attack from its cordoned-off inner harbor.

The next step in Mehmed's plan was to construct a pier in the narrow part of the harbor on which to plant one of his biggest cannons to pound the walls, while his men scanned the fortifications for the most promising place to scale. The double assault on the land and seawalls increased the burden of the city's defenders. After more than a month of pounding, the walls were crumbling. Mehmed offered terms, but Emperor Constantine spurned them.

On May 29, 1453, shortly after midnight, with Turkish cannons blasting, two waves of attacks on the walls were repulsed, the corpses of the slain filling up the deep ditch. The third was by the Janissaries, however, and their ferocity taxed the resources of the weary defenders. When Giovanni Giustiniani, the Genoese military commander of the land defenses, was fatally wounded by gunshot and had himself brought to his ship, the remnant of his seven hundred Genoese troops, assuming the walls had been scaled, retreated through the city and ultimately sailed away, along with a force of Venetian ships.

When the Kerkoporta, a small gate near the northern corner of the land wall, was inadvertently left unlocked, a small group of Turkish soldiers streamed in, and a fight broke out. This breakthrough encouraged a mass assault on the walls that succeeded through sheer strength of numbers. Emperor Constantine, called by Greek poet Odysseas Elytis "the last of the Hellenes," died fighting for his country.

As Turkish troops swarmed into the city, all the gates were thrown open to let in even more, and they were soon joined by their comrades who had penetrated a gate on the harbor wall. Several thousand inhabitants of Constantinople were slaughtered in the aftermath, and the hordes of others who took refuge inside Justinian's Hagia Sophia or in the other churches were hustled back to the camps and fleet to be sold or kept as slaves.

The city—afterward also known as Istanbul, a corruption of Greek words for "to the city"—was plundered briefly but efficiently in lieu of pay for the soldiers, as was customary. Hagia Sophia was immediately converted into a mosque, its icons being desecrated or plastered over, and noon prayers were said there on the first Friday after the conquest, three days later. Constantinople itself was made the new Ottoman capital.

Mehmed extended privileges to the Orthodox Church, restoring the Greek patriarchate early the following year. A grand rabbi was also set up, and Turks, Christians, and Jews were deported from Anatolia and the Balkans to repopulate the city after the human toll of the siege, massacre, and enslavement, as well as the departure en masse of the Italian merchants. Many Byzantine scholars fled to Italy, where their knowledge and manuscripts of ancient Greek literature and philosophy stoked a Renaissance that was already well under way (see Questions 101 and 106).

Though his troops were accused of destroying 120,000 manuscripts, Mehmed gathered Muslim and Christian scholars at his court, amassed a vast library, and left behind a *divan* (collection) of about eighty of his poems in Turkish and a few in Persian. But he was cruel and implacable when thwarted. After the conquest, a Venetian diplomat described him as "of aspect more frightening than venerable, laughing seldom."

Under his rule, the Topkapi ("Cannon Gate") palace complex was initiated in 1459, eventually accommodating two thousand women in its world-renowned harem. In the same year, he began work on the enormous Mosque of the Conqueror and its associated colleges, hospital, medical school, hospice, public bath, and soup kitchen.

The Conqueror went on to take Athens in 1456, though he was temporarily stunned at Belgrade by János Hunyadi of Hungary, losing twenty-four thousand troops and gaining a javelin wound in the thigh. Serbia became a province of the Ottoman Empire in 1459—the same year in which Pope Pius II tried to rally European support for another crusade but was told by Duke Francesco Sforza of Milan that the time for that sort of thing was over (see Question 82). The last Byzantine-associated outposts, the Peloponnesus and Trebizond, fell to the Turks in 1460–61, and Bosnia was conquered in 1463, the same year that saw the completion of Mehmed's mosque in his capital. He extended his rule to all of Anatolia by defeating a Turkmen leader in 1473, and his conquest of Albania was completed by 1479, eleven years after the death of its valiant national hero Skanderbeg.

Toward the end of his life, Mehmed requested a good painter from Venice and got a very good one, Gentile Bellini, who decorated the walls of his palace with erotic murals and painted the bearded and turbaned Grand Turk himself in profile in 1480. The man who called himself *Kayser-i Rum* ("Roman Caesar") died at age forty-nine, perhaps by poison, shortly after setting out for another military venture. At word of his passing, Pope Sixtus IV led Rome—and ultimately all of Europe—in celebration.

110 ∽ Who was the first French *poète maudit?*

François Villon (1431–c. 1463), Parisian thief, pimp, murderer, etc.

THE EXPRESSION *POÈTE MAUDIT* ("accursed poet") wasn't coined until 1832, by French author Alfred de Vigny in his *Stello*, a dialogue in which three short stories are narrated with the moral of how poets, such as the ill-fated André Chénier and Thomas Chatterton, come to bad ends, since they belong to "a race always cursed by the powerful of the earth." In 1884, *Les Poètes maudits* was used as a title by Paul Verlaine for his six brief biographies of contemporary Symbolist poets, including Arthur Rimbaud, Stéphane Mallarmé, and himself (under the transparent anagram of Pauvre Lélian).

But the prototype in French literature of the *poète maudit*—a criminally inclined, seriously unhinged, substance-abusing bohemian artist who tends to die young and whose genius is intricately bound up with his nonconformity—was one of the greatest lyric poets of the Middle Ages or any age: the Parisian François de Montcorbier (aka François des Loges), who renamed himself Villon after the chaplain who unofficially adopted the poverty-stricken young boy—whose father had died—and sent him to school.

Villon fell in with a bad lot, however, his criminal history beginning in June 1455, when he killed a priest with his sword in a drunken quarrel. His sentence, banishment from Paris, was terminated in January by a royal pardon on grounds of self-defense. Toward the end of 1456, when Villon and four others stole money from the College of Navarre, he skedaddled from Paris again. To commemorate his departure, he composed *Le Lais* ("The Legacy"), a poem of 320 lines in the comical medieval genre of the false last will and testament. Among many other bequests, he leaves his heart to the woman who dumped him, a punch in the eye and the right to shiver to the bums lying under the street stalls, snippets of his hair to his barber, his old shoes to the cobbler, and his clothes to the ragman.

We next hear of him in 1461, summering in a dungeon of Thibault d'Aussigny, bishop of Orléans, at Meung-sur-Loire. We don't know what his offense was, but we do know he was subjected to an early form of waterboarding by having large amounts of cold water forced down his throat through a cloth. Luckily for him, the new king, Louis XI, passed through Meung that fall and released all the prisoners in honor of his recent coronation.

Only two years later, in 1463, the poet was sentenced to death by hanging for his involvement in a street brawl in Paris, though he may have been only a spectator. After a legal appeal, his sentence was commuted to banishment from Paris for ten years. At age thirty-two, François Villon was never heard of again and is generally presumed to have died soon afterward.

Villon's poetic masterpiece is *The Testament* (1461–62), in which he returns to the format of the pseudo last will, but here at much greater length—more than two thousand lines—and with an acerbic vehemence born of suffering, especially the water torture, hunger, and other punishments Bishop Thibault had subjected him to.

Once again he leaves what little he owns (and much that he doesn't) to various cronies and foes in highly colloquial and earthy rhymed stanzas, replete with sexual double entendres. Embedded in *The Testament* is "The Ballad of Dead Ladies," in which Villon reprises the ancient theme of *ubi sunt?* ("Where are they now?") to ask rhetorically what has become of all the great beauties and heroines of the past, like Joan of Arc, "the good maid of Lorraine / Whom the English burned at Rouen," and

> *Where is the learnèd Héloïse*
> *For whom they castrated Abelard*
> *And made him a monk at Saint-Denis?* (see Question 84)

English poet Dante Gabriel Rossetti's translation of this poem—with its refrain of "But where are the snows of yester-year?"—has itself become a classic.

The Testament includes several other tour-de-force set pieces, such as the anguished reminiscences of a withered prostitute lamenting her lost youth, which she graphically contrasts with the ravages old age has wrought on her former beauty. Though still a young man himself, Villon feels prematurely old, and thus he empathizes with an old man whose witty stories no longer amuse the young, since "an old monkey is always unpleasant, / And every face it makes is ugly."

Despite the humor of Villon's "bequests"—much of it lost on us through ignorance of why they are appropriate to the legatees—we're saddened by the grim first-person accounts of squalor, imprisonment, sickness, pain, impotence, and drunken rows and sordid copulations with the whore named Fat Margot whose debased pimp he is. Most moving of all, though, in a long work brimful of dissipation, is what he leaves his mother, "who suffered bitter pain for me, / God knows, and many sorrows"—a humble prayer for her to recite to the Virgin Mary, conjuring up the old widow's simple religious faith. Among its lines are these:

> *I'm just a poor little old woman*
> *Who knows nothing and never learned to read.*
> *I see on the walls of my parish church*
> *A painted paradise, with harps and lutes,*
> *And a hell where the damned are boiled—*
> *One makes me scared, the other glad and joyful.*

In a contrite ballade with the refrain "I beg everyone's mercy," Villon makes an exception for the torturers who starved him in prison, saying, "I'd give them farts and belches," and wishes that their ribs might be smashed with sledgehammers and other massive weapons. He ends *The Testament* by imagining his last act on earth—taking a long swig of wine.

While expecting to be executed in 1463, Villon wrote his most famous poem, "Ballad of the Hanged Men," which imagines five or six hanged corpses addressing passersby, urging them not to mock the horrific appearance of their rotting flesh, with their eyes and beard pecked out by magpies and ravens, but instead to pray to God that he absolve us all alike. Here is how it opens:

> *O brother humans, who live on after us,*
> *Don't let your hearts be hardened against us,*
> *Because, if you show pity for us wretches,*
> *Sooner will God have mercy on you, too.*

Nineteenth- and twentieth-century decadents and aesthetes loved Villon. Besides the French Symbolists and Rossetti, there was Algernon Charles Swinburne, who published translations of ten of Villon's poems in 1878. In a poetic tribute, Swinburne calls him "prince of all ballad-makers" and "our sad bad glad mad brother," testifying to the abiding fascination of Villon's scant three thousand lines of verse even four centuries after his death.

As a bawdy hell-raiser, Villon also became a hero of the iconoclastic American poet Ezra Pound, who imitated him in some early poems, wrote an opera of sorts, *Le Testament* (1923), based on the French poet's verses, and ended up as a famed prison-poet himself. Pound evidently appreciated Villon's firsthand acquaintance with his low-life Parisian subject matter, claiming that "his depravity is not a pose cultivated for literary effect."

But "sad bad glad mad" François Villon, the drunken and debauched bottom-feeder, was also an enigmatic scholar-poet who had earned a master of arts degree from the University of Paris at age twenty-one and asserted in one of his ballads, "I know all things except myself."

111 ∾ What was the first voyage of Christopher Columbus?

An exploration of Watling Island, Cuba, and Hispaniola, in 1492

THE OTTOMAN CONQUEST OF CONSTANTINOPLE in 1453 had choked off lucrative European trade routes to the East, which focused on luxury items such as silks, spices, perfumes, and gems (see Question 109). A new way had to be found to obtain the products of the Orient without having to deal with Arab merchants and other middlemen.

Even before the fall of Constantinople, that's what Portuguese mariners had been trying to do. After taking Ceuta in Morocco in 1415, at the instigation of the young Prince Henry the Navigator (1394–1460), the Portuguese continued inching down the coast of Africa and venturing out into the Atlantic until they were masters of the Madeira Islands and the Azores and had established in 1445 their first trading post in West Africa, which enabled them to traffic directly for slaves and gold. Two years after Henry's death, Portuguese sailors explored the coast as far south as Sierra Leone, intent on gradually finding a sea route to India and East Asia around Africa. But then in 1474 King Alfonso V was informed by a letter and map of Paolo dal Pozzo Toscanelli, an elderly Florentine scholar, that the riches of Asia could more easily be reached by sailing west across the Atlantic.

Christopher Columbus (1451–1506) put great faith in Toscanelli's map, which grossly underestimated the distance from Europe to the Orient. Born to a wool weaver in the maritime powerhouse of Genoa, young Columbus sailed the Mediterranean before taking up residence in Lisbon in 1476, where he went into business making sea charts with his brother Bartholomew. He may have sailed to Iceland in the following year and heard stories of a new world to the west, but he also later gained much practical experience of navigation on trading vessels bound for West Africa, Madeira, and the Azores.

Mesmerized by Toscanelli's suggestion, Columbus was also misled by several books that seemed to corroborate the old Florentine's notions. For example, a fifteenth-century Latin translation of an ancient tome by second-century-AD Greek geographer Ptolemy showed the world as only five-sevenths its actual size. The *Imago mundi*, a geography text written in about 1410 by the French churchman and cosmographer Pierre d'Ailly, featured an enormous Eurasia 225 degrees wide (whereas only about 150 degrees separate western Spain from eastern Japan across the Eurasian landmass) and a very narrow intervening Atlantic. The Latin translation of Marco Polo's description (c. 1300) of his sojourn in the fabled kingdoms and empires of the East—including the Cathay (China) of history and embellished legend—fired Columbus's imagination of realms of untold wealth and received his copious marginal comments.

Nonetheless, when he approached King John II of Portugal in 1484 with his idea for a sea voyage to the East by traveling west, he was turned down. This wasn't because people thought the world was flat and you could fall off the edges but because most learned men of the time suspected the earth was a lot bigger than Columbus dreamed. In fact, way back in the third century BC the Greek scientist Eratosthenes had calculated the earth's circumference at about twenty-four thousand miles—less than one thousand miles short of the true value. Though no one suspected the existence of the Americas between Europe and Asia, King John's advisers correctly warned him that Asia lay much farther away than the twenty-four hundred miles Columbus posited between the Canary Islands and Japan (Marco Polo's Chipangu). In fact, it was more than four times farther off.

After the death of his wife, a Portuguese noblewoman, in 1485, Columbus and his five-year-old son Diego moved to Spain, where he tried to interest Ferdinand and Isabella in his enterprise. Three years later, the Portuguese navigator Bartholomeu Dias rounded the southern tip of Africa, newly dubbed the Cape of Good Hope. Columbus, who had returned to Portugal to try again with King John II, was on the docks to greet Dias on the latter's return to Lisbon from his epochal voyage. That finished off the Portuguese king's interest in a westward journey to the Indies, since the eastward approach looked very promising indeed. Bartholomew Columbus then tried, without success, to interest Henry VII of England and Charles VIII of France in his brother's proposal while Christopher returned to Spain.

Columbus had little encouragement from Ferdinand and Isabella—and their expert advisers—for almost seven years. On receiving what seemed to be a definitive refusal, he was on his way to ship out to France and try his luck there again when Isabella's treasurer begged her to reconsider. The Spanish royals had completed their conquest of Granada, the last Muslim kingdom of Spain, and had ordered the expulsion of two hundred thousand Jews who refused to convert to Christianity, so they were in a mood to advance the cause of their religion in the wilds of Asia and perhaps beat Portugal to the wealth of the Indies. In April of 1492 they finally agreed to sponsor Columbus, made him "High Admiral of the Ocean Sea," and promised him the governorship of any new lands he might discover.

After setting out from Palos in southern Spain on the morning of August 3 with a crew of about ninety men, Columbus, sailing in the flat-bottomed cargo ship *Santa María* as his flagship and accompanied by the caravels *Niña* and *Pinta*, dropped down to the Canary Islands and topped off his provisions. On September 6, he set a course due west on latitude twenty-eight degrees north, where he knew the northeast trade winds would bear them along. Despite his practice of keeping two separate logbooks, falsifying one with smaller daily distances traversed so as not to frighten the men, his crews grew restive during the last part of a voyage that involved being out of sight of land for longer than just about any European sailors up to that time.

Slightly more than a month after the little fleet left the Canaries, a lookout on the *Pinta* spotted land at two a.m. of October 12. After daylight, Columbus and his two captains went ashore to claim the land for Spain, naming it San Salvador—"Holy Savior." This is thought to be Watling Island in the Bahamas, about four hundred miles southeast of Florida.

Since Columbus thought he had reached the Indies—the European name for South and Southeast Asia—he called the natives he found *Indians*, but they didn't seem to be the sophisticated people Marco Polo had described. Instead, most of the Arawaks Columbus encountered were stark naked and painted their faces or bodies. They made spears out of cane; spun cotton cloth for their nets, hammocks, and the briefs that only grown women wore; and fashioned huge dugout canoes. They thought the visitors were gods who had come down from the sky in their ships. They loved colored glass beads, hawk bells, pieces of scarlet cloth, and copper coins and would trade almost anything for them. Most distressing of all, the only gold they had was in the form of an occasional nose plug.

Although Columbus never tired of pointing out how handsome, gentle, kind, and affectionate the natives were—"no better people . . . in the world"—already, by October 14, he was writing in his logbook, "Should your Highnesses command it, all the inhabitants could be taken away to Castile or held as slaves on the island, for with fifty men we could subjugate them all and make them do whatever we wish." He appreciated the beauty of his surroundings—"the scent of flowers and trees" and "the singing of small birds is so sweet that no one could ever wish to leave this place"—but the leitmotif of his logbook entries is *oro*—"gold"—which he seeks frantically everywhere he goes.

On October 28, he reached Cuba, where his men saw people smoking massive cigars. Since Columbus's calculations told him he was in the southern Chinese province of Mangi, as described by Marco Polo, he sent his men looking for the Great Khan, unaware that the Mongol dynasty of China had fallen 124 years earlier (see Question 91). Instead, they found a village of about fifty thatched-roof wooden houses, where they were feted with sweet potatoes.

Still no caches of gold, fields of precious spices, or anything tangible to corroborate the vague assurances of captured natives that all the gold was just over the next horizon. The day of December 6 found Columbus in the western part of the large island he named Hispaniola (now Haiti and the Dominican Republic), though thinking it might be Japan. When the *Santa María* was wrecked on a reef on December 25, he saw it as a sign from God to plant a trading post, calling it "La Navidad" in honor of the holy day and leaving thirty-nine men there. A skirmish farther east on the island resulted in a native's being wounded by a sword-thrust in the buttocks and another by an arrow in the chest.

Only three months after arriving, Columbus decided it was time to go back. On January 16, 1493, he set out from eastern Hispaniola with his two remaining ships, soon climbing to thirty-five degrees north to use the westerly trades to waft him back to Spain. After surviving fierce winter storms and a brush with hostile Portuguese officials in the Azores, he was blown onto the coast of Portugal on March 4. He reached Palos, Spain, on March 14, and, in the following month, received a hero's welcome in Barcelona from Ferdinand and Isabella that was to be the high point of his career.

The letter he wrote on his return journey summarizing his voyage contained extravagant claims about the quantities of gold and spices he had observed, as well as promises to bring back as many slaves the next time as their Highnesses might require. He neglected to mention the various near mutinies, the loss of his flagship, and the insubordination of the captain of the *Pinta*, who at one point had sailed off on his own. Columbus had returned with a handful of bewildered natives, a few parrots, some plants he thought might be valuable, and not much gold. We now know that he hadn't even been the first European to venture to the New World, since the Vikings had repeatedly done so many centuries before (see Question 75), but, as historian Samuel Eliot Morison pointed out, "There is no reasonable doubt that Columbus made the *effective* discovery from which all American history stems."

Columbus made three more voyages across the Atlantic. On his second (1493–96), accompanied by twelve hundred to fifteen hundred men in seventeen ships, he discovered the Virgin Islands, Puerto Rico, and Jamaica, and learned that the colonists of La Navidad had all been slaughtered for making off with women and harassing the natives for gold. He established another colony seventy-five miles east of it and named it Isabela, which became the first permanent European settlement in the New World. He also encountered the cannibal Caribs, who raided the peaceful Arawaks, stealing their women and castrating their young men to fatten them up as food. In 1495, Columbus set up a forced labor system and required natives older than fourteen to pay a gold tribute to the king of Spain every three years. Those who refused to work were killed or shipped back to Spain as slaves.

On Columbus's third voyage (1498–1500), involving six ships and three hundred colonists, including thirty women, he discovered Trinidad and the Orinoco River, landing on August 5, 1498, on the Paria Peninsula in what is now Venezuela. His geographic speculations now became bizarre, including the notion that the earth must be pear-shaped or like a round ball on one part of which was "a prominence like a woman's nipple." He also thought he had found the site of the earthly paradise—the Garden of Eden—and that the mighty Orinoco might be one of the four biblical rivers described as flowing out from it. This voyage ended in personal tragedy for Columbus and his two brothers, sent back to Spain in shackles by the royal agent Francisco de Bobadilla for their excessive rigor in suppressing revolts by the natives and colonists in Hispaniola. Meanwhile, in 1497–99, Vasco da Gama had made the long sea voyage from Portugal to India and back by sailing east around Africa, and in 1500 Pedro Cabral claimed Brazil for Portugal.

After his rehabilitation, Columbus made a fourth journey (1502–4), departing from Seville with four caravels and sailing from the Canaries to Martinique in twenty-one days. He scoured the coasts of Honduras, Nicaragua, Costa Rica, and Panama, looking, obviously in vain, for the passage through which Marco Polo had sailed from China to the Indian Ocean.

The results of what is euphemistically referred to as "the Columbian Exchange" were many and varied. The introduction of European plants, animals, and diseases, especially smallpox, practically destroyed the native populations, not to mention the effects of enslavement and the quelling of rebellions. The natives of Hispaniola, for example, estimated as numbering about three hundred thousand in 1492, were extinct by 1550. After most of the natives died off, the Spanish, Portuguese, and, later, the English brought African slaves to work the sugarcane and cotton plantations and mine gold and silver. Europeans found maize, tomatoes, potatoes, sweet potatoes, squash, peppers, chocolate, vanilla, and many other foods in the New World, as well as the bane of syphilis.

Between 1509 and 1511, the Spanish conquered Puerto Rico, Jamaica, and Cuba, and Juan Ponce de León discovered Florida in 1513. In 1519–22, the tiny remnant of Ferdinand Magellan's circumnavigating fleet returned to Spain, finally settling the question of just how far the Indies were from Europe and where Columbus's discoveries stood in relation to them. Hernán Cortés conquered the Aztec Empire of Mexico in 1519–21, and Francisco Pizarro initiated the conquest of the Inca Empire of Peru in 1531. The English and French staked their various and often conflicting claims in North America.

As for Columbus, he died in Valladolid, Spain, on May 20, 1506, far less wealthy and esteemed than he would have liked, feeling he had been cheated by King Ferdinand, and no wiser as to the true whereabouts of his epic meanderings. Luckily, he never lived to see the maps with *America* emblazoned on them, from the Latin name of the Florentine explorer Amerigo Vespucci, who may have been the first of his contemporaries to realize that a "new world"—at least from the perspective of Europeans—had indeed been stumbled on, rather than some outpost of the Orient. The irony of Columbus's dogged insistence that he had found a westward route to Asia was not lost on nineteenth-century Italian scholar Niccolò Tommaseo, who wrote that "the poor Genoese navigator . . . as a reward for his indomitable patience and sublime humiliations, finds more than what he was looking for and thus, by mistake, gives a new world to civilization."

SIXTEENTH CENTURY

112 ∽ Who was the first modern political scientist?

Niccolò Machiavelli, whose treatise The Prince *was written in 1513*

LORENZO DE' MEDICI ("THE MAGNIFICENT"), de facto ruler of the Florentine republic, died in the epochal year of 1492, which the Florentine statesman and author Niccolò Machiavelli (1469–1527) saw as the beginning of the end of Italian freedom from foreign aggression. Two years later, the French under Charles VIII invaded Italy, and Florence rebelled against Lorenzo's inept successor, his son Piero the Fatuous, restoring self-rule after two generations of Medici domination (see Question 106).

At first, the fanatically anti-Medici Dominican preacher Girolamo Savonarola managed to establish a kind of theocracy in which Christ was declared the city's king. But in 1498, the pleasure-loving Florentines tortured, hanged, and burned the friar at the stake in the city's main square. As Machiavelli later observed, "All armed prophets have conquered; the unarmed ones have come to grief."

Rid of Savonarola, the Florentine republic appointed young Machiavelli secretary of the council in charge of war and foreign relations. His work brought him firsthand acquaintance with Europe's crafty potentates, such as Louis XII of France, Holy Roman Emperor Maximilian I, Ferdinand II of Aragon, and Pope Julius II, and required him to send back numerous dispatches from his thirty-odd diplomatic missions over the next fourteen years.

The leader who impressed him most was the young Cesare Borgia, the brutally ruthless warlord and son of Pope Alexander VI. With his father's support, Borgia was carving out a state for himself in the Marches and Romagna in central Italy, which had long languished in the hands of inept princelings and murderous bandits. After his father's death in 1503, however, Borgia lost his pillar of strength and died four years afterward.

In September 1512, Giuliano de' Medici, Lorenzo the Magnificent's youngest son, was placed in charge of Florence by Spanish military muscle. The city lost its liberty, and Machiavelli his job. In February of the following year, falsely accused of joining a conspiracy against the restored Medici rulers, Machiavelli was imprisoned and tortured with six "drops" of the strappado, which involved lifting the prisoner by a rope attached to his wrists, which had been tied behind his back, and dropping him abruptly partway to the ground.

When Giuliano's older brother Giovanni de' Medici became pope as Leo X in March 1513, the new pontiff declared a general amnesty for the prisoners held in Florence's jail. Machiavelli and his wife and children retreated to the modest family farm near San Casciano, about ten miles southwest of Florence. As a respite from arguing over pennies while playing cards with the locals, Machiavelli would change into his court clothes in the evening to spend several hours poring over the books of the ancient historians.

Among the fruits of his studies in his enforced idleness was *The Prince*, begun in July and finished by December, a slender volume that he hoped would restore him to favor and active political life. He designed it as a practical handbook for an aspiring prince, based on his study of ancient history and wide diplomatic experience. Now that the Medici family had regained Florence and achieved the papacy, Machiavelli thought his book would inspire Giuliano or some other young Medici prince to step into Borgia's shoes, create a strong state in central Italy, and put an end to Italy's humiliation.

The book thus reflects the chaotic Italy of Machiavelli's time, in which the French had deposed the duke of Milan, taken the kingdom of Naples, and then lost it to the Spanish. In addition, Venice's mainland possessions, Genoa, and other northern Italian cities had either been pillaged or conquered. German and Swiss mercenaries were streaming into the peninsula in an onslaught against which the small, fractious Italian states were helpless.

Desperate times called for desperate solutions, and Machiavelli never had truck with half measures. Rejecting medieval unitary traditions of political subordination to either the pope or the Holy Roman Emperor, he broke with writers like Thomas Aquinas, Dante, and the authors of books known as "mirrors of princes," who based their arguments on Scripture and natural law. Machiavelli relied only on what had been proven to work, and the musty traditions of rule by an entrenched aristocracy or the church had failed Italy miserably. The need was for a strong secular leader, not necessarily of noble blood, who could seize and hold on to power, inspire confidence, and defend his state against the military might and machinations of the emerging nation-states of Europe.

Because Machiavelli believed that people and their political problems are always essentially the same, he looked to history to instruct the present and help shape the future. He resolved to set forth the "laws" that govern how states are won, maintained, and lost, discovering that these laws have little to do with morality, "right," or religion:

> I've thought it better to set forth the truth of things rather than
> what they're imagined to be. Many have imagined republics
> and principalities that have never been known to actually exist;
> and since the way life is lived is so far removed from how it
> should be lived, he who sets aside what is done for what
> should be done learns how to ruin himself rather than how to
> survive. The fact is, the man who wants to be good all the time
> is ruined among so many who are not good. From this it fol-
> lows that a prince who wants to stay in power has to learn how
> not to be good, and to use this skill, or not, as necessity may
> require.

Machiavelli's cynical view of human nature—men are generally "ungrateful, vacillating, deceitful, cowardly, and greedy"—leads him to deduce that people will do the right thing only if compelled to do so. Thus, if the prince has to choose between being loved or feared, he should choose the latter, because love is fickle, whereas fear is not.

For princes, the end may well justify the means, or, as Machiavelli phrases it in his other political masterpiece, *The Discourses*, "When an action is reprehensible, the result may excuse it, and, when the result is good, always excuses it." Even popes, like Alexander VI and Julius II, were past masters of deceit. Although might may not actually make right, men are dazzled by success, no matter how achieved. It's thus more important for a prince to *appear* to be merciful, loyal, humane, sincere, and religious than to have those qualities in actuality if they frustrate his legitimate ends. Besides the qualities of a man, he also needs those of both the lion and the fox, since a lion can't defend himself against traps, and a fox has no defense against wolves.

While Machiavelli's most famous statements are the very essence of realpolitik, they also reveal his penchant for exaggerating for dramatic effect: "Men must either be coddled or crushed, since they can avenge themselves for petty injuries, but they can't for fatal ones. Any injury should be the kind from which the possibility of revenge is not to be feared." To maintain power in a state with a former hereditary monarch, all the new prince has to do is avoid changing the laws and taxes—and "extinguish the line of the former prince."

Yet *The Prince* was no apologia for tyrants, who, Machiavelli wrote in *The Discourses*, bring on themselves "infamy, scorn, abhorrence, danger, and disquiet." Instead, the prince must reward the good deeds of his subjects, encourage trade and agriculture, and refrain from depriving men of their property and molesting their women, which earn only hatred. He must surround himself with competent advisers and shun flatterers. To defend the state from aggression, the prince must be a capable warrior who understands that citizen militias, rather than mercenary troops, are the sinews of a nation. The overarching goal is to provide the political liberty and stability that make possible a civilized life for all.

The book ends with an emotional appeal to the Medici to liberate the peninsula from the foreign "barbarians"—meaning the French, Spanish, Germans, and Swiss. Italy, "leaderless, lawless, beaten down, despoiled, torn apart, overrun, and subjected to every manner of desolation," needed nothing less than a secular savior, since "this barbarous tyranny stinks in everyone's nostrils."

The shock value of *The Prince*, still strong, derives from its bald statement of unsavory political realities—as deduced from the actual behavior of rulers—in terms of norms that can lead to success. Henceforth, at least in Machiavelli's view, politics was to be equated with expediency. Though published only posthumously in 1532, *The Prince* circulated widely in manuscript.

The book that heralded the arrival of the modern secular state got Machiavelli nowhere with Giuliano de' Medici, who died in 1516. The author then dedicated it to Giuliano's young nephew Lorenzo, whom Pope Leo had just made duke of Urbino, but Lorenzo was more interested in someone else's gift of a pair of greyhounds than in the small volume being presented to him. There was to be no job for Machiavelli from Lorenzo either, who died in 1519 at age twenty-seven.

Machiavelli's *Discourses on the First Ten Books of Livy* (1513–21), another product of his chronic unemployment, deals with republics and the laws by which they are governed. His preface announces that, like a Columbus, he will try to "discover new ways and methods," that is, deduce practical lessons of political behavior from his study of Livy's *History of Rome*. As medieval authors on politics had used Scripture to prove their points about authority, the responsibilities of the ruler, and those of subjects, Machiavelli would use Roman history to reveal the eternal wellsprings of successful republican states.

In this book, we are made to marvel at the heights of greatness achieved by the ancient Roman republic as long as its citizens maintained their virtue (Latin *virtus*, Italian *virtù*—"manliness" with connotations of self-assertion, willpower, audacity, and a thirst for glory). While Christian virtue often produced men who were passive and contemplative, ancient Roman virtue created a nation of warlike men of action who built a stupendous empire.

Republics are the best form of government for societies that are not hopelessly corrupt—a test that many states in his own day, like Milan and Naples, failed. (For these, strong princes are necessary to discipline and marshal their unruly and indolent subjects.) As in *The Prince*, ideal political action stems not from moral principles but from what is known to work best. Since the preservation of the life and liberty of one's country is the highest good, all other considerations must give way when republics are threatened by external or internal foes. Whether writing about principalities or republics, Machiavelli always assumed that the survival of the free state was the prime directive of government.

The Art of War, published in 1521, was Machiavelli's third major book on political life, but he is also famed in Italian literature as the author of *La Mandragola (The Mandrake)*, a bawdy comedy of seduction that's still a favorite with theater fans. Pope Leo X so enjoyed the command performance of the play at the papal court in 1520 that Machiavelli was received back into Medici favor and commissioned to compose his distinguished *History of Florence*. By a new Medici pope, Clement VII (1523–34), he was given the important job of fortifying Florence's walls.

In May 1527, however, after the starving and unpaid troops of Emperor Charles V viciously sacked Rome, a republic was reestablished in Florence, and Machiavelli found himself out of a job again—this time for having worked for the Medici. But he was soon finished with Florence, its republic, and the world, dying in the following month at age fifty-eight after a brief stomach ailment, leaving his family in poverty. Italy had lost "a potent genius," according to Renaissance scholar Federico Chabod, "peerless in the realm of political thought." The legend of diabolical Machiavellianism that arose after his death, especially in France and Elizabethan England, is a story unto itself.

The Florentine republic perished a mere three years after Machiavelli at the hands of Charles V, who handed the city back to the Medici for another two centuries of rule. During the sixteenth century, the strong centralized governments envisioned by Machiavelli emerged in France, Spain, and England, but Italy, hopelessly fragmented, remained the chief battlefield of European power politics until a Spanish and ecclesiastical torpor descended like a miasma over much of the peninsula.

Italian unity was fully achieved only in 1870, after the Papal States and the city of Rome itself had been wrenched from the rule of the pope. A half century later, Italian philosopher Benedetto Croce pointed out that Machiavelli's foundation of modern political science was due to his discovery of "the necessity and autonomy of politics . . . which cannot be exorcised and driven from this world with holy water."

113 ∾ Who was the first successful Protestant reformer?

German theologian Martin Luther, who circulated his
Ninety-five Theses *in 1517*

WITH ITS GOTHIC CATHEDRALS, summae of theology, and emerging universities, the thirteenth century presents an image of Christendom in its wholeness and unity that may have enjoyed a brief reality but was in serious disrepair two centuries later. By the beginning of the sixteenth century, calls for reform and spiritual renewal of the Christian church were sounding from a variety of sources and with a variety of agendas. In most cases, Rome's central hierarchy remained unresponsive or effectively suppressed the complaints.

The efforts of John Wycliffe and Jan Hus, the conciliar movement, the Christian humanism of Desiderius Erasmus, and other initiatives addressed a pervasive discontent (see Question 102). The goals were to remedy clerical abuses, promote attention to Scripture, balance the power of the pope with that of church councils, and infuse what seemed an increasingly worldly, external, and mechanical institution with a renewed spirit of Christian devotion.

None of these earlier efforts had a lasting effect on the church at large. When reformation finally came, it dramatically shattered whatever unity remained, bringing an unprecedented reexamination of Christianity's central message and ultimately a thorough reorganization of Western society along new religious and political lines. To a remarkable extent, that cataclysmic transformation grew from the activity of one individual, a professor of theology at an obscure university who set out with no specific intentions of reform. His agenda, rather, was the defense of specific religious truths he had discovered as his own deliverance from spiritual devastation.

Martin Luther (1483–1546) was born in Eisleben, Saxony, where his father, originally a copper miner, had prospered modestly in the mining industry. He was educated in Mansfeld, Magdeburg, and Eisenach, entering the University of Erfurt in 1501, where he earned both a bachelor's and a master's degree by 1505. In accordance with his father's wishes, he began law studies in May of that year, but within months he abruptly changed course and entered the monastery of the strict Augustinian Order of Hermits. According to legend, the step was precipitated by a vow he made during a terrifying thunderstorm: "Help me, St. Anne! I will become a monk." He took his monastic vows in 1506 and was ordained a priest in the following year.

By all accounts, Luther was an exemplary monk who observed the rigorous routine with great precision. His early monastic career was marked by a chronic spiritual unrest, however—to a degree unusual even in that "age of anxiety" in which thoughts of guilt, death, and judgment were widespread themes in popular consciousness. He was continually preoccupied with questions of God's judgment and his own sinfulness. Neither extreme ascetic deprivations nor compulsive use of the confessional nor the pastoral commonplaces of the prevailing theology ("Do what is in you and God will not fail to give you grace to do more") brought him the assurance of God's favor he had sought in monastic life. An initial breakthrough occurred under the teaching of his superior, Johann von Staupitz, who counseled Luther to withdraw attention from his own performance and the paradoxes of predestination and instead "look to the wounds of Christ" as having been suffered for his benefit.

Recognizing his intellectual promise, Staupitz directed an unwilling Luther to undertake an academic program in biblical studies, which was completed with a doctorate in 1512. Subsequently, Luther assumed the professorship of biblical theology at the newly created University of Wittenberg, a position he was to hold for the rest of his life. Between 1513 and 1521, he lectured on the biblical books of Psalms, Romans, Galatians, and Hebrews, and in 1514 he also assumed pastoral duties for the church in Wittenberg.

Considerable debate exists as to when Luther experienced his breakthrough to an "evangelical" theology focused on a new understanding of the Gospel—the evangel, or "good news." But even in his early lectures it is clear that the sustained encounter with Scripture had resolved much of Luther's spiritual torment and introduced him to a new source of clarity and assurance. This new theology centered on the doctrine of justification by faith alone, which burst on Luther's consciousness as a new discovery, having lain hidden in the pages of Romans and Galatians all the years that "the Bible had been shoved under the bench."

In an autobiographical fragment from 1545, Luther speaks of wrestling with the phrase "the righteousness of God" in Romans 1:17—a struggle resolved in his so-called Tower Experience. How could the righteousness of God be "revealed in the Gospel," as St. Paul says—that is, be part of the "good news"—when it is the very means by which God judges and punishes sinners such as Luther himself? Eventually he came to see this righteousness as a gift: the righteousness of Christ that is credited to the account of the destitute sinner upon believing.

> At last, by the mercy of God . . . I began to understand that the righteousness of God is . . . the passive righteousness with which merciful God justifies us by faith, as it is written "He who through faith is righteous shall live." Here I felt that I was altogether born again and had entered paradise itself through open gates. There a totally other face of the entire Scripture showed itself to me.

Themes of Luther's emerging theology include the inability of fallen man to satisfy God's law, free justification by grace on account of the merits of Christ, and the reception of that benefit solely by faith (that is, trust in Christ). Intrinsic to Luther's stance is an increasing reliance on Scripture as the sole arbiter of Christian life and doctrine—a principle for which he found precedent in St. Augustine (see Question 31), but which also reflected the contemporary humanist impulse behind the slogan *ad fontes* ("back to the sources"). Through a strong emphasis on St. Paul's epistles to the Romans and Galatians, Scripture is understood in a novel way as presenting opposing voices of Law (what God demands) and Gospel (what God has mercifully done for those who cannot meet his demands). "The Law says 'do this,' and it is never done. Grace says, 'believe in this,' and everything is already done."

Luther had no sense of his teachings as clearly dissident and no overarching plan for reform when the indulgence controversy launched his career as a public figure. At issue was a plenary indulgence promulgated by Pope Leo X to help pay for the renovation of St. Peter's Basilica in Rome. Archbishop Albrecht of Mainz had an arrangement with Leo whereby preaching of the indulgence was allowed in his territories in return for a percentage of the proceeds—funds that Albrecht needed to pay the massive debt incurred in purchasing his second bishopric. Marketing was entrusted to a Dominican friar, Johann Tetzel, an experienced preacher of indulgences whose particularly crass approach was scandalous to some purists but undeniably effective. A favorite (and theologically suspect) theme was the opportunity to release one's suffering parents from purgatory for the price of a few guldens. Luther's theses 27 and 28 mention Tetzel's slogan: "When the coin in the coffer rings, the soul from purgatory springs." Very likely Luther's intervention was motivated by pastoral concern for penitents under his care, who had strayed into Albrecht's territory and were being misled by Tetzel's spiritual malpractice.

According to legend, Luther posted the *Ninety-five Theses* (formally, the *Disputation on the Power and Efficacy of Indulgences*) on the door of the Wittenberg Castle church on October 31, 1517—the customary method of proposing a subject for academic debate. The date is celebrated in Protestant churches as Reformation Day, the beginning of the Protestant Reformation. Whether or not the posting ever took place, Luther sent his sharply worded talking points, which were written in Latin, to his own bishop, to Albrecht, and to other interested parties.

The proposed debate never happened, but the *Theses* were quickly translated into German, printed, and disseminated throughout the Holy Roman Empire and elsewhere in Europe. Although they hardly address core Reformation doctrines, Luther's *Theses* soon tapped into a popular current of reformist sentiment, which had both religious and nationalist components. Rome reacted harshly, prompted partly by Albrecht's financial concerns and the machinations of Tetzel's fellow Dominicans. Public interest was intensified by the ensuing drama, as Rome attempted to stifle the insubordinate *fraterculus* ("insignificant little friar").

The next three years saw a series of escalating confrontations between Luther and the Roman hierarchy. Luther's opponents quickly shifted the ground of debate to the issue of papal authority. The pope had authorized the indulgence; that should be a sufficient answer to all of Luther's criticisms. Luther, in contrast, expounded the theological and scriptural issues in tracts, pamphlets, and formal disputations, widening the scope of the disagreements at each new step. He also registered a formal appeal for a general council to decide the case. Rome's representatives simply demanded recantation. Luther expressed astonishment at his opponents' reluctance to engage with him on the basis of Scripture. When they did so, they handled the matter "about as well as an ass knows how to play the lyre."

Rome's opposition stimulated a remarkable phase of productivity in Luther. In time he began to see an irreconcilable division between the teachings of the hierarchy and St. Paul's message of justification. Through the "new media" possibilities of the printing press—which functioned as a sixteenth-century equivalent of the Internet—he shared his rapidly developing thought with a wide audience across Europe (see Question 108). Luther was becoming a theological folk hero; a later woodcut was to depict him as "the Hercules of Germany."

In 1520, he published three pivotal Reformational treatises. The *Address to the Christian Nobility* identified the papacy as "a false, lying specter" and called on German territorial princes to take responsibility for reform in German lands. Luther justified this appeal on the basis of "the priesthood of all believers" (1 Peter 2:9) and outlined twenty-seven specific proposals for reform. *The Babylonian Captivity of the Church* deconstructed the existing Catholic sacramental system, reducing the number of authentic sacraments to two—baptism and the Lord's Supper (with an intermediate status for penance). Luther connected the reception of sacramental benefits with faith, rather than with the mere performance of the sacramental act.

The Freedom of a Christian represents Luther's first comprehensive presentation of the evangelical view of salvation and the Christian life. It contains a lyrical evocation of justification as a "blessed exchange" effected by the marriage of Christ and the believing soul "through the wedding ring of faith." In this marriage, Luther argues, everything is held in common. Thus, "Christ is full of grace, life, and salvation. The soul is full of sins, death, and damnation. Now let faith come between them and sins, death, and damnation will be Christ's, while grace, life, and salvation will be the soul's."

Luther further describes how a theology of grace, in turn, gives rise to an ethics of freedom and gratitude: "Just as our neighbor is in need and lacks that in which we abound, so we were in need before God and lacked his mercy. Hence, as our heavenly Father has in Christ freely come to our aid, we also ought freely to help our neighbor through our body and its works, and each one should become as it were a Christ to the other." In this way, the Gospel brings into being the paradox that opens the book: "A Christian is a perfectly free lord of all, subject to none" and "A Christian is a perfectly dutiful servant of all, subject to all." This service was to be carried out in the ordinary "vocations" of daily life: work, family, friendship, membership in community.

Unimpressed by such passages, Pope Leo issued the papal bull *Exsurge Domine* in June 1520: "Arise, O Lord . . . the wild boar from the forest is attempting to destroy thy vineyard . . . Arise, O Peter! . . . Arise, O Paul! . . . Arise, all saints!" The bull cited forty-one propositions attributed to Luther as heretical and demanded his recantation on pain of excommunication. On December 10, Luther publicly burned the papal document along with some volumes of the canon law, decisively signaling his break with Rome. His excommunication followed in the papal document *Decet Romanum Pontificem*.

The next step was to have been Luther's apprehension and punishment by the civil authorities. Through the intervention of his territorial ruler, the elector Frederick, Luther was granted safe conduct to appear before Emperor Charles V and the imperial Diet of Worms in April of 1521. Pressed for a recantation of his books by the assembled powers of church and state, Luther offered his iconic reply: "Unless I am convicted by Scripture and plain reason (I do not accept the popes and councils, for they have contradicted themselves), I am bound by the Scriptures I have quoted and my conscience is captive to the Word of God. I cannot and I will not recant anything, for to go against conscience is neither right nor safe. God help me. Amen." To nineteenth-century British historian and essayist Thomas Carlyle, this event was "the greatest scene in modern European history; the point, indeed, from which the whole subsequent history of civilization takes its rise."

Charles V honored the safe conduct, and Luther was allowed to set out for home. Shortly afterward, the Diet issued the Edict of Worms, which branded Luther a civil outlaw. On the way to Wittenberg, he was "kidnapped" by retainers of the elector and hidden for his own safety in Wartburg Castle, where he remained for ten months. While there, he completed his translation of the New Testament into German. His translation of the entire Bible, completed in 1534 (and revised several times afterward), had a seminal impact on German language and literature. His translations were made from the original languages, with the assistance of experts in Greek and Hebrew who met with him regularly in committee.

Meanwhile a wave of evangelical reform was taking place in Wittenberg and breaking out in other parts of Europe. Alarmed at the disorder precipitated by his more zealous reforming colleagues, Luther returned to Wittenberg in 1522 to resume direction of the emerging church and act as coordinator of the Lutheran cause in Germany. The Edict of Worms remained in effect throughout Luther's life but could never be enforced for political reasons. These included the emperor's dependence on support from the German princes in his conflicts with the Ottoman Turks, who besieged Vienna in 1529. From 1522 onward, Luther assumed a background role in the emerging Reformation but remained a principal guiding spirit of the revival his work had set in motion. He continued to produce the sermons, treatises, biblical commentaries, catechetical materials, hymns, and other writings that fill more than one hundred volumes in the Weimar edition of his works.

Luther had long attacked Rome's requirement of clerical celibacy as directly contrary to Scripture (1 Timothy 4:1–3). Along with work, marriage and family are central to the affirmation of ordinary life that follows from Luther's doctrine of justification—an affirmation that remains one of the strongest legacies of the Reformation. In 1525, Luther married Katherine von Bora (Katy), one of a group of nuns who had left the convent and taken refuge in Wittenberg. The Luthers had six children, four of whom survived. Their extended family, with whom they occupied the former Augustinian monastery, included the orphaned children of a deceased sister, assorted live-in relatives, student boarders, and the occasional refugee or indigent pastor. Accounts of the Luther household provide an image of pious, affectionate, and hospitable domesticity that became a model of evangelical family life in the Protestant tradition for generations.

When Luther died in 1546, the religious landscape of Europe was vastly different than in the year of his birth, largely as a result of his own influence. Although he was conscious of a prophetic role in rediscovering and proclaiming the Gospel, Luther never attributed his effectiveness to special personal revelation or illumination. Instead, he connected it with simple fulfillment of his assigned vocation as teacher of God's Word to the church. A sermon preached in 1522 offered Luther's own explanation of the power at work in the change:

> I simply taught, preached, and wrote God's Word; otherwise I
> did nothing. And then, while I slept, or drank Wittenberg beer

with my friends Philip [Melanchthon] and [Nicholas von] Amsdorf, the Word so greatly weakened the papacy that no prince or emperor ever inflicted such losses upon it. I did nothing. The Word did it all.

—*Eric Lenk*

114 ❧ Who made the first coherent statement of the heliocentric theory?

Polish astronomer Nicolaus Copernicus in 1543

NICOLAUS COPERNICUS'S MOMENTOUS CONVICTION that the earth moved around the sun wasn't original. He neither provided observational proof of his idea, nor did he discover any general laws of force or motion. Rather, he confined himself to modifying an archaic model of the universe without challenging or correcting some of its large-scale errors, such as the belief that planets moved in perfect circles at constant speeds.

Nonetheless, his book *De revolutionibus orbium coelestium* (*On the Revolutions of the Heavenly Orbs*) exerted a certain pressure on the prevailing model of the heavens. Although his thesis was virtually ignored when it appeared, it eventually revolutionized our understanding of the cosmos, thanks to cascading breakthroughs by Tycho Brahe, Johannes Kepler, Galileo, and Isaac Newton. Along the way, our physical and metaphysical awareness of the universe underwent a radical transformation.

Since antiquity, astronomers had constructed geometrical models to imitate apparent celestial motions. In his *Almagest*, Claudius Ptolemy (AD 83–169), a Greek mathematician, astronomer, and geographer who worked in Alexandria, rigorously distilled the work of previous Greek thinkers—in particular the highly sophisticated observations of Hipparchus (190–120 BC)—into the model that dominated Western astronomy for the next thirteen hundred years. The Ptolemaic system put a stationary earth at the center of the cosmos, circled by the sun, the moon, the five known planets, and the stars.

Later philosophers integrated Ptolemy's model with Aristotle's conception of the universe as a system of intelligent concentric spheres impelled by a prime mover. This elaborate dance of crystalline spheres turning around a single center in which humankind stood at the apex of earthly life remained in full force in Copernicus's time. Such a world-view held potent metaphysical implications. In 1541, two years before *De revolutionibus* was published, the alchemist Paracelsus merely expressed the learned consensus when he wrote, "God did not create the planets and stars with the intention that they should dominate man, but that they, like other creatures, should obey and serve him."

That's not to say the geocentric scheme had never been challenged. Almost six hundred years before Ptolemy, Philolaus, a contemporary of Socrates and follower of Pythagoras, had asked whether "the central fire" was not in fact the intelligent source of light and life around which every other orb revolved. A partial list of those who entertained thoughts of a heliocentric system includes Aristarchus of Samos, Seleucus of Seleucia, Aryabhata of India, al-Sijzi and Qutb al-Din of Persia, the Afghan astronomer Albumasar, and many other Muslim astronomers who professed dissatisfaction with the complexities and imperfections of the geocentric model.

"Ptolemy assumed an arrangement that cannot exist," wrote Alhazen in Cairo in about AD 1000. To match the actual observed movements of the heavenly bodies, Ptolemaic astronomers resorted to small adjustments to orbital positions called equants and deferents. Over time, as more accurate observations were made, the model was overrun by a gaggle of these little compromises. Surely, thought Alhazen—and Copernicus five hundred years after him—a competent Creator would not need such a motley assortment of tweaks to produce the glories we behold.

But how to prove it? In Copernicus's day, the scientific standards of evidence and experiment that command our faith were still in the future. Much of what passed for science was arrived at via mathematics and reasoned argument rather than empirical observation. Copernicus was an amateur who belonged to no learned societies. Obsessed by his idea, he knew it was fodder for scorn or worse: Anyone can see that the earth doesn't move, while the sun, moon, and other celestial bodies do.

So he took his time. As early as 1515, he had sketched out his heliocentric theory in the *Commentariolus*, a manuscript of only a few pages that he circulated to a small circle of friends. When in 1543 *De revolutionibus* finally presented its counterintuitive claim, Copernicus was on his deathbed. His work was the result of decades of rigorous labor that took into account more than a thousand years of astronomical observations. A typical English edition of the tome runs to 330 folio pages, one hundred pages of tables, and over twenty thousand tabulated numbers. Even so, it proved nothing, but merely sought to persuade a reasonable reader that one inference from the available data appears more likely than another, no matter how unlikely it might at first seem.

Copernicus was, first and foremost, a Renaissance humanist. Born in Poland in 1473, he belonged to a Catholic family wealthy enough to send him to school in Cracow and then Italy, where he received a top-notch education at the universities of Bologna and Padua. His formal degrees were in medicine (providing ample practice in empirical observation through dissection) and law (shaping his skill in cogent argumentation). But he absorbed much more: classical literature, mathematics, and astronomy.

At Bologna in 1497 he made his first astronomical observation—a lunar occultation of Aldebaran later recorded in *De revolutionibus*—under the tutelage of Domenico Maria Novara da Ferrara. Novara's thinking was molded by his teacher Regiomontanus, who highlighted weaknesses of Ptolemy's *Almagest* after helping translate it for Cardinal Bessarion (see Question 101). Regiomontanus, in turn, had studied with Georg von Peuerbach ("the father of mathematical astronomy in the West") and with Nicholas of Cusa, a philosopher and mystic who had argued that the earth was not the center of the universe but a star like other stars.

Even as he turned the old system on its head, Copernicus was still working within the Ptolemaic model and its philosophical underpinnings. Here, for example, is his resonant declaration of heliocentrism in *De revolutionibus*:

At rest, however, in the middle of everything is the sun. For
in this most beautiful temple, who would place this lamp in
another or better position than that from which it can light up
the whole thing at the same time? For the sun is not inappro-
priately called by some people the lantern of the universe,
its mind by others, and its ruler by still others. [Hermes] the
Thrice Greatest labels it a visible god, and Sophocles' Electra,
the all-seeing. Thus indeed, as though seated on a royal throne,

the sun governs the family of planets revolving around it.
Moreover, the earth is not deprived of the moon's
attendance. . . . Meanwhile the earth has intercourse
with the sun, and is impregnated for its yearly parturition.

Copernicus the humanist is making a bold scientific claim with a Shakespearean richness of metaphor. Where we moderns expect to be told of a hot mass exerting force on cooler masses, he unveils a mythic realm of animate, intentional, interactive beings that nevertheless obey Ptolemy's model. His goal is not to undo the model but to say that a stronger case could be made for it if the positions of the sun and the earth were reversed. Much of the support for his theory consists of mathematical arguments showing that the heliocentric view is more elegant. In fact, because he insists on perfectly circular orbits, his proposed system agrees with observations less well than Ptolemy's.

Certain facets of Copernicus's argument proved compelling. In Ptolemy's system, for example, the planets were said to achieve their major orbits around the earth by means of smaller, advancing circular movements (epicycles) that necessarily also involved "backward" motions, because that's what they appeared to be doing. Copernicus's system offered a simpler view. Here's theoretical physicist Stephen Hawking's explanation:

As Earth speeds around the Sun in its faster orbit, it periodically overtakes the outer planets. Like a slower runner in an
outside lane at a track meet, the more distant planet appears
to move backward relative to the background scenery.

With the sun at the center, the order of the planets fell into place, and the apparent positions and movements of celestial bodies could more cogently be seen to be complicated by the actual motions of the earth. Despite these luminous clues, the heliocentric thesis of *De revolutionibus* was neither accepted nor decried on publication—except by Martin Luther, who said, "This fool wants to reverse the entire science of astronomy." Instead, it was largely ignored and appeared on no university syllabus other than Salamanca's for a century. Much like today's geeks, professional astronomers of the time cared mainly about practical applications.

The fact that tables derived from *De revolutionibus* allowed for more accurate calendars and predictions of celestial events showed practicing astronomers that Copernicus knew something about astronomy. But it was simply too obvious—even for the young Galileo—that the earth stood still and the heavens moved—until about 1600. Then, in quick succession, three first-caliber scientists made discoveries that, taken together, completed the overthrow of Ptolemy's universe, turning Copernicus's "revolution" into the new common sense (see Question 121).

—Tom Matrullo

115 ∿ Who was the first ruler crowned as czar of Russia?

Ivan IV the Terrible, who claimed the title in 1547

AFTER THE FALL OF THE GREEK ORTHODOX BYZANTINE EMPIRE and Constantinople to the Muslims, Moscow became, in the eyes of the Russian Orthodox Church, "the third Rome" (see Question 109). In 1472, the year of his marriage to the niece of the last Byzantine emperor, the grand prince of Moscow, Ivan III the Great (r. 1462–1505), assumed the title of "Sovereign of all the Russias" and adopted the two-headed eagle of Constantinople as the national emblem. In 1480, when he ceased paying the annual tribute to the Mongols of the Golden Horde (see Question 91), Ivan started calling himself *tsar*. This Russian word (usually written *czar* in English), like the German *kaiser*, derives from *caesar*. It generically meant *emperor*, and indeed Ivan III had almost tripled the area of the principality centered in Moscow over which he ruled until it comprised much of the western part of modern-day European Russia.

Ivan III's grandson, Ivan IV, whose reign extended from age three in 1533 to his death in 1584, was dubbed *Grozny*, usually translated as "the Terrible" but meaning something more like "Awesome" or "Formidable." After his mother's sudden death, probably by poison, in 1538, Ivan experienced neglect and sometimes starvation, while the hereditary aristocrats known as boyars killed one another and bled the country as rival factions fought for control of the state and the young prince. His childhood and teen pastimes were those of a young savage: torturing birds, flinging cats and dogs off the Kremlin walls, and riding

through the streets with gangs of drunken louts, terrorizing his unfortunate subjects.

At age thirteen, Ivan ordered the arrest of the leader of a boyar faction and had him thrown to a pack of starved hunting hounds to indicate
he was ready to govern on his own. On January 16, 1547, sixteen-year-
old Ivan IV became the first grand prince of Moscow to be formally
crowned "czar of all Russia." After ordering a bevy of young virgins
sent to him from all over his realm, he chose from them Anastasia
Romanovna as his bride, whom he later fondly recalled as "my young
heifer."

In 1550, the young czar had the law code revised, and these early
years of his reign also saw him summoning an assembly, establishing a
standing army, strengthening the position of the Russian Orthodox
Church, and introducing other administrative reforms. Trade relations
were established between Russia and English merchants who ventured
to the White Sea port of Archangel, and Ivan also imported European
technical experts.

His childhood hatred of the boyars induced the czar to found his
power on Cossack horsemen, fierce peasants who had established semi-
independent republics in southern Russian borderlands and who were
inured to war by fighting Muslims and Muscovites alike and raiding
caravans. In 1552, Ivan led an army of 150,000 that overthrew the Muslim Tatar khanate of Kazan, which had repeatedly devastated northeast
Russia, and he ordered most of its people massacred. To celebrate his
conquest Ivan built the splendidly onion-domed and spectacularly colorful Cathedral of St. Basil in Red Square across from the Kremlin.
Ivan annexed the khanate of Astrakhan in 1556, gateway to the Caspian
trade route. Both Kazan and Astrakhan were strategic acquisitions for
Russian control of the Volga and the first non-Slavic accretions of the
expanding Russian Empire.

Ivan sent armies west, too, to carve a path to the Baltic through
what are now Latvia and Estonia as part of a strategy to bolster Russian
trade by gaining access to European goods that could be transported to
the Caspian Sea via the Volga. He experienced numerous setbacks and
only transient gains in this so-called Livonian War, which dragged on
for a quarter of a century and plunged Russia into severe economic
distress.

Then, in 1564, Ivan's top general and close friend, Prince Andrey
Kurbsky, deserted to the enemy Lithuanians, claiming the czar was

planning to murder him. In December, Ivan left Moscow for his nearby summer home, announcing he had abdicated because he was surrounded by hostile boyars and churchmen. He came back by thunderous popular demand a few months later, however, with the stipulation that he would now proceed to rule pretty much as he pleased. This involved an elaborate plan to break the boyars' power by seizing almost a third of the country as his personal possession or "separate estate"— the *oprichnina*. The rest he left to the boyars and bureaucrats to administer, though Ivan would tax it and subject it to his control in military and foreign affairs.

To safeguard the *oprichnina*, he enlisted the aid of the *oprichniki*, a sworn personal guard, private military and police force, and all-purpose death squad he formed in 1565. It was drawn from landless and disaffected young nobles, the new military class and service gentry Ivan had created, and serious criminals, who all received parcels of land confiscated from uncooperative boyars or formerly considered crown lands. At first, a thousand *oprichniki* sufficed, but their numbers eventually swelled to six thousand. At one point, Ivan and three hundred of these men ensconced themselves in his fortified summer residence outside Moscow, where the czar presided as their "abbot" while the *oprichniki* masqueraded as black-cassocked monks, alternating between hysterical religious observances and drunken, sadistic sexual orgies with men and women alike. Ivan's new fanatical followers carried out the cruel executions of several thousand boyar opponents of the new regime, and often the victims' wives and children were slaughtered, too.

In 1570, Ivan falsely suspected the northwestern commercial city of Novgorod of planning to join the Lithuanian-Polish coalition against him, so he had several thousand townspeople murdered, many of them by being tied to sleds that were sent hurtling down into the Volkhov River. The *oprichniki* busily burned down shops and devastated houses and farmlands in the surrounding areas. After also pillaging the city of Pskov, Ivan celebrated his quashing of the alleged conspiracy with a masquerade ball in Moscow. The very next year, however, Russia was invaded by the Crimean Tatars, and Moscow itself, with the exception of the Kremlin, was sacked and burned to the ground. The failure of the *oprichniki* to defend the capital led to the demise of the *oprichnina* experiment.

Sweden and Poland teamed up in 1578 against Russian expansionism to the west and forced Ivan to disgorge all his conquests in the

Baltic. He had more success in the east when the Cossack hetman (leader) Yermak Timofeyevich conquered the western Siberian khanate across the Urals in 1582, initiating Russia's very gradual takeover of the vast Siberian landmass.

Despite being an energetic ruler and one of the most vigorous writers and learned laymen—especially in theology—of his admittedly backward nation, Ivan the Awesome has been accused of boiling people in oil, drowning or hanging them, burying them alive, impaling them, quartering them, flogging them to death, ripping their ribs out with fiery-hot pincers, and much more along the same lines. He ordered the metropolitan of Moscow strangled for refusing the czar his blessing during a cathedral service. A traveler noted that Ivan "foamed at the mouth like a horse" at even petty annoyances.

In 1581, Ivan killed his favorite son, Ivan, the heir to the throne. The czar had disapproved of his pregnant daughter-in-law's immodest outfit and had given her a beating, causing a miscarriage. When his son remonstrated with him, Ivan flew into a rage and smashed him in the head with his iron-tipped staff. The young man died of his gangrenous wound a few days later, and his father gave vent to paroxysms of grief and remorse, howling for days on end. After the czar's beloved Anastasia died in 1560—poisoned by the boyars, he suspected—he married seven more wives in succession, having his penultimate drowned the day after the wedding on discovering she wasn't a virgin. When one of his wives was imprudent enough to take a lover, Ivan had him impaled outside her window.

Czar Ivan eventually developed a disease that bloated his body and made him stink to high heaven. He died suddenly at age fifty-three, supposedly while playing chess, on March 18, 1584. Was he poisoned? A few days earlier, Ivan may have tried to rape his daughter-in-law, the wife of his feebleminded son Fyodor and the sister of the boyar Boris Godunov, who intervened during the attempt and may later have killed the czar to save his own skin. When Ivan's body was exhumed and tested about a half century ago, it was found to contain very high levels of mercury. Was this the poison used, or did Ivan self-medicate his syphilis with mercury, a standard treatment for that disease at the time?

Boris Godunov acted as regent for his brother-in-law, the inept and childless Fyodor I, the last Russian ruler of the ancient line of Rurik (see Question 67). On Fyodor's death in 1598, a national assembly chose Godunov as czar (1598–1605). His reign and its aftermath are known as the "Time of Troubles"—fifteen years of civil war, famine, horrific Polish and Swedish invasions, rebellions, and several pretenders to the throne. The country was unified again when seventeen-year-old Michael Romanov (1613–45), a great-nephew of Ivan the Terrible's first wife, Anastasia, was chosen as czar, initiating a dynasty that ended with the murder in 1918 of Nicholas II and his family at the behest of Vladimir Lenin.

In 1906, Rainer Maria Rilke wrote a poem about Czar Ivan IV in which he imagined the life of this psychopathic paranoiac as "nothing but the daily fear of everything." Joseph Stalin was a great admirer of Ivan as a nationalistic hero, and during World War II Sergey Eisenstein made a two-part film about the czar with a score by Sergey Prokofiev. Today, however, most of us would probably subscribe to historian Will Durant's judgment of Ivan the Terrible: "He was one of the many men of his time of whom it might be said that it would have been better for their country and humanity if they had never been born."

116 ～ Who was the first modern essayist?

Michel de Montaigne, whose first edition of Essays *appeared in 1580*

MICHEL EYQUEM DE MONTAIGNE (1533–92) was born in the Château de Montaigne, thirty miles from Bordeaux. His father's family of successful traders was ennobled in the late fifteenth century and moved into public service. Montaigne's mother, Antoinette de Louppes de Villeneuve, stemmed from a prosperous family of converted Spanish Jews who had settled in Bordeaux in the fourteenth century.

Though Montaigne's father, Pierre, had little schooling, he loved the conversation of learned men. This "best of fathers," as his son, quoting Horace, called him, had progressive ideas about education. The infant Michel was held over the baptismal font not by fellow nobles but by "people of the lowliest class" and was sent to live among them for as long as he was nursing. His father's intent, in Montaigne's words, was "to bind me and attach me to them," and the boy grew up in a kind and tolerant household.

His first tutor spoke only Latin to him, and Montaigne himself spoke no French till he was five years old. His father, apparently losing his nerve for these educational experiments, sent the boy off to school, where, Montaigne said later, he didn't learn anything and lost what he did know. His real education came from his extracurricular reading, especially of Roman history, which he pursued secretly and avidly.

The young Montaigne showed no remarkable talent for anything— though he didn't show any remarkable disposition to vice, either: "No one predicted that I would turn out bad, but only useless. . . . The danger was not that I would do wrong, but that I would do nothing." Nonetheless, at age twenty-one he was appointed to a court at Périgueux that presided over all cases relating to taxes and fees. Three years later, in 1557, the court's jurisdiction was transferred to the Parlement of Bordeaux, and Montaigne spent his time between this city and the royal court in Paris. Witnessing how the administration of justice was corrupted by greed, opportunism, and factionalism, he protested against the proliferation of fees and various legal bribes and gifts that put justice out of reach for the poor. He was conspicuous in the Parlement for his impatience with pomp and ornate formality of expression.

Bordeaux was one of the first places in France to see the violence between Catholics and Protestants that would rage, on and off, through-out the country for the next thirty years. Civil wars offer both opportunity and danger. Montaigne did not seek the one and took no extraordinary measures to avoid the other. He kept his house open and unsecured, even when the danger was right outside his own gates. But his good judgment, honesty, kindness, and openheartedness won him confidence, so he was a trusted emissary and negotiator. He noticed that times of civil strife blur the lines between the useful (the politically expedient or profitable) and the honorable (the good that one pursues for its own sake). He would write on this distinction in his late essay "Of the Useful and the Honor-able," especially with reference to the troubles of his own times. The reli-gious wars may also have indirectly influenced the themes of his earliest essays: warfare, negotiations, promises, sudden misfortunes, and people in all sorts of crises.

By the time he retired from the Parlement in 1570, at age thirty-seven, he had had a close-up view of a wide range of human activities and human character under a variety of conditions. He had also had another experience that would be crucial to the development of his ideas: friendship.

Étienne de La Boétie was a fellow magistrate in the Bordeaux

Parlement and, though only a few years older than the twenty-four-year-old Montaigne, was already a married man and a distinguished scholar and writer. The friendship blossomed instantly and lasted only four years. When La Boétie contracted dysentery, he warned his friend away from the possible danger of contagion. Montaigne went to him immediately and stayed by his bedside, listening to his advice, talking with him, giving him comfort, and nursing him to the end.

To speculate about compatibilities and interests in such a relationship can only be impertinent. Montaigne, a man made of the best materials for winning and sustaining friendships, had only this one in his whole busy, sociable life. When he writes of La Boétie in his essay "Of Friendship," he sets this relationship apart. In describing their affection, complete mutual candor, and interest in each other, Montaigne avoids his familiar self-reflecting irony, and his language pulsates with wonder and love: "If someone presses me to say why I loved him, I feel that I cannot express it other than by answering, 'Because it was he, because it was I.'" He mourned this loss for the rest of his life, but it prompted him to set down his thoughts in what he was the first to call *essais*—"trials" or "attempts"—publishing his first edition of fifty-seven essays in 1580 (and fifty additional essays in two subsequent editions).

Montaigne was hardly the first person to write essays: Seneca (one of his heroes) and Cicero both wrote compositions that could be so described. And there were, of course, numberless formal productions of scholarship. Where Montaigne differed from all these—and in this he was an important first—was in his beginning without knowing where he was going to end up.

He furnished a room in his château as a study and had inscribed there, among many other Greek and Latin quotations, the Roman dramatist Terence's famous line, "I am a man: nothing human is foreign to me." These words were not just a nice formula for Montaigne. Educated to wealth, privilege, and a role in public life, he seems never to have internalized differences of class, nationality, religion, or culture. He had a great capacity for fellow feeling—a sympathetic imagination and tenderheartedness that extended even to animals: "I am not afraid to say that the tenderness of my nature is so childlike that I cannot well refuse my dog the play he offers me, no matter how ill-timed his request may be." When papal censors objected to his statement in an early edition of his *Essays* that torture was cruel and didn't work, he left it in and repeated it in a later essay in the next edition.

He wrote, then, from a consciousness of his experiencing self: a self that felt, reflected, judged, acted, and, most important, observed itself. This separateness had occurred to St. Augustine, who responded by building a theology that sought to explain it—or explain it away—by placing the individual in a divine cosmic order (see Question 31). Montaigne was skeptical of all such philosophical endeavors. Matters of divine truth were outside the scope of his undertaking, because they were necessarily outside the scope of human knowledge. God decided what to reveal of himself to humans, and when, and how.

Montaigne's skepticism was set forth in the *Apology for Raymond Sebond*, his longest and most formal essay, an exhaustive catalog of the fallibilities of human reason. It is a sustained attack on intellectual presumption, the failure of the mind to acknowledge its susceptibility to error and to contingencies that influence its capacity to observe, judge, and act rightly.

The biggest of these contingencies was death, which Montaigne had treated in two early essays. In the first, entitled after Solon's statement "That Our Happiness Is Not to Be Judged Until After Our Death," he has already made the subject his own:

> In everything else, we can wear a mask: when our splendid
> philosophical discourses are only a form of posturing; when
> events, not trying us to the quick, give us the option of main-
> taining a serene countenance. But in the last scene, between
> ourselves and death, there is no more making believe—we
> must speak plain French, we must show whatever is good and
> clean at the bottom of the pot.

In the very next essay, entitled after Cicero's claim "That to Philosophize Is to Learn How to Die," Montaigne asserts that the pursuit of virtue, even if human imperfection cannot attain it, is the happiness of life. But the first requirement of virtue must be to overcome the fear of death. It's not renunciation of life that he proposes, but habituation to mortality as a condition of existence, so that the fear of death does not interfere with our ability to lead a life that will enable us to enter that last scene with serenity.

This Stoic detachment also had another use: It made Montaigne unafraid to look into himself with objectivity. Noticing that his mind was as busy and wayward as his body, he asked how happiness, virtue, and wisdom were to be achieved. The answer seemed to consist in accepting one's fallibility as wholeheartedly as one's mortality.

To acknowledge fallibility was not to shut down inquiry; it opened it up. From the admission of Socratic ignorance—"I know that I do not know"—it was possible to determine what might be known. He looks, for example, at the ways in which people hold their ideas: the pedantry of scholars so lumbered up with knowledge that they can't shift it about to make a competent substantive judgment about anything; the softer, more impressionable minds of children and the uneducated. He noted the universal tendency to treat custom and received ideas as ordained by nature: "The chief effect of the power of custom consists in its seizing and taking possession of us to such an extent that we are hardly able to escape its grasp and return to our proper selves, so as to consider its commands and subject them to reason."

To make the effective connection between acquired knowledge, experience, and the will was the purpose of education. The mind so educated could respond appropriately to contingency, discover what it did not know, bring a wider range of experience, information, and reflection to bear on a problem, and be more likely to recognize complexity and less likely to be threatened by difference. Its possessor would realize that "to change his mind and correct himself, to abandon a wrong course at the height of his enthusiasm, are rare, forceful, and philosophical qualities." A large and subtle idea emerges with this view of the mind: that consciousness is not opinions or knowledge but activity, and this activity, this continuous motion—the mind's own movement and its adjustment to continuous change—is what it is to be alive.

> I cannot make my subject stay still. It lurches and staggers
> along with a natural intoxication. . . . This is a record of
> diverse and changeable occurrences. . . . And so, from time to
> time, I may well contradict myself, but the truth . . . I do not
> contradict. If my mind could settle down, I would not be
> writing essays, but drawing conclusions. Instead, it is always
> in apprenticeship and on trial.

In creating a multidimensional portrait of his own mind with the greatest fidelity to the experience of consciousness, Montaigne created an image of the human mind: "I set down a life that is humble and lackluster, but it's all one. . . . Each man bears within himself the entire form of the human condition." The *Essays* don't simply describe the pursuit of self-knowledge and virtue; they are the record of the pursuit itself. The development of Montaigne's thought, over some twenty years from the time he began to write, occurs by means of this activity of sifting, revising, adjusting, and reexamining, and the result is a cumulative portrait; this is part of the reason Montaigne is so difficult to summarize. He portrayed himself by showing his mind at work on his experience and on what he observed, from reading and living, of human nature.

There are no allegories or fictional dialogues in Montaigne. Rather than use these devices, which he rather despised, he referred to experience and observation. He is the most anecdotal of philosophers. Surely no other has more types of people trooping through his pages: kings, cannibals, mountebanks, soldiers, academics, eccentric nobles, judges, clever animals, beggars, prognosticators, peasants, and philosophers, all attesting to the infinite variety of human nature and to Montaigne's own capacious, humane curiosity.

Seven years into his project, he paused to address the reader in one of his characteristically engaging openings in the essay "Of the Resemblance of Children to Fathers." He was afflicted with kidney stones, the ailment that killed his father and the one he feared the most. It subjected him to bouts of horrible pain, and it was incurable. It was another test of his philosophy of detached inquiry into his experience. He had taught himself "to hold to life by life alone" and found not freedom from pain, but freedom from the hold of pain and the fear of it on his imagination. He was able to take a long-desired trip to Italy, where, in spite of the stone, he thoroughly enjoyed himself for a year and a half, reveling in the human diversity he found there and keeping a journal of his travels.

He was summoned back to France by Henry III, who requested him to serve as mayor of Bordeaux. He went on to be elected to two more terms. Here was applied wisdom, but it yielded more than the ability to live with pain. The last essays are written with the fluency and boldness of a mind delighting in its own play over the whole web of experience. He writes unafraid of what will turn up. He had come to understand that everything is connected to everything else. He died peacefully in 1592, survived by his wife and a daughter.

The *Essays* were translated into English by John Florio in 1603 and became part of English literature. The English and American masters of the familiar essay—Addison, Steele, Hazlitt, Lamb, and nameless legions—owe Montaigne a debt. He haunts the pages of Laurence Sterne's *The Life and Opinions of Tristram Shandy*, and the novel as a study of character is almost inconceivable without him. Writers as diverse as Pascal and Emerson acknowledged his mesmerizing influence.

American thinker Eric Hoffer recounted in his 1983 autobiography, *Truth Imagined*, that in his days as a migrant worker he spent a winter alone with a secondhand copy of the *Essays*. He read it three times over. "I felt all the time that he was writing about me," Hoffer wrote. "I recognized myself on every page. He knew my innermost thoughts." At a labor camp in the San Joaquin Valley, he couldn't open his mouth without quoting Montaigne, and it became a standing joke among the men to ask, "What does Montaigne say?" One man flipped through the book for a while and handed it back, observing that it was nothing special—anybody could have written it. Montaigne would have liked that.

—*Kia Penso*

117 ❧ What was the first Shakespearean tragedy?

Titus Andronicus, *first staged in 1594*

THE TRAGEDY OF TITUS ANDRONICUS is generally regarded as the worst play Shakespeare ever wrote. In his 1926 introduction to the play, American scholar Frederick D. Losey observes that it "reeks with revolting and unmotivated horrors," bemoans the fact that it "admits of no moral inference, affords no edification," and concludes that it "seems almost designedly bad." According to literary critic Mark Van Doren in 1939, "monstrosities and absurdities abound," it's the only one of Shakespeare's plays that is "inhuman," and the style is generally "as coarse as burlap." Italian novelist Giuseppe Tomasi di Lampedusa succinctly pronounced it "unreadable." Some scholars, incredulous that the Bard would have stooped to a potboiler like this, have denied his authorship, in whole or in part. Yet *Titus Andronicus* was mentioned by Francis Meres in his *Palladis Tamia* (1598) as a tragedy of Shakespeare's, and it later appeared in the first collected edition of Shakespeare's plays (see Question 124).

William Shakespeare (1564–1616) had already written several chronicle (or history) plays (the three parts of *Henry VI* and *Richard III*) and at least one comedy (*The Comedy of Errors*) before his initial foray into tragedy with *Titus Andronicus*, which was first staged by the Earl of Sussex's Men at London's Rose playhouse on January 23, 1594. The play's remote ancestors are the Roman philosopher Seneca's gruesome tragedies of blood and lust, the first of which was translated into English in 1559. Three years later, the first English tragedy was acted, *Gorboduc*, which showed strong affinities with Senecan dramaturgy. But shortly before Shakespeare himself first began writing for the stage, Thomas Kyd concocted a gory and phenomenally popular tragedy of revenge, *The Spanish Tragedy* (c. 1586), the earliest surviving Elizabethan play of its kind. Other influences on Shakespeare were the larger-than-life mayhem and sonorous blank verse declamations—the "mighty line"—of Christopher Marlowe's hugely popular two-part play *Tamburlaine the Great* (c. 1587–88), which details the conquests of a megalomaniacal fourteenth-century Übermensch.

The Elizabethan revenge play genre developed into an honorable tradition that, despite large servings of rant, fustian, braggadocio, bombast, and rodomontade along the way, saw its sublime apotheosis in *Hamlet*. It usually featured a great deal of lurid (and often gratuitous) violence and a protagonist driven to the brink of insanity because of cruel actions that inspire him to exact a merciless and sensationalistic vengeance.

Shakespeare's play, completely unhistorical, is derived from a chapbook titled *The History of Titus Andronicus*, and there were also apparently three older plays on this subject. Shakespeare's is saturated with a violent poetry of madness and excess, drawing for some of its horrors on Seneca's *Thyestes* and on the legend of raped and mutilated Philomela and her terrible revenge as recounted in Ovid's *Metamorphoses* (see Question 2).

The play opens with the triumphal return to Rome of Titus Andronicus, the empire's greatest general, a veteran of forty years in the field. He has defeated the Gothic barbarians and brought back five prize captives: the queen of the Goths, Tamora (accented on the first syllable), her three sons, and her black lover, Aaron the Moor. Queen Tamora's eldest son, Alarbus, is butchered as an offering to the shades of Titus's sons—twenty-one or twenty-two of them, he's not sure himself—who have died in the wars. Saturninus and his younger brother Bassianus, sons of the late emperor, are contending for the throne, but although Titus is the people's choice for emperor, he defers to the knavish Saturninus.

The new emperor wants Titus's daughter Lavinia as his wife, but no sooner does he free the Gothic prisoners than he begins courting Tamora. When Bassianus seizes his betrothed Lavinia from Saturninus, Titus's four remaining sons help the couple escape, but Titus kills one of them for daring to stand up to him in the fray that follows, in which the old general thinks the "honorable" thing to do is to support the emperor at any cost. Emperor Saturninus now reveals himself as a tyrannical villain, openly renouncing Lavinia, Titus, and his sons, and choosing to marry Tamora, who vows to her husband to exterminate Titus's family for the killing of her son.

Titus behaves like a foolish ur-Lear in this first act. As a simple-minded soldier, proud and headstrong, he doesn't realize who his true enemies are, turning against his sons, his brother Marcus, and the decent Bassianus. In this context, Titus's blind devotion to authority, in the mode of the old-style virtuous Romans, comes across as repellent. His extreme rigidity and outmoded patriotism are out of touch with the sordid realities of his time, and he evinces an atavistic cruelty in insisting on the sacrifice of Tamora's son, not to mention the slaughter of his own.

In Act 2, Aaron the Moor is revealed as Empress Tamora's lover; when her sons, Demetrius and Chiron, confess that they lust after Lavinia, he urges them to rape her. During a royal hunt, in which Bassianus and Lavinia catch Tamora together with Aaron, Tamora's sons stab Bassianus and rape and mutilate Lavinia, cutting off her hands and ripping out her tongue. When two of Titus's sons manage to fall into the pit in which Bassianus's body was thrown, Aaron makes the murder look like their work. (The villainous Barabas in Marlowe's *The Jew of Malta* influenced the characterization of Shakespeare's Aaron, who is a total monster for no apparent reason.) Saturninus accuses Titus's sons of Bassianus's murder and condemns them both to death.

The third act portrays Titus agonizing over the impending doom of his two sons, and his last remaining son, Lucius, has received a sentence of perpetual banishment for attempting to free his brothers. Aaron makes up a story that if Titus wants his sons released, either his son Lucius, his brother Marcus, or he himself has to chop off his hand and send it to Emperor Saturninus as a token of good faith. While Lucius and Marcus both offer to spare Titus and go off to find an ax, Titus tells Aaron he will sacrifice his own hand and asks the Moor to chop it off. Even here, Shakespeare can't resist a pun when he has Titus say, "Lend me thy hand, and I will give thee mine."

Titus's two sons are executed anyway and their heads scornfully sent to him along with his own hand. A thirst for revenge now forms in his poor excuse for a mind as he laughs at how stupid he's been: "Ha, ha, ha!" Like the aggrieved old father Hieronimo in Kyd's play, Titus is tormented by grief beyond what he can bear and descends into semi-madness. While one-handed Titus exits with the head of one of his sons and Marcus with the other, daughter Lavinia must carry Titus's severed hand between her teeth because the poor dear has no hands herself. Titus bids his banished son Lucius to flee Rome and raise an army among the Goths.

More dismal puns are in store for us in the next scene when Marcus rebukes Titus for urging Lavinia to commit suicide with the words, "Teach her not thus to lay / Such violent hands upon her tender life," and Titus counters with, "Oh, handle not the theme, to talk of hands." A piece of stage business that most decidedly does not work occurs when Marcus uses his knife to kill a fly in his dish, and the newly mellowed Titus reproaches him with, "How if that fly had a father and mother?" When Marcus says it was a black, ugly fly—sort of like Aaron—Titus descends to pure bathos by asking for the knife to stab the fly again, even giving it an extra shot for Tamora.

The fourth act gets off to a rousing start when Lavinia uses her stumps to leaf through a conveniently dropped copy of Ovid's *Metamorphoses*, stopping at the tragic tale of Philomela. Titus now realizes what has happened to her, but just in case he doesn't, she sticks a staff in her mouth and uses her stumps to guide it while scratching out in a sandy patch of Titus's garden the word STUPRUM—Latin for "rape"—followed by the names of Chiron and Demetrius.

Apparently unhinged by grief, Titus sends weapons to the rapists, along with a veiled threat—the two opening lines of an ode of Horace—as a "present," though Aaron understands what they really portend. Tamora secretly gives birth to Aaron's black son, sends it to him by a nurse, and bids him kill it so that her husband won't discover her infidelity. Instead, Aaron, planning to have it raised by the Goths, kills the

nurse, whose squeals he compares to a pig's when he stabs her, and pro-
cures a white baby so that Saturninus will think it's his own. Time for a
little comic relief: Shakespeare throws in a silly scene between Titus and
a country bumpkin, whose entry is announced by the stage direction,
"*[Enter a CLOWN, with a basket, and two pigeons in it.]*"

In what is fortunately the last act, Aaron and his infant son are captured by a soldier serving under Lucius, who is marching on Rome at
the head of a Gothic army. In return for a promise of safety for his child,
Aaron regales Lucius with a catalog of his villainies (much as Barabas
does in *The Jew of Malta*), boasting of what he's done to Titus, his two
sons, and Lavinia—and all for laughs. Among the murders and rapes he
throws in accounts of vicious practical jokes, like setting barns and
haystacks on fire and digging up corpses and leaving them on their dear
friends' doorsteps.

This is followed by an absurd and tedious scene inspired by *The
Spanish Tragedy*, in which Tamora and her two sons impersonate the
characters of Revenge, Rape, and Murder to convince the supposedly
mad Titus that they will avenge his wrongs if he will set out a banquet
at his house and urge his invading son Lucius to attend a parley there
with Emperor Saturninus. Titus agrees, though he is now concealing his
nefarious plans by feigning madness, like the avenging Hieronimo in
The Spanish Tragedy.

After Tamora exits, Titus has her sons tied up and cuts their throats
while Lavinia catches their blood in a basin she holds with her stumps.
We learn that Titus will grind their bodies into a pulp, mix in their
blood, and bake it all up in a pie. At the banquet he's laid out for the
royal family and other noble guests, Titus, dressed like a cook, serves
the pie to Tamora—and shortly afterward stabs his daughter Lavinia to
put an end to her shame. Then he informs Tamora that she has eaten her
sons in the pie and kills her, too (as in Seneca's *Thyestes*, in which the
title character is fed the body of his son at a banquet, and in the Ovid-
ian myth of Tereus, who is fed his son Itys by Philomela, whom Tereus
has raped). Saturninus immediately kills Titus, Lucius kills Saturninus,
and "a great tumult" ensues.

When the dust settles, Lucius is acclaimed emperor. Aaron is
planted breast-deep in the ground to starve to death, but he's still his old
self: "If one good deed in all my life I did, / I do repent it from my very
soul." Tamora's corpse is thrown to the "beasts and birds of prey." As in
The Spanish Tragedy, there's a scorecard recital of crimes at the end to

remind the audience how diligently it has been entertained. The fourteen violent deaths in *Titus Andronicus* compare favorably with the nine in Thomas Kyd's *Spanish Tragedy*, and the four violent deaths at the end are no more than the four who die in the final scene of *Hamlet*, though in *Titus* the mechanical quid pro quo of the stabbings makes for a ludicrous effect.

It's no wonder that some Shakespeare scholars have seen *Titus Andronicus* as a comical travesty of the revenge play genre, but that's probably not the case. In this play, the young Shakespeare, overreaching in his effort to "out-Kyd Kyd," may well just have slipped and lost his footing. Moreover, the violence and brutality of the play have a different effect on us than on the original audience that also enjoyed bear-baiting, bullbaiting, and public hangings.

In 1614, Ben Jonson paired *Titus Andronicus* with *The Spanish Tragedy* as plays that only the ignorant were still fond of—perhaps meaning they were both still being performed. At least three quartos of Shakespeare's first tragedy appeared in his lifetime, the last as late as 1611, suggesting that people were eager to read it, and it was staged by at least four different theatrical companies of the time.

In 1678, Edward Ravenscroft adapted the play, seeing fit to increase its horrors by having Tamora stab her child and Aaron be tortured on the rack and burned to death onstage. In contrast, the black American actor Ira Aldridge radically altered the text to allow his sympathetic portrayal of Aaron in East London productions in 1852 and 1857.

When the original play was put on in London not long after the barbarities of World War II, some people got sick in the theater. Since then, Laurence Olivier delivered a virtuoso performance as Titus in a 1955 production directed by Peter Brook in Stratford-upon-Avon, England; Derek Jacobi played Aaron in 1963 in Birmingham, England; and Joseph Papp staged the play as part of the New York Shakespeare Festival in 1967.

An imaginative film adaptation, *Titus*, directed by Julie Taymor and starring Anthony Hopkins as Titus and Jessica Lange as Tamora, appeared in 1999. In a production of the play directed by Yukio Ninagawa in Stratford-upon-Avon in June 2006, the rigid codes of honor and revenge of Japanese samurai warriors were brought to bear on Shakespeare's over-the-top tragic debut, in which "Rome is but a wilderness of tigers."

118 ✆ What was the world's first opera?

*Dafne by Ottavio Rinuccini and Jacopo Peri, performed in
Florence in 1598*

THERE'S BROAD BUT NOT UNIVERSAL AGREEMENT that the first opera
was a short pastoral entitled *Dafne*. The librettist, Ottavio Rinuccini
(1562–1621), called it a "simple trial" and praised the composer,
Jacopo Peri (1561–1633), for developing a new style of speech-song
enabling the entire tale of Apollo's pursuit of the nymph Daphne to be
enacted in music. It was first performed before a small Florentine audience in the home of a nobleman in 1598 and was liked well enough to
receive several more performances over the next few years, though very
little of the music has survived.

Dafne, however, was a pale sketch of what opera would become.
Like other complex media (think of film or TV), the form did not
emerge all at once but took shape through a series of arranged marriages of music and drama, each with its distinct solution to the mani-
fold difficulties of uniting action, poetry, spectacle, and music. We'll
discuss four such moments, but first, a little context.

Much as the fifteenth century in Florence had seen a humanistic
full-court press to recover, translate, and interpret ancient Greek writings and culture, a new group of intellectuals in the sixteenth century
aspired to recapture the power of ancient music. Music for the ancients
must have been a potent art—did they not tell of Orpheus, who could
make trees and stones dance to his song? And did Plato not advocate
banishing certain musical modes from his ideal state because they exercised too much sway over the souls of men and women?

Such clues, along with the belief that Greek drama was performed
with a chanting, dancing chorus, led Renaissance artists and intellectuals to believe that the music of the Greeks united musical form and dramatic meaning with a power beyond anything that "modern" music,
with its complex counterpoint, could achieve.

The goal of fusing music with drama became something of an
obsession for Florentines. Girolamo Mei (1519–94) devoted many
years to researching Greek musical theory, and when a group of
younger artists and humanists began meeting regularly from 1573 to

the late 1580s at the home of Giovanni de' Bardi, they sought to recover the pure Greek style, in opposition to what they considered the corrupt music of their day.

One member of the group was Vincenzo Galilei, the lutenist, composer, and father of Galileo Galilei. Vincenzo wrote to ask Mei, then living in Rome, about his findings, and a detailed correspondence ensued. In 1581, Vincenzo published his "Dialogue on Ancient and Modern Music"—an impassioned indictment of polyphony. "Contrapuntists," he wrote,

> deserve to be reputed coarse idiots. . . . [They] seek every
> opportunity to make sure that when they sing, no one will ever
> make any sense or structure of the thoughts spoken. Indeed,
> one does not ever understand a word, as if they were ashamed
> to be reasoning animals, not to say humans.

Galilei and others in the so-called Camerata de' Bardi envisioned a new music that would simplify polyphony by subjecting all the parts to a single treble voice accompanied by a flexible figured bass. Instead of four equal voices moving against one another in contrapuntal complexity, one voice would articulate the words and, beneath it, a bass line would move, freely adapting its rhythm to the natural emphases of the words and filling in appropriate harmonies as required by the melody.

Vincenzo Galilei did more than theorize. In 1582, he composed a setting of the speech of Ugolino, one of Dante's damned souls, as an experiment in giving aural priority to the text. As an imitation of the Greeks, it may have gone astray, but although the music hasn't survived, it remains a harbinger of what was to come—opera, the cantata, and the Baroque in general.

While theorists continued their investigations, major spectacles requiring combinations of actual music, drama, and dance were being commissioned. None was more colossal than *La Pellegrina* (*The Pilgrim Woman*), a multimedia entertainment devised for the 1589 wedding in Florence of Ferdinand I de' Medici, Grand Duke of Tuscany, to Christina of Lorraine.

Conceived as the high point of festivities that included a mock naval battle in the courtyard of the Pitti Palace (flooded for the occasion), *La Pellegrina* took the form of *intermedi*—six compositions involving music, dance, and elaborate scenic effects that came between the acts of a rather forgettable play. One *intermedio* composed by Cristofano Malvezzi, Peri's music tutor, called for thirty separate vocal parts divided among seven spatially separated choirs.

La Pellegrina is memorable for several reasons: It cost the astronomical sum of 45,000 scudi, it took eight months to prepare, and it combined the talents of Rinuccini, Peri, Malvezzi, Bardi, and many others. More significantly, it is the first work to showcase the *sprezzatura* style—a mode of singing in which rigidly measured rhythm recedes to the background in favor of a freer declaration of text— clearly deriving from the researches of Galilei and the Bardi group. Yet it remained a musical production distinct from the stage play it accompanied, though it's debatable whether the spectacle was incidental to the play, or vice versa.

The next decade saw a race to bring this impending convergence of drama and music to final, blissful fruition. In 1590, Emilio de' Cavalieri, a Roman aristocrat lately summoned to Florence to take charge of Duke Ferdinand's artistic endeavors, produced two staged musical pastorals, *Il Satiro* and *La disperazione di Fileno*. The compositions employed a form of sung declamation that gave Cavalieri sufficient pretext—at least in his own eyes—to claim that he alone had rediscovered the true music of the Greeks.

This development incensed those in the Florentine contingent, who were not about to allow some Roman interloper to abscond with the holy grail they'd been pursuing for so many years. It was then that Rinuccini and Peri, along with Florentine nobleman Jacopo Corsi, began working on *Dafne*. Its production at the Palazzo Corsi in 1598 led to a commission for a more ambitious work of musical drama, which they called *Euridice*, named for the lost wife of Orpheus.

Many historians who refuse to accord pride of place to *Dafne* as the first opera bestow it instead on *Euridice*. The latter work premiered on Friday, October 6, 1600, in a fairly small room in the Pitti Palace before an invited courtly audience of about two hundred. Both score and libretto survive, and nothing in either suggests the fancy stage machinery or extravagance of *La Pellegrina*. The production has eleven characters accompanied by a small instrumental ensemble that included organ, harpsichord, lute, and an ancestor of the cello, all played behind the scenes.

Apart from the fact that the actual music survives, *Euridice* was noteworthy for several other reasons: for one, its successful use of recitative, or monody—Peri's solution for setting to music the sections of a text that are not lyrical in nature but serve only to advance the dramatic action.

Where others had tried but failed—some approaches being too rigidly songlike in nature, others trying too hard to mime the specific words being sung—Peri's recitative was immediately recognized as something special. It offered a middle ground that allowed music to support and gently enhance the text without trammeling it in formal melodic elements that would distract from the free onward movement of declaratory speech.

Another reason *Euridice* was momentous was that it's almost certain Claudio Monteverdi (1567–1643) was present to hear it. If Peri and Rinuccini were focusing on liberating sung speech from fixed geometries of musical form, Monteverdi's genius would not allow opera to remain a mode in which music obsequiously served drama. In his hands it would become an organic musical form, driven by the declamatory needs of speech but structured according to large principles of musical organization and employing all the richness and variety that music had to offer: dance, song, duet, toccata, canon, ritornello, and madrigal, as well as a more potent form of recitative than Peri ever imagined.

Monteverdi was working for Vincenzo I Gonzaga of Mantua when Peri's *Euridice* premiered. His response was the *Orfeo*, based on a libretto by Alessandro Striggio, which had its first performance in Vincenzo's sister's apartments on February 24, 1607. With its forty-piece orchestra, its evocative ritornello that changes mood with the action of the drama, its large and small inspirations, its assignment of specific instrumental groups to characters and locales within the story (cornets, trombones, and organ for the Underworld), and its assured recitative, *Orfeo* ushered in a new, more complex model of what opera could be, replete with all the riches of music balanced against a text suffused with its own internal harmonies and poetic depth. *Arianna* followed in 1608, but the work is lost except for its famous lament. Of nineteen Monteverdi operas, only three survive: *Orfeo* and two late works written in Venice, where he was choirmaster for the last three decades of his life: *The Return of Ulysses* (1640) and *The Coronation of Poppea* (1642).

It wasn't by chance that these early operatic works invoked ancient myths involving Apollo, the god of music, and Orpheus, the poet/singer whose song conquered death itself. Peri, Rinuccini, Monteverdi, and all those racing to bring Greek music back from the dead were consciously creating works about the relative power of words and music even as they strove to reincarnate that power. When Monteverdi articulated his musical goals, in what he called his "*seconda prattica*," he invoked Plato's idea, also stressed by Vincenzo Galilei, that music, for the good of the state, should emulate the well-ordered soul: "Then beauty of style and harmony and grace and good rhythm depend on simplicity, I mean the true simplicity of a rightly and nobly ordered mind and character" (*Republic*, Book 3).

Alas, the subsequent history of the form followed a somewhat different path. Opera soon escaped its courtly precincts and sober theoreticians to enjoy a profligate career in freewheeling Venice. The intent to create a form that would subordinate the passionate extravagances of music to the governance of a nobly ordered mind gave way to a promiscuous genre that strikingly anticipated the worst excesses of disco or American television.

In Venetian theaters, opera became the rage for nobility and commoners alike. From the day the Teatro San Cassiano, the first public opera house, opened its doors in 1637, opera outshone every other musical or theatrical form. Between 1637 and 1700, according to music historian Donald Grout, seventeen opera houses produced 388 operas in Venice alone, and as many more elsewhere in Italy. Gone were the austere monodies of Peri, the noble clarity of Monteverdi. Instead, libretti underwent an endless recycling of dumb and dumber plots that served as mere pretexts for concatenations of showy spectacle, dance, and virtuosic musical display.

Here is John Evelyn, a cultured Englishman, describing a visit to the opera in Venice:

> . . . the Opera, which are Comedies & other plays represented in Recitative Music by the most excellent Musitians vocal & Instrumental, together with variety of Seeanes [*sic*] painted & contrived with no lesse art of Perspective, and Machines, for flying in the aire, & other wonderfull motions. So taken together it is doubtlesse one of the most magnificent & expensfull diversions the Wit of Men can invent: The historie was *Hercules* in Lydia, the Seanes chang'd 13 times . . .

This was in 1645, only two years after Monteverdi's death.

—*Tom Matrullo*

SEVENTEENTH CENTURY

119 ∾ What was the first English dictionary?

Robert Cawdrey's A Table Alphabeticall, *1604*

BY THE SIXTEENTH CENTURY the recovery of the scientific, philosophical, and literary heritage of the ancient world was exercising a profound influence on English, which incorporated many words from Latin and Greek and some from Hebrew and Arabic. These unfamiliar terms, sure to trip up the unsophisticated reader, had begun to be gathered in didactic "hard word" collections, such as the one included in Richard Mulcaster's *Elementarie* (1582). This book, a guide to teaching and an exhortation for the use of English rather than Latin in education, contained a list of eight thousand imported words but provided no definitions. As a prominent London teacher, Mulcaster was primarily interested in standardizing spelling, because "forenners and strangers do wonder at vs, both for the vncertaintie in our writing, and the inconstancie in our letters."[1]

Another early hard-word glossary was embedded in Edmund Coote's *English Schoole-Maister* (1596), which included many of Mulcaster's selections but with brief definitions. His was the first English-only glossary to do so, and he modeled it on the bilingual dictionaries that were already available.

But the first stand-alone English dictionary, appearing in 1604, was Robert Cawdrey's *A Table Alphabeticall, conteyning and teaching the true writing, and vnderstanding of hard vsuall English wordes, borrowed from the Hebrew, Greeke, Latine, or French, &c. With the interpretation thereof by plaine English words, gathered for the benefit & helpe of Ladies, Gentlewomen, or any other vnskilfull persons. Whereby they may the more easilie and better vnderstand many hard English wordes, vvhich they shall heare or read in Scriptures, Sermons, or elsewhere, and also be made able to vse the same aptly themselues.* A single copy of this work survives at Oxford's Bodleian Library.

Born around 1538, Cawdrey began working as a small-town English schoolmaster in 1563. His dictionary, which he compiled with

---

[1] The Elizabethan alphabet comprised twenty-four letters, with *v* and *u* being the same letter; *v* was used at the beginning of words and *u* in other positions. *J* was not a separate letter but was used as the capital of *i*.

the aid of his son, represented an effort to provide explanations of the difficult words that were entering the language so rapidly that he feared English speakers might no longer be able to understand one another. In his introduction, he criticized the increasing practice of adopting "inkhorn" terms, creating an English word out of a foreign one—usually Latin or Greek—without explanation. He dismissed speakers who travel abroad and "pouder their talke with ouer-sea language," just as they dress in "forraine apparell." He called for the use of language that was proper and apt, with grave words reserved for weighty matters, beautiful words used "as precious stones are set in a ring, to commend the gold," and plain words used when straightforward understanding is needed.

Cawdrey relied heavily on Mulcaster's and Coote's earlier works, but he also used many other sources, including Latin-English dictionaries and glosses of legal, scientific, and religious texts. But his dictionary was not simply an amalgam of earlier works—it represented the efforts of a true lexicographer seeking to provide a coherent, practical resource for his contemporaries.

Cawdrey's entries were alphabetized—a novel concept at the time, which he felt compelled to explain in his introduction. The definitions were concise and often simply synonyms, without the explanatory and descriptive components of later dictionaries. He also flagged with *g* or *fr* words derived from Greek or French:

> *arithmeticke, (g)* art of numbring
> *excheaquer, (fr)* office of receits

The first 120-page edition (others appeared in 1609, 1613, and 1617) contained some twenty-five hundred entries. Perusal of Cawdrey's dictionary reveals the sprightliness of the English of the time:

> *blattering*, vaine babling
> *driblets*, small debts
> *garboile, (fr)* hurlie burly
> *maffle*, stammer, or stut
> *snipperings*, pairings

Some words still common have morphed in meaning:

> *climate*, a portion of the worlde betwixt north and south
> *concoct*, to digest meate

fastidiousnes, lothsomnesse, or disdainfullnesse
flagrant, burning, hot
inaugurate, to aske counsell of soothsayers
seminarie, a nurserie, or seede plot for young trees, or grafts

Others have fallen by the wayside and are not greatly missed:

illiquinated, vnmelted
morigerous, well mannered
oblectation, recreation, delight
obnubilate, to make darke
periclitation, ieopardie, or hazarding
pluuiatile, raine

A few definitions might now be considered a tad judgmental:

fornication, vncleannes betweene single persones
sodomitrie, when one man lyeth filthylie with another man

And others reveal the limitations of the science and medicine of the day:

catharre, a flowing of humors from the head
genius, the angell that waits on man, be it a good or euill angell
melancholie, (g) black choler, a humor of solitarines, or sadnes
theologie, (g) diuinitie, the science of liuing blessedly for euer

Some are elegant in their precision and clarity:

desolate, left alone, or forsaken
modest, sober, demure
sympathie, (g) fellowelike feeling

While others obfuscate with perfect circularity:

gentile, a heathen
heathen, see Gentile

Cawdrey's achievement was soon followed by others. In 1616, Dr. John Bullokar published *An English Expositor: Teaching the*

Interpretation of the Hardest Words Used in Our Language, which focused on Greek and Latin loanwords and continued to be published in revised editions until as late as 1775. Next was *The English Dictionarie*—the first to use *dictionary* in its title—published by Henry Cockeram in 1623. Cockeram acknowledged his historical debt to *A Table Alphabeticall* and *An English Expositor* on his title page but added much material of his own and provided far more colorful definitions than those of his predecessors. His explication of *crocodile* contains this zoological lore: "[I]f it see a man afraid of him, it will eagerly pursue him, but on the contrary, if he be assaulted he will shun him. Hauing eaten the body of a man, it will weepe ouer the head, but in fine eate the head also: thence came the prouerb, he shed crocodile teares, viz., fayned teares."

In 1656, barrister Thomas Blount published *Glossographia*, which defined eleven thousand words derived from Greek, Latin, Hebrew, Saxon, Turkish, French, and Spanish, as well as from disciplines like mathematics and architecture. Blount also greatly expanded the definitions and for the first time delved into word etymologies, but his work was surpassed in popularity two years later when Edward Phillips, the nephew of John Milton, published *The New World of English Words* with approximately twenty thousand entries. This dictionary offered "the interpretations of such hard words as are derived from other languages, whether Hebrew, Arabick, Syriack, Greek, Latin, Italian, French, Spanish, British, Dutch, Saxon, &c., their etymologies, and perfect definitions. . . ." Up to half of the "perfect definitions," however, had been copied directly from Blount, without permission, and Blount retaliated in 1673 by publishing *A World of Errors Discovered in the New World of Words*, highlighting Phillips's mistakes and lack of originality.

The popularity of dictionaries continued to increase with the publication in 1721 of Nathaniel Bailey's *Universal Etymological English Dictionary*. Bailey was the first lexicographer to aim for inclusion of all English words, not only exotic or difficult ones, with the purpose of illuminating the derivation of even the most simple and common terms. He also introduced the stress accent to guide pronunciation and, in subsequent editions, added proverbs and diagrams.[2] At Bailey's death in

---

[2] The 1737 edition of Bailey's dictionary served as the source for his slang dictionary, *A Collection of the Canting Words and Terms, both ancient and modern, used by Beggars, Gypsies, Cheats, House-Breakers, Shop-Lifters, Foot-Pads, Highway-Men, &c.* A sample entry: "ARK-RUFFIANS, Rogues, who in Conjunction with Watermen, &c., rob and sometimes murder on the Water; by picking a Quarrel with the Passenger and then plundering, stripping and throwing him or her over board, &c."

1742, the tenth edition of his dictionary was in press, and his remained the most popular dictionary throughout the eighteenth century, ultimately serving as the basis for Samuel Johnson's masterly compilation.

By the mid-eighteenth century there had been an explosion of literacy among the general population in Britain as well as in the availability of books, newspapers, and other publications. Sentiment was growing for an authoritative dictionary of the English language that would reflect the entire lexicon as currently used in writing and speaking, as had been done for Italian in 1612 by the *Vocabolario degli Accademici della Crusca* and for French in 1694 by the *Dictionnaire de l'Académie française*. In 1746, a group of London booksellers contracted with Dr. Johnson to enter into this project for the sum of 1,500 guineas. He went on to labor nearly nine years at the task, aided only by clerks helping with transcription. The resulting *Dictionary of the English Language* (1755) contained almost fifty thousand entries, with many words having multiple definitions—and, for the first time, definitions and shades of meaning were demonstrated by quotations from English writers including Shakespeare, Milton, and Dryden. Also noteworthy was Johnson's occasional injection of humor and personal opinion, as in his notorious definition of *oats*: "A grain which in England is generally given to horses, but in Scotland supports the people." He also ruefully illustrated the word *dull* with the statement, "To make dictionaries is dull work."

Johnson's dictionary remained authoritative for more than a century, but in 1857 members of the Philological Society of London began to plan a truly comprehensive record of the language in conjunction with James A. H. Murray and Oxford University Press. They envisioned a 6,400-page, four-volume work that would include all English words since 1150 and take approximately ten years to complete. But five years into the project Murray and his colleagues had only reached *ant*, and it wasn't until 1884 that the first fascicle appeared.

Murray's team, greatly expanded, continued the gargantuan task for more than four decades until, in April 1928, the tenth and last volume of *A New English Dictionary on Historical Principles* was published. Revision began immediately, however, and a supplement, along with a reprinted twelve-volume edition, appeared as the *Oxford English Dictionary*—the famed OED—in 1933.

Work on the OED continued throughout the twentieth century—with the second edition appearing in 1989 and a CD-ROM version in

1992—and into the twenty-first, with an ever-expanding online version that offers quarterly revisions. At the core of the titanic work may still be discerned the goal of an Elizabethan schoolteacher who hoped that his readers would "the more easilie and better vnderstand many hard English wordes."

—*Nancy Walsh*

120 ∾ What was the first permanent English settlement in the New World?

Jamestown, Virginia, established on May 14, 1607

IN 1580, FRANCIS DRAKE RETURNED to England from his three-year circumnavigation of the globe in the *Golden Hind*, which was sorely laden with stolen Spanish gold. He had set off to find the Northwest Passage to China but ended up as the scourge of Spanish treasure galleons in the war of Protestant England against its great Catholic enemy. Drake was knighted by Queen Elizabeth I on his ship's deck as the nation's most patriotic pirate. England now needed to map the American coastline and establish a supply base there to enable privateering sea dogs like Sir Francis to keep hounding Spanish colonies and shipping in the New World.

Soon the English claimed the Atlantic coastline from Newfoundland to Cape Fear, North Carolina, naming the entire area Virginia in honor of Elizabeth, their "Virgin Queen." In 1584, Elizabeth's favorite courtier, Sir Walter Raleigh, sponsored an expedition that identified Roanoke, an island in Pamlico Sound in what is now North Carolina, as the most propitious site for a settlement, and in July 1585, Raleigh's cousin, Sir Richard Grenville, led more than a hundred men ashore. The men built a fort at the northern end of the island, and the artist John White made exquisite watercolors of the Algonquian natives and the local flora and fauna. After a severe winter and Indian attacks, however, they were all happy to return to England with Sir Francis Drake when he stopped there in June 1586 after raiding Spanish colonies in the West Indies and Florida.

White returned to Roanoke in 1587 as governor of a second colony sent out by Raleigh of about one hundred settlers, including some women and children. White's granddaughter, Virginia Dare, the first child born in America of English parents, saw the light on August 18, less than a month after the colonists arrived. A week after her birth, White sailed back to England for supplies, but the failed invasion of England by the Spanish Armada in 1588 and the ongoing war with Spain prevented him from returning to Roanoke until August 1590. Meanwhile, the entire colony, including White's daughter and little granddaughter, had disappeared. *CROATOAN*, the native name of Hatteras Island, about sixty miles to the south, was carved on a post and *CRO* on a tree. A hurricane prevented White from searching for the "Lost Colony," whose fate remains unknown. Raleigh lost a huge fortune in these unsuccessful ventures.

The first permanent English settlement in the New World was finally established by a joint stock venture, which spread the financial risk. Under a charter granted by the next sovereign, James I, the Virginia Company of London embarked 104 men and boys on December 20, 1606, in three ships headed for Chesapeake Bay, Virginia, under the command of Captain Christopher Newport. After meandering a bit, they set foot on what they variously called James Towne, James Forte, and James Cittie on May 14, 1607.

Now an island because of erosion, Jamestown was then a wooded, uninhabited peninsula with a narrow neck at the mouth of the James River, relatively easy to defend against attack and allowing ships to pull right up to the settlement to dock. It was also a low-lying marshy haven for mosquitoes. Captain John Smith, an experienced mercenary who had recently been enslaved by the Turks, was one of the seven members of the settlement's governing council, though, because of his mutinous behavior on the voyage, he was excluded from the leadership for a month. Another council member, the investor Edward-Maria Wingfield, became the colony's first president.

As soon as the settlers landed, they began building a fort—and it was a good thing, too, because on May 26 two hundred armed natives of the Powhatan Algonquian confederacy attacked, killing a colonist and wounding eleven others before being driven off by the ships' cannon fire. Jamestown's triangular fort, mounted with artillery pieces and surrounded by a stockade, was completed on June 15, but by mid-November almost half the settlers had perished from dysentery, malaria, severe fevers, malnutrition, and (in the case of those who hunted or gathered firewood in the forest) getting picked off by Indians. Wingfield had been ousted as president on September 10 and replaced by John Ratcliffe.

Winter found the settlers dependent on bartering iron hatchets and other goods for the Indians' maize, but the natives of Chief Powhatan's thirty-tribe confederacy blew hot and cold. In December 1607, they captured John Smith. According to his own account, he was going to be executed by having his skull smashed against a stone by the Indians' clubs when Powhatan's preteen daughter, Pocahontas—a nickname perhaps meaning "Little Wanton"—saved Smith's life by shielding his body with hers. Historians have suspected the event may have been a harmless initiation rite—or an incident made up by Smith—but the girl became friendly with the English and sometimes brought them gifts of food from her people. Released in January 1608, Smith met with Powhatan again a few months later. In return for promising to help Powhatan against his enemies, the diplomatic Smith was made a *weroance*—an Algonquian chief.

Since more than half of the first settlers were "gentlemen"—that is, idlers or military men who did the minimal amount of work—they expected to be supplied with food by English ships or indentured servants rather than by growing it themselves. As employees of the Virginia Company, they were supposed to look for gold and silver and the fabled Northwest Passage. It's not surprising that when Captain Newport returned to Jamestown with a supply ship in January—and a hundred more settlers, including five Poles—he found only thirty-eight survivors.

When John "Weroance" Smith was elected to leadership of the colony in September 1608, he enunciated his famous rule, based on a New Testament text: "He that will not worke shall not eate (except by sicknesse he be disabled)." Under Smith's vigorous presidency, the settlers cultivated a hundred acres, intensified their fishing, produced pitch, tar, and glass for export to England, dug a well, and built forty or fifty houses, but it was still tough going for his inexperienced men. In August 1609, seven ships arrived with two hundred to three hundred men, women, and children, but Smith was soon severely burned in an accident and had to return to England in early October.

The winter of 1609–10 was a brutal one called the "Starving Time" for Jamestown. With the intrepid Smith gone, Powhatan refused food to the English colony and ordered anyone who strayed beyond its fortifications killed. The settlers were reduced to eating roots and berries, any and all animals—domesticated, wild, or verminous—they could get their hands on, and even human flesh: "One amongst the rest did kill his wife, powdered her, and had eaten part of her before it was knowne, for which hee was executed, as hee well deserved," wrote Smith in his *Generall Historie of Virginia*. "Now whether shee was better roasted, boyled or carbonado'd, I know not, but of such a dish as powdered wife I never heard of." When two ships with scant supplies finally arrived in May 1610, Sir Thomas Gates found only sixty emaciated survivors of the five hundred colonists who were there at the time of Smith's departure and decided to evacuate them all. Shortly after setting out for England in June, they were met at the mouth of the James by three incoming ships under the new governor of Jamestown, Lord De La Warr, who, bringing supplies and 150 more settlers, ordered the fleeing colonists to turn around.

Besides giving his name to Delaware, the governor established strict military discipline and built two new forts but had to depart within a year because of illness. In August 1611, Gates landed another 280 settlers. In the same year, John Rolfe planted tobacco seeds from Trinidad, obtaining a sweeter smoke than that of the bitter Virginia tobacco. After he exported it to England in 1613, it soon came to be preferred over the Spanish tobacco that had captured the market. Despite King James's detestation of "the blacke stinking fume" of smoking, calling it "a custome lothsome to the eye, hatefull to the Nose, harmefull to the braine, dangerous to the Lungs," Jamestown had hit upon a cash crop.

Meanwhile, Pocahontas, captured by the English in 1613, converted to Christianity, took the name Rebecca, and married John Rolfe in the following year, thus initiating eight years of relative peace between the Powhatans and the settlers. In 1616, she sailed with her husband and infant son, Thomas, to England, where she was the toast of King James's court before dying of a lung ailment the next year at age twenty-one. Her son grew up in England before returning to Virginia to become a successful tobacco planter.

To attract more colonists to Jamestown, the Virginia Company began allowing settlers to purchase parcels of land instead of merely sharecropping. It also directed the inept governor, Sir George Yeardley, to arrange for the election of two men from each of the colony's four boroughs and seven plantations to help him and his small council govern. The twenty-two members of this House of Burgesses, the first

American legislative body, assembled in a church at Jamestown on July 30, 1619.

Malaria and dysentery scattered the burgesses within six days, with one fatality, but not before they levied a tax of ten pounds of tobacco on every male over age sixteen. Though the enactments of the House of Burgesses were subject to veto by the governor and the Virginia Company, at least military rule had been replaced by English common law and a representative assembly—and future members would include the likes of George Washington, Thomas Jefferson, and a fulminating Patrick Henry. To cap things off, the Virginia Company sent a shipload of young women of unimpeachable morals to Jamestown in 1620, allowing colonists to purchase a bride for 120 pounds of prime tobacco.

Meanwhile, the seed of slavery had arrived in Jamestown in August 1619, when more than twenty Africans were bought from a Dutch ship. Since slavery was still forbidden at this time, they were probably treated like white indentured servants, who labored for a set time, usually seven years, to work off the cost of their passage.

After Powhatan's death in 1618, a younger brother who succeeded him as head of the Powhatan confederacy showed increasing hostility toward the colonists. In a surprise attack on Jamestown and nearby establishments on March 22, 1622, the natives massacred 350 to 400 of the settlers, almost a third of the population, initiating sporadic fighting over a decade. The next few years continued to be very difficult. Though many new settlers arrived, including foreign workers to set up sawmills, mortality remained high and many colonists sailed back home.

These setbacks spurred King James to revoke the Virginia Company's charter in 1624. Virginia became a royal colony, and its governor and council were appointed by the king, while the House of Burgesses continued to be elected by freeborn men. Gradually, as more land was made available to settlers, who then took a larger stake in the colony's success, Virginia began to prosper. By 1627, there were a thousand settlers along a twenty-mile stretch of the James River; twenty years later, there were fifteen thousand, and by 1671, forty thousand.

During the English civil wars and Puritan Commonwealth (1642–60), thousands of Anglicans fled to Virginia, but many criminals and indigents were also sent there. In 1644, there was a second massacre by the Indians at Jamestown, and the settlement was burned to the ground in 1676 during the unsuccessful rebellion against Governor

William Berkeley led by Nathaniel Bacon. By this time, King Charles II was squeezing a yearly customs revenue of £100,000 from Virginia tobacco shipped to England. When the more salubrious Williamsburg was made the colonial capital of Virginia in 1699, Jamestown dwindled in significance.

By 1700, all but Georgia of the thirteen original English colonies had been founded, with a population of about a half million. But Virginia was the most prosperous of them all because of its prized strain of tobacco and profit-heavy plantation economy worked by African slaves, who, from the 1680s, began arriving in the southern states at the rate of sixty thousand a decade. The U.S. Congress forbade the importation of slaves in 1808, but the South's "peculiar institution" had already been so long enmeshed with its economic and cultural life that only a massive internecine conflict could put an end to it (see Question 138).

121 ∼ Who built the first astronomical telescope?

Galileo Galilei in 1609

DANISH ASTRONOMER TYCHO BRAHE (1546–1601), lacking a telescope, had spent decades performing the most accurate observations of the heavens up to his time. He'd struggled against Copernicus's conclusions, holding out for a hybrid system in which the earth remained at the center of the universe, but everything else revolved around the sun (see Question 114). In 1600, he met Johannes Kepler (1571–1630), and the two began collaborating near Prague.

After Tycho died suddenly in 1601, Kepler began to analyze the Dane's extensive observations with an eye toward finding general mathematical laws. His massive computations kept running into the same obstacle: Nothing seemed to work as long as one assumed that planetary motions had to be perfectly circular, as Aristotle and Ptolemy had decreed.

In 1609, however, Kepler announced a discovery that would banish Ptolemy's epicycles and bring the rough edges of Copernicus's system into smooth alignment: Planets move not in circles, but *in elliptical orbits with the sun at one focus*. All of Tycho's painstaking observations fell into place under this, Kepler's first law of planetary motion.

In the same year, Galileo Galilei (1564–1642) heard rumors of a Dutch novelty item that could cause distant objects to seem near. Unable to track down one of these "lookers," Galileo, who supported himself partly by making scientific instruments, built a working model in July 1609 that was more than twice as powerful as anything available. It was a fateful match of spyglass and eye. Over the next six months, Galileo made astronomical observations so revelatory that modern observational astronomy can be said to begin with them. Hailed by Kepler for bolstering the Copernican model, Galileo's reports of what he saw through his telescope rocked European society, infuriated Aristotelians, and eventually brought down the wrath of the inquisitorial guardians of the Catholic Church.

Given the simplicity of the basic refracting telescope, it's surprising that it took so long to be developed. People had been using *lesenstein*—naturally occurring, slightly convex, transparent "reading stones"—to enlarge texts for centuries. Magnifying lenses awaited the invention of rather clunky metal frames to hold them before reading glasses began to appear in Florence around 1270.

The idea of a magnifying instrument went back further. Drawing on the sophisticated optics of Muslim scientists, Roger Bacon had written of lenses that could "cause the sun, moon, and stars in appearance to descend here below" in his *Opus Majus* of 1267. Bacon's work inspired Leonard Digges, an Oxford man, to devise "proportional glasses" sometime before 1559 to allow him to see things far off, according to seemingly reliable reports by his son, but these accounts appeared in English at a time when almost no one on the Continent paid attention to our language, so they gained little attention.

Descriptions of similar devices were in circulation, often mingling with tales of fabulous mirrors that could set invading fleets on fire, empower initiates to see anything going on anywhere, or enable instant global telecommunication via images projected on the moon. The first public acknowledgment of a cylindrical tube that magnified objects using two glass lenses was far more mundane, occurring in September 1608, when Dutch lens maker Hans Lippershey of Zeeland filed for a patent. Before the authorities in The Hague could even rule on his application, two other alleged inventors surfaced, one of whom was Zacharias Janssen, a Dutch spectacle maker and former coin counterfeiter, who had invented a microscope in 1590. Very soon there were at least nine claimants.

The Dutch authorities eventually paid Lippershey to produce a few "perspectives" for military purposes but disallowed the patent. The design was so simple, they claimed, it would be impossible to protect the method of its manufacture. The telescope, about twelve to fourteen inches in length, magnified objects only three times and was regarded by many as a toy.

Once Galileo had confirmed the existence of the new device, which was selling in fancy shops in Paris and elsewhere, he made his own model in twenty-four hours. He kept improving it, grinding his own lenses and calculating the optimal angles and lens thicknesses until, on August 23, 1609, he presented to the Venetian senate a telescope that magnified eight times. He wrote:

> It is six days since I was called by the Signoria [ruling council], to which I had to show it together with the entire Senate, to the infinite amazement of all; and there have been numerous gentlemen and senators who, though old, have more than once climbed the stairs of the highest campaniles in Venice to observe at sea sails and vessels so far away that, coming under full sail to port, two hours and more were required before they could be seen without my spyglass.

Venice was an independent state, always on the lookout for defense upgrades, as well as a commercial powerhouse in which profits were linked to the speed of information. Galileo, who as a professor at the University of Padua was an employee of the Venetian state, gave the city rights to manufacture the scope but was less than entirely satisfied with the pay raise he received in return. Besides, the heavens beckoned. Galileo blazed into activity at this point. He knew others were also building powerful telescopes, and it was only a matter of time before everything that these devices could reveal would be discovered, if not by him, then by others.

By late in the year he had developed a fourth telescope—he later called it "Old Discoverer"—that magnified twenty times. About thirty-six inches in length, it had glass that was full of little bubbles and was tinged green by the presence of iron. The lenses were good near the center but poor near the periphery, limiting the telescope's field of view to about a quarter of the full moon.

In November to December 1609, Galileo aimed Old Discoverer at the moon and made detailed drawings. In December to January, he turned to more distant objects, and, according to astronomer N. M. Swerdlow, "He made more discoveries with his telescope that changed the world than anyone has ever made before or since." What Galileo saw was so extraordinary that he quickly wrote *The Starry Messenger*, a short exposition of his key observations that became an instant sensation when it came off the Venetian presses on March 12, 1610.

Kings, princes, and military leaders across Europe clamored for his instruments, and he obliged by supplying over one hundred of them along with his pamphlet to nobles, scientists (including Kepler), cardinals, and at least one queen—Marie de' Medici of France, who reportedly fell on her knees to look through the scope rather than wait for it to be properly set up at a window. Within five years, Galileo's little book was available in Chinese.

The Starry Messenger announced a lunar surface "full of vast protuberances . . . just like the face of the earth itself," it reported that the Milky Way consisted of a vast number of individual stars, and it revealed that four small bodies revolved around Jupiter. (Naming them "Medicean Stars" helped Galileo to a lifetime position in Florence.)

Each of these revelations held portentous implications for understanding the universe. If the moon was rough and mutable like earth, Aristotle's idea of an absolute chasm separating our messy sublunary realm from the perfect, unchanging heavens was fatally undermined. If the Milky Way consisted of millions of stars, then the universe was far larger than Ptolemy thought. If Jupiter had moons revolving around it, then the heavens could accommodate several orbital centers. One by one, the arguments and assumptions of the geocentrists were falling before something more potent than Copernicus's logic: ocular proof.

Galileo didn't openly declare Copernicus to be right, but he articulated the authority that science would use to debunk Aristotle, Ptolemy, and religious resistance to a heliocentric model of the universe:

> In making the celestial material alterable, I contradict the doctrine of Aristotle much less than do those people who still want to keep the sky inalterable; for I am sure that he never took its inalterability to be as certain as the fact that all human reasoning must be placed second to direct experience.

Not that everyone was immediately persuaded. Some major mathematicians and clerics refused to look through the telescope. One claimed that Galileo had cleverly smuggled a fake model of Jupiter's moons inside the instrument—which prompted the scientist to offer a hefty reward to anyone who succeeded in building such a device.

Galileo kept at it, observing the phases of Venus late in 1610, sunspots in 1611, and the puzzling appearance of Saturn. By 1612, almost everything of astronomical import that the Galilean telescope could make visible had been seen, and the initial burst of telescopic exploration came to an end.

Even as his observations—joined with Kepler's computations— began to persuade the world that Copernicus was essentially correct, Galileo's aggressive intelligence was getting him into serious difficulties with the Catholic Church. The man who transformed a mere toy into the tool that helped demolish Ptolemy's universe would be compelled, at age sixty-nine and nearly blind, to kneel before ten cardinals, ask pardon for saying the earth moved, and pretend to retract his scientific statements. Today as the Hubble and other giant telescopes are on the verge of seeing the beginnings of the cosmos, they are furthering Galileo's quest for direct experience of the unknown.

—*Tom Matrullo*

122 ✎ What was the first great novel of world literature?

Miguel de Cervantes Saavedra's Don Quixote, *completed in 1615*

IN HIS 1920 STUDY *The Theory of the Novel*, the Hungarian Marxist philosopher and literary critic Georg Lukács referred to *Don Quixote* as "the first great novel of world literature," which "stands at the time when the Christian God began to forsake the world; when man became lonely and could find meaning only in his own soul, whose home was nowhere." Like many others, Mexican novelist Carlos Fuentes called the book "the first modern novel," while Spanish author and philosopher Miguel de Unamuno considered it "the Spanish Bible." In 2002, one hundred major writers from fifty-four countries voted it the world's best work of fiction.

Long before writing *The Ingenious Gentleman Don Quixote of La Mancha*, Miguel de Cervantes Saavedra (1547–1616) acquitted himself bravely at the horrifically bloody naval battle of Lepanto (1571), in which the Turkish fleet was shattered by Christian allies under Don Juan of Austria. Cervantes permanently lost the use of his left hand, which was hit by gunshot, but he was proud of the nickname he acquired—*El Manco de Lepanto*, "The Maimed Man of Lepanto." On his way home to Spain in 1575, he was captured by Barbary pirates and spent five years as a prisoner at the Casbah in Algiers before being ransomed. Changing trades, he wrote assiduously, especially for the stage, but besides *Don Quixote*, only his *Exemplary Novels* (1613)—a collection of a dozen wry stories—is held in high critical esteem. Imprisoned twice for fiscal irregularities while working as a tax collector, Cervantes may have begun writing *Don Quixote* during his second stint behind bars.

In part I of the novel (1605; part II, 1615), we meet an unmarried fifty-year-old hidalgo, a member of the lowest rung of the nobility, who neglects his humble estate in the arid Spanish province of La Mancha, south of Madrid, preferring to spend all his time reading. Although the narrator is unsure of the man's name at this point—we later find out it is Alonso Quixano, called "the Good"—one thing is certain: His obsessive hobby of reading chivalric romances, like *Amadís of Gaul* (1508) and other Arthurian and Carolingian tales of knights and fair ladies—with their assorted paraphernalia of damsels in distress, wizards, ogres, and dragons—has addled his brains.

Having lost the ability to distinguish between fiction and reality, the tall, gaunt hidalgo decides to rename himself Don Quixote de La Mancha (basically "Sir Thigh-Armor from Sheboygan") and take as his ladylove a zaftig peasant girl he had espied in a nearby village and developed a crush on from afar, renaming her Dulcinea del Toboso ("Sweetie Pie from Rockville"). Accoutered in his great-grandfather's mildewed armor, complete with lance, sword, and shield, he rides off on his emaciated nag Rocinante one July day before dawn (having neglected to inform his niece and the housekeeper) in the guise of a knight-errant to right the world's wrongs and combat injustice everywhere.

After riding all day without encountering any adventures, the newly minted Don, starved and tired, seeks lodging at a sordid inn he mistakes for a castle. The innkeeper, soon realizing he's dealing with a lunatic, agrees to dub him a knight despite Quixote's lacking the wherewithal to pay for his meal and his having attacked two mule drivers in a scuffle over his armor in the courtyard. On his second day of knight-errantry, Don Quixote vainly attempts to prevent a servant boy from being lashed by his master. Then, after trying to force a group of merchants from Toledo to acknowledge the peerless beauty of Dulcinea, he receives a sound drubbing from one of their muleteers. Lucky for him, he's found in the road by a farmer who knows him and takes him home on his donkey, sorely bruised and battered.

The village priest and the barber, concerned friends of the Don, try to weed out the most offensive books from his library of chivalric works, but the housekeeper burns them all. After a few weeks of recuperation at home, Quixote determines that what he really needs is a squire, so he recruits the fat, gullible peasant Sancho Panza ("Holy Belly") by promising him the governorship of an island they would conquer. The unlikely pair set out secretly one night, the Don on Rocinante and huge-bellied Sancho on his petite dapple donkey.

Their first adventure is the archetypal quixotic one of tilting at windmills. Gustave Doré's illustration of the Don and Rocinante smashing hard into the sail of the mill is a fit emblem for Quixote's perpetual clash with recalcitrant reality. When the knight had informed his squire of his intention to rid the world of those "thirty or more enormous giants," Sancho had sensibly asked, "What giants?" Now, as the Don is helped to his feet, he, too, sees they are just windmills but explains that a spiteful enchanter has turned the giants into them to rob him of his victory. And this sets the pattern for the knight's rationalizations for his many future fiascoes, followed by an often hilarious discussion of the incident between the grandiloquent Don, with his head up in the clouds—or somewhere else—and the walking anthology of proverbs, clichés, malapropisms, and rustically shrewd observations that is Sancho Panza.

Cervantes's book starts off as a travesty of the more absurd conventions of literary chivalry—though Jorge Luis Borges claimed it was less an attack than "a secret, nostalgic farewell"—but soon takes off in a compelling direction of its own, raising issues of human identity and fulfillment and of the attempt to impose order and meaning on a world indifferent or hostile to human wishes. Indeed, the death of the chivalric age had given birth to something starker and tawdrier, prompting Lukács to call *Don Quixote* "the first great battle of interiority against the prosaic vulgarity of outward life." An unhinged mind in revolt against such vulgarity may thus easily mistake a barber's glistening brass basin for Ariosto's golden helmet of Mambrino, which conferred invulnerability on its wearer.

In one of his most heroic and idealistic enterprises, the Don liberates a chain gang of condemned criminals who are being sent to work as galley slaves. As recompense, he demands only that the former captives make their way to El Toboso and present themselves to Dulcinea, but the ingrates, who have other travel plans, pelt him with stones instead. After several other ludicrous deeds—including sending Sancho with a love letter to Dulcinea (never delivered), performing harsh penances for his lady in his lovelorn state, and slashing an inn's huge wineskin, mistaking it for a giant with an inordinate amount of blood inside him—Don Quixote is tracked down by the authorities for having freed the convicts. The priest and the barber, who have journeyed out to bring the Don home, convince them not to arrest the obviously deranged old gentleman. They then have the Don tied up in his sleep and concoct a story about how an enchanter has pronounced that he must return home in a cage mounted on an oxcart if he wishes to be joined in marriage to Dulcinea someday. And thus was it done, with Quixote arriving at his village in broad daylight in that deplorable state.

The book was an immediate success in Spain, though Cervantes didn't seem to profit much from it. The novel's most brilliant feature is the prickly relationship that develops between the Don and his paunchy squire, who are often seen as a soul/body Cartesian dichotomy avant la lettre (see Question 125). It is a commonplace of Cervantes criticism that, in this antithetical friendship, Sancho gradually becomes quixotized—learning to use the archaically orotund language of chivalry, for example, to try to influence his master's actions—just as Quixote becomes somewhat more sanchified.

After a rip-off continuation of the book was published in 1614 by a writer who called himself Alonso Fernández de Avellaneda, Cervantes rushed to complete the last fifteen chapters of the sequel he himself had been working on, publishing it in 1615. He thus sent the dynamic duo off on another expedition, in which the problematic nature of literary characters who have become celebrities becomes a major theme and source of humor.

Early in part II, Sancho turns the tables on his master. Entrusted with going on ahead into El Toboso to inform Dulcinea that the Don wishes to pay her a visit, the crafty squire (who has lied about delivering Quixote's love letter to her) convinces the knight that his beatific lady is actually a chunky, moon-faced, snub-nosed, garlic-breathed peasant girl with a trace of a mustache who happens to be riding by with two friends. We and the Don are startled when, thrown off her jackass, the pseudo-Dulcinea remounts by getting a running start behind it, putting her hands up on its rump, and landing nimbly on its back. As expected, Quixote explains her disappointing appearance as the effect of an enchanter's evil magic on his eyes alone—because Sancho claims to see her as wondrously beautiful.

Because many of the characters in part II of the novel have read part I, the narrative mirrors within mirrors multiply. Just as Don Quixote's reading has crazed him, reading about him has caused a craze—even within his own book. The main adventure in part II is the extended stay of Quixote and Sancho as guests of a duke and duchess who humor and deceive the famous pair at their palace for the entertainment of themselves and their court. In one ruse, "Merlin," in the guise of a skeleton, eerily announces that the only way for Dulcinea to be disenchanted is for the pain-averse Sancho to self-administer 3,300 lashes on his fat, naked buttocks (which he later feigns to do out of view of his master while howling convincingly). The snarky nobles prey on Quixote's delusions by having a page disguise himself as Dulcinea, and they also trick the Don and his terrified squire, both blindfolded, into believing they're flying through the heavens on a magical wooden horse.

It is here that Sancho is fooled into thinking he has finally been made governor of an island (actually a town belonging to the duke and duchess, where everyone plays along with the joke). To prepare him for his responsibilities, Don Quixote counsels him to refrain from eating garlic and onions and from belching in anyone's face. In his weeklong governorship, Sancho proves himself "a second Solomon," handing down remarkably sagacious decisions in the cases brought before him. But the noble tricksters put Sancho on a starvation diet for laughs and end up causing him to be trampled underfoot during a simulated invasion of his realm, while they mercilessly tease the sexually inexperienced Don with a saucy servant girl.

Having had enough, Quixote and Sancho make their way to Barcelona. There, Sansón Carrasco, a young friend of the Don disguised as the Knight of the White Moon, challenges him to single combat, unhorses him, and imposes on him the condition that he has to forswear knight-errantry for at least a year. Afflicted with melancholia, the Don speaks to Sancho of adopting the pastoral life as the shepherds Quixotiz and Pancino, but after they're stampeded by a herd of pigs, nothing comes of the plan and the pair returns home.

The mild-mannered hidalgo formerly known as Don Quixote takes to his bed for six days with a fever, then sleeps six hours straight, wakes up sane, renounces his past buffooneries, receives the sacraments, makes his will, and dies, while Sancho weeps inconsolably. Having discarded his idée fixe, Alonso Quixano the Good recovers his sanity, which is also his death sentence.

The book of which he is the heroic antihero has inspired a wide gamut of criticism, from the humanitarian, sentimental, and romantic nineteenth-century viewpoint to the comical and conservative estimate of Quixote as a blundering fool. Herman Melville called Don Quixote the "sagest sage that ever lived," Unamuno thought of him as a saint, and Harold Bloom judged Cervantes's book "the best of all novels." A representative opposing voice is that of Erich Auerbach, who wrote that "the whole book is a comedy in which well-founded reality holds madness up to ridicule," though admitting that, through all his failures, Don Quixote "preserves a natural dignity and superiority."

Literary critic and art historian Wylie Sypher defined high comedy as "a victory over our absurdities . . . won at a cost of humility." But in *Don Quixote*, as in tragedy, the protagonist dies at the end. Like an Ibsen character, the Don remains viable only as long as his illusions persist. Cervantes himself died in Madrid on April 22, 1616, less than a year after describing the demise of a character who, like Faust, Don Juan, and Robinson Crusoe, embodies one of the chief literary archetypes of the modern Western world.

123 ∽ Who first discovered the circulation of the blood?

William Harvey in 1616; his book on it was published in 1628

THE FUNCTIONS OF BLOOD AND THE HUMAN circulatory system were the subjects of much conjecture in antiquity. The Greek physician Hippocrates (c. 460–c. 370 BC) believed that blood was constantly produced in the liver and spleen, whereupon it traveled to the heart to be warmed or cooled by the air reaching the chest via the trachea. Based on his dissections of animals and some human cadavers, the Greco-Roman physician Galen (AD c. 129–200) described both bright and dark red blood. He believed that bright red blood was produced in the heart and propelled by pulsations in the artery walls, that dark red blood was produced in the liver, and that both types were delivered to the peripheral tissues once and totally consumed therein. This Galenic tradition remained influential for more than a millennium after his death.

Several individuals made noteworthy contributions to the transition from Galen's notions to a scientifically correct description of circulation. Ibn al-Nafis (c. 1213–88), an Arab physician born near Damascus who worked in Cairo, described the pulmonary circulation—the portion of the circulatory system that carries deoxygenated blood from the heart to the lungs and returns oxygenated blood to the heart—in his *Commentary on the Anatomy of the Canon of Avicenna*, published in 1242.

Three centuries later, Michael Servetus (1511–53), a Spanish theologian and anatomist, published a description of the pulmonary circulation that may actually have reflected the rediscovery of Ibn al-Nafis's writings. Similarly, Realdo Colombo (1516–59), an Italian professor of anatomy and surgery at the University of Padua, also described the pulmonary circulation in a work that may have reflected extensive use of Servetus's writings without attribution. Colombo's own research was important, however, because it included observations of the functioning of the heart and lungs of small live animals.

Another Italian professor of anatomy and surgery at the University of Padua, Hieronymus Fabricius (1537–1619), conducted dissections of animals and thereby discovered the membranous folds in the interior of veins, which he termed "valves" and are now known to prevent the backward flow of blood. This discovery helped refine the interests of the English physician who would later provide the first scientifically correct description of the circulatory system.

William Harvey (1578–1657), born in Folkestone, Kent, received a bachelor of arts degree from Gonville and Caius College, Cambridge, before traveling to Italy to study medicine at the University of Padua. He remained there twenty-eight months, working under Fabricius's supervision, until graduating in 1602. Harvey did not find Fabricius's explanation of the functioning of the valves in the veins to be convincing, and this eventually spurred him to investigate the larger question of the movement of the blood. His investigations, which employed vivi-sections, noninvasive experiments, and logical calculations, eventually yielded a correct description of both the pulmonary and the systemic circulation.

The results of Harvey's studies were initially presented in a long series of lectures to London's Royal College of Physicians, beginning in 1616. A more influential outlet for his ideas, however, was a ground-breaking work published in Frankfurt in 1628 entitled *De Motu Cordis et Sanguinis in Animalibus* (*On the Motion of the Heart and Blood in Animals*).

The first several chapters of Harvey's book describe movements of intact animal hearts, arteries, and heart chambers as observed during vivisections. Chapters 5 to 8 present the essence of his ideas—that the heart functions by contractility and that the circulation is a closed system—and several subsequent chapters provide further evidence for his beliefs. Chapter 9, for example, presents calculations that use exper-imental measurements of the volume of the left ventricle of the heart, in combination with reasonable, conservative estimates for heart rate and the volume of blood pumped per contraction. The results demonstrated that the hearts of various types of animals pump far more blood per unit time than could possibly be consumed in the peripheral tissues, thereby refuting the Galenist perspective. Chapter 11 describes another famous experiment, in which a ligature is applied to and then removed from an arm. The resulting changes in the appearance of the veins and the tem-perature of the skin supported the concept of a closed circulation.

Late in the book, in his remarkable, two-sentence Chapter 14, Har-vey summarizes his argument for a closed systemic circulation. Here is the second sentence, slightly abridged:

> Since all things . . . show that the blood passes through the
> lungs and heart by the force of the ventricles, and is sent for
> distribution to all parts of the body, where it makes its way
> into the veins and porosities of the flesh, and then flows by the
> veins from the circumference on every side to the center, from
> the lesser to the greater veins, and is by them finally
> discharged into the vena cava and right auricle of the heart,
> and this in such a quantity . . . as cannot possibly be supplied
> by the ingesta, and is much greater than can be required for
> mere purposes of nutrition; it is absolutely necessary to

conclude that the blood in the animal body is impelled in a
circle, and is in a state of ceaseless motion; that this is the act
or function which the heart performs by means of its pulse;
and that it is the sole and only end of the motion and
contraction of the heart.

Harvey's work is particularly impressive in that he inferred the
closed nature of the circulatory system without the aid of microscopy.
The definitive proof was provided by the anatomist Marcello Malpighi
of the University of Bologna, who in 1661 described the capillary
network—the link between the arterial and venous circulations—on the
basis of microscopic studies.

Although William Harvey's work represented a radical departure
from traditional thinking, it eventually attained acceptance within his
own lifetime, at least in part from his publishing a refutation of various
criticisms in 1649 and from the appearance of an English version of his
book in 1653. His description of the circulatory system established car-
diology as a branch of medicine, and his experimental use of all major
classes of vertebrates, including fish, amphibians, reptiles, birds, and
mammals, provided a basis for comparative physiology. In addition, his
use of well-conceived experiments in combination with logical calculations established him as the father of quantitative biology.

—*William A. Walsh*

124 ∾ What was the first collection of Shakespeare's plays?

The First Folio, edited by John Heminge and Henry Condell in 1623

IF IT HADN'T BEEN FOR two of William Shakespeare's friends and fellow
actors, who collected his plays and published them in a single volume
known as the First Folio seven years after his death in 1616, we would
have lost about half of his dramas: *Henry VI (Part 1)*, *The Comedy of
Errors*, *The Taming of the Shrew*, *The Two Gentlemen of Verona*, *King
John*, *Julius Caesar*, *As You Like It*, *Twelfth Night*, *All's Well That Ends
Well*, *Measure for Measure*, *Macbeth*, *Antony and Cleopatra*, *Coriolanus*,

Timon of Athens, *Cymbeline*, *The Winter's Tale*, *The Tempest*, and *Henry VIII*. These eighteen of the thirty-six plays in the First Folio (a folio is a large-size book) had never been printed before, and four other plays would have survived only in garbled form, since they had been printed only as "bad quartos" (a quarto is a small-size book). Of the generally accepted Shakespearean plays, the First Folio failed to contain only *Pericles*. Though a quarto of that play attributing it to him had been published in 1609, Shakespeare seems to have written only parts of it.

When Shakespeare died at age fifty-two, he himself had not taken any steps to have any of his plays printed or collected, and he did not mention them in his will. Plays weren't yet considered serious literature in those pre-postmodernist days, and the first Englishman to publish a collection of his best plays was Shakespeare's ego-enhanced friend Ben Jonson in his *Works* of 1616. While a play was still in its repertoire, the theatrical company that had paid for it to be written (usually about £6) would not want to see it published, because other companies might then stage it themselves when on tour in the provinces or readers of the play would not bother attending London performances. Fourteen of Shakespeare's plays had nonetheless been sold to printers and published in separate quarto versions authorized by his acting company during his lifetime, and *Othello* was first published after his death in 1622. Four other plays had appeared in pirated versions, either reconstructed from an actor's memory (though this theory has been attacked), taken down in shorthand during a performance, or set from a purloined promptbook—what John Heminge and Henry Condell referred to in their preface to the First Folio as "diverse stolen and surreptitious copies, maimed and deformed by the frauds and stealths of injurious imposters." These bad quartos of Shakespearean plays were often abridged versions that were sloppily printed with corrupt texts and many errors.

In his will, Shakespeare had bequeathed twenty-six shillings eight pence each to Heminge, Condell, and the great tragic actor Richard Burbage, his fellow members in the King's Men Company, to buy rings for themselves in his memory. Heminge and Condell did a lot more than that, eventually setting themselves the enormous task of comparing the texts of the company's playbooks and other manuscripts with the existing quarto versions of Shakespeare's plays (some of which had more than one)—all with the goal of bringing out a complete one-volume collection. Besides wanting to honor their departed friend, Heminge and

Condell may have been reacting to an attempt to publish a collection of some of Shakespeare's plays by one Thomas Pavier in 1619.

The First Folio—*Mr. William Shakespeares Comedies, Histories, & Tragedies. Published According to the True Originall Copies*—appeared in London in 1623, printed by Isaac Jaggard and Edward Blount with the backing of several other printers. Despite the obvious reverence of Heminge and Condell for their late friend and his work, the First Folio abounds in errors and sometimes omits passages that appeared in earlier quartos, perhaps because they had been deleted from the company's acting version. If no quarto existed for a play, Shakespeare's original manuscript, as emended for acting purposes, may have been used as the textual source.

Of the First Folio print run of about one thousand copies, almost one quarter have survived. But Isaac Jaggard came out with three different issues that incorporated at least a hundred stop-press corrections made at various stages of printing by as many as nine compositors, who were more or less conscientious about entering proofreaders' changes. These and many other printing irregularities have brought it about that each surviving copy of the book is different from all others.

Nonetheless, the editing quandaries faced by Heminge and Condell were formidable. The First Folio text of *Hamlet*, for example, is missing about two hundred lines that appear in Quarto 2 (Q2) of 1604–5. It also has Hamlet saying

> *Oh that this too too solid Flesh, would melt,*
> *Thaw, and resolve it selfe into a Dew* (1.2.129–130).

In Q1 (a bad quarto of 1603) and Q2, Hamlet's flesh is "sallied" (meaning "attacked," which doesn't make much sense). Was the "sallied" of the two quartos just a misprint for "solid" or someone's uninspired correction for "sullied," a word that was uncommon at the time? For *Hamlet*, modern editors usually ignore Q1 (a pirated version often thought to have been based on the memory of the actor who had the bit role of Marcellus) and create a text that incorporates all the passages found in both Q2 and the First Folio (which has about ninety lines not found in Q2), choosing whichever readings make the most sense.

For *Othello*, the only quarto (1622) features a lot of profanity (e.g., "Zouns" for "God's wounds") and many stage directions, whereas the First Folio text, published in the very next year, has had much of its profanity toned down or omitted (reflecting a law of 1606 muzzling such speech onstage), has fewer stage directions, and includes about 160 lines not in the quarto, including Desdemona's melancholic "Willow Song" in Act 4, Scene 3. The only quarto of *King Lear* is a bad one of 1608, yet the First Folio text (which leaves out about 300 lines from the quarto version and adds several new passages) was based on it—after the extensive ministrations of an unknown editor—so the textual problems raised by this play, usually considered Shakespeare's greatest, are numerous and vexing.

On a more carping level, Samuel Johnson, in the preface to his edition of Shakespeare in 1765, complained that Heminge and Condell, who grouped the thirty-six plays under the rubrics of comedies (fourteen), histories (ten), and tragedies (twelve), "seem not to have distinguished the three kinds by any very exact or definite ideas." He claimed that their notion of a comedy, for example, was any play "which ended happily to the principal persons, however serious or distressful through its intermediate incidents." (Later criticism has dubbed dramas such as *Measure for Measure* and *All's Well That Ends Well* "problem plays" or "dark plays," though the First Folio subsumes them under "comedies." Consider also the ghastly "pound of flesh" bond in another supposed comedy, *The Merchant of Venice*, and the hauntingly somber aspects of late "comedies," such as *The Winter's Tale* and *The Tempest*.) Dr. Johnson also questioned the First Folio's apparent assumption that a tragedy was simply a play with "a calamitous conclusion," no matter how much interpolated tomfoolery had occurred along the way. Furthermore, the history plays were not always "very nicely distinguished from tragedy."

To descend to an even more trivial consideration of the deficiencies of the First Folio, we might mention that some of the plays are divided into acts and scenes and some just into acts. The stage directions, indications of entrances and exits, and lists of characters are done haphazardly, and mistakes occur in the running heads and pagination. Because of last-minute copyright problems, *Troilus and Cressida* doesn't appear in the table of contents, and the play itself is scrunched in at the beginning of the tragedy grouping, with several of its first pages misnumbered and the rest of the play left unpaginated and undivided into acts or scenes. The spelling of the First Folio is wildly inconsistent (as it generally was at the time), with even the name of an editor spelled as Heminge or Hemmings in different places. "Tymon of Athens" in the title of the play yields to "Timon" almost everywhere else.

With all its imperfections, the First Folio, coming in at a bit over nine hundred pages, constitutes one of the very greatest cultural treasures of the human race: the unlikely legacy of a frumpy, baldpated Shakespeare—whose head seems to be floating, severed, on his huge starched collar—in the amateurish woodcut engraving by Flemish artist Martin Droeshout that was prefixed to the collection. It is a far cry from the so-called Cobbe portrait, an anonymous oil painting of a handsome and modish man in his early forties that was judged by some scholars in 2009 to be an authentic representation of the world's foremost dramatist.

The tome sold well. The Second Folio (1632) was a reprint in which a brief poetic tribute by the young John Milton appeared (sample: "Thou in our wonder and astonishment / Hast built thyself a livelong Monument"). The third edition came out in 1663; its second issue, in the following year, included seven additional plays, of which only *Pericles* is usually considered to be mostly the work of Shakespeare. The Fourth Folio was published in 1685.

The first "real editor" of Shakespeare's works was the poet laureate and dramatist Nicholas Rowe, whose editions of 1709 and 1714 carefully marked entrances and exits, standardized act and scene divisions, and added stage directions and place headings. More important, he made significant textual corrections and modernized spelling and punctuation. Alexander Pope's idiosyncratic edition (1725) was mainly characterized by willful tampering with the text. Lewis Theobald, who pointed out some of Pope's mistakes and supplied many excellent emendations in his Shakespeare edition of 1733, thereby earned the title of "King of the Dunces" in the earlier version of Pope's *Dunciad*. Edward Capell, in his 1768 edition of Shakespeare, was the first to collate all available quartos in the attempt to arrive at an authoritative text. Since the late nineteenth century, scholarly standard editions of Shakespeare's complete works have proliferated.

In the years since the First Folio's thirty-six plays were augmented by *Pericles*, the Shakespearean canon has grown, though at the pace of "the whining schoolboy . . . creeping like snail / Unwillingly to school" (*As You Like It*, 2.7.145–147). *The Two Noble Kinsmen*, a comedy dating from about 1612 and based on Geoffrey Chaucer's "The Knight's Tale" (see Question 103), may have been written, like *Henry VIII*, by Shakespeare in collaboration with John Fletcher. *Edward III*, written in the early 1590s, was recognized by some scholars in the late twentieth century as Shakespeare's thirty-ninth play, in whole or in part. Even more recently, a fortieth play may have been admitted to the most exclusive club in dramatic literature: *Cardenio, or the Second Maiden's Tragedy*, another work sometimes attributed to Shakespeare and Fletcher and based on a subplot in Thomas Shelton's translation of *Don Quixote* (see Question 122). For *The Booke of Sir Thomas More* (c. 1600), a play written mostly by Anthony Munday, we have three and a half manuscript pages, thought to be in Shakespeare's handwriting, of a scene of 147 lines in which More calms an unruly London mob that wants to attack foreigners.

A long ode by Ben Jonson with a long title—"To the Memory of My Beloved, the Author Mr. William Shakespeare, and What He Hath Left Us"—which was prefaced to the First Folio, gave rise to several common phrases applied to the Bard, such as his having had "small Latin and less Greek" (at least by comparison with Jonson's prodigious erudition). Addressing his departed friend and rival as "sweet swan of Avon" and "soul of the age! / The applause! delight! the wonder of our stage!" Jonson presciently informed us that Shakespeare "was not of an age, but for all time!"

125 ～ What was the first work of modern philosophy?

Discourse on the Method *by René Descartes, 1637*

JUST THREE CHARACTERS APPEAR IN *Discourse on the Method*, René Descartes's first published work of philosophy: the author, Aristotle, and God. Since God serves mainly as a sledgehammer for demolishing Aristotle, that pretty much clears the field of all cogitators except Descartes.

His *Discourse on the Method of Rightly Conducting the Reason and Seeking Truth in the Sciences*, which he calls "a history, or if you prefer, a fable," announces its modernity in the spare, conversational voice that greets us:

> Good sense is, of all things, the most widely shared; for each
> person thinks that he is so abundantly equipped with it that even

those who are most difficult to please in everything else are not
accustomed to desire more sense than they already have.

The outcome of one's experience of Descartes (1596–1650)
largely depends on the degree of irony one hears in those words. If little
or none, you have Voltaire's Pangloss. Mild irony gives you Jane
Austen, Henry Fielding, or Laurence Sterne. Too much, and you're
verging on Cervantean madness (see Question 122). For Descartes is
up to something strange and bold in his philosophical fable, and the
stakes are high. As science essayist Carl Zimmer recently put it, "No
one's soul would be the same after Descartes."

In 1596, when Descartes was born into a well-to-do family of
lawyers and judges, Kepler hadn't done the math that supported Copernicus, Galileo had not yet looked through a telescope, and William Harvey probably hadn't dissected his first chicken (see Questions 114, 121,
and 123).

By the time the Frenchman introduced his philosophic method
forty-one years later, the learned world had seen the invention and
utilization of logarithms, the slide rule, the pendulum clock, the microscope, the telescope, the air pump, and devices to measure heat. Discoveries by Galileo and Kepler had advanced the case for heliocentrism,
and Harvey had unfolded the complex human circulatory system.

But these breakthroughs were occurring in a cloistered environment
that exerted tight controls over the use of reason. In Paris, for example,
in 1609—the same year Dutch telescopes became faddish—chemists
were legally required to subscribe to the teachings of Aristotle "on pain
of death." Aristotelian concepts of nature and man still dominated science as taught in the schools, much as Ptolemy's system ruled the heavens, and revelation guided theology. The world was torn between active
exploration and institutional surveillance of intellectual endeavor.
Descartes's Jesuit teachers at La Flèche, considered one of the best
schools in Europe, celebrated Galileo's discoveries, even as their order
closely monitored scholarship and censored signs of dangerous thought.

After graduating from law school and savoring Parisian life for
a few years, Descartes decided to see the world, as he recounts in the
Discourse:

> I spent the rest of my youth traveling, visiting courts and armies,
> mixing with people of diverse temperaments and ranks, gathering

various experiences, testing myself in the situations which fortune
offered me, and at all times reflecting upon whatever came my
way so as to derive some profit from it.

In joining the army, he was able to travel and reflect, since volunteers never actually fought and had plenty of leisure—he himself never
rose before ten a.m. He was also on hand for several memorable battles,
including the siege of La Rochelle, a Huguenot bastion, by Cardinal
Richelieu in 1627.

His travels enabled him to gather intelligence across a very broad
spectrum of European science. He met mathematicians, lens makers,
astronomers, and almost certainly a few Rosicrucians, adepts of a
secret society dedicated to dark arts of universal knowledge. By 1628
he had settled in Holland—though "settled" is perhaps not the word for
a spirit that relocated more than thirteen times in as many years.

Over the next two decades he wrote all his major works, and while
today he haunts academic departments of philosophy, the townspeople
of Leiden and elsewhere knew him as the man seen purchasing freshly
slaughtered animals at the butcher's. Visitors to his lodgings recalled
his pointing to dissected calves' heads and saying, "These are my
books." Indeed, a central theme in Descartes's *Discourse* was a rejection of books as primary sources of learning: "I entirely abandoned the
study of letters, resolving to seek no knowledge other than that which
could be found in myself or else in the great book of the world."

Perhaps to drive that point home, his first book was a treatise on
physics called *The World* (*Le Monde*). It cost him four years and was in
the final stages of preparation for the printer in 1633 when he learned
of Galileo's trial and condemnation by the church. Descartes withdrew
it, hoping for a more favorable moment. He explained to his Jesuit
friend and mentor Marin Mersenne that "if [the movement of the earth]
is false, all the foundations of my philosophy are false too."

Because of his impact on metaphysics, Descartes's deep involvement with the physical sciences is often overlooked. In optics, he specified the law of refraction; in meteorology, he furthered understanding
of barometric pressure; his view of animal bodies as machines has
caused him to be called the founder of modern biology; he was the first
to envision contact lenses (although they were conceived by Leonardo
da Vinci, a worthy forebear) as lying directly on the cornea. He did
seminal research and thinking in dynamics, mechanics, psychology,

and cosmology, developing a vortex theory of universe formation famously attacked by Isaac Newton.

Nowhere did Descartes's scientific efforts leave a stronger mark than on mathematics, where "Cartesian" coordinates made possible the convergence of algebra and geometry. His realization that any geometric form can be rendered as an equation, and vice versa, teasingly suggested that the natural world was susceptible to being mapped and ordered in a clear and distinct language that, like the mathematical understanding of ellipses and parabolas, offered objective certainty instead of mere opinion.

Holding back *The World*, Descartes released the *Discourse* as an informal sketch in French of the possibilities of universal knowledge. He believed that all men—and, radically, all women—had enough good sense (he called it the "light of nature") to see the rightness of his conclusions. Possessed of a very large idea about man, nature, and God, Descartes knew he had to be careful. "I hope," he wrote Mersenne, "that readers will gradually get used to my principles and recognize their truth, before they notice that they destroy the principles of Aristotle."

In his argument, Descartes asks what he could know to be true beyond all doubt, apprehending that even if everything he could see, read, or remember could be doubted, he could not doubt that he was doubting: "*Je pense, donc je suis.*"

In what amounts to a Copernican reversal of the assumption that the mind only knows what is first present to the senses, Descartes gives priority to a clear and distinct idea that does not come via the senses, yet becomes the model for all other certain knowledge. The self knows that it is and that it doubts; because it doubts, it must be finite. But one can grasp finitude only if one already possesses a clear and distinct idea of infinitude—something so perfect that it necessarily precedes any finite self both logically and ontologically. In the same instant that I intuit that I doubt, I intuit a Being whose perfection precludes the possibility that it could wish me to be deceived. Thus, I have metaphysical warrant to accept the unclear, indistinct evidence of the senses as a sign that my head, hands, feet, fireplace, books, dissected bodies, and all that I formerly doubted are not merely dreams or phantasms.

Out of Descartes's hyperbolic doubt emerge "self," "God," and "world" like colors from white light or the self-evident properties of the triangle. His method reduces everything that is neither self nor God to mechanical matter in motion, measurable and therefore open to scientific objectivity. He attached three selections adapted from *The World* to the first edition of *Discourse on the Method*—essays on optics, meteorology, and geometry—to illustrate how his method could lead to an integrated system of universal knowledge.

Despite his caution, Descartes's effort to set physics and meta-physics on a new foundation—thinking self, soulless matter, and infinite benign Being—failed the church's bullshit detector. Even as the philosopher contracted a fatal case of pneumonia in Sweden while attending to the demands of his student, Queen Christina, who required her tutor to brave the Scandinavian winter at five a.m., his "fable" was wormwood to the guardians of faith and human knowledge. "In truth, Descartes teaches one to doubt too much, and that is not a good model for minds who are naturally credulous," wrote the Jesuit Jansenist René Rapin.

In the *Meditations*, his other great work of metaphysical speculation, published in 1641, Descartes wrote, "My mind is a vagabond who likes to wander and is not yet able to stay within the strict bounds of truth." Amid the fractious intellectual climate of the seventeenth century, such words were susceptible to stern construction. In 1663, a mere thirteen years after his death, his entire oeuvre was placed on the *Index of Prohibited Books*, and shortly thereafter Louis XIV banned the teaching of his thought. The restless spirit of Descartes vanished until a more adventurous moment, in 1824, when he was republished in France, and he has actively wrought havoc with our good sense ever since.

—*Tom Matrullo*

126 ⌘ Who first published a work on calculus?

Gottfried Wilhelm von Leibniz in 1684

THE ASTUTE OBSERVER OF MODERN LIFE might conclude that under-handed maneuverings and bitter competition are best exemplified by political aspirants, professional athletes, and animals during mating season. In fact, the rarefied annals of mathematics can claim a fierce territorial dispute that outlasted many a political, athletic, and coupling controversy of our day.

The crux of this dispute over priority of discovery is that genius never exists in a vacuum. Only within a scientific landscape of established principles, theory, and practice will the vision of genius manifest itself. Such was the case in seventeenth-century mathematics, when the culture of ideas was ripe for a transcendent intellect to survey the scene and generate from its components a new era in thinking. The calculus controversy erupted because the century produced two towering mathematical geniuses instead of just one.

The first, Sir Isaac Newton (1643–1727), was a posthumous child born in Lincolnshire, England, and raised primarily by his grandmother until age twelve. He attended Trinity College, Cambridge, where he studied Aristotle, as well as the great early modern thinkers, such as Copernicus, Galileo, Kepler, and Descartes (see Questions 114, 121, and 125). Although credited with the discovery of the generalized binomial theorem, he was otherwise an average and undistinguished student.

After graduating in 1665, Newton moved home to Lincolnshire to isolate himself from the Great Plague. It was there that his mettle as a scholar was remarkably realized, for during two years of study he made significant strides in optics, leading eventually to his laws of color; in mechanics, leading to his universal laws of gravitation; and in mathematics, leading to his development of calculus.

In 1669, Newton released to a small group of his peers the first written description of his new method of mathematical analysis, which he entitled "On the Methods of Series and Fluxions" upon revision two years later. In so doing, he introduced the earliest form of calculus ("series and fluxions") to an elite audience. Had Newton sought fame for his discovery—or perhaps even recognized its tremendous implications and potential—he would have published in a scholarly journal.

The other great mathematical genius of the age, Gottfried Wilhelm von Leibniz (1646–1716), was born in Leipzig, then part of the electorate of Saxony. At age seven, on being granted unrestricted access to the personal library of his late father, a professor of moral philosophy, Leibniz taught himself Latin, which he mastered by age twelve. For the next eight years, he immersed himself in the formal study of philosophy and law. On receiving his doctorate in law from the University of Altdorf in 1666, Leibniz embarked on a career in service to noble German courts, including stints as assessor, counselor, historian, librarian, political adviser, and privy counselor of justice.

Despite these responsibilities, Leibniz's predilection for scholarly pursuits and invention proved irrepressible. Fascinated by human thought patterns, he defined what we now recognize as the basic principles of modern logic. He also invented the first four-function calculator, thereby securing membership in the Royal Society of London. Well before the advent of modern geology, he speculated that the earth has a molten core. In opposition to contemporary ideas of the laws of motion, Leibniz devised a theory based on dynamics, arguing from the point of view that space and time are relative rather than absolute and that the conservation of motion, rather than kinetic energy, was the governing principle.

While on a diplomatic journey to France in 1672, Leibniz initiated a profound study of mathematics. Under the tutelage of Dutch physicist and mathematician Christiaan Huygens, he spent a year studying the work of both classical and contemporary scholars before journeying to London, where he exchanged ideas with several colleagues of Newton and eventually with Newton himself. Although the evidence suggests that his interlocutors and correspondents shared with him only vague references to Newton's "series and fluxions," these casual allusions were later thought to have inspired a new way of looking at mathematics that led Leibniz to reinvent calculus independently—or, as some alleged, to plagiarize it from Newton.

By 1675, Leibniz's notebooks reflected the use of his own derivations and conceptions of calculus, which he called infinitesimals, to find slopes of curves and areas under curves, and within two more years, he had defined a rigorous notation for his ideas. Intuiting the revolutionary significance of his discoveries, he published in 1684, in the *Acta Eruditorum* of Leipzig, the first exposition of his methods of calculus, refining his work in several more articles of exposition and application in subsequent years. Thus, at least in the public eye, Leibniz had discovered calculus.

Two decades passed while Newton and Leibniz pursued their distinguished careers in physics and philosophy, respectively. Then, in 1704, an anonymous reviewer of a manuscript that Newton had submitted for publication accused him of pilfering Leibniz's infinitesimals and claiming them as his own. The review was published, thereby raising the issue of priority. Newton's close associates had known of his pioneering work in calculus since 1669 and had been unmoved by its subsequent independent development by Leibniz. On the other hand, scholars outside Newton's group had known only Leibniz's published exposition of calculus and had been using his methods and establishing his notation for twenty years.

In no time at all, friends and representatives on both sides were exchanging accusations of dishonesty and plagiarism, while Newton and Leibniz became embroiled in the dual pursuit of exonerating themselves and vilifying each other. In his incredulity at being labeled a plagiarist, Leibniz defended himself with considerable outrage. Newton contended that it was the besmirching of his character by accusations of dishonesty, rather than concern over who received credit for the discovery, which fueled his own rancor.

The charges, countercharges, and animosity continued for years. Eventually, in 1712, in response to a request from Leibniz, the Royal Society agreed to investigate the history of calculus and publish the findings. It was Newton himself, however, who surreptitiously compiled the report on behalf of the Society, carefully delineating all the allegations against Leibniz. He followed up with an anonymous review of the Society's report in a separate publication, thus broadening his smear campaign.

As for Leibniz, he did not see the report until 1714, when he was more concerned with his declining health. At the time of Leibniz's death in 1716—and for years to follow—Newton remained his vicious adversary. During the last two decades of his life, he inserted a vituperative rant about Leibniz into each of his publications, whether or not the content was related to calculus. Only his own death quelled his fury.

The current prevailing opinion is that Newton and Leibniz developed calculus independently and in different ways. It is also understood that the ideas of many eminent mathematicians, from Archimedes to Pierre de Fermat and James Gregory, laid the groundwork for Newton and Leibniz to make their historic discoveries, and that many thinkers since their time—notably Bishop Berkeley, Baron Cauchy, and Bernhard Riemann—have transformed calculus from its inchoate beginnings into the rigorously mathematical science that it is today. In his own better days, Newton himself demonstrated a broader perspective by writing in a letter of 1675, with reference to another scientific dispute, "If I have seen further it is by standing on the shoulders of Giants."

—*Lisa C. Perrone*

EIGHTEENTH CENTURY

127 ∽ Who was the first British prime minister?

The Whig statesman Sir Robert Walpole, 1721–42

AS AN ENGLISH COUNTRY GENTLEMAN BORN in Houghton Hall, Norfolk, educated at Eton and Cambridge, and elected to succeed his father in the House of Commons at age twenty-five, Robert Walpole (1676–1745) represented the landowning class that controlled Parliament and the nation's destinies. An avid hunter and boozer with a young live-in mistress and a fondness for telling coarse stories at convivial tables, he became leader of the Whig party and Britain's first prime minister despite being a high-living, double-chinned, irreligious squire who had been sent to the Tower of London in 1712 by his Tory enemies on a charge of corruption while serving as secretary of war. His keys to success were hard work, a focus on results, and a knowledge of every man's price.

After the death of the last Stuart monarch, Queen Anne, in 1714, during the latter part of whose reign the Tories were in power, the Whigs and Walpole came battling back. The succession fell on Anne's second cousin, George I (1714–27), the first Hanoverian king of Great Britain—a German princeling who did not speak English. In the next year, the "Old Pretender" (son of the Catholic Stuart king James II, who had been deposed in 1688) unsuccessfully tried to seize the throne in an armed uprising. Many of Britain's Tories had backed the restoration of the Stuarts and thus found themselves on dicey political ground vis-à-vis King George. Soon Walpole took his revenge on the Tory party leaders, impeaching them for treason, while he himself was appointed first lord of the treasury and chancellor of the exchequer in 1715, though resigning after a year and a half because of factional infighting.

During the War of the Spanish Succession (1701–14), the nation had racked up a staggering debt. The South Sea Company, which had a monopoly of trade with the Spanish colonies, agreed to take over three-fifths of the debt by offering its stock in return for government bonds held by those who had lent to the nation. Other speculators soon began gobbling up shares, and the value of the stocks rose more than tenfold on the premise that the company would soon be doing a thriving business with Spanish possessions in the Americas and the Pacific.

Though he himself had at one time invested heavily in the venture, Walpole warned Parliament and the nation about the dangers inherent in the South Sea Company's promises of untold profits to be reaped in the Spanish trade, predicting it would fail. Regarding him as a spoil-sport Cassandra, both houses of Parliament approved the company's proposals in early April 1720.

The bubble burst after stockholders began dumping shares in September, wiping out life savings, inheritances, and pin money. "When the crash came," wrote historian G. M. Trevelyan, "the outcry of the disillusioned and ruined filled the land." Banks collapsed, investors killed themselves. The directors of the company, who had spent almost £600,000 greasing the palms of politicos and cashed in their own shares secretly when the value was still high, were regarded with the white-hot hatred reserved for this particular type of human parasite, and their estates were confiscated.

On the strength of his dire prognostications regarding the South Sea bubble, Walpole was made chief minister of George I in April 1721, once again becoming first lord of the treasury and chancellor of the exchequer, this time for almost twenty-one years. Because George couldn't wait to set out for his beloved Hanover each year, many of his kingly prerogatives, such as steering domestic policy, were gradually taken over by Walpole, head of the ruling Whig party in Parliament and now de facto prime minister. (The title, which Walpole regarded as abusive, was not made official until 1905.) No other British prime minister has ever served longer. Since Walpole spoke no German or French, he and King George communicated in Latin (of sorts) while quaffing punch.

Walpole's so-called Bubble Act forbade the issuing of stock without a government charter, putting a crimp in the style of Britain's incipient CFO types, yet the new prime minister was hardly a foe of financial interests. He even managed to keep the South Sea Company from going belly-up by getting the Bank of England to assume the £7,000,000 debt that the company owed the public. He also kept the government from repudiating any of its debt and set up a system for both interest and principal to be paid periodically.

More important, he became the true founder of the British cabinet system, in which the leaders of the legislature are also the chief ministers of the executive branch—and the prime minister heads both the cabinet and the House of Commons. The cabinet keeps itself in power by agreeing to support policies that can expect the backing of a majority in the House. If it loses that majority, the ministry falls. Walpole appointed cabinet ministers who adhered to his policies and sent the others packing.

He was probably the most colossally corrupt prime minister in British history, but payoffs and purchases were the normal method of doing politics—or any other business—in those unregulated days of institutionalized chicanery. Walpole routinely bribed members of the House, ensuring his majority for more than two decades, and bought seats in Parliament for his cronies in numerous "rotten boroughs"—districts that had become almost depopulated and whose remaining handful of voters could be persuaded to cast their ballots for his cherry-picked yes-men.

Walpole's Parliament comprised five or six hundred extremely wealthy landowners during an era in which property qualifications disenfranchised all but the apex of the socioeconomic pyramid. The government of Great Britain was thus led by about seventy Whig families that constituted "the Whig oligarchy." The heads of these families usually sat in the House of Lords, and their younger members in the House of Commons, and so, "between them both, they licked the platter clean."

The perks and kickbacks accruing from Walpole's position as chief distributor of spoils and patronage in the realm—since he made all the top appointments in the royal household, the armed forces, the Church of England, and the civil service—enabled him to enlarge his ancestral Houghton Hall into a spectacular Palladian mansion designed by Colen Campbell at a cost of £200,000. He adorned his palatial seat and various other dwellings with an art collection that his grandson later sold to Catherine the Great of Russia, where it formed a core collection of the Hermitage Museum in St. Petersburg.

When George II (1727–60) succeeded to the throne, he considered dismissing Walpole, who for years had been a close friend of the politically sagacious Caroline, princess of Wales. The new queen advised her husband to maintain Walpole in power, and the royal pair was rewarded by Sir Bob—he had been knighted in 1725—with a larger allowance. When King George presented 10 Downing Street to him, Walpole accepted only on the condition that it would pass down to his successors as head of government. Industrialization proceeded rapidly during this reign, especially in the coal and shipbuilding sectors, and

Walpole's policies, geared toward free trade, favored merchants and manufacturers, as well as his own class of wealthy landowners.

Indeed, Walpole's motto—*quieta non movere* ("let sleeping dogs lie")—reflected his belief that keeping taxes low on property owners would help ensure that Tory landed magnates would not militate for a Stuart restoration. It also referred to his foreign policy of not antagonizing traditional enemies like France and Spain.

Although managing for many years to keep Britain out of Continental squabbles, such as the War of the Polish Succession (1733–38), even Walpole was powerless against that most virulent of human diseases, war fever. British merchants wanted free trade with Spanish America (and not just the right to control the slave trade—which the Spanish planned to revoke), and thus smuggling became widespread. The Spanish retaliated by stepping up their searches and seizures of British ships, and the British countered by capturing Spaniards in the Americas and selling them as slaves. In addition, the British possession of Gibraltar was, then as now, a sticking point.

In March 1738, Captain Robert Jenkins regaled the House of Commons with his ear—kept in a small bottle—claiming he had been shorn of it by hot-blooded Spanish customs officials (though some prominent British contemporaries judged the story to be bogus). Acceding to the self-interested jingoism of the merchants and the self-destructive jingoism of the masses, a reluctant Walpole and a bell-ringing Britain ("Soon they will be wringing their hands," he said) embarked on the maritime "War of Jenkins' Ear" against Spain in October of 1739.

The British war effort proving generally lackluster, the Commons voted against Walpole on a minor point on February 2, 1742, forcing him to resign. He was created earl of Orford by the king and took his seat in the House of Lords, from which he continued to direct the Whigs in Commons and advise the king. Aside from his flagging popularity, his last years as prime minister were marked by personal griefs. After his wife's death, he married his mistress in March 1738, but she died in childbirth only three months later.

Robert Walpole died at age sixty-eight on March 18, 1745, after a long and painful illness, leaving behind, among other children, his son Horace, whose *Castle of Otranto* (1764) initiated the craze for Gothic novels. As Walpole always feared, a Stuart-led invasion took place under "Bonnie Prince Charlie," the "Young Pretender," in 1745, the year of Walpole's death. The main British army had to be transported home from the Continent to put down the six thousand Scottish High-landers who had flocked to the charismatic prince's cause.

A lover of painting and architecture, Walpole was not a patron of literary men, though he had the honor of receiving Voltaire during the latter's stay in England. Among Sir Robert's political enemies were the most illustrious British authors of the day, such as Jonathan Swift, Alexander Pope, John Gay (who lambasted him and his mistress in *The Beggar's Opera* in 1728), and Henry Fielding (who satirized him in his 1743 novel, *Jonathan Wild*). A newspaper, *The Craftsman*, was started by Walpole's great Tory enemy, the politician and philosopher Henry St. John, Lord Bolingbroke, with the explicit purpose of thrashing the Whig prime minister, who did not, however, take anything lying down. Swift noted that "Walpole hires a Set of Party Scribblers, who do nothing else but write in his Defence"—apparently to the tune of £50,000 a year.

Readers of Swift's *Gulliver's Travels* (1725) have encountered Walpole in the guise of Flimnap, the Lilliputian lord high treasurer who develops an aversion for six-foot-tall Gulliver stemming from jealousy regarding his six-inch-tall wife (the joke being that Walpole couldn't care less about his wife's infidelities). The emperor of Lilliput (read George I) "was indeed too much governed by that favourite."

Gulliver also describes how the highest political offices in Lilliput are filled based on the candidates' dexterity in doing a kind of dance on a high-wire before the emperor, in which the winner is the one who can leap the highest without falling. Since even current ministers are occasionally required to demonstrate that their skills on the wire are undiminished, Flimnap was doing so one day when, though he could outjump "any other lord in the whole empire," he took a nasty fall that would have broken his neck if he hadn't landed on "one of the King's cushions" (i.e., mistresses) that happened to have been left beneath the high-wire—a snide reference to the duchess of Kendal, who is believed to have persuaded George I to restore Walpole to power in 1721, thus initiating his epochal ministry.

128 ∼ What was the First Continental Congress?

An assembly of delegates from British colonies in America,
September to October 1774

IN THE EIGHTEENTH CENTURY, Great Britain defeated France in a struggle for two empires. The battle of Plassey in 1757, which led to British control of Bengal, is usually seen as the beginning of British rule in India. In the fight for Canada and other French possessions in North America, William Pitt the Elder, "the British Cicero," brilliantly directed the war effort in Parliament and as secretary of state during the French and Indian War (1756–63), climaxing in the British capture of Quebec in 1759. France ended up ceding their settlements in Canada to the British, as well as all their territories east of the Mississippi.

The mother country had long pursued a policy of salutary neglect toward the British colonies in America, according them a lavish measure of self-government that they came to interpret as their right. After the French and Indian War, however—which added £100 million to the British national debt, doubling it—Parliament believed the American colonies should help defray the costs of Britain's defending them, especially given the slapdash, halfhearted, and uncoordinated effort the colonial militias and political officials had displayed during the fighting.

The colonists paid only the modest local taxes enacted by their own legislatures, and they routinely resorted to smuggled goods to evade British restrictions on their commerce—such as the molasses they illegally imported from the French or Spanish West Indies for their rum distilleries. In 1761, royal duties collectors in Boston obtained from Britain so-called writs of assistance that empowered them to enter any premises at any time to search for contraband. Resentment against these intrusive measures was exacerbated in 1764, when the Sugar (or Revenue) Act placed duties on Madeira wine, foreign rum, silk, and linen. The catchy slogan "no taxation without representation" was first uttered by Boston lawyer James Otis in protest against this act.

Now the more radical colonists didn't want to be represented in Parliament, since their few votes would be swallowed up by the British majority. They preferred to keep on being unrepresented so that they could claim exemption from parliamentary rule altogether. This minority view, especially during the reign of the thin-skinned, irascible, and autocratically minded George III (1760–1820), was tantamount to treason.

But the majority of Americans resented the British mercantilist notion that colonies existed solely for the economic benefit of the mother country: to supply it with raw materials, snap up its excess manufactures, avoid competition in certain key industries (such as ironware), and use only the empire's ships and seamen as carrying services. The colonies had long thrived under their own political initiative and economic industriousness (enhanced by widespread smuggling), but now even formerly prosperous Virginia planters were faced with massive debts to Britain because of unfavorable trade balances and proliferating import duties.

On March 22, 1765, Parliament passed the Stamp Act, hoping to garner £60,000 a year from the required purchase of revenue stamps to be affixed to newspapers, magazines, pamphlets, legal documents, and even playing cards and dice. As the first direct, internal tax (as opposed to customs duties) imposed on the colonists, this act roused them to fury—and not just in the abstract, but to rioting, pillaging, and tarring and feathering royal revenue agents. The cost involved and the hassle factor were both considerable, but the principle of a direct tax was deemed totally unacceptable.

In the view of U.S. historians R. R. Palmer and Joel Colton, "The British Americans were possibly the least law-abiding of all the more civilized European peoples." Though the British themselves paid a stamp tax, "Sons of Liberty" groups sprouted in Boston and elsewhere to burn the special stamp paper and urge (sometimes force) colonists to avoid paying the tax. Imperial tax agents were strongly encouraged to seek other employment. In October 1765, representatives of nine colonies met in New York City as the Stamp Act Congress, resolving to adopt an embargo on British imports. On the very day, November 1, that the act came into force, the city was the scene of wide-ranging riots.

On March 18, 1766, the Stamp Act was repealed as unenforceable. But a year later, Charles Townshend, chancellor of the exchequer, sponsored four much-hated measures passed by Parliament. Among them was one that, with the prospect of raising £40,000 a year, placed a colonial import tax on tea, lead, paper, glass, and paint.

The Massachusetts legislature, in February 1768, urged the other colonies to resist paying the Townshend duties. The British government countered by dissolving any legislatures, like the New York Assembly, that responded to the call. But when, a year later, the Virginia House of Burgesses rejected Parliament's authority to tax the colonies, and the governor duly dissolved the Burgesses, they met privately to discuss economic reprisals. Soon British exporters were feeling the squeeze of a boycott up and down the Atlantic coast. "The American Revolution," Samuel Eliot Morison reminds us, "was brought about by radical groups in the seaport towns, usually in alliance with local merchants, and with planters of the Southern tidewater."

Just a few months after the inception of Lord North's all-Tory and all-toady ministry in London, an incident took place on the snowy evening of March 5, 1770, on the Boston waterfront outside the despised customshouse, which was being guarded by a single sentry (or "lobster-back," as the locals called the red-coated British soldiers). When members of a crowd that had assembled began throwing snowballs at him, he called for help, and about twenty soldiers came running out. After a half-hour standoff, in which the troops were pelted with snowballs interspersed with stones by a jeering mob of several hundred, one of the soldiers was knocked to the ground with a club. When he got to his feet, he fired his musket. The ensuing melee resulted in the shooting death of five civilians (three immediately and two others from their wounds), including a black man, Crispus Attucks. The fracas was exploited to the maximum as "the Boston Massacre," especially by Samuel Adams and Paul Revere, to turn public opinion decidedly against the British, though the soldiers, courageously defended by John Adams, were acquitted of murder.

Committees of correspondence, originated by Sam Adams, now sprang up to keep fellow patriots throughout the colonies up to speed on the latest disquieting political events. It's ironic that on the very day of the Boston Massacre, the Townshend acts were repealed, except for the tax on tea, which was meant to save face for a vacillating Parliament and symbolize its right to tax the colonies.

Tea, which edged out rum as the most popular beverage in the colonies, was the focus of yet another item of bungling imperial legislation. In the Tea Act of May 10, 1773, Parliament attempted to save the British East India Company from bankruptcy by enabling it to undersell even the smuggled Dutch tea available in the colonies from American merchants. American ports rejected the company's tea—which, cheap as it was, was still being taxed by the last of the Townshend duties—either by sending the ships back or leaving the tea to rot on the docks. In Boston, however, on the evening of December 16, 1773, a large group of men, some using feathers and red paint in a vague attempt to resemble Mohawk Indians, boarded three British ships and flung into the harbor all 342 chests of the company's tea in a flamboyant display of patriotism that was dubbed the Boston Tea Party.

King George was not amused. In the spring of 1774, he approved a series of drastic parliamentary reprisals that the colonists decried as the Coercive or Intolerable Acts. The port of Boston, the city's economic lifeline, was to be shut down in June and remain closed to all vessels, even boats, until the cost of the destroyed tea—and of other assorted property damage—was repaid. No public meetings, especially of the town-hall agitprop variety, could be held without the approval of the new governor, General Thomas Gage. The power of the governor to appoint senior colonial officials for Massachusetts practically rescinded the colony's venerable charter. General Gage himself disapproved of a Quartering Act that allowed British troops to be housed in unoccupied private structures. More British soldiers were to be deployed to Boston. An unrelated law, the equitable Quebec Act, was interpreted by many colonists as pro-French and—horror of horrors!—pro-Catholic.

Outrage over the Intolerable Acts reverberated throughout British America. Several committees of correspondence issued a call for a colonial congress. On September 5, 1774, the First Continental Congress met in Carpenters' Hall in Philadelphia, the colonies' largest city (population forty thousand). Its fifty-six members included those redoubtable second cousins John and Samuel Adams, George Washington and Patrick Henry from Virginia, and John Jay from New York. (Notables such as Benjamin Franklin and Thomas Jefferson first served in the Second Continental Congress [see Question 129], though Jefferson drafted the Virginia delegation's instructions for the First Continental Congress.) Of the thirteen original colonies, only Georgia failed to send a representative—the royal governor was able to prevent it. Peyton Randolph, speaker of the Virginia House of Burgesses, was unanimously elected president of the congress, and it was decided that each colony was to have one vote in the proceedings, no matter how many delegates represented it or how relatively populous and wealthy it was.

As a way of asserting the colonists' full entitlement to the protection of English common law, the congress issued a declaration of ten rights. The first was the right to "life, liberty, and property" (which Jefferson later changed to "life, liberty, and the pursuit of happiness" in the Declaration of Independence). Other traditional English rights insisted upon were "a right peaceably to assemble . . . and petition the king" and a right to trial by jury. The declaration also spoke out against taxation without representation, the maintenance of standing British armies in the colonies without consent of their legislatures, and the Intolerable Acts, which it dubbed "impolitic, unjust, and cruel, as well as unconstitutional."

On October 20, the congress adopted the Articles of Association, which embodied an economic agreement among the colonies that also strengthened their overall bonds. Among its fourteen articles was an immediate ban on the importation of British tea and a law forbidding the importing or consuming of any British or imperial goods after December 1, 1774. All exports to Britain or the British West Indies were to cease after September 10, 1775—giving American merchants extra time to reap profits—unless the Intolerable Acts were repealed by that date. The boycott of British goods was to be enforced on unwilling participants (sometimes violently, as it turned out). Among other provisions were a price freeze and sumptuary laws forbidding money-wasting extravagances and diversions such as gambling, staging plays, and spending too much on funerals.

On the day before the final session of the First Continental Congress on October 26, it petitioned King George to redress colonial grievances going back to the end of the French and Indian War in 1763. In asking him to repeal the Intolerable Acts, it assigned the blame for maltreatment of the colonies on unnamed "designing and dangerous men," rather than, as in the Declaration of Independence, on the monarch himself. The congress voted to convene again on May 10, 1775, if their grievances had not been addressed by then.

Stay tuned (see Question 129).

129 ◆ What was the first battle of the American Revolution?

The battle of Lexington and Concord on April 19, 1775

AS PART OF THE BRITISH GOVERNMENT'S retaliation for the Boston Tea Party in December 1773, General Thomas Gage, the recently appointed military governor of Massachusetts Bay Colony, dissolved its assembly (see Question 128). But in October of 1774, the intrepid assemblymen convened at the village of Concord as an illegal congress of their own—the Massachusetts Provincial Congress, under the presidency of the rich Boston merchant John Hancock—and proceeded to direct the affairs of the colony, with the sole exception of British-occupied Boston.

The British rightly suspected Concord, eighteen miles northwest of Boston, of being the site of an illegal weapons and munitions cache that the local farmers had formed in case the redcoats decided to extend their effective rule into the interior of the colony. Bostonians rightly suspected that seven hundred British grenadiers and light infantrymen—the crack troops of their regiments—had been relieved of their regular duties on April 15, 1775, to receive special training for an assault on the munitions stockpile at Concord.

On the night of April 18, General Gage placed Lieutenant Colonel Francis Smith in command of this force to seize the arms in Concord. The patriotic silversmith Paul Revere had arranged for a signal to be flashed from the steeple of Boston's Old North Church. The presence of either one or two lanterns in the tower's window would inform mounted couriers as to what route the British were taking: "one if by land, and two if by sea"—(that is, by land all the way via Boston Neck, or by boat across the Charles River and then overland)—in the words of Henry Wadsworth Longfellow's 1860 poem, "The Midnight Ride of Paul Revere."

The sight of two lanterns in the steeple that night informed the waiting riders that the British had been spotted rowing across the Charles to present-day Cambridge. Revere and William Dawes took off for Lexington to alert the countryside and to warn rebel leaders John Hancock and Samuel Adams, who were hiding out in the town. Dawes went the entire way by land, whereas Revere was rowed across the river to Charlestown, where he roused the locals (who in turn sent out other riders) before commencing his own fabled ride. Revere got to Lexington first and advised Hancock and Adams to make themselves scarce, while yet more horsemen set out for neighboring towns. Although Revere, Dawes, and a third rider, Samuel Prescott, were later intercepted by British officers, Prescott managed to escape and make it to Concord, from where additional riders fanned out.

By dawn, when an advance British column marched into Lexington, seventy-seven colonial militiamen were waiting for them on the village common under the command of Captain John Parker. The British commander, Major John Pitcairn, lined up his four hundred light infantry troops to face the Americans and issued a dire warning: "Disperse, ye rebels, disperse!" Greatly outnumbered, the Americans were following Parker's command to heed Pitcairn's stentorian voice, when a shot rang out. After the ensuing skirmish, eight Americans lay dead and ten wounded, while only one British soldier was wounded—though Pitcairn had his horse shot from under him.

When the British arrived in Concord, they searched, mostly in vain, for munitions that had already been spirited away or destroyed, thanks to the advance warning the town had received from Prescott. But a covering party of about one hundred British troops on the Concord River was surprised at the North Bridge by almost four hundred minutemen (the strongest and most gung ho young members of the militias, who were supposed to be ready to fight "at a minute's notice") and other militiamen. In their wary retreat across the bridge, the British seem to have fired first without orders, killing two minutemen and wounding four others. The colonials returned fire, killing three British soldiers and wounding about a dozen.

The main British force kept looking for hidden weapons, had lunch, and moved out of Concord at about noon, thus allowing ever-increasing numbers of colonial militiamen to arrive on the scene. On the long march back to Boston, the British were repeatedly fired on by large formations of militia, and their rear guard troops were picked off at a distance by farmers and other guerrilla snipers who shot from behind houses, barns, walls, hedges, and trees. On several occasions, the British broke into shambling runs along the road.

If General Gage had not sent an additional nine hundred soldiers as far as Lexington under Hugh, Earl Percy, to rescue the column on its dismal return, it would have been annihilated. The survivors of the ill-fated mission to Concord staggered back into Boston out of ammunition and seriously demoralized. Casualties for the day were 93 for the Americans and 273 for the British, who began to have a clearer idea of what American resistance on a large scale might mean.

On May 10, 1775, soon after hostilities had been initiated, the Second Continental Congress convened in Philadelphia at the Pennsylvania State House (now Independence Hall). John Hancock of Massachusetts was unanimously elected president of the congress, which was to remain the legislative body of the colonies and the newborn nation throughout the period of the Articles of Confederation, until March 3, 1789 (see Question 132).

On the same day the Second Continental Congress assembled,

Colonel Ethan Allen, in uneasy joint command with Colonel Benedict Arnold, and Allen's Green Mountain Boys captured Fort Ticonderoga in northeast New York, the key to Lake Champlain and the water route to Canada. Congress actually debated giving the fort back, because it seemed such an outright act of rebellion. Nonetheless, it passed measures to raise an army on June 14 and, on the following day, John Adams proposed that Colonel George Washington of Virginia be appointed its first general and commander in chief (see Question 130).

Soon after Washington left Philadelphia a week later to take command of the sixteen thousand New England militiamen who were besieging the British in Boston, he heard news of the battle of Bunker Hill (actually Breed's Hill), where colonial soldiers on June 17 had been dislodged from their high ground in Boston but had inflicted heavy casualties on the British.

With these events as a backdrop, it's not surprising that Congress's "Olive Branch Petition" of July 8 was rejected, unread, by King George III, who, on August 23, ordered his government to suppress the rebellion in the colonies. In late December, an act was passed authorizing British warships to seize any colonial ships and impress their crews into the Royal Navy. In January 1776, Thomas Paine anonymously unleashed in Philadelphia his fiery pamphlet, *Common Sense*, urging total severance from the mother country, ruled over by "the Royal Brute." In touting independence, Paine wrote that "the Sun never shined on a cause of greater worth." In a major victory on March 17, the Continental Army drove the occupying British troops from Boston.

Then, in May, the colonists learned that the king was dispatching twelve thousand German mercenaries—the notorious Hessians— against them. On June 7, Richard Henry Lee of Virginia proposed the resolution in Congress that "these united colonies" were "free and independent states . . . and that all political connection between them and the state of Great Britain is, and ought to be, totally dissolved." It was seconded by John Adams but still opposed by many delegates.

In the meantime, thirty-three-year-old Thomas Jefferson of Virginia was entrusted with drawing up a Declaration of Independence. Two days after Congress voted for severance from Great Britain, a modified draft of Jefferson's eloquent and indignant document was formally adopted on the evening of July 4 and later signed by President Hancock and fifty-five other delegates. It would be a long haul until the decisive battle of Yorktown, Virginia, in 1781, when General Cornwallis surrendered to Washington.

During the American Revolution, Britain had many enemies in the world and no powerful friends. In the year after the Americans won the pivotal battle of Saratoga in 1777, the French came into the war on the American side (followed by the Spanish in 1779 and the Dutch in 1780). These European allies—first and foremost the French, their financial aid, and their army and fleet at Yorktown, including the leadership shown by Lafayette and Rochambeau—were the main reason that the former colonies, with their population of 2.5 million (of whom at least half did not support a war of independence), were able to defeat a nation that was then the richest and most industrialized in the world and that had the most powerful navy and a population more than three times larger than that of British America.

On July 4, 1837, Ralph Waldo Emerson's "Concord Hymn" was sung at the completion of the battle monument there. Here is the famous first stanza:

> *By the rude bridge that arched the flood,*
> *Their flag to April's breeze unfurled,*
> *Here once the embattled farmers stood*
> *And fired the shot heard round the world.*

In *The American Scene*, a book recording Henry James's travels in the United States during 1904–5, the author addresses Concord thus: "You're the biggest little place in America—with only New York and Boston and Chicago . . . to surpass you." James speaks of "the exquisite melancholy of everything unuttered" at Concord that "lies too deep, as it always so lies where the ground has borne the weight of the short, simple act, intense and unconscious, that was to determine the event, determine the future in the way we call immortally." Referring to the later residence there of Emerson, Hawthorne, and Thoreau—a trio of friends who often skated together on the frozen Concord River—James avers that "the vulgar note would in that air never be possible."

130 ∾ Who was the first president of the United States?

George Washington, 1789–97

HE HAD BEEN THE BEDROCK of the American Revolution, but in December 1783, George Washington resigned as commander in chief of the army and retired to Mount Vernon, Virginia, emulating the Roman general Cincinnatus, another legendary leader who had laid aside power after his military job was done. Washington's attempt to live out his remaining days as a gentleman farmer proved ephemeral, however, since within a handful of years his oaklike sense of duty persuaded him to return to public life and serve two terms as the first president of the fledgling United States.

After the Constitution had been ratified by the requisite nine states between December 1787 and June 1788, voting in that first election was conducted in December 1788 and the following January. The fifty-seven-year-old Washington was chosen unanimously by the electors from the various states—a testament to his unparalleled stature as the commanding general of the Continental Army during the war—and John Adams became his vice president.

Sworn in on April 30, 1789, in New York City, Washington delivered his inaugural address from the balcony of the Senate chamber in Federal Hall on Wall Street to the two houses of Congress assembled there. The tone of the brief address—seven paragraphs in all—was contemplative and vaguely religious, revealing Washington's perception of a Providential influence in the founding of the nation and linking its survival to adherence to moral precepts. He closed by invoking the divine blessing on "the enlarged views, the temperate consultations, and the wise measures on which the success of this Government must depend."

During his presidencies, Washington watched the country grow with the admission of five states (North Carolina, 1789; Rhode Island, 1790; Vermont, 1791; Kentucky, 1792; Tennessee, 1796), even as he dealt effectively with many challenges while eschewing grandiloquent titles, refusing dictatorial powers, and, in the end, ceding authority to John Adams, his elected successor. During his first term, the fundamental problem facing Washington was the need for the federal government to be developed in its entirety, and the Constitution offered few specifics. On taking office, the first American president had no treasury or tax collection system, no outline for the relationship between the executive and legislative branches, no judiciary, no navy, and an army of fewer than 650 men.

Habitually surrounding himself with able, intelligent subordinates, Washington did a commendable job in appointing his four-man cabinet. The need to establish a treasury and stabilize the country financially was his most urgent problem, so he selected the brilliant Alexander Hamilton to be the first secretary of the treasury in September 1789.

Although relatively young, the thirty-four-year-old Hamilton was already a famous political essayist, lawyer, and financier. By December 1791, he had completed and submitted five major reports to Congress. Two dealt with public credit, reflecting Hamilton's concern about paying the public debt, while the others covered import duties, the establishment of a mint, and industry. During his tenure, which ran through January 1795, he was also instrumental in founding the First Bank of the United States, chartered in 1791, and in developing several levies and duties to raise revenues, including an excise tax on whiskey that had major ramifications during Washington's second term. When he resigned from the Treasury Department, Hamilton left the nation fiscally sound, having established the federal government's responsibility for major economic initiatives.

When Washington appointed Thomas Jefferson as secretary of state, the primary concerns in foreign affairs were the ongoing European conflicts. Although Jefferson officially maintained a policy of neutrality, his personal sympathies lay with France. He believed that the underpinnings of the French Revolution were similar to America's, setting him against Hamilton, who favored peace with the British to facilitate commerce. Jefferson also regarded Hamilton's economic program as a dangerous projection of centralized power. These differences became so serious that when he left the cabinet on December 31, 1793, Jefferson had turned against Washington, whose views regarding European affairs and economics were closer to those of Hamilton.

Washington picked Henry Knox, who had succeeded him as senior officer of the Continental Army in December 1783, to serve as secretary of war. His responsibilities included the management of relations with the native tribes, and Knox argued that the United States should honor treaty obligations and the natives' rights, becoming the first U.S. government official to advocate this view. Washington worked tirelessly with Knox on these matters during his first term, formulating a policy of peaceful coexistence with the tribes predicated on respect for designated sanctuaries. When this policy soon failed, Washington spoke with bitter distaste of white settlers whose intrusions into the Northwest Territory had caused conflicts that required military responses: "I believe scarcely any thing short of a Chinese wall will restrain land Jobbers and the encroachment of settlers upon the Indian country."

The man Washington tapped to be attorney general, Edmund Randolph, was almost certainly the least gifted member of the original cabinet and may have been the first cabinet official whose selection was largely attributable to personal and political connections. The most noteworthy aspect of his cabinet career occurred during Washington's second term, after Randolph succeeded Jefferson as secretary of state. When it came to light that Randolph had been involved in clumsy machinations that appeared to favor France in violation of neutrality, Washington demanded his immediate resignation.

James Madison, "the Father of the Constitution" and another of Washington's trusted advisers, was an influential member of the House of Representatives who served as an unofficial liaison to Congress. Shortly after Washington assumed office, Madison drafted the amendments to the Constitution that later became known as the Bill of Rights and facilitated their passage by Congress (see Question 132).

In the spring of 1792, Washington wanted to retire, feeling careworn and burdened by age and the bitter rivalries within his own cabinet, especially between Jefferson and Hamilton. When his close advisers argued that he was indispensable, however, he reluctantly agreed to serve a second term, which proved to be a time of several serious threats to the nation.

The Northwest Indian War, the country's first major military involvement after the Revolution, had already begun in the 1780s. This war resulted in more casualties for the United States military than the nineteenth-century wars against the Sioux, led by Crazy Horse, Sitting Bull, and Red Cloud, and the Apaches, led by Geronimo and Cochise, combined. Crushing defeats prompted Washington to recall General "Mad Anthony" Wayne, a skillful officer during the Revolution, from civilian life to active service. The war finally ended in 1795 with the

Treaty of Greenville, following a decisive American victory at the battle of Fallen Timbers in the previous year.

The gravest threat to the nation during Washington's second term was associated with the outbreak of war between Great Britain and Revolutionary France in 1793, at a time when relations between the United States and Britain were still fragile. Although public sentiment strongly favored France, Washington recognized that the true interest of the nation lay in maintaining neutrality, since another war with Britain would have been disastrous. Jay's Treaty, negotiated in London by Chief Justice John Jay and signed in 1794, reflected this perspective. Though its terms favored Great Britain, the treaty afforded the United States an interval of peace in which to strengthen itself and therefore represented a major long-term strategic success.

A separate threat to domestic tranquillity erupted in 1794 in western Pennsylvania, when farmers protested the excise tax on whiskey that Hamilton had proposed and Congress enacted in 1791. Although initially averse to the use of force to quell the disturbance, Washington eventually decided that strong action was required in what was later known as the Whiskey Rebellion. A force of about thirteen thousand men was raised from the militias of Pennsylvania, Virginia, and other states, and Washington assumed personal command—the first and only time that a sitting president went into the field to command troops—but the crisis abated before the outbreak of serious violence.

Washington's farewell address was not delivered orally, instead taking the form of an open letter to the American people published in the *American Daily Advertiser* of Philadelphia on September 19, 1796, and the *Independent Chronicle* of Boston a week later. Right up front, he referred to the upcoming elections and stated his decision "to decline being considered among the number of those out of whom a choice is to be made." He went on to warn against regional factionalism, the influence of political parties, and permanent foreign entanglements. Washington retired for the second and last time to Mount Vernon in 1796 and died there at age sixty-seven on December 14, 1799.

Washington's reputation in his day was unrivaled, as expressed in Henry Lee's eulogy: "First in war, first in peace, and first in the hearts of his countrymen." However, time has revealed aspects of Washington's greatness that his contemporaries could not have appreciated. His cautions about regionalism were prescient in light of the Civil War, his warnings that excessive political partisanship would hinder efforts to conduct national affairs wisely have proven all too true, and his dismissal of Randolph for undercutting official policy exemplified the accountability that is often called for but seldom observed. George Washington was not only the first American president and among a handful of the very greatest, but his legacy of wisdom is as enduring and ageless as his carved stone visage on Mount Rushmore.

—William A. Walsh

131 ∾ What was the first action of the French Revolution?

The storming of the Bastille in Paris on July 14, 1789

IN HIS DIARY UNDER JULY 14, 1789, King Louis XVI of France made the laconic entry, "*Rien"*—"Nothing"—but he was probably referring to his inability to go hunting at Versailles, because of the political turmoil at the time, and to list his kills of the day. Louis was an indefatigable hunter and tinkerer with locks who had come to the throne in May 1774. Although his two immediate predecessors, Louis XIV and Louis XV, had wreaked havoc on the country's finances through incessant wars and luxurious dissipation, Louis XVI's recent aid to the colonists in the American Revolution had saddled France with a staggering and unsustainable national debt. In 1789, the machinery of government finally broke down.

After going through a handful of finance ministers—including a few who had antagonized the nobility by proposing to tax all landowners—Louis XVI called a meeting of the Estates-General at Versailles. This French national parliament, initiated by Philip IV in 1302, was convoked only when the king desperately needed new sources of taxation. It had last met in 1614—175 years earlier.

The Estates-General comprised three estates: the clergy, the nobility, and the Third Estate, which represented everybody else in the country who was neither a cleric nor a noble. In the past, each chamber had met separately—and the first two privileged estates of clergy and nobles could always outvote the Third Estate, two chambers to one. But when the Estates-General convened in May 1789, the Third Estate, led by a gaggle of lawyers who represented a rising bourgeoisie, demanded that the representatives of the three estates assemble and vote as one body. Since the king had already specified that the Third Estate was to have six hundred representatives—a number equal to that of the other two estates combined—the clergymen and nobles feared that, with only a few defections from their own numbers, the Third Estate could outvote them. A stalemate ensued when the king sided with the privileged estates and the Third Estate refused to back down.

Much was at stake, since the Third Estate wanted the other two to start contributing to the support of the nation. The nobles—about four hundred thousand persons, including women and children—enjoyed important tax exemptions, though they practically monopolized the officer ranks in the army, the prestigious posts in government, and the ranks of the higher clergy. As for the Catholic Church, its vast lands were tax-exempt.

It thus fell to the Third Estate to pay the lion's share of the taxes and internal customs. The bourgeoisie resented having to support two large parasitic classes above them without having access to their numerous privileges. These highly literate professionals had long been imbibing the writings of *philosophes* such as Voltaire, Diderot, Montesquieu, and Rousseau, who decried the stranglehold with which the church, the Bourbon monarchy, and the pampered nobility held the rest of France captive. As for other members of the Third Estate, increasing numbers of urban workers found themselves unemployed, locked out of the guilds, and faced with soaring bread prices, while the peasants—about 80 percent of the population—had to pay manorial fees to their lord for the use of his mill, winepress, and ovens. Tied to the land, peasants also had to contribute free labor to their lord for a certain number of days a year (the so-called corvée).

Fired by these grievances, the representatives of the Third Estate declared themselves to be France's true "National Assembly" on June 17, 1789. When the king, prodded by the nobles, locked it out of its chamber, the National Assembly met in an indoor tennis court at Versailles. By the "Tennis Court Oath" of June 20, it vowed not to disband until it had forged a constitution for the nation. The king called out a large number of troops, hoping to stifle the assembly and discourage nearby Paris from stirring the pot.

After the reforming finance minister, the Swiss Jacques Necker, who had become a popular hero, was summarily dismissed by the king and banished, the young journalist Camille Desmoulins, among others, gave a speech in the garden of the Palais-Royal in Paris on July 12, waving a pistol around and urging direct action. That evening, a roving mob clashed with royal cavalry forces and pelted them with stones. They also sacked forty customs posts.

The next day, a Parisian mob pillaged a monastery for grain, wine, oil, and cheese. The people were not only hungry but also panicky, since they feared that the king's soldiers, numbering about twenty thousand, had surrounded the city and would soon quash their tumults. They kept watch at the city gates, erected barricades, and armed themselves by breaking into the shops of gunsmiths and armorers, while not neglecting humbler weapons such as kitchen knives, daggers, and clubs.

On the morning of July 14, a crowd estimated at eighty thousand broke into the armory at the Invalides and appropriated thirty-two thousand muskets and some cannons. When the people learned that 250 barrels of gunpowder had recently been moved to the Bastille for safekeeping, a crowd of about nine hundred, including some defecting soldiers and French Guards, assembled there to demand it. They also wanted the governor of the Bastille, the inept Marquis de Launay, to remove the cannons he had recently mounted in the embrasures of the structure and which threatened the entire Faubourg Saint-Antoine.

The Bastille was built as a fortress in the late fourteenth century to protect Paris against English invasion during the Hundred Years' War. Later, especially under Cardinal Richelieu in the seventeenth century, it served as a prison for enemies of the state. Famous inmates included "the Man in the Iron Mask" and Voltaire (two stints), and in more recent times it was used mainly to house subversive writers and upper-class troublemakers. The Marquis de Sade, for example, a comfortable resident of the Bastille since 1784, had worked away at his imaginatively repulsive *120 Days of Sodom* there until his transfer to the insane asylum of Charenton about a week before the fall of the fortress. But the structure's eight round towers and hundred-foot-high walls loomed menacingly above the Saint-Antoine district, and the king's right to imprison people in the Bastille merely by issuing a lettre de cachet, without any court involvement, remained a hated symbol of tyranny.

With such a large crowd bellowing at him in front of the Bastille, de Launay must have wondered if his garrison of eighty-two old pensioned soldiers and thirty-two Swiss would be able to withstand an armed onslaught. When, at about ten a.m., a pair of delegates arrived from the impromptu steering committee of the city to urge de Launay to withdraw his cannons, he allowed them in and cordially invited them to sit down to an early French lunch that went on and on. Fearing the worst, the crowd, which had penetrated into the Bastille's accessible outer courtyard, grew even more restive. Two men climbed the inner wall and let down a small drawbridge that allowed the mob to swarm into the inner court, where they were faced with a huge raised drawbridge protected by a water-filled moat almost eighty feet wide. Panicking, de Launay ordered his soldiers to shoot, and though the besiegers returned fire, it went very badly with them: Ninety-eight died on the spot or later from their wounds, and seventy-three others were wounded, while only one soldier was killed and three wounded on the defenders' side.

At this juncture, some French Guards arrived with several cannons, which they set up before the drawbridge. De Launay offered to surrender, threatening to blow up the entire fort—and much of the neighborhood—if he was denied fair terms. Since the crowd refused to relent, and de Launay had foolishly provisioned the Bastille for only two days, he finally lowered the main drawbridge. The enraged crowd poured into the fortress, slaughtered six of its nonresisting soldiers, and seized the gunpowder. De Launay was marched toward the city hall but never got there, being beaten and stabbed to death by the crowd. His head, along with that of a murdered politician, was cut off with a pocketknife and stuck at the end of a pike to be triumphantly displayed around Paris.

The seizure of the Bastille was hardly a liberation of political prisoners. Only seven men were being held there at the time: four forgers, two lunatics who soon ended up at Charenton, and a young aristocratic libertine being held at his family's request. But now the king had lost both his nerve and the city of Paris—and the National Assembly was not going to be quelled by military force. He withdrew the troops and even pinned a revolutionary tricolor cockade to his hat when he was brought to Paris with his tail between his legs a few days later. Most of the Bastille was demolished by the end of November.

More important, the National Assembly began dismantling the ancien régime: It abolished guilds, feudal rights, tithes, and internal customs, and it confiscated church property. On August 26, it adopted the Declaration of the Rights of Man and of the Citizen (excerpt: "Liberty consists in the ability to do whatever does not harm another") and began drafting a constitution.

In June 1791, Louis and his queen, the Austrian archduchess Marie Antoinette, were captured while trying to flee the country to join the king's brother and other noble and reactionary émigrés who were stirring up foreign governments to invade France. Although the discredited king agreed to the establishment of a constitutional monarchy in October, revolutionaries feared that while he was alive, he would serve as a rallying point for foreign autocrats and native royalists who would want to restore him to absolute rule. On August 10, 1792, the Parisian mob stormed the royal palace of the Tuileries and arrested the king and his family, initiating a more violent and radical phase of the French Revolution.

The first guillotine had been set up in Paris on April 25, 1792, to put a highwayman to death, but that "compassionate" new instrument of execution would soon be kept busy by a more varied clientele. In the "September Massacres," about eleven hundred priests, royalists, and other suspected enemies of the Revolution were executed in anticipation of an allied invasion in response to France's declaration of war on Austria.

The French Revolutionary Wars began with a French army of fifty thousand turning back an invading force of forty-two thousand Austrians, Prussians, Hessians, and French émigrés at the battle of Valmy in northeast France on September 20, 1792. The allies, nominally led by the king of Prussia, had determined to take Paris, quash the revolution, and restore Louis, but they thought better of it after being on the receiving end of a furious French cannonade (and an outbreak of dysentery). Heartened by this victory, the French abolished the monarchy and went on the offensive, invading several German states and annexing Savoy, Nice, and the Austrian Netherlands (Belgium). A French republic was proclaimed by a newly formed National Convention in 1792—renamed "Year One"—with a new constitution guaranteeing freedom of religion, the press, and assembly, and a motto proclaiming "Liberty, Equality, and Fraternity."

Much of Europe, in seven successive coalitions, would remain at intermittent war against Revolutionary and Napoleonic France until 1814. Revolutionary France extended its boundaries to include German territories west of the Rhine, and it set up client republics in Holland,

Switzerland, and several regions of Italy, spreading its antifeudal doctrines.

The king, officially demoted to "Citizen Louis Capet," was tried for treason and guillotined on January 21, 1793, in what is now Place de la Concorde. Marie Antoinette, called "l'Autrichienne"—"the Austrian woman" with a pun on "the Austrian bitch"—had been the subject of an enormous underground libelous literature depicting her as totally debauched. She was guillotined in October.

The instigators of the infamous Reign of Terror of 1793 were, according to Camille Desmoulins, "mostly young people who, brought up on readings of Cicero at school, were fired by them with the passion for freedom." Indeed, the cult of Roman republican virtue became almost parodic during this time. "The French Revolution viewed itself as Rome incarnate," wrote literary critic and essayist Walter Benjamin. "It evoked ancient Rome the way fashion evokes costumes of the past."

The leader of the most radical revolutionary group, the Jacobins (named for a Paris monastery in which its members met), was the young lawyer Maximilien Robespierre, nicknamed "the Incorruptible" for his imperviousness to bribery. Robespierre claimed that "virtue was always in a minority in the world"—and he definitely considered himself part of that minority.

Under Robespierre, the Jacobins used a revolutionary legislative assembly to rule, leading to successive waves of infighting, extremism, purges, and liquidations. The dozen members of its notorious Committee of Public Safety, dominated by Robespierre, were responsible for executing, in less than a year, about forty thousand French citizens whose "Rights of Man" had not been very zealously respected. In atrocities referred to as the "Noyades [Drownings] of Nantes," two thousand enemies of the Revolution in that city were loaded onto barges which were then sunk in the Loire.

The state, seen as the sacred, concretized will of the people, developed into a cult whose ritual consisted of political murder. Finally, Robespierre's habit of executing his former accomplices led to his own guillotining, in the company of other radical Jacobins, in the so-called Thermidorian Reaction of 1794[1]

---

[1] Thermidor—"hot month"—was mid-July to mid-August in the French Revolutionary Calendar, which had renamed all the months and days of the week and created months consisting of three weeks of ten days each.

For all its excesses, the French Revolution abolished slavery in the French colonies, smashed the remnants of feudalism, defanged the church, and spread Enlightenment ideas throughout Europe. On the other hand, its inspiring of nationalistic agendas, when combined with its other inventions of "the nation in arms" and universal conscription, later resulted in the most dreadful slaughters the world has yet seen (see Question 146).

France's national holiday of July 14, established in 1880, does not commemorate the fall of the Bastille, but the Festival of Federation, held exactly a year later in 1790, to mark a spectacular celebration in which the soldiers of France converged on Paris to swear oaths to serve the king and the National Assembly. At the former site of the Bastille is the 150-foot July Column—topped by a winged bronze male figure symbolizing the Spirit of Liberty—commemorating those who fell in the Revolution of July 1830, which brought Louis-Philippe, "the Citizen King," to power. The Opéra Bastille, inaugurated on July 14, 1989, today sits benevolently at the rear of Place de la Bastille.

132 ∾ What was the first amendment to the U.S. Constitution?

A guarantee of freedom of religion, speech, the press, assembly, and petition, in 1791

THE THIRTEEN AMERICAN STATES that had thrown off the detested yoke of the British crown were understandably wary of the potential for abuse from a strong central government, and the end of the Revolutionary War revealed a schism among the new country's leaders. Some wanted power to remain essentially with the state legislatures, with little oversight from a distant central government that might be less likely to attend to their interests, while others, including George Washington, advocated a strong central government.

The general's experiences in the war, with the states failing to provide sufficient provisions for the army, causing the near starvation of his soldiers, had led Washington to perceive as inadequate the wartime constitution known as the Articles of Confederation and Perpetual Union. Under that document, ratified by the states between 1777 and

1781, the central government, a unicameral legislature, was accorded the capacity to regulate military and monetary matters—to request troops and revenue from the individual states—but provided with no mechanism by which these requests could be enforced, as Washington had seen in the plight of his starving men.

The Articles of Confederation also failed to provide the central government with an executive branch, a permanent federal judiciary, and the power to levy taxes and regulate commerce. Once the war was over, squabbling among the states escalated as they imposed tariffs on one another's goods, claimed lands in the West, and issued various types of paper money. The country as a whole was headed toward chaos, with stagnating trade, crushing debt, increasing disorder, and growing hostility between the powerful moneyed classes and the impoverished farmers.

The farmers who had fought in the war returned home without pay to face escalating state taxes, property confiscations, and debtors' prison. In the summer of 1786, an armed uprising broke out in western Massachusetts that continued into the winter and early 1787, when it culminated in an attack on the Springfield armory by veteran farmer Daniel Shays and his followers. The inability of the government to handle effectively the skirmishes associated with Shays' Rebellion alarmed the young country's leaders. When Washington heard of the rebellion he said, "I am mortified beyond expression when I view the clouds that have spread over the brightest morn that ever dawned upon any country." He added, "Without some alteration in our political creed, the superstructure we have been seven years raising at the expense of so much blood and treasure, must fall. We are fast verging to anarchy and confusion!"

Several months later, fifty-five delegates from twelve of the states met in Philadelphia to write a new constitution—one that would be strong enough to hold the fractious states together. Throughout the hot summer of 1787 the delegates debated the merits of various political systems ancient and contemporary, ultimately adopting an ancient Roman model that incorporated a separation of powers and extensive checks and balances, with a bicameral legislature, single executive, and independent judiciary. The resulting federal constitution, drafted by James Madison, described a "mixed" government and required ratification by at least nine of the thirteen states.

The ratification process pitted the Federalists (as the supporters of the stronger new Constitution called themselves) against the anti-Federalists, who believed the Constitution failed to protect individual liberties, and the latter group began publishing pamphlets and articles opposing ratification. In response, Alexander Hamilton, James Madison, and John Jay began publishing a series of essays explaining the Constitution and advocating its ratification. These *Federalist Papers* were widely read; *Federalist No. 10* was particularly influential, with its notion that representative democracy, rather than direct democracy, would better safeguard individual liberty from the abuses of factional or majority rule.

Delaware and Pennsylvania were the first states to ratify the Constitution, followed by Massachusetts, where a straw poll early in the state's convention showed 192 votes against the Constitution and only 144 in favor. But John Hancock proposed a compromise to his fellow convention delegates: Ratify the Constitution, and call for the addition of a Bill of Rights to be adopted by the first Congress. The Massachusetts anti-Federalists capitulated, giving the state a final vote of 187 for and 168 against, and narrow victories in New York and Virginia followed. By mid-April 1789, the new Constitution and government were in effect, with Washington having been chosen as president (see Question 130).

Although James Madison had not been in favor of a bill of rights during the framing of the Constitution, he had been won over by the time he took his seat in the first Congress. He proposed twelve amendments, all of which were passed by both House and Senate, but the first two, which dealt with the size of the House of Representatives and congressional salaries, were not ratified by the required number of states. What began as the third amendment ended up being the first, following ratification by the states on December 15, 1791. The new First Amendment to the Constitution reads as follows:

> Congress shall make no law respecting an establishment of
> religion, or prohibiting the free exercise thereof; or abridging
> the freedom of speech, or of the press; or the right of the
> people peaceably to assemble, and to petition the Government
> for a redress of grievances.

While many of the precepts formulated in the Bill of Rights were based on English law and the English Bill of Rights of 1689, the First

Amendment was a notable exception.[1] The English monarchy that the colonists had fled and then fought had a highly restrictive view of "speech." First, English law placed strict controls on what could be published, with licenses required for anything to be printed. This practice was assailed by John Milton in his 1644 essay *Areopagitica*, an eloquent plea for the liberty of unlicensed printing. In addition, the law of seditious libel criminalized the publication of any criticism of state or church, even if true, and allowed punishments as harsh as hanging.

Once the states had declared their independence from England they had begun creating their own state constitutions. The earliest, Virginia's, was adopted in 1776 and included this statement: "The freedom of the press is one of the greatest bulwarks of liberty, and can never be restrained but by despotic governments." By the time the federal Constitution and Bill of Rights were drafted, nine states had similar statements in their constitutions.

Despite these rights having been enshrined in both state and federal constitutions, less than a decade after the adoption of the Bill of Rights, Congress passed the Sedition Act (1798), which made it a federal crime to publish "any false, scandalous and malicious writing . . . against the government of the United States, or either house of the Congress . . . or the President." Conviction could bring a prison sentence of up to two years and fines as high as $2,000. Ostensibly intended to prevent developments like the Jacobin Terror in France, the law actually represented an effort by the Federalists, who were in the majority in Congress, to suppress written commentary favorable to Vice President Thomas Jefferson as he challenged incumbent John Adams for the presidency. Fourteen men, most of whom were associated with pro-Jefferson newspapers, were prosecuted under the act.

---

[1] The other nine amendments in the Bill of Rights (1791) deal with the right to bear arms, quartering of soldiers, searches and seizures, rules for prosecutions and eminent domain, the right to a speedy trial and to counsel, trial by jury, excessive bail and cruel punishments, unenumerated rights, and the rights of the states and the people. Among the seventeen later amendments are those addressing a revision of how the president and vice president are chosen (12; 1804), abolition of slavery (13; 1865), citizenship rights (14; 1868) and voting rights (15; 1870) for people of color and former slaves, income tax (16; 1913), Prohibition (18; 1919), women's suffrage (19; 1920), repeal of Prohibition (21; 1933), presidential term limitations (22; 1951), presidential disability (25; 1967), voting age lowered to eighteen (26; 1971), and congressional pay (27; 1992).

The Sedition Act backfired badly on the Federalists, since it was seen as an effort to bring back the tyranny of King George III. Jefferson won the presidency, and his new Republican Party (the forerunner of today's Democratic Party) took both houses of Congress in the election of 1800. When Jefferson assumed the presidency in 1801, he pardoned all those who had been convicted of sedition.

It was not until the twentieth century that freedom of speech once again became a serious legal concern. During World War I, the Espionage Act of 1917 and the Sedition Act of 1918 forbade disloyalty, refusal of military duty, and even "scurrilous" language against the government. In *Schenck v. United States* in 1919, the Supreme Court was asked to strike down a ruling against Charles Schenck, who had published pamphlets criticizing conscription. The Court unanimously upheld Schenck's conviction, with Justice Oliver Wendell Holmes writing, "The question in every case is whether the words used are used in such circumstances and are of such a nature as to create a clear and present danger that they will bring about the substantive evils that Congress has a right to prevent." In *Debs v. United States*, also in 1919, the Court again upheld the conviction of the union leader and Socialist Party presidential candidate Eugene V. Debs, who had received a ten-year prison sentence for speaking out against American involvement in the war.

Restrictive measures continued when, in 1940, Congress passed the Smith Act, which made it a crime to "knowingly or willfully advocate, abet, advise or teach the duty, necessity, desirability or propriety of overthrowing the Government of the United States . . . by force or violence, or for anyone to organize any association which teaches, advises or encourages such an overthrow, or for anyone to become a member of or to affiliate with any such association." The Smith Act was used during the 1940s and 1950s to prosecute socialists, fascists, and, most notably, communists, as in *Dennis v. United States*. In that case, convictions were upheld for eleven defendants who had been charged with conspiring to "teach and advocate the overthrow and destruction" of the government, not with actually attempting it or even conspiring to do so.

But as Red-baiting diminished after Senator Joseph McCarthy's condemnation by the Senate, public sentiment began to shift, and so did subsequent court rulings. In 1957, the Court ruled in *Yates v. United States* that, to constitute a crime, advocacy of violent overthrow of the government must be accompanied by some action toward that end.

The political upheavals of the 1960s and protests against the Vietnam War further stretched the boundaries of protected speech. A law banning the mutilation of draft cards was upheld in 1968, but by 1971, with the increasing unpopularity of the war, the Court overturned the conviction of Paul Robert Cohen, who had been arrested for wearing a jacket emblazoned with the words "Fuck the Draft" inside the Los Angeles Courthouse. Writing for the majority, Justice John Marshall Harlan commented, "One man's vulgarity is another's lyric."

The notion that freedom of speech was invalidated by obscenity had a profound effect on what books Americans could read. Earlier in the twentieth century, novels such as D. H. Lawrence's *Lady Chatterley's Lover* and Theodore Dreiser's *An American Tragedy* were banned, and in 1933 a copy of James Joyce's *Ulysses* was seized by customs authorities when it was brought into the United States. In 1957, the Supreme Court upheld the conviction of Samuel Roth, who had sent a publication deemed obscene in the mail, in contravention of federal law. Justice William J. Brennan, Jr., however, wrote that "sex and obscenity are not synonymous" and proposed a test for censorship: "whether to the average person, applying contemporary community standards, the dominant theme of the material taken as a whole appeals to the prurient interest."

Another landmark ruling took place in 1964, when the Supreme Court overturned a libel ruling in *New York Times Co. v. Sullivan*. Prior to the Court's decision, libel law in the United States reflected that of England, in which the burden of proof rested with the defendant. On March 29, 1960, the *New York Times* published an advertisement by supporters of Martin Luther King, Jr., accusing unnamed southern officials of violence and misconduct in their treatment of civil rights workers and protesters. L. B. Sullivan, commissioner of the Montgomery, Alabama, police force (which had been criticized, sometimes inaccurately, in the ad), sued the *Times*, claiming damage to his reputation, and a state court ruled in his favor, awarding a $500,000 judgment.

Other lawsuits were filed on behalf of southern officials who objected to the way northern newspapers covered the civil rights struggle, until the *Times* was facing fines running in the millions, which would have put it out of business. The newspaper took the case to the Supreme Court, which found decisively for the *Times*. In his opinion, Justice William J. Brennan, Jr., stated "that debate on public issues should be uninhibited, robust, and wide-open, and that it may well include vehement, caustic, and sometimes unpleasantly sharp attacks on government and public officials." The Sullivan ruling went on to say that "erroneous statement is inevitable in free debate, and . . . it must be protected if the freedoms of expression are to have the breathing space that they need to survive." Henceforth, plaintiffs in libel cases would have to prove not only the falsity of statements but also the intent to deceive.

Landmark rulings such as these have not been forthcoming in the first decade of the twenty-first century. The Bush administration's practices of attempting to compel reporters to reveal sources and turn over notes, paying allegedly independent journalists to espouse the government's views, and conducting much of its business far from public scrutiny eroded and hampered the guarantees and safeguards of the First Amendment.

After the passage of the Sedition Act of 1798, James Madison wrote that it asserted "a power which, more than any other, ought to produce universal alarm, because it is leveled against the right of freely examining public characters and measures, and of free communication among the people thereon, which has ever been justly deemed the only effectual guardian of every other right." In *Freedom for the Thought That We Hate: A Biography of the First Amendment*, constitutional scholar Anthony Lewis comments as follows:

> Madison's phrase "the right of freely examining public characters and measures" really expresses the premise of the American political system. . . . It tells us why Americans should scent danger when a government tries to stop a newspaper from disclosing the origins of an unsuccessful war, as the Nixon administration did when the *New York Times* began publishing the Pentagon Papers on the Vietnam War in 1971, or accuses a newspaper of endangering national security by disclosing secret and illegal wiretapping without warrants, as the administration of George W. Bush did during the Iraq War in 2006.

—*Nancy Walsh*

133 ～ What was the first permanent African settlement for freed slaves?

Freetown, Sierra Leone, in 1792

THE YEARS LEADING UP TO the American Revolution saw growing concerns among many southern colonists and plantation owners about their increasingly restive slave populations. Insurrections of blacks had occurred in New York in 1712, on the island of Saint John in 1733, and at the Stono River in South Carolina in 1739. Uprisings were taking place on plantations in the Caribbean and in the South American Dutch colony of Suriname, and rumors were circulating about their spreading north. By the summer of 1775 there was widespread panic throughout the southern colonies that an armed slave uprising, aided and abetted by the British, was imminent. In North Carolina, the Wilmington Committee of Safety banned the importation of new slaves and sought to disarm all local blacks. In July, the British commander of Fort Johnson on the Cape Fear River near Wilmington issued a proclamation entitled "Encouragement to Negroes to Elope from Their Masters" and offered protection to slaves who escaped.

The royal governors of the southern colonies also saw their power, and that of the crown, crumbling, and were growing increasingly desperate for troops to shore up their defenses against the colonists. After the early skirmishes at Lexington and Concord (see Question 129), it was clear that no British troops could be spared from the northern garrisons. As historian Simon Schama writes in *Rough Crossings: The Slaves, the British, and the American Revolution*, rumors spread that the British were about to "play the race card" and that "secret caches of arms were to be off-loaded from British ships and delivered to Indians and blacks. Once the slaves had slaughtered their masters and burned their houses, they would be rewarded with their liberty." Schama also observes that "this nightmare is what Thomas Jefferson meant in the Declaration of Independence when referring, otherwise cryptically, to the king having 'excited domestic insurrections.'"

On November 7, 1775, Lord Dunmore, the royal governor of Virginia, issued a proclamation declaring martial law in his state and asserting that the rebelling colonists were traitors to the crown. It also pronounced "all indentured servants, Negroes, or others . . . free that are able and willing to bear arms." Newspapers published the text of his proclamation, and the local authorities responded by tightening restrictions on slaves and threatening severe punishment for runaways. Nonetheless, many blacks fled to Dunmore's ship on the Potomac and, within a month, three hundred had been inducted into the so-called Ethiopian Regiment and outfitted in uniforms inscribed with "Liberty to Slaves."

One of these runaways, Thomas Peters, thought to have been born in what is now Nigeria in about 1740 and brought to America on a French slave ship, joined up with another regiment of former slave soldiers, the Black Pioneers. Wounded twice and promoted to sergeant, he eventually made his way to New York City, where numerous loyalists, both black and white, had fled in the hope of obtaining safe passage to Canada, England, or elsewhere. Peters and his family boarded a ship bound for Nova Scotia—the beginning of a journey that would ultimately lead him to the west coast of Africa, where he would become one of the founders of Freetown, Sierra Leone.

From the settlement in Nova Scotia, where he lived with some two thousand former Black Pioneers and their families, Peters sought to claim the land allotments promised by the British. A vast tract of Nova Scotia had been set aside by the British government for former loyalists, with the greatest shares going to those who had lost most in America. Free blacks, of course, had had nothing to lose, and thus found themselves at the back of the line. Fewer than half of the black settlers received any land, and these were typically given plots entirely unsuitable for farming. Peters initially brought the black loyalists' complaints to the lieutenant governor of the province of New Brunswick, without effect, and then to the Home Office in London, where he had arrived in October 1790.

Meanwhile, London had witnessed a growing movement for abolition of the slave trade, which followed a triangular route. British-made goods were taken to the west coast of Africa and exchanged for slaves. The captive blacks were then transported across the Atlantic—the horrifying "middle passage"—and sold in the West Indies and elsewhere. Slave-grown products such as sugar and tobacco were then shipped back to England. The slave trade, dominated by Britain, accounted for 80 percent of the country's foreign income.

This situation was repugnant on moral, humanitarian, and political grounds to abolitionists like Granville Sharp and John and Thomas Clarkson and to parliamentarian William Wilberforce. As early as 1769, Sharp had published *A Representation of the Injustice and Dangerous Tendency of Tolerating Slavery*, and by the 1780s Quaker antislavery committees had begun petitioning Parliament. The Clarkson brothers and Wilberforce had established the Committee for Effecting the Abolition of the Slave Trade, which first met in May 1787. This group, which was influential in raising public awareness through a campaign of pamphlets, lobbying, and boycotts, adopted as its logo a kneeling slave in chains above the words "Am I not a man and a brother?"—an image created by pottery designer Josiah Wedgwood.

Thomas Clarkson spent years traversing England, promoting abolition and gathering evidence of the cruelty of slavery, such as the leg irons and branding irons used on slave ships, as well as giving lectures and publishing essays. Wilberforce, who had been giving antislavery speeches in the House of Commons since 1789, introduced in April 1791 the first bill to abolish the slave trade. When it was easily defeated, Wilberforce said, "Let us not despair; it is a blessed cause, and success, ere long, will crown our exertions. Already we have gained one victory; we have obtained, for these poor creatures, the recognition of their human nature, which, for a while was most shamefully denied."

These were the men ex-slave Thomas Peters met with in London. He told Granville Sharp that the failure of the government to provide blacks with the land and provisions they had been promised in Nova Scotia had, in effect, forced them back into servitude after they had risked their lives for the loyalist cause. Peters and Sharp together drafted a petition in which they detailed the settlers' land grievances and requested "some establishment where they may attain a competent settlement for themselves, and be enabled by their industrious exertions to become useful subjects to his Majesty." The petition also stated that while some of the settlers in Nova Scotia wished for land allotments there, others were "willing to go wherever the wisdom of government may think proper to provide for them as free subjects of the British Empire."

Sierra Leone had previously been investigated by Sharp and others as a destination for free blacks, a sizable number of whom had been residing in London. In 1787, Sharp had arranged for four hundred blacks to go to Sierra Leone to establish the "Province of Freedom," otherwise known as Granville Town, on land purchased from a local chieftain. This earlier utopian mission had failed, however, after disputes broke out between the would-be settlers and the locals, ending with another chieftain's burning down the makeshift settlement in 1789.

But Sharp persisted, founding the Sierra Leone Company with Thomas Clarkson to establish a permanent settlement made up of the disgruntled Nova Scotia settlers. With this goal in mind, Thomas Peters returned to Nova Scotia accompanied by experienced sailor John Clarkson and armed with a document from the company promising adequate plots of land and a system of law that would include black juries and "civil, military, and commercial rights" that would be identical for blacks and whites. The men recruited about twelve hundred former slaves from several of the small Nova Scotia settlements, setting out in late 1791 in a flotilla of fifteen ships for a harrowing transatlantic crossing during which many sickened and dozens died. The group arrived at Saint George's Bay in Sierra Leone in March 1792, and legend has it that Peters led the settlers in greeting their new home by singing a hymn with the refrain, "The day of jubilee is come, / Return ye ransomed sinners home."

The settlers soon found that certain of the promises made to them would not be fulfilled. In the interim the company had decided that the land allotments were to be taxed and that the blacks would not be self-ruling; instead, a group of white councillors, skilled in surveying, engineering, and other tasks that would be needed to establish the colony, would act as magistrates. This was hardly the color-blind utopia the settlers had hoped for.

Moreover, the white councillors, who had arrived two weeks earlier, ostensibly to begin work, had simply remained on their ship in the harbor, using up supplies, bickering, and drinking rum. Nothing was ready when the settlers arrived, and the rainy season was approaching. As the leader of the blacks, Peters complained to John Clarkson, who by this time had been appointed governor. Though Clarkson was admired and trusted by the blacks, Peters was outraged by the seeming repetition of the Nova Scotia deception.

Clarkson, who had become ill during the voyage, continued to experience fevers, fatigue, and extreme nervousness while attempting to oversee the clearing of the land and the building of at least temporary housing before the seasonal storms arrived. Despite being an unwilling governor, wanting little more than to return to England, he remained dedicated to the settlers and their cause. Throughout the spring of 1792 he sought to maintain his authority, particularly over the increasingly uncooperative whites, and to placate the blacks by establishing an assembly in which they could air their grievances.

Peters was becoming more strident, seeking a position of authority as speaker general for the settlers and continually haranguing Clarkson, demanding representation for the blacks in the government. As such, he was merely insisting on the same rights of British subjects that the Americans had demanded less than two decades before. In June, however, Peters succumbed to malaria, leaving seven children whose Creole descendants still populate Freetown.

John Clarkson, ailing and feverish, remained in Freetown as governor only six months more, but long enough to award land grants to the first forty settlers and see the first gardens planted. He received gifts of yams, papayas, chickens, and eggs when the entire colony turned out to bid him farewell as his ship sailed on December 29.

The fifteen years following Clarkson's departure were characterized by material progress but political unrest and animosity toward the English directors of the Sierra Leone Company, who were attempting to enforce strict new regulations and impose new taxes. The colonists grew increasingly rebellious, and by the summer of 1800, blacks in the assembly threatened that the white magistrates and company men might be set adrift in the ocean without sails. Back in England, the company directors made noises about a naval invasion to quash the rebellion, but a group of settlers declared the governor to be overthrown and wrote its own laws, setting price ceilings and establishing fines for crimes such as trespassing and theft.

The company dispatched a ship from Halifax, Canada, carrying hundreds of Jamaican warriors, but the worried young new governor, Thomas Ludlum, decided not to wait for its arrival and ordered loyal settlers to surround the rebels, who were encamped outside Freetown. In the ensuing battle, two rebels were killed and many others escaped into the forest, only to be captured; the leaders were hanged.

A new company charter was introduced, eliminating the black representatives in the assembly. While order was restored and trade in coffee, sugar, and rice began to prosper, the company slowly foundered, and funds for administration and defense evaporated. In 1807—the same year that a bill abolishing the slave trade was passed in Parliament—Freetown became a crown colony, remaining such until 1961.

The early years of the nineteenth century also saw a rising tide of abolitionism in the United States. After the Revolution and the abolition of slavery in the northern states, many Americans, including Thomas Jefferson, had begun expressing interest in establishing a colony like Freetown as a solution to the "problem" of free blacks, because it was widely believed that blacks and whites would never be able to coexist peacefully. In 1816, the American Colonization Society was formed with the strong financial and political backing of President James Monroe. Five years later, the first freed American blacks established a settlement south of Sierra Leone, and in 1824 the new country was named Liberia and its capital was called Monrovia in honor of the president's contributions to the cause.

In the decades following the years of struggle in Freetown, the English abolitionists continued their advocacy, and in 1823 the Society for the Mitigation and Gradual Abolition of Slavery was formed. That same year, William Wilberforce published his *Appeal to the Religion, Justice, and Humanity of the Inhabitants of the British Empire in Behalf of the Negro Slaves in the West Indies*, arguing that slavery was a moral disgrace that must be outlawed. Despite his ongoing efforts in Parliament, another decade elapsed before Wilberforce, on his deathbed, learned that the Slavery Abolition Act would be passed.

Thomas Clarkson continued traveling tirelessly to gather petitions demanding emancipation, and after the British Abolition Act of 1833 he advocated for abolition in America. Both Clarkson brothers believed that halting the slave trade would choke off the institution of slavery itself, but the day John Clarkson died in 1828 he came upon an article in the *Anti-Slavery Reporter* detailing the ongoing abuse of slaves in the West Indies. His last words were, "It is dreadful to think, after my brother and his friends have been working for forty years, that such things should still be."

—*Nancy Walsh*

134 ∾ What was the first manifesto of British literary Romanticism?

The preface to the second edition of Lyrical Ballads *by Wordsworth and Coleridge, 1800*

THE PERIOD IN ENGLISH LITERATURE stretching from roughly 1660 to 1798 is often referred to as the neoclassical age because it harked back to the balance, harmony, and themes associated with classical Greek and Roman literature, especially the works of Homer, Virgil, and Horace. Though the era was highly diverse—incorporating John Milton's sublime epics and the birth of Restoration drama and the English novel—it remains preeminent as an age of scintillating satire, as epitomized in the acerbic verse of John Dryden and Alexander Pope (e.g., *The Rape of the Lock* and *The Dunciad*) and the mordant prose of Jonathan Swift.

The poetry of the neoclassical era was aimed at a small, sophisticated readership. It tended to be didactic, rhetorical, decorous, and refined, emphasizing the primacy of reason, the mind, and absolute truths. Allusions to Greco-Roman literature, mythology, and culture abounded, and there was a decided emphasis on the urban lives and interests of the upper crust and the political and literary classes in London. The poetry of the time was often witty and sometimes venomous—Pope was aptly nicknamed "the Wasp of Twickenham." It dealt in polished, elegantly phrased generalities, in "what oft was thought, yet ne'er so well expressed." Poets such as Dryden and Pope perfected the balanced antitheses of the heroic couplet (two rhymed, end-stopped lines of iambic pentameter) to ridicule vices and absurdities with the goal of reforming socially offensive behaviors—or attacking their enemies.

This era was followed in European letters by Romanticism, a label first applied in the late eighteenth century to *Faust* and other works by Johann Wolfgang von Goethe to indicate their kinship with the magically mysterious world of medieval romances. Romanticism grew out of the Sturm und Drang (storm and stress) movement in Germany, whose most influential work was Goethe's epistolary novel *The Sorrows of Young Werther* (1774). German Romantic thinkers such as J. G. Herder stressed that the true culture and genius of a nation arise from the spirit of the common people rather than the effete educated classes.

In Great Britain, the twilight of the neoclassical era was marked by proto-Romantic manifestations such as the rise of the macabre Gothic novel and the so-called Graveyard School of poetry, as in Edward Young's *Night Thoughts* (1742–46) and Thomas Gray's "Elegy Written in a Country Churchyard" (1751). The mentally unhinged Christopher Smart wrote dithyrambs to his marvelous cat Jeoffry, James Macpherson faked translations from wild Gaelic epics supposedly written by a third-century poet named Ossian, and, in 1765, Bishop Thomas Percy published a collection of old ballads—*Reliques of Ancient English Poetry*—that sparked an enormous revival of antiquarian interest in the Middle Ages and its folk art and folklore. Other early Romantic British poets include Thomas Chatterton, who faked medieval English poems and committed suicide at age seventeen in 1770; the Scottish bard Robert Burns (1759–96); and the towering idiosyncratic genius William Blake (1757–1827). Blake's sardonic "Proverbs of Hell" in his *The Marriage of Heaven and Hell* (1790–93) offer nuggets of Romantic lore such as "The road of excess leads to the palace of wisdom" and "The tygers of wrath are wiser than the horses of instruction."

This was the literary environment that saw the appearance in 1798 of *Lyrical Ballads, with a Few Other Poems*, a collection of verse published in Bristol by William Wordsworth (1770–1850) and Samuel Taylor Coleridge (1772–1834). The two young poets had become close friends and neighbors while living in villages near Bristol in 1797 and decided to collaborate on a book. As it happened, of the twenty-three poems in the anonymous first edition of *Lyrical Ballads*, all but four were by Wordsworth, though the opening poem, by far the longest of the collection, was Coleridge's "The Rime of the Ancient Mariner." Even here, Wordsworth's input was not lacking, since he had suggested that Coleridge add the episodes of the mariner's shooting of the albatross and the dead sailors' steering of the ship.

The title *Lyrical Ballads* was an oxymoron that suggested the poets' radical agenda: Their goal was to meld the more learned traditions of lyric verse (often thought to convey strong feelings) with the popular or folksy artistry of ballads (which told a story in rather simple verse). An "Advertisement" prefixed to the volume explained that most of the poems were to be considered as experiments to see "how far the language of conversation in the middle and lower classes of society is adapted to the purposes of poetic pleasure."

Wordsworth's contributions include some notoriously sentimental slop like "We Are Seven," in which a little girl can't understand what it means that two of her six siblings are dead, and "The Idiot Boy," which contains bathetic lines such as "Burr, burr—now Johnny's lips they burr." (Coleridge later remarked that this poem was "rather a laughable burlesque on the blindness of anile [old-lady-like] dotage, than an analytic display of maternal affection.")

In "The Tables Turned," however, we approach the core of Wordsworth's thematic concerns in his conviction that Nature is the supreme ethical teacher:

> *One impulse from a vernal wood*
> *May teach you more of man,*
> *Of moral evil and of good,*
> *Than all the sages can.*

This poem also contains a famous critique of the sterile and analytic scientific mind: "We murder to dissect."

The collection ends (as it begins) with an undeniable masterpiece: Wordsworth's "Tintern Abbey," a poem in blank verse evoking a visit with his sister to a landscape that had moved him deeply five years earlier at age twenty-three, when Nature still "was all in all" to him. Now, his calmer but deeper insight into Nature—its pantheistic divinity and its grave moral effect on us—is made possible by the sobering knowledge of suffering he has acquired, having heard in the interim "the still, sad music of humanity."

But the philosophical and linguistic complexities of "Tintern Abbey" associate it with the "Few Other Poems" of the book's full title. Most of the rest of the poems in *Lyrical Ballads* deal with the lives of uneducated rustics—people unspoiled by the sophistications and sophistries of modern city life. The volume constituted a British counterpart to Jean-Jacques Rousseau's exaltation of primitivism, made all the more cogent by the horrors, crime, and dislocations inflicted on the new urban proletariat by England's Industrial Revolution. Wordsworth wanted to help his readers develop their moral sensibilities by paying heed to the mysterious promptings of the natural world.

In the division of labor for the volume, Wordsworth was supposed to take everyday subject matter and bring out its charming novelty, while Coleridge's task was to deal with the supernatural or exotic in a way that made it seem vividly realistic in order to arouse in the reader, as Coleridge later phrased it, "that willing suspension of disbelief . . . which constitutes poetic faith."

Lyrical Ballads thus presented individual narratives of tragedies and simple joys among the lowly rather than generalized rules of poetic decorum or human behavior, as in Pope's *An Essay on Criticism* and *An Essay on Man*. Concentrating on rural life as Wordsworth knew it from his native Lake District, it took as its subject matter children, peasants, old men, the mysterious, the eerie, and sometimes the supernatural. It emphasized the emotions, the imagination, subjectivity, and spontaneity. Instead of the universal traits that neoclassical literature had focused on, *Lyrical Ballads* stressed the particular, and often the peculiar. (In Blake's words, "To generalize is to be an idiot.") As opposed to poets like Dryden and Pope, Wordsworth treated the lives of humans who were "different" with pathos rather than mockery. He also used freer organic forms—blank verse or balladlike stanzas—rather than the ponderous heroic couplets of neoclassical verse.

The novelty of all this is subject to debate. Whereas the great scholar of Romanticism M. H. Abrams asserts that "no other book of poems in English so plainly announces a new literary departure," Wordsworth scholar Geoffrey Hartman believes the poems of *Lyrical Ballads* "were not original in subject or sentiment, or even in many elements of form." Whatever shading or nuances one prefers to give to these opposing views, one thing is clear: The first reviewers of *Lyrical Ballads* did not care for it very much. In the second edition of 1800, bolstered by an additional volume of poems by Wordsworth, the poet felt obliged to include a preface that explained his (and, to some extent, Coleridge's) aesthetic creed.

"All good poetry is the spontaneous overflow of powerful feelings," Wordsworth asserts, yet "it takes its origin from emotion recollected in tranquillity." This latter qualifying phrase removes poetry from the arena of primal grunts and stresses its requisite quality of contemplativeness. Although people crave sensationalism, poetry can educate them to a more proper sensitivity to the life around them: "For the human mind is capable of being excited without the application of gross and violent stimulants." (This statement is somewhat less true today than it was in 1800.) Citing the craze for Gothic novels, "sickly and stupid German tragedies, and deluges of idle and extravagant stories in verse," Wordsworth decries "this degrading thirst after outrageous stimulation." *Lyrical Ballads* was an experiment "to ascertain how far, by fitting to metrical arrangement a selection of the real language of men in a state of vivid sensation," poetic pleasure may be

produced. Simply stated, poetry is good prose set to meter, which con-
tributes charm to the verse and also restrains the poet's tendency to get
carried away.

The language of "humble and rustic life"—seen as "a more permanent, and a far more philosophical language than that which is frequently substituted for it by poets"—was to be preferred over urban
artificiality and "the gaudiness and inane phraseology of many modern
writers." What Wordsworth means by "the real language of men" turns
out to be poetic speech shorn of the absurd excesses of eighteenth-
century poetic diction and rococo ornament. (Oft-cited examples are
"the finny tribe" for *fish*, because the latter word was considered too
lowly, humble, and pedestrian to use in verse, and the even more ludicrous "household feathery people" as a euphemism for *chickens*.)

Wordsworth and Coleridge had thus determined "to choose incidents and situations from common life, and to relate or describe
them . . . in a selection of language really used by men, and, at the same
time, to throw over them a coloring of imagination, whereby ordinary
things should be presented to the mind in an unusual aspect." As
opposed to the view of the perceiving mind as John Locke's tabula rasa
(blank slate), the Romantics, following the notions of Immanuel Kant,
saw the mind as actively participating in the creation of perceptions in
a way that defines the faculty called "the imagination."

To the question, "What is a poet?" Wordsworth responds: "He is a
man speaking to men: a man, it is true, endowed with more lively sensibility, more enthusiasm and tenderness, who has a greater knowledge
of human nature, than are supposed to be common among mankind."
He also possesses "a greater readiness and power in expressing what he
thinks and feels," but he differs from other men only in degree, not in
kind. The goal of the poet is to give "immediate pleasure to a human
being," though Wordsworth also wants to write the kind of poetry that
will be "important in the multiplicity and quality of its moral relations."

In his *Biographia Literaria* (1817), a hybrid work encompassing
both autobiography and some of the most perceptive literary criticism
in English, Coleridge subjected Wordsworth's theory and practice of
poetry, as embodied in the *Lyrical Ballads* and its preface (which
Wordsworth revised several times afterward), to a sometimes scathing
critique, especially regarding Wordsworth's exaltation of the language
of common men as the fittest for poetry. "With many parts of this preface," Coleridge wrote, "I never concurred." Nonetheless, he continued

to regard Wordsworth as the greatest English poet since John Milton—and who would say he was wrong?

The dour, humorless, and self-obsessed Wordsworth and the feckless, substance-abusing, and bloviating Coleridge became seriously estranged in 1810. Though they reconciled in 1812—and even toured Europe together in 1828—the two never recaptured their old intimacy. When Coleridge died in 1834, his erstwhile friend, who had once referred to him as a "rotten drunkard," did not attend the funeral. But in his famed "Kubla Khan," Coleridge managed to leave the world a much more striking embodiment of the ideal Romantic poet than Wordsworth's "man speaking to men":

> *Weave a circle round him thrice*
> *And close your eyes with holy dread,*
> *For he on honey-dew hath fed,*
> *And drunk the milk of Paradise.*

NINETEENTH CENTURY

135 ∾ What was the first French empire?

The empire ruled over by Napoleon Bonaparte, 1804–14

ALONG WITH GOETHE, BEETHOVEN, AND BYRON, Napoleon Bonaparte (1769–1821) was one of the titans of the Romantic era, but he alone seemed to embody the zeitgeist itself. The man whose conquests made him emperor of the French, master of continental Europe, and the epitome of French military *gloire* was born Napoleone di Buonaparte to parents of Italian ancestry in Ajaccio, Corsica, and to the end of his life spoke French with an Italian accent. French novelist Stendhal went so far as to see Napoleon as the last of the great Italian condottieri—the Renaissance soldier-tyrants who dominated the politics of their age and made up their morality on the fly.

Educated in military schools in France, Napoleon became an artillery officer at sixteen and, after capturing Toulon for the French Revolutionary government, a brigadier general at age twenty-four (see Question 131). In 1795, when a conspiracy threatened the existence of the Republic (which was fighting off enemies at home and abroad), he dispersed the royalist mobs in Paris with "a whiff of grapeshot," according to historian Thomas Carlyle, but actually by shooting down fourteen hundred of the rioters who didn't flee fast enough from Napoleon's cannons.

This exploit induced the new government of France, the Directory, to put Napoleon in command of the French army of Italy. Before he left for the wars, he married a beautiful Creole widow, Josephine de Beauharnais, who was six years his senior.

In Italy, he won six brilliant victories, mainly against the Austrians, in the northern part of the peninsula. After the battle of Lodi in 1796, by which he chased the Austrians out of Lombardy and established the Lombard Republic, he earned his nickname of "the Little Corporal" from his troops, who admired the spunk of their diminutive general (he was about five feet two inches). In 1797, he founded the Ligurian Republic in Genoa and put an end to the senile Republic of Venice (see Question 36). Intending to take the war to Vienna, he got within sixty miles of the Austrian capital when a truce was declared. Apart from his spectacular military successes against larger forces, he also sent

513

shipments of plundered gold, jewels, and artworks back to France, where he was hailed as a hero on his return.

Napoleon's next assignment was to assume command of French forces training for an invasion of England, which (with Austria, Prussia, and Russia, at various times) was one of the chief powers resisting the influx of French Revolutionary armies and ideas. Judging France not quite ready for a direct attack on *la perfide Albion*—"perfidious England"—Napoleon decided to threaten its interests in India instead by sailing an army to occupy Egypt in the hope of conquering the Ottoman Empire.

In 1798, Napoleon's victory at the Battle of the Pyramids against Egyptian forces made him master of the country, but British admiral Horatio Nelson destroyed the French fleet in the Battle of the Nile. Napoleon advanced into Syria and began the siege of Acre but called it off after two months of watching his soldiers die of bubonic plague. He himself left Egypt in 1799, two years before his army abandoned its occupation.

The renown of his albeit unsuccessful Egyptian campaign (during which his men discovered the Rosetta Stone) allowed Napoleon to overthrow the wishy-washy Directory by the coup d'état of 18 Brumaire, Year VIII of the Revolutionary Calendar (November 9, 1799). He established the so-called Consulate (1799–1804), headed by three consuls, while making sure he himself became virtual dictator of France as "First Consul." Appointing the nobleman, former bishop, and perpetual opportunist, dandy, and ladies' man Talleyrand as foreign minister (though describing him as "shit in a silk purse"), Napoleon nonetheless made all the big decisions. These included leading an army across the Alps to chase the Austrians out of northern Italy (again) at the battle of Marengo in 1800 and restoring Catholicism in France—after the Revolution had suppressed it—by the Concordat of 1801.

With the formidable British fleet shutting off easy access to the Atlantic, Napoleon decided in 1803 to sell the enormous Louisiana Territory to President Thomas Jefferson for $15 million—a remarkable acquisition for the United States that almost doubled its size. The dismal remnant of French troops trying to suppress the Haitian rebellion led by Toussaint-Louverture was evacuated in the same year. Of the twenty-five thousand soldiers dispatched to Haiti in 1801, twenty-two thousand had died of yellow fever.

Napoleon took full advantage of a British-backed plot to assassinate him that was uncovered in Paris in February 1804, using it as a pretext for making his position hereditary, so that the success of any future attempt against his life would fail to bring about a regime change. The Senate and the Tribunate of the Consulate duly proclaimed him emperor of the French and king of Italy in May, and Napoleon invited Pope Pius VII to officiate at his coronation at Paris's Notre Dame on December 2. At the ceremony, the pontiff anointed Napoleon's head and hands and then handed the crown to the new emperor, who placed it on his own head and then crowned Josephine. Less than five years later, Napoleon had Pius arrested for refusing to renounce his rule over the Papal States, which were made part of the French Empire. (The pope, held captive in northern Italy, returned to Rome only after Waterloo.)

The famed Code Napoléon was promulgated in this same year, with its core principle of the equality of all before the law. The Code was exported to lands subject to France, which also saw a forced modernization of their economic, financial, and class structures. Aside from codifying the tangled mass of French laws into a condensed and consistent whole, Napoleon unified the French educational system, reinstituted learned societies, introduced the metric system, and created the first modern European civil service.

In 1805, it pleased Napoleon to be crowned king of Italy with the Iron Crown of the Lombards in Milan Cathedral and to abandon the French Revolutionary Calendar, now that he was a proper emperor. Although in October Lord Nelson smashed the combined French and Spanish fleet at Trafalgar, off the Spanish coast, the French army remained supreme. At Austerlitz, north of Vienna, Napoleon shattered the Austrian and Russian armies and, the following year, crushed the Prussians at Jena and Auerstädt, but he could not bring Great Britain to heel.

His Berlin and Milan Decrees thus aimed at waging economic war on Britain—that "nation of shopkeepers," as he scornfully labeled it—by instituting the Continental System, which prohibited the importation of British goods into continental ports of territories under his rule or allied with him. Ships that came to continental ports after calling at British ports would be seized. The British retaliated by blockading continental ports, searching and seizing ships for whatever they deemed as contraband, and perfecting the art of smuggling. Napoleon's strategy backfired, because it created European-wide resentment against him. One coup de grâce he administered in 1806 was his dissolution of the rickety, eight-hundred-year-old anachronism known as the Holy Roman Empire (see Question 73), replacing it with a Confederation of the Rhine, over which he made himself "protector."

Besides creating a new nobility in France, Napoleon unleashed his inner nepotist. He made his brother Louis king of Holland (though later dethroning him), his brother Jérôme king of the newly created German kingdom of Westphalia, and his brother Joseph king of Naples. After taking Barcelona and Madrid in 1808, he moved Joseph over to the throne of Spain and made his brother-in-law Joachim Murat king of Naples while appointing his stepson, Eugène Beauharnais, viceroy of Italy. Small wonder that Napoleon's mother, Letizia Ramolino, who had borne thirteen children and was officially dubbed "Madame Mère," adopted as her unofficial motto *"Pourvu que ça dure!"* ("Provided it lasts!").

Conservative, Catholic, and royalist Spain, however, did not appreciate its new masters and rose in rebellion. England began actively helping native guerrillas battle the French in this Peninsular War, which sapped Napoleon's fighting strength elsewhere—he called it his "ulcer." Another disturbing thought for Napoleon was his lack of a legitimate heir, so he divorced the forty-six-year-old (and fairly promiscuous) Josephine.

Napoleon's star was at its zenith in 1810. In addition to France and Corsica, his French Empire embraced the Low Countries, German lands west of the Rhine, about one-third of Italy, and parts of Slovenia, Croatia, and the Dalmatian Coast. Beyond this core of the French Empire was the "grand empire," which included the rest of peninsular Italy, Spain, the Confederation of the Rhine, and the Grand Duchy of Warsaw. The rest of continental Europe, except for the Ottoman Balkans, Portugal, Sicily, and Sardinia, but temporarily including Russia, Prussia, and Austria, was allied with France. Also in this year, Napoleon married Archduchess Marie Louise, daughter of Austrian emperor Francis I and niece of the guillotined Marie Antoinette. (Their son, Napoleon François Joseph Charles [1811–32], was declared king of Rome.) At the end of 1810, however, Czar Alexander I of Russia announced that his nation would no longer abide by the Continental System.

The result was the major fiasco of Napoleon's career—his invasion of Russia. Believing that forcing Russia back into compliance would succeed in bankrupting Britain and obliging it to sue for peace, alarmed by intelligence reports of a threatened Russian invasion of Poland and the French Empire, and hopeful that his defeat of Russia would enable him to be crowned emperor of Europe, he assembled his international *Grande Armée* of about 610,000 for the largest single military operation before the advent of World War I (see Question 146).

Napoleon set out with only three weeks of supplies, confident that he would soon encounter the Russian army and annihilate it. He crossed into Russia on June 24, but disease was already exacting a horrible toll on his troops. After defeating the Russians at Smolensk, he won the grueling victory of Borodino on September 7 against Marshal Mikhail Kutuzov, in which the French army lost more than thirty thousand killed, wounded, or captured, versus about forty-two thousand for the Russians. Entering Moscow on September 14, Napoleon saw that most of the three hundred thousand inhabitants had fled and stores of food had been destroyed. Because most of the city was torched by order of the departing Russian governor, the emperor realized it would be impossible to spend the winter there with little food or shelter.

Czar Alexander refused to discuss peace terms, so after five weeks in Moscow there was nothing left for Napoleon to do but sound a retreat on October 19 with an army already decimated by typhus, dysentery, the cold, and hunger from the Russian scorched-earth strategy. While crossing the Berezina River in modern Belarus, the tattered shards of the Grande Armée were devastated by flank attacks from the Cossack cavalry and Russian forces, while many others drowned or died in stampedes. Learning of a coup attempt in France, Napoleon left Joachim Murat in command when he abandoned the army on December 5, traveling in disguise in a horse-drawn carriage mounted on a sleigh. While stopping in Warsaw on his way back to Paris, he made his famous remark: "From the sublime to the ridiculous is but a step." Only about ten thousand men fit for combat survived the Russian campaign.

Yet in 1813 Napoleon raised a new army of a half million. Although his old foes now ganged up on him, he defeated the Austrians, Prussians, and Russians at Dresden in August before sustaining a catastrophic blow at the Battle of the Nations at Leipzig two months later. The French armies retreated across the Rhine before the end of the year, and the Allied armies occupied Paris on March 30, 1814.

Napoleon abdicated on April 6 and was banished to the tiny island of Elba, off the Tuscan coast. The brother of the executed French king entered Paris and assumed the throne as Louis XVIII, while the

Congress of Vienna opened with land grabs by the victorious powers—Great Britain, Russia, Austria, and Prussia. France was shrunk to its borders of 1792, but the ever-pliant and protean Talleyrand, the French representative at the congress, pleaded that the common foe had been Napoleon and not France. Many of the French Revolutionary and Napoleonic legal reforms, as well as the abolition of feudalism and manorialism in conquered territories, were allowed to stand, even as kings were being restored to their thrones in Spain, Portugal, Naples, and elsewhere.

But while the French were busily hating their new king and the Allies were quarreling at the Congress of Vienna, Napoleon escaped from Elba and made his way to France, promptly scaring Louis XVIII over the border to Ghent. Napoleon's "Hundred Days" began with his entry into Paris to general jubilation on March 20, 1815, and his being proclaimed emperor once more. He soon recruited an army of 125,000.

The weary British, Austrians, Prussians, and Russians formed yet another alliance, while the Congress of Vienna adjourned. The duke of Wellington, who had defeated French armies in Spain many times during the Peninsular War, was put in charge of ninety-three thousand British, Belgian, Dutch, and German soldiers. He was joined in Belgium by Field Marshal G. L. von Blücher and his 116,000 Prussians. The two commanders were to wait there for the arrival of their Austrian and Russian allies, who would swell their combined troops to six hundred thousand—an irresistible force with which to deliver a knockout blow to France.

Napoleon knew he had to attack Wellington and Blücher before the others arrived, since, as it was, he was outnumbered almost two to one. Advancing into Belgium, he determined to drive his army between the two enemy forces and defeat each in turn—a time-tested strategy of his. On June 16, French troops under the command of Marshal Michel Ney failed to dislodge Wellington at Quatre Bras, but Napoleon resoundingly defeated the Prussians at Ligny, eight miles away, though his men suffered ten thousand casualties.

The next day, Wellington began retreating north toward Waterloo, south of Brussels, but Marshal Ney lost his opportunity to pursue and destroy the British army. On the morning of June 18, Napoleon wanted to force a battle before Blücher could arrive with his forces. Wellington, with sixty-eight thousand men, made a stand against Napoleon's seventy-four thousand troops, knowing the Prussians were on their way. Napoleon's forces attacked ferociously and repeatedly all day, but when a Prussian corps arrived on the field in the late afternoon, the French were seriously outnumbered. Although Napoleon could have retreated into France under cover of his Old Guard, he realized that a defeat would mean the end of his revived empire. Instead, he used these veteran troops in a do-or-die advance supported by French artillery fire. British infantrymen at the crest of a ridge had been ordered to lie prone with their guns fixed on the French first column. When the two forces were about 150 feet apart, the British command to rise and fire rang out, and the French, who had not seen the concealed enemy, were cut down by musket fire and a bayonet charge.

After Blücher sent a second Prussian corps into the field and Wellington led a counterattack against the French line, Napoleon's troops were routed, suffering about thirty-three thousand casualties as opposed to the enemy's twenty-two thousand. Napoleon's dream of a unified Europe under one law, one economic system, and one military command—his own—died that day.

He abdicated for a second time on June 22, and Louis XVIII returned to Paris. The allies now determined to occupy France for three years and impose a war indemnity of seven hundred million francs. The former emperor was exiled to the British-held South Atlantic island of Saint Helena, where he died, officially of stomach cancer but perhaps by arsenic poisoning, on May 5, 1821, at age fifty-one. In 1840, his remains were brought back to Paris and housed in a sarcophagus of red porphyry beneath the gilt dome of the church of Les Invalides.

After the Revolution of 1830, in which the ultrareactionary Charles X, brother of Louis XVIII, was ousted, and the Revolution of 1848, in which Louis-Philippe, "the Citizen King," was toppled, a short-lived Second Republic was established with Napoleon's nephew, Louis Napoleon Bonaparte, as president. But Louis staged a coup and proclaimed himself emperor as Napoleon III in 1852. His Second Empire lasted until its fiery crash in 1870 as a result of the disastrous Franco-Prussian War, in which the emperor was captured at the battle of Sedan and deposed.

Beethoven, an ardent admirer of the ideals of the French Revolution, had intended to entitle his third symphony *Buonaparte*, but when he discovered that Napoleon had been proclaimed emperor in May 1804, he exploded, "Now he too will trample on the rights of man!" Although the word "Buonaparte" was furiously scratched out from the score, he renamed the work *Sinfonia Eroica* (Italian for "Heroic Symphony"), "composed to celebrate the memory of a great man."

136 ⌒ What was the first photograph?

View from the Window at Le Gras, *taken by Joseph Nicéphore*
Niépce in 1826

IN THE SUMMER OF 1826, French gentleman-scientist Joseph Nicéphore
Niépce (1765–1833) successfully produced the first permanent positive
image with a camera—the culmination of years spent tinkering with
engraving and lithography. But Niépce's achievement also reflected the
discoveries of many scientists before him who had contributed crucial
pieces of knowledge about an optical device that could capture an
image and the chemical process that could fix it on a prepared surface.

The device was the camera obscura ("dark chamber"), which was
a room or box with a pinhole or lens on one side through which light
passed. That the image of the outside view was projected through the
pinhole onto the opposite wall of the box, reversed and upside down,
had long been known, from the first description of its principles by Chinese philosopher Mo Ti in the fifth century BC to the first projection of
an outdoor image onto an indoor screen by the Arab "Father of Modern
Optics," Alhazen, in the early eleventh century to the use of the camera
obscura as a safe means of observing solar eclipses by the thirteenth-
century English friar-scientist Roger Bacon. German astronomer
Johannes Kepler (1571–1630), who also used the device for the observation of eclipses and sunspots, first dubbed it a *camera obscura.*

These early cameras merely projected images. Advances in chem-
istry, such as the discovery of the light-sensitive compounds silver
nitrate and silver chloride, would be required before the images could
be made permanent. Thomas Wedgwood of the pottery family and
chemist Sir Humphry Davy were able to make "sun prints" that copied
transient images onto glass treated with silver nitrate, but like other
early camera enthusiasts, they never managed to fix the images. That
remained for the ingenious Niépce, who with his brother had previously invented a combustion engine for propelling boats.

On a bright summer day in 1826, Niépce set up a large camera
obscura by the upstairs workroom window of his estate at Chalon-sur-
Saône, near Le Gras in central France. The camera contained a pewter
plate coated with the petroleum derivative bitumen of Judea, which

hardens on exposure to light. He removed the cap from the lens, which faced out the window, and after an eight-hour exposure to this view of the estate's outbuildings, courtyard, and trees, the plate was removed and washed with a mixture of oil of lavender and white petroleum to remove the unfixed debris. The resulting image on the plate, primitive though it was, with the sun appearing to shine on both sides of the buildings because of the long exposure time, was the first photograph, a term that means "writing with light."

Niépce called his process *heliography* ("sun writing") and brought his pewter plate to England in 1827, where he met Francis Bauer, a noted botanist-artist. Bauer arranged for Niépce to present his findings and show his photograph to London's Royal Society, but he and his invention were rejected because he was unwilling to disclose his methods. Niépce subsequently returned to France but left his photograph with Bauer, who framed it and added an inscription to the paper backing: "Monsieur Niépce's first successful experiment of fixing permanently the image from nature."

Niépce continued his work, experimenting with silver compounds that darkened with exposure to light, and in 1829 he formed a partnership with Louis-Jacques-Mandé Daguerre, who was working with similar processes. Niépce died of a stroke in 1833, leaving his notes with Daguerre, who went on to develop a famous process by which a polished silver-plated sheet of copper was exposed to vapor from heated iodine, making it light-sensitive, and then exposed to an image in a camera obscura. The resulting latent image on the plate remained invisible until the plate was exposed to mercury fumes. The positive image that then appeared was fixed in a bath of hyposulfite of soda and was known as a daguerreotype. A commission of the French Academy of Sciences evaluated Daguerre's process and recommended that the government purchase the rights to it and provide Daguerre with a lifetime pension. The inventor demonstrated his photographic process to the public, with much fanfare, in August 1839.

Daguerreotypes were much more sensitive, detailed, and clear than Niépce's heliograph, but long exposure times of up to forty-five minutes were still required, depending on the time of day and season. Most early daguerreotypes were of buildings and static street scenes because only stationary objects could be "seen" during the long exposure time. In Daguerre's *Boulevard du Temple, Paris*, taken in late 1838 or early 1839, the broad street is lined with trees and buildings but appears empty. In fact, the boulevard would have been crowded with vehicles and pedestrians—all moving too quickly to register on the light-sensitive plate. An exception is in the lower left of the photograph, where a lone gentleman stands with one knee raised and his foot resting on a dark, box-shaped object. He was having his shoes shined and, unlike the crowds bustling around him, had remained still long enough to achieve exposure.

A few years earlier in England, William Henry Fox Talbot (1800–77), a wealthy young scholar, had also begun experimenting with photography, using paper that had been treated with light-sensitizing silver compounds. As early as 1835 he had successfully produced images with this process, although in his initial efforts the areas of light and shadow in the picture were reversed from their appearance in nature. The solution to this problem, Talbot realized, was to photograph the photograph, thereby reversing the lights and shadows back to their natural state. He accomplished this by waxing the exposed, fixed photograph and placing it on a second piece of photograph paper. This was then treated with gallic acid, bringing out the image. Talbot called this the calotype ("beautiful impression") process, and his friend and fellow scientist Sir John Herschel offered the terms *negative* and *positive* for the first and second images.

But in January 1839 Talbot—and the rest of the world—heard of Daguerre's triumphal announcement of the "invention" of photography in Paris. Nonetheless, Talbot obtained a patent for his process and, between 1844 and 1846, published three hundred copies of *The Pencil of Nature*, which included twenty-four tipped-in photographs of landscapes, portraits, and buildings "wholly executed by the new art of photogenic drawing, without any aid whatever from the artist's pencil." The production of this first photographically illustrated book, according to historian Daniel J. Boorstin, "merits a place comparable to Gutenberg's in the history of typographic man" (see Question 108).

Talbot was awarded the Rumford Medal by the Royal Society for his calotype process, which permitted multiple copies of a picture to be produced. It never achieved the popularity of the daguerreotype, however, because the patent required practitioners to pay a fee and because the images produced on photographic paper were blurrier than the precise renderings achieved with metal plates.

By the mid-1850s, both the daguerreotype and the calotype were abandoned by most photographers in favor of the newer collodion process, developed by Englishman Frederick Scott Archer (1813–57). This was similar to Talbot's calotype process but used glass plates instead of paper for the negatives. Also known as the wet-plate process, collodion photography had the clarity of daguerreotypes and, like calotypes, allowed multiple copies to be made. However, this technique required the photographer to repair to the darkroom immediately to develop each picture, and the cumbersome equipment had to be reloaded each time, meaning that only about six photographs could be taken in a day. By the late 1870s, a dry-plate process had been invented, permitting photographers to take multiple photos and develop them all afterward, which meant they were no longer tied to the darkroom and could venture much farther afield. Professional companies that prepared and developed photographs soon appeared.

Meanwhile in Rochester, New York, a young bookkeeper and amateur photographer named George Eastman began to explore the possibility of using a flexible medium that could be spooled within the camera instead of plates, thus allowing multiple photographs to be taken without reloading. In 1888, he introduced the Kodak box camera, which held a roll of one hundred negatives and sold for $25, including the first roll of film. Once the roll had been used up, the photographer sent the film, camera and all, back to Rochester, where Eastman's company processed the film, developed the photos, and returned the camera, reloaded, to the customer. The advertising slogan was, "You press the button—we do the rest." Eastman subsequently went on to develop smaller, cheaper cameras that the user could load and unload, and at the turn of the century he was offering the Brownie camera, intended for young people, at a cost of $1. The popularity of photography as an amateur and family activity was ensured.

During these decades of technical development, attention also turned to broader uses for photography, such as in journalism. In 1855, British photographer Roger Fenton set out for the Crimea, with the backing of the government, to photograph the conflict that would later be memorialized in Alfred Tennyson's "The Charge of the Light Brigade." Fenton's discreet, sanitized pictures of soldiers at leisure helped to ease the British public's outrage at the mismanagement of the Crimean War.

Shortly thereafter, the outbreak of the American Civil War provided a grim opportunity for Mathew Brady, who was already a well-known photographer with studios in New York City and Washington.

Brady assembled a group of about twenty photographers whose tens of thousands of pictures documented every aspect of the war—the enormous weaponry, the young dead of both sides strewn across the fields, and the eerie gutted remains of Southern cities.

Photography was also to play an important role in social reform, most notably in the work of Danish-born Jacob Riis. His depictions of the misery and squalor rampant in the tenements of New York City, published in newspapers and collected in *How the Other Half Lives* in 1890, were so shocking that they led to government efforts to improve the conditions in which urban immigrants were forced to live.

This tradition was carried on during the Great Depression by the Farm Security Administration, whose photographers amassed 270,000 photos documenting the effects on ordinary farmers and their families of the stock market crash and the Dust Bowl years. The most famous of these photographers was Walker Evans, whose work with James Agee in *Let Us Now Praise Famous Men* depicted the daily hardships of destitute Southern sharecroppers.

While photography was increasingly used for chronicling the world, from family life to war, it also began to be viewed as a new art form. In his 1936 essay "The Work of Art in the Age of Mechanical Reproduction," Walter Benjamin noted that "for the first time in the process of pictorial reproduction, photography freed the hand of the most important artistic functions which henceforth devolved only upon the eye looking into a lens."

Prominent among photographers who considered themselves artists was Alfred Stieglitz (1864–1946), whose classic pictures of New York City, such as *Winter, Fifth Avenue*, were widely celebrated. In 1902, Stieglitz founded an organization he called the Photo-Secession, likening his group to the German Secessionist painters, who objected to academic art. He set up his famous gallery at 291 Fifth Avenue, where he showcased not only photographs but also the work of contemporary painters, and from 1903 to 1917 he published *Camera Work* magazine.

Stieglitz was also a proponent of color photography, using the so-called autochrome process, which had been patented by Auguste and Louis Lumière in 1903. This was a screen-plate technique in which the light filtered through dyed translucent particles of potato starch, imprinting a colored image on a photographic emulsion.

While photography was rendering the world and its inhabitants with increasing verisimilitude, painting was increasingly abandoning the representational. Susan Sontag observed that "what photography did was to usurp the painter's task of providing images that accurately transcribe reality. . . . By taking over the task of realistic picturing hitherto monopolized by painting, photography freed painting for its great modernist vocation—abstraction."

Photography particularly influenced the Impressionists, with their interest in the properties of light and experiments with perspective. Sontag noted that these French painters made use of "the camera's translation of reality into highly polarized areas of light and dark," adopting the photographers' "free or arbitrary cropping of the image" as well as their "indifference . . . to making space, particularly background space, intelligible" (see Question 139).

The influence of photography continued with subsequent art movements. In Pablo Picasso's 1907 painting *Les Demoiselles d'Avignon*, a seminal step toward the new pictorial language that would become Cubism, the figures are conceptualized with multiple exposures and points of view in a two-dimensional plane, just as a camera might. Photography might even be said to have gained a limited victory when avant-garde painting became almost totally nonrepresentational in the Abstract Expressionist movement of the 1950s and beyond.

The twentieth century saw the confident emergence of yet another photographic art form, that of "moving pictures" (see Question 143), as well as technological advances including automatic flashes, Kodachrome film, the instant-print Polaroid Land camera, disposable cameras, and the ubiquitous digital camera, introduced in 1975. The ever-changing photographic medium would continue to attract talented practitioners like Edward Weston, who explored the natural beauty of the Pacific coast, and Robert Frank, whose influential 1958 book *The Americans* depicted the social loneliness and despair he had observed during a two-year tour of the country. Another highly influential photographer was Diane Arbus, who, before her suicide in 1971, created portraits of society's forgotten and rejected—the malformed, bizarre, and freakish—that force the viewer to confront and contemplate images that would otherwise be shunned.

What lies ahead for twenty-first-century photography? One prediction was made way back in the 1960s by the elderly Edward Steichen, who had been a member of Steiglitz's Photo-Secession group. Steichen wrote, "In the past few years there has been such a larger number of free-spirited, independently thinking young photographers—seekers, probers, and explorers of new horizons—than we have heretofore encountered. They give ample assurance that the future of photography is richer in prospect and potential than ever before." The end of that decade saw the birth of the first internet (see Question 150), which has gone on to provide photographers of all ages with a limitless venue for the seeking, probing, and exploring products of their sensibilities.

—Nancy Walsh

137 ∽ Who first published a theory of evolution based on natural selection?

Alfred Russel Wallace in 1858

MANY PEOPLE ASSUME THAT THE THEORY of evolution by natural selection—the concept that in its modern development underlies and unifies the biological sciences—was first presented by Charles Darwin (1809–82) in *On the Origin of Species*, published in 1859. The book drew heavily on Darwin's observations as a naturalist aboard HMS *Beagle* in 1831–36, during a voyage commissioned primarily for charting the coasts of the southern regions of South America. After this mission was completed, the ship sailed north—famously putting in at the Galápagos Islands—and then crossed the Pacific, stopping in Tahiti and Australia before returning to England via the Indian Ocean and the Cape of Good Hope.

In fact, Darwin's masterwork was neither the first written expression of his ideas nor was it the first lucid, published presentation of a theory of evolution by natural selection. A younger acquaintance of Darwin, Alfred Russel Wallace (1823–1913), born in Wales to an English mother and a Scottish father, had reached similar insights after extensive independent and self-financed fieldwork as a naturalist in the Amazon basin in 1848–52 and in the Malay Archipelago beginning in 1854. Wallace formally described his views in an essay written on the island of Ternate in 1858 entitled "On the Tendency of Varieties to Depart Indefinitely from the Original Type." In contrast, Darwin's earlier written presentations of his thinking consisted of incomplete or private communications: a draft manuscript begun in 1839 (and revised five years later) and a letter to Asa Gray, a botanist at Harvard University, in 1857.

Wallace was largely self-educated. By his early twenties, he had studied *An Essay on the Principle of Population* by Thomas Malthus, which introduced him to the concept of checks on populations; Darwin's 1839 *Journal and Remarks*, which summarized biological, geological, and anthropological observations from the voyage of the *Beagle*; and *Principles of Geology* by Charles Lyell, which established the great antiquity of the earth. He also benefited from several years of work with an older brother, a surveyor, which had whetted his interest in sciences such as geology and botany.

Wallace's 1858 essay, which discussed processes that affect populations, traits of domesticated animals as special cases with respect to natural selection, and the views of the earlier evolutionary naturalist Jean-Baptiste Lamarck, is striking in several respects. One is his explicit use of language calling to mind the phrase "survival of the fittest" (later coined by the philosopher Herbert Spencer), which has come to epitomize the theory of evolution. Regarding insects, for example, Wallace stated that "those races having colours best adapted to concealment from their enemies would inevitably survive the longest."

Moreover, his paper presaged important aspects of the modern science of ecology, understood as the branch of biology concerned with the distributions and abundances of organisms. He understood that population sizes of predators must necessarily be limited by those of their prey, that mortality during early life or from disease would act as strong regulatory mechanisms of population, and that the characteristics of a habitat, particularly the quantity and quality of its food resources, would ultimately control the number of inhabitants—a concept now termed a "carrying capacity."

Finally, he suggested that "could we become perfectly acquainted with the organization and habits of the various species of animals, and could we measure the capacity of each for performing the acts necessary to its safety and existence under all the varying circumstances by which it is surrounded, we might even be able to calculate the proportionate abundance of individuals which is the necessary result." With this sentence Wallace outlined a simple model of an ecosystem, with its flows of energy and nutrients, and interactions within and among species, all expressed in quantitative terms.

Wallace sent his completed essay to Darwin, with whom he had corresponded since 1854, for the older man's comments. Recognizing the close similarity between Wallace's ideas and his own, Darwin sought advice from the geologist Lyell and Joseph Hooker, a botanist. Because both men were close to Darwin and familiar with his work, they arranged—unbeknownst to Wallace—a public reading of Darwin's and Wallace's writings before the Linnean Society of London on July 1, 1858. An amalgamated article—including an introductory letter from Lyell and Hooker, part of a chapter from Darwin's still unpublished book, an abstract of his letter to Asa Gray, and the full text of Wallace's essay under its own title—was published later that year in the Society's *Proceedings* under the general rubric of "On the Tendency of Species to Form Varieties; and on the Perpetuation of Varieties and Species by Natural Means of Selection." Wallace, who good-naturedly accepted Darwin's modus operandi in this matter, thus became the author of the first published article describing a theory of evolution by natural selection.

The reading failed to evoke strong interest among the Society attendees; the few comments on it were mostly skeptical or even dismissive. Many leading naturalists of the time clearly missed its significance, and the most important consequence of the publication of Wallace's paper may have been that it spurred Darwin to complete his own work. Despite compiling voluminous notes over many years, Darwin had delayed publishing his findings while seeking incontrovertible evidence. Because the basic ideas had now been presented, publication took precedence, and *On the Origin of Species* appeared in the following year, with an initial printing of 1,250 copies. The tremendous controversy that ensued—and the full-length presentation of the material—led to Wallace's being superseded by Darwin. Wallace's involvement with unorthodox thought, which ranged from socialism to spiritualism, probably also contributed to his secondary historical position.

It is important to recognize the substantive differences between the ideas of Wallace and Darwin, particularly regarding the evolution of man. Darwin's mechanistic perspective did not require a supernatural explanation for human evolution, which is why it remains controversial among certain religious groups and the scientifically naive. Even now, however, two hundred years after his birth, Darwin's ideas have withstood intense scientific scrutiny and furnish the underpinnings of much of modern biology. Wallace's view—that human evolution was a teleological process—is not consistent with modern scientific thought. As such, recognition of Darwin as the greater scientist and the father of modern biology is entirely fitting, although Wallace preceded him, at least in a technical sense.

Wallace received far less acclaim than Darwin—perhaps less than his due—but in certain respects his achievements were even more impressive. Wallace was primarily self-educated (rather than being a graduate of Cambridge University), and his expeditions were largely self-financed (rather than commissioned by the Admiralty). He is still regarded as the father of biogeography for his studies of the distributions of monkey species in the Amazon and of plants in Indonesia. At least three extant species of fish, five of birds, two of mammals, and six of arthropods have been named after him, as well as a mountain in the Sierra Nevada, an undersea trench near Australia, and craters on both the moon and Mars. In addition, several prestigious awards commemorate him, either alone or in association with Darwin. Most scientists would call that a significant legacy.

—*William A. Walsh*

138 ∿ What was the first major battle of the American Civil War?

Manassas or Bull Run, fought in Virginia on July 21, 1861

WHEN ABRAHAM LINCOLN WAS INAUGURATED as the sixteenth president of the United States on March 4, 1861, he said to the nation, "In your hands, my dissatisfied fellow countrymen, and not in mine, is the momentous issue of civil war." Secession fever had run high since the previous December, when Lincoln's election was assured and the South Carolina state convention in Charleston declared that the union of that state with the rest of the country was "hereby dissolved." Mississippi, Florida, Alabama, Georgia, Louisiana, and Texas followed suit, and in early February delegates from those states had met in Montgomery, Alabama, to form the Confederate States of America. The constitution of the new nation centered on states' rights and slavery, and Jefferson Davis, a former congressman and senator from Mississippi, and former secretary of war, was chosen as president.

The breach between the North and South over slavery had been widening for decades, as the North became increasingly industrialized and the South had remained largely agrarian and dependent on slave labor. Lincoln had made it clear that he considered slavery wrong, and the Southern secessionists spread rumors that if he were elected president he would attempt to destroy their "peculiar institution." Events such as the lethal 1859 raid by John Brown and his small armed band on Harpers Ferry, Virginia (now West Virginia), with their vague intent of establishing a warlike republic of fugitive slaves, had terrified the South—and hardened its resolve.

Because feelings also ran high in the North, attempts at compromise on the expansion and perpetuation of slavery were doomed to failure. By the time Lincoln assumed office in March, the Confederate authorities had taken control of most of the forts and navy yards of the South. Exceptions were Fort Sumter at Charleston, South Carolina, and Fort Pickens at Pensacola, Florida, which remained under Federal control.

Shortly after the inauguration, Confederate representatives approached Washington with a request for the surrender of these two remaining outposts, and while Secretary of State William H. Seward refused to meet with them, he indirectly assured them that no further provisions would be sent and that evacuation would ensue. The determined Lincoln, however, decided that supplies would be sent to Fort Sumter and, against the advice of his cabinet and General Winfield Scott, who had been the army's top general for two decades, he ordered a relief expedition. In Lincoln's view, the Union had been created in perpetuity by the Founding Fathers, and secession by the states represented an illegal insurrection.

At Fort Sumter supplies were running out. Word of the relief mission had not reached garrison commander Major Robert Anderson, who offered to turn the fort over to the Confederates within a couple of days. But Southern forces under General P. G. T. Beauregard, which had surrounded the fort, demanded immediate surrender, and at 4:30 a.m. on April 12, Confederate guns began shelling the fort. The bombardment continued for thirty-four hours until Anderson lowered the Stars and Stripes and surrendered. According to historian Samuel Eliot Morison, "For a brief—too brief—time, until they realized what sacrifice a civil war would require, almost everyone in the North backed the President, and had only one word for the act of firing on the flag—treason."

The first guns had roared, and while many on both sides clamored for war, there was still hope that some accord could be reached, with four of the remaining Southern states—Virginia, Arkansas, Tennessee, and North Carolina—holding out against secession. But Lincoln called for seventy-five thousand Northern militiamen to report for duty, and by April 25, soldiers from Massachusetts and New York were arriving in Washington. The holdout states promptly seceded and joined the Confederacy, and Jefferson Davis moved his capital from Montgomery to Richmond, Virginia. Lincoln declared that the ports of all seceded states were under blockade.

Neither side was prepared for war. The Federal regular army consisted of only sixteen thousand men, mostly spread throughout the western territories. The looming war would have to be fought, at least initially, by volunteers from state militias, most of whom belonged to small, local companies and who had little, if any, training in combat or within large, coordinated regiments. Many of the leaders of the state militias were political appointees lacking military experience, and many of the West Point–trained officers of the Federal army resigned out of loyalty to their home states.

In the run-up to war, the North held several important advantages, with a population of twenty-two million compared with nine million in the South, including three and a half million slaves. The North had five times as many factories that could manufacture war matériel, while the South would have to import its guns and other equipment from Britain and France despite being blockaded. The North also had a functioning government in place rather than the hastily assembled Confederacy.

But the South had the advantage of position: It was defending "home and hearth" rather than an abstraction—the Union—and the North would have to invade to defeat its armies. Furthermore, in early March, Jefferson Davis had called for one hundred thousand volunteers to serve for a year, and the secession of Virginia, in particular, provided the Confederacy with many highly qualified military leaders. In all, more than three hundred officers—nearly one-third of the regular army's experienced officer corps—resigned to fight for the South.

The reluctance with which some of them made this choice was evident in the words of Robert E. Lee, who in early 1861 was a colonel in the U.S. Army stationed near San Antonio. To his son, Lee wrote, "A Union that can only be maintained by swords and bayonets, and in which strife and civil war are to take the place of brotherly love and kindness, has no charm for me. If the Union is dissolved, the government disrupted, I shall return to my native state and share the miseries of my people. Save in her defense, I will draw my sword no more."

Both sides believed the war, should it come, would be short. Secretary of State Seward envisioned one major foray that would overthrow the Confederate government, and Lincoln's initial call for seventy-five thousand volunteers asked them to sign on for only three months. The Southerners dismissed the threats coming from up North, claiming that the Yankees, whom they considered lowly farmers and citified shopkeepers, would turn and run when they encountered soldiers who had grown up riding and shooting.

Late spring and early summer found soldiers from the Northern states flocking into Washington and those from the South massing in northern Virginia. General Scott, who formulated the "anaconda" strategy, in which the Union Army intended to constrict and suffocate the Confederacy by controlling both the Atlantic seacoast and the rivers to the west, advised against rushing into battle, emphasizing the need to train untested militias. Scott wanted to spend a year drilling troops, setting up supply lines, stockpiling guns and ammunition, and providing standard uniforms to replace the motley assortment worn by the individual state militias.

Brigadier General Irvin McDowell, appointed by Scott as commander of the Army of Northeastern Virginia, also was concerned about his troops' lack of experience. But Lincoln was under pressure from influential, hawkish Northern politicians and newspaper editors who grew increasingly shrill as more and more Southern troops pitched camp practically on the doorstep of the capital. Lincoln told McDowell, "You are green, it is true, but they are green also; you are all green alike."

So on July 16, McDowell led his army of thirty-five thousand out of Washington, heading southwest toward the important rail hub of Manassas Junction in Virginia, where the Confederate Army of the Potomac under General Beauregard was encamped. The days were hot and dusty, and the march was highly undisciplined and leisurely, with soldiers continually wandering off for refreshment or rest. Supplies were slow in coming, and delays ensued. The first contact between the two armies finally took place on July 18, when a small engagement of advance forces at Blackburn's Ford resulted in the Union forces being pushed back.

Meanwhile, an additional sixteen thousand Union troops were stationed up the Potomac near Harpers Ferry, commanded by Major General Robert Patterson, and an additional nine thousand Confederates under General Joseph E. Johnston remained in the Shenandoah Valley. The plan was that McDowell would lead a direct attack on Beauregard's position, and Patterson was to keep Johnston's troops occupied to prevent them from reaching the railroad line that ran from Shenandoah to Manassas Junction, whence they would be able to reinforce Beauregard. Johnston, however, successfully eluded the aging, infirm Patterson, and his men headed for Manassas.

Beauregard knew that McDowell was approaching, so he prepared to execute a flank attack before the Union troops reached his main position, along eight miles of the stream known as Bull Run, striking with his right at the Union left. McDowell, however, planned a similar tactic, aiming to cross Bull Run upstream from Beauregard's men and slam down hard on the Confederate left flank. The result was a fiasco.

The first battle of Bull Run, as it would be known in the North, or Manassas, as it would be called by the South, began early on July 21. Throughout the morning, the Union forces pushed back the Confederates, with two divisions of McDowell's forces crossing Bull Run near Sudley Church, where they would be in position for the flank attack. McDowell sent two of his regular army batteries forward to lead the attack, advancing to Henry House Hill and weakening the Confederate lines, until a stubborn defense was mounted by a Virginia brigade headed by Brigadier General Thomas J. Jackson. Another Confederate general, Barnard Bee, desperately trying to rally his fading troops, called their attention to the brigade's action, memorably saying, "There is Jackson standing like a stone wall!"—providing Jackson with a sobriquet that would stick with him forever.

By four p.m., when Johnston's Shenandoah reinforcements arrived by railway, the situation on the battlefield was "confusion worse confounded." Orders were misunderstood or not followed, soldiers fled, and Union gunners disastrously refrained from firing on blue-clad Virginian soldiers they mistook for their own. A bayonet charge of Jackson's brigade, combined with a flank attack by Johnston, pushed the last of McDowell's troops off Henry House Hill across Bull Run.

The Union retreat was complicated by the troops' inexperience in complex maneuvering, but the primary cause of the ensuing pandemonium was the presence of hundreds of civilians from Washington, who had ridden out in carriages and wagons for a festive day of picnicking and watching through field glasses, from the edge of the battlefield, the expected glorious Union rout of the rebels. The road to Washington rapidly became clogged with fleeing civilians, Union artillery and ambulances, and soldiers on foot or horseback, all growing increasingly panic-stricken as rumors of pursuit by the dreaded Confederate Black Horse Cavalry spread. Union soldiers abandoned their weapons and equipment and simply ran, straggling into Washington through the next day, as news of the dreadful outcome shocked the capital. Of the approximately eighteen thousand men on each side who had actually engaged in battle, Confederate casualties amounted to almost two thousand dead, wounded, missing, or captured, but Union casualties approached three thousand.

Civil War historian Bruce Catton summed up the events of that Sunday as follows: "There is nothing in American military history quite like the story of Bull Run. It was the momentous fight of the amateurs, the battle where everything went wrong, the great day of awakening for the whole nation, North and South together. . . . It also ended the rosy time in which men could dream that the war would be short, glorious, and bloodless."

During the four years of the Civil War, about 110,000 Union soldiers died in battle, and an additional 250,000 succumbed to disease and other causes. Estimated Confederate losses were 94,000 killed in battle and 164,000 by disease. More than 30,000 Northerners died in prison camps, as did more than 25,000 Southerners. Place-names such as Gettysburg, Antietam, and Appomattox would be etched into the collective national memory. Lincoln would be struck down by a fanatic shortly after his second inauguration, at which he exhorted the exhausted nation, "With malice toward none, with charity for all, with firmness in the right as God gives us to see the right, let us strive on to finish the work we are in, to bind up the nation's wounds, to care for him who shall have borne the battle and for his widow and his orphan, to do all which may achieve and cherish a just and lasting peace among ourselves and with all nations."

—*Nancy Walsh*

139 ∽ What was the first Impressionist painting?

Claude Monet's Impression, Sunrise, *1873*

IT'S BEEN CALLED THE MOST IMPORTANT MOVEMENT in the history of art and "the other French Revolution." It's Impressionism, that celebration of *liberté*, *egalité*, and *fraternité* in the Paris art world of 1860–90 that changed the entire world's capacity to accept the individual artist's personal vision. The Impressionist movement began in the stranglehold of academic art and ended in the freedom that would eventually welcome Cubism, Picasso, Abstract Expressionism, and Andy Warhol.

Poetically enough, it began at sunrise. More specifically, it began with a painting of the sun rising over the port city of Le Havre by the young French artist Claude Monet (1840–1926). It was April 1874, and Monet was about to do something for the first time: submit the painting not to the Salon, the huge annual exhibition run by the all-powerful Royal Academy—acceptance to which was the only path to success for aspiring artists—but to a special show consisting of paintings by himself and his friends.

This group formed the core of a new movement in revolt against academic art and its paralyzing insistence on conformity in both subject matter (history, mythology, or religion) and technique (strong outlines and satin-smooth brushwork). The group included Pierre-Auguste Renoir, Camille Pissarro, Paul Cézanne, Edgar Degas, Frédéric Bazille, and one female member, Berthe Morisot. Aware that the foggy, brooding atmosphere of the painting might leave him open to criticism—with its small circle of red-orange for the sun and a few orange slashes for the sun's reflection in the water surrounded by blue-green mists rendering the harbor vessels almost invisible—Monet called his painting *Impression, Sunrise* (1873; Musée Marmottan Monet, Paris).

On April 25, 1874, an article poking fun at the show by critic Louis Leroy appeared in the satirical magazine *Le Charivari* under the title "The Exhibition of the Impressionists." This article first gave the movement a name (and its author the status of permanent footnote in the history of art). Although originally used pejoratively, the label *Impressionism* stuck. At the group's third exhibit in 1877—there would be a

total of eight between 1874 and 1886—the term was officially adopted
for advertising and publications.

In their insistence on painting the living world around them rather
than re-creating past events, the new coalition of renegade artists—then
known as the "Intransigents"—could look back to two distinguished
trailblazers: the painters Gustave Courbet (1819–77) and Édouard
Manet (1832–83). Courbet had elected to paint in neither the Romantic
tradition of Eugène Delacroix nor the Neoclassical tradition of Jean-
Auguste-Dominique Ingres, but in a new genre being adopted by both
painters and writers: Realism.

Manet, who was to become an important figure in the Impressionist movement, had accepted the challenge thrown out to all painters by
his friend, the poet-critic Charles Baudelaire (1821–67), in his essay
"The Painter of Modern Life": Don't look to the past; rather, look for
your inspiration and subjects in the modern world of a fast-changing
Paris. As an artist, Manet turned himself into Baudelaire's ideal flaneur,
the civilized stroller of the Paris streets who observed everyday life. His
large canvas *Music in the Tuileries Gardens* (1862; National Gallery,
London) was an accurate depiction of a well-heeled crowd having a
good time at an afternoon concert.

The Salon jury showed its displeasure with Manet's decision to follow Baudelaire's prescriptions by rejecting several submissions. Two of
Manet's paintings created scandals: *Déjeuner sur l'herbe* (*Luncheon on
the Grass*) (1863; Musée d'Orsay, Paris), in which a nude woman is
attended not by academically approved nymphs but by two contemporary, fully clothed young men; and, in a similar spirit of pleasant
amorality, *Olympia* (1863; Musée d'Orsay, Paris), a depiction of a
recumbent nude woman in a modern setting who is probably awaiting a
visit from her next wealthy customer.

The notoriety resulting from Manet's rejection by the establishment made him a hero to Monet and his friends in the decade preceding the first Impressionist exhibition. They visited the atelier where he
worked and the Café Guerbois, where he held court. To outsiders,
Manet was the group's leader, but the truth was more complex.
Although he offered moral and sometimes financial support, Manet
never formally identified himself with the group and did not exhibit at
any of the eight Impressionist shows.

But who were the Impressionists? At the center of the movement
was Monet, who had been raised in Le Havre by a middle-class mer-

chant family. His precocious gift for caricature was noticed by Eugène Boudin (1824–98), who specialized in painting the seas, shores, and skies of the Normandy coast. Boudin taught the teenage Monet to paint outdoors (*en plein air*) in conditions of changing light and weather. Monet was captivated by the experience and would spend the next seventy years attempting to capture on canvas the changing patterns of light and color found directly in nature, often in series of paintings on the same subject—the Saint-Lazare train station, haystacks in a field, Rouen Cathedral, London's Parliament buildings, the water lilies of his flower garden at Giverny—executed at different times of the day or year.

When he went to Paris in the early 1860s, Monet met several gifted artists: Renoir, Sisley, Pissarro, and Bazille. Pierre-Auguste Renoir (1841–1919), born in Limoges, had shown an early talent for decorating porcelain. When his working-class family moved to Paris, they lived in the slums near the Louvre, through whose halls the young Renoir roamed. Harking back to Manet's *Music in the Tuileries Gardens*, though in a more democratic mode, Renoir went on to paint festive crowd scenes in two of his most famous works: *Dance at the Moulin de la Galette* (1876; Musée d'Orsay, Paris), a lively assemblage of young working Parisians dancing and chatting in the dappled sunlight of a favorite haunt in Montmartre, and *Luncheon of the Boating Party* (1881; Phillips Collection, Washington), in which young weekend excursionists fill a riverside porch with food, wine, and their own exuberant spirits. Both paintings delightfully embody the modern pleasure principle, as do his epicurean depictions of mothers cuddling children, luxuriant overweight nudes, and lush floral arrangements.

Although Alfred Sisley (1839–99) was the son of well-to-do English émigrés, he lived nearly all his life in France. He would be helpful to Monet and others when they chose to flee to England during the brief Franco-Prussian War of 1870–71. Camille Pissarro (1830–1903) had been born into a wealthy Jewish family in the Danish colony of Saint Thomas. He was sent to school in Paris at age twelve and later traveled in South America before returning to Paris to study painting. Frédéric Bazille (1841–70), from a wealthy family in southern France, became a generous colleague who lent studio space, materials, and money to his needier friends. Bazille was the Keats of the Impressionists: His brilliantly promising career was cut short by his death in 1870 in the Franco-Prussian War.

Monet and his friends went on frequent excursions to outdoor sites in the environs of Paris in the 1860s, including the picturesque towns on the Seine that had become easily reachable by train. He and Renoir painted side by side at Bougival, as did Pissarro and Paul Cézanne at Pontoise. It was in these countryside and quayside visits, during which dozens of shimmering masterpieces were produced—such as Monet's and Renoir's twin studies of a popular watering hole downriver from Paris called La Grenouillère—that some art historians believe "classic" Impressionism was forged. Its basic principles were as follows: Paint contemporary subjects from the visible world surrounding the artist; execute paintings in the open air (as opposed to bringing outdoor oil "sketches" back to the studio for completion); and re-create the sensations of light and color visited upon the artist by the scene directly before him with no intermediary act of memory or imagination. This required a technique of rapid, rough brushstrokes with thick paint rather than the smooth, invisible brushwork favored by the Academy and its Salon jurors.

Monet's advice to the open-air painter summarized the Impressionist style: "Try to forget what objects you have in front of you, a tree, a field. . . . Merely think, here is a little square of blue, here an oblong of pink, here a streak of yellow, and paint it just as it looks to you until it gives your own naive impression of the scene."

Through Manet, the group met Degas, Cézanne, and Morisot. Edgar Degas (1834–1917), the son of a wealthy Parisian banker, began his career as a painter of classical scenes but under Manet's influence turned to modern urban subjects, especially the ballet dancers of the Parisian stage. Cézanne (1839–1906) was born in the south of France, where his father was first a factory owner, then a banker. Growing up in Aix-en-Provence, he began a long friendship with Émile Zola (which came to a sudden end in 1886 when he was depicted as an artistic failure in one of Zola's novels). Though moody and unpopular, Cézanne found a friend and painting partner in Pissarro. The socially connected family of Berthe Morisot (1841–95) allowed her to study painting because it was an acceptably "feminine" accomplishment. She met Manet in the Louvre and became his model and protégée; she later married his brother. Morisot combined landscape art with an interest in the modern woman and deftly managed to balance a painter's life with that of an upper-crust lady of the time.

Degas brought two important new painters into the group: the American Mary Cassatt (1844–1926), famous for her studies of women and children, and the Parisian realist Gustave Caillebotte (1848–94).

Caillebotte's name is less familiar than the others, but recent reevaluations of his stunning urban scenes are now giving art lovers an opportunity—rare among the much-studied Impressionists—to experience the pleasure of a fresh discovery.

All the Impressionists faced harsh criticism at one time or another, with their brushwork perhaps drawing the greatest ire. Why learn to paint anymore, asked the critic Leroy and others, since an accurate representation of nature is no longer required, but only an "impression" of it? The Impressionists' brilliant colors—generally lighter than those in the Academy's historical paintings—also came under fire. Critics felt obliged to tell Monet what color the sky was. Renoir's nudes were revolting, with touches of green and purple on their bodies suggesting putrefaction. Cassatt's *Lydia in a Loge Wearing a Pearl Necklace* (1879; Philadelphia Museum of Art) had smudges of dirt on her face.

Despite their many shared struggles and values, it would be a mistake to think of the Impressionists as a homogeneous group, and an even bigger error to think of them exclusively in terms of the enchanting *plein air* landscapes of Monet, Pissarro, Bazille, Morisot, and the early Cézanne. Degas hated outdoor painting and focused chiefly on contemporary figures in movement: ballerinas, horses, and bathing women. Renoir also favored figures and never totally renounced the Salon. The lines of Caillebotte's Parisian scenes were clean and hard. Cézanne was a special case: Even among the radical Impressionists, he was an artist ahead of his time, with many of his paintings having a "modern" look that seemed to anticipate Cubism. Usually classified with Paul Gauguin, Georges Seurat, Vincent van Gogh, and Henri de Toulouse-Lautrec as a Post-Impressionist, Cézanne is considered a bridge from Impressionism to the moderns; Picasso called him "the father of us all."

By the 1880s, the original alliance was coming unglued as a result of personal disputes (usually involving the fractious Degas). The eighth Impressionist exhibition of 1886 was also the last. Nonetheless, Impressionism gradually dazzled the eyes of both critics and the public. In the new century, all the surviving Impressionists—Pissarro, Cézanne, Degas, Renoir, Cassatt, and Monet—would become rich (or richer) from their art. On December 5, 1926, Claude Monet, whose personal impression of a sunrise had given an epochal movement its name more than a half century earlier, became the last of his extraordinary fellowship to depart the world each had captured on canvas with such incomparable grace.

—*Joseph Sgammato*

140 ∽ Who developed the first practical incandescent lamp?

U.S. inventor Thomas Edison in 1879

THOMAS ALVA EDISON (1847–1931), PERHAPS the world's outstanding inventor, is credited with 1,093 U.S. patents, as well as others in England, Germany, and France. As a child, he struggled in the classroom and was homeschooled by his mother. He also developed hearing loss at an early age due to scarlet fever and repeated bouts of mastoiditis. Although Edison's schooling ended at age twelve, he became a fairly avid reader.

Edison's hearing problem ultimately steered him toward inventing. By 1863 he had become an apprentice telegrapher—a profession at which he excelled—but interpreting a series of dots and dashes soon became impossible for him when the receivers switched from printouts to audible beeps. Edison spent the next six years fine-tuning the existing equipment, eventually figuring out a way to send two messages on a single wire at the same time. He also worked on a printer that could type words rather than just dots and dashes (as in Morse code). Because of these developments, he was able to leave his job in 1869 to become a full-time inventor. He would later develop the phonograph as well as the quadruplex, which could transmit four messages simultaneously across the same line, earning more than $100,000 for himself in 1874. Several years afterward, he invented the carbon microphone, which was used in all telephones until the 1980s.

In March of 1876, Edison moved to Menlo Park, New Jersey, where he built a laboratory of two and a half stories and brought with him his assistants, Charles Batchelor and John Kruesi. Batchelor, who had worked with Edison on the telephone and phonograph, was a draftsman and mechanic. He would draw up the plans, and Kruesi, a machinist, would translate them into working models.

No other inventor capitalized on the resources of the wealthy like Edison and his team. In 1878, backed by J. P. Morgan and the Vanderbilts, the inventor formed the Edison Electric Light Company, securing $30,000 for research as well as twenty-five hundred of the three thousand shares. In return, Edison had to relinquish to the company the rights to all inventions and discoveries for five years. After the corporation made its first $50,000, Edison was to be paid $100,000 and royal-ties on all electric lamps, which later allowed him to expand his lab to cover two city blocks, including a glassblowing facility, a machine shop, and an office library.

In December of 1878, Edison hired Francis Upton, a scientist and mathematician, to assist with the technical aspects of engineering and circuitry and to perform some difficult calculations. By the following summer, Edison had grown tired of numerous failed lighting experiments and began to focus on an electrical generator that could be used to create an entire electrical infrastructure. He knew that while lights would be used mainly at night, electricity could be sold both day and night to power motors, ovens, sewing machines, and the like.

Edison's big breakthrough with the electric light finally occurred in October of 1879, when he demonstrated that a carbonized cotton filament would burn for 13 hours. He and his team later switched to a carbon-coated cardboard filament, which burned for a remarkable 170 hours. Edison kept this discovery from the press while quietly obtaining a patent for the carbon-filament lamp on November 4, but the story eventually leaked on December 21. He was soon forced to organize a public exhibition, which he gave on New Year's Eve and New Year's Day. On display were lights as well as vacuum pumps, generators, and the filament-making process. To capitalize on his invention, Edison patented an electrical distribution system in 1880, and by 1887 there were 121 Edison power stations in the United States.

Edison's incandescent lamp—that is, a lamp emitting visible radiation from a heated material (in this case, the filament)—was easily the most influential invention of the nineteenth century, arguably of the entire modern era. He was not without competition, however. Gas lamps had been the primary alternative to candlelight and oil lamps since the early part of the nineteenth century and were widely used until the early twentieth century—some U.S. cities still retain them, as in parts of New Orleans's French Quarter. These gas lamps burned a coal extract before most of them were converted to the use of methane (natural) gas. Gas offered a cheaper alternative to candles and oils but carried risks such as flammability and carbon monoxide emissions. Edison's challenge was to convince investors and the public that electric light could be safe and cost-effective.

The first electric lamp of any kind had been created in Germany in 1650 by Otto von Guericke of Magdeburg, who discovered that a sphere made of sulfur would emit light when rubbed rapidly with the hands, the friction providing the electrical charge necessary to produce a faint glow. Between this primitive device and Edison's first public demonstration of a practical, sustainable, and economically feasible form of lighting, the materials used in the process consisted primarily of vacuum-sealed glass globes with a wide range of filaments. (Removing the air from the bulb prevented oxidation of the filament and reduced the transfer of heat from the filament to the glass.)

Although there were more than twenty previous inventors of various forms of incandescent lamps, Edison triumphed over the others because he

- developed a superior vacuum (combining two existing pumps) that could outperform other models in evacuating gas from bulbs,

- found an effective filament material in carbon fiber (earlier filaments burned out in a matter of minutes), and

- created a high-resistance lamp that could be powered from a centralized generator.

Major improvements included the introduction in 1911 of the tungsten filament, which was coiled two years later to increase the radiating surface. The bulbs were also filled with nitrogen or an inert gas, such as argon. In 1925, the bulbs were frosted with acid to make the light softer and reduce glare. Today's fluorescent lights are not incandescent at all. Instead of filaments, they use two electrodes to excite neon, another inert gas, to the point at which it becomes plasma, a supercharged form of matter that emits light energy.

Many of us are familiar with compact fluorescent lights (CFL bulbs), energy-efficient bulbs that use less wattage to produce more power. Recently, the British company Ceravision has created a super-energy-efficient bulb that works by bombarding aluminum oxide with microwaves. Whereas incandescent lamps convert only 5 percent of their energy into light, and fluorescent bulbs about 15 percent, these microwave-energized bulbs convert more than 50 percent. At least in theory, they can burn for thousands of years—a far cry from Thomas Edison's carbonized cotton filament with its thirteen-hour life span.

—*Dante D'Epiro*

141 ∽ Who developed the first gasoline-powered four-wheeled automobile?

Gottlieb Daimler and Wilhelm Maybach in 1886

FROM SOMETIME BETWEEN 4000 AND 3500 BC to the early nineteenth century, horses, horse-drawn vehicles, and other such animal-powered conveyances were the only means of ground transportation. The steam-powered railway locomotive, invented in 1804 by British mining engineer Richard Trevithick, was actually preceded by several crude forms of automobiles in the late eighteenth century. These first cars were steam powered just like their locomotive counterparts. Their steam engines worked by using coal fed into a furnace to heat water to the boiling point. The steam would then expand under pressure and drive a plunger through a cylinder. The plunger was connected to a rod that was attached to a wheel, which would turn in accordance with the oscillations of the rod.

In 1769, Nicolas-Joseph Cugnot of France built the first automobile: a three-wheeled carriage with a steam engine mounted in front of the lone front wheel. Bulky, cumbersome, and impractical, it had to stop every one hundred feet to make more steam. In between stops, however, the car moved along at a blistering 2.5 mph. In 1771, Cugnot earned the dubious distinction of causing the first automobile accident when he crashed into a wall. A few more attempts to create serviceable automobiles were made by Cugnot and his contemporaries, but the machines could not run on their own power because they had to be stoked constantly.

Although the nineteenth century yielded great advances in the development of the steam engine, the British Parliament, beginning in 1831, made it difficult, if not impossible, to operate steam coaches on roads because of excessive tariffs, requirements, and outright prohibitions. These laws were lifted in 1896, but in the meantime, in Germany and France, interest shifted to internal-combustion engines. These engines utilized the energy released from the combustion of high-pressure gases, which drove pistons that converted the energy to a mechanical form. From 1680 to 1883, numerous combustible substances, such as gunpowder, hydrogen and oxygen, coal gas, petroleum, kerosene, stove gas, and gasoline, were used in attempts to fuel engines.

The first functional internal-combustion engine is credited to the Belgian engineer Étienne Lenoir in 1859, when he converted a steam engine to one that utilized coal gas and an electric spark ignition. In 1863, he modified his engine to run on petroleum and added a carburetor to power a three-wheeled carriage that actually completed a twelve-mile trip, but the inefficient one-horsepower vehicle took eleven hours. In 1864, an Austrian engineer, Siegfried Marcus, built a one-cylinder engine with a carburetor and, six years later, the first gasoline-powered vehicle.

In 1876, Nikolaus August Otto, a German engineer, invented and later patented the first practical four-stroke internal-combustion engine. The four strokes of his "Otto cycle"—downward intake, upward compression, downward combustion, and upward exhaust—drove pistons that converted fuel into mechanical energy.

Two engineers employed by Otto, Gottlieb Daimler (1834–1900) and Wilhelm Maybach (1846–1929), resigned because they felt Otto did not see the benefits of continuing development of the internal-combustion engine. In 1885, the two made significant improvements, creating the gasoline engine that was the basis of today's: an efficient lightweight engine with a vertical cylinder and a fuel-injected carburetor. In 1886, they fitted this engine to a stagecoach, thus creating the first gasoline-powered four-wheeled automobile.

The two inventors continued to tweak engine configurations and, in 1889, produced a belt-driven, rear-engine-mounted, four-speed auto that crept along at 10 mph. In 1890, Daimler founded the Daimler Motoren Gesellschaft (Daimler Motor Company) and, in 1894, won the world's first auto race. In 1901, Maybach designed the Mercedes model, later leaving the company to establish his own airship engine manufacturing company.

Meanwhile, the German engineer Karl Benz (1844–1929) had been working with internal-combustion engine designs as well and, in 1885, created a practical three-wheel automobile for which he had designed the chassis. He received the first patent for a fuel-powered car in 1886 but did not build his first four-wheeler until 1893. His firm, Benz & Cie., became the world's leading automobile manufacturer by 1900. In 1926, the Daimler and Benz firms merged as Daimler-Benz, and the brand name Mercedes-Benz was applied to all its vehicles.

In the United States, John William Lambert, who had been following Benz's work, dreamed of creating a lightweight beltless gas engine for use in his country. He did much of his work in the 1880s and 1890s, receiving a patent for a gasoline engine in 1887 and building the first practical U.S. automobile in 1891.

Electric cars were also being developed in the nineteenth century. Robert Anderson of Scotland invented the first electric carriage between 1832 and 1839, but his and other similar vehicles were far from useful, since they were costly, cumbersome, and extremely inefficient. In addition, they contained batteries that required frequent stops for charging. Designs improved during the latter half of the century to such an extent that electric cars actually led the U.S. market at the turn of the century.

By 1910, although the electric infrastructure needed for charging existed in the United States, electric cars were being outperformed by gas-powered cars. They were able to make only short trips of thirty to forty miles, traveled at only 15 to 20 mph, and took a considerable amount of time to recharge. Electric cars did have one advantage in their electronic ignition (as opposed to the heavy crank on gas cars), but soon this feature was adapted to fit gas cars. By 1920, the electric car was all but dead.

It was Henry Ford's Model T that revolutionized the U.S. auto industry in 1908, because it was useful, affordable, and reliable. Ford was able to achieve efficiency through the assembly-line process, which included interchangeable parts and a sequential fabrication method. His mass production of automobiles, coupled with the high wages he paid, allowed his workers to become customers, too.

The Model T got twenty-five miles per gallon in 1908—better than many modern-day American cars. As the quest for a greener planet continues, manufacturers will need to look at fuel efficiency ever more closely. Hybrid vehicles combine gasoline and electric power, and there were even some models in development that ran on hydrogen fuel cells. These hydrogen cell cars were once considered to be the future of the automotive industry, but programs involving them have been scrapped in favor of more immediate remedies. There are currently several ways of producing hydrogen (including electrolysis, chemical reduction, and thermolysis), but they are all inefficient, because they either require a great deal of energy or emit greenhouse gases, such as carbon dioxide, as by-products. Some argue, in fact, that burning fossil fuels directly produces fewer greenhouse emissions than producing hydrogen. The cells also contain platinum, which does little to make them affordable.

Ultimately, a zero-emission vehicle will be required to curb global pollution. Because of its abundance, hydrogen is still the fuel of choice, and the stars have run on hydrogen fusion for billions of years. We have yet to harness this energy efficiently—fusion calls for extremely high temperatures and requires more energy than it yields—but when we succeed, the possibilities will be limitless. The only way to achieve this goal appears to be via a nuclear fusion reactor, which would run on heavy-water derivatives (deuterium and tritium) and emit only water vapor as its waste product. That technology, however, is not likely to become practical for decades.

—*Dante D'Epiro*

142 ❧ What was the first modern theory of dream interpretation?

Sigmund Freud's The Interpretation of Dreams, *1899*

ON NOVEMBER 4, 1899, A BOOK purporting to present an unsettling theory of dreams was published in Vienna. Its title page bore a line from the *Aeneid* spoken by Juno, the angry queen of the gods, vowing to unleash the powers of the nether regions to accomplish her dark ends. Its thesis: Dreams are bearers of repressed wishes that, when interpreted, cast human nature in a rather unflattering light. The author, an obscure forty-three-year-old Jewish physician and university lecturer, braced himself for the blowback from an outraged humanity.

He needn't have bothered. *The Interpretation of Dreams* took time to fulfill Sigmund Freud's wish: Only 351 copies were sold in its first six years. In due course, Freud's foray into the realm of shadowy messengers was to succeed beyond his imagining. Regardless of what one decides about his methods and model of the psyche, Freud's impact on a broad range of twentieth-century interpretive practices is difficult to overestimate, and this book was his formal debut.

The book's polemic began with its German title, *Die Traumdeutung*, or "The Meaning of Dreams," because at that time prevailing scientific opinion took the position that dreams had no meaning whatsoever. Part autobiography, part picaresque novel, chock-full of peculiar dreams and often more bizarre interpretations, the book gets down to business in its first sentence:

> In the following pages I shall prove that there exists a
> psychological technique by which dreams may be interpreted,
> and that upon the application of this method every dream will
> show itself to be a meaningful psychological structure that
> may be introduced into an assignable place in the psychic
> activity of the waking state.

The author immediately takes the reader in hand as a silent partner while he surveys the thought of previous authors, ponders unresolved questions, and narrates the dream that led to his discovery. We are there when basic hypotheses, such as "Dreams are the fulfillment of wishes," bubble up from empirical data presented in a purposive spirit of collegial openness and scientific neutrality. We witness ingenious feats of inter-pretation and, like Polonius behind the arras, are privy to sexual traumas and familial secrets of the Viennese bourgeoisie—secrets offered in the confidentiality of the doctor's well-upholstered consulting room.

Through seven chapters a coherent argument unfolds, deploying an extraordinary number of dreams, riddles, and literary allusions to illustrate a comprehensive theory of the nature of dreams and the struc-ture of the mind. When our guide discreetly closes the door to protect his privacy, or that of his patients and colleagues, we accept his tactful judgment without hesitation. Although this narrator never identifies himself explicitly by name, location, or professional credentials—he might as well be Virgil guiding us into the underworld—we rely on his confident authority.

What intrigues the narrator is the sphinxlike status that dreams have had for thousands of years. Surveying speculations from the early Greeks to his own day, he finds that they either assume dreams are meaningful but offer no reliable method of reading their meaning, or they simply dismiss dreams as the aimless shadow play of the mind in a relaxed state. No theory accounts for the apparent senselessness of dreams while holding that they indeed make an important kind of sense.

At this point Freud pauses, not to offer his own theory, but rather one of his own dreams: the now legendary "Dream of Irma's Injection." In it, he is receiving guests in a large hall and encounters Irma, a recal-citrant patient, whom he reproaches for not accepting his "solution" to the nervous disorder for which he's been treating her. She speaks of pains in her throat, stomach, and abdomen, causing him to think he must be missing some organic trouble.

> Her mouth then opens wide, and I find a large white spot on the right, and at another place I see large grayish-white scabs attached to some peculiar curling formations, which were apparently shaped like the turbinate bones of the nose.

He calls over several medical colleagues, who proceed to offer patently absurd opinions, calling their medical competence into question. The dream ends with this:

> My friend Otto has recently given her an injection . . . when she felt ill. . . . Such injections should not be made so irresponsibly. . . . And the syringe was probably not clean.

Freud then breaks the dream description into parts and follows the associations suggested by each segment in isolation from the rest. These lead to a ganglion of memories linked with other patients and physicians too complex to summarize, but the upshot, Freud says, is that: "I am not to blame for Irma's persistent pains. . . . Otto is." By representing things as he would like them to be, the dream acquitted him of responsibility. The import of the dream is clear, and Freud states it in italics: *"The content of the dream is thus the fulfillment of a wish; its motive is a wish."*

Much ink has been spilled over this epiphany. Freud himself acknowledges there was more to the analysis than he presents. (This is a recurrent feature of *The Interpretation*—no dream is exhaustively analyzed, and Freud suggests that no analysis can ever end.) It is now understood that "Irma" represents possibly three women, one of whom was a patient of Wilhelm Fliess, Freud's closest confidant during the writing of *The Interpretation*. Fliess had in fact botched an operation on the woman's nose (he left a half meter of gauze in it, leading to near fatal bleeding and disfigurement), but this instance of nightmarish professional misconduct does not emerge in the dream analysis. Biographer Peter Gay sees the dream as fulfilling more than one wish, since it protects Freud both from charges of poor practice and from having to recognize his friend's outrageous oversight.

"Irma's Injection" satisfies yet another wish: the wish of the narrator that dreams possess meaning. No wish is more necessary at this point in the narrative, if the rest of the book is going to exist. Indeed, the title of the next chapter takes the insight from Irma and broadens it into a theoretical principle: "A Dream Is the Fulfillment of a Wish."

The Interpretation picks up steam at this point. If the wish is father to the dream thoughts, it asks, then why are so many dreams filled with anxiety and dread? The reason is that dreams are shaped by "two psychical forces"—one constructs the wish expressed by the dream, while the other "acts as a censor upon this dream wish, and by means of this censoring forces a distortion of its expression."

Dreams, then, are the outcome of a struggle between a creative wish and a defensive, censoring agency that modifies its utterance. Freud elaborates a map of the mind in which the unconscious is the locus of wishes that often derive from our infancy—such as the desire to kill our fathers and marry our mothers. The tale of Oedipus strikes us so profoundly, he says, because in it we recognize an image of our strongest, earliest wishes.

The censor defends against such blinding insights. Freud employs a curious dream to illustrate this process of distortion:

I. My friend R. is my uncle.—I have great affection
for him.

II. I see his face in front of me, somewhat changed. It seems
to be elongated. A yellow beard, which surrounds it, seems
to stand out very clearly.

Freud's analysis showed that the dream was connected with his hopes of professional advancement and his fears that—like R. in the dream—his chances might be sidelined by anti-Semitism, then on the rise in Vienna. The dream likens R. to Freud's uncle Josef, the family's black sheep, who had run afoul of the law many years before. The feeling of affection was entirely an illusion created by the dream to allow the dreamer to have hypocritical warm fuzzies about a colleague he was actually likening to a criminal. The wish being fulfilled was that, since Freud was not a criminal, his chances of advancement were much better than R.'s.

Freud likens the censor to the necessary hypocrisy of polite society, as well as to writers in repressive states who have to resort to talking about Chinese Mandarins when they really mean powerful ministers. But there's yet another turn of the screw. In a footnote, Freud discloses that during the analysis he forgot that he actually had five uncles:

> It is astonishing to note how my memory—in my waking state—narrowed itself for the purposes of the analysis. I have actually known five of my uncles, . . . but at the moment when I overcame my resistance to interpreting the dream I said to myself that I have only one uncle—the one that was meant in the dream.

The compromised position of consciousness is clear and makes Freud's candor all the more impressive—even as he is laying the groundwork for his new science, he leaves us with the nagging thought that the waking consciousness can be spellbound by the force of dreams. If so, do analyses diagnose hidden wishes, or do those wishes construct the analysis?

That dreams are asocial dramatizations driven by infantile desires is the substance of Chapter 5, "The Material and Sources of Dreams." Childhood is a paradise that we reclaim in sleep. But it is Chapter 6, "The Dream Work," that offers the intellectual fireworks that make the book memorable. Over successive editions, this chapter grew like Pinocchio's nose as more and more dream samples were brought in.

If the wish is the motive force of the dream, the "dream work" is the means of its encryption. Freud, whose first published work was about aphasia, guides us through a rich panoply of techniques deployed to disrupt speech and disguise our wishes.

Via *condensation*, dreams condense multiple latent thoughts into one punlike image or may represent a single thought via several images. Another strategy, which he calls *displacement*, shifts the center of a dream from its real subject to seemingly indifferent material, just as magicians use misdirection to divert our attention. The censor will employ rebuslike images, allusions, symbols, calculations, logic, absurdity—even the self-observing effect through which we alter a dream as we dream it.

One brief example will have to stand for many. A woman dreamed she was at a peasant festivity and told her husband: "This will end in a general *Maistollmütz*." Work with the patient's associations divided the last word into *Mais* (maize), *toll* (mad), *mannstoll* (nymphomaniac), and *Olmütz* (a town in Moravia)—all fragments of recent conversations she had had. More words lay behind these: *Meissen* (a porcelain figure representing a bird), *Miss* (her relatives' English governess had just gone to *Olmütz*), and *mies* (Jewish slang for "disgusting"). "A long chain of thoughts and associations led off from each syllable of this verbal hotchpotch," adds Freud.

Whatever one makes of *The Interpretation*'s theory, it can't be denied that its author wrestled long and hard with the angel.

In *Jokes and Their Relation to the Unconscious*, which appeared five years after *The Interpretation*, Freud recapitulated his basic view of dreams and dream work:

> This strange "manifest" content of the dream can regularly be made intelligible as a mutilated and altered transcript of certain rational psychical structures which deserve the name of *"latent dream-thoughts."*

For Freud, the enigmatic face of the dream tries to turn our rational, scheming desires into babble, and his passion lay in reading the babble with careful attention, as though attending to a literary text. In his fusion of the arts of healing with the devices of concealing, Freud was yoking two kingdoms, two practices: medicine and interpretation. His work is an unwitting harbinger of the twentieth century's vast preoccupation with the nature of reason and of signs, from the surrealism of Antonin Artaud to the Lacanian musings of Slavoj Zizek, from semiotics to postmodernism.

The final chapter of *The Interpretation* begins with the haunting dream of the burning child. A father feels a tugging on his arm; it's his son who is saying, "Father, don't you see I'm burning?" The dreamer wakes to find it is no dream—the laid-out body of his son, who had died the night before, is aflame from a candle that has tipped over in the night. The fire's light was in the dream, as was the little boy. Only, in the dream he was alive, trying to speak, to awaken his father. Freud calls this a "transparent" dream, as the wish was not concealed. But which was the father's real wish: to dream so that his son could "live," or to extinguish both dream and son to save his own life?

For Freud, the riddle of human nature never lends itself to transparent reading. "Properly speaking, the unconscious is the true psychical reality," he says late in the final chapter, then shifts to italics: "*Its inner nature is just as unknown to us as the reality of the external world, and it is just as imperfectly reported to us through the data of consciousness as is the external world through the communications of our sensory organs.*" Then comes an admonition that hangs like a baleful oracle over the century about to begin: "It is essential," he says, "to abandon the overvaluation of the property of being conscious."

—*Tom Matrullo*

TWENTIETH
CENTURY

143 ～ What was the first narrative film?

Georges Méliès's Le voyage dans la lune
(A Trip to the Moon) in 1902

THE BIRTH OF MOTION PICTURES in the predawn era of the twentieth century was truly a Big Bang. An explosion of fin de siècle developments brought "animated photography" from the constraints of Thomas Edison's kinetoscope, in which a solitary viewer looked at moving images through a tiny peephole (1889), through the invention of the *cinématographe*, a projector that enabled the Lumière brothers in Paris to show films on a theater screen to large audiences (1895), to a new plateau in the early twentieth century when an ever-growing hunger for films portended a giant industry in the making. In such a frantic era of growth, it is not always easy for film historians to assign "firsts." Nonetheless, a tradition that continues to survive asserts that French producer-director Georges Méliès, in *Le voyage dans la lune*, an adaptation of two best-selling science-fiction stories, gave the cinema its first narrative film in 1902.

Méliès (1861–1938) was a professional magician and a man of the theater. As owner-operator of the Théâtre Robert Houdin in Paris, he produced shows that specialized in spectacle and illusions. When the Lumières began projecting films on a screen for curious Parisian audiences, Méliès was among the first to attend.

What did he see? Scenes from everyday life: workers leaving a factory, a train arriving at a station, a man watering a garden with a hose (albeit with a playful twist in which he gets doused himself), a baby being fed lunch, men playing cards. Today they look like home movies, but in 1895 audiences were entranced.

So was Méliès. It is tempting to say—along with many others—that the magician in him spotted the potential for magic in animated photography. He certainly was excited at the prospect of adding it to his repertoire of illusions. When the Lumières refused to sell him one of their machines, Méliès built his own based on an English model. Almost immediately, he went into film production, at first outdoors like the Lumières, but later in a studio he built, similar to Edison's Black Maria in New Jersey.

Méliès's films were typically not the raw recordings of real activities—*actualités*—being offered by the Lumières in France and Edison in America. Instead, they were elaborately artful fictions, often involving fantasy elements and startling visual conceits. As he had suspected, Méliès found that magic tricks were easier to carry off using animated photographs than on a stage. Through his experiments, he discovered most of the methods of trick photography that would be used for the next hundred years, including the dissolve, stop-motion, double exposure, slow and fast motion, and animation. With these techniques Méliès could depict sudden disappearances, ghostly effects, and magical transformations. In one film, he himself removed his head several times so that four live heads were on the screen simultaneously. These imaginative productions were immensely popular.

Despite their creative use of the new medium's technical possibilities, most of Méliès's films had a theatrical look, with painted backdrops and actors approaching center frame from left or right as if from the wings. Méliès's camera never moved, as though approximating the view of a theater patron in a good seat. In making his films, Méliès used the full range of talents acquired from a life in the theater, serving as producer, director, production designer (arguably the first in film history, and a highly gifted one), costume designer, and actor. Long before the word became familiar in film criticism, Méliès was an auteur to be reckoned with.

In 1902, he produced his most famous work, *Le voyage dans la lune* (*A Trip to the Moon*), basing his story on *From the Earth to the Moon* (1865) by Jules Verne and *The First Men in the Moon* (1901) by H. G. Wells. The fourteen-minute film consists of thirty shots, each of which is an entire scene or, to use Méliès's word, tableau.

Voyage's opening shot is a rich, busy frame that still impresses today: a large set with a painted backdrop depicting the observatory hall of the Astronomic Club, crowded with men dressed in wizard's robes and pointed hats. As a live narrator would have explained to early audiences, they are scientists attending a meeting to discuss a possible trip to the moon. Although the camera never moves, the tableau is far from static. The scientists are never still; each is waving his hands, or turning to a neighbor and talking excitedly, or standing up and sitting down, or removing his funny hat, wiping his head, and putting it back on.

A group of pages—played by attractive women—enter carrying telescopes. They are followed by the club's president, an impressive magus with flowing beard (played by Méliès himself) who enters grandly and walks toward the dais in front of a blackboard. As the president reaches the dais, an apparently unscripted event occurs—his hat falls off. Méliès the actor/producer saves the shot when he quickly swoops up the hat and sets it on the desk in front of him without missing a beat.

The president proceeds to sketch his starkly simple plan on the blackboard: An enormous cannon will fire a shell with live cargo to the moon. Only one of the scientists opposes the plan, but he is angrily attacked by everyone—the president throws books at him—and is silenced within seconds (the same conflict occupies twelve chapters in the Verne novel). Five scientists agree to accompany the president. He comes down from the dais to join them; the pages bring traveling clothes, and the would-be voyagers change into these garments before exiting at screen right. As this delightfully frenetic opening shot dissolves into the next, it is clear that science fiction in cinema, however serious it might become in the next hundred years, will be born as a lighthearted romp. Dystopian nightmares tomorrow; comedy tonight.

Succeeding shots continue to be marked by a sea of movement, often comic. Workmen busily preparing the vehicle (resembling a large bullet shell) that will take the astronomers to the moon are interrupted by the nosy, clumsy scientists, one of whom falls into a pail of acid. On launch day, a sailor pulls a ladder next to the space vehicle to allow the scientists to board. The showman Méliès loses no chance to be diverting: The sailor is female, pretty, and wearing a skimpy uniform. To satisfy the tired businessmen out front, she is joined by a dozen others to push the shell into the mouth of the huge cannon that will shoot it into space. (Given their task, can one resist the urge to dub them the Rockettes?) An officer gives the signal to fire as cheering Rockettes and others give the men a rousing send-off.

The next shot is of a traditional cartoon of the man in the moon. Morphing into the real face of an actor, the moon moves closer. In a sudden stop-motion substitution, we see the shell firmly fixed in the man in the moon's right eye, to his great consternation. This, the most famous shot in *Le voyage dans la lune*, has endured as an iconic representation of the early silent era and is recognizable to many who have never seen the film.

On his surreal moon, Méliès treats us to a dream sequence with a parade of special effects mainly involving comely young women. An underground grotto in a crater contains a beautiful and haunting backdrop depicting rocks, a waterfall, and gigantic mushrooms that grow magically. This becomes perhaps the film's funniest scene, thanks to the attack of the Selenites, nimble moon creatures played by acrobats from the Folies Bergère. As the first attacker enters the scene, he displays for the audience the special contortionist's skill that producer Méliès was paying for, but the performance crimps his scary alien style by allowing him to threaten the intruders only by inching toward them on his buttocks like an itchy family pet. At the last moment he leaps to his feet. The president defends himself with the only weapon he's brought along—an umbrella. It suffices. When he hits the Selenite, the moon-dweller evaporates via stop-motion into a cloud of smoke. So does a second. Finally, however, a crowd of Selenites proves too much for the travelers, who are subdued and marched into the elaborately appointed throne room of the Selenite king.

Developments are swift. The president breaks free from his bonds, grabs the king, and throws him over his head to the ground, where he explodes in a ball of smoke. Other Selenites meet the same fate in the melee that follows, which ends with the flight of the earthlings toward their space vehicle as their enemies from the Folies Bergère remain in hot pursuit.

In the last scene on the moon, the president reaches the vehicle, now sitting conveniently, if inexplicably, on a cliff at the edge of the moon. (The other astronauts are already aboard.) The president slams the door shut, grabs a rope attached to the nose of the spacecraft, and jumps off the cliff. Gravity sends the ship, him, and a Selenite who jumps on the rear of the vessel plummeting back to earth. After a few seconds of rapid descent, the vehicle plunges into the sea. A surprisingly effective underwater shot shows the ship floating to the surface. The travelers are rescued offscreen, and then towed back to shore via animation. In several final scenes often missing from available versions of the film, the voyagers receive a resounding public welcome.

Le voyage dans la lune was an instant hit. Although Méliès made money in Europe, he failed to earn the enormous returns he was expecting from America, because Edison's technicians pirated the film and exhibited it in the United States without paying him. Thanks partly to this and poor business decisions, Méliès ultimately went bankrupt and died in relative obscurity. But his contribution to film is unquestioned: "I owe him everything," said D. W. Griffith, widely considered cinema's first master.

While the Lumières in their *actualités* had chosen to give the world "more matter with less art," the creative Méliès did the opposite. In terms of future directions, he backed the right horse. Indeed, by remaining ever at the service of pleasure-seekers, Méliès helped steer motion pictures toward their predominant twentieth-century roles of entertainment and artistic expression. Of Méliès's more than four hundred productions, only about a third survive. Luckily, these include the film that—besides being a delightfully rococo *divertissement*—marks the birth of storytelling in the movies.

—*Joseph Sgammato*

144 ∾ Who made the first powered flight?

Orville Wright at Kitty Hawk, North Carolina,
on December 17, 1903

SINCE ANCIENT TIMES, HUMANS HAVE marveled at the majesty of birds in flight and their apparent ability to defy the laws of nature. The Greeks embodied both their aspirations and their fears regarding the possibilities of human flight in the myth of Daedalus and Icarus, a father and son who, confined to the island of Crete by King Minos, planned to escape with two sets of wings that Daedalus had fashioned from feathers and wax. Though warned against it, young Icarus, exalted by his newfound power, flew too close to the sun, which melted the wax on his wings, causing him to plunge into and give a name to the Icarian Sea.

During the Renaissance, Leonardo da Vinci spent many long hours observing birds and drawing up plans for flying machines that bear a resemblance to modern helicopters, gliders, and parachutes. He himself made some unsuccessful attempts at flying and, in a note on one of his many designs, wrote, "This machine should be tried over a lake, and you should carry a long wineskin as a girdle so that in case you fall you will not be drowned." The ornithopter, his concept for a birdlike flying machine, had to wait until 1870 for its first working model, which was the size of a pigeon. (The first successful engine-driven manned ornithopter was built by Adalbert Schmid and flown in 1942.) Another great Renaissance painter, Albrecht Dürer, designed a flying machine in 1522.

But the annals of successful human flight begin with the brothers Joseph and Jacques Montgolfier of France, who discovered that heated air contained within a lightweight, bag-shaped object causes it to rise. In a public demonstration on June 4, 1783, they sent a hot-air balloon to an altitude of about three thousand feet before it slowly returned to the ground ten minutes later and a mile and a half away. On September 19 of the same year, before a huge crowd at Versailles that included King Louis XVI and Queen Marie Antoinette, they sent a doubtlessly petrified sheep, duck, and rooster up for an eight-minute, two-mile flight. Finally, the first manned, untethered balloon flight took place over Paris on November 21, lasting twenty-five minutes and safely setting down the young physician and the aristocratic army officer who had volunteered for the mission about five and half miles away from the launch site.

In the mid-nineteenth century, gliders built by the Englishman George Cayley had some success, and toward the end of the century Germany's Otto Lilienthal designed a glider that enabled him to complete twenty-five hundred successful flights before his fatal crash in 1896. These experiments influenced the Wright brothers to take an interest in gliding as a sport.

Wilbur (1867–1912) and Orville (1871–1948) Wright were the sons of a Midwestern Protestant bishop who traveled a great deal on church business. Wilbur's plans of attending Yale were derailed in the winter of 1885–86 by an ice hockey accident, and he spent the next several years at the family home in Dayton, Ohio, caring for his sick mother, who died of tuberculosis in 1889, reading widely in his father's library, and assisting him with church matters.

Wilbur then decided to join Orville in the printing business, which his younger brother had dropped out of high school to start. The pair also found time to edit and publish two local newspapers and to craft their own printing machines, displaying a talent for problem-solving and mechanical devices. In 1892, the brothers opened a bicycle shop as well, which provided further training in the building and repair of lightweight machinery. They also began to conduct experiments related to their real interest—flying machines.

In addition to their knowledge of Lilienthal's glider experiments— their interest piqued by his death in 1896—the brothers had read extensively in mechanics, mathematics, and the literature of flight, particularly the kite-flying experiments by the meteorologist A. Lawrence Rotch and the telephone pioneer Alexander Graham Bell. They requested information on aeronautics from the Smithsonian, including the works of Samuel P. Langley, a mathematician and physicist who published *Experiments in Aerodynamics* in 1891, and they were also influenced by the writings of James Means, who founded the Boston Aeronautical Society in 1895 and began publishing *Aeronautical Annual* that same year. In addition, the Wright brothers sought out the French-born engineer Octave Chanute, a leading expert on aviation who served as their chief technical consultant from 1900 to 1905, the period that gave birth to powered flight.

Before moving on to the first airplane, the brothers conducted many experiments with gliders, determining that a successful flying machine would require wings to generate lift, a propulsion system for movement, and an in-flight control system to steer and stabilize the airborne craft. They realized that Lilienthal's method of stabilization, which relied on the pilot's shifting the weight of his body, was doomed to failure. Instead, they utilized a constant center of gravity system, which maintained stability by varying the air pressure exerted on different parts of the wings and other surfaces by changing their angles. This system, which would give the pilot complete control, was patented by them and came to be known as aileron control.

The Wright brothers then set out to find a suitable venue for their experiments. Dayton's terrain was flat and its winds were light—hardly ideal. The brothers ascertained through the U.S. Weather Bureau that Kitty Hawk, a small village on the Outer Banks of North Carolina, offered windy conditions, sand dunes from which to launch and to land softly on, and relative privacy. In 1900 and 1901, the brothers conducted numerous glider experiments in and around Kitty Hawk, mainly trying to solve the problem of control. Wilbur made all the glides, the longest of which was about four hundred feet. Although the brothers were discouraged with their progress, Wilbur agreed, at Chanute's behest, to address the Western Society of Engineers in Chicago on September 18, 1901, and his remarks formed the basis of an article later published as "Some Aeronautical Experiments" in the society's journal.

After returning to Dayton, the brothers constructed their own wind tunnel and measurement gauges to evaluate lift and drag at different angles, collecting an enormous amount of data during the fall and early winter of 1901 by testing between a hundred and two hundred wing designs in their tunnel. They then went to Kill Devil Hills, North Carolina (about four miles south of Kitty Hawk), to test their full-scale glider in September and October of 1902. It seemed to perform as expected, and this time the brothers shared the flying duties in seven hundred to one thousand flights, the longest of which lasted twenty-six seconds and spanned 622.5 feet. They had achieved stability and even added a movable rudder to the wing-warping system for additional control.

With the wing and in-flight control systems performing satisfactorily, the only remaining problem was propulsion. For this, the Wright brothers enlisted Charles Taylor, a machinist they had employed in the bicycle shop, to help them build their own internal-combustion engine. The result was a twin-propeller-driven, gasoline-powered, four-cylinder engine weighing 200 pounds and churning out twelve horsepower. With their engine in tow, the brothers returned to their camp in Kill Devil Hills in September 1903. It took them about seven weeks to assemble and test the new unit, which they affixed to their 1902 glider. The ensemble of engine, glider, and pilot weighed about 750 pounds.

Wilbur was to make the first powered-flight attempt on December 14, but he stalled on takeoff and damaged the front portion of the plane. After three days, their invention was ready to be retested, the honors this time belonging to Orville, who, at 10:35 a.m. on December 17, 1903, managed to fly his contraption for 12 seconds over 120 feet. This modest first was followed by Wilbur, who covered 175 feet in 12 seconds, Orville who covered 200 feet in 15 seconds, and finally Wilbur again, who flew 852 feet in 59 seconds. All four historic flights, taking place at a dizzying 10 feet of altitude, were witnessed by five locals. The brothers continued their experiments the following year, but it was only in September 1905 that they learned to avoid tailspins during short turns. With this obstacle cleared, Wilbur flew a twenty-four-mile course for thirty-eight minutes on October 5, even performing some circles and other maneuvers.

Convinced their design was complete, the Wright brothers turned their attention to marketing their innovation, securing the patents necessary to sell it. In 1906–7, some doubt still existed as to who had developed the first powered flying machine, but the brothers continued to negotiate with investors and government agencies in Europe and America. In February 1908, they signed a contract with the U.S. Army worth $25,000. They were required to supply a machine capable of carrying a pilot and passenger for at least an hour at an average speed of forty miles per hour. The following month, they reached an agreement with French investors who planned to develop airplanes under license from them.

The Wright brothers returned to Kill Devil Hills in May 1908 and made twenty-two more flights with their 1905 machine, incorporating upright seating and hand controls. On May 14, Wilbur took the world's first airplane passenger, the mechanic Charles Furnas, up for a spin. In August, he went to Europe and made flights in Le Mans and Pau in France, and also in Rome, attracting attention from the kings of Great Britain, Spain, and Italy, while garnering global recognition.

Orville conducted a series of army trials in Fort Myer, Virginia, but on September 17 he took up Lieutenant Thomas E. Selfridge, who became the first passenger fatality as the result of a crash caused by a split propeller. The pilot himself was badly injured, but after visiting his brother in Europe, he returned to Fort Myer to complete the trials in 1909. Despite the lethal accident, the army was sufficiently impressed to award the Wrights an additional $5,000 bonus because they exceeded the speed requirement of forty miles per hour. Afterward, Orville traveled to Germany, flying in Berlin and Potsdam, whereas Wilbur made some distinctive flights as part of the Hudson-Fulton celebration in New York City. At College Park, Maryland, he served as flight instructor for the first three U.S. Army officers who learned to fly.

The brothers incorporated the Wright Company in November 1909, with Wilbur as president and Orville as a vice president. They built a manufacturing plant in Dayton, as well as a flight school at Huffman Prairie. After Wilbur succumbed to typhoid fever on May 30, 1912, Orville presided over their company until 1915, when he sold it to a group of investors. He served as a member of the National Advisory Committee for Aeronautics from 1920 until his death on January 30, 1948.

After airplanes were extensively used in bombing and reconnaissance missions in the latter stages of World War I, the first nonstop transatlantic flight was accomplished by Captain John Alcock and Lieutenant Arthur Whitten Brown of Britain's Royal Air Force, who traveled from Newfoundland to Ireland in 16 hours, 12 minutes on June 14–15, 1919. The first solo transatlantic flight was made on May 20–21, 1927, by Charles Lindbergh, who, to worldwide acclaim, flew his *Spirit of St. Louis* 3,610 miles from Roosevelt Field on Long Island, New York, to Paris, France, in 33 hours and 30 minutes.

Flying has become immensely safer than in Lindbergh's time—not to mention the day when Lieutenant Selfridge lost his life in Orville Wright's plane. By 2006, there was only one fatal accident per 4.2 million flights by Western-built commercial jets, and the average American's life-time risk of dying in a car accident was more than twenty times greater than that of perishing while on a commercial flight. Nonetheless, the fate of Icarus can still give us pause—about 40 percent of us have some degree of anxiety about flying—and as many as 6.5 percent are so afflicted with aviophobia that they absolutely refuse to venture into an element foreign to our terrestrial nature.

—*Dante D'Epiro*

145 ∽ What was the first theory of relativity?

Albert Einstein's Special Theory of Relativity, published in 1905

WHAT WOULD HAPPEN IF WE could strap ourselves onto a beam of light and travel with it—at light speed? What would the world look like? Indeed, what would the beam of light look like from such a perspective?

When riding on a galloping horse, the fixed objects that we pass, such as the trees, the grass, and the fence, may appear somewhat fuzzy because of motion blur. But since we move through space at the same speed as our mount, we can gaze down and get a good idea of equine anatomy. We can observe our horse's velveteen ears folded carefully into aerodynamic position. We can see the coarse individual hairs in his mane undulating with his rhythmic gait. We may even be able to see the steady pulse of his blood as it traverses through an artery in his neck. We can see our horse clearly, because on a macroscopic scale we move in unison with him. Now, what about that beam of light? If we could strap ourselves onto it, traveling just as fast as light travels, what exactly would the light look like? Would we see its form and its anatomic details as if it weren't moving?

At age sixteen, Albert Einstein (1879–1955) pondered these questions. The framework for his inquiry was formed when, decades earlier, physicist James Clerk Maxwell discovered the principles of electro-magnetism, uniting light, electricity, and magnetism with a single mathematical equation. A natural consequence was that all forms of electromagnetism would be clocked at "light speed," regardless of the observer's speed or frame of reference. What this means is that, no matter how quickly we move, light will always appear to be traveling inhumanly fast. It will always appear to be moving at light speed.

This is no small consequence, because in our experience of the world, our own speed relative to an object in motion affects how fast we observe the object to move. For example, suppose we stand outside and watch a boy walking down the street toward a corner. When he reaches it, he stops and hurls a baseball forward. We clock the ball at 40 mph. The next day, we get into a car and drive along the same street. At the moment we pass the corner, we see the same boy throw the same baseball from the same spot as yesterday, aiming it along our direction of travel. This time, the ball doesn't move past us nearly as fast as when we stood still. In fact, relative to our moving car, the baseball is barely making headway through the air. We can see it slowly creep past us, almost levitating outside the car window as we drive down the street. We look down at the speedometer and immediately see why: Our car is traveling at 39 mph. We can assume from yesterday's identical throw that the ball's speed is 40 mph. Thus, relative to us observers, the ball is gaining ground at a mere 1 mph. No wonder it barely appears to move.

Yet according to Maxwell's equation, light will always appear to move at light speed, no matter how fast the observer is moving. Whether we stand still, look out the window of a speeding train, or peer through a porthole on the space shuttle, light will always appear to approach or recede from us at light speed. This is analogous to making the dual claim that, while standing on the street, we see the baseball move away from us at 40 mph, and while riding in the car, we see the ball move away from us just as quickly, exactly 40 mph faster than our own motion. How can that be?

To Einstein, the constancy of the speed of light was perplexing, profound, beautifully simple, and the key to a remarkable understanding that still lay undiscovered. It was in 1905 at the age of twenty-six that Einstein first publicly outlined his Special Theory of Relativity in a scientific paper entitled "On the Electrodynamics of Moving Bodies." (His General Theory of Relativity, published ten years afterward, described how the matter in space-time creates a warp or bend in its framework, causing objects, and even light itself, to adhere to these framework distortions according to the process we call gravity.)

According to Special Relativity, observers in an inertial frame of reference—that is, two different observers experiencing constant, steady motion relative to each other—will obtain different measurements of each other's progress through time and space. The rub is that both sets of measurements will be correct.

Regarding time, a stationary observer will see a moving clock tick more slowly than his own watch. Here's an example. The driver of a speeding car uses an ultra-high-precision stopwatch to measure the time it takes him to travel exactly one mile on a marked highway. A roadside observer of the speeding car also measures the time required by the car to travel this distance, using similarly sophisticated timing equipment. The driver's time measurement is slightly less (on the order of nanoseconds) than that of the roadside observer. Nonetheless, both timing devices are completely accurate in their own frames of reference. The reason for the discrepancy, according to Special Relativity, is that time passes more slowly inside the moving vehicle, and thus the driver's watch should rightfully indicate a smaller number than the observer's timing equipment.

Regarding space, Special Relativity asserts that observers will perceive a moving object as being shortened along its direction of motion. For example, if a roadside observer were able to measure the length of a speeding car as it passed, he would obtain a shorter measurement than if the car were parked.

Were it not for Einstein's acknowledged genius, we would question the plausibility of Special Relativity. Time dilation and length contraction do not jibe with our everyday experience, but the conflict is a result of the minuscule proportions involved. While the astounding effects of Special Relativity are true at all speeds, even the relatively minute ones we achieve while walking and driving, the distorting effects described by the theory become measurable only at speeds that are a substantial fraction of the speed of light. Countless experiments with particles moving at near light speed have demonstrated and numerically matched the predictions of Special Relativity.

Consider A. H. Reginald Buller's amusing speculation on traveling faster than the speed of light in his famous limerick, "Relativity":

> *There was a young lady named Bright*
> *Whose speed was far faster than light;*
> > *She set out one day,*
> > *In a relative way,*
> *And returned on the previous night.*

If this were possible, Buller would have discovered the fountain of youth. Of course, light itself is incapable of traveling faster than light speed, so we humans, woefully sluggish in comparison, are doomed to aging and a much lower speed limit. In fact, only "objects" with zero mass, such as electromagnetic disturbances (including light), are capable of traveling at light speed. Thus it's impossible to formulate an answer to Einstein's original question, "What happens if we chase after a beam of light at light speed?" There's no way to look at light as if it were standing still.

We may ask instead, "What would happen if we could travel through space at 90 percent of the speed of light for fifty earth years?" Such speeds are also impossible for humans, but at the very least we can compute a theoretical answer. According to the Lorentz equations, which quantify the time dilation and length contraction described by Special Relativity, we would return from our journey having aged only about twenty-two earth years.

—*Lisa C. Perrone*

146 ∿ What was the First World War?

*A European bloodbath that involved much of the
rest of the world, 1914–18*

THE ILLIBERAL CONGRESS OF VIENNA (1814–15), which redrew the map of Europe after the convulsions of the French Revolutionary and Napoleonic Wars, sought to satisfy traditional dynastic claims and establish a balance of power (see Questions 131 and 135). The victorious major powers—Great Britain, Prussia, Austria, and Russia—were placated in order to avoid future bloody showdowns, and the weaker nations were used as pawns. To its credit, the congress prevented another general European war for a hundred years.

The two world wars can be seen as successive stages of a massive European civil war that essentially pitted both ends (France, Britain, and Russia) against the middle (Germany and Austria-Hungary), with Italy migrating from the first group to the second. In the twentieth century, linguistic nationalism first played a major role in determining a people's demands to "redeem" territories in which fellow speakers of its language lived under "foreign" domination, as in the Austro-Hungarian, German, Russian, and Ottoman Empires in the Balkans and Eastern and Central Europe. In addition, the rise of Otto von Bismarck's German Empire from the militaristic substratum of Prussia had long alarmed the great powers located at "the ends" of Europe—France and Russia. France had already been humiliated by Germany's might in the Franco-Prussian War of 1870–71, and Russia feared that its buffer-zone possessions—Poland, the Baltic states, and the Ukraine—would be overrun by expansionary Germany under its mushy-brained, big-stick-wielding kaiser, Wilhelm II.

By the time the Great War broke out, mutual rivalries and hatreds had been simmering for decades. The French wanted Alsace-Lorraine back, which Germany had seized in the Franco-Prussian War. Germany resented the worldwide reach of the British Empire and its indomitable navy. In the so-called scramble for Africa that began in the 1880s, the continent was so thoroughly colonized that by 1914 only Ethiopia and Liberia were free of European control. The British and French resented Germany's recent acquisition of African and Pacific colonies, which had long been *their* preserve, and its growing sea power. The Germans wanted more territory to the east, but the Russian Bear seemed poised to swallow up even more of Eastern Europe than it already possessed. The British were furious at Germany's plan to finance the missing links in a Berlin–Baghdad railway, which would threaten British India and their Near Eastern possessions. The Ottoman Empire seemed ripe for dismantling to Russia, Britain, France, and others.

The Balkans, long trodden underfoot by the Ottoman Turks and the Hapsburg Austrian Empire, wanted to rid themselves of both, but Bosnia and Herzegovina had been annexed by Austria as recently as 1908. Russia was eager to assume an overlordship there as a protector of fellow Slavs and Orthodox Christians—and to grab some warm-water ports. The First Balkan War (1912), in which Serbia, Greece, and Bulgaria had defeated Turkey, was followed by a second in 1913, in which Serbia, Greece, Romania—and Turkey—defeated Bulgaria. Serbia began agitating for a "Greater Serbia" that would encompass all South Slavs. Although Italy had a treaty alliance with Germany and Austria-Hungary going back to the 1880s, it had festering irredentist claims against Austria. The European alliance system, whereby France, Britain, and Russia's Triple Entente ("understanding") stood ready to square off against the Triple Alliance of Germany, Austria, and Italy, facilitated the rush to war.

The match to this powder keg was applied by Gavrilo Princip, an impoverished nineteen-year-old Bosnian nationalist and member of a secret Serbian society, the Black Hand, which sought to end Hapsburg rule in the Balkans and unite the South Slavs into a nation. On June 28, 1914, he shot and killed Archduke Franz Ferdinand, the presumptive heir to the Austro-Hungarian Empire, and his wife, Sophie, during an official visit to the Bosnian capital of Sarajevo. Austria-Hungary, which had been seeking to crush Serbia as the nest of Slavic separatism, gave the small nation an ultimatum that was guaranteed to be at least partially refused.

Germany's assurance of carte-blanche support to Austria-Hungary for any military move against Serbia was the deathblow to European peace. Austria-Hungary declared war on Serbia on July 28, 1914, initiating a cascade of irresponsibility. When Russia began mobilizing (including on the German frontier) to protect its Slavic little brother, Germany declared war on Russia on August 1, and on its ally France on August 3, and proceeded to invade neutral Belgium. The British gave the Germans an ultimatum to evacuate Belgium and, when it was ignored, declared war on Germany on August 4. Austria-Hungary declared war on Russia on August 6; France and Britain declared war on Austria-Hungary on August 11 and 12, respectively. In early November, the Allies (France, Britain, and Russia) declared war on the Ottoman Empire. In the following year, the secret Treaty of London promised Italy the South Tirol, Trieste, Gorizia, and other Austrian territories if it entered the war on the Allied side, which it did on May 23, 1915. The Central Powers—Germany, Austria-Hungary, Turkey, and Bulgaria—thus found themselves pitted against almost all the rest of Europe (except neutral Spain), Japan, various other nations around the world, and, later and decisively, the United States.

The Germans were relying on their secret Schlieffen Plan to enable them to conquer France in a lightning six-week strike. The plan, which envisioned a two-front war with France and Russia, was meant to knock France out of the war quickly while merely holding German territory defensively against Russia for the time it would take the relatively backward, lumbering nation to gather any military momentum. After France had sued for peace, Germany's troops and weaponry would be rapidly transported east by the country's extensive railway system to annihilate Russia.

The Schlieffen Plan called for a very powerful German right wing to steamroll its way through Belgium and then sweep past and behind Paris to attack the French armies from the rear and drive them south toward the Swiss border in a gigantic wheeling entrapment. This tactic outraged not only Belgium and France but also Great Britain, whose cardinal principle of foreign policy in Europe since the days of Elizabeth I was based on keeping a major power out of the Low Countries. When confronted with the 1839 treaty that established the perpetual neutrality of Belgium, the German chancellor called it *"un chiffon de papier"*—a mere scrap of paper. Had the Germans known that Britain, beset by serious labor problems and a restive Ireland, would nonetheless enter the war, they may not have been so cocky about their secret plan.

Russia, too, came alive sooner than expected, sending two armies into East Prussia, so that the German right flank aimed at Paris was weakened by a diversion of some troops to the Eastern Front. And after the Belgians put up unexpected resistance (countered with German atrocities of starvation and random mass executions of civilians), the French under General Joseph Joffre were able to halt the German advance about sixty miles from Paris. With the help of the British Expeditionary Force, they were able to push the invading Germans back at the titanic battle of the Marne (September 5–12), in which 2.4 million men fought, and at the first battle of Ypres in October–November. On the Eastern Front, after initial successes against the Austrians, the Russians suffered an astounding defeat in the battle of Tannenberg (August 17–September 2) at the hands of the Germans, who proceeded to gobble up Russian Poland and, eventually, other vast territories of the Russian Empire.

Now both sides realized it would be a drawn-out war, not the early-round knockout both had gambled on when hordes of soldiers all over Europe had marched off exulting in their patriotism and promising to be back home for Christmas. A war of attrition, with six hundred miles of trenches dug from the Belgian coast on the North Sea down to Switzerland, descended on the Western Front, as the artillery-blasted fields of Belgium and northeastern France, cratered with shell holes, bristling with barbed wire, and swept by machine-gun fire, became the scene of meat-grinding offensives and counteroffensives that swallowed up millions of men in an area less than a hundred miles wide. Italy, which joined the Allies in 1915, got bogged down in a war against the Austrians in its own frigid killing fields in the northeast corner of the peninsula, which saw twelve major battles on the Isonzo River alone. Soon, to avoid conscription, men were jumping off tables with huge loads on their shoulders to rupture themselves or blowing off half a foot with shotguns.

Military aircraft were first extensively used in World War I, and the aerial bombardment of civilians became an established practice. The Germans were the first to drop bombs on a city when a zeppelin dropped a few on Liège, Belgium, followed by a larger dirigible raid on civilians over Yarmouth, England, on January 19, 1915. Before the end of the war, Germany's ace fighter pilot, "the Red Baron" (Manfred von Richthofen), had shot scores of enemy planes out of the sky; the Germans had bombed London, Paris, Naples, and other cities; and British bombers had hit cities in Germany from bases in Britain. Other new technologies flourished: The first systematic use of modern chemical warfare was by means of chlorine gas, a choking agent that destroys lung tissue, released by the Germans along a four-mile front at the second battle of Ypres on April 22, 1915.

A major German offensive aimed at the fortress of Verdun and its fortifications on the Meuse River (late February–July 1916) was repulsed by the exceptional valor of French troops under command of General Philippe Pétain, whose phrase "*Ils ne passeront pas!*" ("They shall not pass!") passed into the language, though at the cost of four hundred thousand French and almost as many German casualties. In response, the Allies launched the battle of the Somme (July 1–November 18, 1916), in which twenty thousand charging British soldiers were mown down, mostly by machine-gun fire, in the first twenty-four hours. This futile offensive, devised by General Douglas "Butcher" Haig, commander of the British Expeditionary Force, resulted in 1.1 million casualties for both sides combined. Although armored tanks were first introduced by the British on September 15, the "Huns" or "*les Boches*" (as the Germans were called by their foes) just built new trenches to replace those destroyed by the hulking new war machines. The total number of casualties for the battles of Verdun and the Somme exceeded two million.

The British navy prevented shipments of any kind to Germany or its allies by sea and bottled up the German surface fleet after the battle of Jutland on May 31–June 1, 1916, but the enemy responded by developing submarine warfare into a deadly weapon against Allied naval ships and merchant vessels, including those carrying munitions for the

Allies from supposedly neutral America in 1916–17. American public opinion against the Germans—already inflamed by their torpedoing of the British ocean liner *Lusitania* off the Irish coast on May 7, 1915, in which 1,200 lives were lost, including 128 American citizens—was exacerbated by the Zimmermann telegram of January 1917. This missive, intercepted and decoded by the British and released by President Woodrow Wilson to American newspapers on March 1, was sent by the German state secretary for foreign affairs to the German ambassador in Mexico, instructing the latter to promise Mexico help in regaining its long-lost territories of Texas, New Mexico, and Arizona if the United States went to war with Germany and Mexico attacked its big northern neighbor.

After four American commercial ships were sunk as a result of Germany's recent resumption of unrestricted submarine warfare, Wilson, whose reelection campaign in 1916 had benefited from the slogan "He kept us out of war," went to Congress seeking a declaration of war against the German government "to make the world safe for democracy." He received it a few days later on April 6, 1917.

Meanwhile, Russia was reeling like a punch-drunk boxer. After the abdication of Czar Nicholas II and the fall of Prince Alexander Kerensky's provisional government, Vladimir Lenin and Leon Trotsky, the Bolshevik leaders of the Russian Revolution, pulled their battered nation out of the war in late December 1917. Germany was thus able to transfer a large number of troops to the Western Front and mount a series of spectacular offensives deep into French territory in 1918— coming within thirty-seven miles of Paris on May 30. But all was ultimately in vain, culminating in Germany's final failure to break through at the second battle of the Marne in mid-July and early August. Large forces of American troops under General John J. "Black Jack" Pershing had begun arriving in France in June 1917, and the fate of the Central Powers was sealed after the American-reinforced Meuse-Argonne offensive in the fall of 1918.

The Allies, heartened by a decisive Italian victory at Vittorio Veneto, had started marching on Vienna, the Americans had landed 2 million fresh troops in France, and the Germans realized they could not win the war. Before their homeland was invaded, the Germans (already abandoned by their allies) proclaimed a republic on the day the kaiser abdicated and fled to neutral Holland. The armistice Germany sought on the Western Front went into effect at eleven a.m., French time, on

November 11, 1918. Afterward, blame for the loss of the war was readily assigned to "a stab in the back" by civilian fifth columnists, socialists, communists, Jews, and other supposed betrayers of the fatherland, and the seeds of World War II were thus sown.

The peace treaty of Versailles (June 28, 1919) punished Germany and caused massive resentment but without crippling it enough to remove its war-waging ability for a long time to come. In addition, the Allied fleet blockaded Germany until it signed the treaty, causing the death by starvation of more than 750,000 of its citizens. Germany was obliged not only to pay staggering reparations (mostly negotiated down or repudiated) but also to assume the entire responsibility for the murderous conflict in the "war guilt clause." Alsace-Lorraine was to be surrendered to France, and Germany's African and Asian colonies were variously distributed. Poland, made independent of its former master, Russia, was enlarged at German expense and endowed with a "Polish corridor" to the Baltic that cut off Germany from its province of East Prussia.

Austria-Hungary, stripped of both its emperor and its empire, was dismembered into a tiny Austrian republic and an independent Hungary, Czechoslovakia, and Yugoslavia (comprising Serbia, Croatia, Slovenia, Bosnia, Herzegovina, and Montenegro). Romania was almost doubled in size by the access of formerly Hungarian Transylvania and other territories. Italy received the former Austrian possessions of Trent, Trieste, and the South Tirol. After the collapse of the Ottoman Empire, Turkey was left intact, but Britain and France divvied up most of the remaining Ottoman territories, with Britain receiving Iraq, Jordan, and Palestine as League of Nations mandates and France receiving Syria, which included Lebanon. Arabia became independent.

The number of war dead for the chief belligerents in World War I, out of 65 million mobilized soldiers, was as follows: Germany, 1.8 million; Russia, 1.7 million; France, 1.4 million; Austria-Hungary, 1.3 million; Great Britain and its empire, 947,000; Italy, 689,000; Turkey, 325,000; Bulgaria, 90,000; the United States, 50,000 (and another 62,000 who succumbed to the influenza pandemic of 1918). Two out of every three German soldiers were either killed, wounded, or captured. France's dead and wounded amounted to fully half its men of military age. Romania, which joined the Allies in August 1916, suffered 335,000 combat deaths—45 percent of all the men it mobilized. On average, 5,600 battle deaths occurred every day for the more than four years that the slaughter continued. A conservative estimate is 8.6 million battle dead in all and more than 21 million wounded. At least 6.6 million civilian deaths occurred, including an estimated 1 million Armenians who perished in genocidal persecutions carried out by the Ottoman Empire.

Despite these staggering figures, President Wilson's obsessive project, the League of Nations, which his own country did not join, proved ineffectual in preventing a global bloodbath in the following generation. The result was another 57 million dead in World War II (1939–45).

Two quotations may help put the savage destruction of the First World War in perspective. The first was an observation made by Sigmund Freud in a lecture he gave at the University of Vienna while the war was still raging: "Think of the colossal brutality, cruelty, and mendacity which is now allowed to spread itself over the civilized world. Do you really believe that a handful of unprincipled place-hunters and corrupters of men would have succeeded in letting loose all this latent evil, if the millions of their followers were not also guilty?" And in a 2002 book, *War Is a Force That Gives Us Meaning*, veteran war correspondent Chris Hedges wrote: "In World War I, on the Western Front, the putrefying and decomposed dead lay draped on the barbed wire and rotting in gaping shell holes. . . . They vanished as swiftly as the eternal causes for which they were sacrificed. They were replaced by a new generation and new causes. In the light of time, what looked so momentous then now looks like folly."

147 ∿ Who first transmitted a live television image of a human face?

Scottish inventor John Logie Baird on October 2, 1925

IN 1861, WESTERN UNION BUILT its first transcontinental telegraph line across the United States, but television was something no one had yet even imagined. When an 1880 article in the British publication *Nature* speculated that such a device might be possible, it dismissed the project as too costly and ultimately useless.

At the time, the communications challenge was to develop a reliable transatlantic system, involving the testing of many different conductive materials. One of them was selenium, which seemed to display varying conductivity, but Joseph May, an English telegraph technician, noticed that this variability was related to exposure to sunlight. Nothing would come of this discovery at the time, but it showed that light could be converted into an electrical signal.

Every object or material has its own pattern of absorbing or reflecting light, and our retinas are able to convert this light into meaningful images in our brains. In 1880, eight years after May's discovery, the French engineer Maurice Leblanc published a paper about a system that would capture images piece by piece, convert them to electrical signals, and then reassemble them for viewing. These signals could conceivably travel a distance along a wire, just as in a telegraph. Like the retina, a photoelectric cell converts light into electrical impulses. If these impulses could be transmitted quickly enough, our eyes would view them in such rapid succession that a virtual image would form. Since electricity travels very fast, even a complex image could theoretically be scanned and reassembled—and, indeed, today's televisions still employ this scanning method of image production. Leblanc himself was never able to build such a device.

Another pioneer in scanning technology was a German engineer, Paul Nipkow, who invented the scanning disk, a metallic disk with a series of holes arranged in a single spiral from the outer edge of the disk to its center. As the disk spins, light from an object passes through the holes at different locations and intervals in such a way that every revolution of the disk provides one full scan of the object. Although he patented his disk in 1884, Nipkow, too, failed to build a working model of a television, but his idea would later be used by those who did: Charles Francis Jenkins (1867–1934) of the United States and John Logie Baird (1888–1946) of Scotland.

It's still a matter of debate as to who transmitted the first televised image, Jenkins or Baird. In 1922, Jenkins transmitted a still image using radio waves (which had been pioneered by Guglielmo Marconi and others a generation earlier) and moving silhouette images in the following year, but Baird first successfully transmitted a live human face on October 2, 1925, working in his attic lab in Soho, London. Neither inventor was much acclaimed for his work at the time. Because Baird had little funding, his equipment was made of scrap metal he had thrown together himself, but he nonetheless succeeded in building a working television apparatus.

Baird's first televised image on that day in October was actually the head of a ventriloquist's dummy nicknamed "Stooky Bill," since the lighting the inventor used to illuminate the televised field produced too much heat for human comfort. It's perhaps fitting that Stooky Bill should have been the first head to appear on a device later stigmatized by many as "the boob tube." Baird, however, wanting to try out his device with a real person, managed to persuade an office boy, William Taynton, to pose in front of the hot lights—though at five images per second, his movements must have seemed very herky-jerky on the screen. On January 23, 1926, Baird gave the first public demonstration of a TV apparatus, and from sometime in that year there survives the first photo of a televised human face, the chubby visage of a man in a bow tie—Baird's business associate, Oliver Hutchinson, who bore a striking resemblance to the young Jackie Gleason.

Among Baird's achievements are his transmission of a moving image from London to Glasgow through telephone wires in 1927 and his transatlantic television broadcast in 1928. The following year, he opened the first television studio. Baird also created the first TV recording by transcribing his thirty-line signal onto a 78-rpm record, but he had no means of playing it back. For his part, Charles Francis Jenkins was issued the first television station license, W3XK, by the Federal Radio Commission in 1928, and he also bears the infamy of having broadcast the first TV commercial in 1930.

Jenkins and Baird had modeled their equipment after Nipkow's disk, which was a mechanical apparatus. But another current of TV development involved electronic systems, which made use of cathode-ray tubes (invented in 1897). Electronic systems would eventually win out because of their superior resolution and frame rate, and also because their development was heavily backed by RCA.

As early as 1908, A. A. Campbell-Swinton (1863–1930), a Scottish electrical engineer, made a strong argument for the use of cathode-ray tubes for transmission and reception of images. Cathode rays are electron beams that respond to electromagnetic fields and are contained within a vacuum tube. According to Swinton, the problem with mechanical scanning was the low scan rate and subsequent frame rate (only about five per second), producing choppy images with poor clarity. Since cathode rays could be projected onto phosphorescent surfaces almost at the speed of light, flickering would no longer be an issue. The method of transmission would also be less cumbersome than the mechanical version, which utilized a series of transparent rods to transmit TV images. Failing to see any economic benefit in television, however, Swinton never built a set.

Unbeknownst to Swinton, a Russian scientist and professor named Boris Rosing had already put together a combination model with a mechanical scanner and cathode-ray receiver in 1907, but there is no record that Rosing ever built a working model either. A student of his, Vladimir Zworykin (1889–1982), would soon leave for America, though, and continue to develop electronic TV models at the same time as Philo Farnsworth (1906–71), an American working independently in San Francisco.

In 1923, Zworykin was working for Westinghouse Electric Company when he filed for a patent for an all-electronic television system, but he was unable to build a working model. Six years later, he secured $100,000 in funding from RCA, Westinghouse's parent company, to develop a working system, but Farnsworth had already demonstrated one in 1927. Legal battles between Farnsworth and RCA ensued in 1932, each claiming to have created the first electronic television. Though RCA lost and ended up paying royalties, it nonetheless capitalized on the new invention at the 1939 World's Fair in New York, with Franklin D. Roosevelt being the first televised president. Zworykin also patented the first color TV, his iconoscope TV camera, and the kinescope for picture display (the receiver).

In May 1941, ten TV stations were issued licenses by the FCC. The first to begin broadcasting, on July 1, 1941, was WNBT (now WNBC). The first cable TV system was built in rural Pennsylvania in 1948.

Recently, TV displays have switched from cathode-ray tubes (CRT) to liquid crystal display (LCD). These TVs are thinner and lighter and capable of superior resolution and frame rates up to 120 Hz (120 frames per second). And you can probably buy one now for less than the $600 price tag of TV sets at the 1939 World's Fair.

—*Dante D'Epiro*

148 ⌒ What was the first antibiotic that was safe and effective in humans?

Penicillin, discovered by Alexander Fleming in 1928

IN THE SPRING OF 1928, Scottish biologist Alexander Fleming was at St. Mary's Hospital Medical School in London, clearing up his notoriously chaotic laboratory where test tubes and plates of bacteria typically lay around festering for weeks, when he noticed that one of the plates containing a staphylococcal culture had been contaminated by a mold that he later described as a "white fluffy mass."

This turned out to be a fungal growth, the result of a serendipitous drift by a spore of *Pencillium notatum* from a mycology laboratory on the floor below. Surrounding the mold on the gelatin plate was a halo-like area of destroyed bacterial colonies, and Fleming realized that the staphylococci had been destroyed, or lysed, by some substance secreted by the fungus. Instead of discarding the contaminated plate, he transferred the mold in broth to another agar plate and tested its effects on other bacteria. The result—inhibition of the growth of not only staphylococcus but also streptococcus, pneumococcus, and gonococcus—changed the history of medicine by rendering the scourges of many common and potentially lethal infections treatable at last.

Fleming's work grew out of earlier efforts to develop chemotherapy for infectious disease following the widespread adoption of the germ theory of infection, most notably propounded by Louis Pasteur in the latter half of the nineteenth century. Substances such as mercury, arsenic compounds, and carbolic acid were used to treat diseases ranging from syphilis to gangrene, but these highly toxic materials also killed healthy cells, often leading to debilitating adverse effects.

An important insight was provided by German physician and chemist Paul Ehrlich, who observed that a dye he was experimenting with was selectively absorbed by some bacteria but not others. He proposed that targeting a specific microorganism with a "magic bullet" could provide a less toxic form of chemotherapy, sparing healthy tissue.

During the first decade of the twentieth century Ehrlich worked with various chemical dyes without success but then began experimenting with hundreds of different compounds of arsenic on mice infected with trypanosomes, the protozoa that cause African sleeping sickness. Finally, in 1909, with the 606th compound tested, afflicted mice (and subsequently chickens and rabbits) were suddenly cured, apparently without toxicity. Ehrlich then sought to find a clinical use for compound 606, suggesting that because trypanosomes were thought to be related to the spirochete that causes syphilis, his compound might offer an alternative to the harsh mercury treatments then in use. In 1910 he reported initial successes with his magic bullet in patients with syphilis.

In his best-selling 1926 book *Microbe Hunters*, American microbiologist Paul de Kruif described Ehrlich's experiences in treating syphilis as "healings that could only be called Biblical." One case was that "of a wretch" who "so dreadfully had the pale spirochetes gnawed at his throat that he had had to be fed liquid food through a tube for months. One shot of the 606, at two in the afternoon, and at supper time that man had eaten a sausage sandwich!"

But with time it became apparent that compound 606, or salvarsan, as Ehrlich named it, didn't help all patients, caused severe side effects in many, and even killed some. Still, de Kruif concluded his rather fanciful rendering of the "trail-breaker" Ehrlich's story by claiming the scientist should be forgiven "his fault of not foreseeing that once in every so many thousands of bodies a magic bullet may shoot two ways."

Another important insight that helped pave the way for penicillin was the awareness that certain microorganisms were capable of hindering others. In 1877 Pasteur had observed that some airborne bacteria were capable of inhibiting the growth of anthrax, and other European researchers subsequently found that, in the laboratory, the rod-shaped bacterium *Pseudomonas fluorescens* could inhibit the growth of bacteria that cause typhoid fever and skin infections. But this in vitro "bacterial antagonism" was not considered to have therapeutic potential in vivo.

With the failure of salvarsan, much of the interest in identifying an antibacterial agent or compound faded, but Alexander Fleming continued the search. During World War I, he worked in a research laboratory for the Royal Army Medical Corps, testing substances he hoped would kill bloodborne microorganisms and help heal soldiers' wounds. After the war, he was appointed assistant director of the inoculation department at St. Mary's, and in the early 1920s he reported having identified a substance in human tears and saliva that exhibited antibacterial properties. He had sneezed on one of his cultures, only to observe ten days later that the bacteria on the plate had dissolved. Unfortunately, this substance, which he called lysozyme, turned out to be largely useless because it inhibited only insignificant microorganisms with little pathogenic potential. But Fleming persisted, waiting and watching for "interesting" developments in his messy assortment of culture plates. Penicillin was the result.

In 1929, he published "On the Antibacterial Action of Cultures of a Penicillium" in the *British Journal of Experimental Pathology*. In this paper he summarized his findings by stating, "A certain type of penicillium produces in culture a powerful antibacterial substance," which he named penicillin. He noted that penicillin was nontoxic in animals even in enormous doses and that it did not seem to interfere with leukocyte (white blood cell) function, which he recognized as an important component of the immune system. Finally, he suggested that penicillin "may be an efficient antiseptic for application to, or injection into, areas infected with penicillin-sensitive microbes"—effectively announcing the beginning of the antibiotic era.

Fleming was unaware that penicillin worked by destroying the bacterial cell walls, nor was he ever able to concentrate, purify, and stabilize it in the quantities required for testing in animals, much less in humans. Although few researchers were still looking for the next "magic bullet," a team of researchers at Bayer Laboratories in Germany continued to investigate dyes for their effects on bacteria, reasoning that dyes that stained the pathogens might also interfere with their growth. In December of 1931 they found that a newly patented dye, Prontosil, showed promise in mice infected with *Streptococcus pyogenes*, and clinical tests were undertaken at nearby hospitals during the next three years. The results were published in a prominent German medical journal early in 1935 but were initially met with skepticism.

Yet successful management of infections with this first sulfonamide drug continued to be reported, and Prontosil was catapulted into the headlines when treatment of one of President Franklin Roosevelt's sons, who had developed life-threatening complications from a streptococcal infection, resulted in a cure. Although successes turned out to be limited, Prontosil continued to be used and interest in antibiotics resurged, further encouraged by the discovery of the soil-derived antibiotic gramicidin by French-American microbiologist René Dubos in 1940. Fleming would later acknowledge these developments as having "completely changed the medical mind in regard to chemotherapy of bacterial infections."

In Oxford, scientists Howard Florey and Ernst Chain, who had once again focused attention on penicillin in 1938, ultimately developed methods of extracting and stabilizing the drug. They enlisted the help of the United States Department of Agriculture's Northern Regional Research Laboratories in Peoria, Illinois, to grow large amounts of the penicillin-producing organisms, and pharmaceutical firms were recruited to undertake manufacturing and marketing. By 1941, an injectable form of the drug was available for clinical use.

During World War II, penicillin was reserved primarily for the military. One notable exception occurred in Boston in November of 1942, when a fire tore through a nightclub, killing 450 people and leaving many more with severe burns likely to become lethally infected. Some victims were taken to Massachusetts General Hospital, where a small quantity of penicillin was made available and proved to be lifesaving for these badly burned patients. This first civilian use of the first safe and successful antibiotic was proclaimed a miracle cure, and demand for penicillin skyrocketed.

In 1945, Fleming, along with Florey and Chain, was awarded the Nobel Prize in Medicine. In his acceptance speech, he offered a caution: "I would like to sound one note of warning. Penicillin is to all intents and purposes nonpoisonous, so there is no need to worry about giving an overdose and poisoning the patient. There may be a danger, though, in underdosage. It is not difficult to make microbes resistant to penicillin in the laboratory by exposing them to concentrations not sufficient to kill them, and the same thing has occasionally happened in the body. The time may come when penicillin can be bought by anyone in the shops. Then there is the danger that the ignorant man may easily underdose himself and by exposing his microbes to nonlethal quantities of the drug make them resistant."

That, of course, is precisely what happened. Until the mid-1950s, penicillin was available over the counter and was misused and overused, and there were reports in a London hospital of resistance rates of 14 percent in 1946 and 59 percent by 1950. In subsequent decades, as scientists developed newer and more powerful antibiotics, the ever-resourceful bacteria have continued to mutate and develop new defenses against the drugs. Today, even with our various cephalosporins and fluoroquinolones, a specter haunts the medical community. According to William Schaffner, MD, Professor and Chair of the Department of Preventive Medicine at Vanderbilt University School of Medicine in

Nashville, Tennessee, "We infectious disease specialists have encountered in some of our patients life-threatening bacterial infections that are resistant to *all* currently available antibiotics. This is the sad consequence of prodigal overuse of antibiotics—both in human medicine and in animal husbandry. If we do not substitute prudence for profligacy, we will find ourselves in a post-antibiotic era in which doctors stand at the bedside wringing their hands because there is little else they can do."

Notwithstanding the possibility of such a nightmare scenario, the discovery of the first effective antibiotic by a determined and insightful biologist has saved untold millions of lives. When Professor G. Liljestrand of the Karolinska Institute in Stockholm was awarding the Nobel Prize in Medicine at the close of World War II, he said of Alexander Fleming's achievement, "In a time when annihilation and destruction through the inventions of man have been greater than ever before in history, the introduction of penicillin is a brilliant demonstration that human genius is just as well able to save life and combat disease."

—Nancy Walsh

149 ❧ Who was the first human to walk on the moon?

Neil Armstrong, on the U.S. Apollo 11 Mission, July 20, 1969

THE MYSTERIOUSLY WAXING AND WANING orb in the night sky—"the lesser light" of Genesis—has given rise to countless myths, superstitions, and magical beliefs and practices throughout the ages. Joshua was said to have commanded the sun and moon to stand still so that the children of Israel could have their fill of slaughtering the Amorites: "Sun, stand thou still upon Gibeon; and thou, Moon, in the valley of Ajalon." In Greek legend, Selene (or Phoebe), the Titaness revered as the moon goddess, fell in love with the handsome shepherd Endymion and visited him nightly in a cave on Mount Latmos, where he slept a perpetual sleep in which he never aged—a haunting story that John Keats adapted in a long poem beginning with the words, "A thing of beauty is a joy forever."

Selene, the ancient Greek word for *moon*, gave us the science of selenology and the name of the chemical element selenium. But the ancient Greeks later imagined Artemis (also called Cynthia and Delia), a virgin huntress endowed with a silver bow and ten hounds, as their goddess of the moon, though her temple at Ephesus (one of the seven wonders of the ancient world) was actually dedicated to an Asiatic fertility goddess pictured with several rows of pendulous breasts—more than forty in all.

The words *menstruation*, *measure*, and *month* are all connected with the word *moon*, and the cycle of approximately twenty-eight days associating the female menses with monthly lunations contributed a seemingly naturalistic basis to primitive lunar calendars. The Roman moon goddess was called Diana or Luna, and *lunacy* (from Latin *luna* for *moon*) was attributed to the baleful effects of the moon on human sanity. We still say of a period of time marked by an unusually high number of accidents, crimes, or bizarre behavior, "There must have been a full moon," and *moonshine* can refer either to illegally produced booze or a crazy notion. Men changed into werewolves during the full moon, and the proper time for decanting wine was traditionally determined with reference to the phases of the moon. Its phases have long made the moon an image of fickleness, as when Romeo begs Juliet: "O, swear not by the moon, the inconstant moon, / That monthly changes in her circled orb, / Lest that thy love prove likewise variable."

Lunar eclipses were alarming occurrences for primitive societies, who feared the moon had been swallowed up by a monstrous deity that had to be scared into disgorging it by the clanging of pots and pans or the performance of bloody sacrifices. An early scientist like Aristotle, however, used the curved appearance of the shadow the earth cast on the moon during lunar eclipses as a proof that our planet was spherical. In medieval Europe, the "man in the moon" was thought to be Cain carrying a bundle of thorns, exiled to that cold orb when he tried to excuse himself to God for murdering his brother Abel.

Traveling to the moon has captivated the minds of many writers, who have often treated the theme jestingly or satirically. In the late second century, the Greek skeptic Lucian, in his archly titled *A True Story*—a send-up of the tall tales of historians like Herodotus—tells of his journey to the moon after his ship is hurled forty miles into the air by a whirlwind and then wafted the rest of the way by winds that blow for seven days and nights. Lucian's moon turns out to be inhabited only by males, who mate with one another and get pregnant in the calves of their legs, have removable eyes, and eat by sucking in the vapors from roasted flying frogs.

In the *Paradiso*, Dante and the shade of his beloved Beatrice ascend instantaneously from the earth to the moon as the first stage on their journey to God in the empyrean (see Question 98). In Ludovico Ariosto's *Orlando Furioso* (1532), things lost on earth are said to end up on the moon, which is where the wits of the poem's hero, Orlando—driven mad by his desperate love for the fair Angelica—have wandered. St. John the Evangelist obligingly gives a character named Astolfo a lift to the moon in Elijah's chariot so that he can retrieve Orlando's wits, which he finds stoppered in a vial. Cyrano de Bergerac and Jules Verne are among the many other authors who have written fictitious accounts of journeys to the moon, which have also inspired some highly entertaining films (see Question 143). In his 1969 "Moon Bound," African-American poet Raymond Washington sarcastically speculated that his black brothers and sisters would soon be forcibly transported to the moon to pick "moon cotton" and perform other menial chores.

Although the first-century Roman encyclopedist Pliny the Elder believed that the moon was almost the same size as the earth, the volume of our planet is actually about fifty times greater than that of the moon. By an extraordinary coincidence, the diameter of the sun is about four hundred times that of the moon, and the moon is about four hundred times closer to us than the sun—so that the two celestial bodies appear to be roughly the same size to us. Although the moon's gravity is only about one-sixth that of the earth, it's enough (with a little help from the sun) to cause the twice-daily tides observed on earth.

Earth's sole natural satellite, roughly 240,000 miles away, appears to have been formed from the impact of a Mars-size object with the infant earth about 4.5 billion years ago, which sent molten debris and rock fragments into earth orbit. After about one hundred million years, this detritus solidified and reunited as the moon. Meteorite bombardment and the sun's corrosive effect on a lunar surface unshielded by an atmosphere, in addition to lava pouring up from volcanoes, have pock-marked the moon's face, variegating it with craters, lava basins, and the remnants of rocks ground into fine powder.

Because the moon rotates on its axis once in the same time that it takes to orbit the earth once, it keeps the same side facing us. Its days and nights each last fourteen of our days, and its surface temperature varies from 225 degrees Fahrenheit at high noon to −388 degrees in deep craters at the lunar poles, where the sunlight always falls horizontally.

But back to our story. As part of the International Geophysical Year (1957–58), the sneaky Soviet Union used an ICBM to launch *Sputnik 1*, the first artificial satellite to orbit the earth, on October 4, 1957, setting off a space race with the United States that also had obvious military implications. *Sputnik* (meaning "fellow traveler" in Russian) was a spherical satellite 23 inches in diameter (with four antennas) and weighing 184 pounds. Whipping along at 18,000 miles per hour 150 miles above the earth, it took only 96 minutes to complete an orbit—including over the United States! Its two radio transmitters beep-beep-beeped all the way, so that it could be tracked even by amateur radio operators all over the world. Then on November 3, the Soviets sent up a dog, Laika, in the 1,120-pound *Sputnik 2*.

Not to be outdone, the United States military countered on December 6 with a tiny, three-pound satellite that got as far as four feet above the launchpad before exploding in a televised fiasco that earned it the names "Flopnik," "Kaputnik," and "Stayputnik." Yet soon after, on January 31, 1958, *Explorer 1*—a seven-foot, bullet-shaped satellite—was successfully launched from Cape Canaveral, Florida. NASA, a civilian space agency, was created later that year.

Then, a month before the United States sent up Alan Shepard, its first astronaut, on a 15-minute suborbital flight, Soviet cosmonaut Yuri Gagarin became the first human to journey to outer space on April 12, 1961, when he orbited the earth once in 89 minutes at an altitude of 187 miles. Uncowed, President John F. Kennedy announced on May 25 to a joint session of Congress a national goal of putting a man on the moon before the end of the decade—an undertaking that seemed quixotic at the time.

Several years later, on January 31, 1966, the Soviets' *Luna 9* became the first spacecraft to make a soft landing on the moon, whereas the Apollo manned moon program began disastrously in January 1967, when a flash fire during a ground test killed three American astronauts. Yet on the day after Christmas of 1968, the crew of *Apollo 8*, the first humans to orbit the moon, sent us the gift of the first photos of our home planet taken from seventy miles above our only natural satellite. Meanwhile, the Soviet leadership had lost some of its appetite for putting a man on the moon in light of the exorbitant costs and a recent string of unmanned mission failures that indicated an unacceptably high risk for their cosmonauts.

As commander of its historic *Apollo 11* flight, NASA chose Neil A. Armstrong, who had been born in 1930 in Wapakoneta, Ohio, studied aeronautical engineering at Purdue, and flown missions in the Korean War. He later test-flew aircraft like the X-15 for NASA and served as command pilot for *Gemini 8*, which was marred by an in-flight malfunction requiring an emergency splashdown in the Pacific. On July 16, 1969, he blasted off for the moon, perched atop a huge Saturn V rocket with fellow spaceflight veterans Edwin E. "Buzz" Aldrin, Jr., and Michael Collins. The three components of their craft were the command module, *Columbia* (the flight command area where the crew had its quarters); the service modules (for propulsion and support systems); and the lunar module, nicknamed the *Eagle* (for getting the moon walkers to and from the surface and supporting them while they were on the moon itself). After separation from the command module, which Collins continued to pilot, the other two astronauts descended toward the moon on July 20, with Armstrong at the controls of the lunar module as they sped down toward the Sea of Tranquillity. With less then 17 seconds of fuel left, Armstrong announced to the world at 4:18 p.m. (EDT), "The *Eagle* has landed."

After resting for six and a half hours, Armstrong emerged from the lunar module and began cautiously descending the nine rungs of the craft in his bulky space suit. As he placed his left foot on the lunar surface at 10:56 p.m., he uttered his famous words: "That's one small step for a man, one giant leap for mankind"—some claiming he inadvertently left out the *a* in front of *man*, others saying he just elided it. Like all memorable expressions, it's been parodied endlessly, as when TV's Dr. House inveigled the luscious Dr. Cuddy into giving him a mercy hug with groping privileges and sighed, "One small feel for man, one giant ass for mankind."

Aldrin soon joined Armstrong on the surface, describing it as "magnificent desolation," while Collins continued orbiting overhead. After spending more than two hours loping around, collecting rock and dust samples, setting up scientific instruments, taking photos, leaving a plaque with an inscription that ended, "We Came in Peace for All Mankind," and setting up an American flag (later toppled by the ascent engine's exhaust), the two moon walkers retreated to their module and slept. More than a half billion people all over the globe had tuned in to watch them cavort on the moon.

After a total of 21 hours on the surface, Armstrong and Aldrin blasted off in the ascent stage of the lunar module and hooked up with the command module, which splashed down safely in the Pacific on July

24. The Apollo project to put a man on the moon was an incontrovertibly epic feat, but it had been achieved at a cost of $25 billion (more than $150 billion today). Ten other Americans walked on the moon in five further lunar landings between November 1969 and December 1972 (not counting the near disaster of *Apollo 13* in April 1970), leaving three lunar rovers, much rocket debris, and many scientific instruments on the moon (and also setting up sturdier American flags). But with repetition of the amazing achievement, the thrill was gone, and space exploration moved in other directions. NASA's plan to send humans to the moon again by 2020 seemed all but doomed in October 2009.

The first lunar landing provided an indelible memory for many who witnessed it. This writer, for instance, watched the event with two friends on the little TV of a bar in Manhattan, a year after graduating from high school. (Yes, the drinking age was still eighteen then.) The moon walk as it appeared in black-and-white on the small screen was like an archetypal dream image, and I couldn't shake an obsessive fear that the astronauts would be stranded on the moon with their communications intact, so that we—or at least their flight controllers—would have to hear them gradually perish. (Indeed, President Nixon had William Safire write a condolence speech for this very eventuality.) After the moon walk, our jubilant bartender stood the three of us a round, which may have been bourbon on the rocks—or was it a 7&7?—while we all puffed contentedly on our cigarettes.

But not everybody believed the lunar landings really took place. Consider the remarks of two of my grandparents, for example. One of my grandfathers, who had worked for many years as a laborer in New York during the Great Depression and World War II and had experienced America's devious ways firsthand, told me when I visited him in Italy in 1973 that the moon landings had all been elaborately staged propaganda stunts that had been shot in some Hollywood studio. During the same trip, my grandmother on the other side of the family, a fervent evangelist, explained to me that the supposed lunar landings were ridiculously impossible, since God would never allow mere mortals to set foot on his other worlds.

The year of the first trip to the moon was an eventful one: 1969 was the year in which Richard M. Nixon was first inaugurated and the United States, with 550,000 troops in Vietnam, began the policy of "Vietnamization"—a gradual handoff of the war to the South Vietnamese. It was the year of Woodstock, the Manson murders, the "Miracle

Mets," Hurricane Camille, the first public flight of the Boeing 747, a General Motors recall of five million cars, the first appearances of *Sesame Street*, *The Godfather* (the book), *Portnoy's Complaint*, *Slaughterhouse-Five*, *Oh! Calcutta!*, *Midnight Cowboy*, *Easy Rider*, *M*A*S*H*, and *Fellini Satyricon*, Samuel Beckett's Nobel Prize, the invention of the microprocessor, and the occasion of the ARPAnet's going online (see Question 150). The century in which the lunar landing occurred was, of course, even more astoundingly eventful, and yet as the year 2000 approached and a group of historians and futurists tried to imagine what our history would look like from the perspective of another thousand years in the future, they found it quite likely that the only event and person that would be remembered from the entire second millennium would be Neil Armstrong and his moon landing.

150 ❧ What was the first internet?

Let me Google that for you . . .

FOR HALF A CENTURY THE INTERNET has been figuring itself out on the fly through a cascading series of hacks. Determining its first moment of existence is not simple, making it a fitting last "first." To see why, we'll need a working definition of *internet*.

"An internet is a connection between two or more computer networks," wrote Robert W. Taylor a generation after he began to instigate that connection at the U.S. Department of Defense in 1965.

The key word here is "between": If *an* internet is the successful overcoming of obstacles and incompatibilities between self-contained computer networks, then *the* Internet is what results from the totality of such success across all computers and all networks whose proprietary designs, languages, and networks ought to make it impossible for them to talk to one another.

Composed of bits, digital data arrive intact thanks to a multiplicity of contrivances that enable them to route around all manner of impediments. One after another, roadblocks to communication have fallen before strong motives, diabolic ingenuity, and sheer luck gracing the work of different groups at different times. Three breakthroughs stand out, each contributing a key part of what most people today understand as basic to the fabric of the Net: hardware routing, data hyperlinking, and simple browsing.

First came the hardware—the "series of tubes," as the lamentable former senator Ted Stevens would have it. Mainframes of monstrous size were gradually getting smaller when, in 1957, Russia shocked the Defense Department into Cold War shivers with the launch of *Sputnik 1* (see Question 149). The need for a persistent, decentralized system of communication assumed top defense priority. By its own admission, the Advanced Research Projects Agency, or ARPA ("Defense" was added later, making it DARPA), was set up in 1958 to "prevent techno-logical surprise to the U.S., but also to create technological surprise for our enemies."

ARPA initially focused on time-sharing on a single computer as a means of efficiently multiplying speed and access to costly main-frames. A genius with a background in psychoacoustics had been work-ing on this very problem five years before coming to head the new agency in 1962.

J. C. R. Licklider had long been fascinated by the way a single computer can beguile each of many simultaneous users into thinking it's serving just that one. In a landmark 1960 paper entitled *Man-Computer Symbiosis*, he further explored this peculiar intimacy:

> It seems likely that the contributions of human operator and
> equipment will blend together so completely in many opera-
> tions that it will be difficult to separate them neatly in analysis.

"Lick" went on to describe a network of "thinking centers" that would stretch toward that symbiosis by blending the functions of libraries with advances in information storage and retrieval and in human speech recognition. After leaving the agency for MIT in 1965, he worked on an ancestor of the UNIX operating system and wrote an even more dazzling 1968 paper describing "a labile network of networks," "super-communities," and a personal assistant computer named OLIVER. He also memorably observed that computer technology was "moving in a way that nothing else . . . has ever moved."

Robert W. Taylor followed Licklider and initiated the ARPAnet project, which aimed to implement Lick's program of accelerating sci-entific research by connecting computers and data over networks. Tay-lor has firmly stated that, unlike ARPA, ARPAnet was not driven by considerations of war—its protocols were public, and all its activities were unclassified.

At that time, each mainframe cost a small fortune, and government bureaucrats kept pressing the small agency to save money by sharing resources. Taylor brought in Leonard Kleinrock to design ARPAnet and Lawrence Roberts to manage it. Kleinrock had developed the basic principles of network communication in his 1962 PhD dissertation at MIT. Through packet switching, a single message gets broken into multiple small bunches of bits, each of which is assigned a header. An auxiliary minicomputer called an Interface Message Processor (IMP, now called a router) speeds each packet by the fastest route to its destination. On arrival, the headers are read, the bits are reassembled, and the intact message is presented to the addressee. It all seemed clear in theory.

In 1968, the Cambridge, Massachusetts, engineering firm of Bolt Beranek & Newman (BBN), whose staff included Licklider and famed artificial intelligence guru Marvin Minsky, won the contract to produce the IMPs, and Taylor gave BBN a nine-month deadline to do so. Insanely, two untested machines arrived at ARPA's test sites—Kleinrock's UCLA and Douglas Engelbart's Stanford Research Institute—on time.

At about ten-thirty p.m. on October 29, 1969, ARPAnet debuted its first host-to-host communication via packet switching when UCLA's computer began to transmit the command "LOG IN." Computer operators at both ends were hooked up by telephone to monitor the progress. Kleinrock later recalled the scene, while representatives of government, industry, and academia watched:

> And so we typed in L. And we said, "Did you get the L?" And he said, "I got the L." Typed the O. "You get the O?" "I got the O." "You get the G?" Crash!

A few minutes after Stanford's computer crashed, they did log in, and the world's first computer network was online. Kleinrock celebrated with a bit of verse:

> *We cautiously connected, and the bits began to flow.*
> *The pieces really functioned, just why I still don't know.*

If the Defense Department aimed to save time and money through shared resources, people using its computers had other ideas. They were sharing not only machines and data but also thoughts and enthusi-asms. Other networks were springing up as well. In 1972, BBN's Ray Tomlinson made it easier by creating SNDMSG, selecting the @ sign to identify each user's location or institution. It was "just a hack," Tom-linson said of his effort, which we now call e-mail. His view was typi-cal of the time—early Net architects described their process as "rough consensus and running code."

ARPAnet quickly added new nodes and new host computers, but all spoke the same language and sat on the same network. Many, including Taylor, mark the true beginning of the Internet from the moment when a group of nerds figured out how to move data beyond ARPAnet, stealing across the void between distinct networks, each with its own proprietary architecture—kind of like safecracking.

For this, more than IMPs were necessary. Bob Kahn at ARPA and Vinton Cerf at Stanford began work on a set of layered protocols whose purpose was to create a "gateway" that smoothed out differences (such as packet size) between networks. They proposed their solution in a 1974 paper noteworthy for containing in its title the first recorded use of *internet—Specification of Internet Transmission Control Program—* where the word is an abbreviated form of the adjective *internetwork*, as in "an internetwork packet."

Much like Tomlinson's e-mail, Kahn and Cerf's effort, known as TCP/IP (Transmission Control Protocol/Internet Protocol), was codged on the fly to see if it could work. An analogy might help. If packet switching is like taking data, writing them on a series of postcards, assigning each a sequential number, and mailing them in any order, TCP/IP puts the postcards in "envelopes" that navigate the gateways between networks.

TCP/IP was tested as early as 1975 and received its first public demonstration on November 22, 1977. Data flowing via the new proto-col successfully made an eighty-eight-thousand-mile voyage from a mobile van near Stanford, California, to Norway, then to London, and on to UCLA, successfully traversing three kinds of networks—ARPAnet, the Bay Area packet radio network, and the Atlantic packet satellite network—in about two seconds.

This could be considered the first successful internet moment by Taylor's definition. During the same period, however, Xerox PARC was linking two networks (Ethernet and ARPAnet) using a protocol said to have helped define TCP/IP. Taylor himself has credited PARC with the first instance of an internet, leaving open the question of precisely when network integrity was first properly violated.

The new protocol required a lot of tinkering before it was officially activated on January 1, 1983. Later in the year, Jon Postel created the Internet Assigned Numbers Authority (IANA), the registry for all domains, protocols, ports, and assigned addresses within the newly created Domain Name System (DNS). This chore was essential—no DNS, no registry; no registry, no Internet. Postel maintained the IANA continuously until his death in 1998.

The foundations for internetworking were now in place. Geeks, academics, and text-oriented social moths chattered away across networks on mailing lists, Usenet groups, and bulletin boards. Unless you were at a major university, it was all pretty slow, expensive, and esoteric. Students and hackers began to invent primitive search engines with names like Wide Area Information Server (WAIS), Archie, Veronica, and Gopher to locate specific files, which were downloadable via File Transfer Protocol (FTP). But there was no simple way to know what was out there and access it.

Things got dramatically simpler in 1989 when Tim Berners-Lee, a British contractor at the European Organization for Nuclear Research, or CERN, proposed a method of addressing and accessing documents through hyperlinks. He and Robert Cailliau were allowed to work on a "play" project, cobbling together a few small technologies—most important, the Universal Resource Locator, or URL, which specifies where an identified resource is available and the mechanism for retrieving it. They also developed the code to represent hyperlinks in texts, called HTML (for Hypertext Markup Language).

The virtue of being able to point to any document, wherever it might be, and open it with a single mouse click was not lost on scientists at CERN, which happened to operate the largest Internet site in Europe. Its staff vigorously began using the "WorldWideWeb" (W3) in 1990, and CERN published the code on the Web the next year, free for all to use.

What Berners-Lee and Cailliau had wrought in the simple hyperlink implemented a dream that had captivated many predecessors. Consider, for example, Paul Otlet's Universal Bibliographic Repertory of 1895—a proto-Googleian search engine on index cards. Or H. G. Wells's *World Brain*, published in 1938, which envisioned a storage depot for the organization of all knowledge. Or the landmark 1945 article entitled "As We May Think," in which Vannevar Bush conceptualized the "memex," a device that would rapidly access information via linked microfilm. Or Ted Nelson's first use of "hypertext" in a 1963 project for computer simplicity he called "Xanadu." Or the gathering of geeks in San Francisco who, on December 9, 1968, saw the first live demo of hypertext (and of the computer mouse) at Doug Engelbart's "Mother of All Demos."

In the 1970s and 1980s, new, faster networks like the National Science Foundation's NSFnet had spun off from ARPAnet's aging infrastructure. Finally on February 28, 1990, the government pulled the plug, and ARPAnet entered history as the Model T of computer networks.

In 1991, when the W3 hit the Internet, "cyberspace"—a term first used in William Gibson's 1981 sci-fi tale, "Burning Chrome"—was still a relatively small place, consisting of some 800 computer networks with about 160,000 computers attached to them. Search was in its infancy, and a user-friendly browser with an attractive graphical user interface had yet to be invented.

In April 1992, a group of Finnish students demonstrated ERWISE, a primitive browser running on UNIX, and the race for the interface was on. Other efforts followed: ViolaWWW, Lynx, and, in 1993, Mosaic. Mosaic incorporated Gopher, Archie, and FTP within a graphical interface that used HTML to display hypertext, images, and more. After the hardware and the hyperlink, the browser—the intuitive interface necessary for worldwide whuffie—clicked into place.

Marc Andreessen led the team that designed Mosaic at the University of Illinois at Urbana-Champaign; he then led them to Silicon Valley, where Mosaic became Netscape. "What we were trying to do was just put a human face on the Internet," he said. It was the face that launched a billion chips: Within eighteen months of its 1995 release, Netscape claimed 65 million users. When Netscape Communications Corporation made $75 million its first year, $375 million the next, and $500 million the third, Andreessen became the poster boy for hacker multimillionaires.

The browser wars had not yet subsided in 1998 when a pair of Stanford geeks fired a transformational salvo into the fracas among search engines with such names as Inktomi, Lycos, HotBot, Excite, and AltaVista. Sergey Brin and Lawrence Page worked up an algorithm that judged the importance of any Web page based in part on how often it was used—cited—by other Web pages. No longer did we need to remember complex Web site addresses. What Netscape had done for display, Google did for search, rendering it intuitive, transparent, and simple. E-commerce and -communities advanced exponentially.

As nodes, applications, and users have multiplied, as processors have gotten faster and cheaper, and as broadband and wireless have become ever more widely deployed, the Net can seem a kind of incontinent golem inexorably reshaping lives, industries, and society itself, usually taking its victims unawares.

The rapid disintegration of traditional news and magazine publishing, the profusion of spam and voyeuristic modes of advertising, the proliferation of BitTorrenting and other peer-to-peer file sharing (remember Napster?) with concomitant impacts on music publishing, television, and film are all symptoms of the Internet's seemingly irresistible disregard for the niceties of proprietary systems in the analog world.

Vast fortunes have been made as well as lost on the Web—think of Google, Amazon, eBay. Clever code has sparked vast clusters of creative activity—blogs, videos, and mashups—as well as new social media, dominated for the moment by Twitter and Facebook, and new modes of political organizing, as demonstrated by Barack Obama's 2008 presidential campaign. Mobile operating systems like Google's Android are integrating nomadic appliances—smartphones and such—into the Web. All this, in turn, is feeding the development of "cloud computing," which promises to simplify operations, applications, and storage by assigning many tasks now performed by individual appliances to the network itself.

So, what rough hack now slouches? Even fools fear to predict what the Internet will do ten years out, or five, but here are three provocative candidates for future Internet firsts.

In 2009, Tim Berners-Lee marked the twentieth anniversary of his W3 hack by describing his vision of a new level of connectivity that he calls "Linked Data." The idea is to give every piece of information a unique address. Then when you ask about "the house where Cousin Buddy lives and its fair market value over the past twenty years correlated with houses in three comparable suburbs in Peoria, Duluth, and Camden, New Jersey," instead of a mashup of maps, documents, and data hauled into view by a search engine, you'll get the answer.

In May 2009, British physicist and mathematician Stephen Wolfram launched Wolfram|Alpha, which intends to be neither a Google-esque search engine nor a crowd-sourced database like Wikipedia.

Instead, Wolfram calls it a "knowledge engine" that uses its own library of algorithms and curated data to compute original, reliable responses to queries.

And futurist-provocateur Ray Kurzweil has been expanding on Licklider's observation that computer intelligence is moving like "nothing else has ever moved." Extrapolating from current accelerations takes him to "the Singularity"—a post-human world under the leadership of "spiritual machines." Kurzweil's conviction that artificial intelligence will prevail literalizes Lick's early vision of human-computer symbiosis and turns it viral:

> The emergence of technology was a milestone in the evolution of intelligence on earth because it represented a new means of evolution recording its designs. The next milestone will be technology creating its own next generation without human intervention.

By 2099, Kurzweil assures us, the machines that enable intelligence to flow through the Net will morph, animate, and intelligently assume single or multiple robotic forms. At that point, the network will no longer be the computer, as Sun Microsystems felicitously used to say. Rather, our cyberdescendants may less felicitously declare, "Hacks R Us LMAO! :-) kthxbye."

—*Tom Matrullo*

Suggested Reading

FIRST CENTURY

Berry, Joanne. *The Complete Pompeii*. London: Thames and Hudson, 2007.

Cassius Dio. *The Roman History: The Reign of Augustus*. Translated by Ian Scott-Kilvert. New York: Penguin Books, 1987.

Fox, Robin Lane. *The Classical World: An Epic History from Homer to Hadrian*. New York: Basic Books, 2006.

New Testament (Gospels, Acts of the Apostles, Epistles, Revelation). Many editions.

Ovid. *The Metamorphoses*. Verse translation by Horace Gregory. New York: Viking, 1958.

———. *Metamorphoses*. Verse translation by Rolfe Humphries. Bloomington: Indiana University Press, 1955.

Pliny the Younger. *The Letters of the Younger Pliny*. Translated by Betty Radice. New York: Penguin Books, 1963.

Suetonius Tranquillus, Gaius. *The Twelve Caesars*. Translated by Robert Graves. New York: Penguin Books, 1957.

Syme, Ronald. *The Roman Revolution*. New York: Oxford University Press, 1987; 1939.

Tacitus. *The Annals of Imperial Rome*. Translated by Michael Grant. New York: Penguin Books, 1956.

Wilson, A. N. *Paul: The Mind of the Apostle*. New York: W. W. Norton and Company, 1997.

SECOND CENTURY

Aurelius, Marcus. *Meditations*. Translated by A. S. L. Farquharson. New York: Everyman's Library, Alfred A. Knopf, 1992.

Gibbon, Edward. *The Portable Gibbon: The Decline and Fall of the Roman Empire*. Edited by Dero A. Saunders. New York: Viking Press, 1952.

Lipman, Eugene J., ed. *The Mishnah: Oral Teachings of Judaism.* New York: W. W. Norton and Company, 1970.

Lives of the Later Caesars: The First Part of the Augustan History, *with Newly Compiled* Lives *of Nerva and Trajan.* Translated by Anthony Birley. New York: Penguin Books, 1976.

Oates, Whitney J., ed. *The Stoic and Epicurean Philosophers: The Complete Extant Writings of Epicurus, Epictetus, Lucretius, Marcus Aurelius.* New York: Modern Library, 1957.

Plutarch. *The Fall of the Roman Republic: Six Lives.* Revised edition. Translated by Rex Warner. New York: Penguin Books, 2006.

————. *Plutarch's Lives.* 2 vols. Translated by John Dryden. Revised by Arthur Hugh Clough. New York: Modern Library, 2001.

————. *The Rise and Fall of Athens: Nine Greek Lives.* New York: Penguin Books, 1960.

Yourcenar, Marguerite. *Memoirs of Hadrian.* Translated by Grace Frick. New York: Farrar, Straus and Giroux, 2005; 1951.

See also Pliny the Younger and Gaius Suetonius Tranquillus (first century).

THIRD CENTURY

Athanasius. *The Life of Antony and the Letter to Marcellinus.* Translated by Robert C. Gregg. Mahwah, N.J.: Paulist Press, 1980.

Barrow, R. H. *The Romans.* Baltimore: Pelican Books, 1949.

Dudley, Donald R. *The Civilization of Rome.* New York: Mentor Books, 1960.

Flaubert, Gustave. *The Temptation of Saint Antony.* Translated by Kitty Mrosovsky. New York: Penguin Books, 1980.

Kulikowski, Michael. *Rome's Gothic Wars: From the Third Century to Alaric.* New York: Cambridge University Press, 2007.

Plotinus. *The Enneads: Abridged Edition.* Translated by Stephen MacKenna. New York: Penguin Books, 1991.

Rostovtzeff, M. *Rome.* Translated by J. D. Duff. New York: Oxford University Press, 1960; 1928.

See also Edward Gibbon and *Lives of the Later Caesars* (second century).

FOURTH CENTURY

Ammianus Marcellinus. *The Later Roman Empire (A.D. 354–378).* Selected and translated by Walter Hamilton. New York: Penguin Books, 1986.

Apicius. *Cookery and Dining in Imperial Rome.* Translated by Joseph Dommers Vehling. New York: Dover, 1977; 1936.

Augustine, St. *The Confessions of St. Augustine*. Translated by John K. Ryan. Garden City, N.Y.: Image Books, 1960.

Barbero, Alessandro. *The Day of the Barbarians: The Battle That Led to the Fall of the Roman Empire*. Translated by John Cullen. New York: Walker and Company, 2007.

Durant, Will. *Our Oriental Heritage*. (*The Story of Civilization*, vol. 1). New York: Simon and Schuster, 1935.

————. *The Age of Faith*. (*The Story of Civilization*, vol. 4). New York: Simon and Schuster, 1950.

MacMullen, Ramsay. *Christianizing the Roman Empire, AD 100–400*. New Haven, Conn.: Yale University Press, 1984.

McNeill, William H. *The Rise of the West: A History of the Human Community*. Chicago: University of Chicago Press, 1992.

See also Edward Gibbon (second century) and Michael Kulikowski (third century).

FIFTH CENTURY

Augustine, St. *The City of God*. Edited by Vernon J. Bourke. Translated by Gerald G. Walsh, S.J., et al. Garden City, N.Y.: Image Books, 1958.

Bury, John B. *The Life of St. Patrick and His Place in History*. Mineola, N.Y.: Dover Publications, 1998; 1905.

Cahill, Thomas. *How the Irish Saved Civilization: The Untold Story of Ireland's Heroic Role from the Fall of Rome to the Rise of Medieval Europe*. New York: Nan A. Talese, 1995.

Gregory of Tours. *The History of the Franks*. Translated by Lewis Thorpe. New York: Penguin Books, 1974.

McCrum, Robert, William Cran, and Robert MacNeil. *The Story of English*. New York: Penguin Books, 1986.

Norwich, John Julius. *A History of Venice*. New York: Vintage Books, 1982.

Trevelyan, George Macaulay. *A Shortened History of England*. New York: Penguin Books, 1988.

See also Edward Gibbon (second century) and Michael Kulikowski (third century).

SIXTH CENTURY

Auerbach, Erich. *Mimesis: The Representation of Reality in Western Literature*. Translated by Willard R. Trask. Princeton, N.J.: Princeton University Press, 1953; 1946.

Bede. *A History of the English Church and People*. Translated by Leo Sherley-Price. Revised by R. E. Latham. New York: Penguin Books, 1968.

Benedict, St. *The Rule of St. Benedict*. Translated by Anthony C. Meisel and M. L. del Mastro. Garden City, N.Y.: Image Books, 1975.

Duncan, David Ewing. *Calendar: Humanity's Epic Struggle to Determine a True and Accurate Year*. New York: Avon Books, 1998.

Gregory of Tours. *The History of the Franks*. Translated by Lewis Thorpe. New York: Penguin Books, 1974.

Justinian. *The Digest of Roman Law: Theft, Rapine, Damage, and Insult*. Translated by C. F. Kolbert. New York: Penguin Books, 1979.

Procopius. *Secret History*. Translated by Richard Atwater. Ann Arbor, Mich.: University of Michigan Press, 1961; 1927.

SEVENTH CENTURY

Armstrong, Karen. *Muhammad: A Western Attempt to Understand Islam*. San Francisco: HarperOne, 1991.

Crosby, Alfred W. *Throwing Fire: Projectile Technology Through History*. Cambridge, UK: Cambridge University Press, 2002.

The Earliest English Poems. 3rd ed. Translated by Michael Alexander. London: Penguin Books, 1991.

Kennedy, Hugh. *The Great Arab Conquests: How the Spread of Islam Changed the World We Live In*. Cambridge, Mass.: Da Capo Press, 2007.

Lewis, David Levering. *God's Crucible: Islam and the Making of Europe*. New York: W. W. Norton and Company, 2008.

Mansfield, Peter. *The Arabs*. Revised ed. New York: Penguin Books, 1978.

Miyazaki, Ichisada. *China's Examination Hell: The Civil Service Examinations of Imperial China*. Translated by Conrad Schirokauer. New Haven, Conn.: Yale University Press, 1981.

Partington, J. R. *A History of Greek Fire and Gunpowder*. Baltimore: Johns Hopkins University Press, 1998; 1960.

The Qur'an. Translated by Tarif Khalidi. New York: Viking, 2008.

Ramadan, Tariq. *In the Footsteps of the Prophet: Lessons from the Life of Muhammad*. New York: Oxford University Press, 2007.

See also William H. McNeill (fourth century).

EIGHTH CENTURY

Beowulf. Verse translation by Seamus Heaney. New York: W. W. Norton and Company, 2000.

Einhard and Notker the Stammerer. *Two Lives of Charlemagne*. Translated by Lewis Thorpe. New York: Penguin Books, 1969.

Jones, Gwyn. *A History of the Vikings*. 2nd ed. New York: Oxford University Press, 1984.

Li Po. *The Selected Poems of Li Po*. Translated by David Hinton. New York: New Directions, 1996.

———. *The Works of Li Po, the Chinese Poet*. Translated by Shigeyoshi Obata. New York: Paragon Book Reprint Corporation, 1965; 1935.

Li Po and Tu Fu: Poems Selected and Translated with an Introduction and Notes. Translated by Arthur Cooper. New York: Penguin Books, 1973.

Liu, Wu-chi, and Irving Yucheng Lo, eds. *Sunflower Splendor: Three Thousand Years of Chinese Poetry*. Bloomington: Indiana University Press, 1990; 1975.

Mitchell, Joseph B. *Twenty Decisive Battles of the World*. Old Saybrook, Conn.: Konecky and Konecky, 2004.

See also Bede (sixth century) and David Levering Lewis (seventh century).

NINTH CENTURY

Adamson, Peter. *Al-Kindi*. New York: Oxford University Press, 2006.

Hyman, Arthur, and James J. Walsh. *Philosophy in the Middle Ages: The Christian, Islamic, and Jewish Traditions*. 2nd ed. Indianapolis: Hackett Publishing Company, 1983.

Keynes, Simon, and Michael Lapidge. *Alfred the Great: Asser's* Life of King Alfred *and Other Contemporary Sources*. New York: Penguin Books, 1983.

Longworth, Philip. *Russia: The Once and Future Empire from Pre-History to Putin*. New York: St. Martin's Press, 2006.

Pollard, Justin. *Alfred the Great: The Man Who Made England*. London: John Murray, 2007.

See also George Macaulay Trevelyan (fifth century) and Gwyn Jones (eighth century).

TENTH CENTURY

Boorstin, Daniel J. *The Discoverers*. New York: Vintage Books, 1983.

Brown, Nancy Marie. *The Far Traveler: Voyages of a Viking Woman*. Orlando, Fl.: Harcourt Books, 2007.

Farquhar, Michael. *Royal Scandals: The Shocking True Stories of History's Wickedest, Weirdest, Most Wanton Kings, Queens, Tsars, Popes, and Emperors*. New York: Penguin Books, 2001.

Holmes, George, ed. *The Oxford History of Italy.* Oxford: Oxford University Press, 1997.

Lindberg, David C. *The Beginnings of Western Science: The European Scientific Tradition in Philosophical, Religious, and Institutional Context, Prehistory to A.D. 1450.* 2nd ed. Chicago: University of Chicago Press, 2007.

Siraisi, Nancy G. *Medieval and Early Renaissance Medicine: An Introduction to Knowledge and Practice.* Chicago: University of Chicago Press, 1990.

See also Will Durant, *The Age of Faith* (fourth century), and Gwyn Jones (eighth century).

ELEVENTH CENTURY

Asbridge, Thomas. *The First Crusade: A New History: The Roots of Conflict Between Christianity and Islam.* New York: Oxford University Press, 2005.

Haskins, Charles Homer. *The Rise of Universities.* Ithaca, N.Y.: Cornell University Press, 1957; 1923.

Howarth, David. *1066: The Year of the Conquest.* New York: Penguin Books, 1977.

Lewis, Bernard. *The Assassins.* New York: Basic Books, 2003; 1967.

Pound, Ezra. *The Spirit of Romance.* New York: New Directions, 1968; 1910.

Runciman, Steven. *A History of the Crusades: Volume 1: The First Crusade and the Foundation of the Kingdom of Jerusalem.* Cambridge: Cambridge University Press, 1987; 1951.

The Song of Roland. Translated by W. S. Merwin. New York: Modern Library, 2001.

The Song of Roland. Translated by Dorothy L. Sayers. New York: Penguin Books, 1957.

See also Will Durant, *Our Oriental Heritage* (fourth century), Joseph B. Mitchell (eighth century), and Daniel J. Boorstin (tenth century).

TWELFTH CENTURY

Abelard, Peter. *The Story of My Misfortunes.* Translated by Henry Adams Bellows. Mineola, N.Y.: Dover Publications, 2005; 1922.

Abelard, Peter, and Heloise. *Abelard & Heloise: The Letters and Other Writings.* Edited by William Levitan. Indianapolis: Hackett Publishing Company, 2007.

Andreas Capellanus. *The Art of Courtly Love.* Translated by John Jay Parry. New York: Columbia University Press, 1960.

Bonner, Anthony. *Songs of the Troubadours*. New York: Schocken Books, 1972.

Boorstin, Daniel J. *The Creators*. New York: Random House, 1992.

Gilson, Étienne. *Heloise and Abelard*. Translated by L. K. Shook. Ann Arbor, Mich.: University of Michigan Press, 1960; 1948.

Goldin, Frederick. *Lyrics of the Troubadours and Trouvères: An Anthology and a History*. New York: Anchor Books, 1973.

Haskins, Charles Homer. *The Renaissance of the Twelfth Century*. Cambridge, Mass.: Harvard University Press, 2005; 1927.

Kelly, Amy. *Eleanor of Aquitaine and the Four Kings*. Cambridge, Mass.: Harvard University Press, 1963.

Morton, W. Scott, and J. Kenneth Olenik. *Japan: Its History and Culture*. 4th ed. New York: McGraw-Hill, 2005.

The Poem of the Cid. Translated by Rita Hamilton and Janet Perry. New York: Penguin Books, 1975.

Pound, Ezra. *Translations*. Enlarged edition. New York: New Directions, 1963.

Suger, Abbot. *Abbot Suger on the Abbey Church of St.-Denis and Its Art Treasures*. 2nd ed. Translated by Erwin Panofsky. Princeton, N.J.: Princeton University Press, 1979.

Warren, W. L. *Henry II*. Berkeley, Calif.: University of California Press, 1977.

See also Ezra Pound (eleventh century).

THIRTEENTH CENTURY

Danziger, Danny, and John Gillingham. *1215: The Year of Magna Carta*. New York: Touchstone, 2003.

Huizinga, Johan. *The Autumn of the Middle Ages*. Translated by Rodney J. Payton and Ulrich Mammnitzsch. Chicago: University of Chicago Press, 1997; 1919.

Joinville, Jean de, and Geoffroy de Villehardouin. *Chronicles of the Crusades*. Translated by M. R. B. Shaw. New York: Penguin Books, 1963.

Lane, Frederic C. *Venice, A Maritime Republic*. Baltimore: Johns Hopkins University Press, 1973.

Maddicott, J. R. *Simon de Montfort*. Cambridge: Cambridge University Press, 1996.

Morgan, David. *The Mongols*. 2nd ed. Malden, Mass.: Blackwell Publishing, 2007.

Oldenbourg, Zoé. *Massacre at Montségur: A History of the Albigensian Crusade*. Translated by Peter Green. London: Orion Books, 1961.

Polo, Marco. *The Travels of Marco Polo*. Edited by Peter Harris. New York: Everyman's Library, 2008.

Thomas of Celano. *First and Second Life of St. Francis with Selections from the Treatise on the Miracles of the Blessed Francis*. Translated by Placid Hermann. Quincy, Ill.: Franciscan Press, 1988.

See also John Julius Norwich (fifth century).

FOURTEENTH CENTURY

Alighieri, Dante. *The Divine Comedy*. Translated by Allen Mandelbaum (blank verse with facing Italian text). 3 vols. New York: Bantam Books, 1982.

———. *The Divine Comedy*. Translated by John D. Sinclair (prose with facing Italian text). 3 vols. New York: Oxford University Press, 1969; 1939.

———. *The Divine Comedy*. Translated by Charles S. Singleton (prose with facing Italian text). 3 vols. Princeton, N.J.: Princeton University Press, 1975.

Auerbach, Erich. *Dante: Poet of the Secular World*. Translated by Ralph Manheim. Chicago: University of Chicago Press, 1961; 1929.

Chaucer, Geoffrey. *The Canterbury Tales*. Edited by Jill Mann. New York: Penguin Books, 2005.

D'Epiro, Peter, and Mary Desmond Pinkowish. *Sprezzatura: 50 Ways Italian Genius Shaped the World*. New York: Anchor Books, 2001.

Hartt, Frederick. *History of Italian Renaissance Art*. 6th ed. Edited by David Wilkins. Upper Saddle River, N.J.: Prentice Hall, 2006.

Howard, Donald R. *Chaucer: His Life, His Works, His World*. New York: Ballantine Books, 1987.

Johnson, Paul. *The Renaissance: A Short History*. New York: Modern Library, 2000.

Kristeller, Paul Oskar. *Eight Philosophers of the Italian Renaissance*. Stanford, Calif.: Stanford University Press, 1964.

Petrarch. *The Canzoniere, or Rerum vulgarium fragmenta*. Translated by Mark Musa (verse with facing Italian text). Indianapolis: Indiana University Press, 1999.

———. *Petrarch's Lyric Poems*. Translated by Robert M. Durling. Cambridge, Mass.: Harvard University Press, 1976.

Robinson, James Harvey, and Henry Winchester Rolfe. *Petrarch: The First Modern Scholar and Man of Letters*. New York: Haskell House Publishers, 1970; 1898.

Tuchman, Barbara W. *A Distant Mirror: The Calamitous 14th Century*. New York: Ballantine Books, 1978.

Vasari, Giorgio. *Lives of the Artists.* Vol. 1. Edited by George Bull. New York: Penguin Books, 1987.

FIFTEENTH CENTURY

Alberti, Leon Battista. *On Painting.* Edited by Martin Kemp. New York: Penguin Books, 1991.

Babinger, Franz. *Mehmed II and His Time.* Edited by William C. Hickman. Translated by Ralph Manheim. Princeton, N.J.: Princeton University Press, 1978; 1959.

Columbus, Christopher. *The Four Voyages of Christopher Columbus.* Edited and translated by J. M. Cohen. New York: Penguin Books, 1969.

Eisenstein, Elizabeth L. *The Printing Revolution in Early Modern Europe.* 2nd ed. Cambridge: Cambridge University Press, 2005.

Freely, John. *Inside the Seraglio: Private Lives of the Sultans in Istanbul.* New York: Penguin Books, 1999.

Grafton, Anthony. *Leon Battista Alberti: Master Builder of the Italian Renaissance.* Cambridge, Mass.: Harvard University Press, 2002.

King, Ross. *Brunelleschi's Dome: How a Renaissance Genius Reinvented Architecture.* New York: Penguin Books, 2001.

Levey, Michael. *Florence: A Portrait.* Cambridge, Mass.: Harvard University Press, 1996.

Schevill, Ferdinand. *The Medici.* New York: Harper Torchbooks, 1960.

Villon, François. *The Poems of François Villon.* 2nd ed. Translated by Galway Kinnell. Hanover, N.H.: University Press of New England, 1977.

See also Edward Gibbon (second century) and Peter D'Epiro and Mary Desmond Pinkowish, Frederick Hartt, and Giorgio Vasari (fourteenth century).

SIXTEENTH CENTURY

Althaus, Paul. *The Theology of Martin Luther.* Philadelphia: Fortress Press, 1966.

Austin, William W., ed. *New Looks at Italian Opera: Essays in Honor of Donald J. Grout.* Ithaca, N.Y.: Cornell University Press, 1968.

Bainton, Roland. *Here I Stand: A Life of Martin Luther.* New York: Plume, 1995; 1950.

Frame, Donald M. *Montaigne: A Biography.* San Francisco: North Point Press, 1984.

Grout, Donald, and Hermine Weigel Williams. *A Short History of Opera.* 4th ed. New York: Columbia University Press, 2003.

Kuhn, Thomas S. *The Structure of Scientific Revolutions.* 3rd ed. Chicago: University of Chicago Press, 1996.

Machiavelli, Niccolò. *The Discourses.* Edited by Bernard Crick. Translated by Leslie J. Walker, S.J. New York: Penguin Books, 1970.

———. *The Essential Writings of Machiavelli.* Translated by Peter Constantine. New York: Modern Library, 2007.

———. *The Prince.* Translated by George Bull. New York: Penguin Books, 1961.

Marty, Martin. *Martin Luther.* New York: Penguin Books, 2004.

Montaigne, Michel de. *The Complete Essays of Montaigne.* Translated by Donald M. Frame. Stanford, Calif.: Stanford University Press, 1968.

———. *Essays.* [Selection.] Translated by J. M. Cohen. New York: Penguin Books, 1958.

Shakespeare, William. *Titus Andronicus.* Edited by Eugene M. Waith. New York: Oxford University Press, 1984.

Troyat, Henri. *Ivan the Terrible.* Translated by Joan Pinkham. London: Phoenix Books, 2001; 1984.

Viroli, Maurizio. *Niccolò's Smile: A Biography of Machiavelli.* Translated by Anthony Shugaar. New York: Farrar, Straus and Giroux, 2000.

Whenham, John. *Claudio Monteverdi: Orfeo.* Cambridge: Cambridge University Press, 1986.

COMPACT DISCS

Cavalieri, Bardi, Caccini. *La Pellegrina, Intermedii 1589/*Paradizo. Antonio Fajardo.

Cavalieri, Malvezzi, Bardi. *La Pellegrina: Music for the Wedding of Ferdinando de' Medici and Christine de Lorraine, Princess of France, Florence, 1589/*Vivarte. Paul Van Nevel/Huelgas Ensemble.

Monteverdi. *L'Orfeo/*Archiv Production. John Eliot Gardiner, Anthony Rolfe Johnson, Lynne Dawson.

Peri. *Euridice/*Pavane Records. Anibal E. Cetrangolo/La Compagnia dei Febi Armonici/Ensemble Albalonga.

SEVENTEENTH CENTURY

Cawdrey, Robert. *The First English Dictionary, 1604: Robert Cawdrey's* Table Alphabeticall. Oxford: Bodleian Library, 2007.

Cervantes, Miguel de. *Don Quixote.* Translated by Edith Grossman. New York: Ecco, 2003.

Cervantes Saavedra, Miguel de. *The Adventures of Don Quixote.* Translated by J. M. Cohen. New York: Penguin Books, 1950.

Clarke, Desmond. *Descartes: A Biography.* Cambridge: Cambridge University Press, 2006.

Cooke, Alistair. *Alistair Cooke's America.* New York: Alfred A. Knopf, 1973.

Descartes, René. *Discourse on Method and Meditations on First Philosophy.* 4th ed. Translated by Donald A. Cross. Indianapolis: Hackett Publishing Company, 1998.

———. *The Essential Descartes.* Edited by Margaret D. Wilson. Translated by Elizabeth S. Haldane and G. R. T. Ross. New York: Mentor Books, 1969.

Drake, Stillman. *Galileo at Work: His Scientific Biography.* Mineola, N.Y.: Dover Publications, 2003; 1978.

Gribbin, John. *The Scientists: A History of Science Told Through the Lives of Its Greatest Inventors.* New York: Random House, 2002.

King, Henry C. *The History of the Telescope.* Mineola, N.Y.: Dover Publications, 2003.

Lukács, Georg. *The Theory of the Novel.* Translated by Anna Bostock. Cambridge, Mass.: MIT Press, 1971; 1920.

Morison, Samuel Eliot. *The Oxford History of the American People.* Vol. 1: *Prehistory to 1789.* Revised edition. New York: Meridian Books, 1972.

Price, David A. *Love and Hate in Jamestown: John Smith, Pocahontas, and the Birth of a New Nation.* New York: Vintage, 2005.

Reeves, Eileen. *Galileo's Glassworks: The Telescope and the Mirror.* Cambridge, Mass.: Harvard University Press, 2008.

Shakespeare, William. *Mr. William Shakespeares Comedies, Histories, & Tragedies. Published According to the True Originall Copies. A Photographic Facsimile of the First Folio Edition.* Prepared by Helge Kökeritz and Charles Tyler Prouty. New Haven, Conn.: Yale University Press, 1954.

Sorell, Tom. *Descartes: A Very Short Introduction.* New York: Oxford University Press, 1987.

See also Daniel J. Boorstin, *The Discoverers* (tenth century).

EIGHTEENTH CENTURY

Amar, Akhil Reed. *The Bill of Rights: Creation and Reconstruction.* New Haven, Conn.: Yale University Press, 1998.

Ellis, Joseph J. *His Excellency: George Washington.* New York: Vintage Books, 2004.

Heffner, Richard D. *A Documentary History of the United States.* 7th revised edition. New York: Signet, 2002.

Lefebvre, Georges. *The Coming of the French Revolution.* Translated by R. R. Palmer. Princeton, N.J.: Princeton University Press, 2005; 1939.

Lewis, Anthony. *Freedom for the Thought That We Hate: A Biography of the First Amendment.* New York: Basic Books, 2007.

Mitchell, Joseph B. *Decisive Battles of the American Revolution.* Revised edition. Yardley, Pa.: Westholme Publishing, 2004.

Palmer, R. R., Joel Colton, and Lloyd Kramer. *A History of the Modern World.* 9th ed. New York: Alfred A. Knopf, 2002.

Pearce, Edward. *The Great Man: Sir Robert Walpole: Scoundrel, Genius and Britain's First Prime Minister.* London: Pimlico, 2008.

Schama, Simon. *Citizens: A Chronicle of the French Revolution.* New York: Vintage Books, 1989.

————. *Rough Crossings: The Slaves, the British and the American Revolution.* New York: HarperCollins, 2006.

Wordsworth, William, and Samuel Taylor Coleridge. *Lyrical Ballads.* Edited by R. L. Brett and A. R. Jones. New York: Routledge, 2005.

See also Alistair Cooke and Samuel Eliot Morison (seventeenth century).

NINETEENTH CENTURY

Adler, Dennis. *Daimler & Benz: The Complete History: The Birth and Evolution of the Mercedes-Benz.* New York: Collins Design, 2006.

Asprey, Robert. *The Reign of Napoleon Bonaparte.* New York: Basic Books, 2001.

Brettell, Richard R. *Impressionism: Painting Quickly in France, 1860–1890.* New Haven, Conn.: Yale University Press, 2000.

Catton, Bruce. *The American Heritage New History of the Civil War.* Edited by James M. McPherson. New York: Viking, 1996.

Davis, William C. *The Civil War: First Blood: Fort Sumter to Bull Run.* Alexandria, Va.: Time-Life Books, 1983.

Freud, Sigmund. *The Interpretation of Dreams.* Translated by James Strachey. New York: Avon Books, 1965.

Gay, Peter. *Freud: A Life for Our Time.* New York: W. W. Norton and Company, 1998.

Kapos, Martha. *The Impressionists: A Retrospective.* New York: Macmillan Publishing Company, 1991.

Klein, Maury. *The Power Makers: Steam, Electricity, and the Men Who Invented America.* New York: Bloomsbury Press, 2008.

Kramer, Peter D. *Freud: Inventor of the Modern Mind.* New York: Atlas Books, 2006.

Lacayo, Richard, and George Russell. *Eyewitness: 150 Years of Photojournalism.* 2nd ed. New York: Time Books, 1995.

Morison, Samuel Eliot. *The Oxford History of the American People.* Vol. 2: *1789 Through Reconstruction.* Revised edition. New York: Meridian Books, 1972.

Sandler, Martin W. *Photography: An Illustrated History.* New York: Oxford University Press, 2002.

Sontag, Susan. *On Photography.* New York: Picador, 1977.

Wallace, Alfred Russel. *Infinite Tropics: An Alfred Russel Wallace Anthology.* Edited by Andrew Berry. New York: Verso, 2002.

See also R. R. Palmer, et al. (eighteenth century).

TWENTIETH CENTURY

Bernard, Bruce. *Century: One Hundred Years of Human Progress, Regression, Suffering, and Hope.* London, UK: Phaidon Press, 2002.

Chaikin, Andrew. *A Man on the Moon: The Voyages of the Apollo Astronauts.* New York: Penguin Books, 1998.

De Kruif, Paul. *Microbe Hunters.* San Diego: Harcourt Brace and Company, 1996; 1926.

Edgerton, David. *The Shock of the Old: Technology and Global History Since 1900.* New York: Oxford University Press, 2007.

Edgerton, Gary R. *The Columbia History of American Television.* New York: Columbia University Press, 2007.

Gilbert, Martin. *The First World War: A Complete History.* New York: Henry Holt and Company, 1994.

Greene, Brian. *The Elegant Universe; Superstrings, Hidden Dimensions, and the Quest for the Ultimate Theory.* New York: Vintage Books, 1999.

Hafner, Katie, and Matthew Lyon. *Where Wizards Stay Up Late: The Origins of the Internet.* New York: Simon and Schuster, 1996.

Hawking, Stephen. *A Brief History of Time: The Updated and Expanded Tenth Anniversary Edition.* New York: Bantam Books, 1998.

Howard, Fred. *Wilbur and Orville: A Biography of the Wright Brothers.* Mineola, N.Y.: Dover Publications, 1988.

Judt, Tony. *Postwar: A History of Europe Since 1945.* New York: Penguin Books, 2005.

Keegan, John. *The First World War.* New York: Vintage Books, 1998.

Levy, Stuart B. *The Antibiotic Paradox: How the Misuse of Antibiotics Destroys Their Curative Powers.* Cambridge, Mass.: Da Capo Press, 2002.

Lightman, Alan. *The Discoveries: Great Breakthroughs in 20th Century Science.* New York: Pantheon Books, 2005.

Morison, Samuel Eliot. *The Oxford History of the American People.* Vol. 3: *1869 Through the Death of John F. Kennedy, 1963.* Revised edition. New York: Meridian Books, 1972.

Nelson, Craig. *Rocket Men: The Epic Story of the First Men on the Moon.* New York: Viking, 2009.

Segaller, Stephen. *Nerds 2.0.1: A Brief History of the Internet.* New York: TV Books, 1999.

See also R. R. Palmer, et al. (eighteenth century).

About the Contributors

DANTE D'EPIRO (Questions 140–41, 144, 147) holds a BS in psychology from Fordham University and a BS in accounting from Lehman College (CUNY). He has worked in hospital administration for the past eleven years and is transitioning from health care to the financial sector. His publications include six essays that appeared in Peter D'Epiro and Mary Desmond Pinkowish's *What Are the Seven Wonders of the World?* and *Sprezzatura: 50 Ways Italian Genius Shaped the World*. He lives in Tarrytown, New York.

RICHARD JACKSON (Questions 82 and 90) holds a BA in classics from SUNY at Albany and a PhD in history from Yale University. He is a senior fellow at the Center for Strategic and International Studies, where he directs the Global Aging Initiative; an adjunct fellow at the Hudson Institute; and a senior adviser to the Concord Coalition. Jackson is the author or coauthor of numerous studies on the social, economic, and geopolitical implications of the aging of the population, including *The Global Retirement Crisis*, *The Aging Vulnerability Index*, and *The Graying of the Great Powers*. He lives in Alexandria, Virginia, with his wife, Perrine, and their children, Benjamin, Brian, and Penelope.

ERIC LENK (Question 113) received a BA from Harvard College and his MPhil in comparative literature from Yale University. He is a writer and editor on medical and other topics and editorial director for Apex Medical Communications. He has a grown son, Chris, and lives in Sparkill, New York, with his wife, Mary Anne.

TOM MATRULLO (Questions 72, 92, 101–2, 104–7, 114, 118, 121, 125, 142, 150) received a BA from the University of Rochester and an MPhil in comparative literature from Yale University before teaching literature and writing for ten years at Pratt Institute, Parsons School of Design, and the New School in New York City. After obtaining an MS from Columbia University's Graduate School of Journalism, he worked as a business writer at the *Herald-Tribune* in Sarasota, Florida, where he lives with his children, Mykhal and Sawyer. He has contributed to magazines and online publications and served as managing editor of a City Guide Web site for Sarasota and other Florida cities. He continues to curate Internet news and information resources while blogging, tweeting, and blipping on his own time.

KIA PENSO (Question 116) grew up in Jamaica, studied literature at the University of California's College of Creative Studies, and received her PhD in English at UC Santa Barbara. She taught for two years at Grinnell College and published *Wallace Stevens: Harmonium, and the Whole of Harmonium* in 1992. She returned to Santa Barbara to teach writing and literature for six years before pursuing an MS from Columbia University's Graduate School of Journalism. Returning to the Caribbean, she worked as a newspaper managing editor in Saint Kitts and Nevis. She now lives in Takoma Park, Maryland, where she is writing a book on Caribbean culture and literature.

LISA C. PERRONE (Questions 126 and 145) received her PhD in mathematics from Emory University and currently teaches mathematics to active-duty members of the U.S. Armed Forces at Marine Corps Base Hawaii and Pearl Harbor Naval Station, Hawaii. She balances the challenges of her profession with an aggressive pursuit of activities that promote physical and spiritual health and the joys of lifelong learning.

JOSEPH SGAMMATO (Questions 97, 139, 143) is a freelance writer and teacher. He received an MA in English from Fordham University and an MFA in film from Columbia University. He teaches at SUNY Westchester Community College in Valhalla, New York, and lives in Norwalk, Connecticut, with his wife, Judy, and their son, Gregory.

NANCY WALSH (Questions 8, 30, 34, 47, 74, 93, 99, 119, 132–33, 136, 138, 148) earned a BA in English literature from Salve Regina College in Newport, Rhode Island. She has written for various medical publications in the United States and England, including *Patient Care*, *The Practitioner*, and the *Journal of Respiratory Diseases*, in a career spanning three decades. She now works as a freelance medical writer in Ridgewood, New Jersey, where she lives with her husband, Peter D'Epiro.

WILLIAM A. WALSH (Questions 123, 130, 137) received his PhD in marine ichthyology from the University of Connecticut in 1986 and has been working since 1997 as a biologist with the Pelagic Fisheries Research Program of the University of Hawaii, located at the National Marine Fisheries Service in Honolulu.

SPREZZATURA

50 Ways Italian Genius Shaped the World
by Peter D'Epiro and Mary Desmond Pinkowish

No one has demonstrated *sprezzatura,* or the art of effortless mastery, quite like the Italians. From the rise of the Roman calendar and the birth of the first university to the development of modern political science by Niccolò Machiavelli and the creation of the modern orchestra by Claudio Monteverdi, *Sprezzatura* chronicles fifty great Italian cultural achievements in a series of witty, erudite, and information-packed essays, including: Julius Caesar and the imperial purple; Ovid's treasure hoard of ancient myth and fable; Dante's human tragicomedy; Brunelleschi, Donatello, and Masaccio, inventors of the visual language of the Renaissance; Leonardo da Vinci, eternal enigma; Catherine de' Medici, godmother of French cuisine; and much more.

History/978-0-385-72019-9

WHAT ARE THE SEVEN WONDERS OF THE WORLD?

And 100 Other Great Cultural Lists—Fully Explicated
by Peter D'Epiro and Mary Desmond Pinkowish

A compendium of culturally significant particulars from the fields of mythology, religion, literature, history, science, mathematics, art, and music, this book is a stimulating fusion of facts that makes for an invaluable reference and an entertaining diversion. Questions are grouped in sections according to the number of items in their answer, so that they are in the form of easily memorized lists. And for those who wish to delve deeper, there is a thoughtful essay to go with each answer that includes fascinating details and places the list in its larger historical context. Much more than a book of trivia, it offers a grand overview of the knowledge needed to appreciate our cultural and intellectual life.

History/978-0-385-49062-7

Meet with Interesting People
Enjoy Stimulating Conversation
Discover Wonderful Books

Visit ReadingGroupCenter.com where you'll find great reading choices—award winners, bestsellers, beloved classics, and many more—and extensive resources for reading groups such as:

Author Chats
Exciting contests offer reading groups the chance to win one-on-one phone conversations with Vintage and Anchor Books authors.

Extensive Discussion Guides
Guides for over 450 titles as well as non–title specific discussion questions by category for fiction, nonfiction, memoir, poetry, and mystery.

Personal Advice and Ideas
Reading groups nationwide share ideas, suggestions, helpful tips, and anecdotal information. Participate in the discussion and share your group's experiences.

Behind the Book Features
Specially designed pages which can include photographs, videos, original essays, notes from the author and editor, and book-related information.

Reading Planner
Plan ahead by browsing upcoming titles, finding author event schedules, and more.

Special for Spanish-language reading groups
www.grupodelectura.com
A dedicated Spanish-language content area complete with recommended titles from Vintage Español.

A selection of some favorite reading group titles from our list

Atonement by Ian McEwan
Balzac and the Little Chinese Seamstress by Dai Sijie
The Blind Assassin by Margaret Atwood
The Devil in the White City by Erik Larson
Empire Falls by Richard Russo
The English Patient by Michael Ondaatje
A Heartbreaking Work of Staggering Genius by Dave Eggers
The House of Sand and Fog by Andre Dubus III
A Lesson Before Dying by Ernest J. Gaines

Lolita by Vladimir Nabokov
Memoirs of a Geisha by Arthur Golden
Midnight in the Garden of Good and Evil by John Berendt
Midwives by Chris Bohjalian
Push by Sapphire
The Reader by Bernhard Schlink
Snow by Orhan Pamuk
An Unquiet Mind by Kay Redfield Jamison
Waiting by Ha Jin
A Year in Provence by Peter Mayle